KESWICK'S AUTHENTIC VOICE

HELP FROM EARTH AND HEAVEN

We who are called apart to hills and dales
　　Where in each sunrise God is speaking clear,
　　Where from each sunset's glow we seem to hear
The songs of wreathèd angels, the all-hails
Of bright-winged seraphims—may watch the sails
　　Of yonder boat that steals across the mere,
　　And know that to the haven as we steer
For us the invisible power of God prevails.

Lo! to the mountains, as we lift our eyes,
　　For help we feel th' Almighty arms are spread;
　　To bring us peace, the lake and field and grove
Proclaim a Father's mercy and His love;
　　While, from the tireless stars, at night is shed
The joy of those who watch in Paradise.

                                        H. D. RAWNSLEY

This poem was written by Canon H. D. Rawnsley, vicar of Crosthwaite, Keswick, 1886–1920, and co-founder with Octavia Hill of the National Trust, as the frontispiece of the book *The Keswick Convention: Its Message, Its Method and Its Men*, edited by Dr. Charles F. Harford.

KESWICK'S
AUTHENTIC VOICE

SIXTY-FIVE DYNAMIC ADDRESSES
DELIVERED AT THE KESWICK CONVENTION
1875–1957

Selected and edited by

HERBERT F. STEVENSON

Editor: THE LIFE OF FAITH, THE KESWICK WEEK

ZONDERVAN PUBLISHING HOUSE
GRAND RAPIDS————————MICHIGAN

U.S.A.
ZONDERVAN PUBLISHING HOUSE
1415 LAKE DRIVE, S.E.
GRAND RAPIDS 6, MICHIGAN

LONDON
MARSHALL, MORGAN AND SCOTT, LTD.
1–5 PORTPOOL LANE
HOLBORN, E.C.1

CANADA
EVANGELICAL PUBLISHERS
241 YONGE STREET
TORONTO

AUSTRALIA
117–119 BURWOOD ROAD
MELBOURNE, E.13

SOUTH AFRICA
P.O. BOX 1720, STURK'S BUILDINGS
CAPE TOWN

PRINTED IN THE UNITED STATES OF AMERICA

60,821

CONTENTS

5

INTRODUCTION

SEVERAL books have been written upon the Keswick Convention and its message, but this volume is distinctive from them all in that it presents the sequence of teaching given at Keswick as contained in outstanding addresses delivered from the Convention platform throughout its history. Many of these are taken from the earlier years, when the teaching of Keswick came as a newly re-discovered revelation from God, to a generation hungering and thirsting for holiness of life and power in Christian service. The speakers were men whose lives had been transformed by this message they now so gladly and convincingly proclaimed. Other addresses represent every era throughout the Convention's eight decades, right to our own day. These reveal the consistency of the message delivered, and that Keswick remains unswervingly true to its original vision and commission. Here we have indeed "Keswick's authentic voice."

H.F.S.

REST

My Saviour, Thou hast offered rest:
    Oh, give it then to me;
The rest of ceasing from myself,
    To find my all in Thee.

This cruel self, oh, how it strives
    And works within my breast,
To come between Thee and my soul,
    And keep me back from rest.

How many subtle forms it takes
    Of seeming verity,
As if it were not safe to rest
    And venture all on Thee.

O Lord, I seek a holy rest,
    A victory over sin!
I seek that Thou alone shouldst reign
    O'er all without, within.

In Thy strong hand I lay me down,
    So shall the work be done:
For who can work so wondrously
    As the Almighty One?

Work on, then, Lord, till on my soul
    Eternal light shall break,
And, in Thy likeness perfected,
    I "satisfied" shall wake.

EVAN H. HOPKINS

The Rev. A. T. Houghton, M.A.
Chairman Keswick Convention Council

"The Christian public is greatly indebted to the Rev. H. F. Stevenson for his labour of love in culling from the past records, from 1875 onwards, some of the outstanding addresses, and thus presenting us with this valuable book, accurately described as Keswick's Authentic Voice."

J. Oswald Sanders
General Director China Inland Mission

"This volume gives the Christian world the distilled essence of the teaching of Keswick, a message which for more than eighty years has brought spiritual emancipation to scores of thousands. Here is the theory of sanctification lucidly expressed, but with a guide to its practical experience. The message of Keswick has brought untold blessing to the home churches and has sparked missionary endeavour the world over."

Rev. Dr. Donald Grey Barnhouse
Editor-in-Chief, Eternity Magazine, *Philadelphia*

"The unique ministry of Keswick has been to call the attention of the Christian world to life in the Holy Spirit. A theologian who has followed the reports of the past three-quarters of a century would quickly recognize that many phases of the doctrine of holiness have been presented by a wide variety of speakers, some of them contradictory. Keswick teaching certainly does not have the 'party line' spirit, which is extremely important as the Holy Spirit does not express Himself in rigid legalistic forms which would deliver the individual from full personal responsibility to the leading of the Lord.

"The Editor of *Keswick's Authentic Voice* is to be commended highly for his selection of the sixty-five addresses in this volume, all of which point the believer away from himself to the Lord Jesus Christ and through the Holy Spirit."

Rev. Alan Redpath
Pastor, Moody Church, Chicago

"The emphasis on New Testament holiness of life is more urgently needed than anything else today, in order that the Christian Church may witness both by life and by lip to the power of our risen Saviour in personal living. Only as this is realized can those without Christ be effectively challenged with the message of the Gospel. I trust that this book will have the wide circulation which it so clearly deserves."

KESWICK AND ITS MESSAGE

MOST movements have roots reaching back into the era before their actual inception. So it is with the Keswick Convention. Long before the first gatherings in a tent erected in a field adjoining the grounds of St. John's Vicarage, Keswick, in 1875, which proved to be the initiation of the renowned annual assembly, the teachings concerning the "deepening of the spiritual life" now associated with the name of Keswick had been both exemplified in the lives of Christian people of many races and generations, and set forth in books in various languages. But the most amazing phenomenon of Church history is the way in which vital doctrines have become forgotten and temporarily "lost." It was so with the very central truth of the Christian faith, which was obscured and buried under the teachings and trappings of Rome until Martin Luther re-discovered it in the glorious phrase "justified by faith"; and likewise the equally clear presentation in Scripture of the "life more abundant" in Christ has been strangely neglected—not only in mediæval times, but right until the middle of the last century. Yet Luther himself had gone on from justification by faith to "the fulness of the blessing of the Gospel of Christ"; and in our own country a book published toward the end of the seventeenth century, by a Puritan divine, the Rev. Walter Marshall, contained all that Keswick later re-minted in present-day language. It is amazing that this obscure Fellow of Winchester College should have come through personal study of the Scriptures to so clear an understanding of an aspect of truth generally disregarded. His book has a cumbrous title, characteristic of those days—"The Gospel Mystery of Sanctification, Opened in Sundry Practical Directions Suited Especially to the Cases of those who Labour under the Guilt and Power of Indwelling Sin." This is, of course, customarily abbreviated to its first phrase—*The Gospel Mystery of Sanctification*. Remarkable as this book is, its author had no idea of proclaiming anything new: his purpose was solely to present, simply and clearly, what the Scriptures have to say on the subject of sanctification. And his book ran through several editions. There was accordingly nothing at all original about the message of Keswick: yet it came with a freshness and vitality almost amounting to a new revelation from on high to a generation which had neglected this glorious fulness of the divine provision for holy living.

Keswick was an indirect outcome of the 1859 Revival. Spiritual awakening brings incalculable blessings in its train—far more widespread and remarkable than even the most visionary of the people of God conceive. The life and destiny of nations are profoundly affected by it, as well as the devotion and zeal of the Church. The Revival of 1859 lifted the entire tone of life in both America and Great Britain, and set in motion dynamic forces of social reform, the impetus of which is with us still. One of the most notable effects, however, was to awaken a sense of spiritual poverty and powerlessness in the hearts and minds of men and women who in ordinary times would have been regarded as outstanding in saintliness and spiritual fervour. Such a consciousness of lack could not be ignored or suppressed in times of such intense spiritual conviction and reality—as awareness of shortcoming is too often and too easily condoned today. The quest for victory over every known besetment, and for fulness of power in Christian service, led to a re-examination of the Scriptural teaching concerning holiness. And God, who awakened the sense of need and desire, provided the answer.

It was in America that re-discovery was made of the full heritage of the Church; and Dr. W. E. Broadman gave it early expression in his famous book *The Higher Christian Life*, which made a deep impression and met a widely-felt need. In it he recounted the experiences and teaching of Luther and of Dr. Merle D'Aubigne, the historian of the Reformation, and many others, including Wesley and General Havelock from our own land. The teaching was eagerly welcomed and widely disseminated—at meetings convened for the purpose, and through books; and among its most gifted exponents were Mr. and Mrs. Robert Pearsall Smith, a Quaker couple who had "come into the blessing" and later joined the Presbyterian Church: it was they who became its missionaries to Europe—bringing back the message which America had so gladly embraced from Europe, but long neglected here! Not only were both eloquent speakers, but Mrs. Pearsall Smith—known by her pen-name of Hannah Whitall Smith—was also an able writer, and her book *The Christian's Secret of a Happy Life* is still a classic of "Keswick" teaching.

Among a number of gatherings they addressed in different parts of this country in 1873, was one small in attendance but significant in its outcome, at Curzon Chapel, London; for among the sixteen or so present were two destined to take a foremost part in the future Conventions at Keswick—the Revs. Evan H. Hopkins and E. W. Moore. Mrs. Hopkins tells how on returning

home, her husband was "like one looking out on a land wide
and beautiful, flowing with milk and honey. That it was to
be possessed, and that *it was his*"; while Mr. Moore wrote long
afterwards, "from that little meeting, as from an obscure source
and spring, the stream of Keswick teaching and influence, which
has gone round the world since then, may truly be said to have
taken its rise."

In the following year a six-days' conference was held at Broadlands, near Romsey, Hants, the country seat of the Rt. Hon. W.
Cowper-Temple, M.P. (afterwards Lord Mount-Temple), and now
the home of Lord and Lady Mountbatten, where our Queen and
the Duke of Edinburgh spent part of their honeymoon. Among the
hundred guests were eminent people in all walks of life. So deep
an impression was made by the addresses given, that hearts were
stirred to their depths, and many present entered into a richer
spiritual experience than ever before, transforming their lives
and ministries. Among such was a visitor from the Continent,
Pasteur Theodore Monod, who during that memorable week
wrote his moving hymn, "Oh, the bitter shame and sorrow."
Like water upon a thirsty land, the message came with all the
power and blessing of the Gospel heard in its fulness for the first
time. Here was the answer to the longing for victory over sin;
the provision for holiness of life and power in the Master's service.
Self-accusation in the consciousness of shortcoming and defeat
was silenced in the new-found liberty of the sons of God; angu-
larities of character and conduct were subdued by the Spirit of
grace; barrenness in witness gave place to fertility and fruitfulness.

Like two of old who found great spoil, these privileged few
exclaimed, "This is a day of good tidings . . . now therefore come
and tell. . . ." So they arranged a larger conference, at Oxford,
shortly afterwards—August 29th to September 7th, 1874. A
large and representative company gathered, including a number
of prominent Evangelical leaders from the Continent. Similar
blessing was experienced here as at Broadlands. "God hath
visited His people!" a contemporary report declared; "God has
opened the windows of heaven, and is pouring out a blessing that
there shall not be room to receive it!" It was indeed akin to
Revival—yet not in convicting and converting the unsaved, but
in bringing the children of God into "life more abundant." One
of these was Canon T. D. Harford-Battersby, vicar of St. John's,
Keswick, a devout man who was yet unsatisfied with his own
spiritual life. While the Rev. Evan Hopkins was speaking on
the healing of the nobleman's son, and describing the differences between a seeking and a resting faith, the Canon said to

himself, "*I will* rest in Him." Later he testified, "I got a revelation of Christ to my soul, so extraordinary, glorious and precious, that from that day it illuminated my life. I found *He* was *all* I wanted, I shall never forget it; the day and hour are present with me. How it humbled me, and yet what peace it brought!"

A still larger Convention was held in Brighton in the early summer of 1875, when remarkable scenes were witnessed. That gathering is scarcely in the genealogy of "Keswick," however, although it was one of its most notable fore-runners. During it, with the needs of the North principally in mind, Canon Harford-Battersby and a prominent Quaker, Mr. Robert Wilson, arranged for a series of "union meetings for the promotion of practical holiness" to be held at Keswick, from July 29th, 1875, at which Mr. and Mrs. Pearsall Smith were to be the principal speakers. A breakdown on the part of Mr. Smith not only prevented his keeping this engagement at the last minute, but obliged him to retire from public ministry. Nothing daunted, the conveners secured other speakers for the meetings at Keswick, notably the Rev. H. W. Webb-Peploe—who from that first year became a dominating figure on the Keswick platform, and remained so, for almost half a century.

With the withdrawal of the American couple who had been so signally used of God in conferences held at so many different centres throughout the land, the movement became focused in the Keswick Convention, which grew steadily from year to year in numbers and influence. Canon Harford-Battersby presided until his Homecall in 1883; but perhaps the outstanding personality both on the platform and behind the scenes was the Rev. Evan H. Hopkins, the "theologian" of Keswick, who more than any other man defined its distinctive "message." He was not only a most gifted speaker, but also editor of *The Christian's Pathway of Power*, a monthly paper begun by Mr. Pearsall Smith in 1874. Mr. Hopkins contributed to the very first issue, and soon assumed full responsibility for it. As the organ of the movement from which Keswick sprang, *The Christian's Pathway of Power* naturally became closely linked with the Convention; and as its editor, Mr. Hopkins made it a powerful medium of Keswick teaching. In 1879 the name of the paper was changed to *The Life of Faith*, and in 1892 it became a weekly instead of a monthly. Its early volumes are the primary source of information concerning the Convention in its formative years, and to it we owe reports of the addresses delivered —some in summary only, others in entirety.

There was a spontaneity about the early Conventions which imparted a remarkable vitality to the gatherings. No programme was pre-arranged, but the conveners and speakers waited upon the leading of the Spirit of God from day to day. All the addresses were extemporaneous. Those taking part had all experienced in their own lives the liberating power of the message they proclaimed, and spoke out of glowing hearts. They were "witnesses" to a distinctive blessing they had received, and longed that others should experience; men with a message, ready whenever called upon to speak with burning conviction of what they themselves had found to be so gloriously true. Some of the addresses consequently seem to us rather disjointed: but it is impossible to read them, even after eighty years or more, without feeling the impact of their spiritual dynamic. The speakers were not concerned with homiletical headings and polished periods, but with what they had "tasted and seen" of the power of God available to every believer, for holiness of life and effectiveness in witness.

Spontaneity was never allowed to degenerate into diffusiveness, however: the Convention had a specific purpose, and kept strictly to it. And without deliberate premeditation, a progression of teaching soon took shape—beginning with the exceeding sinfulness of sin, especially sin in the believer; consequent defeat and powerlessness in life and witness; God's provision for the rehabilitation of the sinner, in Christ—sanctification, consecration, and the Spirit-filled life. This sequence of teaching has never been followed in any mechanical way, of course; it is just the underlying pattern, Spirit-given, and developed year by year in the liberty of the Spirit.

Through the years successive generations of speakers have been raised up, maintaining the testimony of Keswick and proclaiming its message. It must be acknowledged that the "fire in the bones" of the early speakers has not been so evident in some of later years; but thousands attend the Convention annually, hungering and thirsting for God—and they still find the answer to their need. In the addresses which follow, then, we have the full range of Keswick teaching, as given by its most renowned exponents; the utterances of the men who spoke with prophetic voice a message which had proved as the water of life to their own souls. Here we have indeed the authentic message of Keswick.

Such a book as this has long been projected, for several of the leaders of the Convention have, at different times, desired to compile a selection of the outstanding addresses delivered at Keswick from the earliest days, to provide an authoritative compendium of Keswick teaching as proclaimed from the Convention platform by its most distinguished exponents. None of them found it possible to carry this intention into effect, however, and the task has fallen into other hands; but in the preparation of the book the advice and recollections of many of the veterans among Council members, speakers and "regular attenders" have been sought and graciously given. The choice of addresses included in the book is the sole responsibility of the compiler, however; yet the selection would probably have differed but slightly had some other hand fulfilled the task, for the "source books" of information concerning Keswick point emphatically to certain messages as being attended by remarkable blessing: and these were obvious choices. Most of the ensuing addresses marked "high-light" occasions which stand out in the records of Keswick.

In some cases, however, the choice was not so self-evident. It was essential to include, not only addresses which had exceptional spiritual impact and effect when delivered, but also representative addresses of speakers who ministered at Keswick over long periods of years, and exercised considerable influence upon the shaping of the "Keswick message." Some of these maintained a consistently high standard, and no particular address seems to tower above the others, as an Everest among the Himalayas, either in its power of utterance or effect upon the hearers: any one of a great number could be selected as characteristic of the speaker and as bringing enlightenment and blessing to many lives. Some speakers, again, have specialised in the delivering of series of Bible Readings, and the choice of one address from among these is therefore difficult. In such instances the selection has of necessity to be almost arbitrary. The supreme moments of blessing in the Convention's history are, however, recalled by the messages here reproduced; its teaching is fully set forth; and most of the leading speakers are represented.

The sequence of teaching at Keswick is observed in the four sections of this book, insofar as this is possible—for some speakers have themselves overleapt the boundaries of the daily themes, so that their addresses might equally well be included under two or even three subject-headings. For instance, several combine both "Conviction Concerning Sin" and "God's Remedy for Sin," while others might come within the category of both "Consecration" and "The Spirit-Filled Life."

Two important aspects of the Convention's ministry and influence are unhappily lacking—the addresses at both the ladies' meetings, which formed an important feature of the Convention in earlier days, and the missionary meetings, have never been reported except in brief summary, and so are missing from this volume. What would one give to recapture "the raciest address ever delivered at Keswick" by Dan Crawford in 1912; Dr. Hudson Taylor's impassioned appeals for volunteers for China;

Dr. S. M. Zwemer's masterly presentation of the challenge of Islam; Dr. Eugene Stock's statesmanlike surveys of the world missionary situation; and messages by such women pioneers as Lilias Trotter and Amy Carmichael! Alas, we have only passing references to these, to tantalize us. The influence of Keswick upon missionary witness during the past century has, nevertheless, been incalculable. Hudson Taylor regarded the Convention as his finest "hunting ground" for missionary recruits of the very best type; and year by year large numbers of young people still dedicate their lives to the Lord for service wheresoever He might appoint; while countless others pledge themselves to give sacrificially for their support.

The outreach of the Convention has, of course, been as effectual upon the Lord's work at home as in the mission field; and one of the most significant gatherings each year is that for clergy and ministers. As a consequence of renewed dedication at Keswick, or fresh vision and power received, scores of men have gone back to their churches and parishes transformed, to minister henceforth in "newness of life." Few of the addresses given at these meetings are preserved; but the two delivered in 1895 were reported and appear at the end of the book. These stirring, heart-to-heart talks to their brethren, by the saintly Handley Moule—afterwards Bishop of Durham—and J. Elder Cumming, are a fitting conclusion to the selection of Keswick's outstanding addresses, pointing as they do to the ultimate purpose that the Convention has ever kept in view—the total dedication of life to the Lord, that, by His Spirit, His glory might be seen in His people, and His purposes of grace be fulfilled through them.

To read and carefully assess all the addresses at all the Conventions at Keswick since 1875 would be an impossible task—at least, for the compiler of this volume. Happily that is rendered unnecessary by the two "histories" of Keswick, which give informative and discerning comments upon every annual gathering from the year of inception up to the time of their publication—*Keswick From Within*, by J. B. Figgis (1914), and *These Sixty Years*, by W. B. Sloan (1935). Both authors wrote with extensive and intimate knowledge of Keswick, for the Rev. J. B. Figgis, a Brighton clergyman, was present at the Oxford Conference and became a member of the "inner circle" at Keswick from 1876; and Mr. Sloan had a life-long acquaintance with the movement and was its first official secretary. Both give vivid accounts of the most notable occasions, and pen-portraits of the leading speakers. Other books which re-create for us the "atmosphere" of the early days include *The Keswick Convention: Its Message*,

Its Method and Its Men, edited by Charles F. Harford, M.A., M.D.—a son of Canon Harford-Battersby; in this, numerous aspects of the Convention's ministry are described by different writers, all closely associated with the movement. This was published in 1907. Dr. A. T. Pierson outlined the history and teaching of the Convention in a little book published in America in 1903, entitled *The Keswick Movement*; and in *Notes from Keswick,* reprinted from *The Life of Faith* in 1890, the Rev. William Haslam gives stories of lives transformed there. The teaching of Keswick is set forth simply and clearly in a volume issued anonymously in the 1930's, but "with the warm approval of the Trustees," under the title *The Message of Keswick and Its Meaning.* The most objective account and appraisement of the movement is *So Great Salvation: The History and Message of the Keswick Convention,* by Steven Barabas—an extraordinarily exact account, by an American scholar who has never visited Keswick, but wrote this book in 1952 as a thesis for a doctorate degree, after exhaustive research. It is based principally upon the foregoing volumes and the yearly reports of the Convention. Biographies of several of the more eminent speakers provide useful information and illuminating side-lights upon Keswick.

Numerous books have been written on Keswick themes by various of the Convention speakers: but none has been regarded as an authoritative and comprehensive statement of Keswick doctrine, except perhaps *The Law of Liberty in the Christian Life,* by Evan Hopkins. The full presentation of the entire range of the "Keswick message" has therefore awaited such a volume as this: and here it is given as from the "fountain head," the choicest and most powerful messages delivered on the Convention platform. Here Keswick proclaims its own abiding message.

Perhaps as remarkable as the story of Keswick itself is the influence it has exercised world-wide, through Conventions which have taken its name: indeed, "Keswick" has become practically a technical term for gatherings of this kind, "for the deepening of the spiritual life." Not that the Keswick Convention Council has sponsored these off-shoots, or has any direct responsibility for them. An attempt was once made to bring those in Great Britain under the aegis of the "parent" Convention: but this proved impracticable and was soon abandoned.

As we have seen, Keswick was originally just one of a number of Conventions held in sequence in different parts of the country; and quite independently of Keswick several annual Conventions were soon afterwards established in Scotland, notably at Perth and a little later in Glasgow: indeed, in the 1880's the reports of the latter, in *The Life of Faith*, were as extensive, if not more so, than those of Keswick. Yet, strangely, these have disappeared from the religious scene; but the Scottish Highlands Convention, at Strathpeffer, though on a comparatively small scale, still flourishes. In other parts of Great Britain "daughter" Conventions were established, over a period of years, through the initiative of local committees: in Wales, at Llandrindod Wells; in Southern Ireland, at Greystones—discontinued, after long annual witness, in the dark days of the last war; in Northern Ireland, at Portstewart—now second only to Keswick in size and influence, in the British Isles; in the Eastern Counties, at Felixstowe; in the Southern Counties, at Weston-super-Mare; and elsewhere.

While administratively independent of Keswick, these all, from early days, have deliberately modelled themselves upon the Convention at Keswick, and derived their inspiration from the great annual gatherings in Lakeland. It is this sense of spiritual relationship, of filial loyalty to the "parent" Convention—even if that figure of speech is not strictly relevant—that imparts a singleness of purpose to all these local Conventions, and preserves in them the essential teaching of Keswick.

Now, while Keswick looked with benignant interest upon these developments in Great Britain, sometimes giving advice and often providing speakers, it engaged in a more positive *missionary* activity abroad. It sent deputation speakers far afield, from very early days—to Australia, Canada, and other lands of the British Commonwealth; to the mission fields, and especially to India and the Far East; and—yes, even to the United States of America, whence Britain had received the teaching which later came to be known as "the Keswick message." Among those who travelled extensively in this ministry were the Revs. George C. Grubb, Hubert Brooke and G. H. C. Macgregor; and a little later, Drs. F. B. Meyer and Charles Inwood. This aspect of Keswick's witness is still maintained, especially in the sending of speakers, in recent years, to the Mandeville Convention in Jamaica and the Hill Conventions in India. Of course, Conventions in both the United States and Canada, taking the Keswick name, have developed along their own characteristic lines—becoming frequently a series of weekly Bible Conferences throughout the summer months, of a more general character, yet with an underlying regard for the distinctive sequence of teaching associated with the English Keswick. These "Keswick" centres have become an integral and most important part of evangelical life and witness, providing summer holidays for Christian families in congenial surroundings, and with Christian fellowship, plus the additional benefit of daily instruction in the deeper things of the Christian life. In the latest

Convention to be established, however, the Mid-America "Keswick" in Chicago, sponsored by the Rev. Alan Redpath, British pastor of the Moody Memorial Church and speaker at the English Keswick, the original pattern of a one-week intensive "holy convocation" has been restored.

"Keswick" Conventions are now to be found, therefore, in many parts of the world: and on the mission field they have a two-fold character and function—for missionaries, and for national Christians. One of the smallest is to be found on "the edge of the world," at Pounawea, the most southerly point in New Zealand, overlooking the boundless Pacific. Thus has the influence of Keswick reached to the very opposite side of the globe.

I
SIN IN THE BELIEVER

Oh, the bitter shame and sorrow,
  That a time could ever be,
When I let the Saviour's pity
Plead in vain, and proudly answered—
  "All of self, and none of Thee."

Yet He found me; I beheld Him
  Bleeding on the cursed tree;
Heard Him pray, "Forgive them, Father,"
And my wistful heart said faintly—
  "Some of self, and some of Thee."

Day by day His tender mercy,
  Healing, helping, full and free,
Sweet and strong, and ah! so patient,
Brought me lower while I whispered—
  "Less of self, and more of Thee."

Higher than the highest heavens,
  Deeper than the deepest sea,
Lord, Thy love at last hath conquered:
Grant me now my soul's petition—
  "None of self, and all of Thee."

                    THEODORE MONOD

SIN IN THE BELIEVER

ANNOUNCING the first Convention at Keswick, in 1875, Canon Harford-Battersby and Mr. Robert Wilson borrowed a phrase from the Conventions held earlier at Oxford and Brighton to declare its purpose—"For the promotion of practical holiness." The following year a slight but significant change was made, to an alternative phrase, also previously used—"For the promotion of Scriptural holiness": and that has been regarded ever since as the most apt epitome of Keswick's objective. Various alternative expressions have been coined, to describe the Convention's *raison d'être*, such as "For the deepening of the spiritual life": but these are really synonymous with the original declaration of the founders. Holiness in character and conduct; the holiness revealed in the Word of God to be His purpose for His children; holiness exemplified in dedication of life to His will and service— this is the primary concern of the Convention. But it was quickly realised that more than the teaching of holiness is essential; *that* must be preceded by a "breaking up of the fallow ground." All that hinders holiness must be revealed and discarded before the work of grace can be fully accomplished in the regenerate heart and life. And since "the heart is deceitful above all things and desperately wicked" there is, alas, in most believers sin to be dealt with before true holiness can be experienced.

Very early in the Convention's history, therefore, the first note to be sounded was that of the exceeding sinfulness of sin—and especially of sin in the believer; so subtle, and often unrecognised to be what it truly is. In this exposure of the ramifications of sin in the human heart, albeit regenerate, the leading of the Spirit was manifest: for it is His ministry—the ministry of the *Holy* Spirit, through whom alone practical holiness can be realised— to convince concerning sin; and surely as much so, if not more, in the believer as in the unbeliever.

Thus in the sequence of teaching at the Keswick Convention the searchlight of the Word of God is clearly brought to bear upon the life of all present, no matter what their previous spiritual experience might be, in order that they should see themselves as God sees them. Sin, in all its range of insidious activity and influence within the life of the child of God, is fully disclosed: and multitudes who had thought themselves to be good Christians, and busy in various spheres of Christian service, have cried out in agony of conviction, "Woe is me! for I am undone. I am . . . unclean!" The wounding is unto healing, of course; the sin is revealed, that it might be cleansed away. But that is the theme of later stages of the Convention's ministry.

To make light of sin would nullify the teaching of holiness and frustrate the Convention's purpose. But it is not usually the gross sins which need to be searched out and expunged from the life in "the fountain opened for sin and all uncleanness"; though it must be confessed that all too often even prominent Christians have to acknowledge sins of which they should be ashamed. More insidious, however, because often unrecognised, are the sins of the spirit—unbelief, pride, lack of love, covetousness, censoriousness, unworthy thoughts and intents of the heart, unwillingness to yield all to the Lord—these, and many besides, are as great a hindrance to holiness as are the more flagrant and fleshly sins. In the addresses which follow, practically every aspect of the theme is touched upon, by eminent speakers from the earliest days to our own.

It is fitting that the first should be one of the most prominent personalities at Keswick in its formative years, the Rev.—afterwards Prebendary—H. W. Webb-Peploe. He had spoken at the Brighton Convention, and attended the inaugural gatherings at Keswick "as a listener," he himself tells us, in *The Keswick Convention*; but in the absence of Mr. and Mrs. Pearsall Smith he was called upon to take a leading part. From that time onward he was a principal speaker, absent only twice in forty-seven years. Of patrician appearance, and wearing always a white bow tie, instead of the customary clerical collar, his erect figure commanded immense respect, and seemed to personify all that Keswick stood for. He had a powerful voice, and an unsurpassed knowledge of Scripture; he would quote prolifically from memory, always word-perfect. His addresses and Bible Readings were delivered extemporaneously: standing with opened Bible in hand, he would pour forth Scriptural teaching like a torrent. His memorable address on "Sin," delivered in 1885, in answer to the teaching of "sinless perfection" which had developed at certain conventions, and was falsely attributed to Keswick, is perhaps the most weighty utterance on the subject in all Keswick's history. It was matched by an accompanying address on "Grace," also reproduced herein—in the next section (p. 144).

Keswick has owed a great deal throughout its history to speakers from America, and foremost among these at the turn of the century was Dr. A. T. Pierson, who took a leading part on several occasions. More about his ministry there is recalled later (p. 405).

Like Webb-Peploe, he too revealed the "inwardness" of sin. His message on "Habitual Unbelief" was the last of a series of Bible Readings in 1907, and its effect upon one listener has been described by Dr. W. Graham Scroggie, who as a young visitor to the Convention sat enthralled, and when it was ended continued to sit as if spell-bound, completely oblivious of the dispersing congregation, until he suddenly became aware of the fact that he was in the vast tent alone!

It was a grief to the promoters of Keswick that some eminent evangelicals, including the saintly Handley Moule, Principal of Ridley Hall—later Bishop of Durham—regarded the Convention with suspicion, and criticised its teaching as "perfectionist." But while on holiday in Scotland in 1884, however, Moule was invited by his host—a "dearly loved relative"—to attend some Convention meetings being held in a barn at Polmont: and he felt he could not decline to do so without discourtesy. In resentful as well as critical frame of mind, therefore, he went to the first meeting: and "it did not please me at all." The following evening "with some difficulty I made up my mind to go again," and through an address by the Rev. Evan Hopkins he was led into "the blessing" —to use a term familiar to those days. "In the meeting of the next night I felt constrained to put pride into the pocket; to rise and say before all the people how the last night had been a great blessing to my soul." He soon went to Keswick and took his place on the platform he had attacked; and concerning his address on "The 'Total Abstinence' of the Gospel," in 1886, the Rev. J. B. Figgis says, "Next morning the Rev. Handley Moule gave his first words, and oh! how many they met! Every word and its tone showed that one was speaking who had the keenest sensibilities, and made one feel that if he could tell of deliverance from being overcome by the things which are peculiarly felt by a finely-strung nature, then there was not only hope but certainty of freedom to be looked for." This first address was the beginning of a most notable ministry which Dr. Moule—as he became— exercised at Keswick until 1919. His support for the movement was invaluable, not only for its own sake, but in the answer it provided to allegations that Keswick teaching was "extremist" and lacking sound Biblical scholarship. One who recalls the Bishop's last visits to the Convention says, "In some ways, the most impressive speaker I ever heard at Keswick was Dr. Handley Moule. His very presence seemed to express the beauty of the Lord. He had a rich, cultured voice, and his spiritual intensity was so great that tiny beads of moisture covered his brow."

Scotland has made notable contributions to the Keswick platform, and among valued speakers at the turn of the century was

Dr. John Smith, of Edinburgh, "a man of most brotherly spirit," says Walter B. Sloan; "and his death, occurring while he was still in middle life, left a blank which has never quite been filled." Of his address on Isaiah 6, the Introduction to *The Keswick Week* of 1901 says, "It was an overpowering revelation of the effect of a near vision of God; and when the next speaker, the Rev. Evan Hopkins, stepped forward in the deep silence which followed, he said, 'God has spoken to us. It will be better to have no second address, but more prayer.' And all felt it was truly a momentary inspiration of God, and the prayer from one and another led us into the deeper reality of the presence of God."

Two men who rendered incalculable service to Keswick over long periods of years, not only at the "parent" Convention, but also in carrying its message world-wide, were the Revs. F. B. Meyer and Charles Inwood—both of whom received honorary doctorates in the course of their peregrinations. Inwood was a Methodist, exercising a powerful ministry in Belfast when he felt called to devote himself entirely to Convention work. Tall, slim, and with neatly-trimmed moustache, he had an impassioned manner of speech; and his transparent sincerity and intense earnestness imparted conviction and authority to all that he said. The crystal clearness of his presentation carried his message to the hearts of all his hearers. Inwood's Bible Reading on "The Unveiling of the Carnal," in 1909, is described by Sloan as "most heart-searching; and it must have left a deep and lasting impression on the hearers." F. B. Meyer, that renowned Baptist Mr. Greatheart, spoke so trenchantly in 1903 on the necessity for restitution for wrongs committed against others, that the local Post Office is said to have run out of postal orders, so great was the demand by people wishing to send "conscience money" without delay! Some doubt has been cast upon the authenticity of this story, however; we can only say that *The Life of Faith* in its report of the Convention observes, "Hundreds were sore stricken by an address of Mr. Meyer's. . . . From all that we heard, we gather that the effects of this one address have been remarkable." And three years later Meyer himself referred to the incident, when speaking again upon "The Need for Restitution." After discussing more weighty aspects of the subject he proceeded, "Then, I should like all the people here who owe money, to make up their minds that they will send postal orders and cheques through the whole country to discharge their obligations. I shall never forget speaking like this, three years ago; and as a result, someone told me that the local Post Office ran almost out of postal orders: they had not enough to satisfy the demand that was made. People could not rest. . . ." So we have here undoubtedly an address making the most notable immediate effect.

It is fitting that these addresses should be followed by one on "Conscience," by the Rev. Harrington C. Lees, delivered in 1911. During his memorable ministry at Christ Church, Beckenham, Lees spoke frequently at Keswick between 1904 and 1920—when he became a leader of Keswick witness in Australia as Archbishop of Melbourne.

We leap the years for our next address, by a beloved Chairman of the Convention Council, W. H. Aldis. Formerly a missionary in China, and from 1928 to 1943 the China Inland Mission's Home Director in Britain, he was a most brotherly man and a helpful speaker; and he never spoke more movingly than when giving his message on "The Neglected Vineyard" in 1947.

Our next selection also comes from that same year—by the Rev. W. W. Martin, who first took part in the Convention in 1920, and became a highly-esteemed "elder statesman" of the movement before his Homecall in 1957. A naturally shy man, he was profoundly concerned that the foundations of spiritual experience should be truly laid in a deep conviction concerning, and utter renunciation of, sin. "With intense fervour," wrote Mr. C. H. M. Foster, one of the Convention Trustees, in an obituary tribute, "yet withal in deep tenderness, he would apply the surgeon's knife to the cancerous growth, only that he might then go on to magnify the cleansing and healing power of the Great Physician." This was especially exemplified in his address on "A Wild Bull in a Net," in 1947.

Among the present speakers, the Rev. G. B. Duncan is outstandingly used of God at Keswick, and his powerful address on "A Peril of Spiritual Maturity," in 1956, pin-points one sin peculiar to Christians. It was delivered with unwonted passion and forcefulness on the part of one who usually speaks quietly and persuasively, with a tender wooing note. Another of the younger men, Alan Redpath, paying a return visit to his homeland from Chicago—where he is minister of Moody Memorial Church— spoke in great power in 1957. His stern denunciation of "The Sin of David" was likewise electrifying in its effect; and not only at Keswick, but also in the scores of relay centres throughout the land "listening in" to the meeting.

It is interesting to observe the change of emphasis in these addresses through the years. The earlier ones are concerned primarily with "the sins of the spirit"—inward defilement, of which the believer might often be unaware; defects of character, conduct or temperament; pride, and the snares of "counterfeit spirituality." It was tacitly assumed that those attending a Keswick Convention would already have victory over "sins of the flesh." As time went on, however, these latter seem to be gradually included within the scope of the theme "sin in the believer," and recently even to be regarded as the most common cause of present-day powerlessness among Christians. Whether or not this change of emphasis reflects a corresponding change in the spiritual state of the Church, as epitomised in the congregations at Keswick, or whether it merely indicates a more realistic facing of facts concerning the sins of Christians, the compiler must leave others to judge. Perhaps both are true.

This section is concluded with two addresses on counterfeit and defective consecration—which rightly are included within the category of "Sin in the Believer." Commenting on that by Inwood—his first from the Keswick platform, in 1892—W. B. Sloan says, "It was a burning message, and surprise was awakened by his boldness and the awful solemnity of his burning words." And the ministry of Douglas Brown, in 1922, was attended by scenes as remarkable as any in the Convention's history. Coming from the Eastern Counties, where he had conducted campaigns touched with fire from on high—the nearest approach to true Revival experienced in England this century—Brown (son of Archibald Brown, of East London fame, and a friend of C. H. Spurgeon) spoke as a man whose lips had been touched with a live coal from off the altar. "I overheard on all hands," wrote Canon F. J. Horsefield, in *The Life of Faith*, "comments such as 'Keswick has had an earthquake this morning,' and 'He's like a tornado' . . ." (see p. 252). When, at the close of his address on "The Bleating of the Sheep," Brown invited those who desired to dedicate themselves wholly to the Lord to follow him to the Drill Hall, almost the entire congregation proceeded thither: so that "not only was the Drill Hall crowded out; but the Pavilion was filled, and in the tent Dr. Meyer conducted an after-meeting for numbers still waiting there. Never before, even at Keswick," Sloan comments, "had there been such a wonderful scene; between two and three thousand people dedicating their lives anew to God, for whatever service He might choose." That is Keswick's answer to the problem of sin in the believer.

SIN

Rev. H. W. Webb-Peploe, M.A.

I wish to put before you what I believe to be the mind of God on the subject of sin, in order that we may realise as believers in Christ what a marvellous blessedness it is for us to have the propitiation that God has given us in His own dear Son; for there seem to be many who do not quite understand what the Lord Jesus Christ has intended to do, or what it is that they really need Him for. They have accepted Christ for pardon; and they think that they have accepted Christ for one more final act of deliverance from all that can be called sin, when they offer themselves to Him for sanctification. All I would say, at the outset, is that if Jesus Christ gives deliverance from sin as a principle, as well as from sins committed, then that man must be living a more or less independent existence from the Lord. The Lord Jesus Christ may be his Keeper; He may be his life; but He is not the same Jesus to that man that He was at the outset: He is not to him the Cleanser; He is not to him the Provider of perpetual acceptance in the eyes of God. Such a man is more or less compelled to live a life of personal self-satisfaction; he cannot centre his soul in Christ as a dependent sinner just from moment to moment.

The man who believes in a sanctification which eradicates sin from his person, as a principle, must be satisfied with his own condition, and be able to take his place more or less independent of the Saviour, even while he may say that he is dependent upon that Saviour for his vital joys and powers from moment to moment. My object is to trace what I believe to be the mind of God on the condition that attaches to man up to the last moment of his existence on earth—that is to say, however much Christians may have rejoiced in the Saviour, and have known experimentally the power of God the Holy Ghost; however advanced they may be in actual personal sanctification, they are, according to my own conviction, and as I gather the truth from God's Word, dependent upon the grace of the Lord Jesus Christ for pardoning power, and for actual acceptance in the sight of God, to the very last instant they live upon earth.

Because I believe this to be true, it seems to be incumbent upon me to meet those who differ from me on this subject, and to put before them the Word of God as clearly as I can trace it; and if, by the power of God, we are enabled to see the actual personal condition of each man, in regard to this terrible subject of sin, to the last, then, and then only, shall we apprehend what a glorious Saviour we have; what boundless tenderness and loving patience there is in the God of heaven toward His children on earth; what a boundless wealth of mercy there is in the Saviour, that He should continue to bear with the sinful condition of those for whom He died to make them God's true children for ever.

What marvellous, unspeakable yearnings of God the Holy Ghost, and what tender workings there must be in the Saviour in reference to those who provoke the Spirit, however unconsciously—for I speak of men who do not know they sin, perhaps, but who, if I gather the truth from God's Word, are perpetually, in that sense, acting as a provocation to the Spirit of God, by reason of their want of actual perfection. Therefore the Father, the Son, and the Holy Ghost must all be bearing and forbearing in a way that ought to enhance the beauty of their provision for sinners all through life, and the intended final perfection of every true child of God.

How is it that we are to write every man in this world down a sinner to the last moment of his life? You shall be the judges of what God the Holy Ghost has set before us in the Holy Word; and then, if, by God's mercy, we come to a right conclusion of what is God's truth in this matter, there shall rest upon each of us the blessed privilege—for I do acknowledge its unspeakable blessedness, even while I recognise its tremendousness—of just taking ourselves instant by instant to God as sinners to the last, saying, "God be merciful to me *the* sinner;" and thanking God that there is not only a once-accomplished justification when I believed in the Lord Jesus Christ, but a perpetually-giving Christ for sanctification; so that without this perpetual action of Christ, I should have to acknowledge myself at any moment to be lost, but that, thank God, I have to rejoice with a joy unspeakable and full of glory if I rightly accept the provision that God has made for me.

There appears to be a great anomaly—a regular paradox, as we term it in theological language—in this statement: that there can be this realisation of sin every moment of a man's life; and yet that there can be an unspeakable joy and calm—for I adopt all that my beloved brethren have said before me with regard to the fulness of the liberty in Christ, and the provision made for us by that glorious Saviour. To say that a man must needs walk and realise himself as a sinner at every moment, and yet walk in perfect liberty, in perfect peace, and unspeakable joy and security every moment of his life.

You ask, "How can these things be?" Before I proceed to trace the mind of the Holy Ghost on sin, and then on grace, I ask you to realise the tremendously vital distinction between the penalty for sin committed and the guilt incurred at every sinful act, and the want of communion that may be realised when the soul is brought into a position of disturbance between itself, and the great God in heaven.

My brethren, I ask you to realise that at the very moment when you first believed in the Lord Jesus Christ as your Saviour, the question of the penalty for all sin, whatever it might be and however much repeated in your daily life, has once for all been settled in God's sight independently of you altogether. You awake to it, and you clearly rest upon the finished fact from the very moment that you believe in the Lord Jesus Christ. The question of the penalty was settled upon Calvary, and has nothing whatever to do with the sinner in regard to the provision God makes for him. The question of the penalty was between God and Christ. Christ satisfied the demand of the law, and granted in God's sight a complete pardon to all mankind, who are willing to accept the provision by faith, for all the sins they have committed; so that they are delivered by their faith, from the penalty they have incurred at once.

But the question of the guilt still being incurred, is another thing altogether; and my affirmation—as I must endeavour to prove—that the child of God, however far he may be advanced, if he be enlightened by the Spirit, may awake to the consciousness that he has been incurring guilt in the sight of God, not because he has committed what are known among ourselves as definite acts of sin against the codes of morality and respectability that man puts forward, but because he has incurred guilt in the sight of God; because he comes short of the standard that God puts up, and it may be brought home to his soul that he has committed an act, or spoken a word, or thought a thought, from which guilt will arise in the sight of God. He should awake, I affirm, night after night, and perhaps all day long, if his soul be sufficiently enlightened by God, to the consciousness that every thought, word, and deed that proceed from him has, in a deep spiritual sense, brought guilt upon his soul by being short of the glory of God, lacking the perfect holiness of the standard that the Lord Jesus Christ accepted in His person.

But you will observe again, independent of the man, the provision that Christ Jesus made for sinners and for sin, keeps the man—if my doctrine be right—moment by moment cleansed from this

B

guilt, altogether independent of his feelings or experience; that is the availing power of the blood, for though the man comes short of the glory, and though he cannot walk in this mortal flesh up to the standard of the Lord Jesus Christ's perfection, and is therefore in that sense, and only in that sense, a sinner, yet he need never have a feeling of depression on account of these unconscious shortcomings, because the blood of the Lord Jesus Christ is cleansing him from all sin. That is the benefit of that glorious text. Moment by moment as the thing proceeds from the man, springing from the sinful nature that lies deep within him, unconscious it may be of guilt, at the moment, yet incurring guilt, the man finds, by the grace of God, that he is kept cleansed, instant by instant, through the operation of the blood of the Lord Jesus Christ, in God's sight. That is the second great question we have to deal with: first the penalty, secondly the guilt.

Now, thirdly, the child of God is conscious of something altogether independent of the question of the penalty of sin, and the question of the guilt. He is grieved at times—we have all found it so; he is disturbed in his blessed sense of communion with God by the fact that he has broken some one of God's perfect enactments: he has come short of the glory of God, he has wandered in thought at least from God, and communion is disturbed. Now, the question of communion has to be settled, and communion can only be restored by an experimental action on your part. There is only one thing we can do as God's children: and what is that? If we confess our sins, He is faithful and just to forgive us our sins, and to cleanse us from all unrighteousness. So that when I awake to the fact of having in any sense broken God's holy law, I may instantly be restored to communion with my Father and my Saviour, and there is perfect peace in the soul again. We have a precious advocate and a glorious propitiation in the presence of God; and therefore, if we discover our guilt and confess it, in that moment the restoration is complete. The blood has cleansed you, I believe, before you confessed, if you are a child of God; but the guilt requires to be taken away before you have perfect communion.

Keep short accounts with God; don't let your bills run up. If the devil entices you away from God, go to Christ at once and settle the guilt and have done with it. Bring your confession to God; take it to the Lord, and in that very instant do trust God and believe that it is done away with. Don't go on burdening your soul with a sense of oppression. That is the devil's subterfuge, to keep you down when he can get you down by sin. He will keep you down by burdening your soul and blackening your life if he can. We have perfect salvation, and that is perfect communion. I want you to keep clear by instantly confessing, directly you discover anything between yourself and your Father in heaven.

If you have followed me thus far, and have at all agreed with the doctrine I have tried to trace as to the penalty, the guilt, and the communion, or want of communion, I am not afraid to trace out now what I believe to be the saddening condition that every man exists in to the last moment of his life on earth, and yet the glorious position we occupy in having such a perfect Saviour as God has made His Son Jesus Christ to be. The fact is, that if there were no sin in a man on earth, I hardly know how he is to take up Jesus every moment and to sing His praises every moment; he would not need to do so, in my belief. He would not be conscious of a perpetual belief in the precious fulness even of the justification doctrine, and the sanctification provision made in Jesus Christ our Lord.

In Romans 5 we find, "Where sin abounded, grace did much more abound; that as sin hath reigned unto death, even so might grace reign through righteousness unto eternal life by Jesus Christ our Lord." Now I am not proceeding or proposing to treat this subject in a general way, in which it would be taken as a great announcement of the justification truth which is supposed to be the close of this great judicial passage of the Epistle to the Romans; but I take the words in v. 20 in their pure assertion, "Where sin abounded, grace did much more abound"; and I want you to realise that sin abounds. Now, I believe that is contrary to many of our ideas. When we think of ourselves as pardoned sinners we fancy *sin* is put away as well as *sins*, and that from that moment we may begin to walk in perfect deliverance from any presence of evil. Are you prepared, as the Lord Jesus Christ has told us, to go to be judged? He is the kindest judge that ever lived; but he is also the most strict and stern that ever was known, and cannot abate one single jot or tittle of the law because you desire to escape from the exact standard that God puts before us. We are here to-night not be to judged by any human ideas, but by God's high standard. It is not what men think of themselves or deem to be kind, but what God deems, what the Holy Spirit deems: it is that judgment that I must accept.

With regard to sin, whether it is a new sin or the acts of a sinner before conversion, the principles laid down remain the same for one or the other. When we speak of sin, you are perfectly aware that it is the inclination of the child of God as well as of the sinner to lower God's standard to suit our own condition. We read in some writings that sin is only what we consciously commit or say against the law of God or the requirements of our Heavenly

Father. Is that to be our standard at a holiness convention? God forbid, I say, with all my soul. I say God forbid that we should ever accept a standard with regard to the subject of sin which lowers God's requirements and our own possibilities, or to our own conception of what God really demands. Let us take the Word of God in all its fulness, and know sin as God has traced it before us.

Let us pass on to some of the passages from Scripture. In I John 3: 4 we read these words: "Sin is the transgression of the law." Now, I suppose you do not admit as Christians that you have escaped from the law of God, or say that because you are saved you are not under the law, but under grace. The law is the expression of God's mind. The law of God is to be the delight of my soul. God has never changed the standard or altered the tone of the language. God has left the law what it always was— the actual expression of His mind and will; and, therefore, the law remains what it ever was. If you and I are under the Spirit, we bring forth fruit as far as God will enable us to bring it forth. In the first place, take the letter of the law and write that before your own souls, and ask whether you can, like the young man, say, "All these things I have kept." Thank God if you can. If you can say that you have kept the letter of the Ten Command-ments since you received sanctification, or since you came to a Keswick Convention. But what of the spirit of the law as Jesus enunciated it in Matthew 5, 6, 7—the look, the inward feeling of heart, these make adultery and murder; for those feelings that the Lord Jesus has declared to be actually as guilty as an open act of the hand. What shall we say in regard to it? Thank God if you can say—though I doubt if your tongue would dare to say the words—"All these have I kept according to the Spirit."

Go a step farther, and look at the tremendous expansion of the law. Go to Matthew 27: 32 and onward, and with St. Paul to Romans 13, on the doctrine of love—"Thou shalt love thy neighbour as thyself." Will any man say he has kept that law? And once more, add to this the new law, the new commandment the Lord Jesus gives in John 13: 34, "A new commandment I give unto you, that ye love one another; as I have loved you, that ye also love one another." Let us think of the meaning of that "as", and then to hear a man say, "I have kept that law"—"love one another as I have loved you." Let me ask you to realise that a transgression of the law is sin, and that if a man has failed for a single instant in loving me while I am speaking (and hurting your feelings, perhaps) as Jesus loves me, that man is a sinner. We never loved each other as the Lord Jesus Christ loves us all.

Turn to a sentence in 1 John 5: 17, "All unrighteousness is

sin." According to the Greek, the word means that everything that lacks the thoroughness and glory of the standard that God lifts up, is sin. What are we to say to this?—everything coming short of the perfection of God, is sin! "The soul that sinneth, it shall die." Go one step farther and look at the sins that may be committed by word. "By thy words," says our Lord in Matthew 12: 37, "thou shalt be justified, and by thy words thou shalt be condemned." And in the preceding verse God says, that "every idle word that men shall speak, they shall give an account thereof in the day of judgment." Now look at Proverbs 10: 19, "In the multitude of words there wanteth not sin." God does not change His standard because that is Proverbs and the other Matthew; God's Word remains the same in Proverbs as in Matthew, and you and I must put Proverbs and Matthew together and have wisdom to see that in a multitude of words there is sure to be sin, and that for every idle word I shall be brought to an account with God.

I would go a step further and ask, What about thoughts? Turn to 2 Corinthians 10: 5. There we are told to "bring into captivity every thought to the obedience of Christ." That is where some of my friends go wrong; they do not study their tenses in Greek sufficiently. Let us turn to Proverbs 24: 9. We are told that "the thought of foolishness is sin"; and remember that the soul that sinneth shall die. And that applies to God's saints exactly as much as to unsaved sinners, until we recognize the blessed truth I spoke of—perfect provision with regard to penalty, and perpetual provision with regard to guilt; that keeps the soul of man from perishing. Sinning is the same as being damned; so that we are perfectly right in saying that a child of God for one sin would pass to everlasting shame if it were not for the precious blood of the Lord Jesus Christ our Saviour.

Now with regard to other sins, we must take a general view of them. And what think you of such words as those in Proverbs 21: 4, where we read, "the plowing of the wicked is sin"—or "the light of the wicked," as it is in the margin? Then go to James 2: 9, "If ye have respect to persons"—I am speaking to the children of God who want to be honest—"If ye have respect to persons, ye commit sin." And what about those solemn words in James 4: 17, "Therefore to him that knoweth to do good, and doeth it not, to him it is sin"? We have read about our passions and our lusts, and there we have the negative side of sin. I remember being more struck with a remark upon sin than with almost anything for a long time—that sin was not so much a positive quantity as a negative one, and the negative side of sin is perhaps the most tremendous judgment of the people of God.

We read in John 16: 9, that the Holy Spirit convicts "of sin, because they believe not on me." That is not only for the world. Then such words as those in Romans 14: 23, "Whatsoever is not of faith is sin." And those words in James 3: 2, "For in many things we offend all."

Let us now take one or two texts affirming the general condition of mankind. In Proverbs 20: 9 we read, "Who can say, I have made my heart clean, I am pure from my sin?" Then go to Ecclesiastes 7: 20, where we read, "There is not a just man . . . that sinneth not." But what is perhaps the passage most solemnly declaratory of the meaning of God's Word is to be found in Job 4: 17, "Shall mortal man be more just than God? Shall a man be more pure than his Maker?" What are the alternative readings of that? "Shall mortal man be just before God? Shall any man be pure with his Maker?" But that, you say, is the Spirit's lips talking before Job. But St. Paul quotes Job 5: 13 in 1 Corinthians 3: 19. He quotes the words as coming from God, and says that God inspired his lips when he spoke those words. Then he says, in Job 4: 18, "Behold He putteth no trust in His servants, and His angels He charged with folly." Now the greatest authority upon Hebrew, Delitzch, informs us that in that passage God is speaking about His angels and servants, and that though not actually guilty of sin, yet their shortcoming in regard to holiness is such as to make them chargeable with folly in the sight of their perfectly holy Maker. I believe that Delitzch is right, as far as I can speak humbly on a matter of that kind.

Every word of God testifies to one fact, that there is not a perfectly just man upon earth; that even when he is just, it cannot be said that he "doeth good and sinneth not." And why? Because Job, the most perfect man we read of, is brought into the realisation of his true condition—of a man of whom it is affirmed, "that in all this he sinned not with his lips"; yet when this man comes before God, with the perfection of God before him, he says, "Behold, I am vile." Yet that is the man who would not let go his integrity, and of whom it was said that all things were bright and clear with him. He calls himself vile when he sees his God and recognises his own condition. If that be the state of a holy servant of God, such as Isaiah, or Ezekiel, or Jeremiah, or Peter, or John, when he comes to the vision of his living God, when they see their inherent corruption, shall we not acknowledge that sin hath abounded? It is abounding and must abound as long as man remains with the inherent principle of evil indwelling their mortal flesh, and they are subjected to the lusts and corruption during the time that we are in a state of probation. I am convinced that it is good for us to be subjected to the presence of evil here; not to be under the power of evil—but its presence, whether it be physical disease or spiritual corruption.

Now many of you will ask, why do I speak thus? Because I love the doctrines of grace, "that where sin abounds, grace doth much more abound." I mean by grace what I find in God's Word, and I have found that though it does not deliver me from the perpetual instigation and presence of evil, and the principle of sin, the indwelling natural tendency and taste which once came from Adam, and which, as I believe, remains somewhere in the being of man to the last; I say, though I do not believe in grace exactly as some do, yet I believe in it as I read it in God's holy Word, that while sin is always abounding, grace is infinitely more abounding: and to what end?

It is a solemn thing to speak of grace much more abounding. There are parallel truths and parallel texts to meet every word that I have spoken on the subject of sin. There are parallel texts to all that I have uttered which proclaim that though God does not remove that indwelling principle, or corrupt thing we call sin, yet He does by His infinite mercy give us a perfect, perpetual, and enjoyable deliverance from the activities, from the power, from the domination of sin, moment by moment, so long as we trust Him and acknowledge ourselves to be guilty sinners at every instant of our lives. I pause at that word, and reiterate it: while we acknowledge ourselves to be guilty sinners every moment, if we take the perfect standard here traced; yet we need never fear while we are doing nothing to offend against God's holy Word.

The doctrines of grace tell me that whatsoever sin hath done, Christ Jesus in His wondrous power hath more than undone with regard to the guilt and the penalty; it tells me that grace bringeth salvation. Look at Titus 2: 11, "The grace of God that bringeth salvation hath appeared to all men"—in the Revised Version it stands "unto all men"—"that denying ungodliness, we should live soberly, righteously, and godly in this present evil world." Then, brethren, what is grace to bring me? That I read with regard to the Lord Jesus Christ in John 1: 16, "Of His fulness have we all received, and grace for grace." Then in John 1: 17, "For the law was given by Moses, but grace and truth by Jesus Christ." And in Romans 5: 1, 2, with regard to the grace wherein we should stand. Then go to Ephesians 1: 7, 14, and 2: 7, where you will see references to the abundance of the riches of grace.

But more than this, what do I read about the daily provision for need up to the end of our lives? Turn to 2 Corinthians 9: 8, "And God is able to make all grace abound toward you; that ye, always having all sufficiency in all things, may abound to every good work," What do I read in 2 Corinthians 12: 9? "My grace is sufficient for thee." That is my much-loved text. It is that which first brought me to Keswick, and taught me the power of God's love. "My grace is sufficient for thee."

A friend said to me, "I thought you preached absolute deliverance from the principle of sin, eradication of the root of sin." I said, "God forbid." "Then," she said, "what is the difference?" My answer was, "You preach a perfect sinner; I preach a perfect Saviour." I thank God for a perfect Christ. Then one said to me, "If Christ was revealed to destroy the works of the devil, how can there be any sin left?" I replied, "Dear brother, do wait a bit; Christ's day is coming." The devil has had his day, and God's is coming. When God sees fit to take us away from this poor corrupt mortal flesh, corruption shall give place to glory, mortality to immortality, death to life and glory with God through all eternity. Saved by grace; kept by grace, when I ought to be condemned every moment for my folly; I shall be glorified by grace—and there shall be glory to God in the highest, and all through the realms of God's great universe, peace, joy, and gladness, for we shall be fully saved unto eternal glory when Christ comes. When we behold Him we shall be like Him, for we shall see Him as He is.

Oh, brethren, don't forget that while there is sin there is grace to meet all evil. O God, if this be true, make me to hate sin that gives Christ so much to do! Give me deliverance from all known sin. Reveal to me more and more what is the latent working and principle of sin. O God, open my eyes, show me more and more of Jesus. I will run the way of Thy commandments exactly so far as Thou in Thy mercy dost set my heart at liberty. Amen.

THE SIN OF HABITUAL UNBELIEF

Rev. A. T. Pierson, D.D.

WE HAVE designedly left to the last[1] the sin, folly, and crime of unbelief, partly because this great sin lies at the basis of every other; partly because it is the one sin that damns the soul; and partly because its removal means the relief of all other forms of spiritual difficulty.

If there were no unbelief, there would be no unsubdued sin, no unanswered prayer, and no persistent darkness. Yet the majority of people rank unbelief among the venial rather than the mortal sins; they apologise for it as at least a very trifling form of offence against God, and some even think of it as in some sense rather attractive because it implies humility of soul, the sense of one's own unworthiness. Many cannot claim God's promises because of such self-abasement. One of the master-snares of the devil is to inspire a mock humility in the place of a true humility. For while it is presumption to believe when God has not spoken, or to hope when He has not given us ground for hope, it is equally presumption not to believe when He has spoken, and not to hope when He gives a promise.

The key-text of this whole subject is Hebrews 3: 12, "Take heed, brethren, lest there be in any of you an evil heart of unbelief, in departing from the living God." The word *unbelief* carries quite a different sense from *disbelief*. Disbelief is properly a denial of truth; belief is the acceptance of truth. One who does not at all disbelieve, may be in everything unbelieving. I am quite aware that the word disbelieve is not found in either Testament, and that the word unbelief as translated is often, in the original, the equivalent of disbelief. But in the majority of cases unbelief does not carry the idea of denial of truth; and in at least one passage the distinction is manifestly drawn—1 Timothy 5: 8, where the apostle says of a certain offender against God that "he hath denied the faith, and is worse than an infidel"—which is not a clear translation, for the first word is emphatic, and the second is a weaker word. It might be translated, "hath denied the faith and is worse than an unbeliever," that is, he is a disbeliever, and has practically said "It is not so." He has affirmed the thing not to

---

[1] This address was the fourth of a series of Bible Readings.

be true; therefore he is worse than one who does not deny that it is true, but fails to make it available to himself—a very important distinction. Three different men may have one offer of blessing. One does not believe there is anything in it, that there is any real blessing offered. He is a disbeliever. Another believes that there is a blessing offered, but does not accept it for himself. He is an unbeliever. The third believes that there is a blessing offered, and he is bound to have it. That is a believer. You are to judge which you are.

There are two strongly contrasted facts. The first is, that man makes so little of the sin and crime of unbelief; and the second is, that God makes so much of it. It is one instance of the striking difference between God's judgment and man's judgment of things. The only way to show this is to examine the main passages of Scripture in which unbelief is brought to our attention, consecutively, from Genesis to Revelation. Turn, first, to Exodus 17. The people have come out of Egypt and have arrived at the wilderness of Sin—a typical place for an exhibition of the crime of unbelief—and they pitch in Rephidim. There is no water to drink, and now the people chide with Moses, and complain and murmur against the Lord, and even find fault with having been brought out of Egypt "to die in the wilderness with thirst." You remember how the Lord interposes to supply them with water from the smitten rock. Here is the remarkable verse, the 7th—the key to all that follows in the Bible—"And he called the name of the place *Massah*," which means *provocation* or, better still, *exasperation*, "because of the chiding of the children of Israel, and because they tempted the Lord." Notice, what was the temptation? The temptation was that God should forsake His people. What was the provocation? It was that God should destroy His people. Keep these two thoughts before you: the unbelief tempted God, on the one side, entirely to withdraw from His people, and, on the other side, finally to destroy them. What a terrific sin and crime unbelief must be, when it tempts and provokes God to such an extreme as that!

Notice, also—for it is most important: In what did this particular crime of unbelief, on this occasion, consist? They provoked and tempted the Lord, saying, "Is the Lord among us, or not?" That was as much as saying, "Is the Lord dead, or is He living? He has promised to go with us from Egypt to Canaan; is He true to His word, or is He a changeable God?" At one time, when a great anti-slavery orator in America, in the crisis of affairs, was finding fault with God for allowing slavery to be continued in America so long, a poor old coloured slave rose in the meeting and said, "Mr. Douglas, answer me this question: Do you think that God is dead?" A singular rebuke from a poor, ignorant coloured woman. She was enduring slavery with the confidence that God was not dead, and that a time of retribution and deliverance would come. And here the children of Israel, just brought out of Egypt with a strong hand and mighty arm, with tremendous judgments on the Egyptians and deliverances for themselves, no more than got to Rephidim than they said, "Is the Lord among us or not?"

Notice, also, the provocation. This was a want of water; and two of the greatest miracles already performed on their behalf had been miracles with water. When they went over the Red Sea, God piled up the waters as a wall; and then He let down the wall on the pursuing Egyptians. And when His people came to Marah, where the water was bitter and they could not drink, He showed them a tree which, being dipped in the waters, turned them to sweet, refreshing draughts. Yet they forgot all about His deliverances. When they come to the third trouble about water, all the memory of the previous dealings with God was cast into oblivion, and they said, "Is the Lord among us, or not?"

Turn now to Numbers 14. There we are just at the crisis of affairs. The people have come to Kadesh-Barnea, so far on the borders of the land of promise that to this day we are not quite sure whether it was not inside the limits of the land. God had "brought them out to bring them in." They were not at the starting-point now; they were rather at the goal; and, if they had been believing, they might have entered at once into possession of that land, and saved themselves the other thirty-nine years of journey in the wilderness, and leaving their own carcases by the wilderness way. They sent spies into the land, and the spies all came back and told the same story—that it was an attractive land, flowing with milk and honey, where the giant Anakim dwelt, with their walled cities and chariots of iron. It is sometimes said that ten spies brought a false report, and two spies a true report. That is a mistake. They all brought the same report, so far as the land was concerned; but that in which Caleb and Joshua differed from the other spies was this: they besought the people in faith to go up and possess the land, to take sides with God and defy those foes; and the other ten admitted the fertility of the land, but advised them not to attempt to cope with the giants. And because Caleb and Joshua had not only set an example of belief in God, but urged all others to believe, the people were going to stone them to death—and would have done so, but for the voice that spoke out of the pillar of cloud. Look at what unbelief can do. Not only did it prompt the people to rebel against God, and refuse His promised possession, and halt on the very borders of the

land, to which He had brought them with such wonderful inter-
position; but it made them ready to stone those who urged them
to the career and conduct of faith. A most marvellous exhibition!

Now see what God says: "Because all those men which have
seen my glory, and my miracles which I did in Egypt and in the
wilderness, have tempted me now *these ten times*, and have not
hearkened to my voice; surely they shall not see the land which
I sware unto their fathers, neither shall any of them that provoked
me see it: but my servant Caleb, because he had another spirit
with him, and hath followed me fully, him will I bring into the
land whereinto he went; and his seed shall possess it." And
not only did his seed possess the land, but the inheritance of Caleb
was the very stronghold of the Anakim; and when he was past
eighty years of age, he still retained his pristine youthful vigour to
drive out those Anakim and take possession of their fortress.
Most remarkable! But every other man that came out of Egypt,
of an age to bear arms, except these two, fell in the wilderness,
so that the entire wilderness way was lined with a double row
of graves, from Sinai to the Jordan. If you will calculate the number of deaths in the wilderness, you will see that they would be
sufficient to line that way on both sides with corpses; and all
because of the sin and folly, insult and outrage of unbelief. The
"ten times" is not simply a chance number used by way of com-
pleteness. This was the tenth occasion on which the people had
tempted and provoked God—at the Red Sea, in fear of the foe;
at Marah, as to the bitter water; in the wilderness of Sin, as to
food; in the gathering of manna on the Sabbath—which they were
forbidden to do—because they did not believe in the providence
of God; at Rephidim, in their complaint of the lack of water; at
Sinai, in setting up a calf as a kind of visible object of worship;
in the cursing by the son of Shelomith, recorded in Leviticus 24;
in their lusting for flesh at Kibroth-hattaavah (*i.e.* the graves of
lust); in the report of Aaron and Miriam against Moses; and in
the panic at Kadesh-Barnea.

Turn now to Isaiah 7: 9. It is only a sentence, but it belongs
to the history of this tremendous crime of unbelief. Isaiah is
bidden to say to Ahaz, on behalf of God, "If ye will not believe,
surely ye shall not be established." One hundred and thirty years
later, Jehoshaphat repeated this to Judah and the inhabitants
of Jerusalem at a crisis of peril—only then he used the positive
form instead of the negative: "Believe, and ye shall be established."
Now, whenever God sets a particular text in the Bible in a peculiar
and unique form of rhythm or rhyme, or a play upon words, He
means that it shall stand out conspicuously. This verse is not
translatable from the Hebrew: it has a rhythm and a rhyme about

it that cannot be easily reproduced. I have tried to reproduce it, but with very little success, in this little couplet—

> If in God ye do not confide,
> Surely in power ye shall not abide.

That comes near to it. Or—

> Surely, if ye will not believe
> Neither blessing shall ye receive.

There is something very striking in the Hebrew of this passage, which shows that God means it to stand out in this prophecy of Isaiah as a permanent lesson to His Church: that an unbelieving soul forfeits blessing, and makes confirmation in holiness, and a further knowledge and enjoyment of God's presence, impossible.

Let us go back to Psalm 78. This psalm is called Asaph's parable: that is to say, it treats the entire history, from Egypt to Canaan, as a parable designed to teach a great lesson. The whole of that career is reviewed, and the main emphasis of this entire psalm is on this temptation, this provocation, this forgetfulness of God, this not believing God, this not remembering God, which constitute such atrocious treatment of Him. You will find, for instance, four times in this psalm, "They provoked the Most High"; three times, "They tempted Him"; once, "They grieved Him"; and over and over again such expressions as these: "They believed not God," "They trusted not in His salvation," "They tempted and provoked the Most High God," "They provoked Him to anger with their high places, and moved Him to jealousy with their graven images."

Read the psalm, and interpret in the light of this parable the whole story that occupies Exodus, Leviticus, Numbers, and Deuteronomy—four books of the Old Testament given to this amazing exhibition of persistent and habitual unbelief toward God, until, under Joshua, they entered into the land of promise, still to repeat their crime and sin of unbelief, until they were finally rejected. Notice in the heart of the psalm that most significant expression, "Yea, they turned back and tempted God, and limited the Holy One of Israel" (v. 41). You say, "There can be no limitation of Omnipotence." Surely there can be. There are two spheres of power—the physical, and the moral. In the physical sphere nothing is needed but energy. But in the moral sphere everything depends upon co-operation. God can do anything in the physical sphere that lies within the bounds of physical power, because He has omnipotent energy. But in the moral sphere, God can do nothing that is not consistent with the co-operation of His moral subjects.

We must look at this: it is most important. If I go along the street and see a man lying in the gutter drunk, I can by physical energy lift him up and carry him home. But I cannot, by physical energy, make that drunkard a sober man, a total abstainer. There has to come in moral suasion and persuasion, the influence of moral force; there must be co-operation. And so Fenelon used to say—and it is a philosophic saying—"In matters of morals, force is a mistake. Force can never persuade. The only thing that force can do is to compel, and that makes hypocrites." It is a remarkable saying, and I pray you, remember it. In the moral sphere of power there must always be co-operation: God scorns to treat human beings as machines. He never made an intelligent being that had not power to sin if he chose; otherwise obedience would be mechanical, artificial, compulsory. The very fact that sin has entered the universe, in the angelic and human realms, shows that both angels and men were made in the image of God, with the capacity for independent moral action.

It is a tremendous thought that even God Himself cannot control my moral frame, or constrain my moral choice. He cannot prevent me from defying Him and denying Him. He would not exercise His power in such directions if He could, and He could not if He would. Is it not an awful fact that there are some matters in which we may limit God? And in so far as we limit Him, we limit ourselves. "Jesus could do no mighty works in Nazareth," where He was brought up, "because of their unbelief." Until you can get out of your way the mountain of unbelief in your own soul, you cannot remove the mountain of unbelief in others who reject your Master. You have got to get the unbelief out of your own soul first, and then you can do mighty works for God.

Turn to Luke 1. Here is recorded one of the most striking cases of unbelief in the whole New Testament. Zacharias was a remarkable man—one of the few of whom it is written that he was "righteous before God, walking in all the commandments and ordinances of the Lord blameless." He is wearing the robes of a priest; he is before the altar of incense, which stood for prayer and supplication, and acceptable offering and worship. Right there in the administration of the duties of his course, in the peculiar and consecrated garments of his priestly office, while engaged in the solemn service of the offering up of incense, God sends to him His own glorious angel, not only to tell him that his prayer is heard, and that Elizabeth, his wife, shall bear a son, but to make un-mistakable His message by giving him in the three verses that follow, an outline of the entire career of John the Baptist. Yet Zacharias, the priest, the praying man, in the office of his course, notwithstanding his righteousness and blamelessness before God, has the arrogance and impudence to ask, "Whereby shall I know this?" as if there were needed any confirmatory sign of God's emphatic promise when announced to him under these circumstances! Then there came upon him a typical judgment. He was, no doubt, from that moment a deaf-mute—not only speechless, but deaf, for you will observe, in the next chapter, how they did not speak to him, but communicated with him through a writing-tablet; which shows that he was a deaf-mute, stone deaf and absolutely unable to speak even in a whisper.

What does that suggest? That unbelief shuts your ear to God, and shuts your mouth to men. The prevalence of unbelief on your part may make you deaf to further communication from God, and absolutely worthless in your testimony to men—a paralysis of your hearing, and a paralysis of your tongue. There are scores of disciples to-day who cannot hear plainly what God speaks, because of a habitual unbelief; and their testimony also has been wrecked. They have nothing to say; they cannot witness, "God has done this for me," because they have not put Him to the test; they have no testimony for their sorrowing and distressed fellow-human-beings, because of their own position of unbelief before God.

Turn to Hebrews 3: 7—4: 11. This whole section of this Epistle is a New Testament review, a parable of that same desert journey treated in Psalm 78. Never study that story in Exodus, Leviticus, Numbers, and Deuteronomy, without putting over alongside of it this remarkable passage in Hebrews. God has given us here an inspired explanation, interpretation, and application of the whole story of the Israelites in the desert. Here again we meet these two awful words referred to already in Exodus 17, temptation and provocation, over and over again. "Some when they had heard, did provoke"; "Take heed, lest there be in any of you an evil heart of unbelief, in departing from the living God"; "To-day, if ye will hear His voice, harden not your hearts, as in the provocation." Study the whole passage, and see how we are taught here, that all those men who left their carcases in the wilderness fell simply through unbelief: and you may leave your carcases in the wilderness if you do not give up the crime and sin of your unbelief. It does not say that you will be finally lost. You may get into heaven as by a back door; but your present rest in this life, for which, I believe, Canaan stands—spiritual liberty and fertility, constant communion with God, abiding in His presence, victory over the enemy—all these things, together with "the peace of

God that passeth all understanding," you may permanently for-
feit, so far as your present life is concerned, simply by the crime of
unbelief.

Turn to Hebrews 6: 6, "Seeing they crucify to themselves the
Son of God afresh, and put Him to an open shame." Compare
Hebrews 10: 29, "Who hath trodden under foot the Son of God,
and hath counted the blood of the covenant, wherewith he was
sanctified, an unholy thing, and hath done despite unto the Spirit
of grace." Both of these passages are essentially an arraignment
of unbelief, in that highest form of crime of which unbelief is
capable. This demands most careful attention, lest we fail to
realise the awful criminality of unbelief.

There are three things that unbelief makes void. First, it makes
void the Word of God. It were as well that God had not spoken to
you and emphasised His promises by such universal terms and
such repetitious forms of statement, if you do not believe His
promises and take and appropriate them as the basis of your faith
and life. This is just as plain as it can be. Of what use are all the
thousands of years of preparation of this Bible, if God's Word does
not become to you personally the basis of your whole trust and
conduct!

Then unbelief also makes void the sacrifice of Jesus Christ. God
gave His only Son a sacrifice for the world; He gave all He had,
He gave at infinite cost, for an infinite ransom was paid. If you
reject Jesus Christ, or fail to make Him your Saviour, it is for you
as though God had not given Christ, and Christ had not died.
This stupendous sacrifice on the part of God you are virtually
flinging away as nothing. We can never appreciate the tremendous
guilt of unbelief if we do not see that thus it crucifies the Son of
God afresh. That is to say, it is as though you crucified Him for
nothing, and put Him to an open shame without any reward for
His sufferings; and, instead of sprinkling the blood on each side of
the door-post, and above the head, as your protection, you are
pouring it out on the threshold and trampling it under foot;
instead of taking shelter under it, you are treating it with contempt.
What an arraignment of unbelief!

More than this, you are doing despite to the Spirit of grace.
There was a probation of law. God said to Adam, "This do, and
thou shalt live." But Adam failed in his probation of law, and the
chance of such probation for ever passed away from the human
race. There can never be a second probation of law, for law must
always regard you as a transgressor. God therefore gave a new
probation of grace. He put His Son before you on the Cross and
said, "You have only to believe in Him, and your sins shall not be
mentioned to you." And so He pretermits your offences—

Romans 3: 25, margin. What is pretermission? It is more than remission. Pretermission is passing by, through divine forbearance. You sin. God passes your sin by. You sin again, and in ten thousand forms. He passes them all by; He puts them behind His back, for the time, to see how you are going to deal with His Son. This is your probation of grace. If you accept His Son, He never returns to those sins; they are swallowed up in oblivion by virtue of the atoning blood. But if you reject His Son, He is compelled, as governmental Judge, to take up every one of those sins that He has pretermitted for the time being, and deal with them in legal justice, giving every transgression its just recompense of reward; and ending up by dealing with you for that greatest of sins, the rejection of Christ, with the offer of pardon—the rejection of the Atonement.

And so, unbelief not only crucifies the Son of God afresh, and puts Him to an open shame, trampling under foot the blood that should have been put on the door-posts on each side, and overhead; but it makes the dispensation of grace by the Holy Ghost absolutely void, nay, worse than void; for the grace that, instead of saying, "This do and thou shalt live," says, "This believe, and thou shalt live," goes for nothing, and worse than nothing, only adding to the condemnation of the transgressor. It needs the tongue of an angel to do justice to this theme. But it is an awful fact that men consider unbelief a trifling sin against God, while it is the one damning sin, the one sin that, if persisted in, has no forgiveness, because it forfeits forgiveness and rejects the Atonement.

We are now prepared to understand why, in Revelation 21: 8, we find in that fearful catalogue of sin and crime against God, unbelief put alongside of the most flagrant iniquity: "But the fearful, and unbelieving, and the abominable, and murderers, and whoremongers, and sorcerers, and idolaters, and all liars, shall have their part in the lake which burneth with fire and brimstone: which is the second death." Observe, and do not forget it!—the same condemnation that awaits the abominable, the murderers, the whoremongers, the sorcerers, the idolaters, is reserved also for the unbelieving. Do not ever think of unbelief as a trivial sin, when God puts it in such an awful category of crime.

Let us review this terrible indictment and argument. Unbelief limits the power of God, and limits the power of man; unbelief paralyses testimony, and makes us deaf to the voice of God; unbelief is a permanent forfeiture of blessing, as when Esau bartered his birthright for a mess of pottage, and could not get back what he had sold, at any price whatsoever. You may lose your life's opportunities and privileges, and even God cannot give them back; for He cannot restore the lost hour, the wasted year, the mis-spent life. What unbelief has forfeited, no power can give back. He may restore the years that the palmer-worm, the locust, the canker-worm and the caterpillar have destroyed, by an extra-abundant harvest to the famished land; but He can never give such compensating abundance to the famished life of an unbelieving soul. If you have lost your time of sowing, you cannot make up for it in your time of reaping; if you have lost your chance of confiding and trusting, you cannot make up for it in the repentance of a dying bed. God gives life, with all its capacities, talents, opportunities and privileges, for service. If it is invested for self, it can never be got back to invest for God; if it is lost through unbelief, it can never be got back by a final act of faith.

The question is, What are you going to do with your life? Unbelief virtually makes void the Word of God, the sacrifice of Christ, and the dispensation and work of the Holy Ghost; and therefore unbelief is represented in the Bible as the one and only thing that exasperates God. That is not too strong a word with which to translate the original. Exasperation means to rub into roughness. The original is a remarkable word, which can hardly be translated by any other term. The idea is that the very grace of God is perverted into opposition and roughness by an unbelieving soul; that even infinite forbearance has a limit, and this limit is reached in unbelief. God is not so much exasperated by the transgression of every command of the Decalogue, as He is by the one form of sin found in the rejection of His promises in the Word, of His sacrifice in His Son, and of His pleading and tenderness in His Spirit.

There is but one thing to do with unbelief: for ever abandon it! Whatever else you do, solemnly covenant with God that you will believe His Word, trust His Son, yield to His Spirit; that you will step out upon His promises, and dare to venture something for His sake, without regard to feeling; and with single-hearted resting upon His immutable Word. The French translation of Hebrews 10: 23 is, "He who hath made a promise, can keep His promise." To do that is faith! Do not look at surroundings, do not ask for signs or wait for further evidence, but walk right out on the divine promise—trust it absolutely, for the subduing of sin, for the answering of prayer, for the dispersion of darkness; and the triumph of faith will also be the victory over sin, the triumph of prayer, the emergence of the soul out of darkness into the conscious light of God!

THE "TOTAL ABSTINENCE" OF THE GOSPEL

Rev. Handley C. G. Moule, M.A.

I therefore, the prisoner of the Lord, beseech you that ye walk worthy of the vocation wherewith ye are called, with all lowliness and meekness, with longsuffering, forbearing one another in love . . . Let all bitterness, and wrath, and anger, and clamour, and evil speaking, be put away from you, with all malice: and be ye kind one to another, tender-hearted, forgiving one another, even as God for Christ's sake hath forgiven you—Ephesians 4: 1, 2; 31, 32.

THE two subjects suggested by the two limbs of this quotation are very simple and homely, but I think they go straight to the needs both of conviction and of comfort of many Christians whose hearts are really toward the Lord. Observe the connection of the first verses. The apostle has, in the first half of the Epistle, led us up to the heights of heaven and back to the depths of eternity, and on to the eternity to be. I will not sketch to you the marvellous contents of the first three chapters of the Ephesians. Now, instructive it is to see that straight from the glories of the third chapter the apostle comes, in the fourth chapter, as his first deep inference from it all, to what?—to lowliness, meekness, longsuffering, and a very humbling word when we think of the things which occasion the need of it—to the forbearing one another in love. Let us take that precious word to ourselves. It speaks, I think, often of deep humiliation to spiritual Christians; but God's humiliations are never discouragements, if they are taken in the light of His life and of His love. This teaches us, then, that the first, deepest, and most genuine inference in practical life, from the reception of the very highest range of eternal truths, is an inference which runs along the ground; an inference which comes down upon the stones and the dust of the common path; an inference which, so far from lifting a Christian off his feet, gives a double watchfulness, an infinitely augmented watchfulness, to his goings in respect of humiliation and humility. Never let us get away from that point. The Gospel never lifts you off your feet in this sense, though if you throw your weight upon the Lord you shall "mount up with wings" in another sense.

I wish, however, to draw most attention to the last two verses of the chapter, to their very simple yet profound lesson on the "Total Abstinence" of the Gospel. We have too much confined these two words to one branch of philanthropic effort. They are as wide and as deep as the dealing of the whole Gospel of the grace of God with the daily and hourly work of His people. It has sometimes been said, mistakenly, that those who earnestly caution the Christian against false inferences from divine promises —as though danger within were to be forgotten as well as temptation without—are guilty of "allowing a little sin." I hope that may never be *truly* said of our moral, spiritual theory, and of our moral, spiritual daily purpose and aim in the presence of the Lord. *Total* abstinence is the watchword of the Gospel about all sinning on the Christian's part; and, true to the divine practicality of the Gospel, it loves to press this totality just where we may perhaps be most easily tempted to forget it: not concerning some great thing; not concerning the absence, for instance, of all murmuring when some crushing lightning stroke falls upon our lives; the absence of all fear when some imagined martyrdom calls us out to the fire; but concerning the little things of the present day; concerning the feelings in general in our hearts at this hour concerning other people, and the manifestation of those feelings in the little, tiny things, which in their millions make up life.

Let us remember this. What does the apostle say to those immeasurably privileged believers in Ephesus and in Asia? "Let all bitterness, and wrath, and anger, and clamour, and evil-speaking, be put away from you, with all malice; and be ye kind to one another, tender-hearted, forgiving one another." The apostle assumes—and how humiliating, but how gracious the assumption is—the necessity of these things all along. "Forgiving one another, even as God for Christ's sake hath forgiven you." Now, dear friends, my few and simple words shall take their whole text from that word "*all*," prefixed to that almost unimaginative list of sins. You remember that striking passage in the first Epistle of St. John, where he says we ought to lay down our lives for the brethren, and that in the very next verse he goes on to question the love of God in one who sees a poor, needy one, without assisting him. I think the apostle means something very special by the collocation of these two verses. There is a poetic glamour in the idea of a tremendous trial; but is there no risk of being caught in the midst of such imaginations by some little trial of our temper; some little request for unexpected troubletaking; and of finding this a little too much? But the apostle means that the two things are of a piece. If you want to be on the road to glorify God in the high place of the field, you ought to begin now with the very small thing at your feet, to do it in the Lord's Spirit and in the Lord's strength, totally abstaining from the opposite.

Now may I—always wishing to hit myself first and hardest—may I just say—God knows it is with self-humiliation—that I think in this divinely-chosen list of total abstinences, the apostle tells of many and many a point which is often found to be weak in those who know the Lord and love Him, and have surrendered with honest purpose their life to Him, and are in a true, deep sense, true-hearted for Him, and are really working for Him. Yes, I think we must own that these things are not unknown in the inmost circles of the Christian world. There is a tendency not unknown there to religious gossip. There is such a thing as the easy, willing, talking over of other people's characters and work. Is there no such thing as a certain relish sometimes felt when, it may be, someone we have disagreed with in Christian doctrine is caught a little tripping in Christian practice? and our pleasure —I will honestly call the thing *pleasure*—is not because here is a vindication of the need of watchfulness over divine truth, but because here is that dear and precious thing, "my opinion" vindicated to myself. Oh! it is one thing to think sorrowfully, prayerfully, reservedly, over the errors of beloved and honoured friends and brethren in Christ, because of the truth of God and the cause of God; and it is another thing to think of them and talk of them in an easy way. Is there no such thing, again, as a jealousy for our own work, cause, and reputation, which does not make it always altogether pleasant to hear of the marked success granted to someone, or another Christian organisation or of another school of opinion, or, perhaps, to someone not divided from us by any such lines, but by that great demarcation that it is not "number one"? Is there no such thing as that? I think there are tendencies to it, which only the grace of God can counteract, in every heart that beats.

Is there no such thing as trifling—subtle trifling, very minute and microscopic perhaps, but real—with absolute straight-forwardness and truth? Nothing can possibly be holy that is not perfectly fair, that is not perfectly true to known fact, that is not perfectly straightforward as well as pious in its purpose. Deep in the foundations of all that is good, the Bible puts down truth in the inward parts. The least shadow of a shade of a pious fraud is black iniquity in the sight of God. The least conscious, or what might be conscious, exaggeration of fact—for instance, of spiritual success granted to ourselves or to our agency—is dark iniquity in the sight of God, who requireth truth in the inward parts. And what is close akin to this is—and, believe me, I say it out of the depth of personal humiliation—the least unwillingness to be brought to book about our own failures, is dark iniquity in the sight of God. I do not know anything more likely to cause whatever resembles grief in the Eternal Friend than to see a soul that He loves entrenching itself behind some spiritual theory—it may be theories very different from one another—against the plain, downright duty of saying, in this or in that, "I have done wrong." There is a great danger of our doing it. I know it. I speak from the depth of my own soul, and I think also from a large consensus of human experience, and from the witness of this Book. We have been told blessed, because intensely searching, things today and yesterday, about that breaking down which is the prelude, ah! and the accompaniment, too, to blessing. Let us take heed, dear friends, that the Lord never finds us, and our neighbour never finds us thus entrenching ourselves behind any position conceivable when in some matter of plain duty—of kindness, of carefulness about our words, of charity in tone and temper—we are found unwilling to say, "Yes; I see it. I am utterly ashamed of it. I need not have done it; but it is done, and now, now at once, must go upon the Lord's head for pardon, and beneath the Lord's feet for victory."

Is there no such thing, again, as an irreverence about God's name and presence creeping into our deepest hours of devotion? I have never forgotten what I once read in a remarkable old book—Jonathan Edwards' account of the great revival at Northampton, in New England, when I suppose the nearest approach to a converted town ever known in the Christian world, was seen. The manifestations of divine grace and holiness were marvellous; but he says, describing the case he selects because of its peculiar spiritual wonders, "I have seen that person crushed under the sense of the sin involved in one mention of the name of God with inadequate reverence." We cannot be too anxious or too watchful when we are speaking of God or addressing Him. There is sin in a carelessly-worded prayer before the majesty of heaven. Sure I am—it is as deep as the depths of divine truth—we cannot afford to let things go loose in this matter of reverence.

Shall I speak, again, of the iniquity of unthrift of time, that mysterious talent which, unlike others, is spent and gone? God gives us other gifts: gifts of body, mind, or whatever it may be, to spend and have; but He gives us the talent of time, and we spend it, and it is gone. How do we use it? I do not say, let us use it with a weary, restless, miserable, divided anxiety, which will only be greater the further we live from the Master. But I do say, let it always be remembered that we and our time are in His hand; and whether it is for perfect rest, or whether it is for exhausting work, it and we alike belong to Him, and only in our "belongingness" are we free and are we safe.

There is need, too, to speak of the neglect of absolutely secret communion with God, for which we must never substitute not only the holy ordinances of the sanctuary or sacred occasions like this, but even the inmost intercourse of a chosen circle of Christian friends. Nothing must take the place of the solitary study of the Word of God, of the solitary opening of the soul to Him in prayer, where there is not even the temptation to let the experience or attitude of others deflect our consciousness of our own.

So, dear friends, I could touch upon point after point, but it is better just to remember again the brief, deep catalogue of the apostle, which excludes the least swelling of internal irritation as much as it excludes the most demonstrative expression of un-governed anger; which excludes the least spur of impure imagina-tion as much as it excludes the act of the adulterer. Yes; it is total abstinence. And the words would be words of despair without that divine, ancient truth, which we are met in these days to accentuate to ourselves. We never forget that there are other sides of truth, any more than we forget there is another side to the mountain yonder, and we see there is by the perspective of *this* side. There are thousands of other sides to the infinite truth as it is in Christ; but our business this week is to accentuate two aspects of one great truth—the truth of personal, practical holiness as regards our need and as regards Christ's supply.

And now let us remember that for this total abstinence there is stored up in Him divine sufficiency. Yes, and we are in Him. The feeblest believer in this tent is in Jesus Christ, and Jesus Christ in the eternal covenant is in him. What we want is to turn the fact into practical realisation; it is to turn what we have into what we use; it is to turn what we know into what we are. Look then, look off, look in, unto the Lord! I will not think of the infinities of my need, except to lead me to the divine simplicity of the infinity of His supply. We are in Him; we derive it from Him. It is not manufactured within; it is derived from above; and it is derived in that most wonderful way—the em-bosoming of Jesus Christ in the very hearts of His own, by faith and by the Spirit; so that we may say, with perfect sobriety, with daylight reality, and with a keen consciousness of the practical aspects of human life—yes, the Scripture does bid me abstain from the whole of this or that besetting sin, which I see now and did not see yesterday, or which I have long seen and thought I might allow a little of; but I know how to deal with it now. I know what it is to lay the whole of it upon my Lord's head, and the whole of it beneath my Lord's feet, and, without over-anticipations of the future, to know that for the next step He is able to keep me from stumbling as well as hereafter, as He will, to present me faultless with exceeding joy.

THE VISION OF GOD

Rev. John Smith, D.D.

ONE thing has deeply impressed me at this Convention. I have never been present on any occasion on which it seems to me that every address, from its own point of view, bore in more directly upon individual need, and had for its one end the lifting of individual souls into liberty and power. It is my deepest desire to maintain that attitude and that aim in whatever I may be enabled to say tonight.

I wish to look not so much at the personal joy, the individual satisfaction, the comfort, the liberty that we may have; I wish to look beyond that—although, of course, we include that—to the great work of witness to which, as children of God, we are called. We are not our own: we are bought with a price, that we may glorify God in our bodies and in our spirits, which are God's.

Let me ask you, Did you ever notice the wonderful connection between chapter 5 and chapter 6 of Isaiah? I believe you will get a light of a most remarkable kind upon chapter 6 from chapter 5. We are being told in this age that the prophets were, first of all, preachers of righteousness. I believe that to be true. In their own day, and to the people of their own time, they brought down the flashing holy will of God and bore it in upon the minds and hearts of men. In chapter 5 we have Isaiah as a preacher of righteousness, Isaiah diagnosing the moral and religious situation in Judah. I do not wish to use the language of exaggeration, because God is not served by the exaggeration of men, but I am filled with admiration—nay, that is not the word—I am filled with awe at the marvellous searchlight thrown upon individual and national life in this 5th chapter. We have here the six signs of national decadence—great universal principles which were manifested at that time in the history of Judah, and have been manifested whenever a nation or a people have been untrue to their calling, and have fallen away under the blighting power of evil. Let me in a word bring out these six woes.

The first sign of national decadence is *the inordinate love of wealth*. "Woe unto them that join house to house, that lay field to field." After all, wealth is a poor talent. A man can eat only one dinner in a day, and wear only one coat at a time. When men are filled with an inordinate desire for wealth, what can they do with it? They can only throw the reins on the neck of their passions and let them drive.

So you have, secondly, the inordinate *love of pleasure*. This and the other great sign which I have just mentioned, manifest and set the fashion of the people.

Thirdly, there are those who have *lost the ideal*, and the high meaning of life; who mock at God, at duty, at conscience; who say, "When will God manifest Himself?" and who throw themselves into light, and trivial, and worldly, and unworthy occupations, "drawing iniquity with cords of vanity, and sin with a cart-rope."

Then there is this fourth sign. Oh, take these words when you go home and sit down as in the presence of God and study them, each one; this is the light of God upon a nation that is falling away from Him. There are wise men with strong intellects and vivid individualities who must form a theory of this universe, who must think out their own view of existence. But, alas! they are so full of worldliness and the love of pleasure, that this ingenuity of their brain is manifested in calling sweet bitter, and bitter sweet; in putting erroneous meanings upon those great problems of life, and writing out their base pessimisms in the face of God.

Fifthly, there is a darker feature still, a more terrible manifestation of the spirit of evil working in individuals and working in nations—when men have become so completely their own masters that they do not want to have any theory. Their will is sufficient. That *towering egoism* of a Herod which makes his own pleasure, and the satisfaction of his own desires his all-sufficient end, is theirs, and they seem to live as if there was no consciousness of God or of obligation to Him.

Last of all, there is *corruption in the seat of government*: the very regulating forces of society are corrupt to the core, men giving injustice for a bribe.

I might apply all this to our own time, but that is not our subject. There is the vision that God gave Isaiah of the country in which he lived, of the people among whom he dwelt, and of their awful declension. And what made the matter far worse was this: they were a chosen people. God had lifted them above all other nations. He had fenced them round about, and He had planted them as a vineyard that they might bring forth fruit to Him; to be His witnesses to, and exert a moral influence through, the whole world of that early day. Not only had they failed to realise this ideal, but falling further still, they had gone down those deeps of moral degeneracy.

I can fancy Isaiah saying to himself, "Why has God permitted this vision of moral corruption to break upon my spirit?" But if you read back into those earlier chapters you will find that while his soul is crushed under this sense of the terrible corruption of Israel, he realises that there is a purpose of mercy in God's heart. It is not to show that in vengeance He might obliterate this people from the face of the earth, that God is causing their sins to break out in blasting enormity before Isaiah's vision; but God is coming in, in a new and glorious purpose of mercy. These were the great thoughts burning in this man's heart. This was the problem that Isaiah faced. This was the work that he had to do. We are in our day greatly taken up with a wide, humane and national view of the moral and spiritual problems presented in the condition of things in England, Scotland and Ireland. We are all being drawn out by God to look at things in this broader aspect, to look at even the great master-question of evangelisation in this wider aspect of national degeneracy and national declension.

Now Isaiah is in the beginning of his career, and what preparation does God give him? It is here that I come into chapter 6 from chapter 5. What preparation does God give this man that he might be a prophet to his generation, and speak the word of God to that great nation; that he might bring down the light and fire of God into the heart of that degenerate people? Do you know what people say about Keswick? They say it is unworldly, that we are going away from the actual problems of life, that we are not facing the burning questions of the day, that we are leaving them aside, that we are going into the wilderness to nurse a mystic meditation that is as unreal as it is futile. Now, "to the law and to the testimony." On this platform and in face of these great issues, we will listen to God and not to man.

Where did God bring that burdened man, that kingly soul—if ever there was a kingly soul on earth—Isaiah, bearing the burden of his nation's destiny, and surrendered even already, although a full consecration had not come, to the service of his people? I want you to realise this: He brought him under the shadow of God, under the shadow of the Eternal. "In the year that King Uzziah died" he saw the Lord, and His train filled the temple. There the glory of God broke upon his vision in over-powering majesty. Do you know the most hopeless feature of the present day? It is that we are so full of ourselves—I mean reformers, the men burning with a great passion for the highest good of the people. Their weakness is this: they are so full of themselves, and their own plans, and their own standpoints; everything is looked at from an earthly foundation, and they have no vision of God. Oh, let us come under the shadow of God! We have come here for that, and if anything has been wrought in many a heart during this Convention, it has brought a new sense of God. I do not know how you feel, but there is nothing that fills my soul with deeper anxiety—that is too strong a word; one should not be anxious, for God is at the helm—the one thing that fills my soul with gravest concern is a denudation of the sense of God. It seems as if the very soul of religious reverence is being washed from the minds of men. Even many of God's people take care to have just as much religion as will give them comfort and harmonise the discords of their life; but their horizons are the horizons of time, they are bounded by the present. Oh, there is an overshadowing, overwhelming vision of God; and if ever we are going to settle these social problems and bring people to the feet of Jesus Christ—great multitudes of them—we must get away from all these earthly standpoints, we must get under the shadow of God, we must feel the overmastering glory and majesty of the Most High—that "the nations are as a drop of a bucket"; that "He taketh up the isles as a very little thing." I shall not dwell upon that.

But God lets Isaiah see the world in which He lives. We are all so much taken up with our own world that we do not think there is another world, a far vaster world than ours, of which our world is only just an appendix at the outskirts of it. The great centre of the universe is the throne of God, and round Him are angels and archangels, thrones and dominions, principalities and powers; and God is living in the midst of this glorious universe, and in this universe they have a light of their own, and a vision of their own, and a conception of their own. The prophet lets us have a glimpse into the glory, and he gives us to understand what they are thinking about up there, regarding the world down here.

Now I bring you to what I consider to be the most striking contrast within the pages of God's revelation. I have already referred to Isaiah 5. Just take one verse. "He looked for judgment, but behold oppression; for righteousness, and behold a cry." There is his judgment of things as he sees them; but the prophet is now looking away up into the face of God, and he hears the seraphim sing, and they say, "Holy! Holy! Holy! Lord God Almighty!" Here is the contrast, the marvel and mystery into the heart of which I want to get tonight: "The whole earth is full of His glory." Isaiah had said, "He looked for judgment, and behold oppression; for righteousness, and behold a cry." Corruption! Yet in the abode of the True, in the face of the Eternal, the seraphim seeing the issues of things, judging the present by the future, are saying in the open face of heaven, "The whole earth is full of His glory." Do you not think that up there in heaven they saw the sinfulness of sin, even as Isaiah did? They saw the enormity of Judah's disobedience; they saw the vileness and the back-sliding and the wandering away. That broke upon their vision as it had not broken upon the vision of the prophet; yet while they saw sin, the vileness and virulence of transgression, while they saw how it had marred the purpose of God, and the wreck and ruin which it was working in the land, yet they had a point of view beyond that.

Sin is a fact; it is an awful fact in the history of the world of men, with its damning, blighting, polluting, crushing power; but, blessed be God, it is not the supreme fact. It is a disease that has been induced by self-will; but the purpose of God is not going to be defeated by the sins of men. Did you ever think of this? —that one great method of God in dealing with the sins of men is to overthrow evil by permitting the self-manifestation of evil. He allows sin in its injustice, and cruel wrong, and pollution, and utter unworthiness, to blaze into manifestation before the eyes of men, that its nothingness may be seen, and that it may be swept away from His presence for ever. "His sword strikes once and strikes no more," and sin is thus being sentenced through its self-manifestation, and mankind is being cast down into new self-abasement, and awakening to realise its own nothingness. Individual souls begin to feel how far they are estranged from God. The blighting and estranging power of evil is being forced in upon mind and heart, and so the way is being opened for God to come in, in a new manifestation of His glory to the sons of men.

That is the view which fills the angelic throng. Even through the sins of man, with all their dreadful temporal and eternal consequences, of which we cannot speak without awful dread—even through these, the purpose of God is being fulfilled; and in overcoming evil, in meeting all the oppositions of evil, in manifesting Himself as against the evil, God is bringing forth into fuller glory His essential love, His essential holiness; is shining in the splendour of His being before the astonished eyes of men. That is the great thought which filled the seraphs, and found expression in their song, "The whole earth is filled with His glory."

I want you now to turn to the prophet. It is a glorious thing to be a prophet; it is one of the most magnificent rôles in the world. Take some of our imperfect prophets in our own day, men like Ruskin and others who had only a very imperfect message. With what stupendous power did they flash all the moral insight they had, right into the thick of present-day evil! What commanding power these men had before their fellows! Isaiah had that, and in a far grander degree. There he was in Israel with men of high estate and consideration in other respects, and God was enabling him to search to the very quick every phase of corruption, and to bring it out into the light and show its nothingness to the people of that day. What a commanding position for a man to occupy!

But notice: now that he has come under the shadow of God, now that he has begun to see from the throne the exceeding sinfulness of sin, and now that God is over-ruling sin for His great purpose of love; what does he say? Formerly he had said, "Woe unto them that join house to house." But listen to what he says now. "Woe is me!" "There was a time when I thought I could be a prophet. When I saw a vision of God in all His glory, and when I saw the corruption of sin in Israel, I felt it was my work to go forth and discover the evil of my time. But now that I have seen God, and have seen the sinfulness of sin in the light of God and have seen Him in His infinite patience, despite the contumely and enormity of human transgression, working out His purpose of love; when I have heard the very seraphs looking forward to the future and rejoicing in the triumph of mercy over the enormity of human transgression, oh, I feel that I know nothing about it; I have no message, I cannot represent what I have seen, I cannot discover to men the glory that has burst upon my vision! Woe is me! I am a man of my own time. I see now that the very evils which I saw in my nation are in myself. I belong to a people of unclean lips. I spoke about their love of wealth and pleasure, but there is something corresponding to that in me. Insensibly and instinctively I find I am tainted with the corruptions of my age. And not only that, but there are my own corruptions. I am a man of unclean lips." The lip is the organ through which we draw the vital air to purify the life-blood of our being; the lip is the organ through which we utter the depths of our souls. And, says Isaiah, "I am a man of unclean lips; I have been living amidst the men of my time, I have been absorbing their opinions, looking at things from their standpoint; I have instinctively been absorbing their earthly and self-centred judgments. Who am I to shadow forth this wonderful glory of God, to bring down to men that divine mission regarding sin, and that solemn, divine, and glorious mission of love? Woe is me! I am undone!"

I wonder if any of us have some of that feeling? We have been talking a great deal about consecration, and about full surrender and submission to Christ; but do you not feel, face to face with this great work which God would give us to do, what a shallow thing it has been with us! Let me ask you, preachers, Are you making the sinfulness of sin, as in God's sight, very living and powerful to the men among whom you live and move? Are your congregations being bowed down under a terrible unveiling of transgression, the exceeding sinfulness of sin? Are you compelling men to realise the nothingness of evil, that it must lead to corruption, that it is mere human self-will in the universe of Almighty God; that it must dash itself against the thick bosses of Jehovah's buckler? Are you humbling men under the idea of the utter folly of sin, and leading them out from this vision of sin to see the glory of God in the face of Jesus Christ, so that it is coming, so to speak, as a fresh message from the throne? Are you not? Well, the fault is in you, not in God; and it becomes us to get deeper down than we have ever got yet: it becomes us to humble ourselves before the Eternal. What is our surrender worth if we cannot carry the testimony of God in this fashion, if God cannot fill us with His message and send us out to unveil His holiness, and His sinlessness, and His love? If we would be the kind of saints that are going to convict the world, we must get down in the dust and we must begin with ourselves—you with yourself, and I with myself, "Oh, woe is me!"

We have been feeling that what has driven many to Keswick is this: they have felt their prophetic mission and that their evangelical mission was not succeeding. What are we going to do? All that even the princely Isaiah could do was to confess his failure. "Woe is me! for I am undone: because I am a man of unclean lips, and I dwell in the midst of a people of unclean lips: for mine eyes have seen the King, the Lord of hosts." God did not say to him, "O Isaiah, you are taking an exaggerated view." Some in this tent may be saying that, but God did not speak thus to Isaiah. No, the confession of the great and princely Isaiah, to whom God had given such a view of the sins of men and of His own glorious purpose, was received, and out from the throne there came a seraph with a live coal. By the power of God the sacrifice of Christ was applied to the soul. Oh, that we could get away from all vain creature confidence, down into the depths of utter nothingness, where we were when we came to Him first of all, but deeper down because we have got a larger vision of ourselves, and of a life that is undone—incapable of this great mission, working no deliverance in the earth, recognising the fact that the Kingdom of God is shrinking and the kingdom of the world is increasing.

Oh, that we might get down in the very dust before God and say, "I am undone! I have been twenty or thirty years in the Kingdom, and should have had such a vision of Christ that I would look at things from the standpoint of Calvary, and not tone down my preaching to the line of things that prevail; yet here I am incapable of witnessing to a great world lying in the wicked one! Woe is me! I am undone." Can you remember when God met us first in our own utter helplessness and brought us into the Kingdom? Well, He will meet us tonight in the very depths of self-abasement, and He will touch our lips with the salvation of Jesus Christ. And with this salvation of Christ there will come into our souls the fire of the Holy Ghost. And the Holy Ghost, as we have to realise, is a divine Being; there is no limit to His power. It does not matter what I am, it does not matter how sinful, it does not matter how limited; if the Holy Ghost in His fulness has an empty man, He can shake a nation. If I have spoken with God bearing me witness, I do hope that every one here tonight will thus abase himself and herself to receive the fulness of Christ's grace and the fire of Christ's Spirit.

And now what comes? We have been looking at that wonderful vision, we have heard the seraphs' cry; but we are rising higher now, beyond the seraphs to God. What does He say? When He has got a man in the dust, consciously anointed, filled with the Holy Ghost, there is no limit to what He can accomplish through him. And so God says, "Whom shall I send?" "Who will stand forth in this modern day my confessed and attested messenger, to make real to men these very things that are so unreal today—the sinfulness of sin, the utter futility of all selfishness and self-will,·and the glory of God's love coming in to fill the nothingness of men with His fulness? Whom shall I send clothed with power for this great end?" We seem to be carried now into the New Testament. There are moments when the clouds disperse and we get a New Testament vision. "Who will go for *us*?" God gave to Isaiah to stand there in Judah, in the midst of that corrupt age, and so to discover God that the very rebels trembled before Him, and so to discover the love of God that a new hope began to dawn in men's hearts. But Isaiah saw further. Not only did he see God, but he saw the servant of God that "shall not fail nor be discouraged, till He have set judgment in the earth; and the isles shall wait for His law." He went for God as His servant to bear witness to the work of redemption that was yet to come. God enabled him for this; and if you and I are absolutely surrendered to God and yielded up to the influence and power and indwelling of the Holy Ghost, God will come in power and give to us the very testimony we need for our day, so that men shall see God; and not only God, but the Christ of God; and not only the Christ of God, but the Spirit of God. Those old realities that dominated the life of this nation in former times will dominate it more grandly than ever in any past day, and will do it through consecrated men and women to the glory of His name.

But what indication had the prophet that this fulness of blessing was to come? Isaiah had a work to do, that I pray God we may not have. Many a time ominous thoughts rise up before one's mind as to what the issues may be. Having gone so far, we may have to go further before we turn. God said to Isaiah, "Now you are going to the people who 'hearing, shall hear and not understand,' and who will go on till one day they shall be carried away captive; and not until the remnant return will the light begin to break." What a sad prospect! But this man was abased before God, and so he was enabled to stand amid that dark outlook preaching of the vision of God with the power of God, carrying home to the hearts and consciences of men the sinfulness of sin and the glory of God's love, almost as if they had seen His face. He was enabled to so utter these things that his prophecies have become a message to all the centuries since.

I cannot tell what God is going to do. We may have to be humbled as individuals or as a people—we cannot tell. The issues are in the hand of God. But whatever the future may be, I long and pray that there may come a mighty revival, partly as the result of this convention, in which God has been so manifestly working. Whatever the issue may be, you and I, empty of self, and yielded up to God, and filled with the Holy Spirit, will stand among men, whether they hear or whether they forbear, with the light and fire of God, which they cannot gainsay or resist.

c

GO . . . THEN COME

Rev. F. B. Meyer, B.A.

Go thy way; first be reconciled to thy brother, and then come—
Matthew 5: 24.

I READ from the Revised Version: "If therefore thou art offering"—note the vividness of the present tense—"thy gift at
the altar, and there remember that thy brother hath aught
against thee, leave there thy gift before the altar and go thy way;
first be reconciled to thy brother, and then come and offer thy
gift." We have here the photograph of an arrested purpose.
Maybe our Lord, as He stood on some occasion in the Temple, had
witnessed a scene in the history of some worshipper that suggested
this marvellous representation of an arrested purpose. Here was
a soul that, no doubt, knew itself to be a child of God—for these
words of Christ follow upon other words that could only be
appropriate to a child of God; a reverent soul, a penitent soul,
for it had to come to the altar; an eager soul, for it had brought a
gift, prompted, we trust, by gratitude and affection; a soul, therefore, in which God's Spirit was evidently at work in the early
stages of its experience, and which trusted and hoped that it might
early enter into a deeper experience of God.

I am almost certain that there are hundreds of people in this
tent tonight who are children of God by faith, who are reverent
and penitent; and we are standing before the altar of self-surren-
der, beside which stands the Great High Priest Himself; and they
have entered this tent with a serious resolution that they will consecrate their whole life to God. And when Dr. Smith spoke about
a human life being a channel through which the torrent of the
divine nature may flow to men, many a one deep down in the
recesses which are not often opened said, "O my God, through
my life henceforth, as I give it to Thee, wilt Thou pour Thy
mighty self upon a dying world?" I see you standing there.
There is a smile on your face, there is even rapture in your expression; you have something which you desire to give to Him upon
the altar that sanctifieth the giver and the gift. But just there and
just now memory does its work, and seems to stand up like a warning figure, and, pointing backward, says, "Remember!" And as

66

He, the Priest, witnesses that sudden revulsion of feeling, He says, "Go your way; before you can make an offer of consecration, there is a previous work to be done." You want to skip tonight, but Christ will not let you. You want to come to the act of consecration, but there is something previous. He says, "Go . . . then come." First, "Go."

It seems to me as if at this moment the Lord is going to send us back to our homes and to our rooms, that in some letter we shall write, or some word we shall speak, there shall be the first necessary preparation for the work of consecration which will follow presently. First "Go," then "come." Be reconciled to thy brother, then yield thyself to God. That is, your attitude toward God is determined by your attitude toward your brother. You love God just as much as, and no more than, you truly love the man whom you love least. You have been thinking that your favour in the sight of God Almighty was determined by the fervour of your prayers, the exuberance of your hymns, and the religiousness and constancy with which you maintain your private devotion. But understand today that your attitude toward God whom you do not see is gauged by your attitude toward your brother, whom you do see: and we have got tonight to settle that.

An American clergyman told me that for many years he had pleaded with God for revival, but no revival came. Finally, in despair he gathered his church around him, and rolled the burden of his anxiety upon his people, saying, "I have done all I could; it is now for you to consider your attitude toward God." Then there rose up in the church-meeting a grey-haired elder, much respected. He said, "Pastor, I do not wonder that there is no revival in this church; there never will be as long as Brother Jones and I don't speak to one another"; and before all the people the old man went down the aisle to where his brother sat, and said, "Brother Jones, forgive me; for ten years we have not spoken. Let us bury the hatchet." They made peace, and he came back to his seat, and bowed his grey head between his hands. There was a great silence on the people, and another officer of the church rose, and said, "Pastor, I do not think there is going to be a revival in this church as long as I say fair things to your face and mean things about you behind your back. Forgive me!" The pastor forgave him, and he said that for the next twenty minutes, in the awful stillness of the place, men with men, women with women, rose and went to square up old accounts with those with whom they were at feud. And then the Spirit of God came down in a mighty rushing wind.

"Thy brother"—someone near you. Has that brother or sister, or that man or that woman, aught against you? You are disposed to say, "I have a great deal against him; he only paid me five shillings in the pound. All the time he tried to do me hurt. He is an ugly, cross-grained, miserable, soul; I cannot get on with him!" The Lord puts His hand over your mouth, and says, "I do not ask you what you have against him. What has he against you?"

What has your wife against you? Have you been intolerant, have you been irritable, have you constantly demanded of her sacrifice that you have no right to ask? Has there been a domineering, tyrannical spirit in your address toward those nearest and dearest to you? Has any girl or woman living aught against you? Have you excited hopes in that girl's heart which you have not realised; have you been tampering with that girl's love, have you been leading her to think that you would be more to her than you meant to be? Has that woman anything against you? Has that servant, that dependant, anything against you? Have you demanded from him that for which you have not paid just wages? Has that poor servant girl a voice against you tonight, because you treat her as a slave? You do not think of her moral need; you do not mother her.

Have those trades-people aught against you? Do they look upon you as hard-fisted? Do they say they would rather serve men of the world than you; that you are always finding fault, that you keep them out of their money, that there is so much parsimony in your dealings with them? Has your brother aught against you? I do not ask if he is a Christian. He is simply a brother man, a man inferior to yourself, a woman or girl, who is altogether below you in position and station, and God Almighty is searching you tonight.

I put it once more, in the most solemn way, to this audience: you want comfort, you say; you want consecration, you say; you want high rapture, you say; you want to be lifted up upon the wings of the cherubim. I know all that. You resent the arrest. You are offering your gift, but God steps in, and says: "Go back and find your brother, your sister, the child, the woman, the man who has something against you."

Now what does Christ say? He says, "Go and be reconciled." But you answer, "Why should I? I am the older, I am the employer, I am in many ways superior. Let them come to me. If they want to get right, I am quite prepared to make it right."

"No," says Christ; "you must go and be reconciled." Is there any cause of offence now between you and some man or woman in this world still existing? You know you took things out of your father's house which were over and above your share; you know that you divided that property unjustly, or at least in a way which you justified to yourself, but which upset the rest of the family; you know that you have done things in your money matters with your customers and creditors which "won't wash." I tell you that it is absolutely impossible to expect that God will accept your gift and baptise you with the Holy Ghost until these things are put right. First go to your brother and tell him you have done wrong; and make restitution. Write the cheque tonight and send it; add the interest. Write the letter of apology, and say, "Excuse me, and forgive me."

Have you been angry without a cause? When a man allows anger in his soul, it makes him stiff and abrupt and cold. Then Christ says, "Have you let anger make you say of someone, 'Vain fellow!' or 'Ungovernable fool!'" Directly you judge another man in that way, you are judged, and by an invisible court the sentence is pronounced on you that you pronounced. If you call a man a "vain fellow," heaven pronounces that you are vain; if you speak of a man as a "fool," the heavenly court pronounces you culpable of folly; and if you count a man as rubbish, you yourself are cast upon God's rubbish heap—Gehenna—which is not for the future but for now. There are scores of men and women in this tent tonight who are on God's rubbish heap. He cannot use them because they are not just and right in their relations to others.

You say to me, "I do not feel like it." No, but that is not the question. You are to *will* it, you are to *do* it, you are to *obey*, and you are to do it in cold blood; and then "come." Now, in this moment, as I close, Christ stands here side by side with the altar, and He looks into my heart and into your heart, and says, "Remember! Has any aught against you?" I never shall forget how He came to me. There was something in my life—God grant it may not be in yours—and at that supreme moment, when I knelt by my bedside and said, "Christ, I surrender my whole manhood to Thee," He absolutely stopped me. I forced on Him the gifts of my heart, and He refused them, and said, "Stop! There is something to be done first." Something had come into my life which was not only affecting myself but my relations to others, and there my whole nature was entrenched; and I said, "I cannot, and I won't!" It was only after He kept me waiting at the altar until I saw that the fire was burning out, and that He was leaving and passing away with averted face, that I called my Priest back, and said, "Come back! Don't leave me here!" and He returned; and there and then there had to be an adjusted relationship with another and with others. Then, when all was done, I came and offered my gift, and on that gift the fire came.

Now, do you remember something to be done? Then do it, and Christ will fulfil: "I am not come to destroy, but to fulfil."

He will fulfil your life as the summer fulfils the spring and the flower fulfils the bud. O Saviour, fulfil our lives; but help us, first, to do what is to be done tonight. I have been told that on this platform Pastor Stockmeyer, before he spoke with wonderful power, said he must confess to a feeling of jealousy toward another minister who was on the platform. I should not be at all surprised if you find out some Christian worker, and say, "Forgive me"; if you find out some man or woman in this tent or at Keswick and say, "Forgive me." Or you will write a letter before you sleep and post it tonight. You will *go*; then *come*.

THE UNVEILING OF THE CARNAL

Rev. Charles Inwood

ONE IS more and more impressed with the fact that our fathers in the work of this Convention were guided by the Holy Spirit when, from year to year, Tuesday[1] was given up to heart-searching in the presence of God; and, guided by that same Spirit, I trust, I want, as He may speak through me, to search and possibly wound, hearts that need it this morning. The theme of this morning's study will be *the unveiling of the carnal*, and I want to turn your thoughts to the first Epistle to the Corinthians. In this Epistle we have a solemn unveiling of the carnal, and we see that the carnal is the deadliest foe of the spiritual, wherever they meet. Satan and the world assail us from outside, but the carnal is the traitor within, and, therefore, to be feared. John Wesley was right when he wrote—

> But, worse than all my foes, I find
> The enemy within.

Now, what do we mean by the carnal? By the carnal I mean the human, as divorced from the divine; just as by the spiritual I mean the human, possessed, indwelt, controlled, and transfigured by the divine. And so, you see, there is a fundamental difference between the carnal and the spiritual; and that difference runs through their entire conception of life, of man, of sin, of religion, and of God.

But, before we proceed, there is one preliminary question of great importance, which is answered by the apostle in the opening verse. The question is this: Has God two standards by which He tests His children? Has He a carnal standard for carnal Christians, and a spiritual standard for spiritual Christians? No! God has only one standard for us all; and so in an Epistle which, as I have said, is a terrible unveiling of the carnal, Paul opens with these thoughts: First, he says, you are sanctified in Christ Jesus; that is God's purpose concerning you. You are called to be saints, and, in v. 9, called to fellowship or partnership with the Lord Jesus Christ. Beloved, God is testing us by what we might be, by what we ought to be, by what He expects and calls us to

---

[1] Tuesday was then the first full day of Convention ministry—see p. 142.

be; and I pray you do not lay the flattering unction to your soul
that your Christian life is fully up to the average Christian's with
whom you meet. That may be quite true; but the law of averages
does not obtain here. No, no, no! God calls you to be a saint;
God desires to make a saint of you; and God is able to do the whole
work from start to finish in you. The real test is this: Are you,
as a child of God, content with something less than heart-holiness?

But now let me pass on to the survey. I think we shall notice
that the apostle unveils the carnal in three spheres. First, *in the
sphere of the intellectual;* next, *in the sphere of ethics;* and then, *in the
sphere of religion.* I want you to look at the light the apostle
throws upon the phases of the carnal, as they appear in these
three spheres.

First, then, *as to the intellectual.* Do I need to pause and
remind you that Paul was not opposed to intellectual life
and activity? In v. 5 of this chapter he recognises the fact that
they were a singularly gifted people. But he does more than that.
In the previous verse he recognises that these gifts all sprang from
the grace of God. Now, the moment you recognise natural
gifts as an expression of the grace of God, two things will follow:
first, you will not undervalue the gifts in your brother, if you see
the grace of God behind them; and next, if you have such gifts
yourself, you will not be likely to misuse them. There comes into
the whole realm of one's natural gifts a sacredness that one can
hardly describe when you see, in and behind them all, the same
free, unmerited grace of God that you see behind the salvation
of a sinner. Paul marks that out clearly, as you see. No, Paul
was not opposed to intellectual activity, but only to that intellectual activity which either shut God out or left God out. I
think it is not too much to say that Paul's intellect was the greatest
in the whole history of the Christian Church. Paul did not
dethrone that intellect as a wicked usurper when he gave his
heart to the Lord Jesus Christ. No, he consecrated his intellect,
in all the fulness of its powers, to the Lord Jesus Christ, who
redeemed him. God alone knows how much the consecration of
that one intellect has enriched the moral, and mental, and spiritual
life of the whole Church of God.

Now, do not call your Christian brother carnal because he
possesses genius, scholarship, learning, intellectual gifts, and
appears head and shoulders above you, and others. There may
be in this tent some young men of more than ordinary culture,
very rich in mental gifts. My dear brother, God wants to have
complete possession of those great gifts of yours, and if you will
consecrate all your knowledge, your culture, your genius, your
scholarship to the Lord Jesus, He will not put them under a

bushel. He will place them on His own candlestick, and they will give light—His light, not yours—to all that are in the house.

Now notice *three features in which Paul traces the carnal in this sphere*. First—and these thoughts run practically through the first and second chapters—he traces the carnal in their reliance upon what he calls the wisdom of the world. Now, what do we mean by the wisdom of the world? By the wisdom of the world we mean wisdom that is begotten and dominated by the world spirit. The Corinthians were relying upon the wisdom of the world; and Paul at once, in v. 21, points out to them that the intellectual has very sharp and well-defined limitations. This is what he says: "The world, by wisdom"—that is, the world by its wisest—"knew not God." In other words, he meant that there was much which even the strongest intellect cannot discover. No human intellect can ever discover God; for God is self-revealed, or we should never know Him at all. You cannot discover God through the microscope, or through the telescope. Some of those who have looked longest and seen most through them have never seen God, never! But if you know Him already, and look through them, you will see such traces of His fingers as will either make your heart dance and rejoice, or else sink into the silence of filial adoration and awe.

I think we are inclined to attach an altogether fictitious value to natural gifts; and we speak and think of them as if they were the be-all and end-all of fitness for the Lord's work. I think that our very ideals are more intellectual than spiritual. You can see the same thing when I remind you that there is many a minister of the Gospel to-day who is being tested by this one single test— Can we draw the crowd? What is that but leaning on the carnal? Then we lean so much, in our work, upon cleverness, upon ingenuity, upon shrewdness, upon clever advertising, and upon ceaseless posing for snapshots. How we depend upon the world and worldly methods for raising funds for the Lord's work—from skirt-dancing to pageants! Label your pageant a theatrical performance, and seven-tenths of the Lord's people would not go; but call it a pageant, accept the methods, the plans, and—if I am correctly informed, and I believe I am—get the personal supervision and assistance of people from the theatre to work your pageant, and then they flock to see it. It is carnal, if anything is carnal. I mention it that you may not fall into the snare— at least ignorantly—after to-day.

And there is another point—the rooted dislike to the cross, to Jesus Christ and Him crucified: "foolishness," Paul calls it. Christ crucified is foolishness to many Christians in our churches to-day. They must have a gospel; the need for a gospel is so clamant that it cannot be denied, even by carnal Christians. But it is a social gospel, or "a gospel of sweetness and light," or a gospel of mere academic culture, or a gospel with the tinge of esoteric Buddhism or theosophy running through it. They will find a place, aye, almost a welcome, for every nostrum, from Mormonism on the one side to the seductive falsities of Christian Science on the other. But the Gospel that rings out ruin by the fall, redemption by the cross, and regeneration by the Holy Spirit, they do not want; ethics, culture, anything but Jesus Christ and Him crucified. They do not object to wear the symbol in the form of a gold cross; but the real cross, the cross that is the most terrible indictment of human nature the world has ever known, and the cross that proclaims salvation only through the atoning work of Jesus Christ our substitute—no, they do not want that! Wherever you find even a veiled dislike to the doctrine of the Atonement of Jesus Christ, there you are on the track of the carnal.

There is another form of carnality in the same sphere. It is brought out in chapter 15 of the Epistle. As you read between the lines, you trace this form of the carnal—*refusal to believe what reason cannot demonstrate.*

That is implied in Paul's answer. But Paul also assumes that those who denied this fact of the resurrection of the body, because they could not understand it, did not see and weigh as they ought the larger risks of the position they took up. They thought they could doubt that one truth, and yet keep all the rest. As though you could surrender the foundation and yet keep the building all the same. That is what is being done in many directions to-day. I think one of the saddest features of our times is the thoughtlessness with which Christian men and Christian teachers fling their doubts broadcast. Beloved, if you have doubt—not second-hand doubt, but doubts of your own—do not get on the housetop and proclaim them. Get alone with God, and wait there until you get God's answer; for God has an answer for every honest doubt that you have. But they fling these fire-brands in all directions, heedless of the conflagrations which are sure to follow, heedless of the sanctities that will disappear, heedless of the thousands of souls who may be led astray through their doubts. I say again that, to me, the thoughtlessness with which so many Christian ministers air their doubts in the pulpit to-day is positively heart-breaking. They may not intend to instil these doubts into others, but they do not see the larger risks involved, and, as Paul teaches, that is carnal.

Now there is *the realm of ethics,* and that is dealt with at very considerable length. Indeed, chapters 6–10 might all be fairly included under that single heading. I want you to notice, first of all, how the carnal always takes refuge in casuistry, when it is brought face to face with the stern ethical teaching of our Lord and Saviour Jesus Christ. That is one thing. Another is this: the carnal uniformly sides with doubtful things. Who are the Christians that defend theatre-going, and dancing, and whist, and bridge? Who are the Christians that defend the nude in art? Who are the Christians that defend the erotic novel, and Sunday athletics, and all the things that look in that direction? Only carnal Christians. Who are the Christians that are so ready to defend themselves with sayings like these: "A man must live"— but he must not, if he cannot live honestly; "When a man is at Rome, he must do as Rome does." "The end justifies the means." I can hear the hiss of the serpent through these axioms. They are born of the carnal, and ought never to be heard on Christian lips.

Further, ever and anon the carnal lapses into the grossest sins; sins that make us blush, not only for religion but for humanity and morality.

One other thought in this connection, and it is lodged in the first sentence of the Epistle to the Church of God at Corinth. A feature of the carnal is this—its susceptibility to evil environment. The carnal is always the easy prey to the latest error or to the most popular sin. Like the sand on the seashore, it is always ruled by the last wave. Place a carnal Christian where spiritual influences surround him, and where all is in his favour, and you keep him a decent member on your church-roll. But let him go to lands where there is no Christian influence, no Christian public opinion, and oh! how quickly your carnal Christian succumbs there! Oh, they go down terribly! I have met moral and spiritual wrecks by the dozen and the score in every land I have visited. It is traceable to this—the man was only a carnal Christian, and was leaning more than he knew upon healthy environment.

But I pass on to say a word or two about the other sphere, *the sphere of religion.* There are three or four features of the carnal in that realm to which I should like to refer, and one is this, brought out directly in chapters 1 and 3, and indirectly and powerfully in chapter 14—the spirit of partisanship. In some cases it was racial, in others it was social, in some it was doctrinal, in others it was what we to-day should call ecclesiastical, and in several cases it centred in certain well-known leaders and became a form of thinly-veiled man-worship. And so there was party prejudice, and party feeling, and party shibboleths; and all the bitterness, strife, and weakness that always follow in their train. Do not misunderstand me. I believe there will always be differences in schools of thought, differences in our angle of vision, differences in the type of our leaders. But the carnal exalts the one to the disparagement of the other: and, as Paul teaches, that means that the carnal overlooks, first, that all types of Christian workers are mutually dependent, as one member of the body is upon another; next, that all of them as a whole are dependent upon God; and next, that all of them find their unity in God and in God only.

But now, to come to ourselves, what about the presence of this spirit of partisanship among us to-day? Do you judge your brother by a badge? If you do, you are carnal. It may be a racial badge, it may be a social badge, it may be a denominational badge; but it is carnal, and you are carnal if you do it.

What about your shibboleth—a little something that you test every Christian brother by; and if they cannot pronounce it with the accent you have chosen, you discard them as if belonging to the enemy, instead of to the Kingdom of the Lord Jesus Christ? Shibboleth—yes, you would wreck your church for that shibboleth; you would break up your little band of mission workers and the work God has been doing through you for that shibboleth: you would upset the convention for your shibboleth. Perhaps your shibboleth is faith-healing—you can make that a shibboleth; or your shibboleth may be the Lord's Coming—not the fact of it, but your particular interpretation of the fact; some of you are in grave peril along that line. With some of you the shibboleth is your idea of "eradication," and if you could only hear that word fall from the lips of some speaker in this convention, you would say that at last we are getting right! Aye, and with some of you— I pray God that you may be delivered—but with some of you the shibboleth is Keswick. And one shibboleth, from the point of view I am thinking of, is just as bad as another.

Now I am going to say a very solemn thing. I dare not say it except under very clear leading and very solemn constraint. It is this: my own firm conviction is that the arrest of the Welsh Revival was largely due to racial pride and the worship of a leader, which developed during the later history of that great movement. God says, "My glory I will not give to another"; and He will not give it to a nation or to a man. You know how the Jews made circumcision a shibboleth, and with what result? God transferred the base of missionary operations from Jerusalem to Antioch, because Jerusalem was carnal at that very point. Now listen: there are a thousand millions of unevangelized heathen in this redeemed world this morning; and their existence is due, as I believe, to the ascendancy of the carnal in the churches of the West. Let us take care—God may shift His base of missionary operations once more; and it almost looks as if He were going to do it. He may shift His base of missionary operations from the carnal West to the spiritually despised East.

I have not forgotten, in the life of Bishop Creighton, one sentence in a letter he wrote to one of his clergy. He said: "It is far easier to be an ecclesiastical partisan than to be a straightforward Christian." And God wants us to be straightforward Christians. Now, one other feature I must touch on—the craving for the abnormal. You have it in chapters 1 and 14—the craving for something which powerfully appeals to the senses, something you can see, and feel, and handle, aye, and photograph; something that will startle people. And I do think the religious Press of our times is somewhat to blame in this matter. The phenomena of the earthquake and the fire make good "copy"; and if there be anything startling, abnormal, or peculiar, it is flashed all over the world. If, during this convention, some extraordinary light fell on the face of any one of us on the platform, there would be more talk about that than about all the body of Christian truth which will be spoken by the lips of His servants in this convention.

Signs, signs! I meet it in unexpected quarters. I read, with pain of heart, of a convention where, to emphasise the presidency of the Holy Spirit, an empty chair was left on the platform in the chairman's place. That is carnal! If there is a craving for something spectacular, that shows it is of the flesh. I know a pastor who, on more than one occasion, in public—and I had to combat it, because it was a question of truth—declared that in that sadly famous prayer meeting of four years ago visible tongues of fire were seen to descend and rest upon the heads of the group who met, and waited, and prayed here.[1] And that went out everywhere, as if God had done some extraordinary thing. I know eminent Christian workers who are getting handkerchiefs consecrated, and these handkerchiefs are placed on the heads of people who are disordered in body or mind, with the belief that they are going to work miracles through them. What is that? The craving for the abnormal.

Now, beloved, one reason why Spiritualism is working such deadly havoc inside Christian circles is that very thing. If you want to see the unseeable and to know the unknowable, the devil will take care that there is somebody to give you something strange to look at, and something strange to hear. In the Acts

---

[1] In 1905, when some visitors from Wales held prayer meetings for "Pentecostal" manifestations at Keswick (see p. 406).

of the Apostles, on one occasion the disciples prayed for certain signs. The signs they sought were not given; God gave them something infinitely better—God filled them with the Spirit. You never hear of their asking for those signs again.

One thing more: chapter 14, with its strange, sad record of what we would call a tongues movement in the early Christian Church. I believe that we have in that chapter the strangest and saddest phase of the carnal presented in the whole Epistle; and if we laid its teaching truly to heart, we should be saved from much to-day. I do not believe there was much in common between the fiery tongues on the Day of Pentecost and the tongues movement in the Church at Corinth. I believe an alien movement had come in, and was working serious havoc in their midst. And what hurts me most is this: that I am forced to the conclusion that there is a painful identity between the worst phase of the tongues movement in the Church at Corinth, and the so-called tongues movement of our own time. If one-tenth of what I have learned from credible Christian witnesses in Australia, in California, and in England, be true, there is nothing in common between the fiery tongues of Pentecost, and the movement of to-day; but this latter movement is the latest child of the carnal, and is leading hundreds of earnest, unwary souls astray. If it only took the worst, one would not grieve so much; but some of the best of souls are caught by that snare who would not be caught by any other.

I want you to lay these statements to heart. First, all animal, and nervous, psychic excitements lend themselves readily to the carnal, but they do not lend themselves to the spiritual. Again, a disordered condition of mind or body is no condition of the fulness of the Spirit, no proof of the presence of the Spirit in power. By a very singular providence, which I did not at the time understand, I was permitted last year to see the howling dervishes in Asia Minor; and one thing I noticed was this—that the psychic laws manifested by those men were the same as those manifested in Australia and some other places I could mention. The dervishes were probably ignorant of the laws, but they obeyed them; and it is obedience to the law, not knowledge of it, that conditions the result.

One other thing. There are natural psychic leaders, and, if they are in earnest, they will lead you far, far astray. Two things have impressed me deeply in this connection, and the first is this—I believe we are on the eve of a new conflict with the forces that come from that quarter; and I believe, also, we are woefully ignorant of their disguises, and their peril, and their power. Will you believe me when I tell you that it is a rare thing to meet a Christian of such unerring spiritual intuition that he can distinguish between the power which is psychic and natural, and the power which is the power of the Holy Spirit alone? Only as you learn to distinguish the carnal in this occult region, will you be saved from the melancholy tragedy of the tongues movement as it appeared in the Church at Corinth.

If, beloved, you have never till now suspected the presence of the carnal in any of these spheres, then I pray you listen to this warning word. Wherever you meet the carnal, under whatever disguise you meet it, it is the deadly foe of the spiritual in your soul. Do not trifle with it, do not give it quarter, do not tolerate it, do not yield yourselves to it. Yield yourself to Jesus Christ, that He may win complete victory in you over the carnal which you have now discovered. There is in Him an abundance of life, there is in His Spirit an abundance of power; and you can be set free, and kept free from the dominance of the carnal by the super-mighty power and dominance of the Holy Spirit of God.

THE MINISTRY OF CONSCIENCE

Rev. Harrington C. Lees, M.A.

W E ARE here ostensibly to learn what is the will of God for every one of us as revealed in Jesus Christ; and to seek from God that power of the Holy Spirit which alone can enable us to live according to His will. We are here to know what are the conditions of surrender, and to ask that we may have grace, not only to lay hold, but also to let go. We are here to catch the notes of the Lord's song, and to find out, it may be, what has been hindering the music.

Now while we have been listening to clear-voiced exposition, and shall be yielding ourselves, I trust, to fervent appeal, there is a third aspect which we are bound to take into consideration in a gathering of this kind. I mean the personal problems that disturb the soul; for it is possible to have the most delightful exposition, and the most heart-searching appeal, and yet to be left perplexed between the two, because of conditions of heart and soul which we are not able to diagnose for ourselves, and which otherwise might be left untouched, unless provided for in a meeting of this kind.

The subject laid upon my heart to deal with is, Conscience and my relation to it, and all the disturbances it can make in my life; conscience and the lack of understanding of it which has often made a shadow where God intended there should be joy.

I take as the foundation of my talk Acts 24: 16, "Herein do I exercise myself, to have always a conscience void of offence toward God, and toward men." Now conscience bulks largely in our convention gatherings, and rightly so. We make our appeal to it, if it be awake; we seek to arouse it, if it be dormant. The reason is not far to seek. It is simply this, that in every human being, whether he be Christian or not, whether he be living under Christian law or not, there is something which we call, for want of a better name, conscience.

When St. Paul is speaking, in Romans 2, about the heathen who have not the revelation of God in Christ Jesus, as recorded in the written Word, or without that written Word, he says that nevertheless they have within themselves a law by which they are called to live; and that according as they live, or do not live, according to that law, their consciences and their thoughts either accuse or else excuse them—tell them to go on doing as they are doing, or tell them to stop what they are doing. Now I say we have got down there to the bedrock from which we may begin to work; for it is obvious that in a gathering of this kind, which is drawn from a professedly Christian country—whether we be really Christians, born again in Christ or not—there is something here to appeal to, if we begin with this question of conscience.

But I think it is desirable that we should ask ourselves what precisely we mean by conscience; for a good many things—and it must be confessed, a good many extravagant things—have been said on the question of conscience. It has been called the infallible guide of man. You will find men whose lives are really not only a reproach to themselves, but a disturbance to their neighbours, saying, "I live according to the dictates of my conscience." Last year a man who was in the holy ministry of the Church of Christ defended the fact that he had taken another woman while his wife was living by saying that his conscience had not forbidden him, and that he was living according to his conscience. I am glad to say that the Consistory Court very quickly stripped that man both of his living and of his emoluments, because while he might be living according to *his* conscience, he was certainly not living according to the law of God. You will find people who, if the law of their land does not go according to their will or idea, will appeal to conscience as a reason why they should disobey.

Wordsworth himself, you will remember, has called conscience "God's most intimate presence in the soul, and His most perfect image in the world." Now I venture to say that if you think at all, and if you look into this chapter from which our text has been taken, you will see that language of that kind cannot really be defended. St. Paul, in speaking of his conscience, says, first of all, that he has to exercise it in order to keep it in condition; and, secondly, he says of it, that it is to be without offence—*i.e.*, it is neither to stumble itself, nor to make other people stumble because of it. But a thing which needs exercise to keep it in condition, a thing which can stumble, or can make other people stumble, is obviously not infallible! I think we shall not be far wrong if we say of it, that while it is a thing by which we judge ourselves and are judged, we shall nevertheless have to admit that it is a fluctuating factor.

The Hindu woman who throws her child to "Mother Gunga," because she thinks she will please the river goddess thereby, is doing it according to her conscience. The Romanist who racked Latimer and burned Cranmer was doing it according to his conscience. What are we to say, then, with regard to a problem of this kind? I think we must say that the fact is that conscience is part of our human, and merely human, equipment. It is spiritual, but it is not supernatural. It is, if I may say so, the telephone chamber into which God desires to speak heavenly messages; but it is not necessarily the voice of God. It is a place, rather, in which God is heard and the medium through which God desires to speak.

If you look here in this chapter I think you will see three conditions of conscience clearly outlined. There is the fearless conscience, which St. Paul has here when he says, "I exercise myself day and night to have a conscience void of offence." There is a fearful conscience. When the great Roman ruler who heard Paul preach about righteousness and temperance and judgment to come was terrified, that was conscience. And there is the uneasy conscience, when St. Paul says, "I appeal to you, ask the men who have heard me and seen me, whether they have seen anything amiss in me. Ah, but I do remember one thing. I am not quite sure whether I was right or not when I said to them, 'Men and brethren, I am being judged to-day because I am a Pharisee, and because I believe what the Pharisees believe'; and I divided the assembly as I did so. Now I come to bethink me, I am not quite sure I was right there." Even Paul says that he is exercising his conscience, and the conscience is exercising him. So we have Paul's fearless conscience, and we have Felix's fearful conscience. Then in the middle we have Paul's uneasy conscience just beginning to stir. It is therefore partly human and partly divine—human in that it is part of our equipment; divine in so far as God gets His chance to speak into it.

But it will follow, also, of course, that it is limited, and will always be limited, by our lack of knowledge or light. The bias of custom will sometimes speak as a voice of conscience, and yet speak badly and imperfectly. You get, for instance, a case like slavery. Our Christian country must not be presumed to have been entirely without conscience because little more than one hundred years ago Christian men kept slaves; but the custom that had held for so long was blinding men, and their outlook was defective. But when the conscience of the country was awakened, slavery became impossible under the British flag.

The blight of prejudice may come and speak in the voice of conscience. I would like to say this: I have known people—and it is just possible that there may be some here to-day—who are members of either the Established Church or of some other Church, whose consciences were not quite easy because they were going to gather in a tent that knew no distinctions of denominations or sects, over which floated the motto, "All one in Christ Jesus." My friends, I have known, not only in the Established

Church, but I have known in the tiniest meeting-room, consciences which told men that they were sinning if they came here. But the conscience was not right that did it. It was the blight of prejudice that came in.

The consciences of some men are not disturbed when a man goes to bed not quite sober on a Saturday night, because generations of men have done it. So I say that on low ground and in poor circumstances, a man's conscience may be dull instead of open and awake, because of the barrenness of his outlook. The Hindu woman throws her child away because she has a defective knowledge of the will of God, but conscience does not correct her; she thinks she is pleasing God. The Jesuit employs the rack and the fire because he thinks such persecution is permissible if you are to save a man's immortal soul. The Mohammedan who will cut your throat quite cheerfully to-morrow, will have his conscience disturbed because a drop of water has passed his lips during the Fast of Ramadan.

So, friends, I want to say this, that the problem of conscience is not absolutely clear. Unaided it is a goad, but aided it is a guide. I think its tendency is infallibly correct when it says, "Do right at any cost," but its direction is not infallibly correct, and we need something to show us what *is* right after conscience has said, "Do right at any cost." It is like the sighting of a rifle. If a rifle had only one sight you would not very often hit the object you aim at, but the rifle must have two sights, and if both come level to your eye there is a chance of your hitting the mark. Now, you have conscience as one sight. What do you need at the other end? You need the revelation of God, as you have it here in our Bible, His written Word; and as these two are brought into line and relation you will find the life which begins to approximate to the will of God.

And now I come to look at it, that is what Paul says, for the text does not say, "I exercise myself," but "*herein* I exercise myself." Now what is the "herein"? I was struck by that fact only half an hour before I came to this meeting. It ought to have struck me long ago. Now, I see there are two things Paul speaks of there. The "herein" represents the judgment with the stirrings of conscience evoked by its memory, and the Word of God, the Word written to our fathers. When these two come into line, "Herein do I exercise myself, to have always a conscience void of offence."

Now, my dear friends, I wonder if there are any of you who have been trying to live merely according to your conscience, and have found that it was an excellent thing in so far as it said, "Do right," but a very unsatisfactory thing in so far as it did not tell you what to do. Its negative properties were splendid, but its constructive work was feeble; and on that account you have been wandering about, not quite sure, and you have come to this convention that you may have light as to what is the will of God. You have tried to do right. You have done the best you can, but you are like the builder of whom Emerson tells. Someone said to him, "Are you not going to have an architect?" "Oh," he replied, "we are having a man come along by and by, and he will put the architecture in; but meanwhile we are putting up the building." I think there are a great many people like that. They are going on with the building and working hard at it, and by and by they want Christ to come along and put the architecture in! Christ will have nothing of the sort. He will begin from the beginning. He is the foundation stone, and if you want your building to be one that will stand the fire, one that will be gold and silver and precious stones, and not wood, hay, stubble, in that day when every Christian is tested, to know whether he is worthy of Christ's crown or not, I pray you awake to this fact, that to-day Jesus Christ seeks you and calls you with the appeal that comes very insistently from the cross and the throne, comes of the love of the cross and the power of the blood, and the intercession at the right hand of God. Jesus Christ is ready to come to you and to me, to the telephone chamber, and speak into it to-day.[1] When He says to you "Are you there?"— I say it quite reverently—are you going to the end of the telephone to say, "Speak, Lord, for Thy servant heareth"? I pray you to understand that He is saying it to you, whether you realise it or not; and that we have come as His messengers to tell you that He is saying, "Are you there?" Is all of you there? And is the whole of you there, your body and your soul and your spirit? No, that is the wrong order; your spirit, your soul, and your body—all ready, bent listening in order to hear what God has to say?

Now there are many kinds of conscience. I have not time to dwell on them all, but I want to consider one or two of them now, that we may get our minds clear on this matter. The conscience that we come into contact with most often—a little later than this stage of the convention, but sometimes at the beginning—is the *restless* conscience, the conscience that St. Paul knew when the Lord said to him, "It is hard for thee to kick against the pricks." I said that conscience was a goad, and St. Paul had found it out; but it wanted the revelation of Jesus Christ as a Guide in order that his conscience might find him pressing on toward the goal.

Now the restless conscience is very easily known. It is always there when the heart is wrong. It does not belong merely to the Christian economy. You will find it right away back in the days when Joseph's brethren found themselves in trouble in the house

---

[1] These were, of course, early days of the telephone.

of Pharaoh, and their conscience was instantly aroused, and they said, "We are verily guilty because of our sin against our brother years ago. We heard his cries and would take no heed of them; and now God is hard upon our track!" What is it that makes a man think of any deed many years after, when it was a wrong deed? It is conscience.

What was it that made Darius sleepless when Daniel was in the lions' den? It may be Daniel was not sleepless; but anyhow Darius was not sleeping. It was because he had an uneasy conscience. What was it that made the widow of Zarephath say, "What have I to do with thee, O thou man of God? Art thou come unto me to call my sin to remembrance, and to slay my son?" Was there a connection between "my sin" and "my son"? Maybe the sin lay just there. Anyway, there was a conscience speaking to that woman, an uneasy conscience. What was it that Herod heard of One who was going up and down teaching and preaching the Kingdom of God, and doing miracles, that made him say, "It must be John the Baptist, whose head I cut off"? It was an uneasy conscience.

As St. Paul says, conscience accuses or else it excuses us. Which is your conscience doing for you to-day? Is it in any way accusing you? Mind you, it can be a bloodhound as well as a watchdog! God keep it ever on our track until it be run down, and we come to Him to have the conscience put right. A great man has said that when on one occasion he seemed very near death, and his mind passed in review most of the events of his life, he heard a voice speaking clearly to him, his mother's voice, a voice he had not heard since he was a little lad, and it said to him, "Johnny, did you touch those grapes?" A young bank clerk saw the manager of the bank and the chairman of directors conferring together one day. They were talking about raising his salary, but what made him bolt from the office? The fact that his books were £1,000 wrong, and he thought they knew it. The voice of conscience is a bloodhound as well as a watchdog.

But oh, thank God there is something more than a restless conscience. There is a *responsive* conscience; the conscience that, when God calls, says, as St. Paul said, "I exercise myself." That is the conscience which, when the telephone bell rings, hastens from its comfortable seat to hear what the message may be. Do you remember that St. Paul came to the point when the telephone call came, when he had to review and revise his life? You must not think that when Paul was persecuting the Church he was doing it because he had an unholy delight in making people uncomfortable, or a blood-thirst for cruelty. He says, "I verily thought that I ought." He was living according to his conscience;

but directly the higher revelation of Jesus Christ came and spoke,
he says, "I was not disobedient unto the heavenly vision." Now
that is just how God finds you, and how Christ will speak to you—
maybe has been speaking to you at this meeting. You have been
doing a certain thing and saying, "I verily thought I ought."
But now here comes a call to consider, Are you right in doing that
thing which you thought you ought? Are there things in your life
that are to be set aside because a higher revelation has come in?
You have not been living guiltily in man's sight. Has it been
guiltily in the sight of God?

Conscience is not absolute; it is progressive. "If any man will
do His will, he shall know of the doctrine." I read a most suggestive thing the other day. A great menagerie had been sold. There
was a good deal of straw that had been at one time or other used
as temporary bedding for the wild beasts. That straw was bought
by a man who owned a livery stable. When he put into the stalls
the straw on which a lion had crouched, the horses that had
never seen a lion in their lives were uneasy and restless and would
not go into the stalls. It was an instinctive dread of the enemy.
Now, friends, I say this: it is possible for a conscience to be so
responsive to the voice of God, so delicately adjusted to the Word
of God and its claims, that when even a thing you do not know to be
a sin, an enemy you have not even come in full sight of, shall draw
near, there shall be the scent of it, the disturbance, the arousing
call of it that alarms you and delivers you from the sin even while
the enemy is putting the trap across the road in front of you. It is
possible; and God calls upon us to so bend and to be so responsive,
that when the temptation comes it shall find us awake.

Now I want to put in a corrective. It is very desirable to have
an awakened conscience, but it is a very undesirable thing to have
a morbid conscience. I think the worst things we have to deal
with in a convention are morbid consciences. I think it must be
owned that the peril of a convention lies just here. We are not on
that account going to close our convention! We are not going to
stop making appeals that God intends us to make in order that
consciences may be aroused. But we cannot get away from the
fact that many people have become so sensitive to the voice of
conscience that they have become martyrs to it.

I have a Christian friend whose wife has been lying ill for some
time. At night he could not sleep, because he thought constantly
that his wife was calling him. Now, though there is a nurse in
charge, and he is no longer needed, that man gets up and stands
and listens outside his wife's door in the middle of the night,
because he thinks he hears her voice. The habit is purely mechanical, of cours , he imagines he hears the call. There are people

here who keep telephones. I suppose some of you have gone to your bell occasionally when you thought it rang and it did not. Now that is true of conscience sometimes; it is thought to ring when it does not.

There is that word in Isaiah, for instance, "And thine ears shall hear a voice behind thee." Do not get into the way of imagining you hear voices. Will you finish the text? "And thine ears shall hear a voice behind thee, saying, This is the way, walk ye in it." When? When the road is clear in front of you? No, but when you are turning to the right hand or to the left. Conscience, in other words, says "Don't." I think it does not very often say "Do." The constructive part lies in the revelation of God; the negative in conscience.

John Wesley in his *Journal* records that one day he vowed he would not speak to a soul unless the Spirit of God definitely prompted him to do so. When he arrived at the close of the journey, I think at Kingswood, he found that he had not spoken to a soul. Then John Wesley made that sensible resolution that when there were souls that needed speaking to, it would be as well for him to do the speaking, and trust that God the Holy Spirit would use the opportunity as he had followed it up.

I know a young man, one of the most conscientious I know, but I cannot always get him to work when I want him, because he says he is not quite sure whether his conscience is leading him or not. I believe with all my heart in asking God for guidance in our work; but I do believe that when there are fields at home and abroad and a man is idle—I do not say lazy—I do believe that the call of God is just there.

I found one of my most devoted men was not praying at the prayer meeting. I said to him, "How is it it is so long since I heard your voice?" "Well," he replied, "you know you have a way of saying, 'Now, will two or three of you lead in prayer as the Lord shall lead you,' and I am not sure whether He has led me or not." I said, "I have not much doubt about it, for He has been making me uncomfortable because you were not praying and the meeting was not being led."

Do beware of the morbid conscience that is always asking you questions. I believe I am safe in saying—I am on dangerous ground, but if God is prompting I must go on dangerous ground— I believe I am right in saying that you would do well to listen to the voice of God, and let Him ask you questions, but that you will very seldom do well to ask yourselves questions. Introspection, as a rule, has made life miserable rather than joyous, and because the holy life is a joyous life I am very suspicious of introspection.

Now let me go further, and say: we are here as God's messengers

88   KESWICK'S AUTHENTIC VOICE

to bid you listen to God's voice. But I do not say that you are not
to listen to man when he tries to awaken a dormant conscience.
On the contrary, we are here because we believe we can awaken
a dormant conscience. A friend of mine was present at a baptism
in Japan the other day, and the questions put to the women about
to be baptised were something like these: "Are you willing to give
up idolatry in every form; to put away idols that are found in your
house; to give up the fox worship, the devil worship, or whatever
it may be? Are you willing to remain unmarried if the Lord does
not find you a partner who is walking in the way of Christ? Are
you prepared to obey your parents in everything, except as touching the service of Christ, and are you prepared to take the consequences and the punishment of disobedience if it means yielding
to idols?" To the men, questions like this were put: "Are you
prepared to give up telling lies in your business?" Now what was
all that? It was the arousing of the dormant conscience, or, rather,
of a conscience that was not necessarily dormant, but might
possibly need instruction along ways it had not yet seen.

When Jesus Christ was going to heal the paralytic man, why
do you suppose He said first of all, "Thy sins be forgiven thee"?
I think because there was a sin at the root of the paralysis, and the
Lord wanted to show him that it was not only healing but pardon he
wanted, as well as intending it as an object-lesson for those outside.

So I beseech you, lay this to heart, those of you who would get
deliverance from known sin. St. Paul says, "I know nothing
against myself," and that shows that it is possible for a man to get
victory over known sin. But it does not say that it is possible for
him to get to a condition where he is not sinning. There are
things unknown in my life and yours, things of ignorance in my
walk and yours, about which God forbid that we should ever say
that we have no sin, and so deceive ourselves, as St. John warned
us long ago. So St. Paul says this: "I know nothing against myself;
yet am I not hereby justified: but He that judgeth me is the Lord.
Wherefore judge nothing before the time, until the Lord come,
who will bring to light the hidden things of the heart." He will
cleanse your conscience constantly, so that things which you knew
not to be wrong may be known to be wrong a year hence, and
that things which you did not know to be wrong when you came to
this convention may be shown to you, and you may put them away,
so that your conscience may not only be restless, but responsive,
and get from the morbid stage to that where it is at rest in God.

There are two more things I want to say. You may have not
only a responsive conscience, but, on the other hand, a *rejected*
conscience. It is possible for you to sleep through an alarm clock;
it is possible for the telephone bell not to arouse you if you keep

on disregarding it; it is possible for the conscience to be dulled, if you are disobedient to the heavenly vision.

There was an Indian in North-West Canada once who was asked about conscience, and he said: "Conscience is a little three-cornered piece of tin inside my heart that turns round and round and hurts; but if I do not listen to it, by and by the corners will wear off, and then it will not hurt any more." Now, that is true. There are some animals in the caves of our earth which have no longer sight, though they have eyes; and some of them have no longer eyes upon the surface, though they have eyes under the surface. The simple story is that they used to be able to see and did not see; they had the chance of looking and did not look. They went where they need not go, they went into the darkness, and now they cannot see.

There are consciences like that: consciences that are seared, consciences that are defiled, consciences into which God has spoken and spoken again and yet again, but we would not listen; and to-day we can go to a thousand meetings and the hidden things of God seem powerless to speak to us. It hurts God, and it harms us. Yes, the other people are wounded too. "Ye wound their weak consciences." Why? All because we say, "I have no scruple in doing that. I used to have, but now I see that I was narrow and Puritanical and fanatical, and now it does not hurt me a bit!"

I remember a man saying to me once, "It does not hurt me at all to see a man bowing down before idols. It does not hurt me at all to go to Constantinople and see the Mohammedans at worship, because I think, 'Well, we are Christians and they are heathen and Mohammedans, and they were meant to be.'" There was a dead conscience that could not hear Jesus Christ say, "Go ye into all the world and preach the Gospel to every creature." There was a conscience that could not hear the dumb voice of heathen or Mohammedan that cried for a Saviour they had never known or seen.

It is quite true, you may have a rejected conscience; and you may lead other people wrong by it. Have you ever heard of a ship that was wrecked, and they could not find the cause until they came to examine the compass? Then they found that a man had been cleaning it with a penknife, and the point of the penknife had broken off and remained in the instrument, and so deflected the compass. When your conscience goes wrong you are leading other people astray as well as yourselves; wandering stars, lightships that have broken from their moorings and gone adrift.

Oh, I pray you, if your conscience speaks no longer as it did, let me give you one thought before I close. I dare not close without it. To leave you here would be to plunge some of you into despair. It would be a message not of the Gospel, but of darkness. So I want to say that you can have a *cleansed* conscience. "How much more shall the blood of Christ . . . cleanse your conscience" (Hebrews 9:14). When I read about the animals that never see because they have lost their capacity for seeing, I went on reading further in the thrilling book in which Darwin tells us about them, and I found this to my joy—because I was reading for your sakes, and wanted to find some comfort in this terrible nature-warning he had brought me. Darwin says that someone had found and observed some rats, not too far within the cave, which had partially lost their sight, but not entirely. When these were brought gradually from the darkness into a little light, then more, and still further, and then fuller light, the eye-sight gradually came back. I thank God for that, because I did not want to tell you that the atrophy was always irremediable, even in nature. I knew it was not in grace, but I did not want it to be complete even in nature. So I find God's message of grace to pass on in this illustration to you.

Is the sight going? May it not be quickened? Would you not like to see the things you used to see, to hear the voice of God as you used to hear it? There was a day when Cavalier, the Camisard leader, was led astray by a Delilah of a woman, and lost his touch with God and His cause. He came to England and was presented to Queen Anne. She said to him this, "M. Cavalier, does God speak to you as He used to do?" The great General's head was bent in shame, because the voice of God was no longer heard.

God has been whispering to you, and if the earthquake, and the wind, and the fire have not stirred you, there may be the still small voice that is sounding in your heart. You are frightened because it is so faint, and so far away; frightened because the telephone is so much more out of order than you ever dreamed. But, thank God, you can just spell out the message; you can just interpret what God wants you to do, and what He is saying to you. I pray you listen, that you may hear more, that you may be brought into fuller subjection, that you may be led on to full surrender. Hear now the first part of the message, and the rest of the messages that are yet to come during this convention shall ring truer and even clearer in your soul. So go out with one further light upon the way, and there may come a light above the sun which shall make you say, "Lord, what wilt Thou have me to do?" and then go out to bring the world to the feet of Jesus Christ. So we shall have learned that there is a pure, and a cleansed, and a vigorous and healthy conscience, which may be the possession of every redeemed child of God.

THE NEGLECTED VINEYARD

Rev. W. H. Aldis

ALMOST from the moment that I knew it would fall to my lot to give the second message on this Monday evening, my text has come to me almost irresistibly—I have tried to put it away, fearful lest it might seem unsuitable, or lest it might be misunderstood. It is something the Lord had to say to me, and having said it to me, I venture to pass it on to you. It is part of a verse in the Song of Solomon 1: 6, "They made me the keeper of the vineyards; but mine own vineyard have I not kept."

I hope that none of you will think of us who are on the platform as being in any way on a pedestal. I think I speak for most of us when I say that we would far rather be down there among you! We do not claim to have attained some spiritual height which justifies us in speaking to you. We are a team of men deeply conscious of our own weakness, recognising that in us there is nothing, and that apart from what the Lord is to us, and gives to us, we have nothing to give. We come as those who know their own frailty, but we come also as those who have learnt something, and are learning more of the secret of the life of victory; and we want to share it with you.

I suppose it would be true to say that the vast majority of those who have come to Keswick are engaged in some form of Christian service. It may be that you have been ordained to the sacred ministry; it may be that your Christian activity is that of a teacher in a Sunday-school class; you may be a leader in a Bible class, or a Crusader class, or some other young people's work. It may be that you are parents, with the responsibilities of children in the home. You may be conscious that all is not well, that things are not what they ought to be, or what you desire they should be, and you have come to Keswick hoping that here you will receive something which will send you back to your work with a new vision, a new passion, a new power, a new expectation. I believe that the Lord has brought us here so that He can put His finger on the thing that is wrong, the thing that hinders, the thing that is rendering us powerless and ineffective in our service. He wants to bring it out into the light. As the Psalmist said, "Thou hast set our secret sins in the light of Thy countenance." Why? Merely in order to expose them? No, a thousand times, no! In order to heal them; for I believe that the bringing out into the light of His countenance all those things which hinder, is like bringing them under the influence of some powerful ray which destroys the corrupt tissue. I believe there is healing power in the light of God's countenance, and He wants these things to be brought out into the light, not for the sake of exposure, but in order that we may be finally and completely healed.

It may be that our very service is our hindrance. It is so terribly possible to be over-busy. Some of you well remember how the late dear Bishop Taylor-Smith used to say that he prayed against "the barrenness of a busy life." We must be about our Master's business, but it is tragically possible to be over-busy, so busy that we have no time for our own vineyard. "They made me the keeper of the vineyards; but mine own vineyard have I not kept." Or, it is also terribly possible to be so occupied with our work, that we fail to realise the spiritual deterioration in our lives. We may be like Samson, who "wist not that the Lord had departed from him." Or like Ephraim, of whom the prophet Hosea said, "Strangers have devoured his strength, and he knoweth it not; grey hairs are here and there upon him, and yet he knoweth it not." Spiritual deterioration, yet so busy that we are lost to all realisation of it.

Is it not also possible to be fully occupied in the Lord's service, and at the same time to be neglecting our own vineyard? Was not that what St. Paul feared? "Lest, when I have preached to others, I myself should be a castaway." Oh, beloved fellow minister, ordained into the sacred ministry, is it possible that you have been so busy that you have been altogether unaware of that spiritual deterioration which your parishioners have seen? I remember how Dr. Meyer, of beloved memory in Keswick, on one occasion, as he was giving an address, took from his pocket a fountain pen and said, "This is my pen; I have had it for years. It wrote all my letters, it signed my name again and again. This is my pen, but I do not use it now, I use this one"— and he took another pen from his pocket, and said, "I sometimes imagine that first pen says to me, 'Master, why don't you use me? You used me all those years. I wrote your letters, I signed your cheques, and I was always in your hand, always being used by you; why don't you use me now?' And I said to my pen, 'Pen, you are still mine, and you are in my pocket, and near to my heart; you are dear to me because I bought you, but I cannot use you now because every time I use you you defile my hands, you are not clean.'" A homely illustration and, like all illustrations, incomplete; yet surely an illustration which reminds us of the terrible possibility that we may, as Christian workers, be unusable.

So we come back to the text, and think of the tragedy of the neglected vineyard of the soul. There is in the Book of Proverbs a picture of a neglected vineyard—"I went by the field of the slothful, and by the vineyard of the man void of understanding, and lo, it was all grown over with thorns, and nettles had covered the face thereof, and the stone wall thereof was broken down." A striking picture of a neglected vineyard. God forbid that it should be, in any respect, a picture of the vineyard of your soul. It is a terrible picture, and while primarily it refers to something material, yet surely there is a moral and spiritual application for each one of us. And, while it is especially directed against the slothful, it could be equally applied to any other cause of neglect— though I am not at all sure that sloth, in one of its many forms, may not be responsible for the neglect which leads to that tragic position in many lives.

What does the Lord of the vineyard see as He goes past the vineyard of your soul to-night? The Lord is here, and His eyes are as a flame of fire—that simply means that they search; and all His searching is the searching of love. What does He see as He passes by the vineyard of your soul to-night? Does He see bunches of luscious grapes hanging thickly in all their attractiveness and beauty—love, joy, peace, long-suffering, gentleness, goodness, faith, meekness, self-control? Is that what meets the eye of the Lord of the vineyard as He goes past the vineyard of your soul? Or, because of your neglect does He see it all grown over with weeds and thorns; and the wall—which surely is meant to represent the divinely ordered moral standards, the cherished safeguards of the soul—broken down? Is that possible? If any of you attempt some gardening, you know the peril of neglect. Any little piece of ground neglected, uncultivated, is very soon covered with weeds, and, if left, it is very difficult to eradicate them. That is true of the soul, and of the moral and spiritual life.

What does my Lord see? Does He see, as He looks with His eyes of searching love, the stinging nettles of jealousy, pride, envy, covetousness, impurity, self-indulgence, lying, dishonesty, bitterness, unforgivingness? Does He see these stinging nettles in the vineyard that ought to be producing luscious grapes—that Christ-like character represented by that wonderful bunch to which I have already referred?

All these things grow up so easily in the neglected vineyard. At first, they are scarcely noticed by ourselves; then they begin to grow, and become so obvious that they are quite impossible to hide. And finally they are visible to all, and lead to open backsliding. That is what is happening to-day in so many lives. That wall, which is the safeguard of the soul, once so strong and clean, is now broken down. Those moral standards, divinely ordered for us, broken down.

You are less careful than once you were, you are less sensitive to sin, and less particular; you say that, in this world of to-day, it is impossible to follow puritanical standards. In matters of honesty, how many Christians compromise? I remember telling a story here some years ago, about a man who professed to be a Christian who, during the first world war, made a lot of money. He did then, what so many have done in order to pay less Income Tax; he juggled with figures, and so presented his falsified returns that he got away with it, and was undetected. Then one day God met him, and he was truly converted. The first thing he did was to take those old books he had tried to forget, and calculate the amount he would have to repay to the Government, with interest, if he was going to be absolutely honest. He drew a cheque, went up to Somerset House, and asked to see somebody. He was ushered into an office where a man of some standing was waiting for him. He explained what he had come for, told how he had cheated, laid the cheque on the table and said, "That is what I owe." The official looked at him and said, "We should never have found this out; why did you bring it?" "Well," he said, "I have met God; I know what God demands of my life, and this cheque is the result." The official took him by the hand, and said, "I have been going to church now for forty years, and you are the first man I have met who ever had the courage to do a thing like this."

In matters of purity, is there in these days, when the moral standards have broken down, coming into your life a laxity in regard to these things? Many years ago the Rev. J. R. S. Wilson was giving an address on the story of the woman taken in adultery, and how the Scribes and Pharisees brought her to the Lord. They said to Him that, according to the law of Moses, she ought to be stoned. You remember the story how our Lord stooped down and began to write. They persisted with their challenge to Him, to see what He would say, and He rose and said, "Let him that is without sin among you first cast a stone at her" —and J. R. S. Wilson continued, "There is a legend that what Jesus was writing in the sand was the names of those men who had brought this woman. They drew near and looked over His shoulder as He wrote, and read 'Rabbi Ben Israel—guilty of adultery': Rabbi Ben Levi, guilty of the very sin for which he wanted the woman to be stoned, and so with the rest of them; and they slunk out."

Is yours a neglected vineyard? "They have made me the keeper of the vineyards; but mine own vineyard have I not kept." A Sunday-school class, a Bible class, a Crusader class, or some other form of work, or it may be parents with their children—have you been busy with this work, and neglected your own vineyard? If so, what are you going to do about it? You dare not leave it any longer; for your own sake this must be dealt with, and for His sake. In the Song of Solomon there is this beautiful word of the Bride to the Bridegroom, "Let my beloved come into his garden and eat his pleasant fruits." If the vineyard of your soul is a mass of weeds, how can the Beloved come into the garden and enjoy His pleasant fruits—you are just a disappointment to Him. He wants to come into the garden of your soul and enjoy those pleasant fruits—love, joy, peace, longsuffering, gentleness, goodness, faith, meekness, self-control—those wonderful fruits.

What shall be done? Just three things: (i) Get rid of the weeds; (ii) Rebuild the wall; (iii) Cultivate the fruit. First of all, *get rid of the weeds*. Oh, I agree with all my heart with what the Bishop of Worcester has said, "Bring these things to the Cross"; but there is another side of truth. I know a gardener whose garden is very prolific; I have watched him sometimes with a good deal of fascination, and I know that if I asked him one of the secrets of a prolific garden, he would say, "Keep the hoe going." He has an eagle eye for weeds and, when one pushes through the soil, you see him putting the hoe right down, and getting it out. That is what we have to do—keep the hoe going. That is what our Lord meant when He spoke those solemn words, "If thine hand offend thee (or, 'cause thee to stumble') cut it off . . . if thy foot cause thee to stumble, cut it off . . . if thine eye cause thee to stumble, pluck it out." Drastic words, yes, but it is a desperate situation, and it calls for drastic treatment; we have to get rid of the weeds. It is a painful operation, but we have to do it. The Lord does not do for us what He tells us to do; and we may spend months of crying to the Lord to do something for us, which He has told us to do. We must first get rid of the weeds, and then bring our sin-stained life and soul afresh to the Cross for cleansing.

Then you have to *rebuild the broken-down wall*. You have to make some acknowledgment that the wall has been broken down, that your conduct has been a stumbling-block to others, that you have gone to places where you ought not to have gone. You have to rebuild the wall, that safeguard of your soul—those moral standards which at our peril we lower.

Then *cultivate the fruit*. If sloth was the cause of the neglected vineyard and the weeds that grew, then deal with that thing. If we are going to cultivate the fruit, well, of course, we have to abide in Christ; but we also cultivate the fruit by more reading and studying of His Word, so that His Word may become a part of our very being. We need to read, mark, learn, and inwardly digest the Word of God; thus we shall cultivate the fruits. Moreover, it is in our prayer-life that we cultivate the fruits. How little time some of us spend in prayer! Yet it is by more time spent in prayer that we shall be cultivating the fruits.

Will you to-night get rid of the weeds, rebuild the wall, and cultivate the fruit, that you may be able to say to your Lord, "Let my Beloved come into His garden and eat His pleasant fruits"? It is so possible to come to Keswick and have what we call "a good time." I remember a young man who came to Keswick on his way to the mission field, knowing full well that there was something in his life which had to be put right away. He went through the whole of the week; he said he had a good time, and he went out to the mission field, living three years of practically fruitless service. He wrote and told me that, and also that he knew what the Lord wanted to deal with. He had brought forward all sorts of other things, except the one thing he knew had to be put right. He went right through the week at Keswick, without getting rid of this thing, so he had three years of fruitless service, until that wrong was confessed and put right. He wrote a letter to me full of joy as well as of contrition—joy that the Lord had begun to use him, and he was seeing some fruit to his labour. "They made me the keeper of the vineyards; but mine own vineyard have I not kept." Pluck out the weeds, rebuild the wall, and cultivate the fruit.

A WILD BULL IN A NET

Rev. W. W. Martin, M.A.

I AM not concerned, at this hour, with the context of this text, Isaiah 51 : 20. It is sufficient to state that in its setting it referred to the tragic condition into which Israel had fallen. They should have had the strength of an ox, but were impotent. Sin and idolatry had issued in their present condition, pictured as "a wild bull in a net."

A wild bull. What a magnificent picture and symbol of strength! Look at those massive shoulders; see him as he shakes his rugged head; see him with his flashing, flaming eyes; watch him as he paws the ground; behold his switching tail. And now look, as he is charging down the street; nothing can withstand his onward way; everybody and everything gets out of his path. Magnificent! Irresistible! But *a wild bull in a net*, tied with bits of string, impotent: what a tragedy, how pathetic! But there is something more tragic than that. Here is a young man, strong, healthy, with the vigour of youth coursing through his veins. He has learned the secret of life; he has made the great surrender to Jesus Christ; they are sharing life together. Magnificent! Oh, how we need young men like that in our country to-day! But such an one *in a net*. A young man in a net tied by habit, fettered in his Christian life, bound with the cords of a besetting sin which is restraining his activities, and conscious, as a young man said to me the other day, of "frustration at every turn." Tragic!

Here is a young woman with all the charm and grace of young womanhood; she has laid her life at the feet of Jesus Christ, she is an influence for God wherever she goes. What an asset to the country. Magnificent! On the other hand, see a young woman "in a net," tied by cords of fashion, fettered by sinful habit, a slave to custom. Tragic!

Here is a man of business, **a** man who puts God first in his life; who has put the candle of his Christian witness on his bushel of business; whose word is as good as his bond. This man is known as one not ashamed of Christ. His influence on all those with whom he comes in contact is good. On the other hand, see the businessman in a net. Tragic! And how the world scorns any profession he may make.

God means all His people to be free. The Bible rings this out again and again—"the liberty wherewith Christ hath made us free." You remember what our Lord said to Nicodemus: "The wind bloweth where it listeth, and thou hearest the sound thereof, but canst not tell whence it cometh or whither it goeth; so is every one that is born of the Spirit." Free as the wind; "glorious liberty" is what the apostle called it. Yet many men and women are "in a net," and Proverbs 5: 22 is right. "He shall be holden with the cords of his sin."

Now Satan is skilled in the use of the net. He is a greater Retarius than ever competed in a Roman amphitheatre, and he has the experience of many centuries on which to draw. Let us remember that Satan is doing his utmost to thwart God, in two ways. He tries to keep the unconverted asleep, and, if he cannot do that, flings his net over the converted. In a mission hall I saw a woman with a baby in her arms, who became restless, and in that exquisite way that mothers have, she gently rocked the little one to sleep. I thought of Satan who, when a man or woman begins to be restless, comes along and says, "Plenty of time yet, don't be in a hurry, don't worry, think it over, go to sleep again." I do not wonder the apostle cries out, "Awake, thou that sleepest, and arise from the dead." If Satan cannot do that, then he tries to put the believer in a net.

How, then, do God's children come to be "in a net"? There are two methods: they may be gradually enveloped or suddenly overwhelmed. Sometimes the cords of the net gradually fetter their feet; instead of running the way of God's commandments, they walk; then, instead of walking in daily life, they stand still. First hindered in their running, they are brought to a standstill; there is no progress or witness in their Christian life, which issues in stagnation. Then we have the other method of sudden entanglement. In an hour of unwatchfulness, of sudden temptation, in a moment of catastrophe, the man becomes entangled all at once. The Bible, that great record of Christian experience, has many illustrations of the two methods. We are going to look at them, because the record of those experiences is probably the same as that of many in this tent.

Joseph, at seventeen years of age. There are two critical ages in everyone's life—seventeen, when a young man or young woman begins to be conscious of physical and mental development, when customs become habits, when life's character is formed—seventeen is a critical age; and forty-five also. Our divorce courts are eloquent as to the dangers of the years between forty and fifty. Joseph was seventeen, that critical age. See how Satan tried to fling his net over him through the agency of

Potiphar's wife; it was flung, but every time Joseph escaped in triumph. Young man, if Joseph escaped from that tremendous temptation, there is not the slightest reason why you should be the slave of this or any habit or custom. Many a man knows from bitter experience what that sudden temptation is, and it always ends in tragedy.

Samson's was no sudden entanglement, however. It was the net of lust which gradually encircled him through trifling with Delilah, listening to the seductions of sin. For a while he could free himself. "I will go out and shake myself," he said; and he did. But there came a day of slavery.

Here is a man trifling with sin, harbouring it—that book, that thought, that suggestion; and all the while Satan, through Delilah, was just making that net until there came a day of hopeless impotence. Men and women, beware of harbouring that sin of lust. It may be only a simple thought, it may be a picture, it may be a companion. You nurse that viper, but it will eventually bite—or, to use the words of our metaphor, some day you will become netted, and then you will realise with bitter sorrow that you are encircled.

Elijah was caught in the net of depression. He had endured a tremendous strain, but his magnificent challenge on Mount Carmel had cost him a great deal, physically, mentally and spiritually; he was absolutely exhausted and had fled away. God was very good to him, and sent an angel to feed him, and protect him from wild beasts. Listen to him: "I cannot go on . . . It is enough; now, O Lord, take away my life." I wonder if there is someone here, perhaps a missionary or some Christian worker, who has been fighting bravely against tremendous odds during the war years. You have just come back after some prolonged strain, you are tired out, and the reaction has come. You are so weary, your spiritual vitality seems to be ebbing away. Dear heart, God understands. Jesus Christ, too, was weary as He sat by the well. "He knows how hardly souls are woo'd and won." "His choicest wreaths are always wet with tears." Cheer up, you are going to get the victory.

David, too, was caught in the net in an hour of sudden temptation. I need not go into the particulars, they are too tragic. You may say it was Bathsheba's fault, she should have been more careful; but you must trace it farther back than that. 2 Samuel 11: 1 reveals the secret. In an hour "when kings go forth to war," David "tarried still at Jerusalem," and in this hour of idleness he fell. David was scarred for life, and his future was one of suffering through the result of that tragedy. Many suffer throughout life from a sudden hour like this.

Jeremiah was caught in the net of despondency. He had a very onerous task; he was told at the beginning of his ministry that Israel would never listen to him; yet he was to go on protesting and warning; but they would take no notice. He flung his words time and again in warning, and there was no result. There came a day of despondency when he thus spoke: "I said, I will not make mention of Him, nor speak any more in His name." Perhaps you are feeling like that. You have been flinging yourself against that great fortress of Mohammedanism, and somehow you do not seem to have made any impression at all. You have been toiling in some hard parish, or other sphere of work, and you are weary, and you are met with indifference and no response. You are feeling utterly dispirited. Cheer up, I have a message for you before we close our talk together.

There came a day when Paul was entangled in the net of conflict. He longed to do God's will, and he found his old fleshly nature striving in the ceaseless struggle between flesh and will. Listen to what he wrote: "The flesh lusteth against the Spirit and the Spirit against the flesh." "What I would, that do I not; but what I hate, that do I . . . O wretched man that I am! Who shall deliver me from the body of this death?" Many of you know that struggle. You want to do right, yet somehow you are overcome. Your experience is an alternating one—defeat and victory, victory and defeat. You have tried your hardest, and to-day you are like St. Paul. But a little later on the net was broken, and St. Paul was able to talk about the "glorious liberty of the children of God."

Simon Peter was caught in the net of an uncontrolled life. He possessed an ungoverned tongue. There was no doubt as to his loyalty to his Master, as the following will show: "I will follow Thee to prison and to death." "Why cannot I follow Thee now?" "Lord, I would die with Thee . . . yet will I not deny Thee." It came hot out of Peter's heart, and he meant every word of it; yet through the agency of a little serving maid he was ensnared in a net. Later, in a private interview with his Lord, the net was broken.

How many of God's people have uncontrolled tongues? Would you like to be free? I have a remedy to tell in a few minutes.

Think of Demas. What a magnificent Christian he was. St. Paul calls him "my fellow-labourer." But there came a day when Paul had to write, "Demas hath forsaken me, having loved this present world, and is departed unto Thessalonica." He was tempted unto Thessalonica, a city full of commerce, a city of pleasure, and the lure of the city weaved a net around him. He is not the only man. Do you remember how enthusiastic you once were for God?

You went out into the wilderness, you were absolutely red-hot for Him, there was nothing you would not do; yet somehow the devil has been weaving a net little by little, and the old enthusiasm has gone, and you are a very commonplace Christian now. "Departed unto Thessalonica"—is that true of you? You say you have gained experience. Your zeal is now tempered by discretion. Nonsense! Don't try to skulk behind that! Let us face up to it. Are you as keen a Christian as you were in those early days when you learned the secret of the forgiveness of sins, or are you like Demas, in the world with all its fascinations, while the devil is just weaving a net around you?

Judas—I expect he used to steal things when his mother was not looking, and his besetting sin was harboured until he sold his Lord for thirty pieces of silver. He was netted and he never got free. Have you a besetting sin? God save you from the sin of Judas.

Now, there are three ways of trying to escape. There is the way of the fatalist who says, we must expect sometimes to be beaten and sometimes to be successful; defeat and victory must alternate. What a miserable Christian life!—very different from the Scriptural picture of it. Then there is self-effort, using the scissors of determination and good resolution, cutting a bit of the cord here and there. This may produce temporary freedom, but before very long you find yourself entangled again.

What is the Gospel provision? In the city of Capernaum that Sabbath morn, the Preacher said: "He hath anointed me to preach deliverance to the captives"—not gradual but instantaneous freedom. Let us put it plainly: whatever be the net which has enclosed you—I may not have touched on it in the illustrations I have given—whatever the net that has made you conscious of frustration, here and now you may become free. The Great Emancipator has been doing it all through the centuries, and for the past sixty years at Keswick. This tent has witnessed such miracles year after year. Fettered souls have heard the words, "Loose him and let him go," and have been set free. Here, by faith, before you leave this tent, you can have freedom. Are you dead keen? If we seek Him with all our heart, we shall find Him. Will you not determine that, somehow, and at any cost, you will be free from this net which is stunting your life and spoiling your work? Are you absolutely determined? If you play with the thing it is no good: God has nothing to do with triflers in this matter. Will you abandon all self-effort? St. Paul in that struggle between flesh and spirit found great deliverance. Our effort means I and God—the emphasis is on the "I." Are you prepared to put the "I" behind, and then it will be God, and you co-operating with Him.

No matter how much you try to struggle, you will never do it by that means; the devil is too smart for you, he has thousands of years of experience. Will you deliberately hand over your life, with all its faculties and its powers, to the Lordship of Christ? This will, of course, mean abandoning everything which is wrong or doubtful, and being loyal to Christ in active co-operation with Him. It means His absolute lordship over you, to control and lead wherever He wills—not that it will make you careless, but it will remove the responsibility from you to Him.

But I have a warning for you: it is possible to be free, and yet to return to the old fetters afterwards. If a dog can return to the vomit, and the sow to her wallowing in the mire, Christians can return to the old fettered life. There are men and women who years ago deliberately crowned Jesus Christ King of their lives, who have lost their freedom and are again entangled with the yoke of bondage. St. Paul well urged the Galatians to "Stand fast in the liberty wherewith Christ hath made us free." What is the safeguard for this?

Joseph gives us the key. Some six times we read, "God was with Joseph." God and he shared his life together. Whether when sold as a slave, or in Potiphar's house, or in false accusation, or in prison, or on the throne, God and he shared all experiences together. How he came into such a wonderful union is not related; but it was this secret which kept him true and free. It was exemplified in the fierce temptation through which he passed scathless. It would have been a sin against Potiphar, against Potiphar's wife, against his own body, against his own soul; but the great factor is found in his words, "How then can I do this great wickedness and *sin against God*?" It is as we are thus linked up with our Lord, that we shall daily and hourly be kept in all the freedom which is our heritage in Christ.

> He breaks the power of cancelled sin,
> He sets the captive free.

A PERIL OF SPIRITUAL MATURITY

Rev. George B. Duncan, M.A.

WILL you turn with me to 1 Kings 13—a passage of Scripture that may not be very well-known; for I want to consider with you some aspects of failure in Christian living which are peculiarly the peril of those who have grown older in Christian experience, and to do so against the background of this story. And if we want a text to focus our thought at the beginning, we shall take it from v. 11, "Now there dwelt an old prophet in Bethel . . ."

May I begin by saying that I know perfectly well that *age has its prerogatives*. There are some things that age has that youth can never have. I think, for instance, of the *wealth of experience* that age alone can enjoy. I suppose that most of us know what it is to meet older Christians who are rich in experience, who have a wealth of memory that makes them seem rich indeed; veterans of many battlefields and conquests; men and women who have walked a long way with God. They have a maturity of judgment, a knowledge of life and of the Bible, a knowledge of God, that seem to make the problems that baffle and perplex us quite simple, and enable them to avoid the mistakes that those of us who are younger so easily make. In this wealth of experience they have a prerogative over youth: and also, I believe, in *the work of encouragement*. Many of us can recall meeting Christians the wealth of whose experience has humbled us, for those same men and women have accomplished a work of encouragement which has helped us along. And how humbly grateful we shall ever be for that ministry and that memory, that set our feet steadfastly on the way.

But while age and experience have their prerogatives, they also have their *perils*: and it is to these that I want to turn your thought.

Years ago I heard a Christian say, "Few Christians end well." You know, if that is true, then it is more than ever vital that the experienced Christian who so rightly thinks that "he standeth," should "take heed lest he fall." May I add very humbly that I address these words as much to myself as to anyone who has been a servant of Jesus Christ for more than a few years, for it is more than twenty-one years since I led my first evangelistic mission, and

I am beginning now to think of some of the perils that the passing of the years can bring.

Let us turn, then, and look into the mirror of God's Word and see there *ourselves*: and as we read I want to remind you that age is a relative term, and God's Word may come to those who are not so very old, but older than others. So let us look at this old prophet who dwelt in Bethel. And first I want to note with you what I call—

I. The Lethargy that Marked His Service.

Here was a man who had spiritually very nearly come to a standstill. Note *the inaction into which he had settled down.* Bethel, where he lived, was the scene of Jeroboam's sin—the setting up of false religion, served by false priests. The details are found in the closing verses of the previous chapter. The action of the king was to become proverbial and legendary in the history of Israel: for Jeroboam was the king "who made Israel to sin." The motive of Jeroboam's sin was political expediency; the action, one of spiritual apostasy. And in the face of this challenge, the old prophet was silent. He had nothing to say, and said nothing. Why was this? Why had this lethargy settled down across his service for God? Was it because of *weariness*? He had fought through many battles in the past: he just could not rouse himself for yet another battle: this time he would leave it to others to fight. Or perhaps it was *worldly wisdom*—for he had a family to look after, and it would not do to incur disfavour in high places. Would it matter if he compromised just this once, and let this thing pass unrebuked? Well, whatever the reasons, the silence remained unbroken, the message unspoken, and the servant of God remained at home. The lethargy that marked his service.

I want to ask, Is this, perchance, true of you? Is your pace slowing down? Spiritually, vitally, you have very nearly come to a halt and a standstill? There was a time when no one was keener than you in the ministry of prayer. In your own prayer-life you prayed with some purpose. In the prayer-life of your church, you could always be relied upon: your prayer meant so much to the church, to God, to the minister, to yourself. But in your praying you have slowed down; and for weeks, for months, it may be for years, "the old prophet" has come almost to a halt in his prayer-life.

In your consecration you were once fastidiously careful: your standards were high, almost intolerably so, in your separation to Christ from the world . . . but it cost so much to maintain that standard, and you grew so weary, and so wise, that slowly and almost imperceptibly the world has encroached, and as far as consecration is concerned, you have almost forgotten the meaning of the word.

What about your service? How desperately keen you were; how unashamedly you used to go out for the conversion of others—and you saw them converted. But that has all stopped now: you are not interested in that; you do not toil for that; you do not labour for that; you do not preach for that; you do not suffer for that as once you did. You are a Christian still; you are a prophet still; you still hold office—you are a deacon; you are an elder; you are a Sunday-school teacher, you are a member of a committee, a chairman of a committee, you are a minister, you are a bishop, a missionary, a Christian parent: you are holding office. Listen, all the spiritual vitality has been drained out of it, and there is a lethargy upon your service, and you have come to a halt, and you are at a standstill. Your testimony? You have none. Your usefulness has practically gone. You are holding on to a position; you have a rank to which you have ceased to have the spiritual right. The inaction into which he had settled.

And then I want you to notice *the intrusion by which He was startled.* The lethargy which was upon the life of this old prophet was suddenly, rudely startled; the silence which he had been careful to maintain was suddenly, sharply broken. His sons rushed in to tell him of the dramatic event: that the king himself had been offi- ciating at the high place that very day, and the man of God, a young man of Judah, had dramatically interrupted the service. The curse of God had been pronounced against the altar; and the king, violently angry, had caused the instant arrest of the man of God—and he had been struck immediately by the hand of God in judgment. Then a cowed and frightened king had pleaded for mercy, before a rent altar, amid the smoke of the scattered ashes. A cringing and conciliatory monarch had offered hospitality and rewards—to find his offer treated with contempt. What had been the words of the man of God from Judah, to the king? "If thou wilt give me half thine house, I will not go in with thee, neither will I eat bread nor drink water in this place: for so was it charged me by the word of the Lord." The long silence had been broken, and like a sudden peal of thunder out of a leaden and sullen sky, the voice of God had spoken; and with glowing faces the sons of the old prophet ended their breathless story, while the old man watched and listened.

What was it that turned their glowing faces into puzzled wonderment? Was it the sudden, stabbing realisation that what had just happened should have happened long ago? And that the man who should have done it was not the man of God from Judah, but the old prophet, their father, to whom they now told their story— across whose face consternation and anger now chased each other, until finally a burning, sullen anger settled there, and the man who had been inactive so long, stung into action, demanded, "Where did that man of God go?"

The intrusion by which he was startled. All I know is this, that again and again, where the lethargy of our service has slowed down to inaction, when an intrusion comes to startle us into amazement and into anger—when a minister comes to the church with a flaming heart; a son or a daughter is converted in their Christian home to God, and with passionate devotion they give their all to Christ; when a man or a girl joins the fellowship of the church with heart afire for God; a Christian comes into the office, a new nurse starts her training in the hospital, a new curate joins the staff —and the silence is broken. The lethargy is startled into alarm. God begins to speak directly, where there was a comfortable security and quietness. All is disturbed and confused. And the "old prophet," amazed, alarmed, angry, is stirred to action at last.

The lethargy that marked his service . . . Is there an old prophet listening to me now? Spiritually you have come to a halt. Has somebody come into your life? Has the voice of God spoken?

Worse followed, for the lethargy that marked the service of the old prophet was replaced by what I call—

II. THE ANIMOSITY THAT SEARED HIS SPIRIT.

Here we face the tragic fact that the man who took no action at all against the deeds of Jeroboam, became passionately and angrily active against the man of God. One of the things that appals me, that shames me, is just this very thing: the ceaseless animosity of Christian against Christian. You find it in churches, you find it in fellowships, you find it on mission stations, you find it in societies, you find it wherever you find Christians: and the tragedy is that those involved are very, very seldom youngsters in the faith. Children do not normally kill children. Men kill men. You do not find it in the Sunday-school, you do not find it among the young people in the Youth Fellowship. You do not find it among the confirmation candidates. You find it at a higher level. You find it among the older Christians, in your deacons' court, among your elders, in your kirk session; you find it among your clergy and ministers, in your committees, among your Sunday-school teachers, in Christian parents; you find it in the "old prophet." This is where you find it: the animosity that sears the spirit.

Then you find that those who have ceased to be active in the vital things of God against the enemy of souls, are tirelessly active against the "men of God." Why? Why was this old prophet roused to action—not against the false worship of Jeroboam: he did not do a thing about that. Why was he roused to action against the faithful servant of Jehovah? I think, first of all, because of *a pride that would not be humbled.* The man's pride was hurt to the quick. The man who remained unmoved when God's name was dishonoured, was stung to the quick when his own actions were condemned. The security and comfort he had gained by compromising his loyalty had been treated with contempt by another. The standards that he had lowered by his slackness had been raised again to the mast by the zealousness of the man of God. The silence he had so carefully maintained had been broken. The message he had ceased to declare had been declared by another. Everything he knew he should have been, and had failed to be, the man of God from Judah had been. And as his own sons told the story of it all, they told the story of his own condemnation; and his pride hated it. A man in his position, a man of his age, a man of his experience, being condemned, being judged! He had been weighed in the balances, and found wanting. Not explicitly, for the man of God from Judah had not said a word about him: but he had been condemned implicitly. He sensed it as he listened to the story told by his own sons. He saw it in the glow that had been kindled, and still shone, on their faces. His imagination ran riot as he followed the telling of the story in a thousand homes in Bethel that day; and with the telling he would have been called "the old prophet, the man who had done nothing, the man who had lowered his standards, the man who had compromised . . ." Condemned! condemned . . . and *he hated it.*

Have you got a pride that will not be humbled? Oh, his wounded, resentful pride writhed and twisted with the pain of it all, until the focus of all the hate and all the hurt was found in *a purpose that would not be halted*—to find the man, and somehow to bring him down; to bring him down to his own level, and to make him swallow those words of contempt, "Neither will I eat bread nor drink water in this place," making himself out to be better than the old prophet—for *he* had been eating bread and drinking water there for these years and months past. So the purpose was formulated and pursued until he found the man of God. The animosity that seared his spirit.

Tell me, are you more active against the people of God than against the enemies of God? Are you? Is it possible? Do you write more, do you talk more, do you think more, do you plan more, against the servants of God, than His enemies? Do you? I'll tell you why. Because the life of somebody has condemned you. Not verbally, but implicitly. Am I speaking to some parents, and your child's love for Jesus Christ condemns your lack of love? Am I speaking to some minister, and the zeal of someone in your church condemns your lack of it? Am I speaking to some Christian worker, and your compromising with the world is condemned by the consecration of your colleague; some clerk or typist, some nurse, and your silence is condemned by the witness of that new girl; some missionary, and the standard of your devotion to Jesus Christ—or lack of it—is condemned by another? Tell me, have you got a pride that will not be humbled? You have come to Keswick, but in your heart you are pursuing some devilish purpose to bring that one down by fair means or foul, that they too may come under condemnation, for having dared to suggest that you, with your position, with all your experience, and at your age, that *you* were wrong?

Listen, my friend, very briefly as I close. You and I have been looking into the mirror of God's truth in the light of this "old prophet." We have seen the lethargy that marked his service, the animosity that seared his spirit; note finally—

III. THE TRAGEDY THAT CROWNED HIS SUCCESS.

For the old prophet succeeded. And listen: you too can succeed. Parent, you can take the love of your child for Christ, that love, that burden for souls, and *you can kill that.* Brother minister, you can temper all the burning zeal of that young fellow, and quench it. Christian worker, you can lower the standards of that other young person, you can silence that fresh and artless testimony. You can. The old prophet did. And to do it, you will use *the weapon that he used.* Do you know what that was? He used his tongue. And with a blend of friendliness, a touch of authority, a suggestion of divine guidance, with his tongue the old prophet —are you listening?—he *lied.* And as he spoke, he knew he lied. You, too, can use your tongue—one of the most powerful and deadly things we possess. That is why it is one of the touchstones of Christian maturity: "if any man offend not in word (in tongue), the same is a perfect man." You can go on talking persistently: you can speak authoritatively, you can even use the language of spirituality; and in the use of your tongue *you can lie.* And even as you are claiming that what you say is right, you know in your heart that you are lying.

The old prophet knew that he lied. Is there some older Christian here, and you are—am I being hard?—in your dealings with the young, whoever it is, with that other servant of God, whether flagrantly, whether obviously, or whether rather cleverly and with just a tinge of suggestion, you are a liar, and you know it. The weapon you used was the weapon the old prophet used. It was the weapon the devil used when he said to our first parents, "Ye shall not surely die!"

The weapon he used: and *the wreckage he saw* . . . for he brought the young man to the path of disobedience. He brought him into the path of danger. He brought him to the place of death. For suddenly, a leap from the lion, a moment of agony, and a life of usefulness was over. The tragedy that crowned his success.

You see, he did succeed. And one of the supreme tragedies of age is that when we succeed, *we kill* somebody's love for the Master, somebody's purpose of obedience, somebody's devotion and surrender. We succeed, and we slay.

Old prophet, how many lives of usefulness have you ended? The life of one of your children? A member of your church? Somebody on the mission station? Somebody who came under your authority? You lied, and you slew. Old prophet, is there somebody you have not killed yet, but are planning to? Come, stand for just one moment as we close, by the wreckage of the life you lied to destroy. Can you see the face, as the old prophet looked on the face of the man of God on the road that day? The love you killed, the devotion you slew, the testimony you silenced, the consecration you destroyed, the usefulness you ended?

Come, stand by the old prophet. I wonder if you have one thing more in common with him? Listen. The lethargy that marred his service; the animosity that seared his spirit; the tragedy that crowned his success; can you share this—*the agony that broke his heart*? "And the old prophet came to the city, to mourn . . ." Thank God for his tears that flowed! Do you know anything of tears like these? If you don't know what it is to weep here, I only hope that God will give you a place in heaven where you can weep, and weep, and weep . . . for the child of God whose usefulness you killed, whose love you extinguished. Ah, there are those alive to-day, but all the testimony, all the usefulness, everything worthwhile is *dead*. And it was an old prophet that did it.

If we share the agony that broke the heart of the old prophet, and know something of the tears that flowed, then possibly we too may share one other thing in the agony that he knew, for we read in the story, not only of the tears that flowed, but of the testimony that fell from his lips. For at last the old prophet would seem to have been brought back to God, and the lips that had been sealed and silent for so long without any real testimony bore this testimony: "The saying which he cried by the word of the Lord shall surely come to pass." And if you know that your experience of the past months, or even years, has been that of the old prophet that dwelt at Bethel, then may God grant that your lips, too, may be unsealed, and that once again a testimony to the word of the Lord may fall from your lips, bringing grace and mercy and salvation to others.

THOU ART THE MAN!

Rev. Alan Redpath

And the Lord sent Nathan unto David. And he came unto him, and said unto him, There were two men in one city; the one rich, and the other poor. The rich man had exceeding many flocks and herds: but the poor man had nothing, save one little ewe lamb, which he had bought and nourished up; and it grew up together with him, and with his children; it did eat of his own meat, and drank of his own cup, and lay in his bosom, and was unto him as a daughter. And there came a traveller unto the rich man, and he spared to take of his own flock and of his own herd, to dress for the wayfaring man that was come unto him; but took the poor man's lamb, and dressed it for the man that was come to him. And David's anger was greatly kindled against the man; and he said to Nathan, As the Lord liveth, the man that hath done this thing shall surely die: and he shall restore the lamb fourfold, because he did this thing, and because he had no pity. And Nathan said to David, Thou art the man—2 SAMUEL 12: 1–7.

I N A very short time this Keswick Convention will be a matter of history. What will its history be? When we look back upon it, will it simply be that we are able to say that we have had a good week, and that God has given us some helpful messages, and has blessed our heart—and we go home to the same job, the same ministry, to the same mission field, to grind away as before? It could be that; or it could be that there has been such a stab, such a penetrating stab, that never shall we be the same again. The question as to what this convention will be depends upon one thing—and I say this without in any sense disregarding the sovereignty of God. It depends upon whether you are *prepared to face sin*: not somebody else's sin, but your sin; not somebody else's downfall, but the downfall which threatens you; not somebody else's collapse in spiritual life, but the collapse on the very verge of which you are living. Everything depends upon whether you are willing to step into the searchlight of God's Word, and look up into His face and hear the Holy Spirit say deep down in your soul, until you cry to God to have mercy upon you, "Thou art the man!"

What do you think saps the vitality of a country like Britain? What do you think causes shame in the ranks of the Christian Church? What is it that causes far more casualties than the appalling list of accidents on roads, in the air, or on the rail? It is the sin of David. And this is not limited to ungodly circles. The toll of blasted lives and ruined homes is not something which we can preach at a godless crowd: it is something that evangelical Christians to-day—you and I—have to take to our hearts, and bow before God in shame. A student disappears from a University, a theological professor quietly resigns, a church is suddenly looking for a new pastor, a deacon is missing from the diaconate, a Sunday-school teacher or Bible class leader has withdrawn. What has happened? "Thou art the man!" And the thing has come to light; the Holy Ghost has revealed it, and it has come before the public eye—and by this deed, as the fourteenth verse of this chapter says, "Thou hast given great occasion to the enemies of the Lord to blaspheme."

And what about all that is undiscovered by the human eye, and all that goes on behind camouflage and closed doors and the smoke-screen of hypocrisy? "He that covereth his sin shall not prosper." Oh that the Lord might have mercy upon us, and lay bare our hearts before Him; for until your heart is broken, until you are honestly prepared to put the label SIN where God puts it, until you are honestly prepared to acknowledge and agree with what the Spirit of God speaks to you about, there will be no breaking through in this convention of Holy Ghost power, and there will be no impact upon the mission fields of the world. And how desperately this world, and how desperately this country, and how desperately this convention, and how desperately my heart needs something more than a series of good meetings! How urgently we need brokenness, how urgently we need revival, how desperately we need Holy Ghost conviction, how desperately we need to come to the feet of our precious Lord in penitence.

Let me speak to you concerning the *preparation* of this man David: the background of his life. I hardly need to remind you that it was the background of the hills and the country, the mountains and the sheep-farms. The lad who kept the sheep, strong and athletic, leaping over a wall, able to tear a lion to pieces and rend a bear; a master in the use of sling and stone; with a face that glowed with health and youthful beauty. A poet, a shepherd, destined to be a king; deeply religious; so sure that the Lord was his Shepherd, that he would never want; afraid of secret faults and presumptuous sin. And one day God sent Samuel to Bethlehem, saying, "Anoint him; this is he." And from that day the Spirit of God came upon David, as 1 Samuel 16 tells us. From childhood he had known the quickening of the Spirit of God; now he was to know the special anointing of the Holy Ghost.

How often we have met those who undoubtedly are born again, who are sound in their doctrine and who know the Lord, but in whose lives manifestly there is something tragically missing. There is no ability to grapple with the heart or conscience of a congregation; no power, somehow, to bring under the very wave of heavenly conviction and authority. The Holy Spirit is in them, but somehow He is not upon them in anointing. But in the life of this young man David, the flame of God the Holy Ghost had fallen in his youth upon the burnt offering of a consecrated life, and he knew the anointing of the Third Person of the Trinity. God was his Rock, his Redeemer, his Shepherd. In weariness he knew how to find green pastures; in thirst he knew where to go for still waters; in perplexity and in pressure he knew the place of quietness. He set the Lord ever before him.

His battle with Goliath, his treatment of Saul—these things are known so well by us all; and in all this he learned to take meekly the spiteful attacks of other people. Never was he resentful, never was he bitter with others: a man who obviously knew the moving, the melting, the authority of God the Holy Ghost upon his life. Such is the man after God's own heart; such was the calibre of the man who one day was tripped up and caught in a net by the devil and crushed in humiliation. Oh, beloved, from what heights of blessing it is possible to fall! From what experience of glow and power and heavenly reality it is possible to crash in shame. There is never a day but that the man speaking to you is capable of David's sin, but for the grace of God and the power of the blood of Jesus; and there never will be until I get to heaven.

So I think of the *passion* of David: not only his preparation, but the passion of his heart—unknown to anyone else except God; but it became revealed. The crash of his life did not happen in an impetuous outburst of passion in a moment. He had sown the seed in youth. For twenty years before the tragedy of David's life, we are told in 2 Samuel 5: 13 that "David took him wives out of Jerusalem," in direct breaking of the law of God which forbade the multiplication of wives by Hebrew kings lest their hearts should be turned from God. Yet no sooner had David risen to a place of authority, no sooner had he been crowned king over Israel at the age of thirty, than he became indulgent behind the scenes. Now he had got somewhere, now he had reached the pinnacle, now he was in the position of authority, he could afford to be less disciplined; he could afford to be a little more indulgent with himself; and he took to himself wives.

The eleventh chapter of this book tells the story of his sin; and it begins by telling us that while David's armies were at war, David tarried still at Jerusalem. Indulgence has led to indolence. He is out of the fighting line now; he is taking his spiritual vacation, a period off; putting other people into the thick of the fight, he is standing at the back and trying to command them, as it were, from his study or from his desk: he is not in the front line of the battle, he is having an easy time at home. And, to quote the word of Nathan the prophet, "a traveller came afoot," and to satisfy the traveller he went to the house of a poor man and took his one little ewe lamb, even though he himself had so much. And my Bible puts the whole blame on David, not a shred of it on Bathsheba. Before a king she was obliged to give in. In a few moments his character was blackened and his kingdom imperilled, and the Lord was his enemy, and his enemies had been given cause to blaspheme.

Soon David knew that the truth could not be hidden. His blood ran hot and cold. Somehow the thing must be covered up: Uriah must come home—send for him! But Uriah, a man of discipline, a man of integrity, one of David's own soldiers, refused to indulge himself as his king had done. All right, then; Uriah must die. Dead men tell no tales, and a dead Uriah can never deny the paternity of this child. I wonder what General Joab thought when he got his master's instructions to kill Uriah? Strange leader, this; strange leader, that he sings such wonderful psalms and plays such wonderful tunes, and yet is capable of this! Uriah died; and David supposed that nobody but he and Joab would know a thing about it. But there was a fatal flaw in David's reckoning—"The thing that David had done displeased the Lord" (11:27). It was known in heaven; but not only was it known in heaven, presently it was to be known in all the universe, and it was to be recounted through all the centuries, and it was to be known in the Keswick tent in 1957 for our admonition, our warning, our learning, that any one in any authoritative position might take heed lest he fall.

Oh, the tragedy, that this man who walked with God—a psalmist, a poet, a shepherd, a great spiritual force, who knew the anointing of the Spirit upon him—had it all trampled in the dust through the peril of indulgence, the peril of indolence and laziness, the peril of leisure hours. Middle life for David, and for you and me, brings no immunity from the absolute dire necessity of buffeting our body and bringing it into subjection, lest, having preached to others, we ourselves be disqualified.

Somebody might say to me, "A very interesting sermon this, to some people; but David's sin is not mine." Are you sure?

Define it in the light of our Lord's words, "Thou hast heard it said, Thou shalt not commit adultery. I say unto you, he that looketh . . . to lust, is guilty." Have you attained to some position in evangelical circles; are you a leader of a missionary society, a preacher, a minister, a teacher in a Bible class, a missionary on furlough? Have you got somewhere in Christian work? Have you? But, because you have got there, you have slackened in discipline; you have begun to say to yourself, "I of course never go to the movies, but I see some wonderful things on television. I spend far more time with my TV set than with my Bible. I would not for a moment encourage a young person to do so, but when nobody is looking I turn the knob, and there are things there that I look at now that I never knew existed years before." Is that you? And you have risen to a place in evangelical circles!

But listen. Years ago you sowed the seed of a habit, and Satan put in your path one of his subtle unseen nets, and he caught you in it, and you have been dragging that net through the years with you; you have been forming habits, and in Christian life you have become indulgent and slack and lazy and indolent. You are not in the front line of the fight now. Oh no; you prefer to direct the work from your study, from your desk, from your office, and send someone else to do the task. You are not in the front line for God now; you have withdrawn, you have come home on extended furlough, you have made some excuse about your health—and why is it your health has broken down? Is it because of this thing? You have withdrawn, and through life there has been built up in you a habit, a sin, David's sin; and it has never been confessed. And, look, the climax is round the corner; the tragedy is about to break, and the thing is about to come out.

The *penitence* of David. For twelve months he wrapped the wretched business up in his heart and said nothing. He stiffened his proud neck, pursed his lips, refused to give in or to confess. But what was that era like for him? I will tell you what it was like. Listen to his language in Psalm 32. "When I kept silence, my bones waxed old through my roaring all the day long. For day and night Thy hand was heavy upon me: my moisture was turned into the drought of summer. *Selah*"—Just think of it! Oh David, the price you had to pay; and oh God, what a price I have had to pay in my life—and so have you—for David's sin. What a price we have had to pay when we have hardened our neck and stiffened ourselves against God's Word, and resisted His will. Oh, how true it is, as we heard this morning in Dr. Culbertson's quotation from D. L. Moody, that this Book will keep us from sin, or sin will keep us from this Book.

For twelve months David hardened his heart, refused to

confess, and the hand of God was heavy upon him. Do you know something about that? Your Bible dead, your prayer-life barren, your preaching fruitless, and your ministry a waste of time: the whole thing a sham and a pretence—but you have got to keep up appearances. "My moisture," the sweetness of His lovely presence, the wonderful dew from heaven in my soul each morning, the wonderful refreshing that comes from heaven, has turned to the drought of summer. Is there somebody like that listening to my voice to-day?

One day Nathan came and told David the story of a rich man who took a poor man's little ewe lamb. "Oh," said David in a flash of anger, "he must die." Oh yes, David, you excuse your own sin by being harsh in your judgment of somebody else. Friend, I say it quietly to you, but I ask it with all my heart: Is that why some Christian people have no mercy on those who fall? The spirit which hides an uneasy conscience flashes out in condemnation of somebody else. We will welcome any old cowboy on to an evangelistic platform that he might give a testimony when there is still a lot of the cowboy in him; but if a brother slips up, he is finished—there is no mercy. May God forgive us! I think we have to remember all over again the word of our Lord Jesus when He said, "Let him that is without sin . . . be the first to cast a stone."

Then as David flashed his sentence, "He must die," the arrow went right home to his heart; the Spirit of God went right into his soul, and struck the blow—"Thou art the man!" And Nathan reminded David, "The Lord anointed you with the Spirit; and He gave you the kingdoms of Israel and Judah. And if that were not enough for you, He has given you this thing and that thing: He was ready to do anything for you. But you saw a woman whom you wanted, and in order to get her you killed her husband; and you said it was love." Have you ever said, "I love somebody"—a very precious thing if it is true; but I wonder if the truth might rather be, "I want somebody and I love myself. And at any cost, even if it means murder, that one is going to be mine." And you did that, David; you did that. Very well, then; from this day the sword of God is in your home and in your family and in your descendants, and it will never depart from you. And David's answer was a broken cry. "I have sinned against the Lord."

I trust that it is not mere emotion on my part, but I tell you that my heart longs that out from this congregation, out from this convention there might reach to heaven a sob, a groan, a tear, a burden, a cry: "O God, forgive me for this thing." "I have sinned against the Lord," said David—and there was a flood of tears, and a great confession, and a broken heart. In the language of Psalm 51, "Wash me, and I shall be whiter than snow. O Lord, restore to me the joy of salvation; create in me a clean heart, and renew a right spirit within me; restore the joy of salvation. O God, spare me that yet in my old age sinners might be converted. Bring me back into the fighting line, back into Thy word, back into the place of blessing. O God, may I not die with this awful damnable thing beating me!"

The first reaction of conviction is to run from God; and the next reaction is to cling to His feet. Peter said, "Depart from me, for I am a sinful man." But one morning he met the risen Lord, and had a personal interview. "It is the Lord," said John; and Peter is out of the boat and at the feet of Jesus. And that is where I want to be: it is the only place I dare be.

In one last minute, *the pardon of God.* "The Lord hath put away thy sin" (v. 13). Possible? Certain, absolutely certain, absolutely sure, immediate. Sin, desperately dangerous, bringing the judgment of heaven; yet it cannot quench the love of God. If we confess, He is faithful and just to forgive. Oh, but somebody says, Mr. Preacher, what is going to happen to me? I will tell you. "Because thou hast given great occasion to the enemies of the Lord to blaspheme, the child shall die" (v. 14). Sin was forgiven, but its consequences had to be paid. God will forgive, but He will use the rod; He will restore us to favour, but we have to drink the bitter waters of chastisement.

The child died. One of David's sons cheated his sister, as David cheated Bathsheba. Absalom became a murderer. David saw his sin reappearing in his own family; and he lost his kingdom. Oh, they were stormy days for him indeed; but he looked into the heart of it all, and he knew that this was the cup that his Father had given him to drink. This was not the punishment of a judge, but the chastisement of a heavenly Father; and as the rod of chastisement cut deep, the Lord poured the balm of Gilead into the wounds. And one day the pendulum swung back again, and voices began to speak more kindly to him, and they wanted David back again to be their king. And at the end of his life David could say, "Many are the afflictions of the righteous, but the Lord delivereth him out of them all." And, in spite of this sin, in spite of this awful blunder and collapse, he says, "I shall be satisfied when I awake in Thy likeness."

Marvellous grace of Jesus! Waiting to be just that to you and me. And it is desperately what we need: to be at His feet. Will you come there with me?

COUNTERFEIT CONSECRATION

Rev. Charles Inwood

I had wholly dedicated the silver unto the Lord from my hand for
my son, to make a graven image and a molten image—JUDGES 17: 3.

IN THE opening chapter of the book of Job we read, "There was
a day when the sons of God came to present themselves before
the Lord, and Satan came also among them." It is so still.
The wolf knows the quiet haunts of the sheep, and where the sheep
gather the wolf is very likely to appear. Satan is present in every
revival of religion, and in every holiness convention. He is there
to tease and to tempt; to criticise and to discourage. He is there to
hinder what God, by His Almighty Spirit, is doing in the hearts
of His own children. And one of the most effective ways in which
the devil hinders the work of Christ in the hearts of God's children
is by putting before them what I may venture to call *counterfeit
consecration*. Almost everything God does among us, the devil tries
to imitate and counterfeit. I venture to think that there never was
a time when the devil was so successfully imitating what God is
doing as he is to-day. And so we have counterfeit miracles and
prophecies, religions and gospels, Bibles and ministries; and there
is such a thing as a counterfeit Christian.

We must feel—I am sure I have felt it very deeply when looking
at these great congregations in this tent from day to day—that
on this matter of consecration it is of the utmost possible importance
that we should discern between the false and the true. If our
conceptions of consecration are faulty, unscriptural, and false,
depend upon it our experience will be the same, and we shall bring
discredit upon our Lord Jesus, upon the power of His precious
blood, and the power of His Almighty Spirit. A false idea of consecration cannot produce a truly consecrated life; and, oh! it will
be very sad after our having taken part in conventions like this,
when we come by-and-by to stand before the judgment seat of
Christ, if we then discover that our very consecration is only wood,
and hay, and stubble—something which God, in infinite mercy to
us, is compelled utterly to consume.

How are we to find out what is true? "Beloved, believe not
every spirit, but try the spirits, whether they be of God." If we

want to be true here, we have to come simply and prayerfully to God's Word. The Word of God applied by the Spirit of God is the only infallible test upon this matter of consecration. Mark that even the possession of the inspired Word itself does not make us in the least independent of the inspiring Spirit. We are as utterly dependent upon the Spirit of God for the right application of the Word of God as we were, in the first instance, for the revelation of the truth itself to us. And if we are going to face this question, we must be prepared to be loyal and submissive to the Word of God and the Spirit of God. May God help us to be that; and may the Spirit burn, and make the word a searching, burning, piercing, God-honouring word in all our hearts.

I want you to look at these two singular chapters—Judges 17 and 18, taking the third verse of the former chapter as the key to them. I do so, because they present to us a very singular and, shall I add, very admonitory illustration of what may be called perverted consecration. That is all I want to speak about—of what perverted consecration leads to. You will notice that the act referred to in this third verse was a very religious act. It was done in a most religious manner, with due regard to the proprieties and conventionalities of religion. This was a religious woman, and there was even an air of self-sacrifice about her act. She was a widow. In all probability these eleven hundred shekels were all the money that had been left her, and she dedicated these shekels to what we call religious uses.

If a poor widow to-day were known to give her little all to religious uses, there is not a religious newspaper in the whole kingdom that would not approve of it, and call it a noble illustration of consecration. And yet this act that had a religious look of self-sacrifice about it was in God's sight wrong, tainted, and spurious, and something with which God could not possibly be satisfied. There are two features in this act of consecration which, I think, will warrant us in that statement. First of all—and I want to deal to-night with elementary truth—in this act there was no such thing, so far as we can see, as personal consecration of herself to God. She gave her silver, but she did not give herself; and the absence of personal surrender vitiated the whole act, no matter how self-sacrificing it might look.

Now, my dear friends, I venture to think that that mistake is a very common mistake to-day, now that consecration is upon the lips of hundreds, and thousands, and tens of thousands of Christian people. We make a mistake in one of two ways: we give up time, or talents, or wealth. We make what we call a sacrifice for religious uses, and call that consecration. We give something we possess, and call that consecration. It is perfectly right for us to place all we have in God's hand. That is one aspect of consecration. But you must not give your substance to God in lieu of surrender of yourself. If you imagine that any gift of yours can be accepted by God as a substitute for, or an equivalent to, your personal consecration, then you are making one of the most solemn mistakes that you can possibly make. In the epistle to the Corinthians you have God's ideal of consecration—"they first gave their own selves to God."

You say, "I have given this to God," or "I have given that to God." You say, "I have come to these conventions for years, and my Christian life has been a series of dedications of this, that, and the other to God." But have you first of all given yourselves— spirit, soul, and body—to God? Has there been first of all a total, absolute, unconditional, surrender of your whole blood-bought nature back to God? If not, then, though you give your body to be burned, and thousands and thousands of pounds to missionary objects, you have not yet learned the first elementary lesson of this important and tremendous subject of consecration to God.

But, perhaps, there is someone here who will say, "I have consecrated myself, not my substance merely." Let us ask you— to what have you consecrated yourself? There are many Christian people to-day, and their consecration is of this kind—they have consecrated themselves to their church, or to some particular form or sphere of their Christian work; perhaps to some very self-denying form of the work; perhaps to some great social or philanthropic movement. I hear people say, again and again, "I have given myself to mission work"—or slum work, or temperance work. Yes, that is all right in its place; but let me remind you that there are thousands of people who are consecrating every energy they possess to some department of God's work who have never yet taken the step of personal consecration of themselves to the Lord. The result is that there is a wrong order—an order that inverts all the rest: and it comes to this, that thousands who are talking about being consecrated are putting God second, and their self-elected mission service first; and that cannot possibly pass muster with God, though it may pass muster with every church and Christian organisation in the land.

I cannot too solemnly or too earnestly repeat the truth, that personal consecration to God is His first demand from you: and that demand must be met fully. But there was a second feature in this case, that made it still more perverted. This woman gave her silver, she said, to God—but for what? She gave it "to make a graven image and a molten image." To make an idol—not an obscene heathen idol, for she was a religious woman—but a religious idol. I venture to think that the religious idol is the most fascinating, the most popular, and most perilous of all idols that you can know anything about. It reads almost like travesty— so it struck me when I read it the other day—a woman giving her silver to God to make a graven image and a molten image. Such travesty, and yet I could not help saying that that, too, is a mistake which I fear many Christian people are making to-day— self lying aback even of our consecration, trying to use God's patronage as a tool to work out its own will.

We think that God's patronage will take the harm out of our idolatry. We think that it makes that idolatry more respectable and more prosperous, and will get us a good position in the world or the church. We give our wealth, or time, or talents, or scholarship, or social position, or ecclesiastical position, and we call it consecration. I want to know in my Master's name, what is the object we have in view? Is it that this wealth, or these talents, or this scholarship, or this position may be used, or flung aside contemptuously? Is it that they may be exalted or trampled in the dust? No, it is nothing of the kind in hundreds of cases. We give what we possess to God, to make a new religious idol. That is it—something that will make us compare favourably with other Christians; something that will minister to our vanity or self-importance; something that we can worship in secret; something of which we can be proud without losing cast among Christian people; gaining for the old self a new religious reputation— another garment in the newest religious fashion. Religious fashions change just as frequently as Paris fashions, and there are thousands of Christian people slaves to the one, who have been delivered from the slavery of the other.

It is a popular cry to-day, and it is getting more popular— this talk about consecration. But remember that the moment consecration becomes a popular thing, it may that very moment become an idol. Reputation for success in Christian work; reputation for evangelistic zeal; reputation for personal sanctity; reputation, shall I say, as a teacher on such platforms as this— it is possible for these things to become idols: and sometimes we feel this so keenly, some of us, that it is almost impossible for us to make up our minds to stand on a platform of this kind. I do not know any form of idolatry so dangerous as this. The religious idols inside the church are bringing more discredit upon the Lord Jesus Christ, I believe, than all the idols found in the unconverted world outside. God save us from such idolatry as that!

You will notice how angry this woman got when she lost the money. The anger was not so much over the loss of the money as over the fact that she could not now get her darling idol. There is such a thing as this. I have discovered it with shame and sorrow in my own heart, and that is the reason why I am talking like this to you. We consecrate ourselves to God, and some opportunity for a bit of Christian work suddenly comes upon us. We fret about it and chafe under it. Why? Because we have not got the opportunity of showing up, and showing off ourselves, and bowing before that darling secret religious idol.

Now, notice what comes of this perverted consecration. The home of this woman's son was cursed by it. If the damage of perverted consecration could be limited even to ourselves, it would not be so bad: but it cannot be. A low spiritual tone in the parent induces a low spiritual tone in the child. I have come to feel that the worst traits of a Christian parent's idolatry are never visible till the child of the parent has a home of its own. Your wealth, your luxury, or your desire to keep up what is called social position, or to get into what is called society, is not only doing harm, but it will become a dreadful snare to your children. You are making idols to fill, darken, pollute, and damage the homes and lives of your own children. This poor mother was a religious woman. She gave her child a religious name, but that idol she put in her boy's home did far more harm for that child than the beautiful name she gave him.

It is possible for you to give Christian names and training to your children, but in subtle forms like this you are making idols to fill and darken their homes by-and-by. Just notice how rapidly this son goes down. First the mother purchases the idol; then the son becomes an idol-worshipper, and worse still, the grandson actually becomes an idol priest—a priest in an idol temple. Oh! if that is not a down-grade movement I have yet to learn what is. It is taking place under our very eyes, where sometimes we have almost no power to arrest it. And so this son must have an idol temple, and of course an idol priest. And we read that he consecrated his own son to become his priest. This suggests to me the fact that perverted consecration, perhaps more than anything else, leads up to and necessitates man-made ministries, and man-made ordinances. It seems to bring the human into undue prominence almost everywhere. And what is done with God? God is simply put on the retired list—on the list of honours and compliments. It is all man—man-made wealth, man-made idols, consecrated priests. And then you have a man-made priest exercising a man-made ministry before a man-made idol; and swift upon the heels of that there comes a further step down.

He has consecrated his own son, but he is not quite satisfied with that—it is not quite ecclesiastical enough. His son is only a layman, and if he could get somebody a little more ecclesiastical it would suit him better. So he finds that a Levite who comes by is nearer to it than his own son, and he drives a hard bargain with this wandering Levite to become his priest. Only twenty-five shillings a year, and his food and clothes! I do not know that there is anything so low as that in England, Ireland, or Wales. Micah drove a hard bargain. There was one redeeming feature in his case. The man was a Levite, but he was from the family of Moses. He was not a priest, but the genealogy was all in his favour. He came of a good family, and that was much for one whose whole thought centred in a new man-made priest or ordinance.

Notice the most complete satisfaction on the part of Micah, so far as such things could give satisfaction. He says, "Now know I that the Lord will do me good, seeing I have a Levite to my priest." In other words, "Because I have got one who is a sort of an ecclesiastic, I have done the right thing; and I have got the right man. I have my own idols, my own church, my own priest; glory be to myself. God will be pleased"—this is the only time he mentions God, mind you—"God will be proud, and I am sure God will give me prosperity, now that I have this idol temple and idol priest." But God did not. I do not know exactly how long this satisfaction lasted, but it came to an end very rudely. One day there came a wandering band of Danites—marauders. They heard of this priest and these idols; and they went, six hundred men with weapons of war, and they captured the gods and the priest, and the gods and the priest were all lost. Poor Micah! He had put all his goods into one basket, and the basket was not in God's hand. So you get in 18:24 the last view of Micah, a very humbling one. He seems to have been crying, like a child over lost toys, because these idols and this priest had been taken away from him.

I do not find any trace of repentance in his grief. He does not seem to have noticed that gods which could be stolen were not worth keeping in his house. Would to God that some marauding band of Danites would come and do something like that to us! If some power came down upon this great congregation to-night, by which every idol were swept away, it would be the beginning of Pentecostal times in your lives and homes.

Why did these people act like this? Why were they guilty of this low and strange conduct? The reason is given in 17:6, "In those days there was no king in Israel." Idolatry is only possible when the inner throne of one's being is not filled by the Lord Jesus Christ Himself. Just as we read that there was no king in the land, later on we find that there was no magistrate there. Every lesser or subsidiary moral authority in a man's soul is weakened, or upset, or destroyed, when the Lord Jesus Christ is dethroned. You cannot have true order any more than true life unless Jesus Christ reigns in the empire of your soul, and is the supreme, unchallenged Lord of every emotion there. I do not see why this last service of ours should not be a glorious coronation service of Jesus Christ the King.

There is not one here to-night who has not often joined in singing that triumphant hymn, "Crown Him, Lord of all!" You have asked angels, saints, martyrs to do it; prophets to do it; Jews to do it; Gentile sinners to do it; that is all very good and beautiful. But oh! brothers and sisters in the Lord, do you not think it would please the Lord Jesus Christ better if you crowned Him King in your own heart? That is why this convention is held. We want Jesus Christ to be King in the cleansed heart through the indwelling of His Spirit. Oh! will you let Jesus Christ come in? The King is outside much of your life, and the result is that there are all sorts of confusion, rebellion, and unrest. Why not let the King in? He is close at the doors; just outside, waiting to come in. He says: "Lift up your heads, O ye gates; and be ye lifted up, ye everlasting doors, and the King of glory shall come in." Fling open the gates, hail the King! welcome Him as King! Tell Him you are ashamed that you have not known Him as King before; but that henceforth, spirit, soul, and body are to be His—Jesus, King, and the Lord supreme—in your whole heart and life! May God make this moment a moment of solemn coronation of Jesus Christ as King in every heart, for His Name's sake.

DEFECTIVE CONSECRATION

Rev. Douglas Brown

And Samuel said, What meaneth then this bleating of the sheep in mine ears, and the lowing of the oxen which I hear?—I Samuel 15: 14.

I WANT God to speak by His Blessed Spirit through the Word of Truth, even through me, this morning. He has a word to say to His people about defective consecration—the tragic bleating of a defective consecration. I can almost picture Him. There is no one more really at Keswick than Jesus Christ. I know He is here; He was in my room this morning, and hundreds of other rooms, and He is here now, and I think He is listening to something that hurts Him, and He is praying the Father that before the end of this day, this particular thing may cease, may become a blessed silence, "the bleating of a defective consecration." The Lord of Glory hears the bleating of sheep that ought to have been killed, and the lowing of cattle that ought to have been slain.

Jesus starts with the platform. All blessing must start there, if it is to last. There are sins of which we are unconscious—Dr. Meyer expressed it in his prayer yesterday, forgiveness for the unconscious sins. Thank God, the blood of Jesus Christ cleanses these, too. Lord, make us conscious of them this morning; daily increase our capacity to appreciate Thy great forgiveness, for we only understand Thy forgiveness in the terms of our own sinnership, as those terms are brought home to us by the bitter experience; that wonderful draught of God handed to us by the Holy Ghost, bitter indeed because it brings me down into unutterable nakedness before God. Then it is that I discover in me, in the hour of my birth-pains into a new chapter of grace in Christ Jesus, that in me, born of the Spirit of God, there is a new conception of God's forgiveness in Christ, even born out of the rubbish heap of my unreality. O Christ, if there are some sheep bleating this morning for the first time, and we never knew they were there, bring us to a place called Calvary and slay them there! We cannot do it, but help us to bring them there to be slain by Thee! Remember, I beseech you, dead sheep cannot bleat.

Now will you turn back to the third verse of the chapter—
God's definite command to King Saul. Our brother who was
praying this morning used the very word in this verse that I want
to emphasise, "Now go and smite Amalek, and *utterly* destroy
all that they have, and spare them not"; go and smite *utterly*.
I want to emphasise that word; it is a word I was frightened of
for thirty years. I used to shy every time I saw it in the distance.
I can pass it now without putting my blinkers on. *Utterly*. Jesus
Christ is waiting to save a poor sinner like Douglas Brown utterly.
I cannot understand it, but I have got it. But if you want to
enjoy the Lamb that was slain with an utter enjoyment, you must
let Him slay utterly. There must be an echo of Calvary in this
temple of the Holy Ghost; the Holy Ghost is only comfortable in
that tent or tabernacle where the fragrance of Jesus Christ is in
every department of the personality. There must be the fragrance
of slaying, there must be the holy deposit of an absolute abnegation
before God, born of the Spirit of God, until we land into the
millionairism and the multitude of His mercies.

These things are not intellectual, but sacrificial. I used to be
frightened of Keswick. I used to wonder what people meant when
they talked about a second blessing. I felt I was all right; what
were people so anxious about? Thank God, He slew me at the
foot of the Cross. I have not got the second blessing yet, I am just
inside the hall door to the first; and it is better further on. If you
want to know Him, you must stop knowing *about* Him, and you
must come to Him and lose yourself in Him, and let Him find
Himself in you—and it will be a bad day for any sheep that is
alive and ought to be dead. There has been a horrible fear of
man abroad in the Christian Church. We want God to raise up
some mighty man of God who will lead us all into absolute reality
without crankism. Many a man of God has longed to abandon
himself to this great work of leading men nearer to God; but the
danger is this, the Church of God has not learned the art of doing
the transcendental quietly. We have got to come to Calvary in a
more dignified way. Revival is not going down the street with a
big drum; it is going back to Calvary with a big sob.

Slay utterly. "But Saul and the people spared Agag, and the
best of the sheep, and of the oxen, and of the fatlings, and of the
lambs, and all that was good, and would not utterly destroy them:
but everything that was vile and refuse, that they destroyed
utterly." Anybody can do that. That may be good enough for a
Communion ticket, but it is not enough for the communion of the
Holy Ghost. If you knew what this morning is costing me in the
presence of God, your criticism would wither at the foot of the
Cross. The biggest curse in the camp of God to-day is spiritual

pride. God has got to break us, brethren; we have been frightened
about being broken. I know there are difficulties, and we have
been frightened lest any great movement should lead in something that is not of God. Cannot we trust God to take care of this
meeting this morning? Is there not a power that comes out from
the throne of God and of the Lamb that can lead you and me into
a sanity of sanctity? God can do tremendous things, and all the
time they are happening we shall be reading the most sublime
thing that was ever written on the screen of God before a wondering and an enquiring and a waiting heart. The Lord write it.
Lord Jesus, write "Mene, Mene, Tekel, Upharsin" all round this
tent, until this tent is a great big blush; and then, when we have
blushed the colour of Calvary, write up, "I have blotted out as a
thick cloud thy transgressions."

Confession. "What meaneth this bleating of the sheep that I
hear, and the lowing of the cattle?" O God, kill the bleating this
morning! Kill it in Douglas Brown. If I have not heard it yet,
unstop the deaf ear of my soul, and then give me courage to lead
that sheep to Calvary, and Lord Jesus Christ, kill it right there!
When there is defective obedience to the voice of God, that means
the beginning of an awful tragedy. Defective obedience always
leads to being a religious deceiver. Look at v. 13, "And Samuel
came to Saul, and Saul said to him, Blessed be thou of the Lord; I
have performed the commandment of the Lord." Have you ever
had a church member look about like that, and say it? Those are
the men that are hard to tackle. It is these horrible hypocrites that
say, "Blessed be thou," and are conscious all the time they are
living on the defensive; and they will die on the defensive if the
Holy Ghost does not shake them out of their hypocrisies. Yes, we
have been frightened of one another long enough. We have got
to be frightened of God this morning. "The fear of God is the
beginning of wisdom." Sin, horrible sin, cultured sin, religious
sin, convention sin, you are most horrible when you come out in
the garb of religion. You are most illusive when you sing the
songs of Zion. You are most difficult to lay hold of when you walk
with the religious gait of a disciple, and yet the Master looks in vain
for the lighted lamp within the soul, the oil of the Spirit that has
brought you out of the kingdom of knowing about Jesus Christ
into the realm of knowing not *about* Him, but knowing *Him*.

Do you know Him? Does He walk up and down the road with
you; and every time you open the Book and you read it, do you
feel somebody is looking over your shoulder, and with such reality
that you put your finger on a text and turn round and say, "Lord
Jesus, what does that mean for me? Please tell me." The Holy
Spirit wrote the Book from cover to cover, and it is written for my

regeneration from start to finish; and the Blessed Saviour is mine
and the Spirit is mine to bring all of Jesus that He can back into
me for this life and for the next: but if I am to enjoy that, I must
be real. We must do away with convention camouflage, and we
must ring in Calvary reality.

It not only leads to being a religious deceiver. Saul said,
"Blessed be thou of the Lord; I have performed the commandment of the Lord." "Saul, are you quite sure?" "Yes, I have
performed the commandment of the Lord." "Oh, that is a funny
noise! Do you know what the sound of the bleating of a sheep is
like?" "Oh, yes." "Well, I can hear one; is that yours?" God
said, "Slay utterly," and here you are at a convention, saying, "I
have." Yes, you have been a hypocrite. Defective discipleship
is the first step to being a religious deceiver; but when you get
there, you never stop. Sin always hustles you on. Deception leads
to lying. Look at v. 20, "Saul said unto Samuel, Yea, I have
obeyed the voice of the Lord, and have gone the way which the
Lord sent me, and have brought Agag the king of Amalek, and
have utterly destroyed the Amalekites . . ." Stop, stop, Saul.
You have just been sinning and being a humbug until you have
lost even your sensitiveness; do stop and tarry a moment. Samuel
said, "Wait." The word that Samuel used is the same as the one
in Psalm 46: 10, "*Be still*, and know that I am God." Literally,
be very still. I have asked you for the second time, Is it right with
you and God; and now for the second time you say, I have done
what God commanded me, I have performed His commandment.
"What meaneth then this bleating of the sheep in mine ears?"
Dead sheep don't bleat, Saul. What does it mean? All the time
that you are lying, your sheep is bleating. Oh, when a man or
woman is led into this slough of deception, it always leads to a
cowardly shirking of responsibility.

Now look at v. 21, "But the people took of the spoil, sheep and
oxen, the chief of the things that should have been utterly destroyed, to sacrifice unto the Lord." Thank God, his conscience is
not dead. He knows what should have been done. You know
what ought to have been done fifteen years ago in this tent, and
it is not done yet. You have come up every year to do it, and
you have done everything else but that one thing. You have made
so many excuses that you have got from top to bottom of yourself,
and now you are wondering if your ancestors are responsible for
your failure, if heredity is responsible, if environment is responsible, if circumstances are responsible. I tell you, Jesus wants to
teach you and me this morning that He is greater than environment, He is greater than circumstances, and He is greater than our
cowardice. It is no good pointing to your home, it is no good

pointing to your relations, it is no good pointing to your partners
in business, it is no good pointing to that part in the ledger that
your partner is mostly responsible for, but you have blinked at.
You will forgive me, won't you, but for eighteen months I have
been working in the midst of men of this country, the rough men
who know nothing about theology, and they come to me and say,
"Douglas Brown, we are going to believe the Christian Church
when she is real." O God, make us real; we do love Thee; whatever it costs us, we want to face the great opportunity with a great
anointing; and if there are any sheep that we do not know how to
kill, and there are lowing oxen that we do not know how to deal
with, Lord Jesus Christ, become the beautiful Calvary Execu-
tioner this morning. All Thou dost ask is our willingness. Let
there be a bringing out of the sheep that you cannot kill. Ask
Him. He will do it.

Thank God there came the moment of conviction of sin. Look
at v. 24, "And Saul said unto Samuel, I have sinned, for I have
transgressed the commandment of the Lord, and thy words; I was
so desperately afraid of the people, and obeyed their voice." I
heard yours all the time; and all the time that I was doing what
the people told me to do, my heart was crying inside. Oh, I
wanted to do what you told me to do. Pilate was never in a worse
hour of agony that I am in, Lord Jesus; helpless look to Thee
for grace—helpless, weak, cowardly, with all the sheep round me
bleating and the oxen lowing. It is the old story elongating itself
in the hours of my fall, and yet the hours of gracious conviction
of the Spirit that shall bring me to see the way of truth, and walk
in it. O God, save any man this morning from being damned,
on the threshold of a new life!

"I have sinned," said Saul. "I have transgressed Thy commandments." I knew what you told me to do, and I wanted to do
it, and when I said I would I meant it, but oh, the voice of the
people, the great tide of the majority, the spirit of the age,
the lethargy in the church; and every step I tried to take for the
Cross, I found these people were just getting away from me, the
majority seemed to think it was wrong, they did not understand
it. No, they did not understand Pentecost; the religious people
said, "What meaneth this?"

Well, it first of all meant that some of them were half dead,
because they did not understand it. God is waiting for this convention to do something. God is waiting for me and for you to
do something definite in His presence. We have asked Him to
let this convention loose in the might of His Spirit for the regeneration of the nation. O God, in Thine ineffable love, deign to do it
—but these sheep must be killed. We must take the first step.

It is no good coming forward to receive the anointing of the Holy Ghost until I have gone back and brought my sins to Bethel and I have built another altar, and I have said, "O Lord and Maker of mankind, my Master, my covenant God, the One who looked down upon me in my dire disgrace and sinfulness, and didst give me an overwhelming promise that Thou wouldst do with me according to Thy grace, if only I would lift up a holy hand and a clean heart, and a strength of integrity, and be utterly Thine; but oh, Lord, I have miserably failed." The sheep that ought to have been slain are still bleating and the cattle are still lowing; and the prophet of the Lord cries, "What meaneth the bleating of these sheep that God hears in His ears, and the lowing of the cattle?" Lord Jesus, slay utterly in this tent this morning, slay utterly in each one of us; let us forget the platform, let us forget the ushers, and let us forget everything, except that the whole of eternity depends upon our relationship to Thee. God, make it a right relationship.

We are asking for the Holy Ghost, but the jug is dirty. We are asking and are longing for power, but our hearts, even this morning, are full of human inventions. We are telling God what we want to do, and we have half a dozen programmes up our sleeves as to the way we are going to do it. God does not turn up and show us the other way. Lord, do away with our way. Make a way for Thyself in the Christian heart and conscience of this country. God is waiting to lift the Church of God to a new consciousness of Himself; and out of a new God-consciousness given to the Church there shall come a new sense of sin among the people. We cannot preach sin effectively because we are slow to have the vision of God's holiness that can cry, "Woe is me, I am undone; I am a man of unclean lips, and I dwell in the midst of an unclean people: but mine eyes have seen the Lord of Hosts." Master, come when we have seen Thee; we feel words fail, but Thou failest not; come and show us something this morning bigger than our unworthiness, greater than our failures, Thyself in mighty power coming right into the life, like holy dynamite in the person of the Holy Ghost, until our cowardice and our feebleness shall all be driven away before the breath of the Spirit of God, and the Skiddaw of the man that we wanted to be shall stand to-day without a cloud over its top, absolutely beautiful with all the glory of God upon it, mingled with fire that comes from the throne of God; of the life that hands itself over for an utter cleansing through the ministry of the Spirit of God. O Holy Dove, you understand, you know; brood over these people! Man can do nothing with them. You moved 3,000 people on the day of Pentecost; move this 2,500!

E

Now come with me to a place called Calvary. Let us repeat
our vow; let us apply this story to ourselves. Be still, said Samuel.
Wait. That is, be very quiet before God. Yes, we did come to
Him. We did trust Him. The Holy Spirit showed us so clearly,
that Jesus stood in my place and bore the penalty due to my sin;
it is by His stripes that I am healed. It is all of grace, flowing
from Calvary. There is nothing but hell apart from the blood of
Christ. There is nothing but eternal filth, misery and disappointment. O Lord, we owe as much to the Calvary face of Jesus as we
owe to the glory of the sun on the brightest day that the world
ever lived through. Make us grateful. Bring us out of our cleverness into a Calvary crushing. Bring us out of our pride to the
throne of penitence. Teach us how to put our tears into Thy
bottle. The true language of every one of us lies in the heart of a
tear, and only God can read it. Lord, be merciful to that tear
bottle, there is something in it precious to us; it tells Thee of sheep
that we cannot slay and of cattle that still low. We have failed,
we have trusted in our own energy, we have trusted in our own
resolutions. We have leaned against conventions, and when we
have gone wrong, we have propped ourselves up at the next.
Lord, forgive us all. Bring us back this morning. Take away
Samuel and put Jesus in his place; and take away Saul, for we all
feel we are Saul this morning; and Lord Jesus, do not let there be
any more lying, do not let there be any more deception, let us just
look Thee in the face and tell Thee all, for Thou hast come
questioning. Lord, there has been reservation in our surrender,
there has been a frontier in our abandonment to Thee, but oh, in
the moment of quiet, we come back to our covenant with Thee.
Lord, we confess we have broken our pledge and our promise.
We said that we would go anywhere with Thee, but we have not
done it. We told Thee we would never be jealous of other people
any more, and with some of us this convention has been spoiled
because others have been more prominent than we have. Lord,
forgive us. We told Thee that whatever it cost Thou shouldst
always have the right place in our thinking and in our conversation; that in our dealings with our fellow men we would rely on
Thee, to make us feel that we were to be conscious of that pierced
hand on ours, making it move deftly, gracefully, tenderly, sympa-
thetically. We have passed through it all, Lord Jesus, these are
only little bits out of a diary that is the history of our failure: but
we want power. We pray Thee, therefore, to give us an absolute
surrender. O Christ Jesus, bring the bleating sheep home, bring
the lowing cattle home this morning; kill them for us; we will
stand silent and grateful and penitent when we see our salvation
accomplished by Thee. Lord, all we can bring Thee is willingness,

and we do that. Come, and have a great victory at Keswick this morning. Write Thy Name of authority across the heart and the life of every one in this place and tent of meeting with God.

Some months ago, after a service, 1,200 people re-dedicated their lives to God. It was in St. John's Church, Boscombe. There are some services we will remember when we get to heaven. After the people had gone home to pray, one remained kneeling, and for over a quarter of an hour she knelt there in another world. It seemed a sin to disturb her, although they were waiting to lower the lights of the church; but we waited—O God, make us very quiet in patience when we see manifestations of the Spirit; have control over us—and as she knelt God said, "Go and speak to her"—and whatever He tells you to do, always do it, however ridiculous it may seem, always do it, because it is highest wisdom. I went and knelt beside her at the communion rail, and I said, "My sister," and she looked up, and her face was just like a little bit of heaven—oh, there are some looks that Jesus puts into faces, well, we treasure them up, and when the battle goes hard, we just bring out that look; Moses is not the only one in that Academy— and I said, "You have something to tell me." "Yes," she replied; "but I could not have told you a minute ago, because it is only just finished."

I tell you, when God takes a photograph, it is perfect. He does it all in one sitting, and there is no doubt about it. It all comes out, and there is nothing hidden from Him with whom we have to deal; but somehow by the alchemy that is known to Him, He produces a new creation in Himself, and it is me when it comes out, but it is like Him—but then, you see, He cannot live without me and I cannot live without Him. I am in Him, He is in me; it is a lovely tangle, and it is going to take all eternity to disentangle it, and neither of us is going to try. "I live, yet not I, Christ liveth in me; and the life that I now live in the flesh I live by the faith of the Son of God, who loved me, and gave Himself for me." Oh, brothers and sisters, that is it. You say, "I would like to step into that this morning, Mr. Brown." Then bring that sheep along and let Jesus kill it. We have to get all the bleating stopped before we get all the blessing down.

I close with this. This dear soul, this sister, was a hospital nurse, who years ago had lived in Luton. She said, "My mother was very ill, and there came to Luton a preacher of the Gospel whom my mother loved dearly. I was a very worldly girl, and she said to me, 'Dorothy, you must go and hear that man who is preaching at the Corn Exchange; and when you come back, tell me all that you have heard'." Dorothy went to the Corn Exchange, and she

heard the preacher, and he preached on "So Great Salvation."
His name was Brown. He preached about Jesus, and that great
salvation which became bigger and bigger and bigger until there
was no room left anywhere for anything else; it was all salvation,
and she found herself in it, and she said, "I don't want to come
out; Lord Jesus, take me." That was years ago, and the preacher
was my father. Now she was nursing a case in Boscombe, and
between that day and the evening of the service in St. John's she
had wandered, and the sheep were bleating and the cattle were
lowing, and coming along the road she had said, "I will either
get right with God, or else I will drop it altogether." She was
bewildered, did not know what to do. As she came up to the church
she stopped; she could not go a step further. Oh, God can stop
you walking just as much as He can make you walk! So she
stopped right in front of St. John's, and a voice said, "Go into
that church and you will hear words whereby you may be
mended," and she came in, and was one out of many that came
forward, and Jesus mended her. And she said to me, "Do you
know what that means, Mr. Brown? When I went home that
night at Luton I told mother that I had given my heart to Jesus,
and my mother put one hand under the pillow and took out a
purse—it was in the old days of purses—and she opened the old-
fashioned purse and took out a gold coin." She handed it to
Dorothy and said, "Dorothy, Jesus Christ has given you to-night
a heart of pure gold; take that; never spend it on yourself, and
whenever you look at it, remember the night when Jesus Christ
gave my Dorothy a heart of pure gold." That mother went to
glory and poor Dorothy went into wandering. All the vows that
she had made had been broken, and in the night of desperation,
while nursing a case in Bournemouth, God stopped her outside
the church and said, "Go and hear words whereby you may be
mended." She said, "Mr. Brown, God has given me back my heart
of pure gold to-night. The Holy Spirit has been sweeping and
sweeping, and He has not only found the coin, but Jesus came.
They just did it together; and somehow I put the coin back in
those pierced hands. It is His treasury. It is His mint. He deals
out the current coin of the realm, but He keeps His face-mark very
clearly day by day when it is His workmanship, and He has handed
me back my life mended."

Then that hand went down under the tunic and there came out
a little gold coin. She said, "Mr. Brown, I have carried that coin
about ever since that night; I felt I could not break my promise to
my mother. I have carried it about, but lately that thing has
nearly burned itself through." She has not that sovereign now.
It was handed to the vicar, and he sent it to Lowestoft to buy

hymn-books for the Anglican converts. O God, give us back the heart of pure gold this morning!

> Often have I wandered from Thee,
>   Often has my heart gone astray;
> Crimson do my sins seem to me,
>   Water cannot wash them away.

> Jesus, to that fountain of Thine,
>   Leaning on Thy promise I go;
> Wash me in the blood of the Lamb,
>   And I shall be whiter than snow.

That is what happened in my case. Why don't you do it? God is waiting for us to do something. First, see to it that you have brought all your bleating sheep to Him. Don't worry about them. Leave them with Him. 'He knows how to tackle them. I have proved it. Then, when you are quite sure that you have brought those bleating sheep to Calvary and handed them to Jesus, and the lowing cattle—which stand for a different thing in each life, mark you; it may be gossip with you, it may be slander, it may be an angry word, a nasty sharp tongue; maybe there is a Christian who would have been at Keswick this year if it had not been for you. Come along, bring that bleating sheep. It may be spiritual pride. It may be the thought, "Oh, but I am in God's work, and I have had such a lot of experience, and this is so absolutely new, and it is the kind of thing we do not have at Keswick." Well, it is the kind of thing you will have in heaven. Don't smile. I want you to come right home to reality. If you want all that God is waiting to give, God must have all that is in your power to give Him.

Now it is very difficult in a big tent like this, it is very different from campaigning, and the whole thing is so important and so solemn that it must be done very quietly. God told me yesterday afternoon what was going to happen this morning, and when He told me I went to Mr. Sloan and Mr. Fullerton, because when God does a thing, He does it very easily, and when He told me I told them—the Drill Hall is open now, and after a season of silent prayer, whatsoever God tells you to do, do it. There are some of you come up to Keswick professors of religion, you are deserters of Jesus Christ: then confess it. There are those in this tent to whom the definite blessing that has come is this: you loved Jesus because of what you had heard about Him, you loved Him because He had done so much for others; you loved Him because the first rays of His love had entered your soul, and you said, "Jesus, I come to Thee." But do you know Him? He is another Jesus to you this morning. He is Himself. Not to you I first appeal. If Jesus has become a living One to you this week, then come out quietly and confess it; and, dear Christians, there are some of you who come up here for definite blessing, and you have had a great searching and the bleating has nearly stopped, but there is something else you want. I know what I am speaking about—I have some letters in my room: you want power, you want to go back to your church with the anointing of the Holy Ghost. Let Him kill all the sheep, and then when all that is done, come to Him for power. You came to Him for conversion, you accepted the Lord Jesus Christ as your Saviour; accept the Holy Ghost for power. I did eighteen months ago. Why do you stop and think about it? O Christ Jesus, kill the sheep this morning. Make us willing in the day of Thy power. Then let there be the coming forward. Just come forward, and then pass out of the door and make your way quietly to the Drill Hall, while we are singing the closing hymn.

Do you want power? Let us go down on our knees for it in the Drill Hall. We want more prayer. Has Jesus Christ brought you a great hunger for power? Then come and claim it, while we sing the closing hymn. But before we do so, a few moments of silent prayer. Do not wonder about anybody else; think about yourself. Ask God to let every bleating that is there just sound right out until it is very distinct—"Thou hast set our sins in the light of Thy countenance." Then, Lord Jesus, give each one of us grace to bring them to Calvary, and hand them over to Thee. Then, Lord Jesus, don't let Satan make us stop there. When all that which is not of God has been taken away, let all that which is of God be granted. Help us to ask God to break down the fear of man; especially, Lord, I do pray Thee for the men in this tent and the 'varsity men, that magnificent body of manhood. Lord Jesus, these young fellows went over the top for their king and country a few years ago; let them go over the top for Jesus Christ this morning. Oh, let there be a fine body of 'varsity life absolutely surrendered to Jesus Christ. Lord, these are the men that Thou art calling, the men who are clever, the men of capacity, the men of ability, men of intelligence, young men of learning and culture. O Christ of Calvary, get hold of the best manhood in this tent this morning, and absolutely consecrate it to Thyself. Some of them have been up all night praying. Answer the prayer now, and let there be the manhood stepping forward for God's own power. No frontiers, Lord Jesus. Come and rule and reign, break down every opposing idol, and lead us right into the realm of that power whereby we shall be able to claim men for Jesus Christ. Lord, do this work now, as we bow in silence in Thy presence.

II

GOD'S REMEDY FOR SIN

"Stand still and see!" yea, see to-day
    New wonders of redeeming grace—
The mighty Potter moulds the clay
    Again within this hallowed place—
Till through the human the divine
Is seen once more to move and shine.

Here, "commune with thine heart; be still!"
    Search all the secret stores of years,
Till silence now unbearable,
    Self betrays self mid blinding tears—
Then fall at Jesu's feet and say,
Thou canst, Thou shalt, cleanse all to-day!

"Be still, and know that I am God!"
    Peace, wounded conscience, heaving breast!
The pierced hand bears the chastening rod,
    His cloud transfigures and brings rest.
Take, Lord, Thy power! Reign, great I AM,
O'ershadowing Guest, all-conquering Lamb!

Then, in the hush of this fair tent
    And solemn stillness of this hour,
Three thousand souls before Thee bent,
    Break forth, O Holy Ghost, in power—
Sweep through, thou Wind of God, sweep through!
Once more, cleanse, consecrate, renew!

CHARLES A. FOX.

Keswick, 1899.

GOD'S REMEDY FOR SIN

GRACE abounding to the chief of sinners—Bunyan's famous phrase might well be adopted as the motto of the second phase of Keswick teaching. Not only to the sinner convicted while still in the City of Destruction; and not only to the one hastening therefrom and caught in the Slough of Despond: there is grace in Christ our Lord to meet every need of every sinner— grace abounding to "sinners saved by grace" as well as to the graceless! If Keswick searches out the hidden sin, reveals the unconscious sin, and explores all the ramifications of sin, it is in order to magnify the grace which provides pardon and cleansing and restoration and renewal to all who come to the Lord confessing and renouncing their sin. "There's a wideness in God's mercy like the wideness of the sea," declares F. W. Faber, in his great hymn: and the magnitude of it is set before the congregations at Keswick, after the ministry of conviction has done its perfect work.

The answer to sin is summed up in one word—Jesus. He, in the vicarious passion of His Cross, has borne the penalty and blotted out the guilt of every sin of every believer; He has opened for His people a fountain of cleansing from sin and all unrighteousness; He has bestowed upon His redeemed the robe of His righteousness, so that they stand before the bar of eternal judgment perfect in the Beloved.

To present the Lord Jesus, therefore, as the one sacrifice for sin for ever; the deliverer from the defilement and power of inward depravity; the Saviour "unto the uttermost" of all who come unto God by Him—this is foremost in the ministry of the second day at each year's Convention. Integral to this, of course, is the fact that the Lord demands an utter sincerity on the part of those who seek Him: a readiness to renounce the sin revealed; a true desire for cleansing, and an earnest intention of walking henceforth "in the light." In a word, there must be *faith*: for none of God's purposes of grace are fulfilled in the experience of His people apart from faith. That is the key-word of the Gospel; that is the measure of true blessing in everyday Christian life. "According to your faith be it unto you" is the Master's admonition to all who seek His favour, as it was to one of long ago. That is often costly: for faith is not a mere reluctant "yes," a half-hearted willingness. Rather, true faith is the unreserved embracing of His will as ours: and that sometimes means surrendering what is dearly cherished. The setting forth of God's remedy for sin is, therefore, accompanied by a challenging call to count the cost—and an equally forthright reminder of the consequences of equivocation.

As in the previous section we have seen the sinfulness of sin fully displayed, so the addresses which follow declare "the full provision of His wondrous Cross." The first, on "Grace," is the complement by the Rev. H. W. Webb-Peploe to his searching analysis of sin, given on page 31. Next comes a characteristic message from one whose Christlikeness impressed all who knew and heard him—Charles A. Fox, whose handsome countenance, framed in side-whiskers, seemed to shine with heavenly light as he spoke. From student days he had been dogged by ill-health; but an inner radiancy illuminated his whole being. He was said to be the "one natural orator" at Keswick in the early days: but his was essentially the oratory of a man who "spoke from the heart." He had attended the Broadlands and Brighton Conventions, but was unable to go to Keswick, for health reasons, until 1879. In that first year he was recognised as among the choicest speakers, and at the close of his message on "The Master . . . calleth for thee" we are told that "uncontrollable assents arose from all around." And the report in *The Christian's Pathway of Power* adds, "Then we sang in unrestrained response to the Master's call—

> All I have I leave to Jesus,
>   I am counting it but dross;
> I am coming to the Master,
> ·   I am clinging to the Cross.

Mr. Fox was the outstanding poet of Keswick; and when called upon to suffer excruciating pain and deformity through cancer of the face—from which he died in 1900—wrote these most moving verses—

The Marred Face

Marred more than any man's! Yet there's no place
In this wide universe but gains new grace,
Richer and fuller, from that marred Face!

O Saviour Christ, those precious wounds of Thine
Make doubly precious these poor wounds of mine;
Teach me to die with Thee the death divine!

All wounds or woes of earth, once made Thine own,
Add colour to the rainbow round the Throne,
And save from loneliness saints else alone.

Pain trims the lamps at nature's eventide,
Ere the King enters to fetch home His bride—
My King, by suffering perfected and tried.

Beloved ones are hastening past, and all
The ground is strewn with blossoms they let fall
In haste to gain Love's crowning festival.

Heaven beckons on—I press toward the mark
Of my high calling. Hark, He calls! oh, hark!
That Wounded Face moves toward me through the dark!

Two addresses by the supreme "Master in Israel," Evan H. Hopkins, follow. Although not one of the founders, nor ever Chairman of the Convention, he was for forty years the undisputed "authority" at and upon Keswick. He was, as we have seen, closely associated with the movement from its beginnings in this country, and from his first visit to Keswick in 1876 was recognised as a foremost figure. He quickly came to exercise supreme influence both behind the scenes and as a speaker, and was the Convention's acknowledged "theologian," guarding the teaching of Keswick from divergencies into side-issues, and from error. A strong, stalwart character, he was a born leader; but his gifts were utterly dedicated to the Lord—sterling sincerity characterised his whole personality. He was not a great orator, yet none excelled him in the clear presentation of the Convention message. His early training in engineering had disciplined his naturally logical mind, and his addresses invariably built up an incontrovertible argument. It was his custom to prepare outline notes of his addresses on a piece of paper divided into a number of small squares, according to the number of his "headings," marking progressive "steps" in his theme. His appeal was to the will rather than the emotions: but no one was more effective than he in conducting the after-meetings which were a prominent feature of the Conventions of those days, and in leading hesitant souls to the point of surrender to the Lord. The two addresses given here are excellent examples of his lucid style and his powers of illustrating spiritual truth in simple, homely fashion. Delivered in 1893 and 1904 respectively, these touch upon the passage of Scripture which is focal to Keswick teaching—Romans 6–8. Over the years he spoke many times on similar themes: these are characteristic of addresses which brought light and liberty to countless numbers through the decades.

Realising how formidable a journey separated Australia from Britain in those days, we are amazed to read of the several occasions on which the Rev. H. B. Macartney came to take part in the Convention, between 1878 and 1908. Of Irish extraction, his father was Dean of Melbourne, and he a vicar in the city, when the "Keswick message" first reached Australia; and he took the initiative in promoting a similar Convention there. From his first visit to this country he became an outstanding figure at Keswick whenever he was present. "Deep Celtic fervour, profound knowledge of the Word of God, intense devotion to the Person of the Lord Jesus, and the practice of private prayer to an unwonted extent, accounted for the influence he wielded," says Figgis. Of his address on "Christ the Cleanser," in 1893, Sloan observes that it was "such an address as could come only from one who knew much of the secret of a life of constant communion with the unseen and holy One."

"The Conditions on which God Cleanses" were clearly stated by Harrington Lees in 1904—given here out of chronological order, because of the similarity of theme to the address by Mr. Macartney. The future Archbishop of Melbourne was one, says Figgis, "who had learnt, perhaps from his former vicar, the Rev. Hubert Brooke, a very interesting mode of comparing Scripture with Scripture." From his first appearance at Keswick his messages were "looked for with eager expectancy."

Like Theodore Monod, Pastor Otto Stockmayer—or Stockmeyer, as his name is sometimes spelt—had attended the Oxford Convention, and was a greatly appreciated visitor to Keswick on several occasions in its earliest years. Figgis tells, very movingly, how he had shared a room with the German-Swiss Pastor during a conference in Basle: "About five each morning—I was supposed to be asleep—I heard my friend calling upon God and reading His Word. Somewhat to my surprise it was the English Bible that he used. But the fervour of his communion with his heavenly King was what struck me most." Figgis goes on to describe Stockmayer as "a teacher who had not quite conquered the English language, and who also was too much of a mystic for his thoughts to be quite accessible to large audiences." Sloan observes that "his message harmonised with that of others, while at the same time it had a feature that was unique and all its own . . . we can (in extracts cited from his addresses) also feel something of the deep impression made by his ministry." The address given here, on "The Sufficiency of Grace," was delivered during his last visit to Keswick in 1896, and is one of two reported in full—although summaries of several others appear in *The Christian's Pathway of Power* and *The Life of Faith*.

Another personality leaving an abiding impress upon the Convention, though ministering there for only a few years, was the Rev. George H. C. Macgregor. "His addresses, so Scriptural and so incisive, caught the ear of the Convention as few have done," says the chronicler of those early days. Like many another, he himself had come into blessing at Keswick. His biographer tells us that he attended the Convention in 1889 "as a matter of purely intellectual interest: but he had not been in the place many minutes before he found that the treatment (on the doctrine of Sanctification) was practical and new. Then he felt very angry, as a Scotsman, at being told anything new in theology by Englishmen! Monday was a terribly cold day, and Tuesday a burning day. Dr. Moule brought him to the crisis, and the conflict was narrowed down at last to one point. When that very point that night was touched by Mr. Hopkins, he felt so stung that he could have sprung to his feet and left. But God led him to do a very different thing—to commit himself wholly into the Lord's hands. Mr. Meyer laid hold of him as he spoke of getting out of the boat of self, and Mr. Hopkins followed with the opportunity 'Will you get out?' It was to him indeed like leaping out of a boat upon the waters. 'How has it been since?' In temper and worry—my weak places—I have found deliverance; not that the capacity for either has gone, but Christ has His hands on me now."

In 1892 Macgregor returned as a speaker, and only eight years later, at the early age of thirty-six, he was called Home; but in that brief period he exercised a ministry of remarkable power. It was in his last year, 1899, that he delivered the address which still lingers in the memories of veterans then present—"God can— God will." "Who can forget," Figgis wrote in 1914, "his application of the narrative of the woman healed by Christ after she had been given up by the physicians? ... Those who have the *Keswick Week* for 1899 should read every word of this wonderful address."

One who served Keswick devotedly for many years, principally behind the scenes, and through *The Life of Faith*, of which he was assistant editor, the Rev. C. G. Moore surprised the Convention of 1908 with an address of exceptional power, on "The God of Jacob." Delivered on the opening Sunday morning, this set the tone of the entire week.

It is appropriate to give here another memorable address by F. B. Meyer, on "Return to Bethel"—a message primarily for backsliders: one aspect of "sin in the believer" never overlooked at Keswick. It was delivered in 1899.

The name of Bishop Taylor Smith conjures up, for all who knew him, cherished memories of a portly figure in ecclesiastical garb, surmounted by a kindly, shrewd, humorous countenance, with twinkling eyes behind rimless pince-nez. Chaplain-General to the Forces from 1901 to 1925, he was greatly beloved at Keswick, where he was as markedly used of God in personal "counselling," especially among young men, as in his public ministry. A bachelor, he loved young people, and was eagerly sought after by them, for the advice on a thousand-and-one matters he was known to be ever ready to give. His addresses had the qualities of his radiant character—crystal clear and intensely practical, they revealed in every phrase his overflowing love to the Lord. In 1913 he "spoke wonderful words on the Monday evening," says Figgis; and this address on "The Blessed Life," was certainly among the best he ever delivered at Keswick. Incidentally, for the benefit of those who know only the Keswick of to-day, it may be explained that before the 1914–18 war the Convention lasted for ten days: the opening week-end was preparatory; one meeting only was held on the Monday, in the evening; and the sequence of teaching proper began on the Tuesday.

It was said of Dr. Alexander Smellie that "all he wrote was literature"—and that included his sermons and addresses, which he prepared in full and memorised. His ministry at Keswick was limited to the years 1914–22, when it was cut short by a distressing disability. But Sloan observes that "there have been few speakers on the platform more gifted in many directions" than he; "one whose humility of heart exceeded all his gifts." He gave "A Summons to Newness of Life" in 1916—a Convention with a comparatively small attendance, owing to the war: but it was "a glorious week," says Prebendary F. S. Webster, in his foreward to *The Keswick Week*; and *The Life of Faith* speaks of Dr. Smellie's address as "deeply affecting."

Quite a large number of Bishops have spoken from the Keswick platform, including many from the mission field: and among the latter, Bishop J. H. Linton, from Persia, spoke in 1919 (before his consecration) and during furloughs in 1924 and 1932. It was in 1924 that he gave the most helpful address on temptation, here reproduced. In this he drew upon his war-time experiences for very pertinent illustrations; and Sloan observes that it "was calculated to bring help to many a young Christian, in enabling them to face the difficulties of life here in the world, where the power of evil still holds sway."

It is fitting that, having given an address on "Sin" by the Rev. W. W. Martin, we should include a complementary message on "The Heavenly Physician," delivered in 1933. In this he penetratingly discusses the function of Keswick as a "spiritual clinic"—a term used frequently of the Convention from its early days.

Our final representative address in this section is by a greatly loved speaker of to-day, the Rev. G. B. Duncan: this presents his characteristically winsome, tender, almost yearning note of appeal to yield heart and life to the grace and blessing of the Lord—or rather, to the Lord of all grace and blessing, in whom alone is found God's bounteous remedy for sin. All who heard this message, on the washing of the disciples' feet, in 1950, will recall the rapt, almost breathless attention with which the vast congregation hung upon the speaker's words. It was as if all were in the Upper Room, witnessing the unforgettable scene between Jesus and Simon Peter. "Washing of the feet" might well sum up Keswick's message concerning God's remedy for sin in the believer.

GRACE

Rev. H. W. Webb-Peploe, M.A.

I WILL read six or seven verses from 1 Peter 2: 1–10, that you may know the sum-total of the doctrine I would desire to put forward as the life that God's children should walk in. "Wherefore laying aside all malice, and all guile, and hypocrisies, and envies, and all evil-speaking . . ." We will apply the words, one by one, to ourselves as we go on. "As new-born babes, desire the sincere milk of the Word, that ye may grow thereby: if so be ye have tasted that the Lord is gracious." It is the *tasting* of the grace of God that Peter puts forward here as the starting-point of the Christian's life. "To whom coming"—the child of God comes again and again to the Lord Jesus Christ—"To whom coming, as unto a living stone, disallowed indeed of men, but chosen of God, and precious; ye also, as lively stones, are built up a spiritual house, an holy priesthood, to offer up spiritual sacrifices, acceptable to God by Jesus Christ." That is the key-note of all I wish to say—"*acceptable to God by Jesus Christ.*" "Wherefore also it is contained in the Scripture, Behold, I lay in Sion a chief corner-stone, elect, precious: and he that believeth on Him shall not be confounded," or "ashamed," as it is in the Book of Isaiah. "Unto you therefore which believe, He is precious"; and it is the intense preciousness of the Lord Jesus Christ that every one of us stands in need of. I speak to you, dear brethren, to enhance the preciousness of the Lord Jesus Christ. Notwithstanding the indwelling corruption which I believe remains to the last in us; and notwithstanding that indwelling corruption does, as I hold, necessarily stain every thought and word and deed of life by which we give expression to our own vitality or being, yet the Lord Jesus Christ is only thereby made more and more beautiful, and more and more delightsome to the soul, until we realise, as St. Peter expresses it, that by virtue of His righteousness—simply because we have none in ourselves—we may present unto God spiritual sacrifices acceptable through Jesus Christ our Lord.

How often that word "acceptable" comes! How often when the term "well pleasing" occurs it is connected especially, by the Holy Ghost, with the name of the Lord Jesus Christ; and how invariably, though it may not be attached to it at the point of its utterance, it is found that the name of the Lord Jesus Christ occurs close by, so as to bring into connection with Him, and to show that the child of God, though helpless in himself, may yet be perfectly acceptable to God in the Lord Jesus Christ.

Now there would be two classes of hearers who might possibly misunderstand some of the things that were put forward last night.[1] First, some might go away with the despairing conviction, which Satan is always ready to engender in God's children, that if sin remains to the last as we walk in the world, we must give up in despair of pleasing God, and that we must be content to live and walk in sin, even till we are delivered from the burden of the flesh. Another line that may occur to another class of persons (exactly, as it were, at the other extreme) is that if we must needs commit sin, then, notwithstanding the fact that the Lord Jesus Christ has really used me, I recognise sin as the natural course of life, and because I like my sin I may keep it. It is against these two misunderstandings that I would now most earnestly defend the Word of God from any misconception at all.

Thanks be to God—let us announce it very clearly—though sin does remain to the very last, we believe, both in the being of the man, and also in the outcome from the man, yet there is no necessity whatever for a child of God ever to commit one single known sin again; and, on the other hand, it is simply a traducing of the whole blessed Word of God for any man to say, because we have sin about us and in us to the last, that therefore we may continue in the sin that we know we have liked. The great teaching that we have come here to put forward is that there is a delivering Lord, a mighty Jesus, who, by His infinite love, has made provision—at the instigation of God the Father, and by the power of the Holy Ghost—for the preservation of every child of God from any one known sin; and to pass through us such thoughts, such words, and such deeds, as shall be always acceptable to God the Father when they are rightly presented to Him through Christ Jesus our Lord.

If that be a statement of God's truth, then it follows that there can be no excuse whatever for any man ever wilfully or knowingly to allow in himself any habit, or thought, or word, or deed— any action contrary to the will of God. There can be no excuse for any man to allow the indulgence of any appetite whatsoever that springs from the flesh, and which is contrary to the revealed will of God. All that we have put before you is the high standard of God's perfect holiness, which makes even the angels to be

[1] The address on Sin, p. 31.

charged with folly; and then to see what a grand provision there is for such miserable worms of earth as we are; *first*, that the Lord Jesus Christ's blood when shed upon Calvary's Cross should have provided for all the penalty that was attaching to sin; *secondly*, that the precious blood of the Cross at this moment, and every moment, is always making provision for the guilt we should otherwise be incurring moment by moment; and, *thirdly*, that such a magnificent provision is made by our Beloved Lord and Saviour that He can keep us moment by moment in perfect fellowship with God the Father and His Son Jesus Christ, with open face to behold the glory of the Lord, adopting all this magnificent experience which God the Holy Ghost has put before us. They are ours in verity, ours in their fulness; and we may enjoy this communion simply and only by virtue of our beloved Lord and Master Jesus Christ.

How can these things be consistent one with the other? We affirm this, that though on two sides error may arise, the Word of God meets the error on both sides. *First*, let me say that God in His infinite mercy has made the provision for the child of God that there shall never be any dominion of sin over us. We are not under the law, but under grace (Rom. 6: 14), "Sin shall not have dominion over you"; and then in v. 22 it is declared, "But now being made free from sin, and become servants to God, ye have your fruit unto holiness, and the end everlasting life." Therefore the dogmatic declarations of God's Word are quite clear. We never can be under the dominion of sin if we are walking as God's children. Let us lay that down very clearly, because I know how Satan comes to some and says that they must sin; that sin is a natural infirmity, a part of our manhood; that we cannot be at liberty from it: but the Word of God puts it so clearly and solemnly, "Sin shall not have dominion over you," and, "Being then made free from sin, ye became the servants of righteousness."

Secondly, I believe there is not a single desire of the heart that is known to a man to exist, which may not be completely quenched by the grace of God that is given us through Jesus Christ, if that appetite or desire or taste be contrary to the mind or will of God. I believe the grace of God is able so to put forward the blessed Lord Jesus Christ, so to exhibit the beauty of the Saviour, so to attract the heart and the will and the feelings of a man, that he can look up into the face of the Lord Jesus as the sweetest and all-absorbing thing, so that the man has no room for naughty appetite or desire. Therefore we sing as we did yesterday—in the sight of God, if we are wise—even the desire for sin is past.

And I believe, *thirdly*, that if there is a single habit or infirmity in man which seems to derogate from the glory of God, and to keep him lower down than he ought to be living, if he can conscientiously believe that the infirmity, physical, mental, or moral, if removed, would leave him a freer man to serve his God, he may go to his Father in heaven, and expect with full confidence that God will loose him from that infirmity; and yet we hold that there is not a single thought, word, or deed, that comes forth from the man, that is not in one sense tainted by sin.

The two statements will appear to be contradictory; but let us ask ourselves where a reconciliation of these apparently divergent statements is to be found. And, first of all, dear friends, with regard to those words and deeds into which I have taken the liberty of dividing the outcome of man's life. Turn to Isaiah 55, and you will find a magnificent declaration there—it is generally taken, I know, in reference to the world at large—"Let the wicked forsake his way," and people generally apply the word "wicked" to the outside world who know nothing of the Lord Jesus Christ at all; but we are at perfect liberty to apply it to backsliding or low-feeling children of God. Then He says in v. 6, "Seek ye the Lord while He may be found; call ye upon Him while He is near." That is the first step we take at these conferences. We get two facts in that verse—"*He may be found*"; that is a fact, or it would not be put so; and "*He is near*." That brings us to the blessed thought that if we come, He is quite ready, and that His holy blessing will not be withheld. Now comes the blessed word, "For my thoughts are not your thoughts, neither are my ways your ways." There you get two things—thoughts, and ways. *Thoughts, ways, and word*, are all brought before you in Isaiah 55: 8–11, and they are God's thoughts, God's ways or works, and God's word.

Now, my brethren, what have we to do with God's thoughts, God's ways or works, and God's word? Thanks be to God, we have everything to do with them. If we look at 2 Corinthians 3: 5 we read, "Not that we are sufficient of ourselves to think anything as of ourselves; but our sufficiency is of God." Then let us take ways or works in Ephesians 2: 10; and then as to God's word, turn to Matthew 10: 20, "For it is not ye that speak, but the Spirit of your Father which speaketh in you." So that we have the thoughts of God, the ways or works of God, and the word of God, put right through us according to the mind and intention of God. Whatsoever comes from God is perfect, and therefore the thoughts, works, and word of God, must all be as absolutely perfect as God Himself; and then they are passed through me or through any vessel of God: and my contention is that when they are put into us, and are about to be passed through us, they are absolutely perfect, because they are all of God. Then comes the question, How shall they be kept, in any sense, as they are passed through me? If I am a defiled medium, how shall I keep that perfect will of God? as St. Paul puts it in Romans 12: 2, "that ye may prove what is that good, and acceptable, and perfect will of God." How shall I do it, dear brethren? I must give myself to God; the inner being of the man, or his soul, must be given to God; and by the grace of God, when a man is really converted, when he is really saved, when he has really given himself to God, really consecrated his thoughts, that man has given over his will, involving with it his affections, to God, so that the will and the affections are passed over to God, as I trust they will be, by every true child of God to-day.

Let this pass over your heart to-day—I *will* to be holy; I will to be for Thy service; I will to glorify Thee, O God! Nothing is so much in my heart as Thee. God sees this will; it is in thy heart. The Lord takes your will, and it begins to pass through your thoughts; "My thoughts to pass through your thoughts. My thoughts are not your thoughts." They are God's high thoughts. Then you see in 2 Corinthians 10: 5, "Casting down imaginations and every high thing"; casting down our thoughts, and bringing them step by step into the captivity of Christ. I can begin to think the thoughts of God. The thoughts of God, though higher than heaven above man, are passed into the child of God through the brain; and then they are coming out into words and works, and God's ways or works are higher than heaven above; so that my ways or works become infinitely more powerful than anything else you have heard before.

How shall they act through me? He passes the thought; He prepares the work; He gives the word, and it bursts forth from the man. My conviction is that the thing comes into us absolutely perfect, but it passes out of us so far tainted, as water passing through a pipe would necessarily be tainted if, though it spring from a perfectly pure foundation, the pipe were in some degree defiled in its composition. It is just slightly tainted by the fact that, though we are perfectly willing that all should be as perfect as God gave it to us, yet we are conscious of that perpetual infirmity, that perpetual indwelling corruption, that just taints the product.

Then, you say, Where is this peace and this blessed rest of soul? Why it is in this: as the thing comes forth from me, as it were through a fountain, the blood of Christ is ever dripping upon it as it emanates from man. I feel that my heart is clear and right with God. But the heart is not everything; the heart does not touch the sole of my foot, except by sinning. There are distinct principles and parts of man. The heart may be given to God; but there is that indwelling thing called sin, and if it taints the thing that passes through me, praise God that the blood of the Lord Jesus is ready, right at the mouth of a man's being, to cleanse away the guilt of everything as it comes out; and then it is acceptable to God through Jesus Christ our Lord. Christ has made it acceptable, not I. People say, "I know we have to depend on Christ"; but I want Him more than that: I want Christ to be for me the One that makes me every instant acceptable to God; and I believe that this will give comfort and calm to the child of God, longing to live without any broken communion; the child of God longing to live well-pleasing and acceptable to God the Father.

It is Christ who does this: it is the gift of God, the thought of God, the word of God, and the work of God; and if I have unwittingly corrupted that blessed gift of God, thank God, He passes it all through His blessed fountain of the blood of Christ, and accepts it in Christ Jesus our Lord: and so I owe to Christ the debt of instantaneous blessing; it is always given. I do affirm, as far as I understand it, that nothing can make Christ so precious to mortal man as our indebtedness to Him every moment of our lives.

How blessedly this gives us courage in the sight of God, because God's infinite love toward mankind is always operating in such a case through and by the Lord Jesus Christ; and though there is infirmity in the child, and "radical evil" in the things that come forth from the child of God, yet God is not a stern Judge now, but a loving Father, and God's delight is in His children. Why should He delight in me or you? Because He sees my heart is right with Him; the soul—the inner being of man—goes out to Him, and you are speaking to Him by the power of the Holy Spirit, "O Father! O my God, I long to please Thee. I would die to please Thee." That moment you are a spiritual sacrifice, acceptable to God through Jesus Christ. Let Christ keep you, moment by moment, acceptable to God the Father. All that you now have to do is to bask in the sunshine of the face of God; to rejoice in the light of the Father's face; and to live recognising the unspeakable debt which you owe to the unsearchable riches of Christ, and to yield yourselves at every point of your being to God, so that you can recognise the existence of the mighty working of God the Holy Ghost, who will sanctify you more and more every moment that you live. Because He will reveal to you fresh needs, and you pass them over to God, and that moment— I again say what I started with—that vileness that we have discovered, that taste, or that appetite, or that thought, may, by the grace of God, be subdued and removed. No child of God can keep a sin.

Oh, dear friends, place that truth deeply down in your hearts, because that is the teaching we wish to bring forward. It is not perfectionism that we teach; but not conscious imperfection, conscious failure, or conscious infirmity—it is conscious acceptance through the Lord Jesus Christ, and constant growth in well-being through God's dear Son. Yes, there is perfect sanctification in the Lord Jesus Christ; there is progressive sanctification by God the Holy Ghost; there is accepted sanctification by God the Father, through the person of the Lord Jesus Christ, and presented to Him by God the Holy Ghost working in us. May God reveal to us more and more what is meant by being sinful in ourselves, yet ever accepted of God, and able to say, like poor Jock, from the depths of our hearts—

> I am a poor sinner, and nothing at all;
> But Jesus Christ is my all in all.

THE MASTER IS COME!

Rev. Charles A. Fox, M.A.

The Master is come, and calleth for thee—John 11 : 28.

DEAR friends, this evening it is permitted to me to speak before the King of kings. We reckon it a great honour to be called on to speak before the Queen, but every child of God, be he minister or not, has the infinitely greater privilege of speaking before the King. His glory was so great that, when Isaiah saw Him sitting on His throne, the very posts of the doors trembled at His presence, and he cried out, "Woe is me, for I am undone . . . for mine eyes have seen the King." To stand before the King; to speak in His Presence; to say "Mine eyes have seen the King!" this may be the blessed expression and experience of every soul here to-night.

"The Master is come!" And such a Master as He was! Such a Master that Martha had before declared it impossible to die in His Presence, saying, "Lord, if Thou hadst been here, my brother had not died"; such a Master who had declared of Himself, "He that liveth and believeth in me shall never die." He "hath *abolished* death!" The death of the believer is here, *now*; death unto sin. What we call death is the entrance into everlasting life.

Yes, *Master* indeed! He proves He is *Master* by the continual display of His power. When the Lord Jesus entered upon His ministry, He was confronted with every possible antagonism.

First, on the very opening of His public ministry, *Satan* thrusts at Him; but the Master overthrows him with three simple passages of Scripture. When assailed, He quotes but one verse and stops, such is His faith in the Word of God. The devil returned again to the charge, and he is met with the same weapon, and is again overthrown; for He is Master—and as the devil leaves the field, even the Scripture quoted by Him is proved true, and the angels have charge over Him, and they come and minister unto Him. Oh, my friends, notice the power of the simple word of God!

The next thing with which the Master is confronted is *sin*, in its most terrible type. After pouring out accumulation of blessing upon His disciples, "Blessed . . . blessed . . . blessed"—for if He only turn round, blessing flows from His lips—He meets the shadow of death in the person of the leper. This was the first shadow of death which had fallen across His path. See how He immediately removes it. "If Thou wilt, Thou canst make me clean." "I WILL! be thou clean. And *immediately his leprosy was cleansed.*"

Again, *want* meets Him. He has power as Master over the devil, and over leprosy: can He also remove this obstacle? See! Mary saith unto Him, "They have no wine." Was it too humble a need for Him to meet? "Fill the waterpots. Pour out now"; and the witness is, "Thou hast kept the good wine until now!"

Do *you* want wine? Is there no Christian heart here who can appropriate that cry of need, "No wine!"—no one who has to own, "No joy, no festival, no jubilance in *my* heart"? Oh, shall we not bring that cry, "No wine", to the Master to-night, and find out how He can fill?

Then He is met by every form of *disease* and suffering—"lame, blind, dumb, maimed." Shall He pass them by? Nay: "He healed them *all*!"

Then you remember how actual *death* meets Him. There came a man pleading to Him, "My little daughter is even now dead." He went with him and lifted the child up by the simplicity of His divine word, "Damsel, I say unto thee, arise! And she arose, and walked."

But you say, she had only just died. This was—

> Before decay's effacing fingers
> Had swept the lines where beauty lingers;

the faint flush was yet over her—it was scarcely death. Then come again, and see Him Master over death. There met Him a young man being carried to the grave, for the devil confronts Him with death at every point and in every stage. Is He able? "Young man, I say unto thee, arise! And he that was dead sat up." He has power to raise even on the way to the tomb.

Then, again, death meets Him in the person of His own friend. There was no one else so dear to Jesus as this one and his sisters. "Now, Jesus *loved* Martha, and her sister, and Lazarus"; and this was the one whom He chose to be the type of His own death and resurrection. He loved all, He died for all, but He let Lazarus die for Him; he whom He *loved* was the one He let show forth His own power, in that within a week of His own death He raised him from the grave where he had lain four days. Was not this a triumph as MASTER?

But again the shadow of death falls on His path. This time it creeps over Himself, and He dies. But oh, divine victory! Who is Master now? "No man taketh it from me, but I lay it down of myself. I have power to lay it down, and I have power to take it again." And being dead, He has power to vanquish death.

Is HE NOT MASTER? Death, disease, want, sin, meet Him in every possible form, and He overcomes all!

Will you not have Him for *your* Master? Then bring all to Him to-night—the sin, the failing, the defeat; bring all yourself. Is there something still you will not give up? Not to such a Master? Oh, surely you will withhold nothing from Him?

We have seen the *power* of the Master; but we must know what the *will* of the Master is. We find it from the four "I wills" of Jesus.

The first "I will" we have already alluded to, the "I will" of cleansing. It was spoken to the leper, when he said, "Lord, if Thou wilt, Thou canst make me clean." He put his whole case into the hand of Jesus, and left it there. I would that every un-converted soul here would do the same, and put his will into the sovereign will of God. I would that every Christian here would do what this poor leper did, and *will His will only*. Do you think that, if you cast yourself at His feet, He will let you perish there? His whole power and love were put forth on him, "I will! be thou clean."

The next "I will" is a very remarkable one. It is in Matthew 20: 15, "Is it not lawful for me to do what I will with mine own?" How blessed to be called His "own." This is the "I will" of the possession of Christ in His people; a claim absolute, irreversible, entire, complete. Are you giving up to it, consenting to His claim? Oh, friends, I beseech you, yield to it. I beseech you, *be at the mercy of Jesus*! Oh, precious place to be, at His wounded feet, at the mercy of the Master, at His disposal completely. Will you surrender to Him? Will you place all at His disposal, the most humble things in your daily work—your children, your house-hold, every common thing? Will you say *now* to Him, "Do what Thou wilt with them!" The will of the Master is absolute with His own. Do you say, "Do as Thou wilt with me," then the blessing to follow can never be exhausted, when you have included all, and answer back, "Yes, Lord, it *is* lawful for Thee to do what Thou wilt with Thine own!"

The third "I will" is to Peter—"If I will that *he tarry*." By it He claims the *whole* of your life. "How long you live, how soon you die, is entirely at my disposal." Just previously He had told Peter by what *death* he should glorify Him. He gave to him to die; He gave to John long life. Then if He bids you live, what is there to do henceforth? Just this, to "tarry till I come"; to be always at the disposal of the Master; to live to show forth the virtues of

Him who hath called you out of darkness into His marvellous light.

Thus the "I will" of Christ covers the whole of the Christian life: the life which begins with cleansing. What is there more? "Father, I will that they also whom Thou has given me be *with me* where I am, that they may behold my glory." Do you see? Do you know this part of His will? "With me, where I am!" He came to where *you* were; and now, Lord, dost Thou raise us to be where Thou art! He saw the poor wounded man by the wayside, and when priest and Levite had passed, He *"came where he was,"* and raised him. And now He places us where He is!

"Father, I *will* . . ." Hear the One able to pray such a prayer against the whole of heaven. Shall we not ask, then, to see His glory, when He said "I *will* that they behold." There is not one present of all the thousand souls gathered here for whom that "I will" is not asked.

Friends, this is the will of the Master, who has "come" and calleth for thee: that you should be cleansed, claimed, at His disposal, and should see His glory.

Is He Master of property, as well as in power and in will?

Just before He died, He made an inventory of all He had, and then gave it all away. Hear Him:

> "My *peace* I give unto you."
> "That my *joy* might remain in you."
> He gave His body—"given for you."
> He gave His blood—"shed for you."

Then He gave what He thought a great deal of—His words. Twice He repeats this legacy, "I have given them the *words* which Thou gavest me." "I have given them Thy *word*."

All He had He gave away. "The glory which Thou gavest me I have given them."

Then, when He was on the Cross—for He was never so rich as when He was on the Cross!—He gives away *pardon*. He gives *home*—"Woman, behold thy son!" He links two of His own together for ever. There are no such friendships as those which are made by the Cross of Christ. Then, on the Cross, He gives *Paradise* away—Paradise, never heard of between Genesis and Revelation, except only at the Cross. "To-day shalt thou be with me in Paradise." Yes, to-day—immediate transition when you take Christ.

His very clothing was given away. "They parted my garments among them." "They cast lots for His vesture." I wonder what that soldier thought as He put on that seamless vesture: a picture of us murderers clothed in the stainless robe of the righteousness of Christ.

Then His very dead body was given away. Nobody cared for it, until one disciple came and begged it, and was allowed to have it for the asking.

Is He not *rich*, my Master? "My peace, my joy, my words, my glory!" All given away!

This is indeed *the* Master! Master in will, in property, in power —Is He yours?

You say He has never "come." But "the Master *is* come!" He came and emptied Himself, He came and poured His life out. He who called God *Father*, does He on the Cross, in the darkness? No! "My God, my God, why hast Thou forsaken me?" He places Himself among the *lost*; He is in the dark; so dark, that even Christ could not see. Oh, friends, the Master is come, and *calleth*!" Oh, dead souls, listen; oh, living souls, listen; He wants you, He calls you. "Come unto me . . . I will give you *rest*." He calls you to *life*, He calls you to glory, His eternal glory—do you know anyone else who does? Oh, will you not listen? Amid the syren voices of the world hear ye not the still small voice of wooing love, feel ye not its divine fascination?

> For oh, the Master is fair,
>   His smile so sweet to banished men;
> That they who meet it unaware
>   Can never rest on earth again.
>
> And they who see Him risen afar
>   At God's right hand to welcome them,
> Forgetful stand of home and land,
>   Desiring their Jerusalem!

Mary "arose *quickly*"—she had such confidence in Him; she came and fell at His feet when she heard His—the *Master's*—call. Will you do now as she did, and arise "quickly"?

Now what will you give Him, for He calls *you*? There is only one thing to give: "present your *bodies*." Oh, to give to such a Master, and for ever! Henceforth may you so own Him as Master that you refer all to Him, that every shadow and every sorrow should be instantly referred to Him. We are the richer for what we give away to Him. We can leave this place richer than we entered, for we may each say, "I have God for my 'own God' now."

"The Master is come, and calleth for *thee*." Oh! heed this appeal of your wounded Lord. He is all love. His whole being pleads for you to surrender to Him as *Master*: His very wounds plead.

May I not present you now, with myself, to Him as "living sacrifices"?

Oh, living, loving Saviour, we present unto Thee our bodies, our souls, our all. We hold not one thing back; but as the woman cast in "all her living" we give ourselves as living sacrifices on Thee, the living altar. Our lips, our love, our all. Take them as Thine for ever, and may we each go out consecrated irrevocably.

> Take my life, and let it be
> Consecrated, Lord, to Thee.

Yes, Lord, let us give Thee all, and love Thee much, for we have been much forgiven!

DELIVERANCE FROM THE LAW OF SIN

Rev. Evan H. Hopkins

For to will is present with me; but how to perform that which is good I find not—ROMANS 7: 18.

THERE are very many who find great difficulty in the seventh chapter of Romans, not because that chapter does not re-echo their own inner experience, but because they find it impossible to reconcile that experience with a life of victory over sin. A key, therefore, is needed to explain that difficulty. Practically, we know that too often this seventh chapter of Romans has been used as a refuge by those who are leading an inconsistent life; and our spiritual enemy would lead us to use this passage as a warrant for *expecting defeat*. Is it not true that too often it has been used, shall I say, as an excuse for sinning? At all events, many of God's children have come to this chapter for comfort and encouragement while pursuing a course of failure. Surely this was not the purpose of the apostle in writing the passage. When we come rightly to understand it, we shall find that this precious portion of God's Word is full of encouragement, not to those who regard defeat as inevitable, but to those who believe there is a way of deliverance, and would know the secret of overcoming sin.

Now, there have been those who, in reading this chapter, have looked at the passage as describing the experience of an *unconverted* man. It is very important that we should, at the outset, clearly understand the spiritual standpoint of the man who utters these words. If we look at it as the experience of an unconverted man there arises this difficulty: we have to assume that the apostle, after having led us on step by step, in the preceding chapters, to glorious heights of triumph, and fellowship with Christ, suddenly goes back to the most elementary truths. There would then be no natural sequence in the line of progress in these chapters. Nor indeed is this necessary. We shall take the passage as true of the child of God.

My first point, then, is that the passage is *descriptive of the Christian man*. The apostle is speaking of himself as a disciple of Jesus Christ. He *recognises the excellency of God's law*. It is true that a Jew also would be ready to recognise this: but the apostle uses terms here in connection with that law which no mere Jew, as such, could have used. His words are strong and emphatic. He says more than any mere Jew could have said: "Wherefore the law is holy, and the commandment holy, and just, and good" (v. 12). Again, "we know that the law is spiritual" (v. 14). He no longer occupies the standpoint of a Jew, because he is not now seeking to be justified by that law. It is by that law that he has been convinced of sin, as we see from the verses which precede our text. It is that law which has pierced him through and through. He has seen the spirituality of that law, and it has dealt a death-blow to all his hopes of salvation by the righteousness of that law. I say that only a man who had been spiritually enlightened could have spoken thus of God's law.

But again, he finds an *inward joy in the requirements of God's law*. Look at verse 22, "For I delight in the law of God after the inward man." That expression is remarkable. It is a strong one. It implies a *sympathetic relationship* between his inmost being and God's law. It indicates an inward harmony with God's commandments. Now, the natural man could never have said this, and the sinner, however deeply awakened, could never have used such language; he could not have truthfully said that he rejoiced in the requirements of God's law, after the inward man—and by the inward man, I take it, we must understand that part of his being which had been born from above. The language, therefore, is the language of a Christian man, of a converted man.

Then, notice again that his *desires and intentions are on the side of the law*. The law is "good." "To will is present with me"—to will the good, to do the good—"but how to perform that which is good, I find not." This cannot be asserted of any soul that has been untouched by divine grace. I say that we have here the description of a Christian man. But a Christian man *regarded in himself*, apart from faith in Christ. "But how can such a condition be possible?" You say, "It is utterly inconceivable."

Well, let us come to the point by considering what is meant by the expression, "in Christ." It is a favourite expression of the apostle Paul. The germ of that expression we have in John 15. What do we understand by our blessed Lord's words when He says in that chapter, "Without me ye can do nothing"? The *standing* of every believer is "in Christ," without any exception. You are accepted "in Christ." God looks at you "in Christ." But there is another aspect; there is another "in Christ," not simply the "in Christ" of *position* or standing, but the "in Christ" of *condition*, or fellowship. There is such a thing as not abiding "in Christ." There is such a thing as being out of communion—out of Christ in that sense. I believe it is to this condition that our

Lord referred when He said, "Without me"—apart from me, outside of me—"ye can do nothing."

And so, in the passage before us, what is it that we have in these twelve verses, 14–25? The passage is a parenthesis in the line of argument, and for a moment the apostle is contemplating himself as a converted man, and yet as apart from Christ. His desire is heavenwards; his will is on the right side, but he lacks the adequate *power* to perform; sin is stronger than the strength of his will, stronger than all his holy tendencies upward, which he has by virtue of his new birth. And if he lacks power, what then? There is failure, fruitless struggle, painful effort, continuous conflict and defeat. "I see not only the law of my mind, which delights in God's requirement. I see another law in my members, warring against the law of my mind, and bringing me into captivity to the law of sin which is in my members" (v. 23). "To will the good is present with me, but the evil is also present, and how to perform that which is good I find not."

Now, I believe there are multitudes of Christians who are practically in that condition. But you say, "Does not the apostle describe here his own present experience?" Not necessarily. "But he is not using the past tense; he is using the present tense." Yes, but he is not speaking from the standpoint of a present *experience*, though I believe he is speaking from the standpoint of a present *conviction* as to the tendency of the two laws. Therefore he uses the present tense. For instance, when I say, "Fire burns me," I do not mean precisely the same thing as when I say, "The fire is burning me." In the first case I am simply describing the property of fire; in the second I am giving a description of the present action of fire within the sphere of my consciousness. But still I use the present tense. And so the apostle, as one has said, is giving us here a "diagram" of the condition of things apart from the divine remedy. As if he said, Look for a moment at what you are as a converted man, as a renewed soul, as a Christian, as a child of God. You have the summing up of the matter in the last verse of the chapter. "So then, with the mind *I myself* serve the law of God, but with the flesh the law of sin." The "I myself-life" is one thing, but the "Christ-life" is another. There are multitudes of Christians who are living the "I myself-life." They know what pardon is; they know what it is to come to the Fountain; they know what it is to look to Jesus Christ in times of difficulty and perplexity, and to come back again to Him with their guilt, and get forgiven; but they are living the "I myself-life" instead of the "Christ-life."

Now let us turn to *God's remedy*. In order to be able to apply a remedy you must, like the physician, make a true diagnosis of

the disease from which the patient is suffering. Now I find in the
fifth, sixth, and seventh chapters of Romans three distinct aspects
of sin; and in order that we may see what is God's threefold
provision, we must understand the nature of sin in this threefold
aspect.

Look at chapter 5. There we see sin as a load of guilt—sin *upon*
us. Come to chapter 6, and there we see sin as a master—sin *over*
us. Then in chapter 7, sin as a law—*within* us. As the Lord Jesus
Christ is God's remedy, we must see the corresponding aspects of
that remedy as meeting these various aspects of sin. We have
three little prepositions of deep meaning. The keynote of the fifth
chapter is, "Christ died *for* the ungodly" (Rom. 5:6); of the sixth
chapter, "I died *with* Christ" (6:6); and of the seventh and
eighth chapters, "*in* Christ." In order that I may know deliverance from sin, as the burden of guilt, I must see that He died
for me. That is *substitution*. Every Christian knows what substitution means, and some of us, who have grasped that thought,
fancied we had grasped the whole of the Gospel as if there was
nothing more to know.

But the Spirit of God leads on in the next chapter, to see another
aspect of Christ. Not only has Christ died for me, and the guilt
been taken away, but I have to see that I died *with* Christ—and
with expresses *identification*. When we grasp the truth contained in
that thought, we understand what it is to be delivered from sin as
a master. And when we have got as far as that, we fancy, some of
us, that we have got it all. No. We are still troubled and cast
down, because we have not been brought to see the secret of
deliverance from *sin as a law* in us. But now we are brought to
understand God's remedy in the meaning of that little word "in."
To be "in Christ" is *not only union, but fellowship*.

You have noticed, have you not, that in those eleven verses to
which I have referred as a parenthesis, more than thirty times
does the apostle allude to himself in one form or other. Not
once does he refer to God the Father, the Son, or the Holy Spirit.
The reason is that he is regarding himself as a Christian apart for
the moment from the remedy; and he says that in spite of all our
good intentions and earnestness, and our will being on the right
side, the law of sin is too strong for us.

I have illustrated the point sometimes in this way. Suppose that
I take a rod and attach to it a piece of lead. I drop it into a tank
of water. By the law of sinking bodies, it descends; that illustrates
the law of sin. Now I get a piece of cork, and fasten that also to
the rod, and placing it in the water I see that by the law of
floating bodies, it has a tendency to ascend. But the lifting power
of the cork is not strong enough to overcome the downward

tendency of the lead, so that it may be kept from sinking. It rises and sinks alternately. There you have the "up and down" life. "I myself" by the cork serving the law of floating bodies, and "I myself" by the lead obeying the law of sinking bodies. "Up and down."

Now turn to 8: 2 and we read, "For the law of the Spirit of life in Christ Jesus *hath made me free from the law of sin and death*." What has taken place? Let us suppose that I place my rod with the lead and the cork into a little life-belt, and I put them into the tank of water. The rod now does not sink. Why? Because it is in the life-belt. There is sufficient lifting-power in it to keep it from sinking; but it is only as it is in the life-belt that it has the benefit of that law. It is the power of a superior law counteracting the other law. The lead is not taken away, but the rod has the benefit of a stronger power so long as it abides in the life-belt.

A working man to whom I used this illustration at once grasped the principle, and in prayer afterwards he said, "O God, we thank Thee for the life-belt, we thank Thee for the Lord Jesus Christ, who is the life-belt. We thank Thee we cannot sink so long as we abide in the life-belt; but may we never forget, O Lord, that while we are floating inside the life-belt, that the lead is there all the same."

Here, then, are the main points to be borne in mind. Sin is a load of guilt, but Christ died *for* me; sin is a master, but I died *with* Christ; sin is a law, but by abiding *in* Christ I am made "*free* from the law of sin and death." It is not an attainment, you see. It is not something that has taken place in you, so that you no longer have the tendency to sin. That is not it at all. The law of gravitation is not suspended when, instead of sinking, you float on the water within the life-belt; but it is *counteracted by a superior law*, and this is "the law of the Spirit of life in Christ Jesus."

It is thus that I read Romans 7. We do not triumph by virtue of our own struggles and efforts to keep ourselves from sinking, but by abiding in the life-belt and letting Christ have the whole weight of our load, which He counteracts by His superior power. Oh, to know the secret of this *abiding*! That is what we have to learn. Let us begin to learn it now. Hence we see we must not only know what it is to be in Christ in the sense of standing for our acceptance and justification, but also in the sense of *abiding*, that is, of fellowship with Him, if we would live in the power of His victorious life.

F

THREEFOLD DELIVERANCE

Rev. Evan H. Hopkins

Having therefore these promises, dearly beloved, let us cleanse ourselves from all filthiness of the flesh and spirit, perfecting holiness in the fear of God—2 Corinthians 7: 1.

Let us lay aside every weight, and the sin which doth so easily beset us—Hebrews 12: 1.

The law of the Spirit of life in Christ Jesus hath made me free from the law of sin and death—Romans 8: 2.

I HAVE read these three passages of Scripture because I want to direct your thoughts to the threefold deliverance which it is our privilege, as followers of the Lord Jesus, to enjoy. I address those who know something of the blessing of deliverance from the penalty of sin; in other words, who know what it is to be forgiven and to be at peace with God. But how many of those who know that blessing have been brought to feel the need of a deeper and fuller deliverance from sin? Surely this is why we have come up to Keswick. We want to know what is really possible in this life in the matter of deliverance from sin.

You will observe in the passages which I have read to you, that we have sin put before us in three distinct aspects—as a defilement, as a habit, as a law or tendency. It is to this subject of deliverance from sin in that threefold aspect that I want now to direct your thoughts.

I. *Deliverance from sin as a defilement.* Where is it that we realise that defilement? It is of the utmost importance that we, first of all, have a clear conception of the region in which the defilement is realised. Take, for instance, your inner consciousness—that little world within you, the world of thought, and emotion, and volition. Sin can bring its polluting influences into these three elements of our being. It can defile our imaginations and desires, it can obscure our spiritual vision, it can pervert our wills; and where we realise the defilement, we may realise the cleansing. There is nothing nearer to us than our inner consciousness. If sin and darkness and misery are there, no amount of improvement in our surroundings can remedy the evil. The cleansing must take place within. The region of our inner consciousness corresponds to that which the Bible calls the heart.

But let me now very earnestly entreat you to mark the distinction between the *heart* and the *nature*. The evil heart is not the evil nature. It is in this connection that thousands of people are making a great mistake. No wonder that they get confused in the matter of sanctification. The heart is capable of passing through varying conditions. The nature remains unchanged. The heart may be cleansed, sanctified, and made the dwelling-place of God. But you cannot sanctify the evil nature. Therefore let us not confuse the heart, the evil heart, with the evil nature. That is a very important distinction, and we ought to be clear about it from the very beginning.

What is the heart? It is the place within you where three things are focused—your thoughts, your desires, and your will. If these three elements are defiled, then your heart is an unclean heart, and needs to be cleansed. But if the mind is pure, if the desires are cleansed, if the will is consecrated, then you have that which the Bible calls a pure heart, a clean heart. Do not confuse the heart with the nature. If you are regenerate, you can never become unregenerate; but you can have an evil heart. If you are once regenerate and you backslide, then you *de*generate. But the two things are distinct—the evil nature and the evil heart.

It is possible to know cleansing in the heart, but though you have that cleansing you are not sinless. Let me illustrate it to you. Here are two concentric circles. Let the outer circle represent yourself or personality, and the inner circle your consciousness or your heart. Within the inner circle you may know the blessedness of God's cleansing. But, remember, there is a region between these two circles that you know nothing about. God sees it, though you do not; and if you say there is no sin there, you deceive yourself. But God knows; He is not deceived. Now I say that it is possible for you to know the blessedness of a cleansed heart. God can cleanse your desires, He can purify your thoughts, and He can sanctify your will. But you need something more than cleansing. That, after all, is a negative thing. You need something that is positive, and what is the positive? Well, your thoughts, your mind, need to be sanctified, and your affections need to be sanctified, and your will needs to be sanctified. How does the Holy Ghost do this? He sanctifies the mind, after the cleansing, by the truth of God. He sanctifies the affections, after the cleansing, by the love of God; and He sanctifies the will by the power of God. You may know what it is to have a cleansed heart. "Blessed are the pure in heart, for they shall see God." Do not confuse the heart with the nature.

II. *Deliverance from sin as a habit.* "Lay aside every weight, and the sin that doth so easily beset you." We all know the power of habit, either for good or evil. We all know it is something like, very often, "second nature." But it is not a nature. You were born into the world with an evil nature, but not with habits. No one came into the world with habits already formed. An evil habit is something in addition to the fallen nature. Now every habit can be laid aside, but I do not say that the evil nature can be eradicated. How is the evil habit to be laid aside? Gradually? No; abruptly, at once. "Let him that stole steal no more." It is not written, "Let him that stole learn to steal moderately." The Spirit of God when He deals with you in reference to evil habits, shows you that God demands an immediate termination and laying aside of it. How do you deal with a man who is addicted to drunkenness? Do you teach him to leave it off gradually? You say, "No, at once!" Well then, if there are evil habits in your life, it is possible for you to lay them aside, and drop them instantly.

There is another very instructive passage. "That ye put off concerning the former conversation the old man, which is corrupt according to the deceitful lusts; and be renewed in the spirit of your mind; and that ye put on the new man, which after God is created in righteousness and true holiness. Wherefore putting away lying ..." (Eph. 4: 22-25). How do you read that passage? How often does that phrase, the "old man," occur in the New Testament? Only three times. Now here let me again very earnestly emphasise the necessity of making another distinction between the "old man" and "the flesh." They are not the same. The phrase the "old man," as I have said, occurs only three times in the New Testament—in Romans 6, Ephesians 4, and Colossians 3. In *The Speaker's Commentary* there is a very valuable sentence connected with Ephesians 4—"The verses do not contain an exhortation to put off the 'old man,' but a repetition and reminder of the teaching which they had received on the subject on the occasion of their conversion, namely this: that they *had* put off the 'old man,' and they *had* to put on the 'new man.'" St. Paul reminds them of that. And because you have put off the "old man," you have now put off the "old man's" *clothes*. What is a habit? Something you wear. In this 4th chapter of Ephesians there are lots of habits mentioned, and the argument is this: "Seeing that you have put off the 'old man,' do not wear his clothes." If a Christian, if one who is a "new man," wears the clothes of the "old man," what folly! Because you have put off the "old man," now lay aside his clothes.

The "old man" is not the *flesh.* I took the trouble some time ago to collect all that the best commentaries say as to what is meant by the "old man." They all argued in defining the "old man" to be the *unconverted self.* I was talking to Theodore Monod once on this subject, and he said, "The 'old man' is the man of old." That expressed it exactly. Well, the man of old—you have done with him, the unconverted man. What do we read in Romans 6? "Knowing then that our old man was crucified with Him." What does that mean? It means that not only were your sins laid upon Christ, but you yourself, as an unconverted person, were nailed on the Cross with Christ; your old self was crucified with Him. Let us bear in mind, then, that the old man is not the old nature; that you have put off the old, the unconverted self, and that you have put on the "new man," and have now to wear the "new man's" clothes.

We read again in Colossians 3: 8, 9, "But now ye also put off all these: anger, wrath, malice, blasphemy, filthy communication out of your mouth. Lie not one to another." Why? "Seeing that ye have put off the old man with his deeds; and have put on the new man." We have seen, then, that the heart is not the nature, the "old man" is not the flesh. Because I *have* put on the "new man" I have now put off the clothes that belong to the "old man," and put on the habits or clothes of the "new man." There is deliverance, then, from the *habit of sin.*

We do not teach that sin as a defilement is simply to be kept under. Some people think that it is a matter of suppressing sin as a defilement. Not at all. Sin, in that sense, must be absolutely cleansed away, removed. What do we teach? Not that evil habits are to be kept under, merely, but to be put off, and *at once.*

III. *Deliverance from sin as a tendency, sin as a law.* "For the law of the Spirit of life in Christ Jesus hath made me free from the law of sin and death." By a law we understand something that acts with the constancy and regularity of a natural law—just like gravitation, which is always in force. There is a force on the side of sin, which is within me. I inherited it through the Fall. We all have that force within us. Do not be deluded: the same evil tendency is in every man and woman in this tent. But you may be delivered from it, though it is constantly there. You may know perpetual deliverance from it. That is the wonderful thing about it. How is deliverance from sin, as a law, to be realised?

By having the benefit of another law, the law of the Spirit of life. "The law of the Spirit of life in Christ Jesus hath made me free from the law of sin and death." But there are certain conditions. If you were to throw me into the sea, I should go to the bottom. How is that? By the law of gravitation. But if you throw to me a life-belt, and I get into it, what then? By the law of floating bodies I keep on the surface. Do I lose my weight? Not at all. The tendency to sink is there just as it was before, and I do not imagine that if I am in the life-belt for two or three hours I shall lose that tendency. Get out of the life-belt, and down you go. The tendency to sink is not removed. What then? It is perpetually counteracted by another law. On what condition? That I remain in the life-belt. "The law of the Spirit of life in Christ Jesus hath made me free from the law of sin and death"; but in the sense only that the law, or tendency toward sin, is still there, but is perpetually counteracted by another law.

Another illustration. Look at Peter walking on the sea. How was this possible? Could Peter walk on water? Had he attained to this? Certainly not. Had the Lord Jesus Christ wrought such a marvellous change upon the body of Peter that he lost his weight? No. Was Peter really as heavy now as before? Precisely. Was the tendency there that made him sink? Yes. How is it that he is walking on the water? Because the Lord Jesus Christ is exercising another power, and thereby counteracting the weight, moment by moment. There is the perpetual tendency downwards, but Christ's power to deliver is greater than that tendency. Why did Peter sink? You know the story. So it is now precisely. It matters not how long you have been a Christian, you have not lost the tendency downwards. Satan will tell you that you have lost that tendency, and he will seek thus to delude you. If a man asks me, "Do you believe in deliverance from sin?"—"Yes; but in what aspect do you speak of sin—sin as a defilement; or sin as a habit; or sin as a tendency?" There is a marvellous provision in the Gospel of Jesus Christ to meet sin in every possible aspect; and let us intelligently understand the nature of the whole provision. Just as pardon is not cleansing, so we know that deliverance from the defilement of sin is not precisely the same thing as deliverance from sin as a habit; although it is all found in the atoning death of the Lord Jesus Christ. Christ died not only that I might know the forgiveness of sins, but deliverance from sin in all these three aspects, and, hereafter, that I may know deliverance from the very presence of sin.

Let us mark these distinctions. Do not believe what I say without searching the Word, and when you see these distinctions keep your mind calm, and do not get into endless controversy and confusion. It is possible for you to enjoy the very fullest deliverance without stepping off the line of Scripture, or turning aside to all kinds of delusions. May the Lord not only keep us in this attitude in which we desire to obtain the fullest blessing, but keep us faithful on the lines of His holy Word.

CHRIST THE CLEANSER

Rev. H. B. Macartney, M.A.

SUPPOSING that the Lord Jesus Christ were now to appear before your eyes, what would be the consequence? You would forget all about yourselves, your infirmities, your spiritual maladies, and there would come a burst of praise from every lip, that would be heard among the stars. I believe that the showing forth of the Lord Jesus Christ as He is, the Image of the loving, infinite, holy, and eternal God, is the cure for all our diseases. All our imperfections arise from an imperfect appreciation of what He is, *to* and *for* and *in* His people. These words, "The God of all grace," on which dear Mr. Moule has just spoken, have been before me since the early morning, and I will tell you in what connection. I have been thinking that all believers have the grace of God; but which believer has the God of all grace living in his soul? For it is one thing to know that God sent His Son, and to get the benefit of His death in the way of pardon; but it is quite another thing to have God Himself coming into the temple of the body. Remember, too, that when He does come in, He comes undivested of any of His glorious attributes. Nothing of His power, His purity, His compassion, His peace, His faithfulness, is left behind. God is God, whether sitting on the throne of the universe, or on the lowly throne of the believer's heart.

I believe that if you have dim and misty views about the Gospel, you will never be clear about sanctification; but the moment you are clear about sanctification, the Gospel will be a thousand times more clear than ever before. For what is the Gospel of peace? It is justice dealing with Jesus instead of with us; it is Jesus dying for us. And what is the Gospel of purification? Just the same thing, only from another point of view. It is our dying to sin with the Lord Jesus, and rising with Him in newness of life. When the great work of Calvary is being done Jesus is alone. Every sinner who is seeking forgiveness has to stand still and gaze upon accomplished salvation, on Jesus' finished work; and every believer who is seeking light and love and victory over sin, has, in like manner, to retire, and to confess that Jesus is All-in-all. Jesus must be the living One, the loving One, the compassionate One in the heart: His must be the intellect, and His the words. I believe that this is the great truth of Keswick, because it is the great truth of the Word of God—"It is no longer I that live, but Christ that liveth in me."

Let me now draw your attention to John 13: 5, "After that He poureth water into a bason, and began to wash the disciples' feet ... Jesus saith to him (i.e. Peter), He that is washed (or as the Revised Version has it, 'He that is bathed') needeth not save to wash his feet, but is clean every whit" (v. 10). "Now there was leaning on Jesus' bosom one of His disciples, whom Jesus loved" (v. 23). Here we have three things. If I may put them in order just to help your memory, we have the *blood* for the conscience, the *bason* for the feet, and the *bosom* for the head. Now, first, how do we get anything about the blood in that tenth verse, "He that is washed . . ."? It seems at first sight as if it had to do exclusively with water and not with blood. But let us look elsewhere and you will see that there are *two* washings in Scripture. You get the "washing of regeneration" in Titus 3: 5, "To Him that loved us, and washed from us our sins in His own blood." But in Hebrews 9: 13 you get the washing with water and with blood together. The apostle is there referring to the ordinance of the red heifer (Numbers 19). The red heifer was slain; part of her blood was "sprinkled before the tabernacle," and after the remainder had been burned (a most unusual thing) together with her skin and flesh, her ashes were gathered up, kept in a certain place, and subsequently, when needed, were mixed with water— a "water of separation, a purification for sin." So the apostle says, "For if the blood of bulls and of goats, and the ashes of an heifer sprinkling the unclean, sanctifieth to the purifying of the flesh . . ." Here, then, we have the washing of water and the washing of blood brought together—a washing so perfect that we are "clean every whit," *except the feet*. Now let me say a word about sin in believers.

Somebody once said that he had not sinned for seven years, and the man to whom he said it instantly jumped up and said with indignation, "How do you know?" He could hardly, except by a text, have given a better answer. He might have added—"Have you the insight of God? Have you looked at your life by the light of 'the seven lamps of fire'? Have you the Holy Scriptures off by heart from beginning to end, so that you fully know God's perfect way? If we say that we have no sin, we deceive ourselves, and the truth is not in us."

Let us never forget that God Himself ordered the Pentecostal loaves, "the first fruits unto the Lord," to be baked "*with leaven*" (Lev. 23: 17), the thing that he hated, the type of sin. It was never, on pain of death, to be mixed with anything typically representing the Lord Jesus; but these loaves "with leaven" were to be a type, or figure, or shadow, representing the Church of Jesus as God meant it to be. Yes—as God *meant* it to be. I know that "worshippers once purged should have no more conscience of sin" (Heb. 10: 2), but there are regions in our being far beyond the ken of conscience which constitute us sinners, still needing the blood which *goes on* cleansing, still needing the daily intercession. In this sense we are totally different from Adam before he fell. He had a nature absolutely sinless; it did not indeed help him very much, for he fell into the snare of the devil after a very few minutes of temptation. Now we too have a nature which in itself is absolutely sinless, a new "divine nature" (2 Pet. 1: 4); but although we dare not say, even when in the most glorious enjoyment of full salvation, that *sin is dead*, yet we can truthfully say, (and we dare not say otherwise) that when abiding in Christ, and fully believing in Romans 6, *we are dead*, dead to sin, dead with Christ. As for this monster, sin, we have such a remedy in the Cross, such a Saviour close at hand, that it need not trouble us, because it need not exercise one particle of power. Jesus has the power now, not it. "Sin shall *not* have dominion over you: for ye are not under the law, but under grace." If the Bible tells me that it is one of God's facts that the "flesh" is to be incorrigibly bad, even to the very end (Rom. 8: 7), I do not grieve over that fact, although it is very humbling; but I fix my eye on God's provision against it, a provision so glorious that I cry out of joy— Jesus Himself, a Saviour, who not only took my sins to the cross and paid my debt, but took *me* to the cross, and nailed up my "old man" to the accursed tree; who has power to keep that "old man" from coming down from the cross; yea, power to enable me to reckon myself as "crucified, dead, and buried" with Himself, and to make the reckoning good. This—"having died unto sins" (1 Pet. 2: 24, R.V.)—is practically *cleansing by blood*. Jesus Himself is the Cleanser, and some of you who are wanting the mighty indwelling of the Holy Ghost will never get it till Jesus has cleansed you thus, to make your hearts fit to be the abode of such a heavenly Guest.

In 1 John 1: 7 we read that "the blood of Jesus his Son cleanseth us from all sin." Now even if I grant you—for the sake of argument —that that passage has nothing whatever to do with causing sin to cease, yet I find in verse 9 that, "If we confess our sins, He is faithful and righteous to forgive us our sins, and to cleanse us from all unrighteousness." That surely involves *cessation from sin*. Combine the two passages, and you get the whole truth. You need the cleansing by blood from moment to moment because you are a sinner, and you get the benefit of the blood, applied by personal power, which enables you to live as a saint. I feel very strongly indeed that we ought clearly to understand that sinfulness is a fact even with the brightest, happiest believer; but when the Lord Jesus Christ comes into his soul, he is there and then delivered. "Whosoever abideth in Him sinneth not" (1 John 3: 6). When I bring a lamp into a dark room the darkness disappears somehow or other; I do not know what becomes of it. But if I put out the light, the darkness re-appears, and where it comes from I do not know. Just in the same way, if I cease to abide in Jesus, sin instantly begins to make itself felt, as cold prevails when heat is withdrawn, or as corruption follows the cessation of life.

The celebrated J. N. Darby once gave an illustration. He said that supposing he awaked at night and heard a commotion downstairs where he had a dark cellar, and he got up and found that a thief had broken through the house and was in the cellar, he might, if he found the key outside, just lock the burglar in; and as long as he knew that the door was strong on its hinges, and that he had the key in his pocket, he might go about the town all day, or even travel into the country, for it did not matter to him whether the burglar was there for a week, or a month, or a year. Even so, he said, we need not vex ourselves because sin is near, if only God is nearer. The fact of the haunting presence of sin should humble us exceedingly, and we should dread the possibility of again falling under its power. You will all see, however, where the illustration fails. A burglar raging and storming within his prison is not the best illustration of our position when cleansed. That position is, *not* the flesh *continuing to* "*lust*" (Gal. 5: 17), but the flesh "*crucified, with its passions and lusts*" (v. 24).

Here is another illustration, against the perfectionist. You go into a nobleman's garden, and say, "What a lovely garden; there is not a weed in it!" But during the next month the nobleman is away, and the gardener has fallen sick, and has not been in the garden for full four weeks. You now find it to be a perfect wilderness. That is something like the garden of my heart. As long as Jesus is there, the weeds of sin do not appear; He "keeps it night and day" (Isa. 27: 3). But if I grieve the Holy Spirit, if anything causes Jesus to cease from abiding in me, there is wreck and ruin, and all sorts of evils spring up in my soul. I cannot help thinking of the three words on the lips of the Lord Jesus Christ when He was going to leave His disciples. He said, "Father, keep." But He put a prefix before "Father." He said, "*Holy* Father, keep." "These people," He seemed to say, "are to be my bride in heaven; therefore they must live on earth a holy life. Holy Father, keep them in Thy name." Yes, I know that this Bible in my hand is now being drawn to the earth by the mighty law of gravitation, but I am interfering with the natural law, and am holding it up in my living hand; and I say fearlessly that I would rather be a sinner rendered *unable to sin* by union with the Lord Jesus in His death, *unable to sin* because of union with Him in His life—I would rather, I say, be a sinner "safe in the arms of Jesus," kept from sin and hating it with all my heart, than change places with Adam and Eve in the days of their "sinless perfection." It is in *being saved* that we get to know the Lord best, and as sinners learn to *keep close*. Yes, God has got a hold of love upon His people. Keep believing, keep receiving, keep obeying, keep abiding, and stand fast, not in Adam-purity, but in Christ, and in the liberty wherewith He makes His people free.

Do ponder carefully. What *must* be the effect of the washing of regeneration—I mean by that, the new birth? When a thing is newly born of God, it must be clean, it must be perfect. It is no every-day, ordinary thing; it is a specimen of His new creation, in conjunction with His own dear Son, and by the power of His blessed Spirit. And, therefore, as far as you are a person born again, so far and only so far, that holy nature of yours is a sinless nature. St. John says distinctly, "Whosoever is born of God sinneth not" (5: 18), and he also says, "He cannot sin, because he is born of God" (3: 9). It is of the first importance to understand this, for if you believe that you have derived from God a nature that is absolutely holy, you will easily perceive that it will work and live on holy lines, and that it will be true to God as a part of His new creation.

I now come to the *washing of blood*, and I wish to direct your attention to this great truth—the Gospel of St. John is the Gospel of Christ's finished work. Christ says in one place (4: 34), "My meat is to do the will of Him that sent me, and to *finish* His work." In another place in the same Gospel (5: 36) Christ says, "The work which my Father gave me to *finish*." Again, He said, "I have *finished* the work which Thou gavest me to do" (17: 4), and on the cross He exclaimed, "It is *finished*" (19: 30). Now, what did the Saviour come from heaven to do? "The Son of God was manifested, that He might destroy the works of the devil" (1 John 3: 8). And when we see Jesus hanging on the cross, we see Him not only dealing with sins committed by believers, but with sin as a whole, in its root and branch; and therefore you who are His people have just to begin at the very point where He ended. Calvary was the great field of decisive destruction. Jesus fought there; Jesus battled there against the powers of hell; Jesus won there, and left the field victorious. The whole question of sin has been magnificently and for ever settled by the Lord Jesus on Calvary. The victory to us is just as sure as the victory of Waterloo. "The faith which is by Him gives perfect soundness in the presence of us all" (Acts 3: 16).

I want you to see that believers, by the Holy Ghost, may reap two great benefits from the Saviour's accomplished sacrifice. One, you of course know, is the *pardon of sin*; and the other is the *power to cease from sin*. The power to cease from sin is wrought in this way by the Holy Ghost—The apostle asks, in the Epistle to the Romans (6: 1), "Shall we continue in sin, that grace may abound?" You think that he should have replied, "We must not sin, because it grieves and displeases God, and because of its disastrous consequences." But He does not say so. He goes straight to the point, "How shall we who died to sin live any longer therein?" and he proceeds to show that you, in the reckoning of God, are dead to sin in Christ, as dead to sin as He is. And he argues later on, "Likewise reckon ye also yourselves to be dead indeed unto sin, but alive unto God." Then he goes a step further. I lost years in reckoning myself dead to sin, and it did no good. I got worse rather than better, because it seemed as if there was something in the Bible the blessedness of which I could not arrive at. But what follows? "Alive unto God *through Jesus Christ our Lord*" (6: 11).

There was a girl in Australia who, after Mr. Hudson Taylor's visit to the Colonies, went out to China. We thought she was a splendid missionary, bright, happy, and entirely devoted; but when in Shanghai she attended some meetings like this, and she was convicted of sin for holiness, and in the anguish of her soul she consulted a dear friend of mine. He gave her an illustration about reckoning herself "dead indeed unto sin." He told her that when the Lord Jesus Christ had said to Jairus, "The maid is not dead, but sleepeth" (Matt. 9: 24), there were three courses open to Jairus to pursue. He might have said, "The Master is not true this time; I know she is dead; He has made a mistake." Then he would have gone home to his dead child, and he would never have seen her alive. Or, secondly, he might have said, "The Master's word is true. He has said that she is not dead but only asleep, so I will say 'good-bye' to the Master, and thank Him very much for His word, and I will go in myself and raise my daughter up." And so he would go into the room and find her there on the couch apparently dead, but he would say, "She is not dead; she is only asleep." He would speak to her, and put his arms about her, and lift her out of bed to make her stand, and—she would drop down a corpse upon the floor. But the third course was the one that brought blessing. Jesus had said that she was alive, and Jesus must see to it Himself that His own word does not fail. He who is the resurrection and the life must come in and *cause her to live*.

What was the effect of that illustration upon my friend? She got liberty there and then. One of our leading Melbourne ministers came back from England by way of China, and he went into the interior by a difficult and dangerous path, and found that girl. And what did he say to us as we were sitting one day at the Council of the China Inland Mission? He said, "That girl has received about as big a blessing as ever was received by a human heart." It came, you see, in this way. Her reckoning was not a mechanical reckoning, but a reckoning that reasoned thus—"Jesus, You have said it; Jesus, You must do it." Jesus will enable us by His power to take the place of death with Him, and we will become dead to all our old sins, as dead as is requisite for God's highest purposes of holiness; only, however, *while abiding in Him*.

I now pass to the second point about the bason for the disciples' feet. This is very important. Water, I believe, symbolises the Word of God; and you will find, even if you are in the happy enjoyment of Jesus as a Saviour, and even if sin has not dominion over you, and even if you have the indwelling of the Holy Ghost, that it will be a necessity of your life to search the Scriptures; and in searching the Scriptures, you will see something fresh every day that is to be dealt with by Jesus' power. That is the way to go on "perfecting holiness" (2 Cor. 7: 1; Ps. 119: 9; Eph. 5: 26). I would like to remind you of Joshua 1: 8, "Thou shalt meditate therein day and night . . . for then thou shalt have good success"; and Psalm 1: 2, 3, "In His law doth he meditate day and night . . . his leaf shall not wither, and whatsoever he doeth shall prosper"; and Job 23: 12, "I have esteemed the words of His mouth more than my necessary food"; and Jeremiah 15: 16, "Thy words were found, and I did eat them; and Thy word was unto me the joy and rejoicing of mine heart." And why? "For I am called by Thy name." The name of God is on the Christian. You are entrusted with His honour—I might almost say with His very Person. God has given you His crucified and risen Son, and you are to take that Son and to manifest Him to the world wherever you go.

Now, just to show you how cleansing is by the Word, we read in John 15: 3, "Already ye are clean through the word which I have spoken unto you." I want to entreat you to get up a little earlier than you have been in the habit of doing every morning, and to meet God over His Word. You sometimes, perhaps, have tried prayer by itself, and found it rather dull and heavy. You have tried the Word of God by itself, and got a little drowsy over it. Now mingle the two together, and while you read, pray; and while you pray, praise, and then you will have a blessed hour with God.

> Shake off dull sloth, and early rise,
> To pay thy morning sacrifice.

As I close I want to refer you to the last thing—*the bosom for the head*. When you have become accustomed to speaking to God, and to God speaking to you in His Word, then there will spring up such an intimacy between you, that your very flesh and your heart will cry out after Him. There are two different expressions here. First, "leaning on Jesus' bosom" (John 13: 23); and then further on, "lying on Jesus' breast" (v. 25). Draw near to Him, and ask Him to let you *lean* your head upon His breast. But afterwards, when you know Him better, you will be able to let your head rest there altogether, as if that was *your* place, as if you knew of no other in the wide, wide world.

Oh, remember that when you lean your head on Jesus' breast, you are leaning your head upon the bosom of One whose head has been accustomed to lie in the bosom of the Father. "The only begotten Son, which is in the bosom of the Father, He hath declared Him." And when you lie in the bosom of Jesus, you will be such an evangelist, such an apostle, such a preacher, such a writer! You will be telling everybody about Jesus. You will "declare" Him because you know Him. Look at that sheep which the shepherd brings home on his shoulder rejoicing! Look at the head of that sheep! It is hanging down just above the shepherd's heart. Get near enough to hear the throbbing of that heart that once was broken in its love for you.

If you live much in the bosom of Jesus, you will hear His voice, and understand His affections, "My sheep hear my voice." This is one of their characteristics, and I charge you all to get such a knowledge of, such an intimacy with the Lord Jesus Christ, that you will not simply be guided by circumstances. I bless God for the circumstances that He Himself ordains, but there is this danger about them, that we can deal more slackly with circumstances than we can with God's spoken utterances. When God says, "Go," you must go; or "Stay," you must stay; or "Die," you must die; or "Bear," you must bear. But if it is only "a circumstance," you may put another interpretation upon it, to suit your own convenience. If you want the higher life, get to the bosom of the Lord Jesus Christ, where you feel His heart beating, and where you hear His lips speaking. Peter could not hear; he had to ask John. John knew because he could hear a whisper. If you lead the life of intimacy and fellowship with Jesus, people will come to you and ask you questions about guidance, and Scripture, and cleansing: and it will be a blessed thing to be so near Him, that you will be able to publish His name among your fellows. That is the place of blessing. You cannot get higher than the bosom of Jesus.

> Wrapt in deep adoring silence,
> Jesus, Lord, I dare not move,
> Lest I lose the smallest saying,
> Meant to catch the ear of love.

THE CONDITIONS ON WHICH GOD CLEANSES

Rev. Harrington C. Lees, M.A.

*Behold, I will send my messenger . . . and the Lord, whom ye seek, shall suddenly come to His temple, even the messenger of the covenant, whom ye delight in . . . But who may abide the day of His coming? . . . for He is like a refiner's fire, and the fullers' soap: And He shall sit as a refiner and purifier of silver; and He shall purify the sons of Levi, and purge them . . . Then shall the offering of Judah and Jerusalem be pleasant unto the Lord, as in the days of old, and as in former years—*MALACHI 3: 1–4.

I DESIRE to speak to you upon the conditions on which God cleanses. "*He shall come.*" We use the phrase, "The coming of the Lord" in three senses. We use it in the past sense, when alluding to His Incarnation; in the future sense, when referring to His Advent; and in the present sense, when we speak of those divine visitations, of which we trust this convention is one, when the Lord comes specially to individual souls, as well as to collective bodies of Christians, and deals with them in regard to their spiritual life.

"*The Lord whom ye seek.*" Is it that with us to-day? What are you seeking here? One says, "I am seeking rest of soul." Another says, "I am seeking victory over sin." Another says, "I do not know what I want, but I know I want something." Shall I change the question, and put it on the lines of Malachi's words—not, *what* are you seeking? But *whom* are you seeking? If you want rest, you can find it in Him; if you want victory over sin, it is hidden in Him; if you want that nameless something which you cannot define, you can receive it through Jesus Himself coming to dwell in your heart by the Holy Ghost. Whom are you seeking—or, as the Hebrew is more exactly rendered, whom are you *groping after*?

In what sense are you seeking the Lord? Malachi compares the people of the Lord to silver, and in God's Word *silver* has a typical significance in relation to redemption. In Exodus 30: 13 we have the silver which every soul of Israel had to give—the redemption money; and in 38: 27, God takes that silver and melts it down, and makes it the basis on which His tabernacle stands. Now St. Peter tells us, in his first Epistle, 1: 18, 19, what stands at the foundation of all spiritual life. "Ye were not redeemed with corruptible things, as silver and gold . . . but with the precious blood of

Christ." Am I addressing any who, so to speak, are not yet silver in the Lord's sight, and who have not found Him as Saviour? It is no good building from the top. There must first be a foundation.

I was once shown over a lead refinery. They showed me how the metal was melted down, and passed from pan to pan, and ladled out. Each time two-thirds of the metal was taken out, and one-third left behind. "What is that which is left behind?" I asked. "That is the dross, the refuse." "What do you do with it?" "We extract the silver from it." That is just what the Lord is doing always, taking the poor dross in our fallen human souls, unsaved without Jesus Christ, when the world has thrown it on one side and said, "We can do nothing with it," and coming to us as a Refiner, and even out of the lead extracting the redemption silver for His household. Will you, who have not done it before, ask the Lord Jesus Christ to make you to-day as silver from the lead, to cleanse you once for all and now by the blood which He shed on Calvary, to put you in the position of a saved soul? For we are called to teach here not only that men may be saved from their sin, but also that they may be glad in the knowledge of it.

But if we know Jesus Christ as Saviour, our text implies a further knowledge. "The *Lord* whom ye seek"—the *Master*. It is the thought in 1 Peter 3: 15, "Sanctify the Lord God (or 'Christ as Lord') in your hearts." If He is there as Saviour, He wants to be there in a new sense. He comes and says to-day, "The Lord whom you are seeking as Master shall suddenly come." It is the revelation that He gave in similar circumstances to Isaiah. Three times over in the sixth chapter, in that wonderful prophetic call to Isaiah, you will find the word Lord (*Master*) used. "I saw the *Master* high and lifted up." "The *Master* said, Whom shall I send?" "Here am I, *Master*, send me." There are many of you here who have been praying for a blessing; you prayed before you came that the Lord would meet you and bless you, and perhaps you took upon your lips those Old Testament words which have been the hope of seeking souls in all ages, where God promises that He will "pour out a blessing, that there shall not be room enough to receive it." But you must put first things first. If you want the blessing of Malachi 3: 10, you must go through the process of the first three verses.

There are four words here which speak of the cleansing process through which God puts His people, and every one of these processes is used now in connection with the refining of metals. The first one you will find in the second verse—"like fullers' soap." It comes from a Hebrew root, which means to cleanse by bringing beneath the feet, just as washerwomen in Scotland wash clothes by crushing them or treading upon them in the water.

We see a like process in the crushing of the quartz before the metal is extracted: the machine is called a "stamp." The thought is that when God wants to cleanse a soul He often has to crush it in order to free the pure metal from the hindrance of its environment, so to speak, and bring it out for His glory. This crushing process is not pleasant, but one thing is clear: unless you and I are willing to be brought to the feet of the Lord Jesus, we may as well say good-bye to all blessing.

A sculptor wrought a beautiful statue, and a man who saw it said, "I do not understand your statue. You can carve, I know, but your statue is all out of proportion." "You cannot see it as I see it," remarked the sculptor; "you will find at the foot of the statue a place to kneel, and when you kneel at the feet of my image of Christ, you will see it in its true proportion." The man knelt there, and he saw at once the statue in its true proportion and glory. Of course, the act was in itself idolatry, but there was a truth stored in it, namely, that there are things in Christ which you can never learn or see, until you have knelt at His feet and allowed Him to put you beneath His feet.

"Who shall stand when He appeareth?" Some of us who think we can stand before the Lord to-day need to be brought beneath His feet, and to have what He is prepared to give us—a vision of our own *sinfulness*: sin in our private life, sin perhaps that others have not been aware of; sin in our business, which is allowed under pressure of the world; sin in our family life, because we are afraid of confessing the Lord to those about us. If you and I see sin as the Holy Ghost is prepared to reveal it to us, it will mean a coming down. Then *shortcoming*—that our holiness is very inadequate, and that our service has been insufficient. Then *self*—that as we in the ministry have preached the Gospel of our crucified Lord, there has been the thought of ambition in our hearts, that we have sought less to glorify our Master than to preach a sermon of which men should speak well; we have sought, it may be, less the salvation of souls than that men should think we have organised a parish in a way that did credit to us. It may be that the Lord to-day comes as a Cleanser who brings beneath His feet the souls for whom He has prepared blessing.

There is a second word that you will find in this passage which brings before us the second line of God's dealing in cleansing. The word translated *purge* means *to cleanse by sifting and straining*, as by the action of water. There are gold diggings in Western Australia where the gold-dust mixed with soil is separated from it by means of water. This is not so violent or so painful a process as the crushing, but it is not less necessary. I believe that the action of water when spoken of in the Bible, usually means the action of God the

Holy Ghost working through the written or spoken Word. "Where-withal shall a young man cleanse his way? By taking heed thereto according to Thy Word." "That he might sanctify and cleanse His church with the washing of water by the Word" (Psa. 119: 9; Eph. 5: 26). It is God speaking to us in His Word; and we desire, above all things, at Keswick, to give not a message from our lips but a message from God's own Word to every individual soul. It may be that there are things in your life which you know are sins, and which God will deal with; and also things that you do not know of, which God wants to deal with; and to this end we desire to bring you to the Word of God.

> Holy Spirit, by the Word
> Save and cleanse.

Some of you may not think there is any sin in worry. But God has given us a command that in nothing are we to be anxious. God's Spirit wants to save you from the worry which is causing difficulty and hindrance between your soul and God. There are some of you who think you cannot help stumbling as the result of your besetting temptations—that it is no sin, for instance, for a man to exhibit bad temper. Yet, when God has given us His word in Jude 24 that He "is able to guard you from stumbling," do you think it is no sin to persist in stumbling? Again, God tells us in 1 Thessalonians 5: 18, "In everything give thanks." Do you think it right for Christian people to grumble at the dealings of God, at their circumstances and failures, at God's weather, and this thing and the other? "These are only little sins," you say. But it is the little sins that make many of the inconsistencies of most Christian lives. He is not a Christian at all who has not learned that God can deliver him from great sins, and he is not much of a Christian who has not learned that God can deliver him from little sins; and what He wants to do is to sift us, to strain us, to purge us of those things as the metal is purged.

There is a third thing of which Malachi tells us. In verses 2 and 3 you have the word *refiner*. The first process was the action of ·the feet; the second, the action of the water; and this third process is the action of *fire*, in order that the dross which is still in may be got out: dross that you never thought was there. When you missed your train, or your fire would not light, or your dinner would not cook, a little hidden temper came up that you never knew was there. That is dross, and the Lord wants to cleanse it out. He wants to make us pliable, ready and willing to be moulded; He wants us to be as good silver, so that we may take this shape. Perhaps some of you may have come under the action of some sorrow or trial, or you have been sorely tempted. He wants to teach you submission to His will. It may be that God is going to bring before you such a crisis here as will be a real fiery furnace to pass through. Is there anyone to whom you must apologise if you are going to be right with God? Is there anyone toward whom you have not been acting as you ought to act, with the result that God has a controversy with you on that point? Is there any restitution that you ought to make that God has laid upon you? It is astonishing how many of these little controversies there are, and God wants to deal with them. Is there anything in your life that you ought to put right this day—some unhallowed love, to separate from which will be a very passing through the fire? If God is to bless you, there must be no controversy between you and Him. God can never come to dwell in you as His temple, until you have yielded to Him in the matter that He has brought before you for that purpose. The Lord help us, as He points to this or that thing in us which is wrong, to go and put it right, so that we may be without offence before Him, and He may fill our whole lives.

Notice something very tender and beautiful in the words "He shall sit as a refiner." Someone asked a silver-refiner once why he *sat* to do his work, and he replied, "Silver-refining is such delicate work that I dare not stand. I sit by the side of the crucible, because the process is so easily overdone or underdone." Did you think the Lord was dealing hardly with you? Believe that God is love. He never overdoes, but He loves you too well to underdo His refining work. How do you know when that silver is purified? Someone asked a silver-refiner that question, and he replied, "I know that the silver is refined sufficiently, when I see my face reflected in it." The Lord loves you so much that He wants to see His image reflected in you, and He will not let you go until that purpose is effected. Most of us have had to say, like the prophet, "Woe is me!" before we could say "Hallelujah!" and even after we have got to "Hallelujah!" we have still to say, as we see ourselves from time to time, "Woe is me!" The Lord make us to shine like Him, even though it means going through the fire.

The fourth process you find in the word *purify*, which means to make bright. When the metal was brought out from the fire it took the shape that the moulder meant it to have. It looked all smooth when it was melted, but now it has cooled it appears to be rough. It had before, the image of the refiner shining in it; but now the image has gone off. The Lord wants to make His image permanent in us. Many people let the Lord deal with them at conventions by the other three processes, but they will not let Him deal with them by this fourth process, and therefore they do not go on reflecting the Master's glory, and people all around say, "That is a Keswick Christian; I do not think much of

them!" The Lord deliver you and me from that. This fourth process
is intended to polish the silver and make it bright, and thereby to
make the reflection permanent which before was only temporary.

How do they polish the silver? It is a rough business to commence with, a file and sand-paper business. The people who
sand-paper you in your lives are people who "rub you the wrong
way." You say that they are a hindrance to you. They are
meant to be a help; they are meant to make you the brighter,
and to take off the rough corners. Every person may be a means
of grace to you if you ask God to make them so. Then there is the
leather as well as the sand-paper, and this we find in the daily
circumstances of our lives. But butlers tell us there is something
better even than leather for making silver shine. "My hand,"
says the butler; "there is nothing like the palm of your hand for
making silver shine." And there is nothing like the Lord's hand
for making the Christian shine. It is by the direct infilling of the
Holy Ghost, and by daily maintained communion with God,
that the soul reflects His image. "We all with unveiled face,
reflecting as a mirror the glory of the Lord, are transfigured into
the same image from glory to glory, even as by the Lord the
Spirit" (2 Cor. 3: 18).

May I remind you again of this definite promise hidden beneath
those four processes?—"He *shall come.*" I look back, and remember that all through the year 1890 the Lord had been dealing
with my soul. I knew I wanted something, but did not know
what. The Lord kept leading me, and yet I seemed to get no
light. But I recollect, when rising early one morning, that God
gave me this promise, "The Lord whom ye grope for shall
suddenly come." "Then," I said, "I am going to hold on, Lord,
till Thou dost come." I got a little light here and there. When
I came to Keswick all seemed darkness at first, and then, thank
God, the light came. And light is going to come for you, if you
will hold on to the Lord's promise that He will come. The Lord
will come as you yield, as you surrender, as you consecrate your
all to Him. He will come, by the Holy Ghost, to dominate and
control your life, and make it a power and blessing to every soul
with whom you come into contact. He wants to deal with you
in these four ways to-day—the process of *humiliation*, when He
brings you beneath His feet; the process of *revelation*, when He
sifts you by the water of His Word; the process of *separation*, when
He puts you into the fiery furnace of the crises of your life; and
the process of *transformation*, when He maintains in you that which
He has wrought, by His indwelling Spirit. Shall we trust Him,
then, that this convention shall be the time of His coming, when
we shall welcome Him into the hearts He has redeemed?

THE SUFFICIENCY OF GRACE

Pastor Otto Stockmayer

LET ME bring before you a word given to the apostle Paul by his Master in a very critical moment of his life. It is in 2 Corinthians 12, where in writing to this Church he goes back to past days in his life, some fourteen years ago, when there was a man so-and-so—it was himself—and that man had received wonderful revelations, and at the same time, or soon afterwards, the Lord gave him a thorn in the flesh (v. 7); the messenger of Satan was permitted to buffet him, that he should not be exalted over much. He did not know at the time wherefore it was necessary, but fourteen years later he rejoiced. He then understood the matter; but knowing not at the time, he besought the Lord thrice that this trial might pass from him, and then came the answer (v. 9): My Lord said unto me, "My grace is sufficient for thee, for my power is made perfect in weakness." It was not want of obedience and submission on the part of the apostle, but how could this man accept that an angel of Satan should buffet him, an apostle, who knew and had testified (Col. 2) that Jesus Christ, on His cross, had overcome and triumphed over all principalities and powers of darkness, over all messengers of Satan? How could he accept that, denying his own preaching and knowledge? He could not, for his Saviour's sake. Three times, therefore, he stood before his Lord and said, "Lord, canst Thou do this?" And the Lord, without giving him any explanation, simply told him, "My grace is sufficient for thee."

There are times in our Christian life in which we have just to do this—accept as children from God things which often seem to be, and are, in contradiction with what appears to us the teaching of Scripture. We have not to make what some call efforts of faith; we have to wait upon God—we shall never suffer from anything that comes from God. And yet it was a messenger of *Satan* who had buffeted him; but even that messenger was sent or permitted, as you may take it. The reply to his prayers was, "My grace is sufficient for thee," and later on, when fourteen years had gone by, little by little the light came, and looking back after new experiences in his missionary life, he saw and understood that with such overwhelming revelations as he had had of

God's glory, he was exposed to self-exaltation, and that the Lord in His grace kept him though permitting even Satan's messenger to buffet him. Oh, let us stand always, and live always, so near to our God, not that He may give us an immediate explanation, for we will gladly wait until He be pleased to lift the veil, but so that in every critical situation, in everything which seems in contradiction with God's own word, and with God's own dealings at other times, we may stand by faith in the attitude which pleases Him, until the thing is taken away. Oh, yes; "My grace is sufficient for thee, but for the moment I cannot explain, nor take away this trial."

The Lord is Sovereign in His majesty; He is "a God who hideth Himself," but in His own time, some years later on, when we have grown up, and look back in new light, we shall see in the light of His wonderful faithfulness, why God had to permit this for our sake, and for His own. "My grace is sufficient for thee." I need not to know why my God has led me to-day as He did lead me, but I can go on knowing that God makes no mistakes, that His horizon is wider than mine; and I can bow down and await the moment in which God may be pleased to justify Himself, and to explain His own ways. Meanwhile, His wonderful grace is quite sufficient for me—and for thee, my brother and sister, whatever be the situation. Should you be not yet saved (is it possible that anyone should be sitting in this hall[1] day after day, and not know we are saved by grace, through faith, which means that God has taken everything upon Himself from beginning to end) there is only one thing to prevent your being saved—your abominable unbelief and disobedience. It is disobedience not to believe, to go round God's grace and make no use of it.

Grace means just this: that the Lord God undertakes to carry out and carry through, and do from beginning to end, what the law could not do, what human effort could not do—for we could do absolutely nothing in our impotence and inability to approach one step to God. Yet He came near to us, down to our platform, our standpoint, to take our very nature. He did all, *all*, just that you this very evening may take the grace that is offered. "The grace of God hath appeared to all men" (Titus 2: 11), to every kind of man, to all peoples, to every person, whatever his situation of soul or of life—it is equal to all captivity, to all pride, to all lust—equal to triumph over and overcome all hindrances.

Pastor Monod, who has just left us, told you the old, old story— God has done everything which belongs to salvation, to conversion, to piety, to godliness, even to becoming a "partaker of the divine nature." Nothing is wanting; it is God who has done it. Every-

---

[1] This address was delivered in the Pavilion (see p. 405, footnote).

thing is provided, and there is the Holy Ghost to carry out in your souls everything which Jesus Christ has carried out for you; and yet you, a miserable sinner, are sitting and hearing us, miserable messengers, as if *you* were to do it, and you forget that behind us there is His own majesty, and that he who rejects the poor, vile messenger, rejects the Lord. You say, "But my dear German Pastor, you don't know in what a situation I am." No I know not, but I know the words my Lord spoke before He ceased speaking to man. With His eyes toward His heavenly Father, He said, "Be of good cheer; I have overcome the world" (John 16: 33). You speak of the difficulties of your surroundings, but you don't believe what is written in the Word of God; and yet you speak against those people, Ritualists and others, who don't recognise the authority of the written Word—and you are quite as bad as they are. You have before you the Word of God, "Be of good cheer; I have overcome the world," yet you look at the world as a world which has power to stop you, and think that so long as your situation is what it is—in the shop, the office, the army, among worldly men—you cannot trust God. Oh, trust Him! I have a God who can do impossible things; I have a God who *has done* impossible things; I have a Lord who has overcome the world, even my Lord and thy Lord. There is a pathway whereby he who looks to the Lord and not to his own things, can pass from prison even as Peter one night went out from between the soldiers, and out from prison.

What a wonderful word that is in Titus 2, "The grace of God appeared to all men." To do what? Just to bring us into a real position toward this world, which had frightened us, or attracted us, or had dominion over us through fear or lust, and to give us the possibility of denying our ungodliness, and of living soberly, righteously, and godly. When? After death? When you are in another world? No, in this present world as it is to-day, and as you find it this evening, and to-morrow, and next week. I am enabled to live pleasing God, like Enoch, with the testimony that I, even I, may please my God, because I live by grace, leaning upon God, trusting God, no longer seeking strength and good influences in that abominable world of my own, never seeking God in places where there is only evil. Do take your place, and more of the grace of salvation will appear before you; leave the dead body, quit your false humility, and the life of Christ will unfold before you, and He will carry you through this life in a wonderful way. The grace which brings salvation brings victory; it is salvation to the uttermost, it is grace to be sanctified, grace to live unto God, and no more for your own miserable self, to be true unto God, and true to yourself as a saved one. All this for you if you look up by faith. Don't look to yourselves to find faith; look up and see the Saviour and thank Him.

There is a second meaning, a second application for the word grace besides that I have referred to. There is a special grace for every special ministry, and every special duty, and every special difficulty, and every impossibility in life—a special grace for special days, as you see clearly in Ephesians 4: 7, "Unto every one of us is given grace according to the measure of the gift of Christ . . ." and then comes the apostle, the pastor, the evangelist, the Bible-woman, anyone who has to do with liberality. For every ministry in the Church (and every saved one is a member of the Church, of the body of Christ) there is a special grace, diversified in its nature according to the diverse ministry. I have not the grace of George Müller, to build orphan houses, and receive by faith all his orphans; I have not the grace of dear Hudson Taylor, nor the grace of a simple housekeeper, a woman, or girl, to manage her ministry rightly; I have just the grace, the special grace, for the ministry which is committed unto me. There is no member of the body, no saved one introduced by God's grace into that wonderful, mysterious organism, the body of Christ, who has not received, besides the general grace, a special gift of grace for a special ministry in the body. Every member has his own grace. The grace is this: to live unto Christ and to be at His disposal, caring no more for your own life, every member of your body being equally at the disposal of your will for the service of the body, the service of the Lord's people, for the glory of the Head.

There is a wonderful passage in the Old Testament in the life of Jonah. It is not quite in your Bibles as it is in our French and German Bibles. We read the wonderful story of Jonah being in that mysterious place, the belly of a fish. The poor prophet had been at last set right. In the night of that mysterious captivity he understood things in their true meaning, and he saw one thing about "lying vanities" (2: 8). The prophet had been frightened by the call to preach in such a city as Nineveh, and he fled. Had the Lord called him to preach in a little village it would have been different, but in a great city! Yet he sees it all clearly now. The Lord had prepared for him a special grace, and he had forsaken his grace. He had been guilty in forgetting this, that our God, the God whom the prophet serves, will never give to a prophet an exceptional task or duty in his ministry without a corresponding equivalent, exceptional measure and gift of grace according to the ministry. It was a grace given to no other man at that time, because no other man had been called to go to Nineveh. When a man is called to a place where no one else is called, he is as sure as he is of his own life, that the Lord who called him has provided a grace absolutely covering and corresponding to everything in the task and in the man.

"My grace!" I had forsaken it, until at last, shut up like the poor prophet, my eyes are opened to see my folly. To be a fleeing prophet—fleeing away from my special ministry—is to regard "lying vanities," lying impossibilities. Be not frightened. There is special grace for special days—not only for prophets, but for the woman, the wife, the child, the servant, the door-keeper. There are days in the lives of women as well as men when the difficulties, trials, and sufferings accumulate; but every day has its corresponding grace. When once you have learned to trust your God, when you have trusted for service and for over-coming the world, then you can get on in absolute weakness and nothingness, looking to God just to know if *He* is sending you to Nineveh, or directing you to visit some one, or to write a letter— no matter what the difficulty, only look to Him, and be sure He cannot send His servant to perform a duty without a correspond-ing, absolutely corresponding, special grace.

And you are spoiling your life and forsaking your grace if you don't see this. One day—it may be the day of judgment—you will look back on your life and see all your graces which had been prepared for you, besides the saving grace and the sanctifying grace: all the special graces and gifts and provisions, prepared for special days and years and circumstances, and that you had been afraid and had shrunk back like Jonah. The day will come when your eyes will be opened, when it is too late to trust God, too late, you have missed the opportunity.

I now come to the last grace: it is the grace of the last days, the final grace—for there is in my Bible a third kind of grace, for the time of the end which is the object of hope. Turn with me to 1 Peter 1: 13—in the R.V. you have it, "Set your hope perfectly on the grace that is being brought unto you at the revelation of Jesus Christ." This first chapter of Peter is a chapter of hope, and here the grace is not only *to be* brought, but it is coming, it is on the way, it is "*being* brought," it is approaching nearer and nearer as the day-star approaches, as the dawn of a new day is breaking in, a new light is pouring on the horizon of the Church. The revelation of Jesus Christ comes nearer and nearer; and just as the sun draws near the horizon before I see it, and the light is clearer, so new light, morning light, new grace such as never before, the grace of the end, is being brought with the revelation of Jesus Christ the coming Lord. We are not waiting for His *coming* (if we translate the word more literally), we wait for His *presence*, for His being here. He is coming, we know He is coming; it is close upon sunrise. You can read in your rooms at four o'clock, even now, but it grows clearer and clearer just before the sun rises. When the moment comes in which Satan can no longer touch our inward life, nor make a break in our life of trust and full surrender, when he can no longer touch the spiritual man, he then attacks the body, because he knows the times and seasons better than we do. If he cannot break down the soul he tries to break down the body, because he sees sanctification threatens to issue in the redemption of the body. Satan knows this and, therefore, he does what he can to break down in an inexplicable way those who are watching for the coming of the Lord, and to whom He shall appear.

As there has been grace for the beginning, for service, for sanctification, and for overcoming, and a special grace for the special task, so there is a grace for the end, for the last days. Learn to hope perfectly for new grace, the grace of the full victory that is coming.

GOD CAN—GOD WILL!

Rev. G. H. C. Macgregor, M.A.

Turn to Mark's Gospel 5: 21–29, the narrative of the healing of the woman with the issue of blood. I take up this story as one of those stories of our Lord's working in the olden times which are such wonderful revelations of His power in dealing with the human body, and which are such marvellous illustrations of His dealing with the human soul. This story is a peculiarly beautiful one, and in the Gospels there is none quite like it. It is the story of what one might reverently call an unintentional miracle; and it is on that account all the more marvellous a manifestation of the Saviour's grace and power.

But before we speak of this woman I want you to look in two directions. First of all, look at the Master. It is always blessed to look at Him. Look at Him now. He has just come from healing the demoniac in the Decapolis region, and is now crossing to the western side of the lake. A crowd is waiting for Him. And among the crowd is one who, as he waits, is tortured with agony. He is watching for the moment when the boat will touch the shores, for on that moment hangs the life of his beloved child. As the boat reaches the shore, Jairus flings himself at the feet of the Master and beseeches Him, "Come and heal my child!" It is as Jesus is on His way in the fulness of His power, to grapple with the very might of death, that we see Him this evening.

Then I want you to look for a moment at the crowd. Crowds are always interesting. If you read the Gospels you will find our Lord Jesus was exceedingly fond of crowds; for the more people He got around Him to bless, the more He rejoiced. But though He loved the crowd, it does not mean the crowd was lovable. Remember these men and women were not anxious enquirers. They were not seeking Jesus Christ for His own sake. They were waiting to see a miracle. They were sightseers, gossip-mongers, rude and jostling, gathering round the Christ that they might have the pleasure of a sensation.

I want you to look at this woman, and, oh, may God open our eyes to learn the lessons she has to teach us! I want to ask you one or two questions about her.

First of all, why is she there? A glance at that woman shows

that she is not the least fitted to be there. She is weak, she is
timid, she is modest—what is she doing in the midst of that surging,
jostling, pushing, crushing crowd? She is there seeking health.
Not life—that she has—but health. For over twelve years the
life she has lived has been one scarcely worth living.

To begin with, it has been a life of *disease*. Day by day her
strength has been drained away, until the very act of living has
become an intolerable burden. It has also been a life of *disgrace*.
Her disease carried with it ceremonial defilement, and caused
her to be looked upon as an unholy and sinful woman. Then
it was a life of deprivation and loss, for that disease shut her out
from fellowship with her friends, and from the holy fellowship of
the house of God. Then, as it is set before us in the story, it was
a life of the most bitter *disappointment*. I wonder if we have
imagination to realise the broken heart, the worry and expectation, always ending in disappointment, that lie behind these
words, ". . . had suffered many things of many physicians, and
had spent all that she had, and was nothing bettered, but rather
grew worse." That woman was not ill because she had made no
effort to cure herself. All her living had been spent in seeking
health, and every course she followed ended in disappointment,
until disappointment passed into despair, and she had no outlook
but death.

But then news reached her of the mighty Healer, and hope
wakened again within her breast, and she said, "Perhaps from
Him I may get what I have failed to get from others. If I but
touch His clothes, I may be made whole." And it was this hope,
this determination to get health, that brought her, timid, shrinking, weak, modest as she was, into the midst of that rude crowd.

Beloved, have you not in that woman a picture of yourselves?
You are here seeking health; not life—that you have. If I asked
those who are Christians here to stand, every one of you would
spring to your feet with a "Glory be to God" for the greatness
of the salvation He has wrought in your case. You know that
His blood has atoned for your sins. You are justified by faith,
and rejoice in hope of the glory of God. But you have not health.
For twenty, thirty, forty years or less, your life has been, like
hers, a life of disease. Day by day your spiritual strength has
been sapped by the sin that dwells within you; day by day your
communion with God and your efficiency in God's service have
been marred by envy, malice, impurity, covetousness, evil
speaking, worldliness, selfishness, self-indulgence. You know it,
and it has so weakened your power that the very living of the
Christ-life has become almost an intolerable burden. Oh, men
and women, what are some of you saying? You are saying it is

so hard to be a Christian, to follow Christ. You have to whip yourselves up to keep at your religion. Your life has been a life of *sickness*.

And then, beloved, in the case of many it has been a life of real *shame*—perhaps not outward shame, although it may be there are men here who have so disgraced their profession as to give cause to many to wonder whether they are Christians at all. But it has been a life of inward shame. You have called yourself all sorts of names, you have been disgraced in your own eyes, filled with bitter humiliation and shame because of the miserable failure of your Christian life.

And then it has been a life of *loss*. How can tongue tell what you have missed through not being filled with the Holy Ghost? Who can tell you what you have lost because you have not known the fulness of life in Jesus Christ? No joy in God, no experience of answered prayer, no continuous victory over the power of sin, no freedom in bearing witness for Jesus Christ, no harvest of souls gathered to His praise and glory. It has been a life of loss.

And it has also been a life of *disappointment*. Beloved, it would take me till ten o'clock to tell you what you have been trying to do to get spiritual health. What a story it would be! You have applied, like that woman, to all sorts of physicians. Some of you have gone to the Ritualist, perhaps; you have taken his prescriptions—many services, confession, fasting, penance, frequent communion. Or some of you have gone to the Salvationist, and tried the excitements of an emotional religion. You have read innumerable devotional books, attended countless conventions, listened to innumerable speakers, pledged yourself in after-meetings time and again. You have entered into all sorts of leagues and unions, and here you are, no better, but rather worse, with a soul more dead than ever, more difficult to rouse, and that finds it harder to respond to the appeals to God.

Oh, what disappointment, what tragedy lies in this meeting! Yet you won't give up the search. The life you are living is so miserable and the life you see yonder is so glorious, you won't give up the pursuit of it. So you are here, like that woman, in search of health.

Now, another question. What is she doing? This question is very easily answered. The great characteristic of this woman is her *definiteness of purpose*. She is not thinking of herself. For the time being her aches and pains are forgotten. No doubt it was because she was suffering and disappointed that she had come there; but now that she is there everything is subordinated to the great effort she is making to obtain healing. She is not like some of you who, when the after-meeting comes, think, if you stand up, what will the person next you think? If the woman had thought of her neighbours, she would have been panic-stricken. But she was thinking of Christ, and all her energy was taken up in getting to Him. She had said in her heart, "If I only touch Him I shall be whole." Her hopes lay altogether outside herself. It was not her longing to be healed that was going to heal her. Her hope of healing was in Him.

Now, beloved, if this night is to end for you as it did for that woman, you must act as she did. You must give up thinking about yourself, thinking even about your sins and your sorrows, your sufferings and disappointments. Some of you have been brought to Keswick by the rumour that has gone out that in this holy convention Jesus Christ was present in mighty, saving, healing power. Concentrate heart and will and thought on Him, not thinking about your neighbour, the speakers, or the addresses. Many people miss the blessing by taking notes of what we are saying. Do not think so much about the address as use the address in order to get to the feet of the Saviour. Think of Him. Think of His power. He to whom you are coming, who in great love and mercy calls you to His feet, is very God of very God. I know it seems utterly incredible that at this meeting the sins that have beset you and conquered you for a whole life should be broken. But it is God who is working!

Then think of His love. Sorrowful, disappointed, broken heart, have you any conception of how much Jesus Christ is longing for your sanctification; of how the heart of Jesus Christ yearns over this meeting? Why, man, you were chosen in Him before the foundation of the world, that you might be holy and without blame before Him in love. He gave Himself for you, that He might redeem you from all iniquity.

Now think of His power until you say, *God can*; and of His love until you say, *God will*. After you have said that, you will find a new hope springing up in your heart, and you will catch yourself saying, "If I can but touch Him, I shall be whole." Then all your energy will be taken up, not with the address or the after-meeting, but in the effort to get Him, that from Him you may draw the healing your soul needs.

Another question: What happened to this woman? Look! do you see her? The crowd is jostling and surging around the great Teacher, and they push her back; but again she returns, and now she is just at His side. She hesitates, and the surging of the crowd sends her to the outskirts again; but at last she presses closer and closer, and puts out her hand and touches Him. Oh, beloved, what a change! An indescribable feeling of health begins to pervade her body, a strange light of gladness and wonder comes into her eyes. She felt in her body that she had been healed of the plague. What all the efforts of earthly physicians for twelve years had been unable to achieve, contact with the living Christ effected in a moment.

About the cure we notice these things. It was a *sudden* cure. It was sudden, because it was God that was working. If she had had to cure herself, it would have taken a long time. She had tried for twelve years, with all the aid of all the doctors, and failed. God did it at once. It was nothing the woman could boast of. That woman's health was the gift of God, and, like all God's gifts, it was received suddenly and by faith.

It was a *conscious* cure. She felt she was healed, and she could bear definite testimony to what God did that day. It was a *complete* cure. Immediately the issue of blood was staunched. Jesus Christ proved Himself that day equal to meet all the woman's need. Then it was a *confessed* cure. It would not have been complete if it had not been confessed; and so Jesus brought that woman, who was just as afraid of speaking in public as some of you dear sisters, into the front of the rude crowd, and made her tell the whole truth. As it was with that woman, so it may be with you.

Do you wonder that some of us feel almost too intensely for words the issues that hang on meetings of this kind? As it was with that woman, it may be, and it shall be, with you, if you act as she did. If, abandoning all confidence in yourself, you will now cast yourself in utter surrender and trust on Jesus Christ, you may be suddenly cured. Do not stagger at it. Remember it is God. If the healing is to come, and the victory over besetting sin, it is not going to come through anything you do, but by the bearing down upon you of the mighty power of God; and when He begins to work, He can work very rapidly. That temper which has bothered you for twenty-five years may be broken to-night, and there will come into your heart such a revelation of the healing power of Jesus Christ that you will never feel it. There may come such a revelation of the love and wisdom of your Father that worry will be for ever a thing of the past. And there may come into your life such a revelation of the beauty of the will of God that the happiest song you will sing to the end of your days will be, "Thou sweet beloved will of God." And this may be suddenly.

Then, beloved, you may be consciously cured. People sometimes ask, "Did you get a blessing at Keswick?" Blessing? Does a man not know when his eyes are opened? "Once I was blind, now I see." There are hundreds of God's people to whom the moment of spiritual healing in this sense is a more conscious

G

thing than the forgiveness of sin. I believe I could take you to the eighteen inches of wood in yonder tent where I consciously came into this experience. These are things far too conscious for a man not to know about them.

Then you may be completely cured. Jesus Christ is equal to any claim we make upon Him. When I say completely cured, do not misunderstand me. The woman came to be healed of the issue of blood, and she was healed of the issue of blood. But that does not mean she was made absolutely physically perfect. When we come to Jesus Christ and give ourselves over to Him, it does not mean that by that one act we become sinlessly perfect. It means that when we come with our need, Christ completely supplies that need. When you come to be healed of your issue of blood, immediately it is staunched. But beyond this healing of the issue, that woman got a method of healing. A discovery was made to her soul, that if ever she was ill with anything else, there was an infallible cure; for by the touch of faith she could bring the healing on to her soul at once. So God will put into your hands a method by which you can draw from Him everything you need for a holy life.

And if it is to be a complete cure, it must be a confessed cure. Men may ridicule us, and even say that we are lunatics! But, beloved, we must confess. If God works, to Him must be the glory. For remember this life is a life of grace, from which boasting is excluded. "What hast thou that thou hast not received?" And if any victory over temptation, over temper, over worry, or self-consciousness is given to you, beloved, how dare you boast of it? Is it not God who has done it all? And if He has done it, and revealed His power and glory in your life, will you not be found ready at the call of Jesus Christ to stand out as a witness to tell the people the truth? Are you going to touch Him to-night?

> She only touched the hem of His garment
>   As to His side she stole,
> Amid the crowd that gathered around Him;
>   And straightway she was whole.
> Oh, touch the hem of His garment,
>   And thou, too, shalt be free;
> His saving power this very hour
>   Shall give new life to thee.

THE GOD OF JACOB

Rev. C. G. Moore, M.A.

I WANT to speak to you about "the God of Jacob," and I will turn you to two passages where we find this great name which our heavenly Father has taken to Himself. The first is Psalm 46: 7, "The Lord of hosts"—the Lord of vast, limitless multitudes who do His will, "is with us"; but "the God of Jacob"—the God of the individual, is also "our refuge." Then Psalm 146: 5, "Happy is he that hath the God of Jacob for his help, whose hope is in the Lord his God, which made heaven and earth, the sea, and all that therein is." Now you will notice that in both these cases this divine name, "the God of Jacob," is given to us in very high and lofty connections. This is not a thing to be passed over lightly. God has honoured this name of His in the very associations with which it is brought before us in these verses.

Now in order to learn the significance of this divine name, the simple and natural thing, of course, is to go back to God's dealings with Jacob, and see what we can discover from them as to the meaning of this name, "the God of Jacob." I will ask your attention to four facts brought before us in the history of Jacob, which clearly illustrate this name of God's; and they are these: First, "the God of Jacob" thought, and planned, and sought the very best for His servant. Second: "the God of Jacob" with infinite wisdom appointed His servant's discipline, and magnificently sustained him under it. Third: "the God of Jacob" was His servant's sufficient help in life's sore dreads. Fourth: "the God of Jacob" redeemed His servant from all evil, and crowned his life with exceeding lovingkindness.

First: *"The God of Jacob" thought, planned, and sought the very best for His servant.* And "this God is our God"; so we may say, "I am poor and needy, but the Lord thinketh upon me." God counts me as one of His problems, to which, by all His resources of power and grace, He will give the highest possible solution. I do not know how this appeals to you, but it is an infinite delight to me that "the God of Jacob" condescends to make my life one of His problems, whose issue, when He has done with it, He will not be ashamed of—neither shall I.

Now let us go back to the history of Jacob, and see how God thought and planned for him. Let us look at the beginning, and note how little else there was of promise for the future in his case. Will you turn to Genesis 25, where we are taken into the home from which Jacob came, from which God led him into all the blessedness He had planned for him. We find here a home where there was very little that prophesied that Jacob would ever be anything, or do anything, or become anything. Let us see where God begins. We read from verse 27, "And the boys grew: and Esau was a cunning hunter, a man of the field; and Jacob was a plain man, dwelling in tents. And Isaac did love Esau, because he did eat of his venison." The father loves his elder son, because he gets his meat for nothing! Evidently we are not among very noble things here in this home. "But Rebekah loved Jacob"— with a fond, partial love that would have ruined him if God had not interfered and planned something better. "And Jacob sod pottage: and Esau came from the field, and he was faint; and Esau said to Jacob, Feed me, I pray thee, with that same red pottage; for I am faint: therefore was his name called Edom (i.e. Red). And Jacob said, Sell me this day thy birthright. And Esau said, Behold, I am at the point to die; and what profit shall this birthright do to me? And Jacob said, Swear to me this day; and he sware unto him; and he sold his birthright unto Jacob. Then Jacob gave Esau bread and pottage of lentils; and he did eat and drink, and rose up, and went his way: thus Esau despised his birthright."

Such were the brothers, the pair of them—the one ready to take mean advantage of his brother's passing hunger, to obtain the birthright; the other, willing to part so lightly with what he should have highly prized. Now take the whole four of them—father, mother, two brothers—will anything great and blessed ever come out of them? No, not unless God steps in! And that is where God generally starts—where there is no promise of anything. Into that home God went, and laid His hand upon Jacob, and led him forth. As Jacob felt the touch of God's hand, he said, "O God, if Thou wilt be my God, Thou shalt!" And He was, and you know what came of it.

It is a grand thing to have God planning for you. God has repeated this miracle ten thousand times. Let me illustrate it by one familiar story—the story of the life of the late Sir George Williams. He was the youngest of eight sons in a farmer's family in an out-of-the-way place in Somerset, on the moors, four miles from the little village of Dulverton. But there were high traditions of farming in this family. Six of the brothers were farmers when the boy, George Williams, left school at thirteen years of age. It was matter of debate in the family counsels whether George was really equal to becoming a farmer. There were considerable doubts about it, for he didn't seem to be shaping well at all. At last things were brought to a climax one stormy day when George was leading home a load of hay along a rutty lane. Through carelessness, or by some mischance, all in a moment hay, horse, boy, all tumbled over into a ditch. Well that, so far as father, mother, and brothers were concerned, settled the future of George Williams. He was not good enough to be a farmer; they would send him into Bridgwater and make a draper of him! They would put him behind the counter—that was what he was fit for. But into that draper's shop "the God of Jacob" came; and one memorable Sunday night, after George Williams came home from a service, at the back of that draper's shop he knelt down and gave his heart to God, and yielded himself entirely to Christ. God took him, filled his heart with zeal and love for his companions, made him a soul-winner yonder in Bridgwater, brought him to London, made him a soul-winner among his associates there, extended his work until he became one whom the whole Christian world delighted to honour; and they buried him in St. Paul's Cathedral.

That is what comes of having "the God of Jacob" to think for you. Who had the highest thought for that boy? His father? No. His mother? No. His brothers? No. It was there, as in the home of old. The best thought for George Williams was in the heart of God, "the God of Jacob." It is an infinite joy to me to think that every man and woman has a God who seeks the best for them. You need not miss your way in life at all. You need not die mourning that life has been a failure. No, not at all. You need not go into eternity feeling you have missed the best. Why? Because "the God of Jacob" will be your God. He will come into your life, with loving thought, with tremendous purpose, and with all the resources of His grace; and He will never leave you until He has done His very best for you. Some of us are old enough now to look back in amazed thankfulness at what God has done. We realise now that no fond mother, no kind father, ever thought for us as God did, but that from the beginning He planned, and hoped, and wrought; and a chief joy of eternity will be this—that in life's brief day "the God of Jacob" was our God.

Second: "*The God of Jacob*" *with infinite wisdom, appointed His servant's discipline, and magnificently sustained him under it.* When God takes us in hand, and plans for us, He proceeds to put us under the discipline whereby His purposes can be accomplished. Jacob's appointed discipline was found in the forty years with Laban— for that seems to be the best interpretation of the chronology here.

Now, who and what was this Laban? Was he "a nice person"—to use a word that is often on our lips to-day? Not at all. He was a keen, shrewd, hard, selfish man of the world, who knew how to value an upright young man in the vigour of his strength, and who appreciated his industry and trustworthiness, just as any worldly business man does to-day. But after all was said and done, as we shall read presently, Laban would have sent Jacob away at the end of the forty years, without a penny in his pocket! That is Laban; and that was the man, who, under God, made Jacob.

Now, what a terrible disaster it would have been for Jacob, so far as we can judge, if he had been put with some very nice and reasonable person. We greatly, I think, over-estimate the influence of "nice people," and what they can do for us. As a rule, the other sort are more important for us. I want to persuade you of that. Take a very selfish man. Suppose you put him with a very unselfish man, what will happen? He will simply bask in the sunshine of the unselfishness of his companion, and will probably, more or less, go on in his own way. But you take this selfish man and put him with a man ten times as selfish as himself, and let him have to wince every hour and every day under the mean selfishness of the other—he will wake up and begin to think there is something very wrong and unpleasant about selfishness! And so, all round; we are roused, educated, blessed, and disciplined, not by the "nice people"—you are going to live with them for ever; don't trouble about them; be content, if God so appoints, to see much of the other sort down here! A military man was talking to me the other day, and telling me how God taught him self-control. Day after day he had to visit a superior officer who provoked him to the last degree; and every step of the way as he went to meet this man, as he said to me, he had to cry, "God help me! God help me!" And God did help him; and under that sore and constant provocation, he acquired Christian self-control.

Now it is very distressing to find so many people wanting to live with and be associated with "very nice" people. I know mistresses who want "nice" servants. I know servants who want "nice" mistresses. I know Christian workers who want the "nicest" associates and fellow-workers. Man! that is not what you need; you need somebody with the right kind of faults, and that is what you should pray for—with the faults, it may be, nay, even the sins, that will discipline you, and make a man of you.

Now let us look at Jacob under Laban. You know how those forty years ended—in that glorious night of fellowship with God. Turn to chapter 31.

First, God was with Jacob all the long years of his discipline.

"The God of my father," he says to his wives, "hath been with me" (v. 5). And, again, in the previous chapter, Laban had recognised this: see verse 27, "Laban said unto him, I pray thee, if I have found favour in thine eyes, tarry; for I have learned by experience that the Lord hath blessed me for thy sake." And in 31: 42 Jacob says, "Except the God of my father, the God of Abraham, and the fear of Isaac, had been with me, surely thou hadst sent me away now empty." And, brethren and sisters, it is better to be with the worst Laban on God's earth, and have God there too, than to live with an angel without His presence.

The second point is this—that Laban was permitted to do Jacob no hurt. Will you turn for this to 31: 7, "Your father hath deceived me, and changed my wages ten times; but God suffered him not to hurt me." Again, verse 24, "And God came to Laban the Syrian in a dream by night, and said unto him, Take heed that thou speak not to Jacob either good or bad." And in verse 29, Laban says, "It is in the power of my hand to do thee hurt: but God——" The one person in the world who won't harm you is your Laban. Go back to him, then, and be thankful that you have got one! We could not give the same guarantee concerning anybody else. God is with us in the presence of our Laban, stepping in in a moment when he is threatening to do us any real hurt. You will be safe with Laban—or perhaps you are a favoured individual, and have more than one—because God will be with you, and He will see that no hurt shall come to you.

Third, Jacob never ran away from his Laban, until God said, "You may go." Verse 3, "And the Lord said unto Jacob, Return unto the land of thy fathers, and to thy kindred; and I will be with thee." Now, friends come to me seeking all sorts of help, which, as I am able, I am delighted to give. But one thing I will never do —I never will help anybody to run away from Laban. I will do you no such unkindness. When it is time for you to go, God will make the way plain; and then, when you go, you will not leave God behind you. God who has been with you in the discipline, will be with you as you go forth, probably into brighter circumstances. But let Jacob be your example, and run not away from your Laban till God says, "Go, and I will be with thee."

Last of all, Jacob never allowed Laban to turn him from his uprightness. Will you turn for this to verse 6, "And ye know that with all my power I have served your father." Verse 42, "God hath seen mine affliction and the labour of mine hands, and rebuked thee yesternight." Now it is a grand thing when you can appeal to God and say, "O God, just look how trying Laban is" —a perfectly right thing to do—and yet also say, "O God, look at my work, the labour of mine hands, and see that it is none the worse for all Laban has been doing." When a man can talk as much and as sincerely to God about the work of his hands, as about his Laban and his trying ways, he is in a high state of grace, I reckon. It is a pity we should be so anxious for God to look at our Labans and deal with them, and save us from them, and forget about the works of our hands.

Now, very hard things have been said about Jacob, and he may deserve a few of them—I am not dealing with that matter, you can deal with that for yourself. My point is this—that through all the long years he never said, "Laban, I will give you as much as you give me. I will pay you back in your own coin." Have you had grace for that? Is there any man or woman who can stand up in this tent and say, "For forty years I have been under the discipline of my Laban—or a series of them—and never once have I been turned from my integrity before God, and retaliated in a manner unworthy of a man who has God for his help and his refuge"? All honour to Jacob that, at the end of the forty years, he could speak to God, not only of the wrongs that Laban had done him, but of his own fidelity, in God's mercy, to his duty, and to his God.

A lady once said to me after we had been talking a little bit about this: "I am going home to gild my Laban!" Don't gild him—leave the gold here for the missionary cause! But do go home to thank God for the hard things in your life, and for the hard people. I owe a great deal to good people, but I owe a great deal to the other sort, too. Don't interfere with God's discipline; don't be running away from your Laban, don't be turned from the uprightness of your heart. It is only through enduring what taxes you to the very utmost, God being with you, that God can make a man of you. These people who are for ever running away from their Labans, always wanting to be with the nice and the pleasant people, what do they ever accomplish for God, or for the world?

Third: "*The God of Jacob*" *was His servant's sufficient help in life's sore dreads.* For this, will you turn to chapter 32. When Jacob heard that Esau was coming, we read that he was greatly afraid and distressed (v. 7). We read also (v. 11) in his prayer, "Deliver me, I pray Thee, from the hand of my brother, from the hand of Esau; for I fear him, lest he will come and smite me." It is part of our appointed discipline on earth that we should all come, sooner or later, into hours of unspeakable dread—hours when heart and flesh fail us, hours when we seem to stand alone on a little stretch of land with great dark waters all round us, where nobody can reach us but God. Sooner or later, I suppose, all of us have to come into some such experience. I hear that one of the great pictures in the Academy this year was one representing a physician face to face with a pale-faced young man to whom he had just conveyed the announcement that he is afflicted with a disease certain to be fatal. Brothers and sisters, it may not take that form, or anything like that form, with you; but we all have to come to critical, tremendous hours when, if God be not our help and our joy, brain will reel and heart may break. What message, then, have we who stand here in Christ's name for frail men and women, called to pass through such experiences? We have this—that "the God of Jacob" will be with you in life's dreads, as He was with Jacob.

You know how, under the influence of this great fear, Jacob got alone with God. He felt there was none but God could help him. He clung to God with tremendous determination, feeling that God alone stood between him and unspeakable disaster: and he came through a prince, having power with God and men. What a joy it is to proclaim this Gospel, that in life's worst dreads, if you will cling to God, God will not only bring you through, but He will bring you through a richer, brighter, better, happier, nobler man, to sing His praises for ever with a note no angel can strike, of triumph in life's worst and darkest hours, through the God of all grace and comfort.

Let me illustrate this. Some while ago I had a letter from a dear friend who was in great anxiety about the health of his wife. No medical treatment seemed to bring any improvement, and, at last, they consulted a specialist, whose diagnosis seemed to indicate the presence of cancer. The physician advised an operation of exploration to discover whether the mischief was of that nature, and, if so, what hope there was of dealing with it. This operation of exploration was performed, and it was found that the cancer in the stomach was so placed that it could not be removed, and that twelve months at the outside was the time she might be expected to live. My friend urged the physician to tell him the whole truth; and then he went to break the news to his wife. When he communicated the tidings to her, he said "she was no more disturbed than I am at this moment in writing to you." She remarked, "Well, dear, if severe suffering is before me, God will give me daily grace to bear it." And then that Christian family settled down to face that prospect. But the happiest, the most peaceful heart in all that home was the suffering mother. I do not know how it was done—God has His own happy secrets—but the weeks, the months, the years passed on, and, instead of getting worse and dying, the beloved wife and mother got better. What an extraordinary God we have! And when my friend wrote to me he said, "She is better than she has been for years." And, mark this, when he asked her permission to send this testimony to me, she requested him to make this addition: "I do not think from first to last, the anxiety about this matter has kept me awake three minutes." What a God we have! How proud we ought to be of Him!

Men and women, when you get into life's dreads, remember "the God of Jacob." He will carry you in peace through the worst, if you will cleave to Him; and you will come out of it all not a poor, broken, battered creature; you will come out of it, as Jacob did, a prince having power with God and with men. "The God of Jacob is our refuge."

Last of all: "*The God of Jacob*" *redeemed His servant from all evil, and crowned his life with exceeding loving kindness.* Turn to Genesis 48: 15, 16. Jacob is dying. "And he blessed Joseph, and said, God, before whom my fathers Abraham and Isaac did walk, the God which fed me all my life long unto this day, the Angel which redeemed me from all evil, bless the lads." Ay, it is grand to die talking like that! I do not know any who can do it but those happy souls that have "the God of Jacob" for their help. "Redeemed me from all *evil*"—how much that dark word suggests. What catastrophes, what tragedies, what sorrow and anguish, what dismay, are covered by that word! And yet Jacob looks back over the long years, and says, "My God hath left me in the grip of no evil. I die with heart unbroken, with vision unclouded, ready to see His face, and through eternity to bless His grace who redeemed me from all evil in this dark world of sin."

Verse 11: "Israel said unto Joseph, I had not thought to see thy face; and, lo, God hath showed me also thy seed." Now, much of life's discipline for Jacob had gathered round Joseph. In connection with Joseph, some of his sorest heart trials had come. Yet there, on the very spot where the fires of God's discipline had burned and purged him, on that very spot his God built the crowning joy of his life! And He will do that for you. You say, "I am in the furnace, I am in sore trial; there is one thing in my life that is testing me to the very uttermost." Hold on to God; and, just there, life's greatest joy will come, before God has done with you.

"The God of Jacob is our refuge." But, brethren, one word more. God has a higher name and title than even this. We thank Him for this, and for all that it means; but He is "the God and Father of our Lord Jesus Christ." And if He could do all this for Jacob long centuries ago, what cannot He do to-day, with all the resources of the Cross of Christ, with all the resources of the Spirit of Christ?

Will you give Him a chance? Shall we go away from this tent wholly and happily yielded up to God, thankful we have such a

God to trust, thankful we have such a God to think for us and to make the best of us, thankful for such a God to carry us through life's hardest, blackest, darkest experiences to a great victory, and who is able to the very last to fill our hearts with joy and peace that passeth all understanding? Who would not rejoice in such a God? "Ah," some of you say, "I wish I had heard this and acted upon it, years ago. There is only a bit of my life left." Give God the bit, and He will astonish the angels and you before He is done with you! Give Him the bit; give Him the bit! Happy the young here this morning—happy, happy they who have the opportunity to give the whole. Oh, how I bless God that He had mercy upon me as a boy, and condescended to come and touch me, and ask me to give Him my all. Not for a million worlds would I that it should have been otherwise! He is willing to take every life here this morning. What possibilities there are if our lives are yielded to Him, to be filled with His presence, sustained by His grace, and crowned with His marvellous goodness and lovingkindness.

GO TO BETHEL, AND DWELL THERE

Rev. F. B. Meyer, B.A.

*And God said unto Jacob, Arise, go up to Beth-el, and dwell there:
and make there an altar unto God, that appeared unto thee when thou
fleddest from the face of Esau thy brother. Then Jacob said unto his
household, and to all that were with him, Put away the strange gods
that are among you, and be clean, and change your garments: And let
us arise, and go to Beth-el; and I will make there an altar unto God,
who answered me in the day of my distress, and was with me in the way
which I went. And they gave unto Jacob all the strange gods which
were in their hand, and all their earrings which were in their ears; and
Jacob hid them under the oak which was by Shechem. And they journeyed: and the terror of God was upon the cities that were round about
them, and they did not pursue after the sons of Jacob. So Jacob came
to Luz, which is in the land of Canaan, that is Beth-el, he and all the
people that were with him. And he built there an altar, and called the
place El-beth-el: because there God appeared unto him, when he fled
from the face of his brother. But Deborah Rebekah's nurse died, and
she was buried beneath Beth-el under an oak: and the name of it was
called Allon-bachuth. And God appeared unto Jacob again, when he
came out of Padan-aram, and blessed him. And God said unto him,
Thy name is Jacob: thy name shall not be called any more Jacob, but
Israel shall be thy name; and he called His name Israel. And God said
unto him, I am El Shaddai*—GENESIS 35: 1–11.

WILL you let me lay my hand upon the cords of memory
to-night? I take you back in your life's story ten, twenty,
thirty years, to the day of your distress when, staff in
hand, a lonely soul, fleeing from the burning heat, you made your
way to the upland and moorland waste, strewn with the boulder
stones, where you laid down to sleep in utter weariness and
exhaustion. And do you remember God appeared to you that
night, that starless night, and how at the foot of the ladder you
vowed to be for evermore His own? Do you remember that
vision of the open sky, that audience of the voice of God, that altar,
and those vows of consecration? Have they been kept? Do you
remember coming here to Keswick? Cannot you find the spot
on the hills, or the little bedroom in the tenement, the lodgings,

where under the pressure of some tremendous sorrow you vowed
you would be all for God?

Ah, but that has all faded away! The light has gone from the
sky, the ladder has gone from the earth, and your vows have
been unkept. Why? Because you entered into a bargain with
God, and you promised that if He would do this you would do
that, and there was a sort of resolution in the energy of your own
nature—and understand that the resolution of our own nature,
though it be in the direction of consecration, will not suffice for
the strain of temptation; and it is because you resolved to be a
consecrated man in the energy of your own flesh that it has been
such an utter and unutterable failure.

Let us pass down the story of your life. Do you not remember
another time—it may have been in this tent, it may have been on
some subsequent evening—you were again alone? Your life had
prospered then somewhat, though the shadow of a great dread
had fallen upon you again; and another time you had a vision of
God, and you thought He said, and indeed He did, that you were
no longer to be Jacob the supplanter, but Israel the prince. It
was a tremendous wrestle; you fought God at first, and then you
thought you yielded; and you began to limp from that time as a
result.

But why is it that your life since then has been again a failure?
You thought that was to be the final act, that never again would
you condescend to be what you had been. But it was not so: why?
In the case of Jacob there were three reasons.

First, the very day after that memorable night he sought to deal
with Esau in the power of his own cunning, and when Esau
suggested that they should march together, he parried the invitation. He said he would follow quietly afterwards, but when Esau
started for Seir, Jacob went in another direction to Succoth. He
never meant for a single moment to go with Esau.

Then, second, Jacob bought a piece of land outside the sinful
city of Shechem, and pitched his tent there. Poor Dinah! How
one sympathises with that lost girl's life! If only her father had
never gone to live so near to Shechem, she would never have been
attracted by the folly and fashion of the city; she would never have
come to a wrecked and ruined life.

And then, third, Jacob permitted the use of idols in his family.
He winked at it, just as some of you are not strong enough to
command your household after you. You wink at and permit,
responsible though God holds you as the head of your family,
things which are inconsistent with your Christian profession. Those
were the three reasons why he failed.

May I just ask you: Has there been any insincerity in your life?

As a business man, in your social habit or speech, have you perpetually been dealing with Esau your brother without the transparency of crystal truth? Have you not been building your house near Shechem, and your children have commenced to go to the theatre, to the dance, to worldly society, and you have been acquiescing in it all? Or may it not be perhaps that you, too, have winked at idolatry in your home? Oh, look at your life and see how insensibly you have been going down, and down, and down from Bethel with its altar. God's call to you to-night is: Arise, leave Shechem, leave your parcel of land there, and leave all the associations which are ruining yourselves and your children, and at any cost arise, go back to Bethel, and stop there, dwell there.

Now, what is Bethel? Jesus said, "Thou shalt see greater things than these; thou shalt see heaven opened and the angels ascending and descending upon the Son of man." And when was heaven opened, and when did the Son of man become the ladder between earth and heaven, and when did the angels come and go? There is but one answer—when Jesus Christ, completing the act of resurrection, ascended, and in ascending opened heaven, and cast the ladder of His ascending glory swaying between earth and heaven as the link, the bridge of communication. And since then surely we may hear words of the writer of the Hebrews when he says that we have "access into the holiest by the blood of Jesus, by a new and living way which He hath consecrated for us through the veil, that is to say, His flesh." And translating the words of Genesis into New Testament phraseology, when we hear God say to Jacob, "Arise, go up to Bethel, and dwell there," surely the New Testament phrase is: "If ye then be risen with Christ, seek those things which are above, where Christ sitteth at the right hand of God." In other words, your failure and mine has too often been our inability, our unwillingness to recognise the position into which Jesus Christ, the second Adam, has brought us in the presence of God. We were born in the first Adam, and our idea when we become convinced of sin is, that this Adam may somehow justify itself before God. Then God comes by His Spirit and puts away all attempts at self-justification, and we have to receive from the hand of God the righteousness which has been achieved by the only Saviour, and which is put into the hand of faith; and we stand before God from that moment, not having the righteousness of the first Adam, but the imputed righteousness of the second Adam.

Then there comes the second act of our life, and we desire to make good the first Adam by our resolutions, by our efforts, by our Bible-readings, by our vows of consecration, by coming here to

Keswick and passing through these meetings. We hope somehow to cultivate from the soil of the first Adam a holiness which will be acceptable to God, and God has to blast it and spoil it by repeated failure, by heart-breaking failure. And then we come to see this—which is almost the most wonderful discovery that can come to a man—that when Jesus Christ rose from the dead He created a new man. May I ask you to look at that, that you may verify this startling affirmation with your own eyes.

In Ephesians 4, from the seventeenth verse: "I say therefore, and testify in the Lord, that ye no longer walk as Gentiles also walk, in the vanity of their mind, being darkened in their understanding, alienated from the life of God through the ignorance that is in them, because of the hardening of their heart: who being past feeling, gave themselves up to lasciviousness, to work all uncleanness with greediness. But ye do not so learn Christ, if so be that ye heard Him, and were taught in Him, even as truth is in Jesus"—the person and work of Jesus—"that ye put away, as concerning your former manner of life, the old man"—put away the old man absolutely, utterly, and for ever. Shall we do that now? That is the meaning of Jacob burying the earrings and the strange gods under the oak; that is the absolute demand of God on us all—that we put away now, here, and for evermore, by an act of deliberate choice and faith—"that ye put away, as concerning your former manner"—your habits—"of life"—this is what Jacob did not do at the Jabbok ford—"the old man which waxeth corrupt"—mark this, *always getting worse*, "after the lusts of deceit; and that ye be renewed in the spirit of your mind, and put on the new man which"—do look at this: of course, as the old man stands for the manner of life, the habits of the old life, so the new man will stand for the habits of the new life—"put on the new man, which after God"—in the likeness of God—"hath been created"—when? Surely in the resurrection of Jesus Christ. As the Son of man, He has created the new man after the likeness of God—"in righteousness and holiness"—righteousness, integrity of character; holiness, sanctification of heart.

Now see, Jacob by a single act buried his idols under the oak, and stepped up to the moorland, and built his altar, and, as it were, walked henceforth on the level of the height. And God says to us to-night, Absolutely, once and for all, give up trying to improve your own nature, put it utterly away by faith in Him who died on the cross, and in the Holy Ghost who makes the work of Jesus Christ efficient in experience. Definitely, absolutely, at this moment have done with it, as it is perhaps concrete in some one distinct evil habit.

Now let the whole of us, who so determine by the grace of God, put on the new creation of the living Christ; put it on here and now. He wrought it for us, but by a momentary act we appropriate it, that from now it shall be the life of our life. Now, that is getting back to Bethel and dwelling there: letting the risen Christ meet everything in your life.

But how about the past, how about Shechem? Shechem was so infuriated that they were prepared to follow Jacob. Is not that just like your life and mine? The natural results of our past mistakes and misdoings follow us. You have brought yourselves into such a tangle, it seems as if there is hardly any hope of your extrication. That is Shechem following Jacob.

What then? The terror of God fell, and was like a rearguard; and as Jacob marched, God was behind. I have seen a mother go into a room where her child has been spoiling the furniture, maybe covering it with the débris of broken toys. The whole room has been in confusion, the child has been sent to bed, and the mother comes after. It seems to me that God is just like that. He is our rearguard. The Holy One shall go before you, and shall be your rearguard; and if you and I will step out into the risen Christ from to-night, God will go behind and keep the results of our mistakes and sins from overwhelming us.

And then, lastly, you say to me: I am sure I cannot live that life! Well, I close with this. "I am"—"Thy name is Jacob." See the contrast—I and God Almighty. I—that is you, trembling soul. You dread to leave this tent, you dread to go back to your life. You say: It is well enough while I am here at Keswick, but when I get home, how then? Hide yourself under the great word —I and God Almighty. Let God keep you in the attitude you now assume, and let God answer all the difficulties that will menace you. Let God keep you—not your resolution to keep yourself on the high tableland of Bethel; but God Almighty who made the arch of the sky, who keeps the stars in glory burning, who holds the ocean as a drop in the hollow of His hand. Believe that the Almighty God stoops to your mean life and makes you more than conqueror.

Oh! soul, get up to Bethel under the open sky, touch the Son of man, keep in touch with Jesus Christ; do not look at difficulty, do not look at your own weak heart, do not trust your own resolutions, do not go back on your past; but look unto Jesus, Jesus the risen Christ above us, in us, with us for evermore.

THE BLESSED LIFE

Rt. Rev. Bishop J. Taylor-Smith, C.V.O., D.D.

It is my great privilege and grave responsibility to strike the tone, to lead the tune, of this holy gathering. I feel the privilege and the responsibility; and I am glad that our Chairman (Mr. Albert A. Head) reminded you that it is your privilege as well as mine, and your responsibility also, to set the tone and the tune. We have no light task before us, then, you and I. Put yourself in my place, and then there will be the believing prayer and the loving sympathy which will make me speak not my words, but His; and if they are His words, they are words of spirit and words of life. I would put myself in your place, and I would seek to say the word that you want saying to meet every need, to answer every quest, to fill every waiting heart.

In the days of old, when our Lord Jesus walked this earth as Man for men, you remember He came to certain towns, and certain villages, where the people were receptive. Their faith was such that they not only brought themselves, but their sick relations, in order that He might lay His hands upon them, and give them the blessing that they needed. Wherever He was met with believing prayer and loving sympathy, we are told that He healed all that had need of healing; and there was great joy and great blessing in that place.

On other occasions He met a cold reception, an atmosphere that was antagonistic; and the Master felt it. He could not do many mighty works, because of the atmosphere of unbelief. So to-night, and at every meeting that you and I attend, there will rest upon us the privilege and the responsibility; and we shall help or hinder, we shall bring blessing to our own souls and to those around us, or we shall prevent the blessing that might have been.

So to-night we gather as the professed disciples of the Lord Jesus. Here we are once more, among the hills, to some of us hills with sacred memories; and the Master is here waiting. We are not the only waiting ones. He was here before us. In that smile and grip of the hand as we stepped out of the train, we felt it was the Master's hand and the Master's love. When we reached the house, and the brother knelt in prayer by the bedside, again it was the Master! Oh, look for Him and you will find Him—not in the

209

meeting only; not only in the Word of God in print, but in the Word of God in picture. He is here; He is everywhere. He has come here specially to meet with you. Believe it! He has come here, if I understand this gathering, in order that He may teach, and in order that we may learn.

As He looked upon the multitudes in the days of old, He is looking upon this great multitude. Need I remind you that unto Him all hearts are open, all desires known, and that from Him no secrets are hid? But He is here in His great name *Jehovah Jireh*, the One who sees, and the One who provides. The night may be dark, as it was on that night when the disciples were crossing the lake at the Master's bidding; and the night may grow darker as the days unfold, as they have done to some in days gone by, until they reach the very fourth watch, the darkest hour of the night; but the next watch is the dawn. Then there shall be the rising of the Sun of Righteousness, and the presence which brings us into the desired haven immediately, and there shall be no more darkness nor twilight.

Beside the Master and His disciples, there is another speaker, another attendant, at Keswick; and that is Satan. He seeth the multitude; he has also come before, and he will be present. He is not one of the invited speakers; but because he has not been invited he will speak perhaps more frequently than those who have been. He will whisper on the mountain-side, and on the lake; and in the loneliness of the wood, where you have gone, as it were, apart from the world, you will find Satan with you.

Then he will speak louder, and he will even go so far as to quote Scripture—but, mark, all his quotations are half truths. He will stop short in the very middle of the sentence. He will tell you of angels bearing up the children of God, that they dash not their foot against a stone; and he will try and persuade you to go in the strength of such a promise; but he will not tell you of the One who shall crush the serpent's head, and trample upon the adder.

Therefore I put you on your guard against that speaker. Watch and pray, for there is victory if you realise that the Lord is nearer than Satan; and though the strong man armed has kept the house in the past, the stronger than he is going to be the future possessor. As you resist Satan by the word of truth, and the exercise of faith, you will find that he will leave you, as he left the Master, coward as he is. When he leaves his victims, or those that might have been his victims, exhausted, he leaves them to the wild beasts, and he leaves them on the mountain-side. But our Master never leaves us: He will stay with us, and on His mountain He will remain. He is with us all the days, not only the days of Keswick, but the days which will follow. "Lo, I am with you all the days." "All power is given unto me." Therefore all is well.

Now what is the purpose of Keswick? Is it a spiritual picnic, where believers from all parts of the world may come and have a happy week together? No. That may be included: but that is not the purpose of Keswick. Is it a place for teachers to bring their class-members, that they may be converted? No. Yet there are many who shall realise the precious blood in this convention. There never has been a convention at Keswick without many conversions taking place. Why, it was only on my last visit, two years ago, that I met two young fellows who are now officers of the British Army. As they were coming from the station, making the foolish mistake that all who come to Keswick know the Lord, I said, "And what do you expect Keswick to do for you?" They stood aghast! They had been invited by friends, but they had never considered why they had come, and for what purpose; but before they left they were rejoicing in the Lord, and testifying to His saving grace and keeping power. Their history will be repeated in many a soul this year.

Is this a gathering where the clergy may take in a stock of spiritual truths and sermons for the coming winter? Ah, you smile, but I understand by that it is the smile of sympathy. Not the clergy only, I think, but the laity and the ladies, will carry away material for their classes and mission rooms. But that is not the purpose of Keswick. It is one of the blessings thrown in; it is one of the other things that are added, but it is not the kingdom and the righteousness. Oh, friends, put first things first; first now, and all the time. You will not miss the other things, but you may miss the better things if you put those matters first.

If I understand the purpose of Keswick, it is to tell those who have ears to hear, the secret of rest; to tell the secret of joy; and to tell the secret of power: rest from struggling, joy in struggling, and power for struggling. There is not time to develop those points, but the rest which comes from the knowledge of sins forgiven, through simple obedience in coming unto the Lord and hearing His voice, and realising what He has done: that is the rest we are here to learn. And joy in struggling, not for holiness, but struggling in the fight against sin and wickedness; and power for struggling, the power of the Holy Ghost.

You all know what it is to be in a gale or a storm. You have seen a storm playing havoc with people's property, perhaps your own. Why is the storm? It is because the balance of nature has been upset. You have all seen also the very opposite of a storm, when the sea is as smooth as a mill-pond, and the clouds are stationary, and the leaves on the trees are still. And whence this peace?

Because all the powers are evenly balanced; the powers are there, but they are in right relationship to one another. So it is in regard to the peace of soul. It is when we are in the right relation with Jesus Christ that there is the calm and no longer the storm.

Too often we say, as we look upon one who has entered into this rest of soul, "He is not tempted as we are, or he would be struggling as we are struggling and have struggled for a long time past. That Christian has an easy life; he is not tempted and tried as I am." Oh, friends, is that so? God is no respecter of persons, and Satan is no respecter of persons; and the trinity of evil—the world, the flesh, and the devil—is against everyone, whether they have the clerical collar, or the nurse's garb, or the deaconess's hood. Then what makes the difference, as we have found it at Keswick, and seen it in others? It is that the balance of powers unseen is working there, and that causes the great calm.

People say, if you are going to Keswick, "You will have a great blessing," as though there were magic in the air of Keswick and healing in Derwentwater. But if it were so, then those who climbed the most, and those who bathed the most frequently, would have the greatest blessing. It is just as they might have said in the days of old, "Are you going to Bethesda?" and the man who had been ill for thirty-eight years said, "I am, and I am expecting a great blessing; in fact, I am hoping to be cured." But, friends, the blessing was not in the place; the blessing was in the Person. Get that well into your minds. It is not the holy associations of Keswick, nor even the atmosphere of a meeting like this, however deeply and intensely spiritual. None of these things can save us. Only in proportion as we come into touch with the Lord Jesus, only as we realise His presence, His Person, shall we go from this place with a blessing. Apart from Him, nothing; but in Him, and with Him, all things necessary for the present and the future are ours.

How will it come? That is a very practical question. Not by looking in, though there will be much looking in—but by looking up and by looking out. You must see His face, and you must hear His voice, and you must do His bidding. That is the threefold secret of blessing. You must see the King first; and in His hand the sceptre, and the crown of that sceptre is the cross, and underneath is the orb. You will realise that the King must be seen first on the cross, the King of the Jews, before He becomes the King of your lives, and the King of heaven. Look up, then, and see Him as your own personal Saviour, the representative for the new Adam, the new race, as it were, introducing a new creation into the world. You will realise that as in Adam we all die—such is our relationship with the first Adam by the flesh—Jesus Christ has come, born at Bethlehem, the Child born, the Son given; Bethlehem, the house of bread, that satisfies the whole hungry world. He is the ladder which Jacob saw in a dream, and Nathanael meditated upon under the fig-tree, which rests on earth in His humanity, and reaches up to heaven in His divinity. All other earthly ladders come short, whether it be the ladder of Confucius in China, or Buddha in India, or works in England. Here is the Christ of God, Jesus Christ, God-man, who was born of our flesh, who has come to make us partakers of the divine nature, and to impart His character, that we may be one with Him for ever: "As in Adam all die, even so in Christ shall all"—that does not mean all creation; it is a technical expression, meaning those that are in Him by grace, through the Holy Spirit, the Lord and Giver of life, and in Him by faith and will surrendered—"even so in Christ shall all such be made alive." To use the old Puritan expression, "Once born, twice to die; twice born, once to fall asleep."

We come back again, then, to our first thought. We are here, and Jesus is here, and at this first gathering He is speaking to our hearts. So I say to those who are yet in their trespasses and sins, blind and unforgiven, "Arise, He calleth thee." It is true. There is not one blind soul here to-night that the Lord does not call. He has brought you here; take that as a token of His love; take that as an assurance that He is here to bless you. He has brought you thus far, not to confound, but to save. "Arise, He calleth thee."

And to those who have followed Him but afar off, and like all who follow afar off, have denied Him, not once, nor twice, nor thrice, He says, "Wilt thou be made whole?" He has looked with pity and followed you as you wandered far from His presence, even beyond reach of His voice, it may be, lured by this and that, but away from His Person and His presence, and now brought in through this convention. He says, "Wilt thou be made whole?" Oh, arise; He calleth thee, and He shall give sight to those blind eyes, and sight to that blind heart. You shall look, and you shall live; and you shall look, and you shall love, and that is the key of Christianity.

And to you who have come, perhaps, more than once to Keswick, and have not yet received that wholeness which He came to impart, oh, answer His voice to-night. "Wilt thou be made whole?" "Lord Jesus, I will."

He waits to give sight; He waits to give strength; He waits to give liberty. Who is there among us who does not need a keener sight, a clearer sight? Who is there among us that does not need strength —strength to worship, strength to pray, strength to witness, strength to serve—and that liberty of lip and life that enables us not only to walk, but to run in the way of the King's commandments? Friends, this is to be your place of anointing, just as much as Jordan was the place of the Master's anointing. What happened to Him then is what may happen to you here, and will, if you are willing to go down into the waters and be buried and rise again.

What was the result of that holy baptism in Jordan? Three things. First, the heavens were opened; and I tell you, you shall see what you have never seen, and further than you have ever seen. The heavens shall be opened unto you, and unto me, if only we will die that we may live. Then there will be the descending power. There descended upon Him the Holy Ghost in the form of a dove. It has been said that had there not been that Holy One on earth, the Lord Jesus, the Holy Ghost, like the dove that was sent forth from Noah's ark, must have returned never to come back. But there was that holy place, that Holy One, and the Holy Ghost descended and abode. And if we are in Him, then the same Holy Ghost abides in us; and as He was to the Father, we shall be to the Father. Thirdly, there was the commending voice, "This is my beloved Son." And He will say to us, "This is my beloved son," "This is my beloved daughter." These are the results of the anointing: dying unto sin, and rising into newness of life.

But you must be prepared also, after such a gift, to be led into the wilderness. The testing follows the enrichment. You who come from manufacturing towns know that everything after being made is tested, whether it be the tweed suit of Leeds, the cotton of Manchester, or the steel of Sheffield; and as surely as you receive the blessing here, you will find the testing there.

Then there will be the life-work, following the testing, which ends in triumph, if you have been anointed. First the gift, then the conquering of Satan, and then the overcoming, and then the winning of souls. That is the programme of Christianity.

But there will be other results in this convention which you and I are called upon to experience. We shall have a new vision of work. The work will be delightful in a sense in which it has never been in the past, however delightful may have been our experience. Faith will take the place of fear when you are called upon for any service and every service; and you will realise that whom God calls He equips. Rest will take the place of struggle; gladness will take the place of sadness; victory will take the place of defeat. You will no longer say, like Moses, "I am not eloquent," because you have heard the voice of the Lord saying, "I *am*. Who hath made man's mouth?" You will realise that because He is, you can be, and you shall be. And you will no longer say, as you cringe and shrink from responsibility—for remember, to whom much is given, from them much will be required—you will no longer say, like Jeremiah, "I cannot speak; for I am a child"; for the Lord will say, "Say not, I am a child: for thou shalt go to all that I shall send thee, to peers and peasants, to cultured and uncultured, to wise and ignorant. Thou shalt go to all that I shall send thee, and whatsoever I command thee thou shalt speak. Be not afraid of their faces, lest I confound thee before them. See, this day did I not at Keswick make thee a defenced city, an iron pillar, brasen walls?" Language fails to tell what God has in store for you, and the provision He has made for all the future, whatever the service may demand.

Now, the message of Christ to-day for us is the same as for His first learners on another hillside to that of Skiddaw. It was a delightful message. All His messages are delightful, brimming over with delight. Do not our hearts burn within us when He talks with us by the way? How did His message begin? It began with the word "Happy"—"Blessed." I like that message. Do not worry—wait; and you shall prove as others have proved—psalmist as well as the prophet—you will be able to say in their words: "I waited patiently for the Lord; and He inclined unto me, and heard my cry." Is it not a happy thought that the divine ear is inclined toward your cry? "He brought me also out of a horrible pit, out of the miry clay, and set my feet upon a rock, and established my goings." No longer the darkness of the pit, of the earth, earthy; no longer the striving to climb up and out, and the sinking deeper, like poor Jeremiah, who sank up to his armpits; but brought into the light, the feet upon the Rock, established not only to stand and withstand, but established to make progress in life, and to sing the new song, which "many shall see, and fear, and shall trust in the Lord."

You ask, How can they see a song? Well, true thanksgiving is thanksliving. Then they can *see* the song, and they are led to follow on and learn the tune. So the band of singers, the ransomed of the Lord, increases in size, in number, and in song.

The Beatitudes tell of a limitless mercy above; they tell of a limitless possibility within. I will read these words; let them be, as it were, the message with a new meaning to-night: "And seeing the multitudes, He went up into a mountain; and when He was set, His disciples came unto Him; and He opened His mouth, and taught them, saying, Blessed are the poor in spirit, for theirs is the kingdom of heaven." We are all poverty-stricken in regard to spiritual matters; but it does not mean only that we are poor in spirit, but that we know we are poor in spirit. "Blessed are those who know they are poor in spirit, for theirs is the kingdom

of heaven" at this Keswick. "Blessed are they that mourn,"
mourn for their failings, mourn for their sins, "for they shall be
comforted. Blessed are the meek, for they shall inherit the earth"
—not coming to Keswick with preconceived ideas, and wanting
every speaker to toe the line to their "doxy," but "Blessed are the
meek that place themselves at the feet of Jesus; they shall inherit
the earth." "Blessed are they which do hunger and thirst after
righteousness"—and who is there among us, speaker and hearer,
that does not hunger and thirst to know more of the Lord? He
is our righteousness, and He says: "Happy children, ye shall
be filled." "Blessed are the pure in heart, for they shall see God."
Amen.

A SUMMONS TO NEWNESS OF LIFE

Rev. Alexander Smellie, M.A., D.D.

Come, and let us return unto the Lord; for He hath torn, and He will heal us; He hath smitten, and He will bind us up—HOSEA 6: 1.

IT is possible to interpret these familiar and haunting words from one of the tenderest books of the Old Testament in two entirely distinct and almost contradictory senses. You may read in them—many of the scholars of to-day are reading in them—the expression of a superficial and totally insufficient sorrow for sin. It is the people of Israel who are speaking, a people who are shallow and careless and unreflective and self-satisfied. They have some little glimpse into their disobedience. They have some slight grief for the wounds they have inflicted upon their Lord. But the pain does not penetrate far or deeply. They know how they can regain a contented mind. "Come, and let us return unto the Lord," they say to one another; "He hath torn, and He will heal us." That is His way. That is His manner and habit. That is His *métier*, as poor Heine said when he lay dying in Paris. But whatever may have been the case with Heine, the men of Israel had no proper conception of the strange and blessed truth which they were announcing. They were glad that they had to do with a God who hated putting away, and who multiplied to pardon; glad that they had to do with Him, because, in fellowship with such a God, they could speedily settle the question of transgression and punishment; they could very readily get rid of their temporary vexations and annoyances; and then they would be free to revert to their accustomed selfishness and sin. That is the one interpretation; and you have only to study the vivid portrait which Hosea draws of those fickle and flippant citizens of Northern Israel, in order to see how much likelihood of truth there is in the interpretation.

And yet, beloved friends, I cannot bring myself to read the words in that way. I prefer what is the older view, that in them we are listening, not to the voices of disappointing people, but to the voice of the great-hearted, patient, and pleading prophet of God Himself. He knew too well the instabilities of his fellow-countrymen; but he knew still better the immeasurable love of his Lord; and out of this knowledge he pleads with them to put his Master really to the test. "Come," he prays, "let us return unto Jehovah, for He hath torn, and He will heal; He hath smitten, and He will bind us up."

When we regard the verse in this light, it becomes a summons to our own land, and to the Church in our land, and to every individual disciple of the Lord Jesus Christ among us. It is a call to repentance—a call that is as modern as it is ancient; a call that is being emphasised and underlined by the terrible sorrow and chastening through which we are passing in these days[1] a call to which we cannot pay heed too soon or too profoundly. I wish that we may listen to it to-night in its personal aspect and accent, as addressed to each one of ourselves. For, surely, it is only as the separate Christian is determined to get right with God, that the nation will be on the high road to the understanding and the abhorrence and the renunciation of its sins, and that the Church will be quick to shake itself from the dust and put on again its beautiful garments. It is we who have been wrong. It is we who have been turning from our true Shepherd and our first love. It is we who must be rectified and led back once more. Do let us seclude ourselves from the crowd. Do let us feel that we are alone with God—the Lord whom we have grieved, but who is here to lead us afresh in the paths of righteousness for His Name's sake.

He calls us to *repentance*. And what is repentance? In that Westminster Catechism, which left Westminster so soon after its birth to make its home in my own northern country, I have a definition of it: "Repentance unto life is a saving grace, whereby a sinner, out of a true sense of his sin, and apprehension of the mercy of God in Christ, doth, with grief and hatred of his sin, turn from it unto God." There is more in the answer, but that will be enough for our purpose. Repentance is my turning from sin unto God. It is my facing right round, so that I am looking no longer hungrily and hankeringly towards those evil things and those questionable things which fascinated me before; so that the Lord, whom I have been forgetting and disobeying, is now my chief desire and my one delight.

Two main motives, the Catechism declares, lie at the back of this change of mind: a true sense of sin, and an apprehension of the mercy of God in Christ. But I think you will agree with me when I say that, for the vast majority of us, the second of these motives is first, both in the order of time and in the order of influence. It is the sight of Him whom we have misunderstood and maligned—His character, His affection for us, His gift of

[1] The Great War of 1914–18.

His only begotten Son, His free and full redemption, His ability and His willingness to perform in each one of us that good work which He has begun: it is this vision of God which alters the entire trend of our lives, and which attracts us irresistibly, like a magnet, home to Him. Do not suppose, beloved, that there is no sense of sin. There is. In evangelical repentance it is keen; it is deep; it is permanent. But it follows, rather than precedes, our apprehension of God and His mercy. It comes when we recognise what sort of a God He is whom we have been neglecting and forsaking. Then we condemn ourselves. Then we abjure the thoughts we have been cherishing, and the ways in which we ran with greedy feet. He so loved me, and this is how I have recompensed Him—it is that which breaks me down; it is that which makes me ashamed; it is that which kindles the grief and hatred; it is that which shows me the exceeding sinfulness of my sin.

Oh, brothers and sisters, let us ask for ourselves a new, and an intimate, and a constraining, and a conquering disclosure of God. For then we shall repent in spirit and in truth.

Now, Hosea will help us to this disclosure. Nobody, I think, before the Lord Jesus Christ came, drew closer to God than the prophet Hosea did. He literally lived and moved and had his being in Him. Sons and daughters of the New Testament although we are, he will acquaint us with our God, that we may be at peace with Him.

This is one thing that Hosea says: *God is near.* It was his constant anxiety to awaken in his erring countrymen the belief that they had not to travel any distance to find God; that He is at hand, that He was brooding over them already and waiting to bless them. "After two days will He revive us; in the third day He will raise us up"—so brief is the interval, so short is the journey, between us and our sins and God and His overflowing salvation. We need that message. The name of God is often on our lips; but actually He is at times little more to us than a vague rumour, an unfigured immensity, something exceedingly undefined and exceedingly remote. We are kept far off from Him by the feeling that we have to fit ourselves for the reception of His restoring mercy; there are moods and dispositions which we must cultivate, there are lessons which we must learn, there are pieties and righteousnesses which we must carry through. And then we are hindered also by the sight of the obstacles, invincible and insuperable obstacles we imagine them to be, which divide us from God. Our character is set, we say, in a groove which is unalterable. Our associations and our habits are fixed. The far country is not geographically far; it is spiritually far: and that is a gulf which is harder to bridge. "A lustful heart," Augustine said—and he knew what he was talking about—"a lustful heart is the far country." Ay, a lustful heart, or a sceptical intellect, or a worldly mind, or a sullen and violent temper: these are the things which seem to make the chasm between us and our God complete.

But no, Hosea says, God is near. He is not nebulous and vague, but more real than we ourselves. He does not exact any elaborate preparations and any attempted equivalents. He wants us just as we are, that He may do for us, and in us, from the beginning to the end, His own work of rectification and renewal. He is not frightened by the trammels in which we have bound ourselves. Let us return to Him, let us trust Him, and the Lion of Judah will break every chain. God is near. Each one of us, here and now, can transact with Him.

There is another truth of which Hosea is even surer—that *God is kind*. He announces it with a singular wealth of gracious imagery. God, he affirms, is like the surgeon: His knife and His scalpel may wound us, but His one intention is to effect a cure—"He hath torn, and He will heal." He is like the fathers of our flesh; they corrected us, but no one wished us well half so unmistakably as they did—"He hath smitten, and He will bind us up." Or if you leave the world of men, Hosea says, for the world of nature, you will discover parables there just as remarkable and just as winning, of the goodness of God. "His going forth is certain as the soft grey of the dawn," which prefigures the sunlight and the warmth of the day. "And He will come to us as the latter rain that watereth the earth," to assuage our thirst, to end our barrenness, to evoke our harvest. These are beautiful pictures of the chastening, and life-giving, and fruit-bearing love of God. And we who have Him painted for us by evangelists and apostles, as well as by the Old Testament prophet, can be more unassailably confident of their truth.

Well, but Hosea is not content with announcing the fact of God's kindness in His words; he illustrates and commends it by his own example. You see how he identifies himself with the sinners he is persuading to repentance. You see how he puts his hand into theirs. He does not say, "Go you, and return"; he says, "*Come*, and let *us* return unto the Lord our God" —you with me, and I with you. It is only a step, only a true inclination of the soul; and the breach is at an end, and the Father is singing His song over His child who was dead but is alive again, who was lost but is found. That is Hosea's way, as it must be the way of all of us who desire to entice our brothers home to be forgiven. And, beloved, the men of Israel had simply to look up into the face of the prophet who talked with them in this fashion, to be convinced how very real it all was to him. This great-hearted, simple-hearted, self-forgetting man, whose own home had been stripped and emptied, whose own home had been devastated by tragedy—his features carried peace stamped on them, and manifestly his heart was tuned to quiet and irrepressible melody. Why was that? It was because, morning and evening, he dwelt in the love of God. If anybody could prevail on other people to believe in that love, it was he. Oh, but the Lord Jesus Christ is far better! He has become one of ourselves. He has been tempted in all points like as we are. He has taken our scarlet sin upon Him. He went to Calvary, and with a great price He bought our redemption, and by His death He opened for us the new and living way of access to God. My brothers and sisters, it is Christ who says, "Come, and let us return—you with me, and I with you." And when we go to God in His company, we shall be greeted with nothing but the loving-kindness of the Lord.

That God is near, and that He is kind—these are weighty motives to repentance; but Hosea adds something else—*God is unlimited and illimitable.* "Let us know," He counsels; "let us follow on to know the Lord." It is just as if he said, "There is no possibility of setting a boundary to His understanding, His power, and His grace. It may seem to you as if your case was altogether unprecedented; and you may feel as though, in all the generations of those who have sought and found Him, there never was a necessity to parallel yours. But that is not to deter you. There are surprises waiting for men and women in the Lord their God: His resources are not yet exhausted. Come and let us return to Him, and He will work a fresh miracle for us; let us follow on to know Him, and He will unveil novelties and ingenuities of wisdom, of compassion, and of renewal, which no eye has seen, no ear has heard, no heart until now has been able to conceive.

The endlessness of God! The Bible is proof of it. Patriarchs tasted that He is good; but psalmists and prophets succeeded patriarchs, and their discoveries were vaster, and their witness nobler. When the old convenant reached its close, it looked as if it had left nothing untold; but then came the fulness of the time, and with the fulness of the time, our Lord and Saviour Jesus Christ; and it appeared as if only at long length man had begun to know the Lord. The endlessness of God! Your life, my life, if God is ours and we are God's, are evidence of it. *Secretum meum mihi,* said Dante—"My secret remains with me." "To him," Christ promises—and it is a solitary and individual experience—"to him will I give of the hidden manna, and I will give him a white stone, and upon the stone a new name written, which no one knoweth but he that receiveth it." The limitlessness of God—oh, brothers and sisters, do not let us, any of us, think that we are disqualified because the demand we have to make upon our Lord is an unequalled demand, or because our wanderings and sins are different from all previous wanderings and sins. The riches of God in Jesus Christ are unsearchable riches. Let us follow on to know the Lord.

God's nearness, God's kindness, God's limitlessness—these are ample incentives, these are appealing invitations to repentance. I had a letter the other day from a friend, and in it a printed leaflet with these lines—

> Absolutely tender, absolutely true;
> Understanding all things, understanding you;
> Infinitely loving, exquisitely near,
> This is God our Father:
> What have we to fear?

It is good tidings of great joy, and yet, beloved—and yet—we have something to fear. Not on His part, but on our part. The last word I have to say to-night is this: God is in serious and awful earnest, and some of us are scarcely in earnest at all.

Hosea, as I have hinted, had his private heartbreak, but he had his public heartbreak too, and it was this: that the repentance of Israel was too superficial, too facile—a fleeting emotion, a "goodness like a morning cloud, and as the dew that goeth early away." Many men are touched into momentary regrets, many men are moved and melted to tears, but the deep places of their souls and the strong currents of their daily lives are not changed. I remember a shrewd sentence of William Guthrie, the Scots Covenanter: "Esau grat his fill"—do you know the meaning of "grat"?—Esau wept his fill—"Esau grat his fill, but he never grat himself into repentance." There are such numbers of people of whom Esau is the representative; and, I dare to say, these people are the despair even of the God of unfathomable power and infinite love. He can do nothing with them.

But, beloved, we are not Esaus. We are children, we are God's Jacobs, whom He has redeemed for Himself with the precious blood of His Son, and whom He has called unto His Kingdom by the almightiness of His Holy Spirit. God is near to us; God is kind to us; the God to whom we come is, as we are finding out, a limitless God. But do we all remember this: that He is also a holy God, and the heavens are not clean in His sight, and He charges His angels with folly? We long to see our country confessing its national sins. We long to see the Church in our land forsaking its bloodless Christianity, its worldly conformity, its selfish indifference toward the millions who are dying without God. But let us commence with ourselves. We return to the Lord because He bears and forbears and forgives; but let us recognise that we return to One who hates our sins with a perfect hatred. We come to Christ because Christ is the Lover of our souls; but do let us recognise and be very sure that we are coming to the Christ of Gethsemane and the Christ of Calvary, to whom those questionable things and those contaminating things which we have been tolerating, for which we have been making excuse, meant the bloody sweat and the accursed tree and the hiding of God's face. Coming back to such a Father, back to such a Saviour, we must abhor every sin; we must hate ourselves because of our traffic and our friendship with sin; and we must continually trust our Lord to keep us from tampering with sin any more. God is in serious earnest, and you and I have to be in serious earnest too.

Many, O Lord my God, are my infirmities; many they are, and great: but Thy medicine is mightier. Search me, and know my heart; try me, and know my thoughts; and see if there be any way of wickedness in me, and lead me in the everlasting way. "Come, and let us return unto the Lord; for He hath torn, and He will heal us: He hath smitten, and He will bind us up."

ENDURING TEMPTATION

Rt. Rev. Bishop J. H. Linton, D.D.

Blessed (or, *happy*) *is the man that endureth temptation*—JAMES
1: 12.

TEMPTATION is one of the inescapable facts of life. Temptation was a fact in the life of the Holy Son of God when He tabernacled with us men; it is a fact to be reckoned with in the life of every man and woman seeking to serve the Lord Jesus Christ; and, as you read the record of the temptations of our Lord Jesus Christ, if you write that down as being only allegory, then you wipe out the inspiration that leads us men on to victory. It was not only during those forty days in the wilderness that our Lord Jesus Christ suffered, being tempted. There was one occasion on which He was talking to His disciples, and He summed up His whole three years' ministry in just two words—"my temptations." He said, "Ye are they who have continued with me in my temptations," and we know that He could not there have been referring to the forty days in the wilderness, for then He went through alone. So that, at any rate, we may begin with this word of consolation for ourselves, that even the Holy One of God, even Jesus, Very God of Very God, knew what it was to go through the fires of temptation, though He went through without sin.

It is not possible for any one of us to go very far through life blind to the awful, insidious force of temptation that besets us on every hand in our Christian life; in our boyhood, in girlhood, in the full vigour of young manhood and young womanhood, the trail of temptation lies right across our lives. Am I not speaking out of my own experience? Is it not true in the life of every one of us here? There have been times in the lives of all of us when sometimes we have felt that escape seemed almost impossible. And I know this, that when you get out into the world, and perhaps more especially when you get out abroad, away from all the restraining influences of home, then the force of temptation is certainly not lessened. Perhaps once, when you were a good deal younger, you came to this convention and listened to some of those grand old saints of God who spoke to us here of sanctification and victory, and perhaps you wondered whether they knew just

what you were going through in the way of temptation. But I
know that one of the saintliest men that ever spoke on this platform, when he was nearing the end of his life wrote to a friend to
ask for prayer, because he found that as he grew older the force
of temptation was growing ever stronger and more insistent, and
he felt the need for continual prayer that he might get the victory.

Now I want to make it quite clear that I am speaking specially
for those who are the Lord's own people. You have come to this
convention because you wanted to get victory over sin in your
life; and to all such I say, Let us go back to the Gospel record of
the life of our Lord Jesus Christ Himself, and we shall see there, in
His experience, what you and I are proving over and over again
in our own experience, that the time of greatest spiritual uplift
is the time when temptation is most intense. That was so in the
life of Jesus Christ, and that is so in the life of every one of us.
I can only stop just to indicate such times as: (i) At our Lord's
baptism, after the Spirit of God had descended upon Him;
then immediately we read that He was driven of the Spirit up
into the wilderness to be tempted of the devil. (ii) Again, as
He faced Jerusalem for the last time, oh! which of us can realise
the awful agony as He cried out to one of His own beloved disciples,
who tried to dissuade Him from all that the Cross meant, and He
said, "Get thee behind me, Satan!"? (iii) Then, in the Garden
of Gethsemane, in that awful paroxysm of the fury of the evil
one, when the sweat burst through as great drops of blood. There
was our Lord Jesus Christ's experience.

Oh! I say, let us be sure of this, that we who have come up here
to this convention, and are going to get, please God, a great
spiritual blessing, if we crown Jesus as King in our lives, then we,
too, are bound to come into conflict with the devil, and he will
seek to win the victory over us. There is no use in shirking that.
And when the Spirit of God comes upon us in this convention,
as He truly will if we let Him, then let us be prepared, too, to be
led up by the Spirit into the wilderness. We will have our testing
just after this, "for the disciple is not above his Master." And
as we go up to our Holy City, with all that is going to mean for us
in separation, and misunderstanding, and self-crucifixion, we,
too, will have our friends who will try to dissuade us from all that
the Cross is going to mean in our lives. We, too, will surely have
our Gethsemane. Only then let us remember that we shall also
have the angels of God standing by to strengthen us. We are not
so alone in our Gethsemane as we seem to imagine.

One is compelled to speak on this subject of temptation with
a deep sympathy born out of hard experience. It concerns the
innermost secrets of the lives of every one of us. I know that

H

temptations do not cease when, at the foot of the Cross, you receive the Lord Jesus Christ as your personal Saviour. They do not lessen when you get out into service for Him, and give Him your whole life for whatever that is going to mean. No, temptations do not lessen then. And when you try to let the principles of Jesus Christ rule in your business life, or when you go out to work for God as a foreign missionary, Satan never relaxes his efforts. Sometimes I think his attack comes in the nature of a barrage, when he seems to rain upon us all the explosiveness of his fury, until we seem bound to be overwhelmed with it. We have experienced that—I have, and you have. Sometimes it is in the nature of sniping from some hidden place; or else it comes in the nature of poison gas, secret, silent, deadly, paralysing, vitiating the very air you breathe.

I think there is a danger sometimes least we think of the Christian life far too much in terms of some catchy hymn-tune, whereas I know, in the experience of my own life, it is a contest in which I feel I can never afford to be caught off-guard. It was not for reclining on couches of scented rose-leaves that we were bidden to take unto us "the whole armour of God." But, men and women, here is the inspiration that comes into my life, and here is the inspiration that comes ringing down from our victorious Captain Himself: that no matter how fierce, how overwhelming the forces that are arrayed against us, these are not greater than the forces that can lead us on to victory. Right into the very heat of the furnace there stands beside us One like unto the Son of God, and He says to you and to me, "Oh! brother; oh! sister; I, too, have felt the scorching flames. I know what it means; I, too, have suffered being tempted, yet without sin—I was tempted in all points like as you are." Can that be really true? Can that mean just what it says, that the Lord Jesus Christ, when He lived as a man on this earth, was really tempted in every point just as we are? Of course it means it; for this Word of God means just what it says, and all that it says, and nothing else than what it says.

So I say, blot out for ever from your mind the thought that because Jesus was God, that therefore in some mysterious way temptation did not have the same power, the same force for Him as it has for you and me. It is this that inspires us to endure when we are feeling the force of temptation: "He was in all points tempted like as we are." Often and often I have thanked God for those words, "in all points." Then it means just this: that Jesus Christ, my Saviour, when He was a boy, was tempted just as I was when I was a boy; it means that as He grew up to be a young man, those temptations that attacked me and that attack you too, attacked Him also. But here is the glory of it for us—He came through victorious, without sin. So to myself, and to every other child of God, I say, Take those words for strength, and consolation, and encouragement to your heart, these words of power, and just hold on to them in the hour of temptation. They are the very word of God.

It is written again, "In that He Himself hath suffered"—oh! thanks be to God for that—"being tempted, He is able also to succour them that are tempted." Oh! men and women, there is a wonderful power in sympathy, even in human sympathy. It is a tremendous power; it wins its way right into the very heart of the one who is suffering. Sympathy means "suffering with," and the one who truly sympathises with another suffers along with that other in the moment or the hour of his suffering. Sympathy is just a stream of love flowing out from the one heart into the other heart, and binding the two together in a bond of love and fellowship. True sympathy can only come from one that has truly suffered.

A lady, who is now experienced in work for her Master, told me that once in the early days of her service she was visiting a woman who had lost her little child; she tried to sympathise with that mother with just such loving words of sympathy as she knew how, and that mother looked up and, through blinding tears, said to her, "Thank you so much; but, then, you are not a mother, and you cannot understand." Oh! how true it was, in the depths of her grief that mother missed something; she missed just the tone, the look, the feeling, that would come from someone who had suffered as she had suffered. The soul that has truly suffered goes out in sympathy; you must know, if you are really to sympathise. Now that is human sympathy. And Jesus Christ, our great High Priest, the Man Christ Jesus, knows what it means to be tempted. He, too, suffered being tempted. And because He knows to the full the power of the tempter as he seeks to win his victory over the soul, the heart of the Eternal God goes out in love, and in sympathy, and in fellow-suffering with every child of God who is enduring temptation. Thank God, Jesus is a God who is able to sympathise to the full.

But, now, He not only knows, He not only suffers with us when we are tempted; but it says, "He is able also to *succour* them that are tempted"—"for in all things it behoved Him to be made like unto His brethren, that He might be a merciful and faithful High Priest . . . for in that He Himself hath suffered being tempted, He is able also to succour them that are tempted." That is the crux of the whole thing for you and for me. He overcame, and His power is available for us, if we will use it, if we also want to overcome.

I feel I am speaking to some who have been almost as long in the Lord's service as I have been in the world. You can look back and say, "These forty years hath He led me, and there hath not failed one word of all His good promises which He hath promised," but there are others, perhaps, who have only just recently begun to follow Jesus Christ. You were realising the need of a Saviour who could save to the very uttermost in your life; you knew that you needed power if you were to live on the higher levels of life; and, perhaps, last year you came to the convention, and you heard a message of God here that just suited your need, and you trusted God for full salvation; and you went away filled with a joy and gladness that you never before had realised. All was joy—for a time; and then somehow temptation seemed to come upon you so thick and fast that you began to despair of ever getting the victory. You seemed to be more tempted than ever before. Out of your own heart there seemed to proceed a raging torrent of evil imaginations, and from around about you temptations seemed to become more intense, more fierce, more insidious than ever they were before, and you began to despair of ever experiencing the victory over sin. Yes, and then a horrible dread came over you lest, after all, Jesus Christ was not the victorious Saviour that you had been led to believe.

Now what does it all mean? I think this: first of all, it is true that you are being tempted more than ever before. I think that probably is true, for the devil will not easily part with his slave, even though the redemption money has been paid. I think also this, that before you gave your life to Christ, you were drifting; you were just going easily down the stream, and you were not conscious of the terrific force of the current that held you in its grip. Now you have begun to pull against the stream, and you are realising how strong the current is. You cannot drift against the stream. Or, if I may put it in another way, you can shut off your engine and trolley downhill with the engine off—and the steeper the hill the more swiftly you go; but it takes a good engine, well tuned, to go uphill on top, and sometimes it is conquest if you creep up at all. But perhaps this is the most encouraging fact of all, that God has allowed you to go into the wilderness to be tempted, because God knows that you are going to win through. In the war the trusted regiments were put in the place where the battle waxed hottest and the fighting was strongest; and, the very enduring of temptation is going to be a blessing—God says so. Sometimes when we are weary, the voice of the Captain comes, and He says, "But do you really want to give in? Would you really like to give up the contest, and leave the devil triumphant?" Oh! you ask the youngest soldier in the King's army! And "we wrestle not against flesh and blood, but against principalities, against powers, against spiritual wickedness in high places." God calls us to a fight in which we never lay down our arms this side of victory. "Blessed is the man that endureth temptation."

"The trial of your faith worketh patience"—worketh patience? Yes, but not that passive idea that so often we connect with the word. The word has a military ring about it; it is the idea of holding out to the end. Here is a little band of soldiers, and they are out there, in a difficult post, with the enemy all around them. Help is long in coming; the enemy call on them to yield, and those soldiers just think of that king whose flag they defend, and they know that behind them they have the whole might of his forces: so they stiffen their backs to the struggle; they dig in deeper than ever, and hold out to the end. There is patience. And "the trial of your faith worketh patience," that sort of patience.

Now, again, temptation is not sin, because the Lord Jesus was tempted. It is giving in which is sin. Oh! men and women, I want to say this now, that the Christian man or woman, with all the resources of God to draw upon, has no right to give in to the evil one. That is treachery to the Master whose name you bear. The promise of God in His Word is, "Sin shall not have dominion over you"; and where sin has had dominion over the child of God, then it just means that the child of God had not used the resources which God has meant us to use. I think sometimes, perhaps, we need to emphasise that to our own hearts even more than to preach it. The Word of God gives no authority whatever for any Christian willingly to consent to a standard of life in which sin gets the upper hand. If we do so consent, then we are deliberately betraying our Master, and we are daring to set up a standard of life lower than that which God summons us to in His Word. It just amounts to this: Here is God's own Word, that liveth and abideth for ever, and the testimony of the Word of God is this, that God calls us not to a life of defeat, but to a life of victory. And when we speak of renouncing the devil, what does it mean? It means throwing back the challenge to the tempter, and saying, "Come along, Satan; I will fight." That is renouncing the devil.

Again listen to the Word of God: "When he is tried he shall receive a crown of life." That crown is promised to the man who is tried and tested, and who triumphs. I suppose in the days of the war we should have looked doubtfully at the soldier who came out of the fray with a clean tunic, and not a splash of mud on it, and we reserve our cheers for the little drummer boy who went out into the zone of danger to rescue his officer. The Victoria Cross is not given to the man who stops at home, but to the man who dares death in the path of duty; to the man who comes, scarred, it may be, and maimed, through the battle, but triumphant. "Blessed is the man that endureth temptation."

Now I want to be practical. The vital question is this: Do we want to triumph? Do we want to have sin done with for ever in our lives, or do we want to go back occasionally to the old sins and the old haunts, back to the pleasures of sin for a season? Then let us be quite frank with ourselves about it; let us tell God what we mean to do. We may go back occasionally to the old sins and to the old haunts, and we may listen to the voice of the tempter when he says it does not matter to give in just once in a while; and God knows there are pleasures in sin—that is the fascination of it. And then we give in. Oh! but then we hear the thunder of God saying, "Know thou that for all these things God will bring thee into judgment; whatsoever a man soweth, that shall he also reap." If you sow wild oats, you cannot expect to reap good grain; if you sow to the flesh, you will reap corruption; if you sow the wind, you will reap the whirlwind.

So we come back now to the question: Do you want to win? You have come up here because you want to win, have you not? Now do you want it at any cost, at anything it may mean in self-crucifixion? Then let us ask ourselves now, Am I willing, this very hour, to make a clean cut with sin? "Willing?" you say. "God knows I am willing, but I cannot." Then I ask you, if God were to empower you now, would you be willing to face all that it means, all that a full deliverance from sin would mean in your life? Would you be willing to face the consequences of that? Then will you take God at His word, that word that never fails? Do you know these lines? I think they are A. B. Simpson's—

> There are some who believe the Bible,
>   And some who believe a part;
> Some who trust with a reservation,
>   And some with all the heart.
>
> But I know that its every promise
>   Is firm and sure always:
> It is tried as the precious silver,
>   And it means just what it says.

Will you come out on that word of God, that means just what it says? Will you plead the promises of God, and put God on His honour to fulfil them in your life?

Here is, then, the promise of victory: "There hath no temptation taken you but such as a man can bear, and God is faithful and will, with the temptation, make also a way of escape, that you may be able to bear it"—and I think that means that every temptation carries with it its own way of escape. This is the promise of victory; I have already referred to the promise of sympathy which we get in the verse: Jesus Christ "was in all points tempted like as we are, yet without sin," and, "in that He Himself hath suffered being tempted, He is able to succour them that are tempted."

Then there is the promise of reward to him that overcometh. Oh! men, it would be the most cruel mockery of God to hold out the promise of reward to the man that gets the victory if conquest was impossible. You cannot believe such a caricature of God as that. "To him that overcometh." Then thanks be to God, it means that conquest is possible. Will you take that as a pledge from God that you may attain unto this life of conquest, and then you will be able to look up with the apostle Paul, and say, "Thanks be unto God who always causes us to triumph in Christ Jesus." I ask you, will you take it? Do you want that life of victory to-night? Will you face up to the consequences? Will you take God at His word, put Him on His honour, and go out, knowing victory over sin in your life?

THE HEAVENLY PHYSICIAN

Rev. W. W. Martin, M.A.

Wilt thou be made whole?—JOHN 5: 6.

KESWICK! What memories this word awakens in men and women the world over! It is not alone the surpassing beauty of the place. Neither is it the hallowed intercourse which God's children have enjoyed these many years. Nay, rather, it is that God has here revealed Himself in numberless cases to individual souls. Here the weary and the disconsolate have found fresh inspiration for life and service. Here the despairing, tired out with life's failure and the unequal struggle with habits and temptations, have learned the secret of victory. Here those whose horizon has been limited have seen the great vision of God's plan for the world. Here young men and maidens have heard the challenge concerning this world of ours, which has made them follow their Lord and Master to the very ends of the earth. Time would fail to tell of the changes and the miracles wrought in this place. To many this tent is the most hallowed spot in the whole world. Not alone have there been revelations of need and sin such as have made men cry out with soul pain; but there have been experiences as instantaneous as conversion issuing in a life triumphant, buoyant, and instinct with joy unspeakable.

To this place God has gathered us this year. Yes, attenders of many years are present: there are faces always familiar at this Keswick Convention. May I say a word to you? Is there no danger lest your very familiarity with the truths for which our convention stands may be a tremendous snare? "He that heareth my words and doeth them not . . ." Beware lest ye are hearers of the Word, and not doers. You who have been here twenty, twenty-five, thirty years, are you living a more victorious life than others? Are you, by the very witness of your daily life, revealing the fact that you have learned the secret of victory? Remember your multiple attendance should have issued in a more holy life in the home and in business. Does it? I want you to ask yourself that question to-night.

Tired workers are here from sordid scenes in town and village, from work difficult and often disappointing, from heathen lands where constant contact with sin and degradation has somehow paralysed the finer instincts of their soul.

Men and women are here who—the tragedy of it!—have lost their first love, and are crying out, "Oh, that I were as in months past! Oh, that I knew where I might find Him!" Yes, but before you find Him again you have got to find out the cause of the failure. God grant that His Holy Spirit may reveal it.

First attenders, how gladly we welcome you among us here! Perhaps some of you have been persuaded to come almost against your will. You are wondering what all the talk and enthusiasm about this yearly gathering of many years' standing can mean. You are somewhat fearful lest emotion might carry you off your feet, rather than that reason should prevail. Yes, and some of you have for years been praying that the way may be opened for you to come. Have we not here even to-day some such? For in a very wonderful way God has made it possible, and you are here.

Critics may have come. They cannot shut their eyes to the extraordinary transformations that have here taken place. Yet this movement has never received the recognition of church leaders; it has never been influenced in its message by modern outlook on spiritual truths; its messages have never been appeals to the purely intellectual part of thinking men: it has never catered for the ease of its audience; it certainly has never ministered flattery to human nature. Few of its speakers are known very much beyond the confines of this movement. And yet it has exerted a power and an influence unequalled in the history of conventions. There is no movement which has so insisted on Christian ethics as Keswick. There is no movement which has so translated and transfigured the whole outlook on life as Keswick. It has possibly driven more people to the mission field than any other movement in the world. It has, I suppose, had more to do with the consecration of life than anything else the world over. There must be some reason for that. Critics, would you kindly defer your summing up of the movement until the end of next week, and then ask yourself the secret of its power?

I want to emphasise something else. The foundation on which this movement stands is, first of all, *conversion to God*. We do not declare that souls find salvation in service, nor that we discover the secret of real Christian living by labour. It takes for granted that every one who comes to this place has known what it is, in the words of Scripture, to be "born again." It will not, therefore, be essentially evangelistic. It will assume that all who are present have had a vital experience of pardon and forgiveness of sins.

You ask, then, what is the characteristic which essentially belongs to this place? I would say it is a spiritual clinic, and this is the line upon which I wish to develop our subject to-night; a spiritual clinic in which each of us, quite definitely, as solitary units, goes into the surgery of the Great Physician to discover whether we are in good health, and if not, to discover what ails us, with a view to present and future betterment. We know the danger of continually haunting the doctor's consulting-room. Spiritual neurasthenia is terribly common. It is not well to be always feeling one's spiritual pulse, or to be anxious about one-self. But doctors tell us we all ought to be overhauled at least once a year. Keswick is the place for the yearly spiritual inves-tigation. I suggest that every one of us should pass into the Physician's consulting-room this year.

I want to say something about the Heavenly Physician. He has never failed in a case that He has undertaken. You may have come here suffering from a series of complications. He has never failed in a single case which has been definitely handed over to Him, and which He has undertaken. Therefore there is not a man or woman here to-night that need despair. Of course it means that His instructions are to be implicitly obeyed and carried out. It is not fair to Him to come up to Keswick, and to get a prescription from Him, and then not to carry it out. No complication is ever a challenge to His skill. We may have a complexity of spiritual ailments, but they are all perfectly simple to Him, and He can easily diagnose them. He cures instantaneously. The enquiry is not, "Wilt thou be relieved?" but, "Wilt thou be made *whole*?" We glory in that part of our message. On this first night the Great Physician may reveal to you the cause of your spiritual malady: and you can be cured on the spot to-night ere you go forth. He never orders a long course of remedial treatment, but He does lay tremendous stress on the need of care in after-living. When He had healed the man at Bethesda's Pool, He said, "Go, and don't do any more sinning." There is tragedy connected with Keswick. So many come to the Great Physician here; they get cured of their malady, and then they go out and live a life careless of His instructions as to the future, and the last state is worse than the first. Some of us could tell sad stories of these who had hopes raised here, and who had experience of the Great Physician's power, but they have gone back again. If only they had obeyed His instructions, "Go, and sin no more," and had implicitly carried out His directions, their cure might have been the entrance into a new life of health and power, without the old maladies causing trouble. He has an infallible cure called "the balm of Gilead." I want to say this quietly. The balm of Gilead was only obtained by piercing the trunk of the tree. The balm of Gilead, which heals spiritual diseases, is only obtained (let us say it quietly), by His piercing and His bruising. In other words, it was obtained at a place called Calvary; and Calvary, therefore, is the centre of our theme, as it always supplies the healing balm for every sickness.

Now, what will be some of the results of His examination? It may disclose that you are in perfect health, and only need *a spiritual tonic*. God grant that you may get it here! It may be He will reveal, as a result of His examination when you and He get alone (you must do that), the fact that your spiritual life is functioning correctly, and that you are living a "whole" life, and there is no need for drastic treatment, but that you only want some of the breath of heaven, such as is here experienced, to invigorate you for future service. Thank God, if that be so. It may be that He will tell you there must be less activity and more quiet in your life. "But," you say, "there is so much spiritual work needs doing." Wherever you go it seems as though duties crowd in upon you. It is not the amount of work, but the quality of it, that tells. There may be, for each of us, need of readjustment of our spiritual time-table. To use another figure, it may be that you have "forgotten Him." He made that complaint years ago— "My people have forgotten me days without number." It may be that you and I have been so busy that we have had little time for His companionship; and perhaps there has got to be a re-adjustment of your whole spiritual life. You were not made, first of all, to tell the Gospel to the heathen whether at home or abroad. You were not made, first of all, to try to win your companions for Jesus Christ. "This people have I formed for myself." That is the first reason why He redeemed you and me: to be His friends. "Ye are my friends." How many times in an ordinary day do you talk to Him? Ten minutes in the morning, and five minutes in the evening? Is that treating Him as your friend? Yet we were created, and re-created, first of all, to be His companions. "I have called you friends." "He chose twelve . . . that they might be with Him," that they might be sharers with Him in His life, and then that He might send them forth. It may be that that will have to be readjusted in your life.

Perhaps the Great Physician will order you *a change of dwelling*. He may say to that young man, "If you want to maintain your spiritual life, China is the place for you." He may say to some young woman, "There are women experiencing new conditions who till now have been shut up in zenanas, and are now feeling their new freedom. If you want to maintain your spiritual vitality, India is the place for you"—or it may be Japan, or Africa, or South America. That will mean the sundering of home ties, which hurts. It may mean the surrender of ease. It may mean giving up some position of wealth or authority. Many a time He has so instructed His patients. There is never a year in the history of the convention when He does not say the same thing to some who gather here—"If you want to maintain your spiritual life, you must go abroad." And, thank God, they have risen up and gone.

He may have to use the surgeon's knife, and sever some friendship, cut off some cherished habit, separate us from some loved treasure. But, remember, the surgeon's lancet is always held by a pierced hand. It is all right. His examination will be thorough, and perhaps painful. I wonder what the stethoscope will reveal? Your *heart*, is that functioning correctly? Does it quicken at the name of Jesus? Is it a "clean heart"? Is it a united heart? Is it a heart that is always loyal to Jesus? Remember, if the heart, the centre, is not healthy, the whole body is going to suffer. What about your heart?

Thoughts. I suppose thoughts react on the heart. Your thought-life, is it clean? *He* is asking these questions. Your thought-life, is it pure? Is jealousy allowed to burn in it? Are the unclean birds allowed to lodge in the chambers of your imagination? If your thoughts were written on your forehead, would you have to wear a veil? Yet some of us on Sunday pray, "Cleanse the thoughts of our hearts by the inspiration (breathing in) of Thy Holy Spirit." That is the prayer that we always have to pray.

Then I think the Great Physician may have to examine our *tongues.* They are so expressive in many ways of health. We remember how Scripture compares the tongue to a ship's rudder. "Whose hand is on the tiller?" Scripture compares it to a fire, and that fire may spread, and there may be a terrible conflagration. Is it to be set on fire of hell, or is it to be a tongue of fire lighted by the Spirit of God? The tongue is able to defile, so we are told, the whole body. A little member, but oh, so potent! If a man can rule his tongue, there is not much fear about any other of his possessions. Your tongue, is it a "sharp tongue"? Have you paid the other person back in the same coin in which by his tongue he hurt you? A hasty tongue, bitter words, sarcasm —how these hurt! "Their words do eat as a canker." Is that true of you? Oh, the agony that has come through hurtful words! I want to ask you to-night in God's name, has Christ unlimited control of your tongue? Will the Great Physician have to deal with that part of your life? The tongue can no man tame, but God can control it. The Great Physician has a wonderful remedy for sharp speaking.

Hands! Do they hang down? Do they clasp in friendship that which is displeasing to Him? Do they express fellowship with the world? Are you "hand in glove," in league with, the world? He has definitely said that there is to be a fine dividing line between that which is opposed to the world and Himself. The powers of the world are always antagonistic to the powers of Jesus Christ. Have you drawn for yourself that fine line? I do not say where the line is. Are those hands holy hands, able to minister to Christ?

Knees! are they often bent in prayer? You never read a book on the spiritual life without insistence being laid on prayer. Is your prayer-life satisfactory? I believe one of the wonders of heaven will be the discovery of what we could have wrought through prayer, and of how little we used it. You can do far more by prayer than by effort, but better still is a combination of prayer and effort. It may be that the Great Physician will have to deal with you and me about our prayer-life. He may have to say some very stern things, but they will be said with infinite love, and a great winsomeness in their tone.

Ears! Are our ears dull because they have not been used? Can we hear the whispering of God's voice? He generally speaks in a still small voice. Do you know that we are all a kingdom of priests, and that, as a priest of God, those ears of yours have been touched with the holy oil: they must never listen to scandal, to things not clean, or to the "doubtful" story?

Appetite! The Great Physician may have to ask us whether our appetite for spiritual food is good, or whether we have to be pampered? Whether we live on slops or little dainties dished with spices? Do we know how to carve from the joint of God's Word and enjoy it, or do we have to be spoon-fed all our lives?

Feet! That is a great message in the Epistle to the Hebrews: "Make straight paths for your feet, lest that which is lame be turned out of the way." Has it been easier for the other person because you have made straight paths? Your example, does it help or hinder?

The Great Physician may have some big disclosures to make to many this week. Will you have the courage to face anything He tells you is wrong? Are you prepared for that? There has been many a sob uttered in this tent, because when souls have come face to face with the Great Physician He has had to reveal something that hurts. These hill-sides here, the lake shore, can tell of many an interview between the Great Physician and individual souls. Do you shrink from consulting Him? Remember that He has infinite skill, He has infinite pity, He has infinite love, He has infinite gentleness. I think He is asking you to-night, "Wilt thou be made whole?" You say, "I scarcely know what is wrong." That does not matter. Will you deliberately here in

this tent to-night, or somewhere alone, get an interview with
the Great Physician? I know what He will ask you: "Do you
wish to be made whole this very night, before Sunday dawns?"
Not merely go down from here relieved, with symptoms a little
less painful. No, not that! One of the wonderful things about
the message we have here is this, that the very moment any soul
faces Jesus Christ, and puts himself or herself unreservedly into
His hands, and says, "Lord, heal me here and now," He will do
it immediately. It is a great word concerning the Great Physician's activity. Shall I tell you the secret? You say that you
are very lonely. For thirty-three years the Great Physician was
a very lonely man when He was preparing to become the Great
Physician of the world, and He can have compassion on your
loneliness. And if you come face to face with Him you will go
out, He and you, both of you together. There is no need to wait
until the end of the week. What will you do to-night? You say,
"This is rather hurried." It is: yet it would be very wonderful
if on this first night of our convention He brought "health and
cure" to some soul.

Shall we just think it over in silence? He asks us each individually, "Would you like to be made perfectly whole to-night?"
And the answer will have to be, "Yes, Lord Jesus!" or "No, not
to-night, some other time." Think what He did on earth.
One touch, and people were made whole. And it is true to-day
that "Thy touch has still its ancient power." One touch from
Him, and you may go out whole to-night. "Here in this solemn
evening hour"—with the hush of God upon us—"Oh, in Thy
mercy, heal us all!"

IF I WASH THEE NOT

Rev. George B. Duncan, M.A.

*And supper being ended . . . Jesus . . . laid aside His garments;
and took a towel, and girded Himself. After that He poureth water
into a bason, and began to wash the disciples' feet, and to wipe them
with the towel wherewith He was girded. Then cometh He to Simon
Peter: and Peter saith unto Him, Lord dost Thou wash my feet?
Jesus answered and saith unto Him, What I do thou knowest not
now; but thou shalt know hereafter. Peter saith unto Him, Thou
shalt never wash my feet. Jesus answered him, If I wash thee not,
thou hast no part with me. Simon Peter saith unto Him, Lord,
not my feet only, but also my hands and my head. Jesus saith to
him, He that is washed needeth not save to wash his feet, but is
clean every whit*—JOHN 13: 2–10.

YESTERDAY we were concerned with the failure and sin that
mark our Christian experience; to-day we are concerned
with the way of cleansing and enablement which we find
in Christ, and which is ours by virtue of our union with Him.
But I do not think it is much good considering the *way* of cleansing until we are quite certain that we are *willing* for it. So I
want to seek by God's grace that you and I may ascertain together
whether we are really willing. May I, then, share with you three
simple thoughts which God has laid on my heart arising out of
the incident recorded in John 13.

As so often in the Gospel story, the interest of a scene which
begins in a crowd suddenly narrows and is focused upon an
individual. I suspect that your experience has been very similar
during these days of convention. Your first impression was of a
vast throng of people; but as you have sat listening to God's Word,
has it not seemed to you as if the throng has disappeared, and the
light of God's presence and truth has narrowed in focus upon
yourself, till sometimes as you have sat listening in this tent you
might have thought that there was nobody else here at all except
you—and the Master? In this story the light focused suddenly
upon Simon Peter and picked him out; and as we look together
at him it may well be that some of us may see something of our
own hearts.

The first thing to note about Simon Peter is, that he was—

I. A MAN WITH DEFILED FEET. And the action of Jesus Christ, and His words, would indicate that the dust of the highway which had defiled the feet of Simon Peter, was symbolical of an inner defilement of heart and soul.

Will you note first of all *the nature* of this man who was defiled. He was a man of *privilege*. Peter was no ordinary disciple. For days, for months, for years, he had accompanied his Master; he had heard His words and witnessed His power and seen something of His glory—just as so many of us can look down the years and down the way by which God has brought us to Keswick, to this very hour; and you and I can see that we too have been privileged by the goodness and mercy which have followed us all the days of our life, not only since our conversion but even before it. We, too, are men and women of privilege.

But Peter was more than that: he was also a man of *prominence*. Peter was a leader. Other disciples remained unnoticed and unknown, but Peter was prominent and conspicuous in the company of those who followed Christ. Have some of us felt that in some small measure we share this in common with Simon Peter? Are you a leader in the Christian circle in which you work; are you a fairly prominent member in your church? It may be that you are an office-bearer, an elder, a deacon, or a member of the church council. It may be that you are a Sunday-school teacher, a Crusader class leader. It may be that you are a missionary, or a minister. Whatever you are, you share with Peter some degree of prominence in the company of those who follow the Master. You are not only a man of privilege but also of prominence, and thus share something in common with the nature of Simon Peter.

What of his *need*? This man was defiled: that was his need. I wonder how many of us who share the nature of Simon Peter share also his need? The defilement of Simon Peter was a defilement which he shared at that moment with the other disciples— the defilement which we were hearing about last night, which we are concerned with at this moment. The pride of the disciples had been touched—the question in their minds was, which of them should be the greatest?

I wonder how deeply that message last night probed down to the very root of the trouble of your life and mine?[1] I wonder how many of us went out of the tent shocked and almost startled at the discovery of some trait of sin permeating almost every relationship of life, a sin of whose existence we had scarcely been aware—the sin of pride. Henry Drummond used to say something extraordinarily significant: he said, in effect, that the sins that the

---

[1] The address referred to was delivered by Mr. Fred Mitchell, upon the sin of pride.

world can see to be sins, are not the most important sins just
because the world can see them. I think some of us Evangelicals
are far too much taken up with sins that the world sees, instead of
those that God sees.

Defiled! Proud! Do you remember the words of St. John
concerning his Lord, words which men ought to be able to say
of us who claim to represent that Lord—"We beheld His glory,
the glory as of the only begotten of the Father, full of grace and
truth." Grace and truth! Are you concerned passionately with
the proclamation of the truth of God's Word? Have you considered that the world takes not so much notice of the truth of
your words as of the tone of your voice? I have felt very much
in my own heart that God has had to deal with me along this
very line. I have preached the Word for quite a time now, but as
I look back I sometimes wonder if Christ would ever have spoken
to men as I have spoken. Not that there has been anything
lacking in the truth of the message. But the Word will never get
as far as the hearts of men if people are put off by the tone of your
voice. Grace and truth! Do you profess a concern for the needs
of others, and yet in your own mind you are constantly critical
of them? May I suggest that your outward concern will not cut any
ice with men in the light of your obvious criticism of them. Grace
and truth! I do not think that we can say that the breakdown
in spiritual work among Evangelicals is due solely to the lack
of knowledge of Christian doctrine. In many cases it may be so;
and I know that ignorance is one of the greatest sins of the Church.
Nor do I think we can say that it is entirely due to the presence
of gross sin or immorality in the Church, although in some cases
even that is true. I want to suggest to you that the breakdown
seems to lie far more often than we like to think in the realm of
the relationship of the heart of the Christian both to other
Christians and to the world.

I would suggest to you that from the spiritual point of view, the
greatest dearth in the Church to-day is a lack of grace, which from
the worldly point of view may be regarded as a lack of evidence.
May I suggest to you that until people see the grace, they will
not listen to the truth? When John looked back on the witness
of Jesus Christ he said, "That which we have *seen and heard*. . . ."
You and I so often expect people just to listen to a message.
Permeating your thinking of others, permeating even your relationship with God, damaging your witness and mine, there has been
this sin of pride. Peter was a man with defiled feet, but he was
more: he was—

II. A MAN WITH A DEFIANT HEART. Christ had moved round
that upper room in a silence that could be felt. Men were looking

away from each other, not daring to meet each other's eyes. Then the silence was broken; a voice sharp with suppressed emotion, harsh under an almost intolerable strain of intense feeling, spoke. It was Simon Peter's voice; and with the hurt of his heart in the sound of his voice, incredulously he spoke, "Not my feet!" Then came the quiet, unhurried tones of the Master's voice: "What I do thou knowest not now; but thou shalt know hereafter." Then a sharp, almost explosive, word: "Never! Never!" Do you know anything of what that refusal of Simon Peter's meant? I know that the motive behind Peter's refusal, and the motive behind yours and mine, may be totally different; but the issue is the same. "My feet? Thou shalt never wash my feet!" Have you been saying the same thing to Christ concerning your life and His will? "Never!" Like Peter you have been during these days of convention nearer almost to anger in your refusal, than to any other emotion. How many of us have felt the tide of anger and resentment rising until we could have walked out— resentment against the speaker, anger with God, resentment against the person who persuaded us to come to Keswick; and like the elder brother in the story of the Prodigal Son, we have heard the sound of music and dancing, we have seen the faces of those enjoying the feast, but we have been angry and "would not go in."

Do you, as you listen, know that you are defiled? You are defiled, are you not; and you are defiant, too, to the very depths of your soul. Your attitude to the Master who would cleanse you is this—"Never! Never! Not my feet; not Thou." Listen; if you echo the refusal that Peter made, you must run the risk that Peter ran.

Listen quietly with me. Christ is speaking, and I think He spoke quietly, don't you? "If I wash thee not, thou hast no part with me." Of course you are a Christian, and you will still be a Christian if you maintain your refusal. Of course you are a worker for God, and you will still be a worker. But I suggest to you—and it may be that this is God's word to some hearts to-night—you may find that you have no part with Christ. I think the tragedy of the Church of Jesus Christ to-day is that great company of converted Christian men and women who have no part with Christ. The tide of Christ's work flows strongly and quietly on, but they are to be found in some stagnant backwater of almost forgotten experience, having no part with the living Christ in His work! The vital issue for you to-day is not whether you are an Evangelical Christian, or whether you are a staunch Protestant in your Churchmanship, or whether you are keen for souls in God's work, or whether you delight to stand in the open-air and give your testimony. The vital issue for you and for me is, what part have we with Christ? You see, if we have no part with Christ, then everything else is of no value. It does not matter how orthodox you are, or Protestant, or keen, or if you stand in the open-air and speak: it all goes for nothing unless Christ is with you. I want to ask you now—what part have you with Christ?

I wish I could paint the scene. That word "Never!" is still echoing faintly round the room. The figure of Peter is tense, the face is flushed, the eyes stormy, and the hands clenched. The kneeling figure of Christ has stilled. He had been busy, but now with that word "Never" He has stopped and is quiet. His face is upturned; He had been looking at Peter's feet, but now He is looking into his face, and the eyes, the quiet untroubled eyes of the Master, gaze into the soul of Peter. Then He speaks: "If I wash thee not, thou hast no part with me."

Angry, resentful, guilty Christian, it is Christ you have to deal with! He knows, with you, the nature of your defilement. And the quarrel and the argument which are raging in your soul even now, are not with the views of any speaker on the platform: your argument is with Christ—"If I wash thee not, thou hast no part with me." Defiled, defiant; can you come with me to the last step? Peter was a man of defiled feet, a man with a defiant heart, but he became—

III. A MAN WITH A DESPERATE CRY. "Lord, not my feet only, but also my hands and my head." When Simon Peter heard the truth, it was utterly unbearable. "No part with me"? That just broke Peter—to have no part with his Lord, when he had had such a part; to be shut out while others were shut in; to know nothing of the unfolding of the heart of Christ, as he had known it in the days of the past; to have no part with Christ, to look down the future days and months and years and to have no part with Christ in His work and in the fellowship of His Spirit; to have no part with Christ—he just could not stand the thought of it, and it broke him!

Can you stand the thought of the future, having no part with Christ in fellowship with Him in that quiet, deep, strong, eternal work of redemption? "No part" with Christ? Can you bear the thought? If you can, I question whether you are a Christian at all. If you cannot bear it, then may God make that truth break your pride to-night; because if Christ does not cleanse us from this evil thing, if we maintain our refusal, He will maintain His rejection—not so far as salvation is concerned, that is settled, we have been bathed; but as far as fellowship and usefulness are concerned, we shall find that we have "no part with Him." As you go back to your church, is the record of these coming weeks and months to be—no part with Him? I know you will be busy, you may be very complacent, you may feel very important, you may maintain your part; but, as far as Christ is concerned you will have "no part" with Him. "No part with me."

Moreover, it will mean having no part with His people. Some of you have had a taste of that already since you came to Keswick. It may be that you are in a house-party, and everybody else seems to have such a quality of common interest and such a depth of friendship that you know nothing of, and you are feeling out of it. You have no part with them. Do you know why? Because you have no part with Christ; you are shut out, aren't you? Yet Christ wants to bring you in.

It was *a truth which was intolerable*, and Peter could not stand it; so that his defiance broke, and instead that desperate cry went out, and Peter offered to Christ *a trust that was unreserved*; and, as so often happens, he was much harder on himself than Christ was. You know, we are sometimes like that: but there is no virtue in being harder on yourself than Christ is. Peter cried out, "Lord, not my feet only, but my hands and my head"—every bit of me, Lord. Peter just gave everything, as the Master knelt in humility at his feet. We often talk about kneeling at Christ's feet, and that is quite true; but I do not think that is the complete picture. He will, and does, ask us to kneel at His feet; but the almost unbelievable thing is that He is kneeling at our feet, saying, "If I wash thee not, thou hast no part with me." On that occasion he took a towel. He took much more to cleanse us; He humbled Himself and took upon Himself the form of a servant, He became obedient unto death, even the death of the Cross; to cleanse you and to cleanse me from pride and sin, He did not take a towel, He took a Cross!

We shall gather round Him in the closing minutes of this meeting, at the Cross. Christ is at your feet; oh, unbelievable grace! You are defiled, defiant, and now, it may be, in the mercy of God, desperate.

III

CONSECRATION

My glorious Victor, Prince Divine,
Clasp these surrendered hands in Thine;
At length my will is all Thine own,
Glad vassal of a Saviour's throne.

My Master, lead me to Thy door;
Pierce this now willing ear once more:
Thy bonds are freedom; let me stay
With Thee, to toil, endure, obey.

Yes, ear and hand, and thought and will,
Use all in Thy dear slav'ry still!
Self's weary liberties I cast
Beneath Thy feet; there keep them fast.

Tread them still down; and then I know,
These hands shall with Thy gifts o'erflow;
And pierced ears shall hear the tone
Which tells me Thou and I are one.

H. C. G. MOULE.

CONSECRATION

In this section we come to the distinctive "message" of Keswick. Foundational to it, as we have seen, is the Scriptural doctrine of sin, and that doctrine searchingly applied to the life of the believer—leading on to the glad declaration of God's remedy for sin in Christ our Lord. But that is not essentially "Keswick" teaching: it is common ground to all who earnestly seek after godliness. It is in the teaching of holiness that Keswick has its characteristic note and emphasis—"glad tidings for saints," Evan Hopkins delighted to call it; sanctification being an extension of the "glad tidings for sinners."

The subject of holiness embraces many facets—dedication to God, on our part; and the consecration by Him of what we present; resulting in sanctification of heart and life. All this is realised through the ministry of the Holy Spirit: so the fulness of the Spirit is the believer's highest good—and the Lord's purpose and provision for him. To present these vital truths, and to press home the issue in the lives of all attending the Convention, is Keswick's purpose. These great themes inter-twine, and many messages embrace the whole range of them. But let Keswick speakers themselves declare the "Keswick message." In this section the twin themes of dedication to God, and consecration by Him, are especially emphasised.

Once more Prebendary Webb-Peploe leads the way—most fittingly, with an address delivered at the very first Convention at Keswick, in 1875. No verbatim reports were taken in the early days; but someone evidently made good use of a notebook, as summarised versions of four of the addresses at the initial Convention appeared belatedly in *The Christian's Pathway of Power* in January and February 1876. These are of such obvious interest that we reproduce three of them: in addition to Mr. Webb-Peploe's, one by the Rev. G. R. Thornton, and the other by an American speaker, Mr. Murray Shipley—who presumably had been associated with Mr. Pearsall Smith in his ministry in this country. The fourth address reported was also by this speaker; and Figgis refers to both his addresses and illustrations as "striking." Of Mr. Thornton the same chronicler writes: "The Rev. George Thornton, the essence of kindness and geniality, did a good work in Bengeo, and then for years at his beautiful church in Kensington. As one of those whose words at Oxford brought Canon Battersby into liberty it is natural to hear of his being at Keswick."

Next comes a message of exceptional interest, by Canon Harford-Battersby, founder of the Convention. Yet it is not a "Keswick" address—for not one of his is reported! Apart from the fact that he was chairman rather than a speaker, the selection of addresses reproduced was very limited before the publication of *The Story of Keswick*, 1892–4, and the fuller report, *The Keswick Week* from 1895 onward. Brief summaries are often given; but these are not very satisfying! So we are grateful for this article, appearing in *The Christian's Pathway of Power*, December 1877, in which the Canon sets forth lucidly the secret of holiness. It may be added that he exemplified in his own life all that "Keswick" proclaimed. A very reserved man, he was truly saintly even before his liberating experience at Oxford. His very presence was a benediction. In his student days his tutor said he "had the ten commandments written on his face." And Dr. J. Elder Cumming, writing in *The Keswick Convention* on "The Founders and Some Leaders," says of him: "I remember some of his short but glowing words spoken from the chair. I saw something of the home life at the vicarage. Most of all I remember his face, which continually brings back to me the language of Acts 6: 15, they 'saw his face as it had been the face of an angel.' No other face I have ever seen has expounded for me that verse; but his did!"

We have already given an 1879 address of Chas. A. Fox, but must include another, concerning which his biographer, Miss Sophia Nugent—herself an important figure at Keswick in those formative years, and a leader of the ladies' meetings—writes: "Perhaps some will remember an hour in the Keswick Convention in 1879 when, in dwelling on the verse, 'Except a corn of wheat...' a moment nearer to the opened heaven of Pentecost than any other we can recall seemed to break over the bowed audience." Miss Nugent later quotes an anonymous visitor to that year's Convention: "Then one day there was granted an hour, as near what the Upper Room must have been on the Day of Pentecost as any I have ever known, when he spoke on 'Except a corn of wheat . . .' New yielding to the Master for the 'much fruit' solemnised that day."

Another honoured name associated with the pre-Keswick Conventions is that of Pasteur Theodore Monod, from Paris. Small of stature, with an aesthetic appearance and vivacious personality, he spoke fluently in English—but with many a quaint turn of phrase. On his several visits to Keswick he exercised a great influence. Of the address entitled "With the Whole Heart," delivered in 1882, Figgis says, "The teaching that rung in most memories after that Convention came from the voice of Theodore Monod. So eager were people to hear him that when the editor of one of our religious papers was asked if he would send a reporter to Keswick, he answered, 'If Pasteur Monod is coming, yes; otherwise, no.' I am not sure that it would be easy to indicate this unique charm. Yet two or three extracts may suffice to illustrate the force and freshness of his words . . ." and he quotes from the message here reproduced in full.

The Rev. George Grubb was one of the several—like George Macgregor and Harrington Lees—who first went to Keswick rather suspicious of its teaching, and there "entered into blessing," and later became speakers on its platform. He was the first to be sent abroad as a "Keswick deputation" speaker—a most fruitful aspect of the Convention's ministry from those days right up to the present. Mr. Grubb travelled widely as an "ambassador at large" of Keswick, and was greatly used of God, especially in India, Ceylon and Australia, where scenes akin to Revival attended his ministry—for he was a fiery evangelist as well as Convention speaker. It was said that over two hundred young people went to the mission field from Australia as a result of his ministry there. On his infrequent "return home" visits to Keswick he invariably had a stimulating effect; and his message on "The Soul-Thirst of Jesus" in 1889 made a profound impression. Figgis describes it as "one of the most notable utterances of these years."

"Phenomenal" is not too strong a word to describe the influence of Dr. Andrew Murray upon Keswick. For the extraordinary fact is, that this influence—as powerful as that of any man upon the movement—was exercised in one year's ministry only. He had attended the Convention as a visitor in 1882, while a student in this country; and a testimony to blessing received appeared over his initials in *The Christian's Pathway of Power*. He was then, however, unknown. Afterward, through his books—written in Afrikaans and translated into English—he became renowned as an exceptionally gifted exponent of the same teaching as at Keswick, and accordingly his visit of 1895 was keenly anticipated. It is an understatement to say that he stirred the hearts of all: such was the impression he made that, at the Saturday morning prayer-meeting, the whole congregation stood in a spontaneous token of respect and honour, as he left to catch his train. It was, says Sloan, "a unique expression of gratitude for a ministry in which to a wonderful degree the power of God had possessed and overshadowed the human instrument."

In his introduction to *The Keswick Week* of that year, the Rev. Evan Hopkins says concerning Dr. Murray's ministry: "One address stands out beyond all others. It was on 'The Way to the Higher Life. . . .' In the silent after-meeting which followed many said there, 'We can, we can'" (i.e., drink the cup of death to the self-life). Both Figgis and Sloan consider, however, that Friday's address surpassed even this. "Friday was the crowning day; and Mr. Murray's, surely, the crowning address," says the former; while Sloan observes, "In the report of that year the first of these addresses, 'The Pathway to the Higher Life' is described as the one address that stands out beyond all others. Certainly the power of God was wondrously present that evening; but the writer in looking back forty years feels that the crowning impression came on the Friday evening, and through the words, 'That Christ may be All in All.' It was an unforgettable night; the heavens were opened, and we saw visions of God!" Both addresses, accordingly, are reproduced here—the first in this section, and the second in the next (p. 425).

Another address by Evan Hopkins, "The Path and the Power," from the Convention of 1897, might be called "Keswick in a nutshell," for the very essence of Keswick teaching is here summarised in masterly fashion.

Canon W. Hay Aitken was renowned as an evangelist who specialised in conducting parochial missions within the Anglican church. It was therefore a surprise to some when he became a Convention speaker: nevertheless on several occasions at Keswick his messages were in great power. Of his message on "Thirsty Christians," in 1902, *The Keswick Week says*, "His words came clothed with the living fire of the Holy Ghost."

Like Evan Hopkins, the Rev. E. W. Moore was one of the small gathering at Curzon Chapel in 1873 which had such momentous results. He was present also at Oxford and Brighton, and was greatly valued at Keswick, although "his condition of health prevented his attending with the same regularity as that of some of the other leaders; but there was always a remarkable power and freshness in his ministry when he did come." In 1905, the year of the Welsh Revival, when its wider outreach was profoundly felt at Keswick, he gave the message on "Ordeal by Fire," after which Dr. Pierson, who was to have given the second address, rose and said that it was no longer the time for addresses; it was the time for confessions. "And sacrificing his own address with a self-forgetfulness that seems ever more and more to characterise him, he himself led the way. The effect will never be forgotten by those who witnessed it. It seemed to give an outlet long desired to the pent-up feelings of the preceding days. From all parts of the great tent men and women, young and old, gentle and simple, professional and lay, rose to their feet to confess the convicting power of the Spirit of judgment and the Spirit of burning. . . ."

A scholar whose books are still highly valued, Dr. Griffith Thomas had been vicar of St. Paul's, Portman Square, and Principal of Wycliffe Hall, Oxford, before his departure from this country for Canada, in response to a "missionary call" to become Professor of Systematic Theology at Wycliffe College, Toronto. He continued to visit Keswick fairly frequently, however, and his addresses always appealed strongly to both heart and mind. His sermon in St. John's Church, Keswick, on the opening Sunday of the Convention week in 1907, "Knowing and Showing," emphasises two essential elements in the Keswick message.

Evan Hopkins delighted to declare that santification is a "crisis followed by a process," and his teaching is most explicit in the address on this theme delivered in 1907. He spoke in very similar fashion scores of times: here is the quintessence of Keswick!

One of the few Methodists—other than Dr. Charles Inwood—to take a prominent part at Keswick, the Rev. J. Gregory Mantle spoke on several occasions between 1901 and 1911, after which he took up a ministerial appointment in America. He had accomplished a remarkable ministry, especially among men, in one of the "toughest" districts of south-east London; and his Convention addresses were frequently illustrated by incidents or experiences from this work. In 1908 he spoke on "Identification with Christ"—a characteristic Keswick theme.

It is fitting to give next another address by Charles Inwood, "The Transfigured Life," delivered in 1913. Concerning this, the Rev. Hubert Brooke—revered veteran from the early Conventions of 1881 onward—said at the Thursday evening meeting: "This morning in this tent some of us had a vision that seemed to reach further up and further out and further in than any of us had seen before. . . . I speak for myself, and I am pretty sure I speak for many, when I say that this morning God showed us things we had scarcely dreamed were possible, that they should be just real. . . ."

As the name of Evan Hopkins dominates the first four decades of the Convention, so that of J. Stuart Holden became paramount in the subsequent score of years. Indeed, for a time he occupied an even greater eminence, by presiding over most of the meetings, as well as over the Council—a dual responsibility Evan Hopkins had eschewed, exercising his authority rather as "the power behind the throne," as Chairman of the Council. It might be explained that, for the first eight years of the Convention, Canon Harford-Battersby acted as Chairman at all the meetings, as convener: it was not until later that a Council was formed. After his death, a succession of eminent laymen served as Chairmen of the Convention, until Dr. Holden's time, when the duty of presiding over the gatherings was vested in the Council, being shared between the Chairman and certain Council members—a practice still followed.

Dr. Holden—as he became—was a most keenly appreciated speaker from 1902 until 1934, and Chairman of the Council from 1924 until 1930. He was a man of engaging personality and exceptional gifts, with a mellifluous voice and persuasive manner. He exercised a most influential ministry in the West End of London as vicar of the renowned St. Paul's Church, Portman Square; and as a Convention speaker he was widely known in America as well as throughout Great Britain. Two addresses reveal his keen understanding of the spiritual problems and situations confronting many Christian people—"The Faith Christ Seeks," delivered in 1912, shows penetrating discernment between true and spurious faith; and "But If Not . . ." created a stir in 1914, and the outbreak of war a few weeks later seemed to impart a prophetic quality to it.

To W. Graham Scroggie belongs the distinction of having delivered the Bible Readings at Keswick more frequently than any other man in the Convention's history—not even excepting Hubert Brooke, whose especial province was the Bible Readings (see p. 409). No fewer than twelve times did Dr. Scroggie fulfil this arduous and responsible ministry at Keswick. He first spoke at Keswick in 1912, and ten years later delivered the pertinent admonition "Now, Then, Do It!" This was the year when Douglas Brown's message on "The Bleating of the Sheep" evoked so remarkable a response (see p. 30); and Graham Scroggie's stimulating exhortation proved very apposite. Canon F. J. Horsefield, himself a widely-known Convention speaker of those days, wrote in *The Life of Faith*: "There could hardly be a greater contrast between two speakers than exists between Mr. Douglas Brown and Mr. Graham Scroggie—the one so fiery, so passionate in his presentation of the truth; and the other so quiet, so logical, and withal so forceful. And yet both were mightily used to bring hosts to a definite decision for Christ on the same day." Tall and slim, with a didactic manner and dry Scots' humour, this eminent Baptist excelled in exposition of "the Word." Sometimes the born preacher in him took command, however, and he spoke with compelling fervour—as he did on this memorable occasion.

We have already acknowledged Keswick's debt to speakers from America, and during the past three decades none has come to its platform more frequently than Dr. Donald Grey Barnhouse of Philadelphia. A veritable giant, with a voice to match his

magnificent physique, he is exceptionally forceful and contro-
versial for a Keswick speaker. Always enthralling to hear, he has
a startling way of expressing spiritual truth—and after the meetings is invariably surrounded by eager young people, arguing and
explaining! He has frequently delivered series of addresses—
either the morning Bible Readings, or in the afternoons—during
the past quarter century. In 1938 he scrapped what he had
prepared for his final message, and spent all night writing—for
he usually wrote out and read his addresses—what proved to be a
most challenging portrayal of the truly Christian life. No more
stimulating address, no clearer presentation of the practical outworking of the Keswick message, has ever been given by this
dynamic visitor from the United States.

To complete this section, a complementary address on "The
Everyday Christian Life" recalls the ministry at Keswick of one
whose career there was meteoric—Mr. Fred Mitchell, a chemist
from Bradford, long recognised as a layman of exceptional spiritual
gifts. Very soon after his first visit to Keswick he became a
speaker, and within a few years was Chairman of the Council.
In that capacity he succeeded the beloved W. H. Aldis, as previously he had succeeded him in the office of Home Director of the
China Inland Mission. Of middle height and rounded figure,
Fred Mitchell consciously modelled himself on Stuart Holden,
whom he greatly admired, and whom indeed he resembled, in
person and manner of speaking. Alas, his ministry was untimely
cut off, at the zenith of its power and fruitfulness, when he lost his
life in a plane disaster. His series of Bible Readings on "The
Lamb upon His Throne," in 1952, marked the peak of his ministry
at Keswick; but these are so inter-related that no one of them
could be reproduced alone. Several others of his addresses linger
in the memory; but the one selected, from the Convention of
1948, has proved of greatest blessing to the largest number.

Like all Keswick speakers, Mr. Mitchell would stress that consecration is not merely an act to be looked back upon; a date to be
cited as a landmark in one's spiritual history. Consecration is
essentially a matter to be expressed in the everyday life; in the
trivial round, the common task. Consecration which has not
abiding effects is spurious. Keswick insists that the crisis must be
followed by the process—a growing, deepening consecration unto
life's end.

THE CHRISTIAN'S WALK

Rev. H. W. Webb-Peploe, M.A.

S
T. PAUL shows us, in 1 Thessalonians 2: 11–13, the *object*, the *measure*, and the *ground* of the Christian's walk in this life, and sets forth clearly the purposes of God in calling us into His Kingdom now and into His glory hereafter. We are told in this passage to "walk worthy of God"; and when God speaks through His Word, it is for us to obey. St. Paul says of the Thessalonian Christians, "When ye received the Word of God, which ye heard of us, ye received it not as the word of men, but as it is in truth, the Word of God, which effectually worketh also in you that believe." Are you ready to bow before the Word of God? I ask you to let God speak to your souls now, directly from His Word, with every prejudice and preconceived opinion laid aside; and then that Word will effectually work in you that believe it.

In verse 12 the apostle says, "Walk worthy of God." This is the whole object of our teaching in these solemn gatherings, because we believe that God has called us to this. It is for this we come to exhort and comfort and charge every one of you (v. 11). We believe there is something far better to be had, even here upon earth, than most people think of, though they may be God's children. St. Paul speaks here of God's "calling" now. What did God call His people for? (See Rom. 8: 29, 30.) To absolute conformity to the image of Christ. Nothing less than this did He purpose, and with nothing less than this should we be content.

How far has this been fulfilled in us? Of course, *perfectly* it cannot be, until we stand before Him in glory. But we have yet to learn how far it may be attained in this life. Again we read, in 1 Corinthians 1: 9, that He "called us to fellowship . . ." that is, even now, upon earth. He has called us into fellowship with His Son, both in His sufferings and in His joys. There is something wrong with us if it is not so. Men kick against this teaching; they do not like to find how far below God's standard of holiness they are living. In Ephesians 1: 4 we are told that God called us to be holy *now*. This is God's great object in calling us. "And without blame"—not without spot, but without reproach of conscience. Colossians 3: 15, to "let the peace of God rule in your hearts." 1 Thessalonians 4: 7, God hath called us unto holiness; 1 Thessalonians 5: 23, 24, unto full sanctification; 2 Thessalonians 2: 13, 14, to the obtaining of the glory. This passage sets forth all the three—salvation, sanctification, and glory—as the purpose of God in calling us; while in 1 Peter 1: 2–15 we are absolutely called to be holy after the manner and standard of God himself. And that, surely, not only in heaven (for we *must* be holy there) but *now*, or why these exhortations?

In almost every epistle I find a command to be perfect. But people seem as much afraid of perfection as though it was some deadly disease that it is folly to seek after! All the apostles speak of perfection, and it is quite clear that God would have us "go on unto perfection," moment by moment, "until we all come in the unity of the faith . . . unto a perfect man, unto the measure of the stature of the fulness of Christ" (Eph. 4: 13). How nearly we may reach it, I cannot profess to say; but that almost all Christians have been hitherto living infinitely below their privileges and calling must be clear to every honest student of Scripture. 1 Peter 2: 9 is clearly not a prospect for heaven, but for earth—"to show forth the virtues (see margin) of Him who hath called you." And consider 1 Peter 5: 10, "The God of all grace . . . *make you perfect*." The meaning of this word is, restoring, or setting straight, or mending—a broken bone, or anything else (see Mark 1: 19; Gal. 6: 1, etc.), *i.e.*, establishing in you a fitness for labour. This is quite a different word from that which speaks of Jesus "being made perfect" in Hebrews 5: 9, and of which St. Paul speaks in Philippians 3: 12. There *is* a perfection which is the starting-point of all true service of God, and this is the proper meaning of the words "make you perfect," after which there are three things which God will do for you—"stablish, strengthen, settle you."

There are three Greek words used for "perfection" in the New Testament, and they are all very different in their meaning. The first means setting the man upright and adjusting him for labour, which is the perfection spoken of in 2 Corinthians 13: 9–11; 2 Timothy 3: 17; 1 Peter 5: 10, etc., and is the preliminary gift of God, without which you cannot "walk worthy of God": and this I believe you may have at once if Christians, and without it you cannot get the others. The second, is that perfection of manhood which makes you fit for hard work and fighting—able to take your part in "the good fight of faith," and to "press toward the mark," etc. (see Phil. 3: 15; Heb. 5: 14; 6: 1, and other references). The third, is that absolute perfection to which we are bidden to look forward, and which can only be attained to when "we shall be like Him, for we shall see Him as He is." But with "this hope in *Him*," are we "purifying ourselves even as He is really pure"? What a glorious thought for the believer, that he is called to "walk worthy of God," and that "faithful is He that calleth you, who also will do it" (1 Thess. 5: 24). What do you know about it in experience? God help you to search and see why you have never had this walk in you.

So much for the purpose of God the Father in calling us. Let us proceed to mark, secondly, what was the purpose of the Son in dying to redeem you—so that here again we may exhort you to "walk worthy of God." Did He die simply to take away your guilt, and then leave you to walk with a sort of shuffling gait through the world, which should make the godless ones mock at your claim of salvation? No, an upright walk was His purpose for His people—a walk that should bring glory to His name. Read 2 Corinthians 5: 15, "He died . . . that they which live should not henceforth live unto themselves, but unto Him who died for them." See! universal dedication of all to Jesus is His will concerning you—a life that tells plainly whose you are, and by whose power you live from moment to moment. He "gave Himself for our sins, that He might deliver us from this present evil world" (Gal. 1: 4). Oh, study the purposes of God, for He would have you study them; and when you have studied them, yield yourselves to be conformed to them. For if you knew the purpose of God in giving His Son Jesus Christ, and the purpose of the Son in giving Himself to die, we should not have young ladies asking, "*May* I go to balls and theatres?" and "*Must* I give up this and that pleasure?" and young men trying how far they can possibly go with the world and yet be Christians. What do you know of deliverance from the world? Again, look well at Titus 2: 14 and Ephesians 2: 10, and then ask yourselves the solemn question, how far you are "walking worthy" of God the Son, and fulfilling the purposes for which He *gave* Himself for you?"

We now pass on to consider, thirdly, the purposes of God the Spirit in descending to earth to take possession of our souls. When Jesus passed into the heavens, He sent down the Holy Ghost, and He has taken the place of the Saviour among men, but with this distinction, that He works *in* us, as well as *for* us. And what was to be His work? What was the object of the Holy Ghost in coming down at Pentecost? Consider these things on your knees, and I fear many of you will soon come to the cross and say, "O God, I have utterly failed to apprehend the riches of the glory of Thine inheritance in the saints," and you will, moreover, have found out the cause of your failure.

Romans 5: 5; 14: 17; 15: 13—here are the *gifts* of the Holy Ghost to those who receive Him as they ought. "The love of God shed abroad in your hearts." "Righteousness and peace and

joy"—and then "full joy and full peace in believing," and all
these through the power of the Holy Ghost. 2 Corinthians 3: 17—
here is liberty for the believer now; liberty from fear, from wrath,
and from the power of sin; liberty to worship, to know God, to
serve Him and follow Him—yea, liberty such as no tongue can
describe: not merely salvation from hell, which some poor
Christians seem satisfied with. And then what follows? Why!
that we are to be "changed into the same image. . . ." (v. 18) as
by the Spirit of the Lord.

But even that is not all, for 2 Timothy 1: 7 takes us one step
further, and tells us that "God *has given* unto us the Spirit of power,
and of love, and of a sound mind." What do you know of all
this in your daily experience, and of that "unction from the
Holy One" of which we read in 1 John 2: 20? Surely if all these
things were in us and abounded, they would make us that we
should be "neither barren nor unfruitful in the knowledge of our
Lord Jesus Christ," but we should walk worthy of God, who hath
called us unto His kingdom (here) and His glory (hereafter). God
intended me to be *so close* to Jesus, when He bought me, as to have
my whole heart taken up with Jesus. He meant me to have no
cares, because Jesus would deliver me from them all (1 Pet. 5: 7);
and no trials, but such as Jesus would sweeten and support me
through. And now the Spirit is come, and there is power, joy,
liberty, peace, love, and a sound mind, all for *us*, in Jesus. This
is the Father's call; this the Son's gift—yes! the *blood-gift* of the
Son of God to you and me, for it took the blood of God to purchase
it for you (Acts 20: 28). And it is the Spirit's power which makes
it all ours to enjoy. But, alas, you and I have slandered the blessed
Word of God, by doubting whether such things were possible;
doubting whether our Father ever purposed such joys; whether
our Jesus really purposed such inestimable blessings for us; and
whether the Spirit could ever make them to be ours in this life.
But such are the solemn declarations of Scripture, and as St.
Paul says of the Thessalonians, so may it be said of all now present,
"When ye received the Word of God, ye received it not as the
word of men, but as it is in truth, the Word of God, which effectually worketh also in you that believe."

THE DEPENDENCE OF FAITH

Murray Shipley

WE HAVE heard of Christ as the Healer of sin; now let us speak of Christ as a present Saviour from sin. Turn to Exodus 33: 12–16. When God would have Moses go and walk a new life of faith, He said to him, "I will be with thee." It is the stepping out upon the untried experience of a new nature, that is the step of faith. When Peter stepped down from the ship to walk on the water, he stepped out upon an unstable element, which he had not proved, simply on Christ's word, "Come." And while he looked to Christ, and expected to walk, he was upheld. Moses in the same way stepped out on God's promise, "I will go with thee." We want to be a separate people; it is the presence of Christ that makes us a separate people (Exod. 33: 16).

Look at Joshua 1: 4–9. When Joshua enters on a new experience, the great promise was "the presence of the Lord"; and the great command to him was, "Be strong, and of a good courage." In these verses the necessity of being strong and of a good courage is proved by the frequent repetition of the same command. Observe the simplicity of the command and the promise. If the Lord went with them all would be well; and if Joshua was strong and courageous in doing the Lord's work, all would also be well. For this success, a full surrender is needed. Joshua was a consecrated man; he followed the Lord fully. We have to take the fact, the blessing, the power, and the experience. See him, again, before Jericho (Joshua 5: 13). Like Abraham, he was fully persuaded that what God had promised, He was able also to perform. Look at the last chapter of Joshua, and note the way in which he spoke of the Lord's dealings with him, after his beautiful life of trust and faith. After his long life, he gathered all the tribes together. How solemnly would they listen to his last charge! "Thus saith the Lord God of Israel, *I* took . . . *I* gave . . . *I* sent . . . *I* brought . . . *I* destroyed . . . *I* delivered . . ." I believe in a *Christian theocracy*. I believe in the Kingdom of Christ; and that Christ intends to rule over us as a King by His power.

God sometimes gave Joshua the victory entirely by His own

power, and sometimes He gave it in making use of an instrument. We cannot over-estimate the importance of realising the presence of Christ not only to meet our great needs, but also our little ones. You have, it may be, visited the large machine-shops, and seen there, moved by hydraulic power, the great sledge-hammer which, when at work, can flatten either a bar of iron or crack an egg-shell. So, also, the Lord's power is calculated to overcome great or small obstacles. Christ's power will not be put forth once for all, but He must be taken as a present Saviour to meet present trials and temptations, moment by moment. Theodore Monod, of Paris, said lately, This is an age of materialism and of logic; modern science seeks to trace everything to its causes. So we, as Christians, need to give the enquiring world a holy life, which it can read at a glance, and it will trace it up to its first cause— God. I must ever look to the smitten Rock for power, and trace up all deliverance to the death and resurrection of the Lord Jesus Christ.

We may have wanted a clearer mental conception of how we are delivered, but I have learned that I have greater strength and victory by realising Christ as my present Saviour *this* moment, and then the *next* moment, without thinking how it is so—not relying on *thought*, but on *Him;* not taking up as it were a sponge full of water in the morning, to last through the day, but realising Him as the living spring in my heart, moment by moment, delivering me from this little temper, or that great temptation. We must choose whether we will trust the Lord as did the children of Israel, or as Joshua trusted Him. The children of Israel trusted the Lord in part, and their leader Joshua in part; but Joshua trusted in the Lord, and in Him alone. The Man with the drawn sword came to fight *His own* enemies.

From one of the headlands of our American coast, during a great tempest I saw the wrecks of ten vessels, while not one of the ships in the harbour was damaged. This was owing to their anchors. In a great storm, if the anchor "is sure" in that it does not break, and "steadfast" in that it does not move, then the vessel is safe. So of our hope, "for we are saved by hope." If our whole being, body, soul, and spirit, is anchored on Jesus, then self will abdicate the throne, and give place to Jesus that He may take possession, and reign in and over us as a present Saviour from sin—and we shall live in independence of the world.

There is one trait in our character which we must be ready and glad to yield up, and that is—our cherished independence. The word *independence* is a favourite word in these modern times. It is written on the heart of every child of Adam: but God is going to teach us the blessings of *dependence*. We are going to give up our impulsive and strong will, and be taught by the Lord His gentleness. *We* are going to abdicate the throne, and accept Christ as our king to rule over us all the time. Joshua knew he could not trust a nation of slaves; and I know I cannot trust this weak will, this mental understanding. I forgot to apply this truth, but I trust Jesus keeping behind His truth. We hold the "shield of faith" between us and the enemy, and send up songs of praise from behind it. We must be utterly and entirely dependent on the Lord, if we would have His strength instead of our weakness. The Lord teach us this close *intimate* dependence of faith in Himself, which knows in whom it trusts while independent of the world! He will then lead us gently. Our lips must cease to talk about people; we must leave off gratifying self; our feet must walk in His very footsteps; and, as we say, "Crown Him Lord of all"; let us put Him on the throne, and, yielding the sceptre to His own hands of wisdom and love, let us crown Christ as our abiding Deliverer from sin; and then, though *without* Him we can do nothing, with our King enthroned in our heart we shall have complete and constant victory.

TRUST AND OBEY

Rev. George R. Thornton, M.A.

Whatsoever He saith unto you, do it—John 2: 5.

SOME people think that a life of full trust means a do-nothing life. Instead of that, it means a life of implicit obedience. It is not to do *some things*, but to do "whatsoever He saith." Jesus has "learned obedience," and knows the blessedness of it; and we shall, too, if we follow these words, "Whatsoever He saith unto you, do it." Who said it? His mother, who knew so much about that dear son of hers that He would never ask them to do anything that was not for their good. She knew it was well worth doing what He said. When we know as much of Him as His mother did, we shall not only long to do everything He saith ourselves, but we shall wish to lead others to do the same. To obey is such a happy thing, when it is to obey Jesus! *Obey at once*, and it will be comparatively easy; but if you wait a moment, it becomes hard. Wait a little longer, and stop to reason about it, difficulties are sure to arise, and it will become very difficult indeed; therefore obey at once.

His command was, "Fill the waterpots with water." Mary did not know what He would say; but in verse 7 we read that the servants, following the apparently strange command of Jesus, "filled them up to the brim." Look at those 18-gallon waterpots! six of them. Think how long it would take to fill such large vessels. It was a great deal of trouble, no doubt; but they thought of that word "whatsoever," and they did not mind the trouble; off they went, and could not help filling them "up to the brim." Would not some of you have only half filled them? Oh! let us follow them in this. Let us not obey Jesus in part, but with a "brimful obedience."

Then He said, "Draw out now!"—what! this water? How strange to draw water for the governor of the feast! "Whatsoever He saith—do it"; they did it. They took the water, nay, the wine, "and bare it." If they had reasoned or refused, there must have been delay, or no wine at all. If they had only half filled the waterpots, they would only have had half as much. They were able to trust a stranger! Oh! Christians, won't you trust your Friend?

Now about obedience. Dwell upon that word "He." "What-soever *He* saith." If asked to do "whatsoever" some people told you, you would say, "I would rather not." But of another you would say, "I would do anything for that man." The more you do what *He* saith, the more you will long to do it, and the more you will find service worth doing. Oh, we need to make so many apologies to our heavenly Father, to the loving Saviour, and to the tender Comforter for speaking—as if this were such a difficult thing to do. The angels don't think so. I think the archangels in heaven must say, "Why are these people speaking so much about consecration? It is such a simple and happy thing to obey Jesus." The attitude our soul ought to assume is well expressed in Hebrews 12: 2, "Looking unto Jesus, the Author and the Finisher of *the* faith "—not of "our faith." The Lord Jesus Christ has lived and walked this life before us. As He had faith and trust, He wants us to have it too. We fathers know very well how to manage our children. We see that little girl with an unripe apple; we know that it will do her harm, and we wish to take it away; but that apple is the most precious thing she has got just now. We take a ripe peach, and hold it up for her, and say, "Look here!" She will drop the apple, and gladly clutch at the peach. The child does not remember what is gone. She has got something better now. Just so the Lord Jesus Christ offers you His own dear self, and as you look by faith to Jesus, the things that thus are so precious to you, shrink into nothing. Talk of surrender, of giving up! look to Jesus, and what you thought would cost you so much, you will scarcely think of at all. "Looking unto Jesus" so satisfies all our desires. We see His beauty—His altogether loveliness, and our hankering after worldly things goes.

We need to keep "looking unto Jesus," moment by moment. You must look moment by moment if it is to be an effectual "looking." You cannot take a look which will last for the future. If we want to know the time, we look at the clock, but that look will not avail in a few minutes—we have to look again. And so we must keep looking continually to Jesus. The Psalmist says of the good man, "He shall not be afraid of evil tidings, his heart is fixed, trusting in the Lord" (Ps. 112: 7). The man who trusts in the Lord will have "evil tidings," but he will not be afraid of them. There will be trouble, but he will not be moved. I have had more trouble since I knew Jesus better, and have trusted Him more, but, oh! what a happy year it has been. We do not say whether there will be more trouble or less, but this we say, "He that trusteth in the Lord shall not be afraid of evil tidings." It is such a blessed experience, that if an archangel were to tell us we were to have no more trouble, we would not thank him. Christ

learned obedience by suffering; should you shrink from it? You
never will be a machine, and if you wish to be, I do not. Why
not? Because I hope for the companionship of God throughout
eternity, and I trust He wants for His companion one who, after
being freely pardoned, has been disciplined down here in His own
sweet way.

"His heart is fixed." We can't have a stock of grace; we want
our hearts just fixed on Him who gives grace. What the Lord
wants is to keep us "chronic beggars." All you have you receive
from Jesus. It ought to be like this—I am a poor beggar, but I
have my hand on the open purse of a true friend by my side, who
is both able and willing to supply my need, and he keeps telling
me to take as much as I want. The more I take, the better he likes
it. We shall always have enough moment by moment, but we
shall never have more than enough for the moment. We should
keep our hand on the open purse. If our will is given to Jesus,
and our heart is fixed, then when evil tidings come we shall say
it is all right, because God sends them. The moment a Christian's
heart is *un*fixed, and he begins to doubt and murmur and regret
God's will, he is on the high road to distrust and unbelief. But
you say, "I think if the speaker knew my circumstances, he would
not speak like that." Dear friend, the more trouble I knew you
had, the more I should tell you to repose on Jesus. If you had
very many troubles, and the Lord was to say, "I only can undertake half of them," your case would indeed be a sad one. But
He is willing to take every trouble from you, and He does it with
such love. If one were to come and say to us, "I owe £10,000,"
we should be anxious on his account; but, if he added, "I can
put my hand on £20,000 at any moment," we should cease to be
anxious. Jesus says, "Let me undertake all." But perhaps you
say, "I have no faith." This is not true, though you may have
very little. Perhaps you think you must wait until you have
strong faith. Where do you find this in the Word of God? "If
you have faith as a grain of mustard seed . . ." Jesus says.

It is with the faith you have got you are to trust Him. Perhaps
you say, "I pray for faith." Quite right. "Lord, increase our
faith!" But never use that prayer in the way that some of you
have done. It is a responsible thing to pray, "Lord, increase my
faith." It implies that you are using all the faith that you have,
and desire more. Look at that porter standing among a heap of
luggage; he says to you, "Help me to move this," but he is doing
nothing himself. Would you help him? You would feel, his
business is to do it himself. You answer him, "No, my friend;
let me see you use your two hands first, and I will gladly help
you." So is it in asking the Lord Jesus to increase our faith; we

must make use of the faith we have, then we may pray that prayer; but if we do not exercise the faith we have, we are almost mocking God in asking for more. Put all in the hand of Jesus. Do you still say, "I can't trust." Remember, unbelief is *sin*. You may bring it as sin to Jesus for Him to remove. He will undertake even this. Throw yourself at His feet, with little or much faith, with emotion or no emotion, but do it now.

HOW TO WALK MORE CLOSELY WITH GOD

Canon T. D. Harford-Battersby, M.A.

THIS is, and ever must be, the question of questions to an awakened and converted soul. To others it may be enough to get a glimpse of God now and then, if that can be called a glimpse of Him which is only the bare reflection of His glory in the mirror of the mind, from those revelations of it which are to be found in His works and in His Word: but if we have indeed tasted of His grace, and understood something of His love to us in Christ, and been brought into real personal communion with Him by His Spirit, we cannot any longer be content with any such glimpses or glances of His glory at a distance; we must be brought nearer; the cry of our hearts must be—

> Nearer, my God, to Thee:
> Nearer to Thee.

It is a bad sign when this ceases to be our quest. There is a condition of soul, indeed, which is not only attainable, but which is set before us in the Scriptures as the only proper condition of the believing soul—that of rest in Christ, when we have found Him for whom our soul longed, and know that in Him we *have been* "brought nigh" (Eph. 2: 13); that "in Him we have eternal life" (1 John 5: 11); perfectly reconciled to our offended God by His precious blood, and covered by His spotless righteousness. This is one thing: and how great a thing those only know who have been brought out of their weary wanderings and tossings to and fro, in the vain search after justification by their own righteousness, thus to rest, in perfect peace with God, because of what the Lord has done for them. But it is another thing altogether, after having found this peace, to walk with God closely in the path of daily life. When we started out on this course, our minds enlightened by that measure of spiritual light which enabled us to see Christ as our justification, and our hearts set on the attainment of the heavenly prize, we thought that the gratitude we felt at that moment, for the great mercies of God we had experienced, would be enough to carry us onward always in an even course, following our Master Jesus, and obedient to the will of our heavenly Father. But soon we found that our "first love" was apt to get chilled, and that the world and sin, which we thought we had renounced for ever, were constantly asserting their claim to come back into our hearts; and our communion got broken, and we lost that blessed peace and joy and comfort which we felt when first we "saw the Lord"; and so, again and again it may be, many of us have been brought to cry out with that sweet singer whose hymns have been so often our solace and delight—

> Oh, for a closer walk with God,
>   A calm·and heavenly frame;
>   A light to shine upon the road
>   That leads me to the Lamb.

And yet, on the other hand, it ought not to be supposed that such failures as that expressed by Cowper in this beautiful hymn, are a necessary part of the experience of every Christian. Can it be necessary for us, after we have started fair on the heavenly road, with a well-grounded assurance of our acceptance, and a clear consciousness of the divine favour, to lose all this, our comfort and our joy, and go along pining for—

>   A calm and heavenly frame;
>   A light to shine upon the road
>   That leads me to the Lamb.

Is it a part of the divine appointment that we should so fall back from our first faith, and our first love; that we should in whole companies and congregations be asking, in melancholy despondency—

> Where is the blessedness I knew
>   When first I saw the Lord?
>   Where is the soul-reviving view
>   Of Jesus and His Word?
>
> What peaceful hours I once enjoyed!
>   How sweet their memory still;
>   But they have left an aching void
>   The world can never fill.

God forbid! The beauty of the words, the accuracy with which they depict a condition of soul with which we and many others are familiar, ought never to make us fall in with the supposition that this is an essential part of Christian experience. The commonness of it should not be allowed to blunt our sense of the dishonour it reflects on the character of our God and Father, that His children—the children of such a King—should "go mourning all their days." It is not from Him surely, but from Satan, His enemy and ours, that this grievous state of things proceeds, either that Christians should be found, so many of them, in the condition described in this hymn, or that they should attempt to palliate their sin and failure by ascribing to it an assumed necessity—in other words, to God, the author and cause of holiness alone.

Thus I desire at the outset of our enquiry to guard myself and my readers against two opposite errors: the one of assuming that we have reached, or can reach, a state of such absolute perfection as that we should go beyond the condition of desiring a more perfect walk with God; the other of assuming that we must necessarily fall back, after conversion, like Israel in the wilderness, instead of going onward in a steady progress from strength to strength, in the direction which God would lead us. The one error is as great, I believe, as the other; and there can be no question as to which is the most common at the present day.

To return now to our question, "How to walk more closely with God."

In the first place, it will be necessary to define more particularly what is meant by "walking with God." The expression is a Scriptural one. It is used of Enoch and of Noah (Gen. 5: 24 and 6: 9); and of the tribe of Levi, in the days of its first consecration to God: "The law of truth was in his mouth, and iniquity was not found in his lips: he walked with me in peace and equity, and did turn many away from iniquity" (Mal. 2: 6). We also find the expression in that memorable passage of the prophet Micah, when, in answer to the question, "Wherewith shall I come before the Lord, and bow myself before the high God?" this answer is given: "He hath showed thee, O man, what is good; and what doth the Lord require of thee, but to do justly, and to love mercy, and to walk humbly with thy God?" (Micah 6: 8). It is evident that what is meant by the expression in all these passages is, to lead a life of constant communion with God, in which God is made our intimate associate and friend, in which we consult Him upon everything, and in which all is given up to His direction and control.

None will deny that this is what we are called to in Christ. For this purpose the Son of God was manifested; for this purpose the Holy Spirit has been sent; for this purpose the Holy Scriptures have been given, and the sacraments of God's grace. It is for this that God deals out His benefits and His chastisements to us. All, all are for this end, to lead us into closer fellowship with our God, to know Him, to serve Him better; never to go away from His side, but to share in the loving communications of His grace all our days. And, let me add, what would the Church be if its members were thus habitually walking with God! What would some of us be if this were more the attitude and posture of our souls day by day, hour by hour, moment by moment?

But the practical difficulties which we all feel in the way of such a walk are many and great. To laymen and clergymen alike it is a path beset with hindrances, which seem often to make it impossible to continue steadfastly in it. The layman is oppressed with the cares of his family and of his business: a thousand things have to be attended to every day, which seem to have no connection with religion or with God's service; and these things dissipate the mind and draw it, in spite of every resolution and many prayers, away from Him who is truly acknowledged to be the centre and the life of the soul. The clergyman, on the other hand, may seem to one who superficially looks at his position to be far more hopefully placed in regard to such a walk. The duties of his calling impose upon him an obligation to be constantly occupied with matters which belong to God's kingdom, God's worship, God's service. He is a teacher and preacher of God's Word. He is bound by his ordination vows to be "diligent in prayer, and in reading of the Holy Scriptures, and in such studies as help to the knowledge of the same, laying aside the study of the world and the flesh." Surely then, he, if any, can walk with God all the day and every day. But every clergyman knows that the sacredness of his office, and the solemnity of his ordination vows, do not hinder the world and the flesh from constantly harassing and afflicting him, and that he is—certainly not less than others, in many cases much more—tempted to be "cumbered about many things," and in the cares which oppress him—the cares and burdens, it may be, connected with his family, or those which attend upon the due fulfilment of his ministerial office, among rich and poor, high and low—he often feels "sore let and hindered in running the race which is set before him."

But still, whether we be clergymen or laymen, let it never be said by us that such a life of communion is impossible. If the profession or occupation with which we have to do is a lawful one, if it falls under the head of those occupations which are necessary or useful for the good of men, or for the glory of God, it is possible, while abiding in that calling, to walk with God, and to bring forth the fruits of practical holiness.

Therefore the question, How to walk more closely with God? does not certainly imply of a necessity that you should exchange what is commonly called a secular calling for a spiritual one; all lawful callings may be spiritual, and what is looked upon as spiritual may be essentially secular, basely, palpably secular, under the garb of fancied spirituality.

Again, then, we come to the question, How can those who feel that their walk with God has been sadly too broken and intermittent, and that in this respect they have fallen very far short of their high calling as God's children, attain to a closer and more perfect walk?

The first thing must evidently be to go and tell God that you want this, and to ask Him to show you how it can be.

This is the first thing, I say, and I would lay stress upon it, as the *sine qua non*, because it is so easy to read books of devotion, study treatises upon the spiritual life, and go to one man after another for instruction as to the theory of holiness, and read your Bible too with diligence, and yet never go, in thorough honesty and simplicity, to God Himself, and say, "Lord, show me how I may walk more closely with Thee." Yet this must be done. No reading, or hearing, or meditation upon what you have read or heard, can do what even one hour's direct personal intercourse with God can do, in showing you where you have erred in the past, or what you need for the attainment of more perfect communion with Him. And when God has been thus honestly approached and His guidance sought, it may be He will show you either that the method you have been using for maintaining a holy walk is deficient, or that there is some cherished idol which needs to be given up, or that there has been a want of watchfulness and prayer.

Let us consider each of these points separately.

I. It may be that *your method has been defective*.

There is but one "way of holiness." It is that which God hath set up from of old. Its boundaries are clearly marked in His Word, so that "the wayfaring men, though fools, shall not err therein." But it is just here that we fail, that we are not willing to be as fools, but like to try our own hands upon this work, and construct a way for ourselves, of our own wisdom, instead of taking God's way. That way is a way of faith from beginning to end. We entered upon it when we came, guilty and vile, to Christ, and found pardon and cleansing through His blood. But we did not see then the extent of our need, or the sufficiency of the supply God has provided for our need; we did not know then the inveterate evil of indwelling sin, or the power of natural corruption; but as we went on we learnt this by sad experience. We saw God's law, holy, just, and good, and we saw that it was to be our rule of life. We struggled to keep it, but in vain; we were forced to say with the apostle, "To will is present with me, but how to perform that which is good I find not" (Rom. 7: 18). What then? Did we, in despair of self, yield ourselves to Him who is "able to make all grace abound toward us"? Did we give ourselves up to Christ, as "dead to sin" by His death, and "alive unto God" by His resurrection? If so, we took God's way of securing that which we needed; and I venture to assert, on the warrant of God's Word, that we were not disappointed in so doing. The Tenth Article of the Church teaches plainly, "We have no power to do good works pleasant and acceptable to God, without the grace of God by Christ preventing us, that we may have a good will, and working with us when we have that good will." This witness is true. "*We* have *no* power"; but in *Christ* we have *all* power. If, then, we are not looking to Christ and abiding in Him, we cannot but fail. We come again "under law," and sin gets the dominion; but let our motto be that of St. Paul, "Not I, but Christ" (Gal. 2 : 20), then how easy it is to please God! To walk with Him, how delightful!

Everything, in short, has been provided in Christ, through the foreknowledge and love of our heavenly Father, for our walking closely with Him (2 Pet. 1: 3). "His divine power," says the apostle, "hath given us all things that pertain unto life and godliness, through the knowledge of Him who hath called us to glory and virtue." The whole secret of a holy walk is here disclosed. First, there is an inexhaustible fountain from which our help comes—"His divine power." Second, a supply which is equal to all our needs—"all things that pertain unto life and godliness." Third, the method by which the supply is reached—"through the knowledge of Him who hath called us." This, then, is the great thing needed in order to attain a closer walk with God: it is to know more of Jesus Christ and the infinite resources which are treasured up in Him for our need. This, no doubt, is a knowledge which admits of continual increase. We knew but very little of the Lord when we went to Him at first for the pardon of our sins. We knew Him in one aspect of His character, in one of His many offices: but of all that He is to the saved soul, which rests and abides in Him day by day, we knew nothing, nor can we know, unless we make trial of His grace—ever fresh trial as our needs arise; going to Him with the same simple faith with which we first went to Him, and saying, "Lord, I need Thee: Thou art my strength and my salvation: I am nothing; Thou art all: Lord, I trust Thee now." Thus acting, our souls cannot but make ever fresh discoveries of the love and power of Jesus to save. We are kept in perfect peace in the most distracting circumstances, and He enables us to do His will and keep His commandments in such a way as to draw forth our wonder, while at the same time it brings us to His feet in adoring praise, as feeling that it is indeed

His presence within to which all the blessing, and so all the glory, is due.

This is God's method of walking with Him. May we each of us learn it more and more perfectly!

II. But God may show you that you have been *cherishing some idol in your heart.*

Cowper recognised this as a most common hindrance to the soul's communion with God when he wrote—

> The dearest idol I have known,
>   Whate'er that idol be,
> Help me to tear it from my heart,
>   And worship only Thee.

It is evident that this must be done if we are to have God as our Friend and Counsellor. "Can two walk together, except they be agreed?" (Amos 3: 3). The question answers itself—If sin is willingly entertained, God's company must be given up. He will not dwell in a heart defiled with idolatrous associations, where Mammon, or human praise, or sensuality, or some earthly love, is usurping the place which He is entitled to occupy within us. "If we have forgotten the name of our God, or stretched out our hands to a strange god; shall not God search this out? For He knoweth the secrets of the heart" (Ps. 44: 20, 21). Entire surrender to Him: the presentation of our whole being to Him, to be searched by His all-seeing eye, to be purified by the cleansing blood of Christ, to be sanctified to His service alone, and be kept by Him from all sin, is the essential condition of a holy walk. Obedience must ever be coupled with faith, if it is not more correct to say that it is an essential part of faith, as the apostle speaks of "the obedience of faith." To walk with God we must please Him. Enoch's walk with God is thus described in Hebrews 11, "that he pleased God"; and then it is added, "without faith it is impossible to please Him." His careful attention to God's requirements, which is implied in the expression "pleasing God," sprang, as it always must, out of perfect trust in Him. It was a saying Yes, promptly and cheerfully, to all that God said to him. If we are to be followers of holy Enoch we must do the same. Is there an Achan in our hearts, coveting and appropriating the "accursed thing," and so bringing "trouble" into our camp, and staying us from victory and from progress? The enemy of our peace must be slain without mercy. With our own hands, with all our heart and soul, we must put him to death, in the strength and under the inspiration of that Holy Spirit which "worketh mightily" in those who believe. And then once more will God, our God, be content to use us, and we shall go forward successfully under His will and favour.

III. Again, it may be God may show you that you have failed through *unwatchfulness*.

Your method may have been right, and your consecration complete, and you may have experienced many happy times of conscious fellowship with God, in service and in daily life; yet you have to acknowledge with shame that there have been sad seasons of dullness and spiritual gloom, when God, you felt, was grieved with you, and your joy in Him was impaired. And when you have gone to Him and asked Him the reason of this, He has shown you that it has sprung from carelessness and want of circumspection. "See then that ye walk circumspectly, not as fools, but as wise" (Eph. 5: 15), is an admonition we need often to remember. The enemy is ever at hand, watching for our halting. If he can draw us on into the indulgence of levity and trifling, or of bad temper, or any of our "old sins," he knows that the Holy Spirit will be grieved, and our communion broken; and then our usefulness is gone, and he is better able to make us his prey. We must do, then, as those who know that they are in an enemy's land, and not relax our watchfulness even when we know that we have an Almighty Guardian who never sleeps. It is true that it is written, "Except the Lord keep the city, the watchman waketh but in vain" (Ps. 127: 1), but let us never for a moment think that therefore it is meant that the watchman need not be awake—that he may sleep upon his post. The fullest assurance of our interest in the Lord's love, and in His watchful providence, should encourage us indeed, and take away all anxiety from our minds, but must not supersede the continual exercise on our part of watchfulness and prayer. The very next chapter in the Book of Joshua after that which relates the capture of Ai, tells of Joshua and his people being entrapped by the wily Gibeonites; and the reason given for their falling into the trap was that they "asked not counsel at the mouth of the Lord" (Joshua 9: 14). "Watch and pray, that ye enter not into temptation" (Matt. 26: 41), ought to be ever sounding in our ears. However long-standing our faith, and however many our past successes, we are never safe except so far as we keep humble, asking counsel every day, remembering our weakness, never daring to do anything apart from Jesus and His grace.

And now my task is done, and I have answered, to the best of my ability, the question proposed, "How to walk more closely with God." But before I end, let me put another question, "What is to be the issue of the solemn investigation here made?" Will any be satisfied with asking it, and finding mentally a solution to it? Or, will they go on to put to the test practically that method which has approved itself to their judgment and conscience to be God's way of maintaining a holy walk? Will they yield up the last vestige of their legal strivings and throw themselves simply upon Him, for Him to work in them to will and to do of His good pleasure? Will they ask Him without delay to show them what idol of vanity, or impurity, or covetousness, has been keeping them at a distance from Him? Will they implore Him to give them more of the spirit of watchfulness and prayer, that the enemy may not be allowed to get the advantage over them?

I feel, and have felt for very long, that the snare, if I may not call it vice, to which the members of what is called the Evangelical section of the Church are most exposed at this day, is that of being zealous for doctrines without being careful enough to know the power of the doctrine of Christ in their lives. This, depend upon it, is what is wanted, what men are asking for at our hands: to show them not only in word but in our own examples, that, as ministers, we have the seal of God upon our ministry, or, as men, that His presence is with us in our daily lives, enduing us with a grace and a power which the world does not possess. And for this we *must* walk closely with God. Soundness of doctrine and correctness of moral deportment cannot supply the want of this. This is the "one thing needful." Let it be our aim at any cost, to attain to it. Then, though men may despise us, we shall, like Enoch, have this testimony at the end of our lives, that we "pleased God," and this is a testimony above all price. Then, too, though conscious that our talents are few and our sphere an insignificant one, we shall be certain to know at last that we have not lived in vain; for the light which will be reflected from our lives cannot fail to be useful to some poor souls who are groping their way heavenward, or to others who are discouraged by the burdens of life, and need our taper to cheer them on their onward road.

May God Himself teach and enable each one of us to walk more closely with Him!

EXCEPT A CORN OF WHEAT . . . DIE . . .

Rev. Charles A. Fox, M.A.

The hour is come, that the Son of man should be glorified—John
12: 23, 24.

THE whole object of our meetings here is precisely this, that
we should learn what it is in our own experience to be
glorified; and if we are true to Him, and are willing to
follow His way of being glorified, namely, by passing through
death, we, too, sons of men as we are, shall leave this place
"glorified."

But let us see what it is for any son of man to be glorified—
what does consecration mean, in a word.

Friends, the very first thing consecration means is—*death*. "The
hour is come that the Son of man should be *glorified*. Verily, verily,
I say unto you, Except a corn of wheat fall to the ground and *die*,
it abideth alone; but if it *die*, it bringeth forth much fruit." Are
you ready to be glorified at such a price; are you willing to "fall
to the ground and die"?

Some of you have come here from far; some of you have been
seeking it for years; now you are at the very point of being glorified
—*are you willing*? The hour is come—the hour that you shall be
glorified through death; "for except a corn of wheat fall to the
ground and die, it abideth alone." The words are true of Christ
first, but after Him of all who follow. They, too, must "fall to the
ground and die," if they would, like Him, be glorified.

Consecration is death, first. You thought, perhaps, that it was
some high place, far above you, to which you were looking up,
hoping to attain. But it is the very lowest place; it is death. Are
you then willing for this?

If you are not willing, then you "abide alone." Your fruit is
absolutely *nil*. Life is solitude; death is fruitfulness. Did you ever
hear of such awful solitude as this? Yearning to win souls for
Him, yet not willing for the death which is the one way of escaping
this most awful solitude under heaven. "It abideth *alone*,"
because it will not fall to the ground and die. "Abideth *alone*!"
Can you face that solitude?

On the other hand, to *die* is fruitfulness. "If it *die*, it bringeth forth much fruit."

But that is just the point—*what is it to die*?

In the Word of God we read of three who were transfigured—glorified. And in each case the transfiguration was in connection with dying. Moses was transfigured, his face shining with the light the Israelites could not look upon, as he came down from the Mount, bearing from God the tables of the Law, which were condemnation to death. The Lord Jesus was transfigured while speaking of His decease. Stephen was transfigured in the very act of dying. To die is to be transfigured; to be transfigured is to die.

Are you willing?

But how was it they were transfigured? It was *in seeing God*. To see Him is to die the death which means transfiguration. But to die thus takes time. It is not merely being at consecration meetings, nor merely singing hymns of self-renunciation; it is *by looking at God*, and seeing what He is; through the Holy Ghost— "*being* filled . . . he said, I see the Son of man standing at the right hand of God!"

Job knew this: Job—the very earliest Christian, yet from whom every one of us may learn—Job says, "My eye seeth Thee. *Wherefore* I abhor myself, and repent in dust and ashes." If you want to die, it is in *seeing God*. It is always so. It was so with John, who knew his Lord so well: John, the nameless disciple, who writes himself down over and over again with proud humility as "that disciple whom Jesus loved." Yet when afterwards Jesus appeared to him, he writes, "When I saw Him, *I fell at His feet as dead*"—he literally "fell to the ground and died." Nothing will make you "fall to the ground" but the near sight of God in Christ —you cannot fall to the ground of yourself.

I ask you, Are you willing to see God and die? Are you ready to *take the time* to do it? I say it solemnly, few take the time to see God. Many there are who ask of Him many petitions, but terribly few who wait in silence before Him long enough to see Him; few that obey His word, "*Be still*, and know that I am God." If you thus see God, and die, you shall be no longer in that awful solitude of abiding alone, but you will work for Him, and win many to Him.

But you ask again, "What *is* consecration?"

Consecration is *confession*. This is a point which has not been much touched yet, but it is one which needs to be fully dwelt upon and explained. "*If we confess* our sins, He is faithful and just to forgive us our sins, and to cleanse us from all unrighteousness." Confession is a very constituent part of consecration. For we live surrounded by an atmosphere of sin: it is above us, around us, within us. The only safe place, then, for the Christian to live in is the confessional; the blessed, open confessional; in Christ Jesus. It is not only that you confess to-day's wrong and sin, and leave it. That will not do. You must live there continuously, or you cannot know the continuous cleansing of the blood. You remember the poor woman who sought Jesus, and who with that wonderful grasp of faith was healed immediately. She gained what she needed, and she was leaving healed, thinking to slip away as silently as she had come. But that would not do. The Lord Jesus said "No," and made her return, and made her tell out there before Him in the very street all about it, "for what cause she had touched him, and how she was healed immediately." How hard to have to confess all the shame and pain! But thus, telling Him "all the truth," there was won from Him one word which more than repaid all—the word which He never before or after used to any other—"*Daughter!*"

Oh, friends, live in constant confession; as simply and unreservedly as if just converted. Tell Him "all the truth," in childlike assurance; make to Him your bold, free, simple confession; your "humble confession." Some confess as if they were quite pleased over it: that is not what He means. He looks for a *contrite* spirit: contrite meaning "bruised together."

And then, having thus confessed, be as sure you are forgiven as that you have confessed. The Lord Jesus is Priest for the very purpose of giving absolution. So few take this in; and the reason why so many are seeking to hear absolution from a human voice is because they know so little of the Priesthood of Christ. There is no priest but Him: we are not priests, we are but presbyters, as you know. The Lord Jesus is the one Priest for this purpose.

Use Him as your High Priest. Tell Him "all the truth." Confess to Him out loud; speak out the sins. It is very humbling, and lays us where we should be, in the dust. Say at each, "That's me; the *Christian*; it is I, the consecrated, the cleansed, who am yet capable of this and that." It is in confession that the blood cleanses, not without. You may sing of its cleansing power, but it is the confessing one who *wins* the absolution. He gives it *surely*, and then bids you return, having restored you immediately. For do believe that He is at least as good as you are; that He *does* keep His word to you as faithfully as you would keep yours to another; that He means it when He says, "If we confess our sins, He is *faithful and just to forgive* us our sins"; yea, and to "cleanse us from all unrighteousness." And thus we become consecrated by His own Priestly consecration. Believe that if you have the frankness to confess all, He has the generosity to forgive all, and with tender hand to put you up in your place again, restored at once, as He did with Peter, meeting him with, "Lovest thou me?"

Yes, consecration is confession. But it is also *separation*—see Exodus 10: 26, "We know not with what we must serve the Lord, *until we come thither.*" God was speaking through Moses to Pharaoh, commanding him to let His people go. You remember the four compromises to which they were tempted before they were let free.

The first is, "Go ye, sacrifice to your God *in the land.*" "Yes, you may serve Him, you may sacrifice, but stay in Egypt." Do you know this? "Stay in the world and sacrifice there. Be as religious as you like, but do not leave; do not make yourself peculiar." Is not this constantly said around you, and has it not been said within us?

The next is, "I will let you go, that ye may sacrifice to the Lord your God in the wilderness: only *ye shall not go very far away.*" "Yes, you may sacrifice; but do not go far; be of a neutral tint. Run out and sacrifice, and then return. You are a busy man; live in the world all day, and then return to God in the evening, when you get home." And so they continue, running out to sacrifice, and then coming back to the world. On Sundays they sacrifice, then all the week are in Egypt; for they go such a little way out—just a Sabbath day's journey; it is no effort to them to return.

Friends, let me speak simply and plainly, you *cannot* live in the world and serve God. "We know not with what we must serve the Lord, until we come thither!" If you want to be consecrated, you must be separated.

Then another compromise is tried. *You* must go, but your children must be kept back. "Let the Lord be so with you, as I will let you go, and your little ones. . . . Not so; go now, ye that are men, and serve Him." Oh, yes, father and mother may go—they may be consecrated and separated; part may go, but the children must live in the world, and then go into the church if they like. Strange fitting for the church! and strange that fathers and mothers can do this, and the children whom they love with whole heart, given up to the things of the world. Strange infatuation! You are a Christian, you are saved, you go out to serve the Lord, but the children may go as they please! I believe that Christian parents have a right to bring their children with them. I know one who asserts that every child of Christian parents should be converted at three years old. But, anyway, I believe that given to God in baptism, and trained up in accordance with that giving, that the children *will* follow. Oh, Christian parents, do believe that God will be as careful about your children as *you* would be, and as willing to provide for them when wholly given to Him. Will He care less for their interest than you?

The fourth compromise is—"only let *your flocks and your herds* be stayed." This arouses a very solemn thought. Your property is wanted by God as well as yourself, and you say, "Yes, He shall have all, and the little ones, but not this!" This question of property is a crucial one; it is not by any means the greatest or the most important thing, but it is generally the *test* question. If you give the property to God, we may be very sure that all the rest has gone over first. We can see our whole-heartedness or not as we treat this question.

Yes, then I do bring all; I can withhold nothing from the Master! I bring everything, little ones and all my property, talents, time, influence. Why? Because we do not know with what we must serve God until we come thither; so all we have must come with us. Until you are wholly consecrated, you do not know how He will use your talents; all must be brought in to Him first, yourself entirely divested, *all* placed in His hands.

Oh, the blessed freedom of this life! All given over to God, He having the care of all. Do you notice the three times on which the word "Take no thought" occurs? The first is in connection with common necessities of food and clothing; of them He bids us take no anxious thought. It is joined to that blessed word, "Your Father knoweth." Children, is not your Father *bound* to feed you, and to provide you with raiment? Oh, I love to say to Him in simplest way, "Father, I want this and that."

The second time is, "Take no thought for the morrow": for the future is in His hands too.

Are you not free? The *past* all cut off, under the blood: the *future* all cut off, in His hands: and you stand in the *present* in God?

Once more. When we are free we want to work for Him, and all may do that. Even a little child may. In the fishing villages it is often the little children who let down the net. Do not say, "I do not know what to say." He will teach you as the time comes. Now comes in His word, "Take ye no thought how or what thing ye shall answer, or what ye shall say; for the Holy Ghost shall teach you in the same hour what ye ought to say." Now this does not mean no preparation. I have known those who have spent years of fruitless toil, because they have vaguely expected Him to provide them at the minute for work they knew of beforehand. The promise is for those who may be called on suddenly to speak or testify for the Master; and it is a sure one, and you *need* "take no thought," but that when God calls you, He will provide you.

Oh, is it not a life of freedom? that even in this you need have no anxious thought. Only live in the Spirit, and you will be always prepared, and you will have for every occasion a holy unpreparedness in the Lord.

Oh, my friends, may *He* teach us fully what consecration means! *Death, confession,* and this *separation,* that we may know the blessed freedom of this life.

We shall then need to live in the perpetual presence of the King. To *see Him* is the secret of consecration. That is the secret of every prayer-meeting. Give God room, and then it matters little who else is there. Then place yourself with the gaze of your whole soul upon Him, intense beyond expression, and fill yourself from the fountain. How God mourns that His people care so little for this. "My people have committed two evils; they have forsaken me, the fountain of living waters, and have hewn them out cisterns, broken cisterns, which can hold no water!" And do you not know how often we have done this? hewn out, with great labour and toil, cisterns of prayers, long prayers full of words, and they have held no water, and we have not *seen God!* I say again, solemnly, how few there are who take time to *see God!* A question was put in my hands this morning, which I had not time to answer—"How to subdue wandering thoughts in prayer?" This is the answer. *See God!* Take time to fix your whole gaze on Him, and *seeing Him,* you cannot wander, when He is holding your eye. *Then* you can give Him definite requests, and the answers will come; for, *seeing Him,* you must ask what is according to His will. You can never be distracted in prayer when He is before you holding your eye, and your eyes meet in earnest gaze of intense love.

Friends, may I plead with you yet? Give all to God, for "we know not with what we must serve the Lord, until we come thither." It will be with anything and everything. Therefore have all ready. Some day He will say, "I want that," and lay His finger on something of yours—*is it given?* Your talent for speaking—He will want that. Your talent for singing—oh, He often wants that. He wants you to follow Jesus in your singing; leading the praises of His brethren. Do you not long to hear Jesus in every hymn—*He* the leader! Oh, how sweetly above He leads the praises. Do you not long to hear *Jesus singing!* I think, as one of His little ones, sitting in the furthest corner of heaven, where the echo of His voice shall break, I shall hear the reverberation of it so overwhelmingly sweet, that it will break my soul over again in renewed adoration at His feet! To hear *my Lord singing!* "In the midst of the church will I sing praise unto Thee."

Soon we shall see Him—see Him where no more sorrow is, or trials, and where the very wounds we have fixed in our Christ shall shine out with glory. That was what *we* gave Him—*wounds!* Can you, will you now, give Him yourselves, and all you have, and say, "My Beloved is mine," and yet further, "I am His"? Let this now be the time of your betrothal to Him, giving over all; losing yourself in Him; dying, and thus being "glorified."

"Master, we give Thee all! We can withhold nothing—spirit, soul, body, all our property, our dear ones, our children. We give them now, before Thou takest them. We give all irrevocably. Take all, Master; and oh, *keep* what we give. Let us not have it back, even if we should plead with Thee to have it back. Be a prudent Father to us Thy weak children; and if we should wrestle with Thee for it again, and long and crave for it, yield not to us. We give now all. We are in the mood to give, the mood of God. Keep, Master, for ever!"

WITH THE WHOLE HEART

Pasteur Theodore Monod

With my whole heart—Jeremiah 32: 41.

WHO speaks thus? Is it Moses, or Samuel, or David returning penitently to his God? Is it one of the prophets, or one of the apostles? Nay; it is God Himself, announcing the blessings of the Gospel dispensation. "I will make an everlasting covenant with them, that I will not turn away from them to do them good; but I will put my fear in their hearts, that they shall not depart from me. Yea, I will rejoice over them to do them good, and I will plant them in this land assuredly, with my whole heart and with my whole soul" (Jer. 32: 40–41). Even the measure of the heart of man we are not able to tell; how much less that of the heart of God! It is the fulness of His heart, of that heart that gave us His only Son, which He is ready to lavish upon us in streams of blessing, if we will but seek Him with *our* "whole heart."

To whom is it promised? To such as cease to rob God. Let us not separate the promise from the command, obedience to which is the very condition of its fulfilment: "Will a man rob God? Yet ye have robbed me. But ye say, Wherein have we robbed Thee? In tithes and offerings. Ye are cursed with a curse: for ye have robbed me, even this whole nation. Bring ye all the tithes into the storehouse, that there may be meat in mine house, and prove me now herewith, said the Lord of hosts, if I will not open you the windows of heaven, and pour you out a blessing, that there shall not be room enough to receive it" (Mal. 3: 8–10). God, who oftentimes proves us, to show us what is in our heart, invites us to prove Him, that He may show us what is in His heart. Only let us come in the path of obedience, giving Him His due, devoting ourselves and all that we have to His service. Then shall we be blessed, exceeding abundantly above all that we ask or think. As has been well said, "Give to God as much as your hands can hold, and He will give you as much as *His* hands can hold."

You have asked for a blessing, you have expected it, you have kept back nothing, and yet, you seem to yourselves to be still

unblest. It remains for you to *take*: "Let him that is athirst
come. And whosoever will, let him take the water of life freely."
"This is the record, that God hath given to us eternal life, and
this life is in His Son." Take it, as freely as it has been given.
But, you enquire, "Have I a right to take? Is eternal life truly
mine? Is Christ mine? Am I His? As far as I know myself, I
give myself to Him; but how can I know that He accepts me?"
Oh, fearful heart! Oh, foolish heart! What would you think
of a maiden who, being entreated by her lover to give him her
heart and hand, would make reply, "I am quite willing; but how
can I know that he will accept me?" Does she forget that he
spoke first, and *asked* her to be his?

Or we will suppose that a ship has been wrecked on the rocks.
The waves are beating it to pieces. But here comes a life-boat
through the surge, and the brave men, at the peril of their lives,
reach the doomed vessel, and beckon the crew to jump into the
boat. "But how can I know," says one of those ready to perish,
"how can I know that they will receive me into that life-boat?"
If they did not intend to receive him, would they have come for
him? Thus, when Christ has come "to *seek* and to *save*" sinners,
to forgive them, to cleanse them, to make them happy, let them
never be so unreasonable as to enquire whether He will accept
them.

Being, then, accepted of Him, boldly claim and take all that
belongs to Him, and call it yours. Just as the young bride, who
has left her father's humble home for her husband's stately man-
sion, has to learn that all that belongs to him, now belongs also
to her. She has but to call it all her own, and use it as such. Let
us simply do the same. Make yourself at home with God. In
Christ all that He has is yours. *Take* it; that is to say, *use* it. Is it
strength that you need? Dare to say, and rejoice to say, "The
strength of Christ is mine." Put forth that strength in your
weakness, and you will find it to be yours indeed. So of patience,
of purity, of peace, of joy, of any blessing, "all *are* yours, and ye
are Christ's, and Christ is God's."

"Thou sayest, I am rich, and increased with goods, and have
need of nothing; and knowest not that thou art wretched, and
miserable, and poor, and blind, and naked. . . ." At this point
many Christians leave off the quotation, as though the following
lines had been torn out of their Bibles; whereas they ought simply
to say, "Here endeth the first lesson." Now let us go on to the
second, as the Lord proceeds in these words, "I counsel thee to
buy of me gold tried in the fire, that thou mayest be rich; and
white raiment, that thou mayest be clothed, and that the shame
of thy nakedness do not appear." He does not want His people

to be a set of paupers in rags, but to be rich and well clad. Otherwise, what will the world think of them, and of Him they call their Father? What would we think of a man supposed to be immensely wealthy and whose children could be seen wandering about the streets hungry and naked? Surely we would doubt either that he was truly rich, or that he was indeed their father. Thus do we not only harm ourselves, but dishonour God, when we fail to possess and to manifest the abundance of peace, of strength, of holiness, of happiness, with which He is ever ready to supply all our need, "according to His riches in glory by Christ Jesus." Let us, then, take heed to the Lord's counsel, and buy of Him.

But why should He speak of *buying*, when we can do nothing more than to ask, to receive, to take freely—when the buying, in short, must needs be "without money and without price"? The point brought out by the word "buying" is, it appears to me, the necessity of coming to a definite decision. All shop-keepers understand this perfectly. You enter, for instance, into one of the shops, numerous in this place, where a great variety of views of the Lake District are to be found. You look them over, talk them over, compare the one with the other, go into ecstasies, pronounce them beautiful, admirable, exquisitely lovely—and move out without having *bought* anything. I doubt whether the shopman will be as pleased with your long and amiable visit as with that of a rough customer, it may be, who hastily walks in, points out a picture, hands over the price, and carries it off. He may have been undemonstrative, but he has thought the thing worth the price, and has bought it.

Thus with the treasures offered to us by the Saviour. We may gaze at them, admire them, desire them, talk and sing, and rejoice in nice addresses, nice books, nice conventions on the subject, while we finally buy nothing—that is to say, we part with nothing, and obtain nothing; we do not come to the point of letting go our hold of ourselves, and taking hold of Christ.

Oh, will we now buy of Him? What does He ask but ourselves —our guilty, polluted, helpless, blind, naked, miserable selves? And what does He give but Himself, the very brightness of the glory of God? He gives gold for garbage, and white raiment for filthy rags. It costs us nothing (for surely we are not *paying* Him when we cast ourselves at His feet); it cost *Him* Gethsemane and Calvary. It was there His gold was "tried in the fire"; and it stood the test. *That* gold He now counsels us to buy of Him that we may be rich.

If there be one here that is not at peace with God, I would simply tell him that "God was in Christ, reconciling the world unto Himself, not imputing their trespasses unto them; and hath committed unto us the word of reconciliation." What have you, then, to do? Just to take hold of what Christ has done—"Be *ye* reconciled to God."

So about the power of sin. How are we separated from sin? By the death of Christ. "If one died for all, therefore all died." Then what have you to do in order to die to sin? To take hold of that fact, to believe it; believe that Christ by His death has created a separation between you and your sin; that the old man (that is, the man you used to be) is on His cross, and the new man is fully free to be used for God by His Spirit.

And *then*, what shall we have to do? To remember that He has redeemed us from all iniquity, and purified us *unto Himself* (Titus 2: 14). He has redeemed you unto Himself, to be His especial property, and you have no more right to take yourself out of the hand of Christ as your Redeemer, than out of the hand of God as your Creator. We belong to Him, and all we have belongs to Him; and it is a perfect shame that we should take hours and days to decide whether He shall have us or not.

We belong to Him, and *all things* belong to us. We take our abode in Him, or rather we refuse to leave it; for He has said that it is our place. "I *am* the vine; ye the branches; abide in me and I in you." Let us, then, remain one with Him in simple faith; He will fill us with His love and make us fruitful to His glory.

How did the apostle Paul enter the Christian life? In Acts 9 we read that Saul of Tarsus, having resisted the first strivings of the Spirit (for the Lord reminds him that he had been "kicking against the pricks"), falls upon the earth, and hears a voice saying to him, "Saul, Saul, why persecutest thou me?" and he says, "Who art Thou, Lord?" How encouraging this is for us all! The very man who was afterwards to say that he counted all things but loss for the knowledge of Christ, inquires, when Jesus Himself speaks to him for the first time, "Who art Thou, Lord?" Whoever you may be, then, the very weakest of believers, if you even hardly know who the Lord is, He can yet make an apostle of you.

Then he goes on to say, "Lord, what wilt Thou have me to do?" In Acts 26 we find a fuller account from Paul's own lips. "And I said, Who art Thou, Lord? And the Lord said, I am Jesus, whom thou persecutest. But rise and stand upon thy feet, for I have appeared unto thee for this purpose, to make thee a minister and a witness both of these things which thou hast seen, and of those things in the which I will appear unto thee; delivering thee from the people and from the Gentiles, unto whom now I send thee, to open their eyes and to turn them from darkness to light, and from the power of Satan unto God, that they may receive forgiveness of sins, and inheritance among them which are sanctified by faith that is in me. Whereupon, O King Agrippa, I was not disobedient unto the heavenly vision." Did he at once, after hearing that magnificent programme of his life's work, start on his mission as the apostle of the Gentiles? Was there nothing between? Look at Acts 22: 10, and see what intervened. "I said, What shall I do, Lord?" As much as to say, "I understand that I am to be the ambassador of Christ to the Gentiles, but it is a great task; where shall I begin?" The answer is, "Arise, and go unto Damascus, and there it shall be told thee all things which are appointed for thee to do."

How simple the Lord's method: Go on to Damascus, pursue the very journey which thou hast undertaken, although thou shalt now enter the town in another spirit and with another purpose; yea, and not as an honoured Pharisee, the delegate of the high priest, at the head of his escort, but as a blind man—no uncommon sight in Eastern countries—(unable to see, he tells us, from the glory of the light with which he had been dazzled)—thou shalt enter it, as a little child led by the hand. This, then, was the thing, the only thing, for him to do at present. The next thing was to remain in Damascus three days, neither seeing, nor eating, nor drinking; but not without praying (Acts 9: 9, 11). Then he heard the door open, and hands were laid gently upon him, and an unknown voice addressed him as "Brother Saul." He recovered his sight, was baptised, was filled with the Holy Ghost, "received meat and was strengthened," and "straightway preached Christ in the synagogue of Damascus, that He is the Son of God." Thus, at the time of his conversion, and ever afterward, the Lord showed him, from day to day, "the things appointed for him to do."

The Lord will not deal otherwise with us. He has great things for us to do (ought we not to say that there is true greatness in anything that is done for God?); and while we try to view our work as a whole, we are likely to be perplexed and disheartened. Let us, then, confine ourselves to the one question: Lord, what wilt Thou, upon this day, at this hour, have me to do? The morrow shall take thought for the things of itself. The appointed task and the appointed grace will be found ready.

The Lord appoints to every one his work, and the measure of grace needful for it (Mark 13: 34). It is a common mistake, and a grievous one, for Christians to be claiming a blessing that is not ready for them because they are not ready for it, or in need of it. In a large household, does every child receive the same food? Do the parents give the same portion to the babe, the boy, the lad of fifteen, the youth of twenty? If they did, would there not

be suffering, either from lack, or from excess, of nourishment?
So does our heavenly Father know what kind or measure of grace
we are fit to use, and therefore able to receive.

While coveting earnestly the best gifts, and ever reaching
forth unto the things that are before, let us trust our Father's love
and wisdom to feed us with food convenient for us, and thus go on
from strength to strength, not in the footsteps of our brethren,
but at the bidding of our Lord.

THE SOUL-THIRST OF JESUS

Rev. George C. Grubb, M.A.

And David longed, and said, Oh that one would give me drink of the water of the well of Bethlehem, which is by the gate! And the three mighty men brake through the host of the Philistines, and drew water out of the well of Bethlehem, that was by the gate, and took it, and brought it to David: nevertheless he would not drink thereof, but poured it out unto the Lord. And he said, be it far from me, O Lord, that I should do this: is not this the blood of the men that went in jeopardy of their lives? therefore he would not drink it. These things did these three mighty men—2 SAMUEL 23: 15–17.

I WANT to find out the reason why the Holy Ghost has been so careful to record this act done by these mighty men. We may be well assured that there are divine and eternal principles of action to be found underneath this deed. Bethlehem was in the hand of the Philistines: Bethlehem, the place where David was born, where the Christ was to be born King of the Jews, in the hand of God's enemies! The land of Israel was in a sad state. The enemies had encroached upon that which was the king's possession, and David was hemmed in by the Philistines, though he was also surrounded by a band of faithful followers. The battle had been very great, and David was tired, and, perhaps half forgetting what he said, he gave expression to the wish, "Oh that one would give me drink of the water of the well of Bethlehem, which is by the gate."

Great David has had a greater Son than himself, the Lord Jesus Christ, and I would wish you to notice what it is that your Lord and Saviour longs for. I am deeply anxious that every one of you should have such a loyal heart as to be willing to go through the opposing host of the Philistines to try to get a cup of cold water for Jesus, to satisfy the terrible thirst that is upon His soul.

What would please Him most for you to do this morning? What are His unutterable longings? Jesus, we read, came to Jacob's well, and there came a woman to the well to draw water. He said to her, "Give me to drink." "How is it that Thou, being a Jew, askest drink of me, which am a woman of Samaria? for the Jews have no dealings with the Samaritans." The Lord Jesus thirsted for the salvation of a single soul. And I want you to learn this, that the blessing you have received is of little use if, when you see a single soul passing you on the road, in the railway train, or in the tram-car, you do not thirst for that soul's salvation. Learn, then, that the Lord Jesus wants to save every single soul; that a great thirst lies upon the soul of Immanuel. Does the great blessing of holiness that you have professed to receive, result in soul-thirst? If it does not, I fear you delude yourself.

The time came when Jesus lay stretched between heaven and earth, a shameful spectacle to angels and devils and men. Here also an awful thirst lay upon the soul of the Christ. "Jesus, knowing that all things were now accomplished, that the Scripture might be fulfilled, said, I thirst. And they filled a sponge with vinegar, and put it to His mouth. Jesus . . . having received the vinegar, said, It is finished; and He bowed His head and gave up the ghost." There Jesus thirsted, not for the salvation of one poor harlot soul, but for the salvation of the whole world. There "God was in Christ, reconciling the world unto Himself, not imputing their trespasses unto them." There Christ "was made sin for us . . . that we might be made the righteousness of God in Him."

Have you ever thirsted for the salvation of the whole world? This convention will do you little good until your soul is restless; until in your dreams at night, it may be, you hear a voiceless cry echoing from the millions in India, China, Africa, and the islands of the sea. Has the salvation of the world ever cost you a single tear in your prayers? Have you ever lain in agony before God, because the whole world lieth in the wicked one? Have you sympathy with Christ, or are you still going to give Him a draught of vinegar? He has got enough of that already, and He would like a cup of cold water from you now. The only thing the world ever gave to Christ was a draught of vinegar. You have given the Lord the bitterness of your sins, your selfishness and your lusts. Will you not, this morning, take and present to Him a cup of pure cold water, saying, "Lord, endow me with a quenchless thirst for the salvation of souls." Your holiness is a delusion, a mockery, and a snare, unless it results in the desire to save everybody you meet. When will our hearts be so loyal as this?

Now notice some of the eternal principles of action that underlie the drawing of this draught of water for David. The first thing is this—*An expressed wish is law to a loyal heart.* These men supremely loved King David, so his longing for the draught was enough for them. They did not begin to argue about the difficulties of going—about the Philistines in the valley: they just went and did it. Is there any expressed wish of Jesus to you that you are refusing to obey? Shall I keep silent a moment while we think it over? Has my Lord expressed a wish to me about any one thing in which I am slow to obey? If that be the case, I am not yet one of Jesus' mighty men; my heart is not really loyal to Him.

Another principle is this—*Love does not wait for orders*, but anticipates the desires of the loved one. It is a blessed thing to love like that, when you can tell by instinct what will please the person whom your heart adores. Oh yes, you can tell what will really please them. Love never waits for orders. What, then, are we to say of the love of the universal Church toward her heavenly Bridegroom? Christ has given most distinct orders about preaching the Gospel to Jews and Gentiles. The Church averts her eyes from the marching orders that have been written in letters of Holy Ghost fire. Indeed, her one *raison d'être* is to go to the uttermost parts of the world to witness for her Lord and Saviour Jesus Christ. God turn our averted eyes toward our marching orders!

Another thing is this: that *Christ values our gifts according to the motive, and according to the labour.* According to the motive: "If ye shall give a cup of cold water in the name of a disciple, ye shall in no wise lose your reward." Then according to the labour: "For my name's sake thou hast laboured and hast not fainted" (Rev. 2: 3). Why do Sunday-school teachers take up work, and a month afterwards come to the pastor and say, "I have made a mistake; please take back my class"? Because they are not labouring for Christ's name's sake. When you do that, you do not grow faint and weary of the work. You know, fainting usually proceeds from weak action of the heart. A great many Christians are suffering from weak action of the heart toward the Lord Jesus Christ; and that is a very dangerous thing. Many Christians have heart disease and do not know it. Let us ask God to reveal to us the secret diseases of our hearts. But He only reveals them that He may heal them. One touch from the hand of Jesus heals the fainting soul. "Consider the Apostle and High Priest of our profession . . . lest ye be wearied and faint in your minds." If there is any person inclined to faint at what lies before you, the reason is, you are not considering Jesus.

God values our gifts according to what they cost us. These three mighty men poured out their lives at the feet of David. "Shall I drink the blood of these men?" said David; and he poured the water out for the Lord. Have you ever poured out your life at the Master's feet? Since I have come up to this convention a great many people have said to me in one way or another: "I feel the want of love toward God, and I do not know how to get it." I will tell you how. "Therefore doth my Father love me,

K

because I lay down my life for the sheep." When you have laid down your life at the feet of God, you will know that you have done it. I really do not think a person can do that without being conscious of it. The Holy Ghost will testify with your spirit that the deed is done. When the deed is done—not when you pretend to do it—then the love of the Father will come in and flood your soul in a way you never knew before. All the theories about holiness will be explained in having the reality.

You remember how often Paul uses the metaphor "poured out." "Yea, and if I be offered up (literally, 'poured forth') upon the sacrifice and service of your faith, I joy, and rejoice with you all. For the same cause also do ye joy, and rejoice with me" (Phil. 2: 17, 18). We are not to be sorrowful because a Christian has to go through great privations, or persecutions, or destitution for Christ's sake. It is to be a cause of joy to the universal Church. Says Paul, "I count not my life dear unto myself, so that I might finish my course with joy, and the ministry, which I have received of the Lord Jesus, to testify the Gospel of the grace of God." Why do we see so many downcast believers? Because, we greatly fear, they have counted their lives dear to themselves. When the believer counts not his own life dear to him, whether he is thirty or eighty years of age, he will be as happy as the day is long. Oh that you older Christians might finish your course, not with gloom, but with joy, by testifying the Gospel of the grace of God. As Paul was about to lay down his life, what did he say? "I am already being poured forth (literally), and the time of my departure is at hand." From the beginning of his ministry to the end, he lived in the spirit of being continually poured out—his life-blood being poured at the feet of his divine Master.

Have you done this? Are you willing to be a drink-offering to Jesus to-day? What was to be done with the drink-offering? Where was it to be poured out? Look at Numbers 28: 7, "In the holy place shalt thou cause the strong wine to be poured unto the Lord for a drink-offering." In the place of communion and prayer, of holy intercession, of heart-communion with Jesus, pour out yourself. "The strong wine": He would like the best you have. Do not give Him weak, washy stuff; He would like the strong wine of your life. Young man, give God your best!

I close by referring to one more thing that Jesus would greatly desire to get from you. He longs for something else besides the salvation of souls. "Jesus said unto them, With desire I have desired to eat this passover with you before I suffer" (Luke 22: 15). That passover was symbolical of the intimate communion, of the holy fellowship, of the constant intercourse that is to obtain between my soul and my Saviour's heart. There is nothing that the Lord desires, after the salvation of souls, more than to have constant realised communion with your soul. If this convention is to be a blessing, we must learn the secret of living in this constant communion with our Lord and Saviour; unbroken communion from the time the morning sun awakes us till the going down thereof. For the Lord's name is to be praised from the rising up of the sun to the going down of the same. Oh, soul, there is such a thing as living in constant, unbroken communion with Jesus, without a shadow on your soul.

> I've reached a land of corn and wine,
>   And all its riches freely mine;
> Here shines undimmed one glorious day;
>   For all my night has passed away.

"There shall be no night there." Wherever Jesus is, He is the light of the world, the light of the heart. "If thine eye be single, thy whole body shall be full of light"—not having two or three quarters of it dark. The light of God shall be in every corner of your being. Oh, a single eye means a great deal. Do not think that a single eye is a very easy thing to get. It means that you are to be searched until you are dead. "I fell at his feet as dead." Then search me, O God, and lead me in the way everlasting.

Then with this single eye upon the person of my glorified and once crucified Saviour, the smallest wish that comes from His holy will, becomes eternal law to me. I will dart off as did the mighty three, in the alacrity of faith (for the King's business requires haste), to do His holy will; and the Spirit of God will be with me; the chariots and horses of fire will be round me, to protect me from the hosts of the Philistines. Though you may be scarred and wounded in the battle—your life-blood poured forth—you will bring your gift to the feet of your David, and give it to Him. He will in His turn pour it out to Jehovah. Then when He comes in His glory He will say, "This my servant was faithful to me in the world. Now I write upon his forehead my new name, and I confess him before Thee, O Father." Thus He will manifest Himself to you, and bid you enter into the joy of your Lord. And thou wilt rest thy weary head upon the breast of Him who has loved thee all along.

"These things did these three mightiest."

THE PATHWAY TO THE HIGHER LIFE

Rev. Andrew Murray, D.D.

THE words from which I wish to speak to you, you will find in Mark 10, from verse 35, "And James and John, the sons of Zebedee, come unto Him, saying, Master, we would that Thou shouldest do for us whatsoever we desire." It looks very bold, but they remembered that those were the words that Christ had used, and so they avail themselves of His promise. "And He said unto them, What would ye that I should do for you? They said unto Him, Grant unto us that we may sit, one on Thy right hand, and the other on Thy left hand, in Thy glory." This last verse gives us our subject—*The way to the higher life.* Here we have two men asking for a place on the throne of glory. And we have our blessed Jesus teaching us what the real way is to the higher life. Oh, let us all yield ourselves to His teaching, and every heart say, Blessed Lord, teach me to-night!

Or, I might give as the subject of my address, *The path of consecration.* We talk so much about it. Let us to-night study in the words of Jesus, and in His presence, what the path of consecration is. And our first thought is this: *The blessing which consecration seeks.* What is that? You cannot find it put more beautifully than in the words of the Bible: "Grant unto us, that we may sit . . . on Thy right hand . . . in Thy glory." Three things they ask—nearness to Jesus; likeness to Jesus; power for Jesus.

Nearness to Jesus—is not that what your heart longs for, when you talk of consecration? Oh, if I could only be having Him all the time with me, always near, and be every day conscious of His presence! And more; they desired not only nearness to Jesus— to be with Him on the throne—but *likeness to Jesus.* This is not beyond His heart. He has promised it. But they asked not only for nearness and likeness to Jesus, but for *the very power of Jesus,* that they might use it for Him. What a blessed answer it was that they gave Jesus! It meant more than they knew. There were elements in it that were not good, but what a large answer it was to the Saviour's request, "What would ye that I should do for you?"

And Christ comes to every one of us with the same question. Come now and formulate your petition, and tell Jesus what you want. Are you ready to whisper to Jesus as your answer, "Lord, perfect nearness to Thee; Lord, perfect likeness to Thee; Lord, perfect power for service for Thee"? Is that your heart? Are you content with the grovelling life of a man who is only just saved, who is just a Christian and nothing more? Or, do you want to aim at the very highest? Do so, my brother, and I pray God to give it you.

And now, as to the second point. The first is, the blessing that consecration seeks. The next is, *The mistakes that consecration makes.* Jesus says at once, "Ye know not what ye ask." Yes, this petition of the disciples was an ignorant one. And oh, remember that in our prayers and consecration there are often terrible mistakes, and much ignorance; but it is ever our comfort to know that Jesus spoke very kindly and tenderly to those disciples, and that for our ignorance and errors He will not cast us off.

What were their mistakes? One was that they were asking for the fruit, and the root had not been planted. They were looking above, and Christ said, as it were, "Look downward; I must have the root." A child sometimes plants a branch, with beautiful fruit upon it, at the seaside, in the sand, and makes a "garden." And we are always wanting only the fruit and the blessing, but Christ wants us to have the root deep down.

Another mistake was this: They did not remember that what they wanted was not His to give. He had not the position to give it. The Father alone could give it—to them who were prepared for it, and for whom it was prepared. How careful Christ is to honour the Father. He wants to bring us to God. He took great trouble to draw the disciples to believe in Himself, but He took infinite trouble to say, in other words, "I am only here to take you up to God." May we all learn that Christ says, "It is the Father that has got the blessing, and you must go to Him through me." Some people think that if we talk too much of God, Christ will lose His place. Brethren, Christ will then become doubly precious, for the more I long for heaven, the more I find I cannot get there without Christ. God help us to seek God in Christ!

And there was still more ignorance. They did not know that their desire for glory was *carnal.* It was mixed up with the idea of a temporal kingdom; and therefore the Saviour said, in effect, "You do not know what you are talking about." Further, there was selfishness in it. They wanted to have the best places, and be above the other disciples. "My disciples, you do not know what you ask." And, dear friends, just at the time when one is dealing more earnestly with souls about salvation, one wants to say, Remember, you do not understand it all. One dear sister said very earnestly yesterday, "Explain to me what it really means, that dying in Christ." And another spoke to me to-day about being filled with the Spirit. I have so often to say to such, Do not try to understand it perfectly, but go, in your darkness, and ask for something beyond what you can understand, and then let God deal with you in the glory of His love. Confess your ignorance and say, "O God, this thing is too great, I cannot comprehend it; but I will trust Thee for it."

Oh! The mistakes we make in our consecration! There is often selfishness, and there is often pride, and there is often carnal apprehension, and the desire for being very happy and holy and useful; and self is at the bottom of it.

Now, Christ does not want His disciples to be deluded by an unsatisfactory consecration, and He helped them. And that brings us to the next point—*The consecration that Christ demands*. "Ye know not what ye ask: can ye drink of the cup that I drink of, and be baptized with the baptism that I am baptized with?" This is the consecration which Christ asks us as the path to the higher life.

Think what it means. What is the cup? You know that refers to Gethsemane. And what was that cup, concerning which He asked the Father that it might be taken away? You know, if you study your Bible, that the Bible speaks only of two cups— *the cup of wrath*, and *the cup of blessing*—the cup of the wrath of God, and the cup of blessing and thanksgiving. Which cup was it respecting which Christ had to say, "Father, if it be possible, let this cup pass from me"? It was the cup of wrath on account of our sins—that accursed death upon the tree of Calvary. But, oh, thank God! He drank it, and He comes now to give it to us to drink; but the curse is out of it. And what is it to us? Nothing but this—you know what Gethsemane means—*the surrender of the will*. That is the cup. It cost Him a struggle to say, in other words, "Thy will shall be done; I will drink it up": but He conquered. And Jesus comes and says to us, too, "Can ye drink of the cup that I drink of, and be baptized with the baptism that I am baptized with?" You know what that means? Did not He say, speaking of His death, "I have a baptism to be baptized with, and how am I straitened till it be accomplished"? He felt, long before, the agony in His soul that was Calvary, that was the Cross, that was His baptism; and He asks the disciples, "Can ye . . . be baptized with the baptism that I am baptized with?" Christians, you want the higher life, you want the glory, and you want the nearness and likeness and power of your Lord; but He asks you, Can you drink my cup, and are you willing to be baptized with my baptism? Do remember that there is no path to the glory but through death! Why is it some Christians are unwilling to surrender themselves to it? Because they do not see the need of it, they do not see that it is a righteous sentence that sinful nature should be condemned to death, and that, in the very nature of things, it is an absolute necessity that, in order to get rid of their life, they must die before God's life can come in.

Someone said to me yesterday, when talking of these things, "And must we then die every day?" As if the thought was, Is it not enough to die once for all with Jesus, in order to live the resurrection life? My brother, would that I could help you to see that the death of Christ is a thing for every day, as really as His life is! They are inseparable.

I cannot make it plainer than by pointing you to some splendid oak tree. Where was that oak born? In a grave. The acorn was pushed under the ground. It had its grave there, and in that grave it sprouted and sent its buds upwards. And that tree—I ask you, was it only one day that it stood in that grave? No. That oak for a hundred years had stood every day in that grave, in that place of death; and in that place of death it has found its life and its beauty. And so, let us learn the lesson that death and resurrection are inseparably combined. You cannot get the resurrection life anywhere, or live it, or enjoy it, except in the grave of Jesus. But as that oak tree spreads its dark roots under the cold, black soil every year, farther and farther, and lives in the grave, so the stem and the branches and the leaves come upward into the sunshine; and it is the reward of the roots down in the grave that the tree is so beautiful and so bright in God's creation. I pray you to learn that it is not a transaction once for all. No.

Bless God! there is a divine beginning, a glorious, sudden beginning, when God opens our eyes, and we have seen the crucified One as our life, and counted ourselves dead, because we see we are dead in Christ. But let that be the disposition of every day —dead to the world, dead to sin, dead to all that is not God's. That is the grave, out of which the glorious life of resurrection joy and power shall grow. And I come with the question to-night, Can you be baptized—can you bear it, are you willing for it— with the baptism with which Jesus was baptized? There was for Him, as "the Apostle and High Priest of our profession," no gate to God or to heaven but through death; and there is no gate for us but in the crucified One and in fellowship with Him.

Now comes our next point. What was the answer of these disciples? There you have—*The consecration yielded.* They answered, "We can." Simple disciples! They little knew what these words meant. Yet, blessed be God! Jesus *accepted the consecration.* For what was His answer? Look at its fulness and tenderness. "Jesus said unto them, Ye shall indeed drink of the cup that I drink of; and with the baptism that I am baptized withal shall ye be baptized." Oh, do you not love this tender Redeemer? There were those poor, foolish disciples saying to Him that they could drink that cup, and yet they knew nothing about what it was going to be; and that they could be baptized with His baptism, and yet they did not understand it.

And how did they carry out their vow? All the eleven in that last night "forsook Him and fled." And at the very supper table they were quarrelling again about who was to be chief. How they misunderstood, and grieved, and at last forsook Him! But, thank God, Jesus accepted that consecration.

But how could He do it if it was so untrue? At bottom it was true. The heart was right; they clung to Him. It just meant this, "Lord, we are ready for anything"; and in His loving heart He seemed to say, "I know you are." And, dear friends, if I come to you and plead that you should drink of the cup of Jesus, that you should drink it out to the very last dreg, can you say, "I give my will utterly to God, never to do my own will"? If I come to you with the question, "Can you be baptized with the baptism that He was baptized with?" can you say, "Jesus, I will live as a crucified one in Thee; Jesus, I will follow Thee to Calvary, I will not rest until my life is spent in the fellowship of Thy cross"? Are you ready to give the answer, "We can"?

I know you tremble, and it is right you should. In the light we have in this text, it is not wrong if we say, "Lord, *I* cannot, *I* am impotent"; but rather say, "Lord, in *Thy* strength I can, in *Thy* strength I will, drink Thy cup, and will be baptized with Thy baptism." Then, when you leave this meeting, or Keswick, for home, get with Jesus and sign your covenant: "Thy cup, O Lamb of God, is my cup; Thy baptism is my baptism." Jesus will carry you through it. His kind answer to those disciples meant more than this—"Oh yes, foolish children, you do not know what you say, but you mean it. I know how your vows will fail, but I will take it from you." That was not so much His meaning. He had another thought—"Yes, my disciples, you shall. I will carry you through it all, and lead you from Gethsemane and Calvary onward to Pentecost."

Beloved, come and make yourselves ready, prepare yourselves for that word, "We can." That is consecration. We can in *Thy* strength. Oh! what joy there would be in heaven if this great company were to fall down and say, when Jesus asks, "Can ye drink the cup, can ye be baptized into my death?"—"Yea, Lord, we can." Let our hearts even now say it.

And what comes next? Something very interesting. Our fourth point was the consecration yielded by them, and accepted by Christ: now comes—*The contention of the disciples about it.* Is it not a terrible thing that every "higher life" movement awakens contention and division? Here are these two disciples. Their hearts are for Jesus, and their longings are for the glory, and it was not unnatural that they should say—for they had been His special friends—"Lord, give us a place on Thy throne." But there are the other disciples, and how quick they are to condemn the two! They do not know that in doing so they are revealing, by the jealousy of their hearts, that they are just as unfit for the throne as James and John.

And let me say, Keswick lifts up the standard of holiness; but if there is one thing that is heavy on my heart, during my stay in England, it is that God's children in England are not as near each other as they should be. Oh, brethren, is not it a terrible thing that this holiness banner is becoming a mark of separation, and that there are people who say, "Yes, this is right," and "That is right," and "This is wrong," and "That is wrong"; and unconsciously there comes a separation? I pray you, call upon God fervently and unitedly that He will pour out such a spirit of love on His people in England that they cannot help coming together. I do not want them to compromise truth or disguise their differences, but I want them to come together and say, "O God, we are one, and we want to show it to each other." In the spirit of love we want to say, "We shall bear with your differences, even when we think them wrong; but *one* we are." God grant that the power of holiness may come among us, and that the spirit of those disciples may pass away from us! God grant that the spirit of Jesus the crucified, His love, may fill us with devotion, not only to the heathen and the unconverted, but to our brethren who are near to us in Christ Jesus, though separated for a little while by earthly distinctions!

And then comes my next thought, and that leads us still deeper down. We read, "But Jesus called them to Him." The Lord Jesus cannot bear division; it grieves Him terribly. You know how He said, in effect, "This is to be a mark that ye are my disciples: that ye love one another as I have loved you." Jesus cannot bear division. Get that deeply into your heart, and every time you think of anybody that differs from you, do make it a point to love him intensely before you talk about it.

But we read, "Jesus called them to Him, and saith unto them, Ye know that they who are accounted to rule over the Gentiles exercise lordship over them. . . . But so shall it not be among you." Now listen! "But whosoever will be great among you shall be your *minister* (or *servant*); and whosoever of you will be chiefest shall be the servant of all." What teaching! But then comes: "For even the Son of man came not to be ministered unto, but to minister, and to give His life a ransom for many." Now just let us look at this.

Look first at its connection with the preceding test that Christ proposes—"Drink of my cup, and be baptized with my baptism": that is something spiritual *in their relation to Him*. But now He brings them down, in the path of their consecration, to their *relation with their fellow-men*. He says to them, in other words, "Not only like me must you give up your will in Gethsemane, and be baptized on Calvary, but, remember, your consecration must be proved in your intercourse with each other every day, and by one consent you must all be servants." Is that what He expects? Yes, it is. Humility is the test of discipleship, and humility is the only path to glory. God says, "He that humbleth himself shall be exalted." You cannot climb to the throne; but climb down, ever deeper down, and God will exalt you.

Let us take in this thought. Jesus came and "made Himself of no reputation, and took upon Him the form of a servant." Every attribute of Jesus, and every circumstance of His life, and every feature of His character is preached upon, and you delight in Him; but have you studied this one—"The form of a servant"? Have you said in your heart, "What divine beauty! My God taking the place of a *servant*." Have you learned it? If not, may you learn it to-night! The path of consecration is the path of humility. Jesus says that he who wants to be chief must be the bondslave of all. The least will be the chief.

You talk of the "primacy" in the Church, of the "primate of all England." Christ says that the primate of all the churches is the very humblest. I wonder if we shall not have to be astonished in heaven at some poor, humble woman, who will there take the first place. Just ask God, for Christ's sake, that the primate in the Church may indeed be the very humblest in your circle. In your prayer meeting just ask God to make him the very humblest, and then you will not get the spirit displayed by those disciples.

William Law gives some earnest advice about praying every day for humility as one of the most essential things we need, and he uses this strong expression: "Pray to be delivered from every vestige of pride as though you were in torment." Oh, let us be afraid of pride, and let us live the life of humility. Jesus wants to bring us down.

"Even as the Son of man came not to be ministered unto, but to minister, and to give His life." Oh, that wonderful word! "*Even as the Son of man*," that is our law, that is our rule to live by. How are we to live? He lived as a servant, entirely to help others and make them happy. That is the work of the honest servant. Shall we not say to Jesus, "In Thy name we take all God's people, and become their servants, and ready we shall ever be to help them in any way"? Oh may that spirit come upon us!

Ah! His death can do it, and you will need the power of His death to do it; for if we are to serve our brother—some one who worries us, and with whom there is friction—if we are to serve him every day and to keep the place of a humble slave, nothing less than the power of Christ's death will enable us to do it. We must live in the grave of Jesus. God bring us there, and keep us there, even as the Son of man gave His life. And then you will be able to say increasingly, "Even as the Son, I drink the cup; and even as the Son, I am baptized into death; and even as the Son, I give my life. I do not leave all the work to the missionary in the foreign field, but I say, Here is my life, Lord; every hour is at Thy feet and at Thy disposal."

There we have the path to the higher life. It began with the prayer, "Nearness to Thee, likeness to Thee, power for Thee, O Jesus." Then came the words from Jesus, to this effect—"You do not know what you are asking." Next is proposed the test of consecration: Can ye drink of the cup? Can ye be baptized with the baptism? And then, after the disciples said they could, the loving answer came, the loving assurance, Yes, it shall be. Next followed that sad picture of the sin of contention. But, praise God, even that has turned out for our good; for we have the blessed lesson coming out of it, that we must learn to be the very least of all.

If, therefore, you want the steps in the path of consecration, they are these: Fellowship with Jesus; absolute and entire surrender to His death; fellowship with one another in love; a humility which gives itself to be the servant of all. God make that the path of our consecration!

And now, I have yet to come to the very best part of my message. You will very naturally ask the question: The teaching of Christ, did it help much? Did it make Peter and James and John what they ought to be? I answer, Not a bit; they remained just as they were. That teaches me the solemn lesson that Christ's teaching, or convention teaching, cannot cast out the devil. The contention went on from this chapter down to the Last Supper. Pride and self-confidence were there, and in the hall of Caiaphas Peter denied his Lord. The teaching of Christ helped them very little, and yet, praise God! it did help them infinitely, for it prepared them, by the consciousness of failure, for something better. Did this ever come? It *did* come. At Pentecost everything was changed. Christ conquered sin and death, and rose to heaven, and sat on the right hand, and received from the Father— yes, from His God and Father—a new gift, a new inflowing of the

Holy Spirit; and by that Holy Spirit—though His teaching could not change them—came within them His own life, and then everything was changed. Where did they get the power to "drink the cup"? Why was it that Peter was ready now for anything? Where did they get the power not to be afraid of imprisonment, to count it a joy to suffer, and to give their lives even unto death—where did they get it? At Pentecost the living Christ, the power of Gethsemane, the power of Calvary, the love that had died, entered into their hearts. Christ dwelt there, and from that day and onward began a new life, a new era in the Church of Christ.

And, O friends, I say that that is the best part of the message, for what I have to tell you in conclusion is—*all this is a divine possibility.* The previous speaker spoke of a plan of life in the case of a man who is half-hearted; I speak of a plan of life for a man who is whole-hearted, and I say to you, take the life-plan of Jesus, and come to-night to Him and say, "Lord, I will accept it; I can be baptized with Thy baptism." Let us, ere we part, join in such an act of consecration.

THE PATH AND THE POWER

Rev. Evan H. Hopkins

I WANT you to look at these words in Colossians 1: 11—
"Strengthened with all might according to His glorious
power." Now here is power for the walk. When God calls us
unto life, He calls us to walk before Him. And when He calls us to
walk before Him, He provides the power that we need in order
to do so. But we need something more than power in order to
walk before God: we need a *path*. Many seem to think it is only
a question of power. "Oh, if I had only the power!" But there is
something before the power: it is the path. How many want the
power to follow their own path. We map out our future; we know
what we should like, and we say, "Lord, give me the power to
follow this path." The power does not come, and then we learn
that God promises His power only along His own path. Let us
take these two thoughts—the path and the power.

I. What is the PATH? There is the path of His will. "Filled
with the knowledge of His will." The path of His favour, "unto
all pleasing." The path of His fruitfulness, "fruitful in every good
work."

First, there is the path of His *will*. It is a beautifully simple life,
the true life of trust, simply following the will of the Lord. It
may be a very humble life, but there is nothing higher than doing
the will of the Lord. The way to do the Lord's work is to walk
along the path of the Lord's will. All the work is in the path of
the will. And what a blessed thought it is, that God has a will
concerning each one of us individually. He has a gracious purpose
concerning each one of His children.

And another thing let us remember: that that will may be
ascertained, may be known, and that it may be done. "Filled
with the knowledge of His will," "understanding what the will
of the Lord is." "Thy will be done."

Now we know that to do the will of the Lord is utterly impossible for us: it is not only difficult, it is impossible. But then,
the Lord calls us to do the impossible work, and to walk the
impossible walk. We have it in the gospels. You remember when
the Lord told His disciples to do an impossible work: "Give ye
them to eat." Was that possible? They were in the wilderness with

five thousand people. How many loaves had they? Just a few,
and two or three little fishes. "Give ye them to eat." That is a
hard command, but they did it. You say, "But they didn't do
it, the Lord did it." Precisely; that is the thing we are teaching.
Before the Lord wrought the miracle things had to be adjusted.
There was the multitude who were to sit down, that was the outer
circle; then the disciples were to come within, there was the inner
circle; but there is only one centre, that is Christ. Now things
are adjusted. Where are the loaves? "Bring them to me." They
were not to work from themselves, they were to work from Christ,
the centre. There is the secret of all work. So the loaves were
brought and put into the Lord's hands, and He looked unto
His Father, and then the stream flowed from Him through the
disciples to the empty vessels, and it went on till they were all
filled. You say, "The Lord did that." Yes, and yet the disciples
did it. They obeyed the Lord's command.

Apply that to the difficulties of daily life. The difficulties arise
because you have a wrong centre—*yourself*. You take the centre
"enable me," and of course you break down. "Believe ye that
I am able?" When the Lord takes the centre, it makes all the
difference in the world. Where there is this adjustment, and you
let the Lord take the right place, then the will of the Lord is done.

Then there was the impossible walk of Peter stepping out upon
the water. "But Peter attained to that," you say, "and what a
wonderful attainment! I have not attained to that." You make
a great mistake. It was impossible for Peter to walk upon the water,
utterly impossible. When he came upon the water, he had his
eye fixed upon Christ, and Christ had His power underneath
Peter, and it mattered not how heavy Peter was. There was the
adjustment. But the moment He looked away the connection was
broken, and he sank. And so the power is in Christ, not in attainment; it is moment by moment, the communication of divine
power meeting our tendency to sink. You say, "I do not think
the blessing I got could be a real blessing, because I lost it." That
does not follow. You got out of it. It will continue so long as you
keep trusting. And so I say, the work before us can be done if
we bring the Lord into it; it all depends upon that. "All things
are possible unto God," and so you see the power is found in the
will of the Lord. Do not be afraid of the will; if you have the
Lord He gives the power.

Then another thought: it is the path of His *smile*. How blessed
a thing it is to be walking "in the light, as God is in the light." It
is our privilege to live in constant communion with God. You
say, "Give me a passage of Scripture to prove that." "I am
the light of the world: he that followeth me shall not walk in

darkness, but shall have the light of life." Now if we believe such passages as these, our faith will grow. "The path of the just is as the shining light, that shineth more and more unto the perfect day." But it depends upon what you are looking at. If you are looking at your work, your progress will be little. There was a certain ploughman, a good man, an excellent servant in many ways, but I heard a farmer say he was a miserable ploughman because, while he was driving the plough, he was continually looking back to see if he made a straight furrow; the consequence was it was always a crooked one. There is only one way to drive a plough—steadily to look before you. Do not look at your attainments, but to the Lord, walking in His smile. And in proportion as you know the true life, you will find it is a simple life. "Unto all pleasing." Not pleasing all people. Did you ever try to please everybody? You cannot do that. It means pleasing the Lord in all things; and when you please the Lord you have His smile, and that is enough.

Again, it is the path of His *fruitfulness*. "Fruitful in every good work." Must I be occupied with all kinds of good work? That is what many Christians are trying to do. It does not mean that. There is a difference between work and fruit. Work is the result of action. Fruit is the outcome of life; there is an organic connection between fruit and the believer. Fruit is the overflow of the sap. Now there are some people who seem to have only just enough sap to keep them in existence, and certainly not enough for fruit. What they want is fulness of life. You have life, so you are a Christian; if you had fulness of life you would be a fruitful Christian. A Sunday-school teacher says, "I have laboured for weeks and months, and I see no fruit." But does not the Lord see fruit? "No; there are no conversions." Ah, but I am not talking about conversions. What is this fruit? Love, joy, peace, long-suffering, gentleness, meekness . . . While you are engaged in the work, be fruitful in these things. Some are murmuring, some are jealous, some are envious. They are not fruitful. This fruit is "the fruit of the Spirit." You may be fruitful wherever you are. All of us can be fruitful. Every moment of the day, we may bring forth the fruit of the Spirit. "Ye are the branches; the branch cannot bring forth fruit of (from) itself"; it is "the fruit of the Spirit." Do not grieve the Spirit, and the first thing He will do will be to fill your heart with love, joy, and peace; and when the inner condition is right, then the outward conduct will be right. We see here then the path in which we have to walk; the path of His will, of His smile, of His fruitfulness. And every moment we can be fruitful: that is the grand thing. "Herein is my father glorified"—that "ye are the means of converting many souls"?

No; but "that ye bear much fruit." Leave the conversion of souls to the Lord, and if you are fruitful there will be conversions.

II. There is the POWER. I like to notice that it is in the passive voice: "Being strengthened." It is not the result of your own struggles. It is like that other passage in Timothy: "Be strong in the Lord, and in the power of His might." Be willing to be empowered. That is the force of the exhortation. You cannot strengthen yourself; capacity to receive belongs to you, ability to accomplish belongs to the Lord. You can receive the strong One, and then you are strengthened. This is the way the blessing comes. There is a kind of toy fountain which, when wound up, plays beautifully for a time, and then runs down. So sometimes souls seek conventions to wind them up. That is self-centred; there is the resolution, there is the effort. You have the winding up, and then the running down. "The water that I shall give him shall be in him a well." How beautiful it is in the Revised Version, "The water that I shall give him shall *become* in him." "Shall *become*" as a fresh experience of an old gift. You have the water. Yes. But now it has become to you a spring overflowing, and the friction and strain have been taken out of your life. We want strengthening "with all might according to His glorious power." First notice it is *divine* power. You say, "of course, every blessing that comes from God is divine." But I want you to notice that it is divine in this sense: we speak of the life of God, the life that He gives; but the life that He *lives* is another thing. God gives me life, but He comes into my heart and lives His life. So here is His power; God is not going to give me power. God gave power to the first man, and man failed, and He is never going to give power to man again. He gives power to Christ. You want power, then you must have Christ. That power is something that He exercises. A weapon has no power in itself. Supposing a giant lays hold of it, the power in the arm of the giant is now in the weapon. "And I was strengthened as the hand of the Lord my God was upon me" (Ezra 7: 28). That is the secret of the power. Again, it is *sufficient* power. "Strengthened with *all* might." I love that little word "all." I like it to stand as it is: "all might." Then there is enough, there is sufficient power. He might promise *much* might, or *some* might, but it is "all might," then it is enough.

And notice it is "*glorious*" power. Take it as it may be translated literally, "strengthened with all might according to *the power of His glory*." What does that mean? In Ephesians 1: 7 I read, "the riches of His *grace*," but when I turn to 3:16 I read, "according to the riches of His *glory*." What is the difference? "Riches of His grace"—Christ on the cross. "In Him we have redemption through His blood, the forgiveness of sins, according to the riches of His grace." We all have that, if we are Christians. Now in the third chapter we read, "That He would grant you ... according to the riches of His glory to be strengthened ..." It is a prayer for converted people, for saved souls, a prayer for fuller blessing, the very thing we have come here for. What are the "riches of His glory"? Christ on the throne. Christ on the cross—pardon, redemption; Christ on the throne—anointing, power for service, the gift of the Holy Ghost, the fulness of the Spirit. We see, then, that it is the power of His glory—the Holy Ghost. The coming of the Holy Ghost was prophetically revealed in the Old Testament, and historically fulfilled in the New. And what is the next thing? That the blessing should be experimentally realised. That is what we want; we want this power in us, working in us. Are you willing? Have you yielded yourself for this? What keeps you back? You say "Yes, but I am not ready to follow His will. I must think about it first." "Am I willing to give myself wholly to God's will?" "Am I ready?" and you draw a deep sigh; as Frances Havergal said once: "God's will was once to me a *sigh*; now it is a *song*." And when we get a view of God's will, we fall in love with it. We see it is a blessed thing; it is something joyous. This is the true spirit of consecration.

Then observe, as to the power—it is *practical*. It is "unto all patience." Is it not wonderful, after all these heights of grace, that we come down suddenly to such a commonplace duty as patience? One of the commonest of sins among Christian people is impatience. You are engaged in some Christian work, and somebody forgets some important duty. You say, "I have no patience with that man!" You need not feel thus, for there is power for this—"all patience." You needn't be afraid of the divine requirement, because there is the divine provision of power. You observe, there is the "all might." Link that with the "all patience." The power is sufficient to meet the requirement. You know, difficulty is a relative term; it depends whether you have power enough. "But can I be patient always?" Certainly. "But must I not make a desperate effort?" No. Let the Lord possess you, and you will discover, as the Lord takes His right place within you, that you become strongest on your weakest side. The impatient man then becomes gentle. Remember this, then, that we have a divine provision to meet the divine requirement. The power is divine, sufficient, glorious and practical.

Now, dear friends, we see all this; but there are certain conditions. We cannot enter into these blessings unless we are in the right relation to God. Are we all really consecrated to God? Have we handed ourselves right over to Him, that we may be at

His disposal? Are you prepared for that? Someone says, "I feel that I am not prepared for this. It is no use saying that I am. I do not want to be a decided Christian." Lots of such thoughts come into our heads. But for myself, I can say that it was a blessed moment when I made no reserves. I just handed myself over to the Lord, and then I discovered that His holy will was not something terrible and dark and dismal. I never knew what true soul-rest was till that moment. I knew the joy of conversion, I mean of pardon; I knew that that had been a marked crisis in my life; but it was some time after that before I saw the glorious privilege of walking with God, as Enoch walked, and having the testimony that we please God, walking in fellowship with Him, and having all one's needs supplied, realising that there is an all-sufficient provision. For every "I need" in self, there is an "I am" in Christ—man's emptiness and God's fulness meeting.

Now, each soul may be brought to this point: *the last thing may be yielded*. And the last thing is very often *unbelief*. We have dropped this and that and the other sin, we are willing to give up worldliness, but we do not *believe*. No, we are waiting to realise, we want to *feel* we have faith. There is seeking faith, and there is resting faith. The nobleman of Capernaum had seeking faith when he went fifteen miles to find Jesus; but he carried a heavy burden. "Except ye see signs and wonders, ye will not believe." "Lord, come down ere my child die." Jesus saith unto him, "Go thy way, thy son liveth." Here was the critical moment. "And the man believed the word that Jesus had spoken unto him, and he went his way." That was resting faith, and the burden was dropped. What did he believe? That his son was healed. He went back at his leisure, and the servants met him and said, "Thy son liveth." "When did he begin to get better?" "Yesterday, at the seventh hour," at the very time the Lord had spoken.

A great many people have a faith that seeks, but they have not a faith that rests. Now we want them to rest; the Lord is here, rest on Him, let the burden go. "Lord, I trust Thee now; I cast myself on Thee now. Lord, as I think about my home troubles, my business troubles, my own individual difficulties in every sphere of life, I bring them all, and commit them all to Thee and rest in Thee; keep me." And believe that He keeps you. I am sure this rest of faith is the centre of all true activity. You cannot work without friction until you have this rest of faith—perfect dependence not only on what the Lord has done, but on what He is to you this moment. Rest in Him. "God is able to make all grace abound toward you, that ye always (not sometimes) having all sufficiency in all things, may abound unto every good work" (2 Cor. 9: 8). Is that really so? Then away with every anxious thought. "Lord, I trust Thee; I hand myself wholly over to Thee; and as Thou has pardoned me and saved me from the penalty of sin, so now be Thou my keeper." The responsibility of keeping you belongs to Him: but the responsibility of trusting Him to keep you, belongs to you. Now let us trust Him.

THIRSTY CHRISTIANS

Canon W. Hay H. M. Aitken, M. A.

I AM not about to take a text so much as to present a subject.
I will read words which are better than any of mine that I
can possibly conceive or present to you; because the words
that I read come from the direct inspiration of the Holy Spirit of
God, as we believe. Let us begin by reading Isaiah 55.

How many of us have preached upon the first verse? We have
told the weary, wandering tribes of earth that there is a Fountain
somewhere near them, and that they need not die of thirst, as
so many seem like to do. We have heard the message pealed forth
from the evangelist's lips over and over again, and we have seen the
blessed results when seeking souls have gathered round the cross,
and with tear-dimmed eyes have gazed into the face of the
Crucified, to discover new life and new joy there—the living
waters of salvation.

Perhaps, as we read the passage, some of us are thinking within
ourselves, "Surely this is not for Keswick! You forget where you
are; you are a mission preacher, and you cannot be anything else.
We do not require the Gospel to be preached to us here; we have
it already, and we know the blessedness of justification by faith."
I know you do. But it has long been borne in upon my mind that
there is a wonderful analogy between the experience of awakened
souls seeking after pardon and salvation, and the experience of
hungering and thirsting souls seeking after a fuller knowledge of
the Lord Jesus Christ and what He can do for us.

I very often find that, when I am trying to conduct consecration
meetings in my own missions, I use very much the same language
in dealing with the Lord's people, as I do on other occasions in
pleading with the once careless and worldly who have ceased to
be careless and have begun to seek after God. I find, not in-
frequently, that the acts of decision I claim from those who are
awakened by God the Holy Spirit to feel their need of a Saviour
are closely parallel, though not identical, with the acts of decision
which yearning hearts have to make who are longing to know
more and more of the power of God's Gospel, and to rise to the
full enjoyment of their spiritual privileges in Christ Jesus. And

so we are going to take this dear old chapter—such a friend of the evangelist—as the Gospel in the largest sense; for it is a Gospel to saint and a Gospel to sinner, a Gospel to those who are far off and to those who are nigh.

I cannot help thinking that probably a very large number of us have come up to Keswick because we are thirsty. I am sure that, wherever I go, I find any number of thirsty Christians—thirsty, not satisfied, apparently not quite sure that they are possessed of the secret of satisfaction. Possibly some of you are saying, "Surely we all ought to be thirsty; and we all shall be thirsty, if we are right, to the very end." I quite agree with you. The beautiful words of St. Bernard are true of us all, and, I think, must awaken an echo in all our hearts—

> Fountain of pleasure unalloyed,
> Who eat Thee hunger still;
> Who drink of Thee, still feel a void
> That only Thou can'st fill.

But it is one thing to feel thirsty, and yet to know that the water is near and that we may go and drink, and it is quite another thing to feel thirsty and to have to say, "Oh, dear me, where is it? I cannot find it, I cannot get hold of it. It must be somewhere, but it is not where I am!" Hagar in the desert looked here and there in the agony of her heart, laying her child under a bush and saying, "Let me not see the death of my child"; and all the while the water was close to her, though she did not see it. She would have died for the want of it, if the Lord had not opened her eyes. Lord, open our eyes to-night—may that be the prayer of every believing heart.

Now many of us are thirsty in this first sense. Our thirst is the desire to know more and more of God. We cannot be satisfied to-day with yesterday's blessing. We need to get closer and closer to God; to feel more of His love, to realise more of His power, and to live in His life, and to taste the joy of communion with Him more and more. I believe that, throughout eternity, it will still be "more and more."

That is all very blessed; but it is not the thirst I am thinking of. It is a very different thing to find our religious life a disappointment, to look back wistfully upon the early days of our first love, and say within ourselves, "Why is it not with me now as it was then? I was zealous then, my zeal is flagging now. I felt as if I could carry all before me then, in the joy of that first love; but I am beaten again and again to-day by almost every foe. I seem not to have the same interest in spiritual things. I look at my worldly neighbour, and I say within my heart, am I really a happier man than he? Does what I call my religion do more for me than his worldliness does for him? I know a good deal about it in my head; but is it to me a something that altogether differentiates my life from his?"

Oh, the thirsty Christians, up and down the broad land and all over it! Thank God, they are thirsty; but can it be His will that we should remain in this condition of unsatisfied thirst? Surely, Isaiah 55 says, "No." Surely we are reading here a description of satisfaction. Jesus Christ does not say to us, "Ho, all ye thirsty, come, and I will give you one good drink; then you may go into the desert again, and spend your life in sighing for the draught you once enjoyed." It is not that; but He is inviting us to a feast, He is drawing us nearer to Himself because He intends to feed us. He seems to use the strongest language that could possibly be employed, in order to impress upon our hearts the fact that He intends His royal bounty to satisfy all the desires of our hearts as they arise, to keep us in a condition of plenitude and not of starvation, because we are drawing upon the boundless wealth of an infinite God. How the words thrill us, do they not? "Come ye to the waters, and he that hath no money, come ye, buy and eat; yea, come, buy wine and milk without money and without price." He does not intend to treat us badly, and to keep us upon starvation fare. It is all there for us, and God must needs wish us to enjoy it.

I think there is something very pathetic in the motive that brings a good many people to Keswick. It is not, I am sure, at all uncommon for a disappointed Christian, a jaded Christian, a weary-hearted Christian, to say within himself, "I'll go to Keswick." You have heard it said, haven't you? "I'll go to Keswick." If he had said, "I'll go to Jesus," it would have been a shorter cut everyway! But when he says, "I'll go to Keswick," he means something. He has heard about the wonderful meetings, how believers gather from the four corners of the world and cast themselves down before God; and how, from time to time, there is, not an angel stirring the waters, but something grander—the Holy Spirit Himself stirring the waters of the human heart, so that again and again benediction falls upon this one and upon that. "You remember so and so? Well, he went to Keswick last year, and he has been a different man ever since! I would give anything if I could get my face to shine like that; but my poor dowdy religion seems all the meaner and poorer because it is cast into dark relief by the brightness of God's vessel over yonder. I almost envy my brother his bright face. I'll go to Keswick, and perhaps I'll get it, too."

Thank God for the yearning desire for a fuller enjoyment of what God is, and that we feel this state of continuous dissatisfaction and of chronic thirst that seems to have nothing to answer to it, no divine draught lifted to our lips to assuage it. But while we thank God for it, we surely feel that this spiritual state cannot be the thing that God intends for us. He must intend something better for us than this life-long thirst. And, remember, it is not only we who are thirsting. I believe that most of these monstrosities of modern thought we hear so much about are the product of nothing else than spiritual thirst. Some who find the Gospel story quite incredible can still swallow all the comedy of Theosophy; those who cannot believe in the supernatural readily accept "Christian Scientism"; and those who speak contemptuously of the Resurrection believe in all the paraphernalia of Spiritualism.

Very wonderful, is it not? No, not a bit! It is just this—we believers have shown so little of the supernatural in our lives, that people have come to the conclusion, "As for Christianity, that is played out; it is little better than humbug; because, while it promises so much, it fails utterly in so far as the meeting of our need is concerned. But the thirst is here, it is a fact of our moral experience. It is no use going to our parochial clergyman, for we can see by his life and teaching that he does not know the secret of satisfaction himself. It is no use going to those who make a loud profession of religion, for they are just as incapable of finding a supply for thirsting humanity as we feel ourselves to be." When one theory after another is presented to men they will take their choice; they are not bound by the traditions of the past, nor are they terrorised from making their choice by the horrors of the Inquisition. Not having seen others enjoy in Christ Jesus what the Gospel has to give, men come to the conclusion that it is no use looking for what they want there— so they look elsewhere.

Thus it is, I believe, with nominal Christians, and with real Christians whose reality is very limited. The latter know enough to feel their sins have been forgiven; but they have never gone on to take hold of and enjoy their heritage in Christ Jesus. They are playing into the hands of false systems, and are leading people to say, "We must look elsewhere for the water to quench our thirst; for as for that Prophet of Galilee, His store seems to be exhausted." It is not exhausted; but we who ought to be enjoying it, alas! how little many of us know about it.

The old seer's voice, speaking for his Master, rings out among the ranks of thirsty Christians, if we are thirsty, "Ho!" It is the exclamation of a man who has made a great find. You are out on the mountains, desperately thirsty, feeling that you must drop if you don't get water soon; and your comrade walking with you says, "I'll have a look around here, and you search there." Presently you hear him cry, "Ho!" and you know what that means—water! You come running up, and there it is; you do not need to be asked twice to drink.

Even so, God is speaking to us. This convention, what is it? It is God's cry—Ho! believe it; respond to it now!—It is God saying "Ho!" to thirsty souls. And what does that "Ho!" draw us toward? To what does it call our attention? I want my first message to be this: Brethren and sisters in Christ, the water is here; it really must be here, or else this New Testament is a lie, and Christianity is a delusion.

I heard of a dear soul saying only to-day, "Yes, but they don't get the power, after all. They talk about being filled with the Holy Ghost, but what can they do? Can they work miracles?" Well, my friends, I find that there were a very large number of persons in New Testament times who received the Holy Ghost and yet did not work miracles. St. Paul expressly says so. He says, "Are all apostles? Are all prophets? Are all teachers? Are all workers of miracles?" At the same time, and in the same chapter, he tells us that the mere power to teach is the product of the Holy Ghost, provided it is the right kind of teaching—teaching in the Spirit. The power to be "a help" is not a "very large order," as the phrase runs; but to be a real help—one who does this helpful work in the power of the Holy Ghost—this surely is a gift of the Spirit.

There may be—I am inclined to believe that there are—such supernatural manifestations made to-day, from time to time, as were made 1800 years ago. I cannot for a moment deny that multitudes of people—people whose words I am prepared to accept—have been cured by trusting Jesus Christ to cure them. Why not? I am stating no theory as to what we ought to do when we are sick. I feel, for my own part, that it has been so much God's way to work by means that, until I am brought to a very different mind, I shall think that I am doing God's will in using means. But there are certain persons who bear circumstantial witness that God has done this for them—only a day or two ago I heard a dear friend say . . . "and God did heal me." I don't dispute it for a moment.

But what I want to press upon you is this—it is not only in what man calls supernatural phenomena that we are to see the work of the Holy Ghost. Suppose that a minister is in the habit of preaching dry and ineffective sermons, sermons that you could not expect to be the means of converting anybody. He tells God that he is weary of his ministry, that he feels he has no power;

and, in his weakness, he throws himself upon the Lord. Suppose that God the Holy Ghost touches his lips, and next Sunday his congregation is electrified. "What has come to the parson?" they say; "he is speaking in a new tongue." One and another are broken down, and a great work of grace begins. What is that? The world will not call it a miracle, but I do! It is the intervention of God in the ordinary course of human events; and that is what we mean by the supernatural.

Let us not say that there is no reality in the divine gift, because not every one who professes to receive the Holy Ghost can work a miracle; but let us believe that, when God pledges Himself, in a distinct and specific revelation, to do something for His people, He intends to do it. Now, what has He pledged Himself to do?

The voice of the ancient seer is re-echoed in the Temple at Jerusalem by a greater than he. "Jesus stood and cried, saying, If any man thirst, let him come unto me and drink." He had a thought for the thirsty ones. He had a heart of sympathy for the thirsty ones. He Himself already anticipated His own great thirst; for He took our thirst upon Him. By-and-by, upon the pitiless cross, Jesus was to say, "I thirst." He knows our thirst; it was part of the curse of sin that He Himself was to bear. My friends, He who Himself was to be thirsty—to know all the weariness of thirst that human spirits know—He cries in the Temple, and He cries still, "If any man thirst"—any man—"let him come unto me and drink."

Our Lord improves upon Isaiah. He does not stop just where Isaiah stopped. He does not tell us about the wine and milk without money and without price, but He goes on to say something dearer than even that to a heart that has any humanity in it; something that must make my spirit rejoice more than even quaffing deep draughts of bliss from the very hand of God. What is that? "He that believeth on me, as the Scripture hath said, out of his belly shall flow rivers of living water." Thank God, that is an improvement upon Isaiah. Jesus said it, Jesus meant it, and Jesus is going to do it! Now, thirsty souls, get this clear before your minds. We have come to Keswick. No! You are here; indeed, this is an actual fact. But there is something more important than that to be realised. We have come to Jesus! At any rate, He is here. He is here, just as surely as He was in the Temple of old; here, pledged by the Temple utterance, to say the same thing to-night. And why? Because He is the same yesterday, and to-day, and for ever. If He said it to the thirsty ones 1800 years ago, He is saying it to the thirsty ones now!

Backslider, are you thirsty? Are you wailing out your woes in those sad words of Cowper—

> Where is the blessedness I knew
> When first I saw the Lord?
> Where is the soul-refreshing view
> Of Jesus and His Word?

My soul is athirst for God—God—*God*! I thirst, I thirst, I *thirst*! Backslider, He says "*any* man." Thank God, there is room in that word for the backslider. Inconsistent Christian, you who have been trying to serve two masters—to live for the world, and for God, too. You feel ashamed of yourself. You sit in God's presence self-condemned, saying, "I know my religious life is a failure, and serve me right. I have not been thoroughly true to God: I have been leading a self-pleasing, self-indulgent life; and I feel very far from God to-night. I have not altogether lost religion, but a distance has crept up between my Lord and me." You are one of the "any" men. "If *any* man thirst, let him come unto me, and drink." Oh, thank God! Let us get this thought into our minds, that we really may come. The blessing that I need is actually here for me to-night, and God intends me to have it. He does not mock the desire of the heart that He has made by empty rhetoric, by sounding phrases, by beautiful poetry, by the imagery that charms our fancy. Ah, no! God does not deal in mere tropes when He offers to us the realities of the Kingdom of heaven—"If any man thirst, let him come unto me, and drink."

Now, have we got that thought thoroughly into our minds? Yes. But stay—I want it to go deeper: have we got hold of it *in our hearts*? If any of us are thirsting to-night, Jesus is here. He is just calling to the thirsty one, and He is saying, "You are not only going to drink—you are going to do that—but I am going to so fill you with myself and with my Holy Spirit, that forth from you the living water shall flow." So that you who have said in your heart, "I never can do any work for Christ, that is the trouble; my lips are sealed," you are going to find those lips of yours unsealed. And you who have been surrounded by worldly influences, who have never been able to take up your cross and confess Christ—you are going to be able to confess Christ. You who have said, "I have no sort of influence," are going to find a new and wonderful influence, working through your weakness, for the glory of God and the salvation of man. Do you believe it?

"If any man thirst, let him come unto me and drink. He that believeth on me, as the Scripture hath said, out of his belly shall flow rivers of water." *"Believest thou this?"* I will put it as definitely as possible—Jesus is here; is He going to do for you as He has promised? Do not evade it; don't take refuge in orthodox platitudes, but keep your eye upon the point and your mind brought up to the question, "Believest thou this?"

Dear friends, if you are fully convinced that Jesus Christ is here to do just what wants to be done, what are the conditions under which you may claim and make sure of the blessing that you need?

We will go to that grand text in verse 7, "Let the wicked forsake his way, and the unrighteous man his thoughts." Hush, don't quote that! You are speaking in an assembly of believers—dear, good, earnest Christian people. Ah, but are you sure that your disappointment in life has not arisen from the fact that you have a way of your own? Not wicked, no; yet when a man wanders from God's way, and begins to take his own way, surely the seed of all wickedness is there. Not "unrighteous"—justified by faith, and at peace with God; but when I play with a besetting sin, when I trifle with an impure desire, the seed of all unrighteousness is there.

Now, what is demanded of us? Not that you should overcome the sin that doth so easily beset you, but forsake it; there is a difference between these two processes. If I am a man of small stature and insignificant power, and I have a friend who is a perfect Samson, I may wish to cease to have any friendship with him, and may say, "You and I part company; I forsake you." But he may say, "Stay, not so fast," as he puts his arm round my shoulder, "*I* am not going to forsake *you!*" This is the trouble. Even so, in order to overcome sin, I want a power greater than my own. But in order to forsake sin, I need a decisive act of my will in response to the claim and the influence of the Holy Ghost.

Has there been some sin you have been trifling with, some secret impurity, some worldly ambition, some quarrel or controversy between you and God, which constitutes your way? It may not be a very bad way, but it is a perverse way, a disobedient way, not the way God wants you to take. Forsake it. You say, "I cannot master it." I dare say not; that is not what I am asking you to do. I am asking you to say, in your will, "I forsake it, if only Thou wilt master it for me."

When we forsake our way, and put aside thoughts of evil we have harboured, and evil thoughts of God that we have permitted to enter and lodge in our souls—when we put them away, what then? "Let him turn to the Lord." It sounds very simple. What is the first word? "Ho, everyone that thirsteth, *come.*"

What is Christ's word? "If any man thirst, let him *come*"—very simple, surely! "But is there something much more elaborate than that," say some of you. "I have to go through a process, haven't I? One must go through the mill if one is to be turned out properly." "First of all I must be purified, then sanctified and consecrated. Each experience must come in its due course, and all will take time, in order that the thing may be rightly done; and after that has all been realised I may begin to think about being filled with the Holy Ghost." Don't you think there is something of money and of price in all this? Is it not getting oneself up to a certain point, so that I may say, "Now, Lord, I have done so many excellent things, and have been through so many excellent experiences, that I am in a position to make a bid for something higher. Give me the Holy Ghost to crown and complete it all."

There is nothing of all that in "Come." "Come" is only the equivalent of "Believe." It is only another way of God's saying, "Take me at my word." You remember what Jesus says, "He that *cometh* to me shall never hunger; and he that *believeth* on me shall never thirst" (John. 6: 35). He uses the words as synonymous, in two parallel clauses. "Coming" is bringing our own weakness and helplessness into touch with the divine fulness, so that the supply from God shall dovetail into the emptiness of my humanity —that is "coming."

Christ just says, "Come"; and I want you to come, if—I must insist upon that—if you are willing that the refining fire shall consume the impurities of a desecrated temple. Then, once the will is thus yielded, there is nothing to prevent you, without waiting for process or for experience, just coming forward and saying, "Lord, I am weary of myself. Lord, I'm sick and tired of my futile efforts to make my life something a little better than it is. I am a poor failure, in myself; but now"—yes, it is an instantaneous and immediate transaction between you and God, to occur just now—"I do what Thou tellest me to do. I come, I come, I come! I get a little nearer, and still a little nearer to Thy pierced feet; and I dare to touch Thee, to grasp Thee by the feet as did women of old, and to look up into Thy face and say, 'Jesus, Thou wilt not mock me; Thou hast said it.' By faith I rest upon Thy word, Thou wilt be true to me; and so I claim that which Thou givest, not by the works of the law, but by the hearing of faith. I hear Thine own sweet voice, and I just believe it; I leave Thee to give me the proofs—let them come in Thine own way and time. Give me prophecy, gift, power of helping, what Thou wilt—I leave all to Thee. But Thy promise, Thy promise, Thy promise—I have claimed it, I hold on to that. Thou canst not lie, Thou dost not lie. O God, Thou wilt not deceive Thine humble suppliant as he lies here at Thy feet."

By-and-by you will be able to say what I was going to say two years ago, after that wonderful Thursday night meeting. The ministers round the platform were just giving their texts. I had preached Christ for years, and had known the power of the Holy Ghost working with me and in my ministry for years; but when dear brother Inwood asked that heart-searching question, "Have you ever definitely *claimed* to be filled with the Holy Ghost?" I felt that I hadn't—I am ashamed to say it. But when, next morning, the texts were going round, they stopped at the platform, and so I had no opportunity to give mine. But I was ready with it if I had had a chance of giving it: "He satisfieth the longing soul, and filleth the hungry soul with goodness." Glory be to Him!

ORDEAL BY FIRE

Rev. E. W. Moore, M.A.

WILL you open your Bibles with me at 1 Corinthians 3: 14, 15, "If any man's work abide which he hath built thereupon, he shall receive a reward. If any man's work shall be burned, he shall suffer loss: but he himself shall be saved; yet so as through fire." We are all builders, whether we will or no. Not a day but sees the structure of our life-character rising.

> For the structure that we raise,
> Time is with materials filled;
> Our to-days and yesterdays
> Are the blocks with which we build.

"There is not a thought in us," said a great writer, "that is not doing mason's work." Point by point, storey by storey, the invisible structure is going up. One day it will stand revealed before men and angels. If that be so, what a dignity it lends to life. We often say it is a solemn thing to die. It is. Even our Lord Himself felt this, when He commended His spirit into the hands of His Father. It is a solemn thing to launch into the unseen. But rightly viewed, perhaps it is almost as solemn a thing to live.

> No service, in itself, is small,
> Nor great, though earth it fill;
> But that is small which seeks its own,
> And great which seeks God's will.

Yes, and in that view, life is all great. The minutest incidents in life have their bearing on the future. It is this wonderful conception of life as a building that the apostle seizes and presents to us in this memorable chapter. We will endeavour, for a few minutes, to follow it out.

First, *we have the foundation laid*. Ministering, some years ago now, in Switzerland, I was sorry as I left the beautiful little mountain church to observe that the rock upon which one of the buttresses of the chancel was built, was crumbling. My friend said to me, "You could not quote that as an illustration of the safety of the house built upon a rock." I replied, "No; but I can

quote it as an illustration of the insecurity of a house built upon
what looks like a fair foundation. That rock looked fair and strong,
or it would never have been chosen." I need not to-night dwell
upon the one foundation. We know how St. Paul had built for
many years upon the fair appearance of morality and ceremonial
observance, and how at length he cast them to the winds, "not
having his own righteousness which is of the law, but that which
is through the faith of Christ, the righteousness which is of God by
faith." The foundation, he says, you have nothing to do with,
except to build upon it. It has been laid for you. "Other foundation can no man lay than that is laid, which is Jesus Christ." It
was laid in the counsels of eternity, it was laid in fulness of time, it
was laid in the sufferings of Calvary, it was laid on the Resurrection morning, when, we may truly say, the sons of God shouted for
joy. Yes, there is no other. "There is," said John Wesley upon
his death-bed, "no entrance into the Holiest but by the blood of
Jesus." How important to be on the right foundation! There is
none other.

> On Christ, the solid Rock, I stand;
> All other ground is sinking sand.

But this passage deals not merely with the foundation, but with
the superstructure; and the second point that it brings before us
is—*the builders at work*. Now, the apostle tells us that very different
materials may be worked into the same foundation. No doubt
he is referring to two things—first, to doctrine; and then, to life.

He is referring to *doctrine*. There were teachers in Corinth who
were leading the people astray. What a responsibility attaches to
teachers! It is a solemn and an awful thing to have to seek to lead
others in the ways of God. I suppose that in the days in which
we are living, the great battle of the builders has been upon the
all-essential subject of the inspiration of Holy Scripture. There
are many gifted leaders who have been led astray, and who are
leading others astray, on this solemn subject. There is one consideration which I cannot forbear adverting to, and that is, that
in questioning the endorsement of Holy Scripture by the Lord
Jesus Christ, men are not merely speaking against the Son of man,
but are coming perilously near to speaking against the Holy
Ghost. It is often forgotten that Scripture expressly asserts that
our Lord, through the Spirit, gave commandment to the apostles
whom He had chosen. He Himself declares that He spoke not of
Himself, but the Father which sent Him gave Him a commandment what He should speak. In Isaiah 11: 2–5 we are expressly
told that the moral and mental ability of our Lord was guided
and controlled by the Holy Ghost, in His sevenfold gifts, in the

plenitude of His power. And whereas it is sometimes said that our Lord, during the period of His *kenosis*, during the period of His ministry as a man upon earth, associated Himself with the ideas of the time, yet it is in that chapter expressly asserted that He will not judge after the sight of His eyes, nor reprove as men reprove; but His ears were open to the voice of His Father. Therefore when our Lord endorsed Psalm 110, the prophecy of Daniel, and the prophecy of Jonah, was the Holy Spirit mistaken? Who suggested to Him that authorship? Who was the Author of the Old Testament Scriptures? Moses? Daniel? Jonah? Nay, they were the writers. Who was the Author? "Holy men of old spake as they were moved by the Holy Ghost." The Holy Ghost was the Author of the Old Testament Scriptures; and the Holy Ghost dwelt in Jesus without measure. For my part, I tremble when I think of these bold theories launched upon the Church to-day; not that they influence me an iota, but I see how they do influence many, and I wonder at it. "Let every man take heed how he buildeth thereupon."

But the words have reference, not only to doctrine, but to *life*. It is a sad reflection that base materials may be worked in upon a good foundation. Here we have them; they are contrasted, the good and the vile: "Gold, silver, precious stones; wood, hay, stubble." Ah, we have been building to-day! Have we been building gold, silver, precious stones? Or have we been building wood, hay, stubble—

> Worldly thoughts, and thoughts of pride,
> Wishes to Christ's Cross untrue.

Base, or double, or mixed motives, entering into Christian life and work—are these the materials that have been built into the wall? If they have the self-seeking mark upon them, they are doomed.

Now the passage goes on: it tells us that *the building will be tested*. Corinth presented a strange contrast in its buildings in the time of St. Paul. There were the magnificent marble palaces, adorned with gold and silver, and the shrines of the gods; and, side by side with them there were the poor tenements of the people, built of wood and thatched with hay and stubble. Now, we can readily understand that, in a city so strangely constituted, if a conflagration should arise the tenements, the cottages of wood, hay and stubble would perish, and only the more solid structures of marble would survive. It is thought by some that the Apostle had in his mind a great conflagration that had swept through the city of Corinth in the time of Mummius. I know not how that may be; but I know that a greater fire than any that has laid low London, or Chicago, will one day test and try not only the fair but also the feeblest houses in the city of God. "The day shall declare it," says the apostle.

The day! We are living here in the night. While Christ is absent it is still night to His believing people; and in the night time, perhaps, the builders may think that they can work in, unobserved, some of these materials that will scarcely bear the light. Ah! the daylight, how it shows up many an illusion! We are living largely in a world of shams; we are taken in by appearances. But the day is to come when "the fire shall try every man's work, of what sort it is." Observe, it has been said that the test is not quantity; it is quality: "Of what sort it is." Will it stand the certain flame of the presence of the Lord? I think that, at the judgment seat of Christ, there will be some wonderful surprises. Many a gilded palace will be reduced to ashes; and many a poor obscure life that no one has heard of, will suddenly be ablaze with the glory of God, and will shine like the sun for ever and ever. Then the words will be fulfilled—

> With jasper glow thy bulwarks,
> Thy streets with emerald blaze;
> The sardis and the topaz
> In thee unite their rays;
> Thine ageless walls are bordered
> With amethyst unpriced;
> The saints build up the fabric,
> And the Corner-stone is Christ.

If that is the prospect, how severe we ought to be upon ourselves, and how tender we ought to be toward others!

> In the elder days of art,
> Builders wrought with equal care
> Each minute and unseen part;
> For the gods see everywhere.
> Let us do our work as well,
> Both the unseen and the seen;
> Make the House where God should dwell
> Beautiful, entire, and clean.
> Else our work is incomplete—
> Standing, in these walls of time,
> Broken stairways, where the feet
> Stumble as they seek to climb.

"Yes," you say, "it is all very well to sing about it; but how can it be done? Is there any means of anticipating the test?" Now,

L

that brings me to *the test anticipated*. The work of our lives shall be tested with fire.

Is there a fire to-day that will test them? Now it is a wonderful thing that men forget that building must conform to a plan. Bricks and mortar do not make a house; you must follow the architect's plan. I say it is a strange fact that many of God's saints thoroughly understand His way of peace, but they do not equally clearly understand His way of holiness. You see, you have before you character as a building. That is all right. You tell me, "I have always believed that it is a very slow work. Rome was not built in a day: neither is character." That is just what I believe. I should say that tier upon tier, brick upon brick, gradually it rises. "Quite true; but, then, what is this that we sometimes hear about—an immediate work in sanctification? Do you believe in an immediate work in sanctification?" Certainly I do, or I would not be on this platform. If I had not experienced it, I would not be here. What does it mean? An immediate work—how is that consistent with a gradual and progressive work? Let us look at it for a moment.

There is a passage, Malachi 3: 1-14, which contains God's secret, God's method of purification. Let us look at it. "The Lord whom ye seek shall suddenly come to His temple. But who may abide the day of His coming? and who shall stand when He appeareth? for He is like a refiner's fire, and like fullers' soap." Where does He come? To His temple; and we are told that *we* are now the temple of God. Certainly that is where He comes. It is not to the world, it is to the Church; it is not to Babylon, it is to Zion. When He was here upon earth, hadn't He a temple among His people; and didn't He come to it to purify it—the first thing and the last thing that He did? To-day, He has His people for His temple; and what is the answer to the longing of hundreds of hearts in this convention to-day? What is the definite blessing that you are wanting? The definite blessing is the sudden coming of Christ to the temple of your hearts. That is it. "The Lord whom ye seek shall suddenly"—what is that? Do you dare to limit God to one way of acting? "Suddenly there came a sound from heaven as of a rushing, mighty wind." What was it? It was the Refiner's fire that purified the temple. He descended in a shower of sanctification, or in the fire which purifies the dross—it does not matter which emblem you use.

To whom does He come? He comes to His "priests." We are not sacerdotalists on this platform, but we are all priests. There is not a man or woman who loves Jesus Christ who is not a priest; and, my brother and sister, to discharge your office you need the purifying flame. "Be ye clean, that bear the vessels of the Lord."

Where does He come? He comes to those whom, in His mercy and condescension, He calls gold and silver. Ah, we know pretty well how poor the output of the gold and silver is in us! There is alloy; but He comes to purge it away. How wonderful that He should deem us precious, as those metals are deemed precious, among men!

Brethren, I know well that it is thus He comes sometimes. I mean that there is a fire in Zion, there is a furnace, there is a falling flame. In a moment there is an overwhelming sorrow, there is a crushing trial. I know, for instance, that the fuel for the fire is drawn from the besetments of life; it is drawn from the crosses, the network of our existence, perhaps from the inconsistencies of those around us, and from ten thousand other causes and circumstances. I know there is a fire in His providences which He Himself uses as an instrument—I know His afflicting hand does it. But, over and above that, it says, "Our God is a consuming fire;" and the Pentecostal power is a purifying fire. It is that we need. If God does something in you, it will abide. Mark that. If a man persuades you into something or another, a little cleverer man will persuade you out of it. But if God does a work in you, neither earth nor hell will persuade you out of it. And the promise here is that "*the Lord*, whom ye seek, shall suddenly come to His temple." Brethren, I admit it is a sifting coming. "Who shall stand?"

I have sometimes felt in my heart, in thinking of the Second Advent in glory, the hope of the Church, that yet it will be a sifting experience. Oh, shall I not be ashamed to meet Him—not afraid, but ashamed? And I think that if He, by the Spirit, comes to your heart and to mine, it is a sifting experience. But isn't this a strange thing—that any should rejoice in the Second Coming in the clouds, and yet shrink from the spiritual coming in the heavenly fire that prepares them for it?

Now, the passage speaks of two things. It speaks about the work rewarded. "If any man's work abide which he hath built thereupon, he shall receive a reward." We do not know what it is to be, but we know that not a cup of cold water given in His Name will pass without a reward. Oh, what a day that will be! The welcome of the Master, the acclamations of the angels, and the toils and sorrows of life forgotten in a moment! But there is another side. "If any man's work shall be burned, he shall suffer loss." What, in heaven? Dread and ominous words! "Suffer loss." That life-work that all men admired, that all men applauded, that looked so fair—is that doomed?

"Fire! fire! fire!" Do you hear it—the hoarse murmur of the crowd, gathering volume as it rolls up the street? "House on

fire! Stand back; here come the engines." See the horses
specked with foam, lashed into a gallop, clatter by, none too soon.
What an awful thing it is! that daring fire, I see, has climbed the
columns and wreathed them with smoke and flame. Nothing can
save the house; but is there anyone there? Look again, there is a
man there—the owner roused from sleep! He rushes to the window, calls for help. Oh, that was well done! Did you see him—
the fireman? He scaled the ladder, and went into the smoke in a
moment. Will he find him? Yes, there he is! He is on his shoulder, poor fellow! How pale he looks, dazed, his clothes burnt off
his back. Down the ladder with him! The crowd cheers. His
property lost, his clothes burnt off, but he himself is saved, yet so as
by fire. Brethren and sisters, do *you* want to be saved like that?
If not, take care that the materials you use are fireproof now.

> Refining fire, go through my heart,
>   Illuminate my soul;
> Scatter Thy life through every part,
>   And new-create the whole.

KNOWING AND SHOWING

REV. W. H. GRIFFITH THOMAS, M.A., D.D.

And he said, The God of our fathers hath chosen thee, that thou shouldest know His will, and see the Righteous One, and shouldest hear the voice of His mouth. For thou shalt be His witness unto all men of what thou hast seen and heard—ACTS 22: 14.

WHEN Saul of Tarsus was met on the way to Damascus by the Lord Jesus Christ, he asked two questions: "Who art Thou, Lord?" and "What wilt Thou, Lord?" The first question referred to a desire for a personal knowledge of the One who had appeared to him; the second expressed readiness to do His will.

These two questions which were thus closely connected at the time of the conversion of St. Paul, were inseparately associated with the rest of his life on earth. So must it be with the life of every Christian. The first step in the Christian life is to be followed by a life-long relationship to the One who has revealed Himself to us. The second of these two questions, "What shall I do, Lord?" according to the version in this chapter, practically sums up everything from the moment of conversion onwards. It was in the life-long willingness to know and to do what Jesus should reveal to him that the apostle Paul found the secret of peace and power, of satisfaction and of service. Surely this message has a special bearing upon the gatherings of this week. What does Keswick mean? It means the Christian life in its fulness of power, of privilege, of responsibility. It means that we have come up here to learn more deeply what it means to be a Christian, whether from the standpoint of character or of conduct, of privilege or of responsibility, of life or of service. I desire to take this text as giving to us some at least of the reasons why we are gathering at Keswick, and as revealing some of the aspects of that Christian life which we desire to study afresh.

First of all, we have here the *divine purpose*. "The God of our fathers hath appointed thee to know His will." This is the divine purpose for every one of us—to know His will. The will of God is the first and last thing in His revelation to us. To know and to do the will of God is everything. In the Psalms we hear the coming

Messiah using these words: "Lo, I come to do Thy will, O my God." When God would describe the ideal man, it is in these words: "A man after mine own heart, who shall fulfil all my will." When we think of that model prayer for all disciples in all generations, the culminating point of the first part, which has to do with the divine glory and purpose, is, "Thy will be done." If we are concerned with the salvation of mankind, we read, "It is not the will of your heavenly Father that one of these little ones should perish." "God willeth all men to be saved, and to come to the full knowledge of the truth." If we are concerned about the sanctification of the believer, "This is the will of God, your sanctification." And if, looking forward to the future, we think of the home above, we at once recall the words of the Master, "Father, I will that they may be with me where I am." So that in everything, and from all points of view, to know God's will is everything. The will of God—it gives joy, it gives dignity, it gives power, it gives glory to life. When we realise that everything in our daily affairs is included, in some way or other, in the will of God, what inspiration it gives us for what we are accustomed to call the most trivial and commonest of our duties.

> Teach me, my God and King,
> In all things Thee to see,
> And what I do in anything,
> To do it as to Thee;
> A servant, with this clause,
> Makes drudgery divine,
> Who sweeps a room as for Thy laws,
> Makes that and th' action fine.

We have been singing "Thy will be done"; but there is one note running through that exquisite and beautiful hymn which is untrue, in the sense of being inadequate in its teaching concerning the will of God. We remember the sufferings of the authoress, and we know that for her the will of God was expressed in suffering. But the will of God is for action, as well as for suffering. There is no need for us to wait for that "happier shore" before we *sing* "Thy will be done." We may sing it here and now, as we pray here and now, not merely "Thy will be suffered," but "Thy will be done."

God's purpose, then, is that we should know His will. What a startling lesson and revelation this must have been to Saul of Tarsus. To know His will? Surely he knew it? The Jew, the scholar, the leader, the member of the Sanhedrin—did he not know God's will? And yet this humble disciple Ananias comes to him and speaks of "The God of our fathers." Saul had been on the wrong tack. He thought he knew God's will; but he did not. And there are many to-day who are just in his position. They have been professing Christians, it may be, for years; they have prided themselves on their knowledge, their orthodoxy, their churchmanship, on their standing among their fellows. And yet all the while they have not known His will! It may be—yea, it shall be—that this week there will be a revelation of God's will to such, which will come with all the startling features of a perfect surprise. "Except ye become like little children," that is the condition for knowing His will. Like Naaman we say, "Behold, I thought"; and that is where we make our mistake. "I thought Christianity was so-and-so; I thought that the Evangelical doctrine of Christian holiness was such and such a thing; I thought that church membership was such and such a thing; I thought that Christian life, and work, and preaching, and practice, in the pulpit and parish, were such and such things." "Behold, I thought!" And this week will come with its revelation. "The God of our fathers has appointed" many of us this week to know His will. Before next Friday night is passed there will be scores and hundreds who will know God's will as they have never known it before. The divine purpose will have come into our life.

Second, the *divine plan*: "To see the Righteous One, and hear the voice of His mouth." For the realisation of the divine purpose, this was the divine plan. First, personal contact with Jesus Christ —"To see the Righteous One." The sight of Jesus Christ was to be everything to Saul of Tarsus all through his life. But will you notice in what respect Saul was to see Him? To see Him as "the Righteous One." What is this sight of Jesus as the Righteous One? You will remember that on the eve of His crucifixion our blessed Lord told the disciples that the Spirit was coming to convict the world of righteousness, "because I go to the Father." The world's impression of Jesus Christ at that time was that He was an "unrighteous" One, and they put Him to death. They were determined to believe that He was unrighteous, a blasphemer, and so they rejected Him. But God raised Him from the dead, and He would not have been allowed to go to the Father had He been other than righteous. So He said that the world should be convicted of sin because "I go to the Father."

And Saul of Tarsus was convicted of that very thing. "I am Jesus of Nazareth, whom thou persecutest." If the voice had said, "I am the Son of God whom thou persecutest," Saul would have been able to say, "I never persecuted Him!" So the word came, "I am Jesus of Nazareth"—that hated word—"whom thou persecutest." Jesus of Nazareth was thus revealed to be with the Father, and therefore, righteous.

"That Righteous One"—this is only another way of saying "The Lord our Righteousness." Personal contact with Christ as "the Lord our Righteousness" is still God's plan for the life of every one of us. The sight of that Lord, our Righteousness—it purifies; the sight of the Lord, our Righteousness—it sanctifies; the sight of the Lord, our Righteousness—it qualifies; the sight of the Lord, our Righteousness—it glorifies. I wonder whether this is true of everyone here? Have we all had a vision of the Lord as our Righteousness—our Righteousness for a guilty past, our Righteousness for a sin-stained present, our Righteousness in view of a perfect future?

> Jesus, Thy blood and righteousness
> My beauty are, my glorious dress;
> 'Midst flaming worlds, in these arrayed,
> With joy shall I lift up my head.

"To see the Righteous One." I have no doubt whatever that during this week there will be many who will see the Righteous One. They will see Him, perhaps, first of all for their justification, and they will see Him also for their sanctification.

See Him for their justification. And yet someone says, "Surely that is not why people come to Keswick!" No, but I am perfectly certain that there are those who come to Keswick for the second step of sanctification who have never taken the first step, that of justification. You and I will never learn a single lesson about sanctification unless, first of all, we know the Lord our Righteousness for justification. Romans 3 and 4 must come before 6 to 8. That is the gateway—justification, not sanctification; not justification through sanctification, but the opposite; sanctification through justification, through the vision of the Lord our Righteousness.

But a part of the plan was also a personal communication from Jesus Christ—not only to "see that Righteous One," but "to hear the voice of His mouth." What a blow to the pride of Saul of Tarsus this must have been—to hear the voice of His mouth, the voice of the One of Nazareth, the One whom he had been persecuting: to hear the voice of God's will, the word from His mouth. There were more things in heaven and earth than were dreamed of in Saul's philosophy that morning on his way to Damascus. God had a new way of revealing His will; Saul was to "hear the word from His mouth." And so it must be to-day. Doubtless we shall hear, this week, many a word of Christ through His servants. But this will not suffice. We must hear the voice of *His* mouth, we must have contact with Christ through His Word, we must come face to face with Christ direct, and hear the voice of God speaking by the Holy Spirit. We shall probably hear it in the tent; we shall hear it as we come to the services and celebrations in this church this week. We shall hear it in our own rooms. We shall hear it, it may be, at the lakeside, or on the hillside. But wherever we are, Keswick will fail for us if we do not hear the voice of His mouth. The vision and the voice of the Lord this week—this is the divine plan for the realisation of the divine purpose.

Third, the *divine project*: "For thou shalt be His witness unto all men of what thou hast seen and heard." This is the culminating point. The purpose and the plan lead up to this project. What does it mean? "Thou shalt be His witness." Not a judge. Saul had been attempting the work of a judge, and the issue was disaster. Not an echo, vague, empty, and practically useless; not a philosopher, not even a theologian; but a witness. This is the meaning of Keswick this week. Everything that God says to us, everything that God gives to us, is for the purpose of witnessing to Christ, rendering our testimony to Him. There is scarcely any other word in the New Testament more frequently used than this word "witness" to express what the Christian has to be and to do.

A witness—one who has direct knowledge; a witness—one who has personal experience; a witness—one who speaks and lives with the knowledge of experience, truthfully, frankly, fearlessly always. Are we parents? We must be witnesses. Our authority as parents will fail in proportion as we are without the authority of the witness. Are we teachers? We shall teach with authority when we teach as the result of our personal experience. Are we writers? Our pens must be dipped in our personal experience. The reason why so many books to-day upon the Bible and theological subjects are dry, dull, unprofitable and unconvincing, is that they have no note of personal testimony behind the aspects of truth they bring forward. Are we philosophers—has God given to us powers for thinking, and writing, and speaking? Our philosophy will be as nothing unless it is based upon personal experience. Are we leaders in Church or State? Has God given us great gifts of organisation? Everything will count for nothing except so far as all our life is permeated with the glow of a personal experience.

"Thou shalt be His witness." Where? "Unto all men." Our first witness will be in our home. Those who are nearest and dearest to us will be watching us, and scanning us more closely than ever when we go down from Keswick. They will want to know what Keswick has been to us, and what the Lord Jesus has been to us; whether we have had the vision, whether we have heard the voice.

Then we shall have to witness in our church. I should not be at all surprised if many a sermon next Sunday in parish churches and elsewhere will be transformed as the result of the vision this week. We shall have to declare that which God has done for our soul; and whether in preaching, or in parish organisation, or in our methods of church life and work, this great personal testimony to Christ must run through everything.

It may be we shall have to witness in the town in which we live, on behalf of morality, social righteousness, municipal purity. And I am perfectly certain that to some the "all men" of my text will be realised in foreign missionary work, and this will be primarily the work of witnessing. Not only the work of teaching and training, but of witnessing to all men of those things of which we have heard and seen. And the power of this is incalculable. The power of personal testimony—it is a power to *ourselves*. St. Paul was telling this story in Jerusalem a good many years after his vision, but the facts were coming back to him as fresh and fragrant as ever. So it will be with us as we look back. And although five, ten, twenty, thirty years after our conversion, we shall not be living merely on that, we shall be glad to go back to the foundation and to the facts of personal experience, and find in them the promise of everything in our Christian life. We shall be able to say, "I know whom I have believed." As we tell the story of what God has been all through those years, our own faith will be strengthened, our confidence rooted and grounded in Christ: and, in spite of all temptations to doubt and despair, we shall look up to Him and say—

> Whoso hath felt the Spirit of the Highest,
>   Cannot confound, nor doubt Him, nor deny;
> Yea, with one voice, O world, though thou deniest,
>   Stand thou on that side, for on this am I.

And the power of it to *others*. It is an unanswerable argument for Christianity, the testimony of personal experience. Paul was in Jerusalem among his old friends. He had a great crowd around him. "Now is the opportunity for ability, thought, eloquence"? No, nothing of the kind; but for a personal witness of what Jesus Christ had been to him. There is no greater foe to Christianity to-day than mere profession. There is no greater discredit to Christianity to-day than to stand up for it, and yet not to live it in our lives. There is no greater danger in the Christian world to-day than to stand up for the Bible, and yet to deny that Bible by the very way we defend it. There is no greater hindrance to Christianity to-day than to contend for orthodoxy, whatever the orthodoxy may be, and to deny it by the censoriousness, the hardness, the unattractiveness with which we champion our cause.

Oh, this power of personal testimony—with the heart filled with the love of Christ, the mind saturated with the teaching of Christ, the conscience sensitive to the law of Christ, the whole nature aglow with the grace and love of our Lord Jesus Christ! This is God's purpose, this is God's plan for us.

Not happiness but holiness, not happiness but helpfulness, is the keynote of Keswick this week. And when holiness and helpfulness are realised, then happiness must of necessity come. So it is for us to know, to see, to hear, and then to show. Are we doing this? There are people in the world around us who never open, who never read this Book. But they are reading us. Are they able to see God in our lives? Are they able to say of us to others, "That man"—or that woman—"reminds me of Christ"? Do we let our light so shine that men may see, not us, but our Father, our Saviour in us; and glorify, not us, but our Father in heaven? This is the real test of a gathering like this. So let us live in the presence of God, let us surrender ourselves to the Christ of God, let us keep very close to the Word of God, let us welcome into our hearts the grace of God, let us seek the fulness of the Spirit of God, and then live evermore to the glory of God.

CRISIS AND PROCESS

Rev. Evan H. Hopkins

OUR subject is: "A crisis with a view to a process." There are few things connected with the Keswick movement which have so much puzzled people as the apparent contradiction, that the blessing is both instantaneous and progressive. Those who have been brought into definite blessing, along the line of sanctification by faith, have borne witness to the fact that they had been brought into an experience of what the Lord Jesus Christ can be to them for holiness, with a suddenness that has been as striking as the change has been blessed and soul-satisfying. The sense of rest, the sense of all-sufficiency of grace in Christ, has come to them with a wonderful instantaneousness. But this has been followed by an experience of its progressiveness that they never knew before. Sanctification in the sense of conformity to the life and character of Christ is a process, a gradual process, a continuous process, an endless process. But sanctification, in the sense of a definite decision for holiness, a thorough and whole-hearted dedication to God, the committal of the whole being to Him, is a crisis; and the crisis must take place before we really know the process. Before you can draw a line you must begin with a point. The line is the process, the point is the crisis. Have you come to the point? Have you come to the point that you are decided to-day, now, here, that you will be holy? Or, are you only earnestly praying that God will enable you to come to the point? Some people have been doing that for years. Do you see the difference?

Two men were arguing upon this subject. One had been brought to understand it not only theoretically but practically, experimentally, and the other one was fairly puzzled—he could not see it. The first man said, "How did you come from London to Keswick?" "I came by train." "Was it by one sudden jump into Keswick?" "Oh, no, I came along more and more." "Yes, I see; but first you got into the train. How did you get into the carriage? Was it more and more?" "No, I just stepped in." "Exactly: that was the crisis; and as you journeyed along, it was more and more. There is the crisis; there is the process."

I want to show you different passages of Scripture, and to

indicate where we have the crisis, and where we have the process. We will begin with *the crisis*, and we will take, first, the act of (i) *separation from all defilement*. Will you turn to 2 Corinthians 7: 1? We have in that verse an act of separation from all defilement. "Having therefore these promises, dearly beloved, let us cleanse ourselves from all defilement of the flesh and spirit." Look at that act. Is it to be done gradually by degrees, or instantaneously? The tense shows us that it is definite and decisive. There is the crisis. God has given you light; the light has shone into your heart. You are conscious of defilement. How will you deal with it? God says, "Cleanse yourselves"—a decisive act of separation from all that you know to be evil. There is the crisis.

Then there is the act of (ii) *putting off evil habits*. Ephesians 4: 31 —of course there are many other passages; I am only giving you a few—"Let all bitterness, and wrath, and anger, and clamour, and evil speaking, be put away from you, with all malice." It does not mean that you are to be a *little less* censorious to-day than you were yesterday. The force of the exhortation is that you put it off, as you put off a coat, so that you are separate from it. Here in this passage we have a list of evil habits. Remember we were not born into the world with evil habits. The evil nature is one thing; the evil habit is another. There we have, then, a crisis—how we are to deal with evil habits.

Take, again, the act of (iii) *"laying aside every weight"* (Heb. 12: 1). Are there any weights in your life impeding your progress, marring your influence? How are you to deal with them? Shall we pray about them? Well, that is good; but praying of itself is not enough. God says, "Lay them aside." How shall we lay them aside? Very gradually, by degrees? Not, if we obey the word that we have before us, remembering the force of the tense. If you have a weight, you know what it is to drop it. That is not a gradual act, but a decisive, definite act. Are there any weights in your life about which God has a controversy with you? Now here is the point. God has brought us up here for this purpose, that we should deal definitely with these things. The act of laying aside is a definite act—not a process, but a crisis.

Further, there is the act of (iv) *handing our bodies over to God*. We little realise that while the spirit and soul are right with God, we may still keep the body in our own hands. I suppose the body is the last thing that the Christian really gives over to God. His gifts, his possessions? Yes. Spirit and soul? Yes. The body? Well, we have not done with it; it is useful, we think, we want to use it for ourselves. Romans 12: 1, "Present your *bodies* . . ." That is what we have to bring. Take the words just as they stand.

You are a Christian; the Holy Spirit has touched your spirit, you have eternal life. The citadel of our being is the spirit, the city the soul, and the walls of the city are the body. The five senses, the five gates, are in the walls, and the evil one gets through the gates. You cannot keep the body, you cannot keep the walls. "Except the Lord keep the city, the watchman waketh but in vain." Therefore, "present your bodies," hand them right over into God's hand—a definite, not a gradual act. There is a crisis; the tense in the original points clearly to that. What you have been trying to do gradually God wants you to do suddenly, immediately, up to the light you have.

Then, take the act of (v) *being divinely adjusted*. Hebrews 13: 20, 21, "The God of peace . . . make you perfect in every good work to do His will." Here is God's act. He makes you perfect. What is the meaning? He adjusts you; you are in a state of spiritual dislocation, you are out of joint, and the prayer is that God should put you into joint. He does not do it gradually; it is done instantaneously. This is what has taken place in the case of hundreds of souls in this very tent. In a few brief moments the whole inner being has been adjusted. First, spiritual adjustment, and afterwards spiritual enduement. There we have again the tense that points to an immediate decisive act, God's act. When we present ourselves to Him, when we yield our whole being to Him and lay ourselves at His feet, then He takes us and puts us into joint, He adjusts us, He brings us into harmony. What we have been trying to do gradually, all our life, now that we hand ourselves over to Him, He does immediately. After those words in Hebrews which I have just quoted, we have "working in you." There is the part that is progressive. Or, again, "to do His will." Doing His will is the progressive part. Being put into joint, being made perfect, adjusted, is the crisis.

Take another passage. There is the act of being (vi) *divinely appropriated*, or wholly sanctified. 1 Thessalonians 5: 23, "The very God of peace sanctify you wholly," that is, sanctify not your spirit and soul only, but body also: the whole man, spirit, soul and body. Sanctification on our side is giving ourselves to God. Sanctification on God's side is appropriating us unto Himself. That is the positive side of sanctification, when God Himself, the Holy One, takes possession of us, appropriates us to Himself. Here is God's act, and the remarkable thing is that it is still in the aorist, pointing to a crisis. The blessing that so many people have realised as a sudden blessing—here it is put before us as God's act, and pointing to a crisis.

Take one more text under the head of crisis, and referring, this time to the act of (vii) *enthroning Christ as Lord*. 1 Peter 3: 15,

"Sanctify in your hearts Christ as Lord." (R.V.) We have here a beautiful thought. Your heart is looked at as a sanctuary—not only as a city. Christ is within, and you know Him as Jesus, and you know Him as Christ, but how imperfectly you have known Him as Lord! It is not that a new Person has to enter in, but it is a new revelation of the same Person to your soul. And when you see Him as Lord, you enthrone Him. To sanctify Christ as Lord is to enthrone Him in your heart. He who is on the throne in glory is now to be on the throne in your heart. That is not a gradual process. The tense here points to a decisive act. It is a crisis. Is not that wonderful? I want you to bear it in mind. So that we not only look at the verb, but at the tense, and this shows us the duty of immediate response, immediate obedience.

What have we seen? That separation from all defilement is an immediate act; that the putting off of evil habits is an immediate act; that laying aside every weight is an immediate act; that handing over our bodies to God is a definite immediate act; that being divinely adjusted is a divine act, and God does it at once, immediately; that being divinely appropriated, or wholly sanctified, is God's act, an immediate act; that enthroning Christ in our hearts as Lord is an immediate act, the act of a moment. All those passages that I have quoted point to a crisis.

Shall we turn now to *the process?*

(i) *Spiritual conformity.* 2 Corinthians 3: 18, "But we all, with unveiled face beholding," or reflecting "as a mirror the glory of the Lord, are changed." Here is the present tense, here is the process, gradual, continuous, endless. This is what you perfectly understand. And the process follows the crisis. "From glory to glory." There is the growth, the advancement, the process.

Take another. (ii) *Spiritual renewal.* 2 Corinthians 4: 16, "The inward man is renewed day by day," is being renewed. That is progressive.

(iii) *Spiritual strengthening.* Colossians 1: 11, "Strengthened with all might, according to the power of His glory." That is Christ on the throne. "The riches of His grace" is Christ on the cross; "the riches of His glory" is Christ on the throne. From the throne came the gift of the Spirit, a stream perpetually flowing. "Being strengthened." There is the process. You do not get the power put into your hands that you may use it independently of Him; it is always in the Lord's hand, and it is always flowing from the throne. "Being strengthened with all might." Are you in the stream? A perpetual reception. There is the process.

(iv) *Progressive purity.* There is such a thing as an instantaneous cleansing. But, remember, there is the other side of the truth— progressive purity. 1 John 3: 3, "Every man that hath this hope in Him," that is, in Christ, "purifieth," is purifying, "himself, even as He is pure." An endless process.

(v) *Spiritual growth.* 2 Peter 3: 18, "Grow in grace." I need not dwell upon the fact that all growth, of necessity, is progressive.

(vi) *Progressive sanctification.* Hebrews 10: 14, "For by one offering He hath perfected for ever them that are sanctified," or "are being sanctified."

Lastly (vii) *transformation of character.* Romans 12: 1, 2, "I beseech you . . . that ye present your bodies . . . And be ye transformed by the renewing of your mind." We have both here put together. The crisis, "present"; the process, "Be ye transformed." How closely they are connected there! I have given you, then, the crisis and the process, and, I trust—I am speaking especially to my younger hearers—you have marked these places in your Bibles to distinguish between the one and the other.

Now we come to the practical question: *Is the crisis to be repeated?* If I have once consecrated myself to God, am I not to consecrate myself to Him again? My answer to that question is this. Take, for instance, the act of consecration. Is it to be done over and over again? or is it done once for all? I say, Yes, it is to be done again *in the sense of restoration.* You have slipped back, your attitude of consecration has not been maintained; you have to come back again, you have to repeat the act undoubtedly.

But, I say again, Yes, it has to be repeated *in the sense of confirmation.* You consecrated yourself to God yesterday; you did it thoroughly, honestly; you wholly gave yourself to Him. You woke up this morning, and what was the attitude you took, if you took the right attitude? Just one of confirmation. I did that act yesterday, and I say "Amen" to the act this morning, not because I have to do it over again, as if I had never done it before; and yet I do do it as an act of confirmation.

Let me close with one little illustration. A beautiful copy of *Aesop's Fables* was presented to a certain family that I know, and that book was very much used in the nursery. After many years, when the children had grown up, you can imagine that the leaves got loose and scattered, as the book had been a good deal pulled about. An artist called at that house, and his eye was attracted by the beauty of the illustrations. He saw that they had been done by a man who knew how to draw. He asked the head of the household, "Would you have any objection to giving me that book? I should prize it much." The head of the family took the book and gathered up all the stray leaves, and put them all together, and taking the book in his hand, he said to his friend, "You are welcome to the book; it is yours. I give to you." The artist took away the book.

Two or three days afterwards one or two more stray leaves were discovered. What did the head of the family say? Did he say, "Dear me! I never gave that book thoroughly to my friend after all! I suppose I must have him back and go over the whole process again; I must tell him that now I give him the book afresh because I did not give it wholly to him yesterday"? No; he says, "I gave the book to my friend, and the *whole* book; therefore, I will pass these leaves on to him; they do not belong to me." There was a fresh discovery, but he remembered that he gave the whole book, and those leaves were all included in the gift, and so he passed them on to his friend.

Do you see how that applies? When you consecrated yourself to God, you gave the whole book, so far as you knew. But, as the Spirit has been leading you on to make fresh discoveries, what are you to do? The devil says, "That was not a genuine act of consecration; you must do it all over again." But you say, "No; I knew I could never do anything perfectly, but I can do it up to the light that God gives me. I can do that thoroughly. In that sense I did give myself wholly to the Lord yesterday, or last week, and now I discover fresh things, and pass them on at once, immediately." In that sense the crisis is repeated—but it is an act of confirmation. See that, every morning, and every day, and many times during the day, you can say "Amen" to the fact that you have handed yourself wholly to Him. In that sense it is repeated, and you need not backslide in order to do it over again.

IDENTIFICATION WITH CHRIST

Rev. J. Gregory Mantle

For in that He died, He died unto sin once: but in that He liveth, He liveth unto God. Likewise reckon ye also yourselves to be dead indeed unto sin, but alive unto God through Jesus Christ our Lord— Romans 6: 10, 11.

I TAKE it for granted that everyone in this tent knows that the great doctrine of this chapter is the doctrine of spiritual identification with the Lord Jesus Christ in His death and in His risen and ascended life. It is worthy of notice that this doctrine of identification is peculiar to Christianity. You will find in non-Christian faiths the idea of death to the fleshly self as the end of the human and as the beginning of a divine life; but that thought has never worked out in practice, because there has not been coupled with it this great doctrine of identification with a living person.

I remember standing one day on the platform of that wonderful pagoda in Rangoon, the pagoda of the Golden Sword, and I saw large numbers of Burmese women prostrating themselves before the Buddha. I said to the friend who was with me, "What is it that these people are praying about: what is the burden of their prayer?" I learned that the burden of their prayer was this: looking toward the Buddha, and praying to the Buddha, they said, "Make me as good as you were; make me as gentle as you were; make me as holy as you were." And there they stopped. They could not sing the hymns that we have been singing: especially that glorious hymn that we have just sung, where our gentleness, and our patience, and our holiness become possible, because of our identification with our crucified but risen and ascended Lord.

You will notice that over and over again the apostle says to these Roman Christians, "Do not you know this?" In verse 3, "Know ye not, that so many of us as were baptized into Jesus Christ were baptized into His death?" Verse 6, literally, "Getting to know this"—the most important thing that you could get to know, the thing the enemy does not want you to know, the thing Satan dreads that you should know—"getting to know this, that our old man was crucified with Him, that the body of sin might be destroyed"—a word that is translated in some places "abolished," in some places "done away"—"that the body of sin might be done away, that henceforth we should not serve sin." Then again, in verse 9, "Knowing that Christ being raised from the dead dieth no more; death hath no more dominion over him." Then in the beginning of chapter 7, "Know ye not, brethren . . .?" How anxious the apostle was that these Christians should know these things.

The truths are so profound, so marvellous, they have such a wonderful influence upon the life, revolutionising it, transforming it from defeat into victory, from weakness into strength, from gloom into gladness and glory, from death into life, that Paul felt the great thing for Christians to whom he wrote was to know these truths. And unless we know them, how can we live in the power of them? You may have this wonderful truth in your New Testament—as you have: but unless you have entered into the power of it, of what value is it to you? Just at this moment part of this building was flooded with electric light. It is a comparatively recent discovery; but there was just as much electricity in this land of ours when it was inhabited by painted savages as there is to-day, only they did not know of it, they did not know how to harness it. We have been living for centuries on the edge of the profoundest secrets, and we are just beginning to discover things which have been hidden from us for centuries. And you have this wonderful truth in your Bible. Oh, may God help us to enter into the power of it, to utilise it, to live it out, so that men may see that, in glorious reality, we are identified with our crucified, and risen, and ascended Lord.

I want you to follow me as I suggest four lines of reckoning. I want you, first of all, to reckon on the fact of death; then, to reckon on the fellowship of death; then, to reckon on the continuity of death; and finally, on the realisation of death.

First of all, reckon on *the fact of death*—that is to say, I am going to reckon myself dead with Christ. And you will notice that is what this wonderful chapter tells you that you may do. Notice the repetition of the word. In verse 6, "crucified *with* Him"; in verse 8, "dead *with* Him"; in verse 4, "buried *with* Him"; in verse 8, "live *with* Him." Crucified with Him, dead with Him, buried with Him, living with Him; identification in crucifixion, in death, in burial, in resurrection. And if we are to rest our faith unwaveringly upon this great fact, we must remind ourselves once again that it is gloriously true that "our old man," that is our fallen, unregenerate nature—not as God created it, but as sin defaced and defiled it—"our old man" was crucified with Christ, that the "body of sin"—so called because every part of our being has been corrupted by sin—might be done away, or abolished. It is important for us to remember, I say, that Jesus Christ took this to the cruel cross, and that it was condemned in the death of Jesus Christ.

There is one verse that has helped me perhaps more than any other in the realisation of this great truth. It is in this epistle, at the beginning of chapter 8: "There is therefore now no condemnation to them which are in Christ Jesus, who walk not after the flesh, but after the Spirit. For the law of the Spirit of life in Christ Jesus hath made me free from the law of sin and death. For what the law could not do, in that it was weak through the flesh, God sending His own Son in the likeness of the flesh of sin"—look at your margin, where you have the Greek words literally given, "God sending His own Son in the likeness of the flesh of sin, and for sin, condemned sin in the flesh; that the righteousness," the righteous requirements, "of the law might be fulfilled in us."

Now, it is that expression that has been so wonderfully helpful to me—"God sending His own Son in the likeness of the flesh of sin." When our blessed Lord hung upon the cross, He hung there in the likeness of the flesh of sin. He took this flesh of sin to the only place where it can ever be taken for us to be delivered from its power: He took it to the cross. You remember what is said about that which is taken to the cross: "Cursed is everyone that hangeth on a tree." Cursed is that which hangs on the cross. So that this flesh of sin, in the sight of God, is an accursed thing. Am I going to fondle it, am I going to encourage it, am I going to pamper it, am I going to give it a new lease of life, this thing which is accursed because Jesus Christ took it to the place where that was ever accursed which hung upon it?

Have you ever done this, have you said to your sinful self—that self which cannot be improved; that self for which there is no healing medicine except death—have you ever said to that sinful self, "My sinful self, thou hateful thing, breaking out now in pride, and now in passion, and now in jealousy, and now in indolence, and now in selfishness, breaking out in a thousand hateful forms; my sinful self, I put thee where the sinless Christ put thee, on the cross; hang there, for God has put thee there: I choose, of my own will, that thou shalt hang in the place where God has chosen to put thee—on the cross of Calvary"?

Here is the secret of victory! Reckon on this glorious fact, reckon yourself dead in the death of Christ, and dare to say, "In Him I am dead to sin." He appeared once to put away sin. Whose sin? Not His own; He was the sinless One. He appeared once, in the end of the world, to put away sin: my sin, blessed be His name; your sin; and it is my privilege to-night, and yours, to say, "I reckon myself dead to sin, because I identify myself—by an act of daring faith—I identify myself with Christ in the fact of His death."

Reckon, secondly, on *the fellowship of death*. You will notice how the apostle insists upon that, in this chapter. He says, "Therefore we are buried with Him by baptism into death; that like as Christ was raised up from the dead by the glory of the Father, even so we also should walk in newness of life. For if we have been planted together in the likeness of His death, we shall be also in the likeness of His resurrection . . . If we be dead with Christ, we believe that we shall also live with Him: knowing that Christ being raised from the dead dieth no more; death hath no more dominion over Him. For in that He died, He died unto sin once: but in that He liveth, He liveth unto God. Even so reckon ye also yourselves to be dead . . ."—reckon on the fellowship of death.

What a wonderful argument that is at the close of chapter 5, that magnificent contrast between the first Adam and the last Adam. I only want to say this—that every living soul is identified either with the first Adam or with the last Adam. We are lost in the one or saved in the other; defeated in the one or victorious in the other; weak in the one or strong in the other; dissatisfied in the one or gloriously satisfied in the other. "Now none but Christ can satisfy" we were singing just now, because we have changed our relationship; because of our own choice we have identified ourselves with a new race, the Christ race.

Reckon on the fellowship of death. Remember that all that happened to Jesus Christ, as the Head of the new race, happened in the purpose of God, to you. When He hung upon Calvary's cross, I hung there, in the purpose of God; the nails that pierced His sacred hands and feet, slew my old life. Say to yourself again and again, "I died with Christ; when He hung on the cross, I hung there. When He rose in triumph over death, I rose with Him."

Our relationship with the first Adam is not a relationship of choice; we are identified with him apart altogether from our choice; we are born in sin. But our relationship with the last Adam, the Lord Jesus, is a matter of choice; and our choice is our probation. We may say, every one of us, whether we choose any longer to be identified with him with whom identification means sour grapes. "The fathers have eaten sour grapes, and the children's teeth are set on edge"; and it will always be "sour grapes" as long as we are identified with the first Adam. We can, of our own choice, identify ourselves with Him who said, "I am the true vine," and we can begin to bear the sweet, luscious fruit which is the outcome of this identification with the Lord Jesus Christ. We become the branches, and make it possible for Him to express His life, His beauty, the winsomeness, the gladness and the victory that is in Jesus Christ, through us who are the branches. How He longs for men and women, branches through which to express all that is beautiful and victorious in His life. Reckon on the fellowship of His death.

Reckon also on *the fellowship of His resurrection*; because there is not only a stream of death running throughout this chapter. I have in my Bible a railway running through this chapter. There is the death railway, first of all. I have underlined and railwayed all the passages relating to death. But it would be an imperfect railway system if I did not railway something else. I have another railway of all the passages that relate to life: "If we have been planted together in the likeness of His death, we shall be also in the likeness of His resurrection." There is the Easter glory, on the other side of the cross. Have you ever noticed verse 4: "Like as Christ was raised up from the dead . . ." By what? By the mercy of the Father? No. By the justice of the Father? No. By the *glory* of the Father. There is more glory gathering about the empty tomb of Jesus Christ than about any other incident in the life of the Saviour. It is the most glorious event in the history of our Lord. "The glory of the Father." I wonder whether Jesus Christ was thinking of it when He said, "Glorify Thy Son, that Thy Son also may glorify Thee"?

Peter says that God raised Him from the dead, ánd gave Him glory. I love on Easter day to dwell on the glory of the resurrection. You have only to read the passages which describe it, and the salutations of the risen Saviour, to see how much glory there is in it. When He came out of the tomb His greeting to His disciples was, "All hail!" It was the shout of a conqueror; the shout of One who had triumphed over death, hell, and Satan; of One who had rifled the tomb, and of whom it was written by Paul, "Death hath no more dominion over Him." He hath conquered gloriously the great enemy of man. "The glory of the Father!" I dare say that you used to think, as I did when I was a boy, that what happened in the empty tomb was this—that Jesus Christ folded up those linen clothes that were wrapped around His sacred body, and put them in a corner of the sepulchre, as a mark of leisureliness and tidiness. That is what I used to think; but I have learned, since then, that that is not what happened at all. What happened was this: Jesus Christ left those yards of linen cloth, in which there was a hundred pounds weight of spices, undisturbed in any of their windings. There was the napkin that was wrapped around His sacred head; it was not disturbed in a single convolution, but the head was gone; and of all the yards of cloth wrapped around Him, not a single winding had been disturbed, but the body was gone. I do not wonder that when the disciples looked in and perceived the stupendous miracle that had been wrought, they believed. Is there not some significance there? Ought we not to leave behind us the old life, corrupt and ever growing in corruption? Ought we not to leave it behind us in the sepulchre, as the Master did?

That manly Christian and stalwart teacher, Dr. Dale, of Birmingham, tells us that, towards the end of his life, he began to ask God to forgive something for which he had never asked forgiveness before. He asked God to forgive him for the sins of gloom. He felt that his face had been gloomy, and he wanted forgiveness for the gloom that had overshadowed his life. You remember the story of how, as he was getting ready for Easter Day services, there flashed upon him with new meaning the thought, "Jesus Christ is alive!" He walked up and down his study and said, "Jesus Christ is alive!" And in the glory of that risen life, he went to preach; and his sun nevermore went down. In the gladness of that resurrection vision, in the glory of that Easter morning, he lived; and his congregation sang every Sabbath morning the Easter hymn, "Christ the Lord is risen to-day, Hallelujah."

A lady came to me in Japan last summer and said, "I am a missionary here, and have to make a sad confession to you. I have come to tell you this, that though I came out from America to teach the people here in Japan, I have never had a single hour of joy in my Christian life. And," she said, "I feel so ashamed of it. Can you tell me the secret of joy? Can you tell me how to get some gladness into my life? I feel that I cannot commend the religion of Jesus Christ to people while I have a joyless experience." I said, "I do not know any secret of joy like this—I am alive in the risen, victorious, indissoluble life of my risen Lord. The glory of that Easter morning is mine. Why, I cannot think of that for five minutes without being glad, without saying goodbye to sorrow and sighing."

> Buried with Christ, and raised with Him too,
>   What is there left for me to do?
> Simply to cease from struggling and strife,
> Simply to walk in newness of life:
>   Glory be to God!

We did not sing that half so jubilantly as we ought to have done. There is triumph there. If we knew the experience more fully, we should sing more jubilantly. That is the secret of victory and of joy. You cannot have a sad face and a defeated look if you are living in the glorious, victorious, risen life of Jesus Christ. And what God did for Jesus Christ He is ready to do for you to-night. He is ready to raise you from the dead, not by His mercy or justice, but by His glory. He will give you a glorious resurrection, if only you will let Him do it.

Reckon, moreover, on *the continuity of death.* Do you notice the alteration in the Revised Version? It is not simply "once"; there are two other words there: "In that He died, He died unto sin once *for all*: but in that He liveth, He liveth unto God." Is there not need to emphasise the continuity of this resurrection life? I know I have been disheartened at times, when I have gone back to some place where there had been a gracious visitation of the Spirit of God, and many men and women had by faith identified themselves with Christ in His death and risen life. It has been a great discouragement to find that they had gone back; and that, when I have gone to the place again, they have had to renew this great act of identification with Him. All our dealings with God are dealings for eternity. Do not let us play at identification with Jesus Christ. Do not let us trifle with these tremendously solemn truths. "Once for all" let us determine, in the strength of God, never to go back. "Once for all" remember that it is written, "If any man shall draw back, my soul hath no pleasure in him." "Once for all" reckon yourselves dead to sin and alive to God.

I had on my table some time ago a beautiful plant. I think it is called an india-rubber plant, and I used to admire its glorious leaves. One day I noticed the green leaves losing their brilliance. I watched the plant closely, and presently the green turned to yellow. One morning I noticed that these leaves, in which I found such delight, had fallen off, just at the least shaking of the table. What was the matter? Take a microscope, and look at the point of union between the leaf and the plant. What has happened there? This: all those little canals and arteries through which the sap has been flowing into the leaf have been what botanists call "silted up," all closed, every one of them. You do not wonder that the leaves have lost their verdure, have become yellow, and have fallen off, because they were starved to death. All the strength and the sap of the plant were being thrown into new life. Bursting out at the top of the plant were new leaves; and the lower ones were dispensed with. What I want to point out is this: when the plant decided (if you will forgive me for putting it like this) to dispense with the lower leaves, and began to silt up the arteries, the plant never went back on its resolve, never said, "Well, these leaves are admired, they are very useful and beautiful; I will keep them after all." No, having once begun the silting up process, it went on until every avenue was closed, all resources were completely cut off, and the leaves dropped off because no life was any longer afforded them.

Beloved, let us show the same spirit with regard to everything in our life that is not of Jesus Christ. Let us begin to "silt up," to put the cross of Jesus Christ between ourself and that passion, to put the sin-killing cross between ourself and that lust, that jealousy, that indolence, that spirit which is not of Jesus Christ—put it there, and keep it there; and what will happen? Why, it will happen, by and by, that the old habit will drop off. Every Sunday night I look into the faces of men we know as "Deptford miracles"—once the greatest scamps in Deptford. They have lost their desire to drink away their wits, and to do unholy things. Don't you see what has happened? God has graciously honoured their faith, their reckoning; and these things have dropped off. They can pass by a hundred public-houses without any desire to go in. Instead of the blow, when they go home, there is the kiss for the wife and for the children. Why, I know men in my congregation who were such a terror in the home that the children would hide in the cupboard, or behind mother's apron if they could not get to the cupboard fast enough, because they knew that father's advent meant kicks, curses, and brutal treatment. But they run up the street to meet father now, and fling their arms around his neck, because the old father has become a new father, and a wonderful change has been wrought.

Last of all, let us reckon on *the realisation of death*. God will make it real. Why are we authorised to reckon on these glorious facts? Simply because God does it. God reckons me to have died with Christ, and I am going to reckon myself to be where God reckons me. God reckons me to be living in Christ, and I am going to reckon myself to be living in Christ. Dr. Pierson pointed out, in this convention, that the word in Genesis about Abraham is this—not "Abraham believed God," but "Abraham amen-ed God." He staggered not at the promise through unbelief, but said "Amen" to it. It seems akin to madness for you to reckon yourself dead to the foul things in your life that have mastered you a hundred times, so that you have come back to this convention with the overwhelming sense of defeat. My brother, say "Amen" to God. Then God will honour your faith, and make these things real in your life, and your Amen to God will please Him as Abraham's did, for God was so pleased with Abraham's Amen that He counted it to Him for righteousness.

THE TRANSFIGURED LIFE

REV. CHARLES INWOOD

He was transfigured—MARK 9: 2.
Be ye transfigured—ROMANS 12: 2.

THE life of our Lord and Saviour Jesus Christ was the most unique life ever lived under human conditions. From first to last, it stands absolutely *alone*. It was a revelation and a challenge to all who saw it; it was a benediction to those who recognised and yielded to its charm. It touched our human lives at so many points, and its touch was always the touch of grace and power. No other life ever lived was so utterly human. Think of His love of the open air and the sunshine and the flowers, the lakes and the mountains. Think of His love of babies and little children. Think of His sensitiveness to hatred; think of His yearning for human trust and human love. Think of His noble scorn of ostentation and unreality and conventionality. Then think of His passion for the damaged, for the smirched, for the handicapped, for the ostracised lives. Think of His passion for the derelicts, and the wrecks, and the flotsam and the jetsam of society. Of Him it was said, "Never man spake like this man." Of Him it may be said with equal truth, "Never man lived like this man." Oh, it was a wonderful life, and the older one grows and the more one looks at it, the more one is amazed at the grace and glory that break out from it in all directions.

Yet while that is true, I think we shall all admit that the Transfiguration was the most unique and other-worldly event in that unique life. It was an event which belonged to another order, an event which seemingly could have no correspondence with anything in ours. Remembering that, does not the juxtaposition of these two texts almost amaze us? "He was transfigured."—"Be ye transfigured."

Now we have been speaking and thinking of the separated life and the consecrated life, we are asking that somehow we may get a vision this morning of the transfigured life which may be ours in Him. So we must look at His Transfiguration and see what light it sheds upon the possibility of transfiguration with us.

What was the Transfiguration in His case? It was evidently

an irradiation of His whole being. It was a glory which did not shine upon Him from without, but which broke outward from within. It was an invasion of the physical and the material by a glory which was spiritual. It was the inner glory of Christ becoming so intense that it silently broke out through the veil of the flesh, making the veil and its covering lustrous with a glory which was not theirs.

My dear friend Dr. Campbell Morgan, speaking on this, said that he thought that the glory was not the glory of Christ's Deity, but rather the shining forth of the essential glory of His perfect humanity. That may be so. Certainly the sphere that was transfigured was the human; but the glory was also ineffably and transcendently divine. May it not have been—I put it in that form—may it not have been an instalment of His resurrection and ascension glory, and a preparation for the Cross and the Passion that lay between?

But now for ourselves. You have doubtless noticed, shall I say, four classes of texts that all refer to soul illumination, some of them familiar. I will quote them.

"Unto you that fear my name shall the Sun of righteousness arise with healing in His wings."

"The Lord bless thee, and keep thee; the Lord make His face shine upon thee, and be gracious unto thee."

"God who commanded the light to shine out of darkness, hath shined in our hearts, to give the light of the knowledge of the glory of God in the face of Jesus Christ."

"We have also a more sure word of prophecy; whereunto ye do well that ye take heed, as unto a light that shineth in a dark place, until the day dawn, and the day-star arise in your hearts."

Shining unto—shining upon—shining into—and then shining from within; these are the four stages of soul-illumination, and the Transfiguration is the latest and the crown of all the four.

Now, beloved, you will see at once that *transfiguration therefore implies and pre-supposes Christ's indwelling in us.* He can and does enlighten sinners; He transfigures only saints. The Lord Jesus Christ must be in us before He can shine out from us; and, mark you, He must be in us not only as Saviour from sin, but specially as our crowned and radiant Lord and King. He cannot transfigure any life from which He is shut out, of course, nor can He transfigure a life which is keeping back part of the price from Him. There is no transfiguration for the soul that is at cross-purposes with the Lord. He can transfigure Stephen; He cannot transfigure Ananias. No mental, nor physical, nor temperamental thing can hinder the transfiguration; but any moral wilfulness can hinder it in any one of us. He must be crowned and radiant King before transfiguration is possible to any one of us. But when we have received Him as the King of Glory, the first condition is fulfilled; and then from Him—for the glory is never ours; it is His, His only, His always, His alone—then from within the glory can and does stream.

Let us see how far it streams. First of all, as St. Paul teaches in Romans 12: 2, *the transfiguration must begin within.* You remember the words of the apostle, as Dr. Weymouth translates them: "Be transformed by the entire renewal of your minds." The apostle says elsewhere, "the spirit of the mind," but the thought is this, that the irradiation is the irradiation first of the human personality and then of all that expresses that personality to men.

I am not going to pause to define personality, because for all practical purposes, when we speak of the personality we mean the man himself; we mean that which makes him man, in distinction from the angels above him or the beasts below. So the first thing is the transfiguration of the personality, the spirit, the soul, inside. And that includes all this; and let every word be weighed. It means that all your thoughts, all your imaginations, all your emotions, all your motives, and joys, are radiant with the glory of your Lord. It means that all your soul's yearnings, all your soul's ambitions, all your soul's satisfactions, all your soul's loves, are radiant with the glory of your Lord. It means that all your speech, all action, all influence, all example, all consciousness, are radiant with the glory of your Lord. Beloved, the transfiguration of a human personality with the very glory of the Lord Jesus is the supreme miracle of personal experience.

That *transfiguration which begins within,* slowly *moves outward.* Notice first, when it does, how *the face becomes transfigured.* Some of us have known faces that had no natural beauty, very ordinary, very plain, very dull; and we have seen them grow so beautiful as the light shone through them! Some of us in our Christian work have seen faces growing pure and sweet, calm and radiant and beautiful as the Lord Jesus shone through them. We have known beloved Christian brothers and sisters, and we have had some of them on our platform, whose faces were so lighted up with the glory of their Lord that, with the love that likes fun, we nicknamed them "Glory-face." I think of our beloved brother Paynter, and James Robertson, my beloved brother minister in Ireland.

Then I have seen a face whose features were contracted by fierce, long physical agony, and deeper anguish of soul, a face with scars, pale with suffering, pinched by want, and I have seen those scars and those furrows and those pinched cheeks, those sunken eyes, shine on a sick bed with the calm, sweet glory of my Lord.

Who would call dear old Amanda Smith[1] naturally beautiful? She had such thick lips, and such high cheek bones, and a skin so black! But those of us who remember her will never forget how that eye sparkled, how those thick lips quivered, how that quavering voice crooned, and how that black face shone with the glory of the Lord. *I* shall never forget it, at any rate!

And not only the face; I think it means that the *whole body is to share in the glory of the Lord*. I believe that every physical instinct can become transfigured with the glory of the Lord. I believe— you young men, listen to it—I believe physical recreation and physical culture and physical strength can be so brought under the supremacy of the Lord Jesus, that they will show His glory. If sin and Satan can disfigure and degrade the body, surely the grace and the glory of the reigning King inside can ennoble the body.

But notice next, *transfigured garments*. There you have the realm not of the physical so much as the material. You know, it is the nature of the material to obscure the spiritual; but the glory of the indwelling Christ can capture the material and triumph over it, and a common garment, such as our Lord wore that day, can become a new medium for the manifestation of the glory of our Lord. You study your Old Testament on this subject, and you will find there how often the material was glorified, the garments of glory and of beauty too; the Tabernacle and the Temple filled with glory.

The food eaten, the table spread—oh, yes! all these things can come under the range of the glory of the Master. A Christian once went to breakfast with the saintly John Fletcher. It was very plain fare, but afterwards that Christian man said to another, "Do you know, taking breakfast with John Fletcher was like taking the Sacrament!" Oh, think of that!

Then, again and again in Scripture, and indeed with us in our common talk, *garments are the symbols of habits*. We speak of a "walking habit" and a "riding habit." Now, beloved, I want to plead in my Master's name for *transfigured habits*. There are some habits found among Christian people which the Lord cannot transfigure, and the sooner you claim deliverance from them the better for you. But there are habits that can be transfigured. By that I mean simply this, our way and manner of doing things; and I want the way and manner transfigured. They may be. The way you blame people when you have to blame them; does

---

[1] A former slave, whose radiant Christian personality had made a profound impression upon all, when she visited Keswick.

glory shine through it? The way you correct your children; do they see His glory dominating? The way you treat your servants; do they see the glory of the Master in the way you do it? The way you praise when you have to praise; does His glory shine through it? What about your way of conducting family worship; does His glory always break out? What about the way you ask a blessing at meals? Seven times out of ten in my wanderings—it is a sad thing to say—I have heard grace asked in about as mechanical and formal a spirit as can be. Then I think of others, like our dear brother Dr. Elder Cumming, and oh, the grace and glory that break over the meal, just through the grace asked at the beginning. What about your habit of spending your leisure; does His glory break through that? What about your habit of correspondence; does He shine through the way you do that? Does His glory break upon your soul through your habit of reading? What about the way you discharge the commonplaces and common duties of life, the way you answer questions, the way you speak of Christians who do not agree with you; does His glory break through the way you do it? Oh, life becomes new when it is so.

Then next, the glory not only illuminated the face and transfigured the garments but, as St. Matthew at least teaches, *the cloud was transfigured*. It was not banished; it was transfigured. It is not the banished cloud, it is the transfigured cloud, that shows to others the glory of your Lord.

I have been thinking, especially in this neighbourhood, of a beautiful illustration of this by Southey the poet, who lived near here. These are his words—

> Methinks if thou wouldst know
> How visitations of calamity
> Affect the pious soul, 'tis shown you there.
> Look yonder at the cloud, which through the sky,
> Sailing alone doth cross in its career
> > The rolling moon.
>
> I watched it as it came,
> And deemed the deep opaque would blot her beams;
> But melting like a wreath of snow, it hangs
> In folds of wavy silver round; then passing
> Leaves her in her light serene.

That is more than poetry, or I would not quote it here.

Oh, beloved, there are some Christians who lose all their brightness when clouds gather around them. Then there are others, and there is just a faint glimmer of light through the cloud.

Half apologetically it comes, almost, as if it were an intruder. Then there are Christians who sing—

> The inner side of every cloud
> Is bright and shining;
> I therefore turn my clouds about,
> And always wear them inside out,
> To show the lining.

A lot of people got hold of that a few years ago and thought they had gotten the best thing. There is something far better than that; it is to have the cloud transfigured, inside and out, through and through; then you do not need to turn them to show the light, for there is no place dark in them.

What do I mean by clouds? Well, first of all, *clouds are often the symbols of trial and trouble and sorrow.* But, oh, those clouds get transfigured. Let me give a case or two. We should call imprisonment a dark cloud as it came to Madame Guyon, a refined, brilliant, clever French lady, flung into that gloomy dungeon in the Bastille, and kept there for years, a dark, dirty, damp dungeon. Yet she writes of it: "Even the very stones in my prison floor shine like rubies in my eyes." Then she sang—

> A little bird am I,
> Shut out from fields of air;
> Yet in my cage I sit and sing
> To Him who placed me there;
> Well pleased a prisoner to be,
> Because, my Lord, it pleaseth Thee.
>
> Naught else have I to do;
> I sing the whole day long,
> And He who most I love to please
> Doth listen to my song.
> He caught and bound my wandering wing,
> But still He loves to hear me sing.
>
> Oh, it is good to soar
> These bolts and bars above,
> To Him whose purpose I adore,
> Whose providence I love;
> And in His mighty will to find
> The joy and freedom of the mind.

That is a transfigured dungeon.

And what about calamities? A beloved brother minister of mine in Ireland, only a very few years ago, went to America in the interests of the Lord's work in Ireland. He had only reached it, I think, a day or two. He had with him his daughter, a girl of seventeen years of age. They were standing at one of those railway junctions in New York, I think near Brooklyn. A train came by and somehow caught his garment, and dragged him underneath it, and crushed and mangled and all but killed him. He was carried at once to a hospital, and there he lay for two or three days unconscious. Then, just before the end, the Lord gave him back a moment of consciousness and he opened his eyes. There he was in a strange ward, in a strange hospital, with all the faces strange but that of his own child. With a smile on his poor battered face he looked up to her and said, "Rosie, be brave; the will of the Lord be done!" and then his spirit went home. Those who stood there saw the glory of Jesus breaking through that dark cloud.

And if it is true of the clouds of trial, let me, for the comfort of somebody, say, it is true of the *clouds of mystery*. There are so many mysteries in life. Every fact of life leads up to a mystery, the mystery of being, the mystery of the soul, the mystery of pain, the mystery of death, the mystery of the future. Yes, and there are the mysteries of the Christian faith too. Every fact in Scripture, and every truth in Scripture leads up to a mystery; of course it does! The mystery of the Godhead, the mystery of the God-man —oh, yes, these are mysteries; but, beloved, every mystery is a challenge and an opportunity for faith; and I have seen the glory of my Lord transfigure the mystery. I have stood and gazed in adoring silence; and then, when silence was no longer possible, heart and lips have broken out into a Doxology: "Holy, Holy, Holy, Lord God of Hosts. Heaven and earth are full of Thy glory: glory be to Thee, O Lord Most High."

Now for a moment or two only, for the time is almost gone, as to *the impression on the beholders*. First, as St. Paul clearly teaches in Romans 12:2, the *transfigured Christian can see where others cannot see*. He possesses the power of habitually discriminating, and knowing the will of God, where others are in darkness and doubt; a great result! Another is this: the *transfigured Christian can always be seen in the dark*, and the denser the darkness becomes, the easier it is to see him and find him. Some of you say you are in such a black environment; but the darker the environment, the more the glory can show itself, if you are shining.

One other thing. The outstanding impression was that of *awe*. Beloved, in a transfigured life there is a majesty and aloofness, an other-worldliness, a nearness of the presence of God, a revelation of depth and height and distance that appeals to men. It is this transcendent element in Christian experience which is so alluring and yet so awe-inspiring. We often complain that there is so little of the element of awe in men's attitude toward religion. Why? Perhaps because there is so little radiant holiness in us to produce that awe. The man is so much in evidence, and there is so little of God. I tell you, beloved friends, no gifts, no knowledge, no scholarship, no power of intellect, no achievements, no personality, can do more than interest your fellows. It is only when they see His glory shining out through you that they begin to ask, "What meaneth this?" Of Percy Ainsworth it was said by one who knew him well, "He made goodness and holiness so radiant, and he made one so sure of God."

A word as to the *conditions*. One, as St. Paul teaches, is *separation from the world* (Rom. 12: 2). Another is *union with the Lord*, for transfiguration comes only to those whose habit is to be alone with the Lord. If you allow the pressure of duty, or of so-called Christian work, to hinder you from getting alone with your Lord, you will never be transfigured as the Lord desires to transfigure you, never!

But the real conditions are these: "with open face beholding the glory of the Lord." "Open face"—openness of soul, transparency of soul. It is *only the transparent soul that can become the transfigured soul*. "Open face"—transparency. "Beholding"—not the look of the penitent, precious though that is, but the fixed, adoring gaze of the transparent soul upon the glory of its Lord. You will never be transfigured by continually looking at your own shortcomings, never! Nor will you ever be transfigured by looking at the shortcomings of your fellow-Christians. You will only be continually transfigured by continually looking into the glory of your Lord; for they who live looking and beholding, though they know it not, are being transfigured from glory into glory by the Spirit of the Lord.

THE FAITH CHRIST SEEKS

Rev. J. Stuart Holden, M.A.

Now when He was in Jerusalem at the passover, in the feast day, many believed in His name, when they saw the miracles which He did. But Jesus did not commit Himself unto them, because He knew all men, and needed not that any should testify of man; for He knew what was in man—John 2 : 23–25.

THESE words form part of the record of a set of circumstances analogous to those in which we find ourselves—a large company gathered round about the Lord Christ, expressing their attitude to Him, and revealing His responsive attitude to them. And, if I am right in drawing this analogy, these are words of very solemn import for every one of us who have come hither at His own invitation to meet with Himself.

It is a singular fact that Christ has no faith in some men's faith. It is a startling consideration that many believe in Him, while He has no belief in them. It is a strange and solemn truth in its implicate of warning to every one of us, that there is a faith to which He makes no response; a professed belief, in the presence of which our Blessed Lord is strangely and significantly silent. I say, these words come to us with a strong message of warning, lest, gathered together as we are around Him, anything of this kind should be the record of this convention, as far as we individually are concerned—that many believed on Him, "but Jesus did not commit Himself to them." The thing above all others to be guarded against, not only now, but right along the whole of the pilgrim pathway, is that kind of so-called faith, to which Jesus only responds by silence.

These words contain at least three things which I want to bring to you. Firstly, the *discrimination* which our Lord exercised; secondly, the *disqualification* which He found in these professed believers; and, thirdly, the *distinction* by which He ever seeks to seal and assure our relationships with Him.

The discriminating Christ! How discriminating He is; and how characteristic this is of His entire dealings with men! He draws men, and then divides them. He wins men to a hearing of His message, and then winnows them. Christ, wherever He is lifted up, draws all men to Him; and then each man as he comes finds himself at a judgment-seat. There is that in the Lord Christ which causes all men who come in contact with Him to reveal themselves. No man can long be insincere in the presence of Christ. For there is that in Him which penetrates and pierces his every disguise. Let a man come into the presence of Jesus Christ, and ere long he finds himself, against his own will, it may be, utterly sincere with regard to his own personal state, and both judged and condemned. Life declares itself, when brought into contact with Christ, very much as that which is written in so-called invisible ink is revealed when subjected to the action of heat. You may write with invisible ink on your paper, and it is as though you wrote in water—no stain or record is left. But bring your paper in front of a fire, and silently but certainly all that has been written will be seen. Let a man come into the presence of Christ, and all the fluid tendencies of his life will crystallise into concrete qualities which express themselves. Let a man come into the presence of Christ, and all that is in solution in his nature will precipitate so as to be easily recognised. In the last analysis of things no man misquotes himself when he comes into Christ's presence. What a man is in the deepest depths of his being gets itself expressed when he comes close to the Son of God.

It was so here in Jerusalem. I pray God it may be so with every one here in Keswick. "Jesus did not commit Himself to them, because He knew!" Right through His life this quality of discrimination characterised the Lord Jesus. For instance, "Not everyone that saith unto me, Lord, Lord, shall enter into the Kingdom of heaven, but he that doeth the will of my father which is in heaven." For instance, again: "They brought young children to Him," and the disciples would drive them back; but "Jesus rebuked" not those who brought them, but those who would exclude them—and rebuked them not for their action, but for the inner impulse which prompted it. "Forbid them not." Or again: "Master, we saw one casting out devils in Thy name, and we rebuked him." "Rebuke him not," saith Jesus, the discriminating Lord, who saw moral qualities in that anonymous worker which were hidden from every other one; who saw a free and living faith expressing itself in one whose language was not harmonious with that of His followers. Again, when our Lord stood before His questioners, and "answered them not a word," we find the same quality in Him which we are to find in these gatherings, revealing itself—unique and absolutely reliable power of discernment. "Many believed on Him in that day, but Jesus did not commit Himself to them." There is no realm of our being in which this discriminating power of Jesus Christ is so entirely important, not only for our notice, but for our obedience, and for the guidance of our moral and spiritual actions, as just here in the realm of faith. For Christ regards faith as the beginning of new life. Christ regards faith as the only adequate supporting and sustaining power of all moral enthusiasm and energy. Christ gets to the root of the whole tree of life when He discriminates between faith which is true and faith which is not true.

Therefore, I beg of you, as we gather together in this convention, submit yourselves not to any man's mind; bow yourselves not to the force of any man's word, which, after all, is but the expression of that man's conception of the truth of God in Christ; but rather draw near to Him who knows what is in man. I cannot judge you. I would not if I could. My knowledge of any human being is entirely inadequate to enable me to form a judgment which has for one moment any weight or power. But He knows the push of heredity. He knows the handicap which is variously imposed upon each individual as he begins life's course. He knows the conjoint powers of circumstances in which we have lived our lives up to this present. And I say it as the deepest conviction of my soul, that, knowing everything, He makes allowance for all as none other could do.

A man said to me only yesterday, "I am convinced of this, sir, that the human love which brightens my life is only possible of existence because of ignorance; that if those who love and respect me knew me as I know myself, love would be impossible." I said to him, "My brother, it is true. But listen to the other side of it. The love of Christ is based not upon ignorance, but upon fullest knowledge. He knows what is in man; He knows all the hindrance to faith; He knows all those mental distrusts to which you are afraid to give expression. He estimates them at their fullest and most accurate moral or spiritual value or demerit." Blessed be God for that! I say these things to you—especially to you, young men and women—that you may be entirely assured that Jesus Christ knows you completely; and that He deals with you not in the mass, not according to a code of hard, iron-bound theological rules and tenets, but according to His own infinite, manifold, grace. Jesus knows what is in man.

Let me pass on to *the untrusted faith*. "But He did not commit Himself to them." Why? Mark you, this is of the utmost importance to us, standing where we do on the threshold of these days of conference. Many believed on Him when they saw signs! That is a kind of faith that Christ does not respond to—sign-supported faith; the faith so-called which refuses to believe Him unless it sees signs and wonders; the faith which is not the sincere assent and consent of the will, but the mere satisfaction of curiosity;

the faith which is either disguised unbelief or naked emotion; the faith which is for ever seeking to overcome God instead of submitting itself to be overcome. That is the faith to which Jesus makes no response, the faith which is entirely based on a man's subjective experience of God's wonder-working power. "Many believed on His name when they saw the signs." Compare that with Christ's ideal of faith, always remembering that grand and comprehensive phrase of the apostle Paul, "the simplicity that is in Christ."

I am certain that everything that makes faith hard, or the way of holiness complex and unnatural, is of the devil. I am perfectly convinced that we are going to get into a track of blessing which shall land us in a mighty flood-tide of reviving grace, the extent of which we have never begun to conceive, if we will only get back to the simplicity that is in Jesus Christ. What is Christ's ideal of faith? Read again the record of His dealings with men for answer. True faith begins in stimulation of conscience which we call conviction of sin. It recognises the utter impossibility of refuting the contrast between the standard of God and the state of life. It expresses itself in penitence, in sorrow for sin, and not only for its consequences. It realises an utter sense of emptiness and weakness, of insufficiency and need. And it means the utter and entire surrender to the Christ who is revealed as meeting all the sin-created need of life, as the only One who can do helpless sinners good. Faith is thus not merely an act, but rather a series of acts. Faith is a maintained attitude of heart, an unquestioned obedience, an established loyalty at whatever cost. That is the faith to which Christ always responds—a faith which works by love; a faith which is, in effect, moral sympathy with Christ Himself; a faith which is responsive to His every call; a faith which leaps out to obey every increasing apprehension of His will. How simple it is! Faith which is just entire heart-sympathy with Christ as He reveals Himself. Compare that ideal of faith with the so-called faith to which the Lord Jesus makes no response whatever—faith which is sign-created and sign-supported.

Now I want to say a few simple and unimpassioned words upon the great need which we have in this convention to seek, to obtain, and to exercise that sort of faith. It has been true in every age, and it is true essentially in our own present age, that there is in faith's name a recrudescence of a curious seeking for signs. There are large numbers of people who will only believe in Him to-day if their faith can be somehow buttressed by some visible sign. There are many among us who tempt Him, asking signs from heaven—signs which, when they are granted—and I will speak to you in a moment as to the origin, as I believe, of many of them

—have little, if anything, to identify them with the simplicity that is in Christ, or aught approaching it. When we know of God's own children being led aside into believing that physical contortions, unintelligent jabberings, hysterical screamings, often leading to gross and impious immoralities, can be signs which support faith, it is enough to make angels weep. Anything which elevates subjective experience above Scriptural expression is not from *above*, but from *beneath*. Yet that is the kind of sign that men and women are being deluded into seeking after to-day, derogating from the glory of Christ by setting up another authority of proof; believing Him not for what He is, but for what they feel; believing Him not for His own glorious self-revelation, but because forsooth of the temporary stirring of their emotions often to very muddy depths. The Lord save us in His mercy! Beware of it, young men and women. Beware of him who comes as "an angel of light," not to repel but to deceive the very elect. Beware of anything which tends to remove you from the simplicity that is in Jesus.

I come to what is the most solemn thing I have to say to you to-night. This kind of faith, so-called, is untrusted by Christ for this very reason: that He knows that if He disappoints these seekers for signs, they will turn unconsciously in the frenzy of their emotion to another source which will respond. There is an anti-Christian supernaturalism which is responsive to the emotional stirring of men after the abnormal. You can get signs, you can get tongues, you can get all kinds of gifts. But beware of the source of your getting! This is the reason for Christ's distrust of this so-called belief in Him. He knows that when a man's heart and mind is set upon the supernatural, the supernatural he will have somehow. He knows that the condition of heart, and the morbid state of mind, which will not be satisfied with anything less than these subjective experiences, will push through everything to be gratified, even though it means tearing asunder all the veils which God in His mercy and love has put between our gaze and the unseen. I do not need to say more on this head, but to remind you that Christ's mistrust of that kind of professed faith is prophetical. For He lifts the veil Himself into the future, and saith, "Thus and thus it shall be. In that day many shall say unto me, Lord, Lord, open to us. In Thy name we have done many mighty works, in Thy name we have prophesied, in Thy name we have cast out demons." And Christ will not say, "You did nothing of the kind." He will tacitly admit their claims, and yet say, "I never knew you." "Many believed on His name, but Jesus did not commit Himself to them."

You will permit me, before passing on to the last section of my message, to read you the words of my friend, Sir Robert Anderson:

"No one may limit what God will do in answer to faith. But we may dogmatically assert that in view of the revelation He has given of Himself in Christ, He will yield nothing to the petulant demand of unbelief."

Let me pass from these considerations to that committal of Himself which these words record as being withheld by Jesus Christ. What is the whole object of our gatherings? What is the blessing we have come together to seek—but just that Jesus should commit Himself unto us? There is a dual committal of which the apostle Paul writes to Timothy: and with which we are already well familiar—"I know whom I have believed, and am persuaded that He is able to keep that which I have committed unto Him," and in the next breath, "Keep that which has been committed unto thee"—a reciprocal committal. When I commit myself entirely in a simple faith to Christ, Christ commits Himself—how poor our words are to describe the mystery of it all—Christ commits Himself to me.

What do we mean by that phrase? We talk of committing ourselves to our friends. My friend and I know each other; we trust each other, we love each other, and we commit ourselves mutually. He opens his heart to me, and I open my heart to him. I disclose my aims to him, and he discloses his aims to me. And so we join interests; we commit ourselves. And there is a sense in which this word completely describes that blessing, for the personal realisation of which this convention stands as a witness: that Jesus commits Himself to men as friend unto friend. He commits Himself to us for the protection of His reputation in the world. What a wonderful thing it is that we go away from gatherings like this charged with the responsibility of guarding Christ's reputation; charged with the responsibility of so living that our lives emphasise and set forth in brilliant conspicuousness the characteristics of the Lord's own perfect love, perfect generosity, perfect sympathy, perfect understanding of men. Wonderful calling! Well does the apostle speak of it as "the high calling in Christ Jesus."

Not only for the protection of His reputation in the world, but also for the interpretation of His intention toward the world. He commits to us the work that angels cannot do—to interpret His intention to men and women who know Him not, or, knowing Him, spurn Him; to interpret His intention, as being put in trust with His glorious Evangel. Think of it! This is what Christ does in response to simple faith. He makes His word of such vital and vitalizing influence in our lives, that it expands into an obvious and plain interpretation to all with whom we come into contact.

And, further, for the completion of His ministry in the world. Not in any propitiatory sense, for that has for ever been completed; but day by day to carry on His work of saving men; day by day to use these hands of ours "to pluck them as brands from the burning"; day by day to use all the life with which He has entrusted us in that great and wondrous work of reclaiming those who have strayed from the fold and the home. This is what it means for Christ to commit Himself to men; that men may bear His name before the world, that men may interpret His Word to the world, that men may carry on His work in the world. Oh, see to it that there is nothing in the nature of your faith which makes it impossible for Jesus so to commit Himself to you.

How is it effected? How is it possible? Such ones as we are, with our limitations and discrepancies, with our stained record, with our vitiated powers—how is it possible? Blessed be His name, when He commits Himself to men, as He waits to do in this place to-night, He liberates the transforming energies of His Spirit in our lives, and the miracle of re-creation is effected. And day by day the area of the government of the Lord increases, and the work of transforming us to His likeness, the work of inspiring to the requisite self-effacement, self-sacrifice, self-forgetfulness goes on. He is prepared to carry on this wondrous work in our souls. If He commits Himself to us He commits Himself, not only to its commencement, but to its continuance and completion. Sign-supported faith is not adequate to the life that is involved in so protecting His name, and interpreting His Word, and completing His work in the world. For the man who sets out to fulfil that commission will find himself opposed by a thousand antagonising influences. And the faith which has not its anchor within the veil, the faith which clings not, though it sees Him not, to "Him who is invisible," the faith supported by the merely subjective and external—such faith will never be able to stand the shock of the world's opposition and the devil's malignity.

Lastly, let me say one word as to the kind of men and women to whom our Lord does commit Himself. For, after all, that is of supreme importance to you and me. Is it possible, you are saying, that I am the kind of man whom Jesus will trust, whose faith Jesus will recognise as being genuine, sincere, and well-founded? Listen! Take His Word again; read through the record of the days of His flesh, and you will find that the kind of men and women to whom He commits Himself are these: men of unstable resolve, but fervent love; women of stained reputation, but earnest devotion; men of secular habits, but simple trust; men of slow understanding, but dauntless courage; women of slender attainments, but grateful loyalty to Him. The poor, broken, stained, and maimed life which has somehow come to realise itself and to realise its Lord—to such an one will Christ commit Himself. And what He doeth, it shall be for ever!

And the test which I propose to myself and to you to-night is just this one—Have I an unsleeping zeal for His glory? Have I in my life a dominating passion for holiness? Have I an increasing impulse to soul-saving service? If not, is it because Jesus has never committed Himself to me? If He has not committed Himself to me, is it because my faith is of the wrong order? Oh, search your' hearts! And may there be effected at the very commencement of these convention days that reciprocal committal which shall mean to you the life more abundant in all its unspoken and unspeakable implicates, for His name's sake.

BUT IF NOT . . .

Rev. J. Stuart Holden, M.A.

I suppose it is safe to say that the majority of us have been led by the proclamation of God's truth, and in all the illumination of His Spirit in these gatherings, to expect large changes in our experience, large renewals of strength and grace, large openings of fruitful service: and with these expectations we are leaving this place of vision, to return to the valley of duty.

I want to speak as simply—and God knows I want to speak as tenderly—as may be to those who, in the days to come, may not realise these expectations; to those who in days to come, and not many days hence, are going to be sadly disappointed because their experience does not reach out to their expectation. I want that each one of us shall see that God has larger meanings in life than we are now able to read, that God has larger answers to our prayers than we are able to anticipate, that God has a thousand ways of fulfilling His promise in human lives that trust Him; that so, forewarned by this knowledge of God's wondrous greatness and transcendence, we may be forearmed against the perils of disappointment, forearmed against that disheartening of soul which makes our hearts the ground, the fruitful ground, for the most noxious seed the devil can ever sow there.

Therefore I want to speak to you on three simple words, as you find them in Daniel 3: 18. Let me read with you from verse 16, which will recall the incident, of which this is part, to your minds. "Shadrach, Meshach, and Abed-nego answered and said to the king, O Nebuchadnezzar, we are not careful to answer thee in this matter. If it be so, our God whom we serve is able to deliver us from the burning fiery furnace, and He will deliver us out of thine hand, O king. *But if not*, be it known unto thee, O king, that we will not serve thy gods, nor worship the golden image which thou hast set up."

You remember the story well. Challenged not to worship God at all, challenged to bow down to the popular idol, challenged to join the fickle multitude in acclaiming an earthly king, to the degradation of the King of their hearts, with a burning fiery furnace in front of them as an alternative to obedience, this is the answer of the three Hebrew children—"Our God is able to deliver us. More than that, our God will deliver us. More than that, if He does not deliver us, we are still not going to worship your idol. If He does not deliver us, our faith is not at an end. If He does not deliver us, our resolution is entirely unshaken: we still believe God."

Now, beloved, it may be for you and me that the experiences we have sought here, that the prayers we have offered here, the hopes that have been aroused here, are none of them going to be realised just in the way we have imagined. It may be that you who have claimed a deliverance which you have seen as part of God's plan in your life, are going to find that God works by human co-operation with His divine Spirit, and that your way of deliverance is a *Via Dolorosa*. It may be that you, my brother, who have claimed a Pentecost from God, are going to find that it leads you not to a revival, but to tremendous Satanic opposition. It may be that in your church or mission you are not going to see a great ingathering of souls at all, but a great revolt of worldly Christians and church officers. It may be that from Keswick you are going into a pathway which is dark with the mysteries of God's dealings with you. And let me say to you here, that if your faith has not got an alternative, you are going to be worsted. If you are going to be bowled over because of the things which, in some shape or form you are bound to meet, then the world which is looking on, and which is taking its measure of Jesus Christ from the loyalty and fidelity of your witness to Him, is going to be staggered. Oh, blessed be God, our gracious God, who teaches our hands to war and our fingers to fight, who is our Hope and our Fortress, our Battle-axe and our Deliverer. Blessed be God who speaks to us ere we go from this place into the unknown life of peril and danger and opposition. Let us see to it that our faith has an alternative to our present expectation. Blessed is the man who goes down from Keswick saying something akin to that which these three Hebrews said to the great king who vaunted himself against God: "We will not serve thee; we will not bow down to thine image, even if God does not do for us as we have trusted Him to do." O God, give us a faith like this!

Do not think that this is faithlessness on the part of these men. Read their protestant words: "Our God is able and He will; *but if He does not*, we still recognise His will as entirely supreme. If He does not, we still reckon God as greater than our hearts and all their imaginings. If He does not do just what we thought He was going to do, we still believe, though we have no evidence of sense to support our faith." This is the faith which accepts God's will not merely with equanimity but with positive enthusiasm. This is the faith which relates itself not only to the commands of

God, but to His contradictions; and if you and I go on with Him
we shall find that pathway to be one of constant contradiction:
Christ contradicting my conceptions; Christ my Teacher contradicting my impulse and my aims; Christ my Master bringing all
things within me into conformity with His holy purpose. Oh,
this is not faithlessness; it is faith, which says, "But if not, my
course is already clear; if not, my determination has already been
made; if not, my resolve is entirely unaltered, for it has been made
in the conscious presence of God, and on the warrant of His own
sure Word."

Beloved, it is by these contradictions oftentimes that God teaches
us in ways which otherwise were impossible either to Him or to us.
There are words which I often read to my own enlightening and
comfort, and you will allow me to repeat them to you now—

> If all my years were summer, could I know
> What my Lord means by His "made white as snow"?
> If all my days were sunny, could I say,
> "In His fair land He wipes all tears away"?
> If I were never weary, could I keep
> Close to my heart, "He gives His loved ones sleep"?
> Were no griefs mine, might I not come to deem
> The life eternal but a baseless dream?
> My winter and my tears and weariness,
> Even my griefs may be His way to bless;
> I call them ills, yet that can surely be
> Nothing but love that shows my Lord to me.

In these days which lie ahead of each one of us, with their
perplexing experiences, remember that His meanings of life are
essentially larger than ours; and it will fill our hearts with peace
and put stability into our lives to be able to say, "But if not,
Lord, I still trust Thee; and if not, I am here as truly Thine as
ever I was; as truly Thine in the darkness of London, of the
slums, of the mission field, of the unsympathetic home, as truly
Thine, my God, in the darkness as I was Thine in the light at
Keswick. But if not——!"

This alternative to disappointed faith tests the entire quality of
the man who professes the faith of God. I know the man—I have
him in mind to-night—who, being disappointed in his experience,
nervously begins to pity himself; the man to whom self-conse-
quence is everything. When God contradicts his expectation and
longing, his faith is staggered and his backsliding begins. I know
the man who is willing to accept the shallow answer to a great
question, the man to whom disappointment becomes disbelief,
the man who measures God in the tiny scales of his own self-

consciousness. Many a one such has gone from Keswick to be utterly disheartened, utterly despondent, and ultimately a deserter. He had never learned to say, "But if not, my God; but if not!"

There is a subtle interaction in the life of every one of us of courage and conscience; and the man who does not stand firm with God and for Him, who loses his integrity, loses also his power of vision, because one experience of his faith staggers him. On the other hand, I know the man who has learned to say courageously with these three Hebrews, "But if not . . . there shall be no deviation from my duty; its dominance shall be entirely unaffected in my life. But if not—if no ecstatic joy fills me, if no revival fruits appear in my work, I mean to go on and do the next thing. If I do not get the sunshine in all its full-orbed light upon my life, I mean to follow the gleam which I have already seen. If I cannot see the distant scene, I can see at least one step. God has given me enough light to walk by, and therefore, if not, I am going on with my work. If not, there shall be no cessation of hostility to evil, no begging out of the conflict with all the forces of the devil in the world. There shall be no lowering of my aim, even if I am conscious of repeated failure." The crime of our lives is not failure, but low aim; and by the grace of God, forgetting the things that are behind, I press on toward the mark for the prize. Even if the battle seems to be going against me, there shall be no desertion of the colours.

My friend there, the business man, has come to a determination to seek first the Kingdom of God in his business, that all things else may be added to him; and he finds not additions, but subtraction; he finds that his profits are not greater, but less each year. He finds that the pathway of the cross is no sentimental, emotional thing to sing about, but that the cross is heavy and the way is narrow and the positions innumerably difficult for the man who says, "But if not, I do not intend to pull the flag down; if not, I do not intend for a moment to desert my Lord, for I can never unsee what I have seen in Him, and I can never unlearn what I have learned from Him, and I can never lose that which He has begun to work in me. Therefore, be the consequences of my fidelity what they may, I am going on with God."

After all, beloved, if you have the real faith of a child as you leave Keswick, and in consequence of God's drawing near to you here, it is founded not upon a subjective experience, but upon God Himself. My faith does not stand in the wisdom of men; my faith does not stand in the memory of an emotional thrill which came through me, lifting me on to a higher life in this place; my faith does not rest upon anything that is visible, but upon that which is within the veil, where Jesus is. Therefore in the calm confidence of a child I may say with these three young Hebrews, "I am expecting God to do wonderful things for me; I am expecting God to break down iron gates before me, and to beat down my foes all around me. I am expecting God to give me great and wonderful power in His work, manifested by souls gathered in and wondrous revival all round. But if He does not, I am still going on with Him, persuaded that He doeth all things well, and that His wisdom is my sheet-anchor."

Now, beloved, let me point out to you that God's response to this spirit is to do a bigger thing than we trust Him for, not a smaller. These men said, "Our God is able to deliver us from your fire. What do we care about your old furnace, heated seven times? It does not affect us; it does not even make us perspire with fright: we are absolutely calm in front of it." But, mind you, God did a far bigger thing for them than they thought He would do. He did not deliver them from the peril at all, but He delivered them in it: and that is an infinitely greater thing. He did not effect their escape from the furnace, but He gave them an experience of fellowship in the furnace that they had never dreamed of, for Jesus Himself came to walk with them in that furnace. I wonder what they talked about! They did talk, and they heard words there which it is not lawful for men to utter or to imagine; and they learned more in that furnace with Jesus than they had ever dreamed it possible for men to know of God. That is the kind of thing God does to the men who have this spirit. They said, "He is going to check your hand, O king"—but He did not do it at all—He did something greater: He changed the king's heart, He brought the king to a knowledge of His almighty power and grace. And, beloved, great though your expectations are, they are not great enough; great though the promises are to your conception to-night, that conception is not nearly great enough. God is going to do an infinitely larger and more influential thing in our lives, if we will stand with Him.

Very briefly, let me point out to you that this is not an isolated instance. I find this principle running right through the Word of God. Let me give you an illustration or two. God said to Abraham, "Take now thy son, thine only son Isaac," and he took him, and together they mounted the hill. I hear the boy saying to the father, "Father, here is the wood for the sacrifice, but where is the lamb?" And I hear Abraham say to him, "My son, God will provide Himself a lamb; *but if not*, the programme is going to be carried out. But if not, there is going to be a sacrifice. My purpose is entirely undeterred; my obedience to God is entirely unaltered; my devotion to God is entirely unmoved, even if He does not provide a lamb, and if I have to put my son to the knife and to the fire.'' That is the secret of Abraham's fruitfulness—his faithfulness; that is the secret of God's blessing to the nations through that man.

I see it again in a man who has lost everything. His home is gone, his friends are against him, his health is gone. He sits there mourning, and under the mourning there is a note of triumph. "God shall bring me forth to the light, and I shall behold Him." Then he says, in effect, "*But if not*—though He slay me, yet will I trust Him. Even if He does not bring me out to the place where I behold His face in righteousness, I shall still trust Him. I know that my Redeemer liveth."

I remember another man. He is in prison—a man persuaded of Christ's identity and mission, a man who stands for the most wondrous self-effacement this world has ever seen, a man who cried to others, "Behold the Lamb of God," and rejoiced when his own disciples left him to go with Jesus; a man who knew the power of God in his life, for he was filled with the Holy Ghost from his birth; a man who saw in Jesus the great Baptizer with the Holy Ghost and with fire; and a man whose faithfulness was put to such severe test as you and I have never known, in the prison-house on the shores of the Dead Sea. He sent his disciples to Jesus —the Jesus who said He had come to liberate the prisoners, and here is one of His loyal friends whom He does not liberate. Here is the One whom he has proclaimed as the mighty Messiah of God, but He seems so slow at coming to the victorious side of His work. John sends his disciples to Jesus and he says, "Master, have I, after all, been mistaken? Art Thou He that should come? I thought you were; *but if you are not*, I am still going on to look for another, for the promises of God cannot be broken."

I think of Paul, too. Oh, those wonderful, those magnificent declarations of Paul's faith. Listen to them above the howling of the tempest. "I am persuaded that neither death, nor life, nor angels, nor principalities, nor powers, nor things present, nor things to come, nor height, nor depth, nor any other creature, shall be able to separate us from the love of God, which is in Jesus Christ our Lord." "In all these things we are more than con- querors, through Him that loved us." "Thanks be unto God, which always causeth us to ride in triumph in Christ." And he ended—where? In a prison; not in a great burst of praise and victory, but in a prison, chained to two Roman soldiers. But Paul had this "if not" spirit in him; and if you want to read its expression, turn to his prison Epistles; turn to the words that came from his heart in that prison-house in Rome, and you will see the indomitable spirit of the man who was filled with the Spirit of God.

But before I close there is Someone higher, greater than Abraham, and Job, and John, and Paul; there is the Blessed One Himself. Oh, beloved, listen for a moment. Away there yonder in the Garden He cries, "Father, if it be possible, let this cup pass from me; *but if not*, Thy will be done." That is the spirit that made the world's redemption an accomplished fact; and that is the spirit in you and me which will invest our lives with redemptive value, as we go out from the throne of God down to the gutter of sin to do the work of the Redeemer. This is the spirit, and the only spirit, which means victory beyond anything we can conceive.

So as we turn from Keswick in these few closing moments, may God make this your spirit and mine, in view of all the future may hold, in view of all the mystery that may becloud your pathway, in view of all that may stagger you for a moment as God's greater thoughts are brought into conflict with your own inferior and unworthier thoughts concerning His purpose. When your prayers, instead of being speedily answered, are delayed of answer; when those things you thought God must do for you He still keeps you waiting for, O God help each one of us to say in some such words as these, "But if not"—

> I'll follow Thee, of life the Giver;
> I'll follow Thee, loving Redeemer;
> I'll follow Thee, deny Thee never;
> By Thy grace, I'll follow Thee.

I will say just one thing more, and it is this: that the world is perfectly helpless before that kind of Christian; the world is perfectly helpless before the man who positively laughs at its shams, because he knows what they are worth. The world is perfectly helpless before the man who goes into the fire for God with a song in his heart. It cannot light a fire, however vehement its flame, that can do more than burn up a man's bonds and bring him into greater liberty.

> Across the path of night leads on the path of God;
> Not where the flesh delighteth, the feet of Jesus trod:
> What though the path be lonely, and dark, and bleak,
>   and lone,
> Though crags and tangles cross it—
> Praise God, we will go on!

That is the spirit in which to leave Keswick. And as the world is helpless before a man of that kind of faith, God cannot be otherwise than truly faithful to such a one. Therefore, as in a few minutes we shall go out into the night, and will never all meet again until Jesus comes back again, beloved, would it not be a blessing to us to bring our Keswick week to a close by solemnly, gladly re-affirming this same glad note in the presence of God to-night: "O God, I am expecting so much from Thee. Correct all my misconceptions. I am expecting Thee to do such wonderful things. My God, I am expecting Thee to make all things new with one word of Thy power. But if not: if Thou keepest me waiting, if Thou dost discipline me into patience, I here and now covenant with Thee, my Lord, that I will stand by Thee. I here and now covenant, my Lord, in all the nakedness and sincerity of my soul, that I am Thine utterly, absolutely, to the last crust and candle-flicker of life. I am Thine, Lord Jesus, for time and eternity." O God, bring us there to-night!

NOW, THEN, DO IT!

Rev. W. Graham Scroggie

I MUST confess that in anticipation of this meeting to-night I have been considerably perplexed, and I am trusting now that the words I am about to utter are His words to us all.

I have been endeavouring, as others no doubt have been, to get our perspective since this morning.[1] Paul had such a vision of Christ, and such blessing flowed into his soul, that he had to go away for three years to get his perspective. Mr. Langston[2] has said that there may conceivably be those here now who are greatly perplexed, who do not exactly know where they are. That is probably true. There must be large numbers of people in this tent to-night who have come thus far through the week, they have listened to the messages, in a way they have appreciated them, and yet nothing tremendous and nothing definite has been done. You have had the word of exposition, and I would venture upon the word of exhortation yet further. I am assuming the presence here to-night of very large numbers who have never been to Keswick before, who have been trying to understand the meaning of it during these days; the presence also of large numbers who are in just for today, perhaps, and have not had the benefit of what has gone before, and are going back to-night. Only the Lord understands the complexity of the situation, and only He can so frame a message that everybody may get something.

I would turn to some words in 2 Samuel 3 : 17, 18, "And Abner had communication with the elders of Israel, saying, Ye sought for David in times past to be king over you. Now, then, do it."

The previous speaker has shown what is necessary to be done. Now, then, do it. After the exposition comes the action. All such gatherings as these must be productive if they are to be of any use at all. We must come to what is practical, intensely practical and personal. There are some blessings that are collective; there are some that are intensely individual. It will be a poor thing for any of us to be in the midst of a mighty movement of the Spirit of God, and to see others blessed, if we are not blessed; to see others having great things that we do not have; to see others making choice and

---

[1] See page 252.
[2] The Rev. E. L. Langston, who had just spoken.

decision if we do not make choice and decision. "Now, then, do it." You say, Do what? And how do it? I would attempt briefly and simply to answer that double question.

Whatever is done, must be done intelligently. We are suffering to-day from a lack of definition, and perhaps still more from a widespread use of terms that are variously interpreted, some people meaning one thing and other people meaning another. We must distinguish things that differ. We must think clearly if we are going to act soundly. There were saints in the Church at Corinth that thought the less they had of intelligence, the more they were likely to have of the Spirit: and they have a large posterity. But that is a fallacy. I am not asked to close down my intelligence in order to exercise faith. Faith is not credulity; faith is not ignorance: faith is intelligent; faith is open-eyed; faith has a reason as well as an emotion, and that man is in grave peril who is resting on emotion rather than upon intelligent understanding. What we do must be done intelligently.

We must make some distinctions; we must distinguish between Christ as Saviour and Christ as Lord. No person has ever known Christ as Lord who has not first known Him as Saviour, but there are multitudes of Christians who know Christ as Saviour who do not know Him as Lord, and we must distinguish. If you are a Christian at all, you know Christ as Saviour. Do you know Him as Lord, as Master?

We must distinguish between the work of Christ for us and the work of the Spirit in us. They are not the same; they are related. The work of Christ for us on Calvary is a finished work. Nothing can be added to it. Nothing can be taken from it. That is historic and outward and visible. The work of the Spirit within us is spiritual, invisible, progressive: and the Spirit cannot even begin that work until we have entered by faith into the meaning for ourselves of the work of Christ for us. But there are many Christians who never get beyond Calvary.

We must distinguish between cleansing and holiness. You cannot be holy without being cleansed, but you can be cleansed without being holy. The Book of Leviticus is divided into two parts: the first part is about cleansing, and the second part is about holiness. Cleansing is the basis for holiness. There can be no holiness until there is cleansing, but we may come to that cleansing without proceeding to holiness. Cleansing is by an act, holiness never is. Cleansing is never progressive, holiness always is, and they are intimately related.

We must distinguish between our standing and our state, between what we are in God's sight in the Person of our risen Saviour, and what we are in actual experience down here among men; between our position in Christ and our actual condition: and it is the purpose of God that our state shall approximate ever more closely to our standing, and our actual condition draw ever nearer to our wonderful position in our risen Lord.

We must distinguish between union and communion. A man and a woman take one another for better, for worse; for richer, for poorer, till death them do part. They are united, there is union; alas, there is not always communion. If Christ is our Saviour, there is union; but is there communion, free intercourse, happy fellowship between our hearts and Him every day and every hour? We are to become what we are. In 1 Corinthians 5 the apostle says, "Let us become unleavened." There are two kinds of knowledge; there is the knowledge that is objective and the knowledge that is subjective. One is the knowledge of apprehension, and the other is the knowledge of appropriation. Now we may apprehend, of course, without appropriating. We may "see" a thing, as we say, without acting upon it. We may understand a text with our minds without abandoning ourselves to that truth with our whole heart. It is this experimental knowledge to which attention is called so much in the New Testament; not the knowledge of mere understanding; not the knowledge that is derived by reading and by hearing, and by accumulating facts in the mind, but the knowledge that comes by commitment, by trust, by faith; the knowledge that is experimental; the knowledge of apprehension and appropriation. It is not ignorance that is productive of faith, but knowledge. Faith must have a firm foundation, and what we do must be done intelligently.

Our Lord again and again refused the commitments of men and women, because He knew that they did not understand what they were doing. A great crowd followed Him, and I can see Him putting up His hand and saying, "Wait a moment, all you would-be disciples." Then He laid down the conditions of discipleship: if a man hate not his father and mother and wife and children and brothers and sisters and himself, if he take not up his cross and follow Christ, he cannot be His disciple. It was not that He did not want the crowd, but He wanted them to understand what they were doing. He taught them—Christ never got anybody by a trick; He put the case before them, and He appealed to intelligence, to will, to common-sense, and to their own higher interest as well as for the glory of God. He called for a choice, for a decision. "Lord, I will follow Thee whithersoever Thou goest." "You will? All right. Foxes have holes and the birds of the air have nests, but the Son of Man hath nowhere to lay His head. Are you coming now?" We never hear anything more of that man.

We read in the second chapter of the fourth Gospel that there were many people who committed themselves to Jesus, but He did not commit Himself to them. Why? Because He knew what was in men. He knew about them; He saw through them. They were enthusiastic; they were eager; they went with the rest; they were ready to do anything, to say anything, to go anywhere all at once; and God knows we are not suffering from over-zeal to-day, but zeal must be according to knowledge if it is to last. Oh, I plead for it. It is the only thing that will endure, that will stand the test to which you and I are going to be put when we go back. We have not come to live here for the rest of our natural lives; to hear addresses and to have these delightful times with one another. We are going back. Back to what? Some of you know. Back to be tested; back to be tried; back to be proved; back to achieve, I trust; yes, but back to endure. The result of that trial that awaits you when you get home will depend upon whether you do what you do here intelligently. Action must proceed from knowledge, and acts from facts. Nobody can cheat me out of my position, because I know my title to it. No one can argue me out of my conviction, because it is resting on a broad, sure foundation. I have not had to prostitute my intelligence to believe what I believe and to be where I am. "I know whom I have believed," and I know what I have believed.

"Ye sought in times past for David to be king over you; now, then, do it." Do it intelligently. Do it deliberately. Knowledge must be obtained and carefully considered. Think it through. Do not perish thinking it through. There comes a time for action; believe me, there comes a time when to pray any longer about a thing becomes a perfect blasphemy; there comes a time when to beseech Almighty God to do something for us is blasphemy, when the hour has come for you to act with the knowledge you have got. But we must be deliberate. There is a man who would build a tower; he starts and it goes part way up; he runs out of material, and it sags and sinks and collapses, and he is a laughing stock. Another throws down the gauntlet and challenges the devil, and on the way to the fight he sends an ambassage and asks for conditions of peace. He miscounted the cost. Life is made up of building within and battling without; the tower and the war; construction and destruction; achievement and endurance. There is a building going up within us all, and we are all battling; we are all fighting; we are all struggling. Who is in charge? Are you your own architect and your own captain? Are you finding your own materials? Have you strength enough of your own to meet your enemy? Or have you thought this thing through, and have you come to the conclusion that our materials anyway are no good, even had we enough, but we have not enough. We cannot build our own characters. All this talk about character-building apart from Christ and His Cross is nonsense. The tower will remain unfinished, and we cannot come to grips with our sin and with ourselves, and with the world and the flesh and the devil, in our own strength. The day will come when we shall have to send an ambassage and ask for conditions of peace: and the devil is always ready to give them.

There are people here to-night who started to build and failed, who started the battle and have not got on with it for lack of intelligence and deliberation. Now, then, do it intelligently, deliberately, definitely. There is a distinct shore line between land and sea; there is a clean-cut horizon between sky and mountain-top, and there is a distinct and unmistakable line of demarcation between the self-life and the Christ-life, and we have to cross it. I was a Christian for thirteen years, and I was in my first charge as a minister of the Gospel before I found that out. "If any man will come after me, let him say 'No' to self." I had preached a sermon on denying oneself this thing and that thing and the other thing, and the Spirit of God brought the thing right into this realm, and He said it is not that, and that, and that; you have to deny *yourself*; it is *yourself*. The last stronghold to fall is the stronghold of self; and the most difficult self to break down is the religious self. We are willing to die. Christ does not ask us to die; He asks us to recognise that we are dead. "I have been crucified with Christ. I live, nevertheless not I, but Christ liveth in me."

All acts are definite, and making Christ Lord in the life is an act and not a process. Will you remember the distinction between instantaneous and progressive operations. This distinction is made abundantly clear in the New Testament by the use of the aorist and present progressive tenses, in 2 Corinthians 7: 1, "Having therefore these promises, dearly beloved, let us cleanse ourselves from all filthiness of the flesh and spirit, perfecting holiness in the fear of God." "Let us cleanse ourselves," aorist, something definite, something instantaneous, something thorough-going; an act, not a process. And, further, not something that Christ has to do for us, but something we have to do for ourselves. "*Let us* cleanse ourselves." Now, then, do it. "From all filthiness of the flesh and of the spirit." For what purpose? "Perfecting holiness in the fear of God." That is the process. The foundation is laid in that cleansing, and the superstructure goes up in holiness. Holiness proceeds from cleansing, not cleansing from holiness; cleansing by an act, holiness a progressive experience in Christ.

Knowledge and deliberation call for decision, and decision is always definite. "Faith is an affirmative and an act that bids eternal truth be fact." "Ye sought in times past for David to be king over you; now, then, do it." To dally with solemn issues is to miss God's purpose, and nothing is so fatal.

If we are to do it intelligently and deliberately and definitely, we are also to do it thoroughly. There must be no reserves; Christ claims to be Lord of all, or He will not be Lord at all. He asks for the throne-room in our life. He will not consent to be a guest at your table: He will be the Master; He will be at the head; He will control the house: that is His claim; He has a right to make that claim—no one else has. "Ye are bought with a price . . . ye are not your own." We admit the one part of the declaration, and we do not admit the other. It is easy enough to sing Gospel songs, but more than that is required. "Ye are bought"—blessed be His name—ye are bought, and the price was blood. But what does that imply? "Ye are not your own." The thing you buy in the shop no longer belongs to the shopkeeper; you have paid for it, and you have a right to take it away and use it as you will. Christ has bought you, and you are not letting Him have you. "Ye are not your own; ye are bought with a price; glorify God in your bodies, which are His." There must be no sin allowed, neither doubtful indulgence. There is a wide line between the bad and the best: bad, good, better, best. On what plane are you living? Are you going to be content if you can get into heaven as by the skin of your teeth? That will not satisfy Him who died for you.

God has His best things for the few who dare to stand the test. God has His second choice for those who will not have His best. The good it is that keeps us too often from the better, and the better it is that is robbing us of the best. Christ calls us to go clean over Jordan. You have been through the Red Sea. Have you been through Jordan? You came out of Egypt. Have you gone into the Land? He brought us out from thence that He might bring us in. You have come out. Have you gone in? Abram and Terah started out of Ur to go into the land of Canaan, and Terah died on the way; but Abram came into the land of Canaan. His purpose was accomplished. Is yours; and God's for you? "Ye sought in times past for David to be king over you; do it!" Crown Him King in your life; do it intelligently, deliberately, definitely, thoroughly, joyfully, immediately. Do not wait for tomorrow morning; do not wait for tomorrow night. Do not wait. This is your hour of opportunity; opportunity vouchsafed unto you and unto me to act in the light of what He has revealed.

We have reason to hope and expect that everybody who has come to this Keswick will be blessed, but you are not all roped in yet. Some came this morning, many; some came on previous days, many; some must come here and now, those who have been hovering on the border, those who have been waiting and wondering. This is your hour. You know enough now to act upon. You know Christ as your Saviour; He comes and claims to be your Lord. He is your safety; He wants to be your satisfaction; He is your righteousness; He wants to be your holiness. He wants to lead you on and lead you out and lead you up. Cannot you trust Him? Won't you go with Him? "Will a man rob God?"

As a blood-bought and blood-washed soul, I have no further right to myself; I have no right to do what I like, to go where I like, to be what I like, to say what I like, to read what I like, to form companionships I like, to choose the career I like. I handed myself over in that great hour of my regeneration to Jesus Christ, and I belong to Him by every right—creation, preservation, and redemption; and unless you can give a reason to the Risen Christ to-night for not surrendering yourself absolutely to Him, you have got to do it. "Ye sought in times past for David to be king over you; now, then, do it."

THE DAY-BY-DAY CHRISTIAN LIFE[1]

Rev. Dr. Donald Grey Barnhouse

They that wait upon the Lord shall renew their strength; they shall mount up with wings as eagles; they shall run, and not be weary; and they shall walk, and not faint—Isaiah 40: 31.

THE truths which we have considered in our earlier studies may be likened to flying and running. Our gifts from Christ, our high position in Him, the glorious privileges that are attached to our title as His sons, the gracious provision for our constant cleansing from sin; the absolute assurance that we stand His, and His alone for ever—these are truths which take us into the heavenlies and keep us there.

All of that, however, will be but head knowledge if we do not come to the final step in our practical studies, and see how we can live moment by moment under the power of the Holy Spirit, so that there will be less frequent outbursts of the old nature to bring to the Lord in confession. We consider, then, our day by day walk in Christ, as the practical maintenance of experimental holiness.

I propose, that we consider a day out of life, with all that a day brings to your life and mine. In this way we shall be able to bring our studies out of the realm of the theoretical and the theological into the domain of the intensely practical and experimental, though we shall be in the Bible at every moment of it. Our calendar day begins at midnight; the Jewish day began at sundown. I may be permitted, therefore, to begin the recital of

[1] In the official report of the Keswick Convention for 1938, the following note by the speaker is given as an introduction to this Bible Reading—

During the past few months I prepared the material that was to be given as the Bible Readings at the Keswick Convention. In Bible conference work in one American city I delivered four addresses which I thought would be the Readings here. Some weeks later in another city I delivered the first three addresses, but an entirely different one for the fourth address. This I brought to Keswick, expecting to deliver it on the Thursday morning. In the early days of the Convention I could get no peace about the fourth message, and finally, leaving the small tent in the middle of the Missionary Reception on Wednesday afternoon, I went to my rooms with the certainty that I must prepare an entirely fresh message for delivery on the morrow. With a natural reticence that was almost repugnance I prepared the very personal message that follows, and which came to me with impelling force. It was received in such a way that I knew that it had been blessed to many hearts. Undoubtedly, the Lord had a special purpose in it.—D.G.B.

our experimental day somewhere between the two of these, and, for a reason that will soon be manifest, I choose the moment when we are about to go to sleep for the night. Someone may wonder why I should begin the account of my day at that point, and the answer rises from a psychological truth that many of us know from experience. I frequently noticed that I awoke in the morning thinking the same thoughts that had been in my mind at the time I closed my eyes in sleep the night before. Many people know from sad experience that the mind frequently drifts to thoughts that are utterly of self, and its interests and desires, in those half-asleep, half-awake moments that end our day and that begin our night. I discovered, therefore, that it was of great importance to capture this half-world of the mind for our Lord Jesus Christ.

One morning when I awoke trying to solve a chess problem that had filled my mind as I had put my head upon my pillow, I became conscious of this law and determined that, henceforth, I should go to sleep thinking of Christ. As the months passed, I discovered that there was much more than a habit involved in this. Here was a proof of the presence of the Lord Jesus Christ in my heart and mind, controlling even the subconscious element of my life. Then I learned that I must not merely go to sleep thinking *about* Christ, but that I must go to sleep in communion *with* Him. I began memorising verses of Scripture at night, and reciting them as I fell asleep. At first these truths were merely objective. "His Name shall be called wonderful . . ." might be my verse on a certain night. At first I would meditate on this, in terms somewhat like those in which I might expound them to an audience. His Name is full of wonders. His Name is the name Jesus, that of the Saviour. He shall save His people from their sins. . . . Then there came a change that He brought in my procedure. Those same sentences were altered to the person, number, and tense of fellowship. *Thy* Name is full of wonders. *Thy* Name is Jesus. *Thou* art my Saviour. *Thou* shalt continually save me from my sins. Soon He became more real than the inside of my eyelids. I could not see them though they were close to my eyes; Him I learned to know in everything but the touch. And closing one's eyes with Christ takes away all fear of sleepless nights. Let others count sheep jumping over a wall; I shall talk with the Shepherd. "He giveth His beloved sleep" (Psa. 127: 2). "I laid me down and slept," says David, "I awaked; for the Lord sustained me" (Psa. 3: 5)

> When sleep her balm denies,
> My silent spirit sighs,
>   May Jesus Christ be praised!

The night becomes as day,
When from the heart we say,
May Jesus Christ be praised!

Then, when I awake to a new day, I wake to hear Him *speak*
to me, and I to Him. David knew this when he said, "When
I awake, I am still with Thee" (Psa. 139: 18).

Still, still with Thee, when purple morning breaketh,
When the bird waketh, and the shadows flee;
Fairer than morning, lovelier than daylight,
Dawns the sweet consciousness, I am with Thee.

Alone with Thee, amid the mystic shadows,
The solemn hush of nature newly born;
Alone with Thee in breathless adoration,
In the calm dew and freshness of the morn.

Still, still with Thee! As to each new born morning
A fresh and solemn splendour still is given;
So does this blessed consciousness, awakening,
Breathe each day nearness unto Thee and heaven.

Oh, how important are those first awaking moments! To
live them with Christ will save us, perhaps hours of our day. We
will not have to come back later to confess that we have lived
in the flesh instead of the life of faith in Christ. And the verse
which we were learning as we fell asleep comes back afresh to our
hearts and minds, and our fellowship is fed with the wonder of
His Name and all that it conveys.

And then the heart naturally turns to *praise*. For Christ,
recognised, exalted, and enthroned in the life, will live the same
life of praise and intercession within us that He is living in heaven.
Have you seen that beautiful picture in the Epistle to the Hebrews
of Christ leading the praise, the music if you like, that rises from
the hearts of the redeemed? Because He has set us apart for
Himself, He says He is not ashamed to call us brethren, saying, "I
will declare thy name unto my brethren; in the midst of the
Church will I—Christ—sing praises unto thee" (Heb. 2: 12).
My heart loves that picture of the singing Christ, and I find that,
as the springtime calls forth the song from the birds, so the indwelling life of Christ, exalted and owned, calls forth praise from
my redeemed being.

Robert Murray McCheyne has given us a wonderful passage
in his memoirs, in which he tells how he learned to banish temptation with praise. When Satan moves up with his forces, the Lord

within raises the cry of triumphant praise to God, and the hosts of the enemy must flee. McCheyne found that the devil could not resist a psalm of praise. There is, of course, a profound spiritual truth behind this, because the believer cannot be living in praise unless he is yielded to the Lordship of Christ. A true psalm cannot rise from lips that have not been fully cleansed. So—

> When morning gilds the skies,
> My heart, awaking, cries,
> May Jesus Christ be praised!

Then, there must be a swift, sharp *prayer* that the Lord shall take hold of my being, my mind, my tongue, as I greet my loved ones. This is for their sake, not mine, for they are easy enough to get along with. How many of us must realise that those who live in the house with us must have a special blessing from God to get along with us! There are some dear women and children that would rather go into a bear pit than have to meet some of you before you have had your morning cup of tea or coffee. Were there some folk at home who sighed with relief when you left for Keswick, knowing that they would have a week of peace in the house, with you away? The Lord never meant that any Christian should have to growl a later apology to husband or wife, saying, "Perhaps I did roar a bit, but I wasn't fully awake, and you know I am not responsible until half an hour after I am out of bed." The Lord will do away with all of that for you, and every side of the bed will be the right side of the bed for you to get out of, when you have committed your mind and your tongue to Him for those first moments of contact that you will have with others.

Now, I have learned experimentally, that the best thing for me to do is to have my day marked off in sections, and *to come to God* for a constant renewal of life as I go on. David says, "Seven times a day do I praise Thee because of Thy righteous judgments" (Psa. 119: 164). You may find it necessary to mark your day into longer or shorter sections, but there must be a constant coming to Him in the midst of the activities of life. When I was in South India, I visited Miss Amy Carmichael at Dohnavur. One of the customs of what is perhaps the most beautiful mission station in the whole world, is to pause at the striking of the hour. In the tower of prayer that rises, flower-covered, above the chapel, there are chimes which can be heard throughout the compound. The whole outward activity of the mission ceases when the chimes begin the hour. The older girls, in their beautiful saris, walking along the flowered pathways, will stop and bow in meditation.

The children in the playing fields will cease their games for a brief moment. The big brothers will get down from their bicycles as they go on some errand, and will stand a moment in silence while the chimes play. It is all like a moving picture that turns, for a moment, into a stereopticon slide, and then it resumes its motion. Unhappy the Christian life that does not have its chimes in it somewhere during the day, to stop the earthly activities while we listen to the heavenly peal, think upon the Saviour a moment, talk directly to Him, listen to His voice in some verse that He will recall to mind, and then step on into the work and the activity of the moment.

God has taught me to look ahead like one who walks along a road, asking God to keep and sustain until the next tree, the next milestone, the next bend in the road, at which point I draw the breath that comes from another atmosphere than this, and step out towards the next point. At home I look ahead, in the morning, to the breakfast table. There we gather first of all around the Word of God, with our children and the servants, for a few moments with the Book. We like to have our family worship before eating. I remember that Leland Wang, of Hong Kong, gives his people the slogan, "No Bible, no breakfast!" If you must go without one of them, skip the porridge, but do not let your soul starve through a morning. Your body can live on the stored-up strength, but the manna from yesterday spoils if we try to use it over again today. There is many a Christian who could find the whole secret of a life of defeat in a neglected Bible.

And then, somewhere at the close of the prayer, perhaps even silently, after the audible words have ended, I look forward to the next bend of the road and commit the table conversation to the Lord and all that must happen until the children go out of the door to school. So much can be taught to children by the incidental and indirect conversation of the father and mother, while they pay attention to their food. We can pick out incidents from the daily press or the life of the parish, and point out some one's failure or success and see the basis for it. To say that John Smith got into trouble because he did a certain thing may leave a more lasting impression than to say, "Now Donald, mind you never do such a thing." The discussion of some verse in the Scripture may bring out a truth which father and mother will know needs strong application in the life of one of the children, and they are quicker at catching the point than are many grown folk.

Then breakfast is over and they are about to be off to school. I often wonder when I sing "Like a River Glorious," if Miss Havergal, who wrote the words, ever listened to four children, full of health and vigour, as they rose from the table and prepared to leave for school! She says,

> Not a surge of worry,
>   Not a shade of care,
> Not a blast of hurry,
>   Touch the spirit there.

I am afraid that there are times when we have "a blast of hurry" in our household. We manage well with the worry and the care, for we have long since learned that if we are worrying we are not trusting, and that if we are trusting we are not worrying. You cannot have a cup of water and a cup of milk in the same cup at the same time. Nor can you have a heart that is resting in Christ that is filled with care. This covers all of the events in the life of the home: sickness, trouble, death, money, discipline, or whatever may be the emergency that may arise. He is faithful to His promise and supplies the strength, meets the need, comforts the heart, and keeps us looking to Himself. This goes for your home-life and your circumstances, whether you are responsible for the home, or whether you are going off to school or to work. The Lord is faithful and able, and He will continually keep us. This is the walk of the life that is lived by the faith of the Son of God.

And now that the children are off to school, I sit at my desk for a quick glance at the newspaper. Just here I must commit myself to the Lord. I must know the Lord in my heart as I read the paper these days. Look at those black headlines. What city is being bombed today? What dictator is destroying more of the liberties of God's dear children? What new persecution is breaking out against the Chosen People? What preacher is making a scandalous utterance in denial of the faith? And in communion with my Lord I hear Him say, as I read the newspaper, "See that ye be not troubled: for all these things must come to pass" (Matt. 24: 6). Does this seem impossible? It is the Lord who has spoken it. But do you realise that we are having to take measures of air raid precaution? Do not forget that the first half of that verse is, "Ye shall hear of wars and rumours of wars." It is of this that He says, "See that *ye* be not troubled."

And of late, as I read my newspaper, I find that the Lord who dwells within my heart leads me in the same work that He is doing in heaven; for there He is interceding for His people. It would be strange that He should do otherwise when He is given full control of a life here below. "In all their affliction He was afflicted" (Isa. 63: 9), and that affliction must be in our hearts as we see this poor, sick world today. I never see the news from China that my heart and mind do not go over that land in prayer. Do I read of Peiping? My heart says, Lord, bless Wang Ming Tao as he preaches, and keep him safe from the enemy. Is it Changsha? There are Marcus Cheng and Ch'eng Chi Kuei. Or Nanking? What has happened to Jonathan and Lena Cheng, and Calvin Chao? Or Shanghai? Lord, what of John Soong and Watchman Nee? Or Hong Kong? Lord, bless Leland Wang as he preaches. And so on, across China and across the world. You may not know all of these particular people, but you should have a list of those for whom you pray. In a drawer in my desk there are three books, filled with the names of missionaries, and national Christian leaders the world over. I love to go over the map with these books and these names, bearing them up before the Lord.

Just here somebody is going to say, "Oh, but you are a minister, and have time to do this! We have our housework or our office work, and cannot spend time like this in prayer, or stop to read the Bible." I am not sure that I believe you, quite. Granted that I have more time for this than many of you, I am convinced that most people spend much more time on unnecessary things than need be, and that they neglect the important things. You sleep eight hours, you work eight hours, and in the remaining hours there are many moments which you could give to the business of intercession and the joy of feeding on the Word of God, if only you would surrender your wills to the Lord for this purpose. It is far more necessary than you know.

I want to pause here to illustrate this with a story. My four children are very keen on stories and riddles, and frequently ask me to bring forth fresh ones for their entertainment. One day I told them this one. A baby was born in New York just a few months ago, and it weighed almost four stone at birth. They fed it on ten gallons of milk every day, and in a few months it weighed almost seven stone. There was a moment of silence, and then Mr. Nine-year-old replied, "Why, daddy, that can't be so! We weighed less than ten pounds when we were born, and here Donny is over eleven and he doesn't yet weigh seven stone." After discussion and the display of much incredulity they at last asked for the explanation, so I replied that the baby was born at the Zoo, and that it was a baby elephant! Then I said to them, "Suppose that the keeper at the Zoo was making his rounds with the food one morning, and found the ten gallons of milk heavy to carry. Suppose that he said, 'I will give these ten gallons of milk to these little birds in this nest in the bird house, and take these worms down to the elephant.' What would happen? Why, of course, the birdlings would drown and the elephant would starve!" We understand that every member of the animal kingdom must have its own particular nourishment, without which it cannot live.

Then we can draw this analogy. We have a new nature which is the life of Christ, and we have an old nature which is the life of sin within us. Saul and Paul dwell together in the same body of the Christian. Saul has a voracious appetite, and the whole organisation of the civilisation of this world is keyed to the feeding of this old nature. So many of the books, the magazines, the trivialities of conversation, the pictures on the hoardings, the cinema—I think that it may be more tolerable for Sodom and Gomorrah than for Hollywood—in short, the whole of life round about us is food for the old nature. On this food the old nature waxes fat and flourishing, and the only thing is to bring it to be crucified. There is but one food for the new nature. "Man shall not live by bread alone, but by every word that proceedeth out of the mouth of God" (Matt. 4: 4). O Christians, why will you starve your spirits till you have no strength to resist the enemy when he comes against you! He, the devil, will never flee except before the Word of God, and the Word of God which has been freshly appropriated and assimilated and flashed forth in the power of the living presence of the Lord of the Cross of Calvary. There is the place of victory. "They overcame him by the blood of the Lamb, and by the word of their testimony" (Rev. 12: 11). And in the course of my day there must be many fresh appropriations of the Word of God to meet the subtle and varying attacks of the enemy.

And now we come to the business of the day. One of the secretaries comes with mail and business. Here is another one of my milestones. A swift prayer must be sent heavenward. Lord, all praise be Thine for the life of the past hour, and I go to the next hour utterly relying upon Thee. Let every letter and every item of business be considered and acted upon in the light of Thy holy presence and in accord with Thy will. Here, again, I have an analogy with your business, whether it be the directing of an office, the performance of some employment, the studying, the ordering of the household, or whatever your particular occupation may be. We publish a monthly magazine, we have a large radio correspondence, there are the problems that arise in connection with some of the families of a city parish. There are more than three hundred pounds to find each month to pay the radio bills. There are manuscripts to consider, and much religious poetry to reject! Yet every detail has to be done in the strength of the Lord, in a moment-by-moment looking to Him.

Christ has promised power for every need. Recently I came across a paragraph on the varieties of power furnished by the Holy Spirit to men in the Bible. "What a range of enduement for special purposes! For instance, the Old Testament tells of Joseph, the shepherd lad, who is made adequate to rule the mightiest kingdom in the old world and save countless lives in a time of unprecedented famine. Bezaleel is given the ability of 'craftsmanship' to bring into being the divine plan for the Tabernacle in the wilderness. Samson is endued with physical strength sufficient to slay a thousand Philistines with the jawbone of an ass. The sweet psalmist of Israel is taught the songs, so rich in deep, spiritual experience, which have been the heritage of God's people down through the ages. Prophets are given boldness to stand before the backsliding people of Israel, and rebuke in plainest terms their idolatry and sin. The remnant, returning to their land under Zerubbabel and Joshua the high priest, are given that purpose of heart which, in the teeth of bitter opposition, sees the new Temple slowly, but surely, erected on the ruins of the old." I believe that it is quite in line with the teaching of the Bible to say to you women that God the Lord can furnish you the Holy Spirit of household order, whether your place is in the scullery or the drawing-room. The Holy Spirit of executive ability can be given to men who need it. The Holy Spirit of faithfulness to humble tasks can be given to those who are employed. The Holy Spirit of skill can be given to doctors and nurses. I know of young Christians who have asked the Lord to give them skill in their arts of music and painting, and whose prayers have been answered. The Spirit of God is provided to meet many kinds of needs in our lives.

In the course of the years we have had scores of thousands of letters in connection with our radio work. A very few are from cranks, and the Lord furnishes my secretaries the patience to read those, and the wisdom to keep them from me. I have come to the place where I never take one of the letters that are brought to me without a quick prayer to God for the ability to meet the need that is therein expressed. I have come to realise that these letters are almost pieces of the human spirit. I know of letters that have been copied because there were too many tear marks over the writing. I know of one letter that was written and placed in a drawer for several months before the courage was found to post it. We need the Lord Himself to answer those tender questions that come from the very depths of torn souls.

Then suddenly with the jangling of a telephone bell, there comes a sharp attack of the enemy. We never know the avenue which he will choose. We never know which envelope may contain his approach, which telephone call may conceal his darts. Here is a friend on the 'phone. Have I seen such and such a paper this week? No, I have not! Do I know that I have been bitterly attacked by some Fundamentalist, and that the leading article in the paper tells people that I am bound up in apostasy and false teaching because I do not leave the denomination I am in? Have I heard that it has been intimated that I am staying in because of my salary, and my unwillingness to leave buildings and pension in order to step out with the little flock, who are now saying that *their* work is the very cause of God? I had neglected to pray about this telephone conversation when the bell rang. I had not asked the Lord to give me the Holy Spirit of answering the telephone when it comes rudely into my work. And so I answer: "These men are cowards, and they are doing the work of the devil, the accuser of the brethren!" Then, when the receiver is back on the hook, I find I am restless. I turn to my letters, but there is something wrong. I read a paragraph two or three times and cannot get the meaning.

Listen carefully, now. Just here the Christian soul stands in the greatest peril that confronts us in the Christian life. There are two courses of action before us. We can say to ourselves, "This work must be done," and we can drive ahead into the correspondence and can get the letters answered in the energy of the flesh. These are the letters that will commit us to meetings that are not blessed. These are the letters that cause us two or three other letters later on to explain what we meant, and then to explain our explanation. The other course of action is to say, Lord, what is wrong? Have I offended Thee? What have I done in my strength that should have been submitted to the Holy Spirit? The secretary who waits, pencil poised, may think that the answer to the letter is being formulated, but in reality, a child is getting back into fellowship with One who is truly holy, and who will not permit answers like that on the telephone. Then, swiftly, I say, Lord, there was that old nature again. It broke out! Wilt Thou crucify it right now, and restore me to the fulness of Thy fellowship?

And now the cloud has gone, the sun shines through and there is light again; there is the clear recognition of the fact that I should have spoken otherwise; there is the opportunity for examining the whole course of my actions in the light of these accusations. Lord, would I sell Thee for buildings, salary, and pension? Is this brother right? Have I missed a turning? Should I have gone out with noise and clamour? And the Holy Spirit brings to my heart the memory of the peace after the long struggle in coming to a decision. I turn again in my mind to that page of the Scripture where the risen Lord spoke to the Church at Sardis. And though He was forced to say that they had a name to live and were yet dead, He told His messenger to "Be watchful, and strengthen the things which remain, that are ready to die" (Rev. 3: 2). He reassures me that there has been no change in His orders, and I remember how I received and heard, and I rest my heart upon His Word and go on. And I remember that the Lord turned the captivity of Job when he prayed for his friends who probably hurt him more than his boils, and I ask the Lord to give me an honest prayer for this brother who has written the attack, and that he may be blessed in the sphere of his labours, in so far as he exalts the Lord Jesus Christ. And joy flows in my heart once more.

There are moments when we need more power than we need at other moments. Yesterday the young men who operate these amplifiers told me that on a fair day like this they need very little power to take the voice to the thousands of people in this tent, as well as beyond to those who sit on the grass. When it is raining and the tent is wet it takes three times as much electricity to carry the same power or voice. There are wet days in life when all the canvas seems saturated with troubles, and we must come much more constantly to the Lord, in order to receive the increase of His power that must be turned on to overcome all of these circumstances that come in life. But the power is there with Him, and He is always ready to flow through to meet any need.

Thus the day goes on. There may come stabs of sorrow, moments when His compassion is needed to meet some soul who has lost a job, who has had death come in his circle. There may be moments of joy, high and wide, when some penitent sinner kneels down by the desk to receive the Lord Jesus, as many have done by my desk. There may be hours of calm meditation when the Spirit causes the words of the Book to glow and the messages for the hungry sheep who are to look up and be fed. He is in it all as the day wears on. There are moments when the cheque-book is in hand and the careful scrutiny of every item must be submitted to His searching gaze. One tenth is Thine, yea, ten-tenths are Thine, O Lord, when this relationship has been established, and the same Holy Spirit of writing cheques must come upon us for the grocery bill and for the missionary cause. He will see to it that the proper balance is maintained, in both senses of the word, the balance between His work and the necessities of life; what I am to spend on myself and the balance at the first of the month to pay the bills.

The afternoon wears on. The children come home from school, and it is their place and privilege to come in and sit on father's knee to babble forth all that may come to the child mind, for the study is in the heart of the home. There are questions to be answered, or little nothings to be told; and the children are seldom to be told that father is busy. The Holy Spirit of family relationships guards them. They have their rights, and this is their privilege especially since father must leave soon to go to a meeting, and there hold forth the Word of life to those that will be gathered together.

And just here there is special need for communion with the Lord and submission to the Holy Spirit. There has been prayer watering every part of the preparation of the message, and now there must be a special anointing for the delivery of the message. How dare we stand to preach when we have not received power from the Lord! How dare we speak to an individual in conversation without looking to the Lord, and asking Him to control that conversation! How dare we carry on any work without Him! Has He not said, "Without me ye can do "—just exactly—"nothing"? There are times when I have leaned against the wall of the vestry of some church with a profound sense of physical weakness, the weakness that must be most like the weakness of a mother who is delivering a child. I do not know who it was who first applied the word "delivery" to a sermon as well as to a child, but I believe that the Holy Spirit of preaching must have given him the idea. Paul knew this when he wrote, "I was with you in weakness, and in fear, and in much trembling. And my speech and my preaching was not with enticing words of man's wisdom, but in demonstration of the Spirit and of power: that your faith should not stand in the wisdom of men, but in the power of God" (1 Cor. 2: 3–5). What joy!

We must have such relationship with Christ, such *constant communication* with Him, that no matter what difficulty may arise in the course of the preaching or the meetings of the day, we can turn to Him and know that we have met Him, and that our problems have been fully dealt with. Let me explain by an illustration that is very, very precious to me. I suppose every good family has a private vocabulary that is unknown to anybody else. You have been in a group of people, when someone mentions something with an added significance that means nothing to anyone else but you and one other person in the group. You turn your head and glance across to where that other person is, and you say in that glance, "Did you get it?" and you get the response, "Yes, I got it." No one else knows that there has been a touch that brings a whole experience to your memory. We have a private vocabulary like that in our home. We have incidents that call up certain experiences in life.

In the early years of our married life, when our eldest child was almost a year old, Mrs. Barnhouse and I were living in

Southern France, where I was studying at the University of Grenoble. We went to Greece one autumn for several months, and while we were there we went out on certain field trips in connection with my work in archaeology. One day we left Corinth and went down to Nycenae, where lie the ruins of the city of Agamemnon. We got off at the little station and walked the mile or two to the mound that was the ruins of the ancient city. There I installed my wife and the baby in the shade, and I proceeded with my work. After a while, as I came over on the other side of the mound, I fell upon a field of wild cyclamen. I had never seen this flower growing wild, and I gathered a large bunch and came back over the mound with them behind my back, and finally presented them to my wife. We often talked about their beauty, and in after years frequently had similar ones growing in our home. Years passed, and every time we saw cyclamen of that particular hue, we would glance at each other and remember those experiences of our early life. One evening, just before Christmas a few years ago, we were walking down the street of Philadelphia with a friend between us. The spirit of Christmas was in the air, snow was falling, it was a crisp, winter's evening. The three of us were talking about something far removed from Greece, or from flowers. We passed by a florist's shop, and there in the window was a great pot of cyclamen of our particular pastel lavender shade. We both saw it at the same time, and leaning forward my wife said, "Oh!" and I leaned forward and said, "Oh!" We went on, continuing with our interrupted conversation, but what we had really done in that moment was to draw up our chairs by the fireside and say, "Do you remember those days, that walk, the dusty road, the fragrance and the sweetness of those flowers, and all the joy of those days?" All that was said by one word and in a flash of a second.

Life is made up of thousands of such experiences and memories like that. In the same way our spiritual life must be filled with experiences that the Spirit of God can recall to us in moments of need. We know times, for example, in the midst of a sermon when it may be necessary to glance to God, and in one flash look into His face and to recall some thought or experience that He once gave to us, to remember that there was once a battle in the soul that settled for ever certain points that the devil might now bring to our minds. For instance, you give some point, and you see it has gone home to the minds of your listeners and it has been used. Every man on this platform knows that the old nature of pride can rise and seek to take the credit for something that God has been pleased to do through the human instrumentality. It becomes necessary to flash a quick look to God and to remember, "Not many wise men after the flesh, not many mighty, not many noble, are called: but God hath chosen the foolish things of the world to confound the wise; and God hath chosen the weak things of the world to confound the things which are mighty; and base things of the world, and things which are despised, hath God chosen, yea, and things which are not, to bring to nought things that are; that no flesh should glory in His presence." You may remember some long battlefield experience in life when you determined to go His way and preach the preaching that He bid you. You can get all that in a glance, in one flashing moment, as your spirit is taken to His, and you can go on in the power of the Spirit in the midst of your work.

New strength and vigour has come with the preaching. He so abundantly supplies that there can be no doubting that His own strength has been poured into the body. And then home at last, to that sanctuary upon earth where there is a companion living this same life of the Spirit and making home a refuge from all the strife of tongues abroad.

The evening comes to a close. The Book is taken once more and the day is brought into review beneath the eyes of Him who is naught but holy. How sad it is to look back and see the things that have displeased Him. Just last night as I brought my day before His gaze, His Spirit convicted me of a sin of omission. I had luncheon yesterday noon with a group of young men. It is not necessary to identify them. They will understand. After the meal we sat for an hour and talked of the underlying principles of the ministry of the Gospel of Jesus Christ. I had a strong feeling as I left that some of you were not yet born again, even though you may be looking forward to a life of religious work. I did not ask you to give diligence to make your calling and election sure. I did not ask you if you had been born again. Last night I asked the Lord to forgive me for my neglect, to forgive me for not pleading with you to forsake the ministry rather than stand in any pulpit of the land with some ethical message that rises from the naturally good elements in the old nature which is, nevertheless, alien to the life of God as it is in Jesus Christ. The Lord tenderly forgave me for that and other sins of the day, and now graciously gives me the opportunity of making this plea to your heart as well as to all others here. There have been days, however, where the confession of missed opportunities brought with it the shaming sense that it could never return, and that some soul had been touched by the old nature without the Spirit of God reaching through me to its need.

And just before retiring for the night, I turn once more to find Him in His Word and worship Him there. I read for my closing meditation that description of the throne of God where the redeemed of earth are gathered. There we are seen, our position already guaranteed by all that our Saviour is, seated with Him in the heavenly places. "And before the throne there was a sea of glass like unto crystal." I remember that the sea, in Solomon's temple, was the laver where the priests of the Lord washed, after they had offered up the lamb. I know that it is the symbol of my daily cleansing through the Word, even as the altar is the symbol of my justification. But here in the passage I am meditating the sea is of glass, like unto crystal. The Word has taken its eternal form, there is no more need for me to come to God for cleansing. How the heart is filled with praise, with adoration, with worship in the Spirit and in truth. There shall come a day without an evening that brings the time of confession. There shall come a time when I stand before God in all the holiness of Jesus Christ, in my condition as well as in my position, with my old nature gone for ever, with the root of sin then destroyed for ever, since it passes from me with the death of this body, or its transformation at the Coming of my Lord. And as I read my evening Word, I look around in that heavenly scene, and see that moment of eternal triumph. For I read: "When those living creatures give glory and honour and thanks to Him that sat on the throne, who liveth for ever and ever, the four and twenty elders fall down before Him that sat on the throne, and worship Him that liveth for ever and ever, and cast their crowns before the throne, saying, Thou art worthy, O Lord, to receive glory and honour and power; for Thou hast created all things, and for Thy pleasure they are and were created" (Rev. 4: 9–11). And I look again, before my eyes shall close in sleep, and see myself there among them, as one day I shall be, and I am able to join in their devotion, as I know that the wonderful provision for my momentary cleansing will no more be needed in that day.

> Holy, holy, holy! all the saints adore Thee,
> Casting down their golden crowns around
> the glassy sea;
> Cherubim and seraphim falling down before
> Thee,
> Who wert, and art, and evermore shalt be.

I know of no truth more calculated to bring forth our deepest devotion than the certainty that the day shall come when I will never have to look into the past and say, "Lord, there is this to confess, and that to be forgiven."

Then quietly to rest, thinking of Him, talking to Him, with meditations that even He has called sweet. And I know that, whether I wake to a day of storm or of calm, I shall wake with Him. Whether I am to know the calm sunny days of work and blessing, or the battles of illness and troubles that beset all members of this race, I can, none the less, pillow my head upon the promises of God, with the certain knowledge that all things will work together for my good, and that nothing shall ever touch me until it has been passed through the loving will of my heavenly Father, who knows the thoughts that He thinks toward me, thoughts of peace, and not of evil, to give me this expected end (Jer. 29: 11).

THE EVERYDAY CHRISTIAN LIFE

Fred Mitchell

THIS is the last evening convention meeting, and the last of our teaching meetings. To-morrow morning we look out upon the world in its need; to-morrow evening we look up to the Lord upon His throne; but to-night we are to think about ourselves in His presence, and to contemplate His resources for us. Therefore, I feel we should seek to gather up the threads of thought which have been brought to us during the week, and then to relate them to the future.

I can remember now very vividly the sinking feeling I used to have as a convention or a conference began to draw to its close; it was almost a nightmare to leave the holy atmosphere in which we had been spending some privileged days, when everything was conducive to holy thought and action, and to contemplate going down again into the valley. It may be that some of you, especially young people, have a measure of anxiety as to how you will go on when you get back to college, office, factory, or home. So I want to speak a word especially calculated to help you as you face the future, and the word which has been laid upon my heart is from Galatians 2: 20. Out of that wonderful text so often quoted at Keswick, "I am crucified with Christ: nevertheless I live; yet not I, but Christ liveth in me: and the life which I now live in the flesh I live by the faith of the Son of God, who loved me, and gave Himself for me," I take this phrase, to interpret it in its context and in our own immediate circumstances: "the life which I now live"—and that as distinct from the life which I have been living this week, which in some measure is an unnatural life. I would not care to spend fifty-two weeks of the year at a convention, would you? It would be too exhilarating, and there would be an experience of the grace of God in the valley which we would never have by remaining here on the mountain top. So I am thinking of these words, "the life which I now live," as expressing the ordinary life we are called to live.

Now, the phrase in the text has behind it and before it certain facts upon which the apostle Paul makes the statement. Those are quite simple facts, which have been brought home to us more than once during the convention—"I have been crucified with Christ," that is the first fact which is in the background; it is the basis of this description which St. Paul gives of the life which he is now living, and which you and I are, please God, now to live when we go from Keswick. If we are to live a life which is truly Christian it must be lived on the basis, first of all, of this fact that you and I have been crucified with Christ; that is to say, that we have died to sin.

Now, that is very easy to say, and in some measure very easy to believe, intellectually; but intellectual belief of the truth of God never saved a soul from sin, and never introduced a saint into victory. It is right and necessary that we should have some clear mental apprehension of the truth, but it is the truth apprehended mentally and then experienced practically which brings the sinner into salvation, and the saint into the glorious experience of sanctification. When the mind has accepted the truth, then the will must accept the implications; and it is the implications of that truth often brought home to us this week which specially concern me at this point. It is not a question of whether I have got the terms of Keswick teaching right, but am I committed to a life which is an expression of them in practical experience? Am I committed to the life of one who has actually died to sin? Am I leaving Keswick as one purposing in the power of God to live the crucified life, actually dead unto sin? If we have been, in the providence of God, brought to that place this week, then we may count upon it that the Spirit of God will bring us into places, positions, and experiences which will give us every opportunity of putting that life into practice, in home, office, shop, factory and mission station; there will be plenty of opportunity for proving the cross and of dying to self. So it is not merely that we have apprehended the truth here, but that we are going forth actually to live this life in the power of God in our own appointed circumstances, and no other.

Now, when such a decision has been made and such an attitude adopted, then it will not surprise us when we are slighted and overlooked; that is part of dying to sin. We have accepted that, have we not? If we have been led so far in our study of God's Word this week, many of us have accepted the truth that we have died to sin, so that when next Monday in the office someone treats us very shabbily, well, that is not surprising; we accepted that this week, and our reaction to that will either be victory or failure. It matters little what happens to us, it matters everything how we react to what happens to us. Shall I next week be misrepresented? Then I accept that as involved in the life of death to sin, and I will not be surprised or perturbed. Shall I be persecuted? So was the Lord, and so shall we be; and here in the quiet of this privileged week, we accept for life or death, for better or worse, whatever the Lord our God shall appoint or permit. We are committed to it, and whatever comes of slighting, misrepresentation or persecution, we accept it as our appointed lot, and we triumph over it by dying to it as it comes to us. It was saintly William Law who said, "Take every such occasion with both hands as a blessed occasion of dying to self." There will be plenty of occasions next week and the week after of dying to self. Are we going to take them with both hands? If so, we are committed to a life of victory. Once that attitude is taken up, and in so far as it is maintained, nobody can do any one of us the slightest harm; they can only do us good. They slight us, and they give us a fresh occasion of dying to self, and proving the glorious victory into which we have entered this week. They persecute us, and they give us an occasion for triumphing in it through the grace of the Lord mediated to us in these particular circumstances. That is victory: dying to self and not reacting adversely to the misrepresentation or the persecution when it comes, as it most surely will come.

Some of my young friends may be saying to me, "This is a terrible price to pay; I had no idea I was being committed to such a life, to lie down and let people walk over me, to be quiet and let people misrepresent me." But it is to such a life that we are committed. That is the life of victory, and that is the life of blessing. It is costly, but it is worth it. It is the way God will enrich our character and perfect our testimony; so receiving the persecution or the slight, we shall preach the most eloquent sermon and give the most convincing testimony to the ungodly.

But I suggest to any who feel this is a very heavy price to pay, that not paying it you will be committed to paying a heavier price. A young man came to an evangelist and said, "It costs too much to be a Christian," and the evangelist wisely replied, "It costs too much not to be one." It costs much to be a truly sanctified Christian walking in the light and life and power of God; but none of us can afford not to be such a Christian. If you have seen anything—as doubtless you have this week—of the awful nature of yourself, the awkward member which springs up at the least provocation with its biting bitter words that once said can never be withdrawn, that takes a pen and writes those burning letters that once sent can never be brought back, if we have seen anything of the nature of self, I doubt not that some of us are willing to pay the price, and receive the grace, and reign in life over this cruel self. When once we have seen the nature of sin in the believer, of self in the man of God, then surely we can pray such a prayer as I came across recently in a book—

> Give me the grace to let my rag-rights go
> In the great wind that from Thy throne doth blow.

There is nothing in self worth holding on to: it ought to be handed to death. And we have committed ourselves to a life such as that: and God is going to give us every opportunity to allow Him to put it to death, with the glorious end in view that, as self is put out of the way, the ever-living, glorious, lovely Lord Jesus will take the pre-eminence and be continually given the pre-eminence, to our joy, and to the saving of many souls. When once this attitude is clear and maintained, the sting is taken out of the dealings of others; that is because, as we are expecting nothing except the way of the Cross, we shall not be disappointed; and we shall enter into a life of rest, getting exactly what we expect and glorifying Christ in it.

That is the first basic fact on which we are to live "the life which I now live." The second is this: "I am crucified with Christ, and I *live*." I am no Greek student, but anyone who knows even a little Greek will see that the translator has put "nevertheless" in to make it vivid. "I am crucified, and I live." I should have thought the apostle would have written, "I am crucified and I am dead." No. I am crucified and I *live*. You see, dear friends, at Calvary there was something which perished and something which persisted, and when God showed me this truth it was a great comfort to my heart. There was an "I" which died, and an "I" which lived. That is important, because God does not by the cross mean the destruction of individuality or personality, but only of sin and sinful self. The "I" which died was a master; the "I" which lives is a servant. The "I" which died loves to be ministered unto; the "I" which lives ministers unto others. The "I" which died was a source; the "I" which lives is a vessel. And when the old "I" is renounced and put to death, then we are able to sing—

> I am an empty vessel, not one thought
> Or look of love, I ever to Thee brought;
> Yet I may come, and come again to Thee,
> With this, the empty sinner's only plea—
>   Thou lovest me,

or more suitably here,

> Thou fillest me.

There is an "I" which God wants out of the way and which you and I want out of the way, and which brings disaster and sorrow everywhere it is manifested; and there is an "I" which is to persist as an empty vessel for the manifestation of the glory of God. It is not the empty vessel which is to die, but the sinful self which fills it, and which when knocked falls over with bitter words and biting sarcasm. The sinful "I" sometimes manifests itself in the prayer meeting, and indeed in other circumstances. When it prays, it says, "I thank Thee, Lord, that I am not as other men are"; it sometimes seeks power, praying, "Give me this power, or that," but the command is, "That ye may receive the Holy Ghost." God deliver us from that "I" in the prayer meeting where it is evidenced; it ought to be put out of the way. God has put him out of the way, we have consented that he be put out of the way, and God is going to work in us His grace that he be put out of the way day by day.

But there is an "I" which God, the Master Craftsman, has made to be an empty vessel which He purposes to fill with living water which will run over and flow out everywhere and every day. That "I" which God has preserved, and will preserve, and which perhaps some young believer may have been a little anxious about, is to be like one of the stones in Aaron's breastplate catching the Shekinah light and reflecting it in a thousand hues and different manifestations. Oh, my dear young friends, your true individuality was wonderfully made by God, when He took the woof of your parentage and wove into it the warp of your circumstances—God has made that to preserve it, in order to show forth His glory; and you will never be your real self until the sinful self is put to death, and Christ fills your own individual personality. That is the second fact. There is the "I" which is to die, and there is the "I" which is to live filled by the glory of God, and shining through it the light from God.

The third fact is that we have been introduced to a new Master —"Yet not I, but Christ liveth in me." I supply the vessel, and He fills it. There was a notice in a missionary magazine some years ago, which read something like this: "Wanted: wicks to burn for God, oil provided free" in lavish, overflowing supply. Wicks needed, empty vessels needed, and Christ to fill them fully. I am an empty vessel, an earthen vessel, but I may be filled and can be filled by the sparkling, ever-fresh water of life which takes the shape of the vessel that holds it: "yet not I, but Christ liveth in me." This is to be the new principle on which our life is to be lived as we go down from Keswick, "the life which I now live." It is to be lived in the faith of the Son of God; we are to live by faith, not by sight as the unregenerated live, not by feelings as the unsanctified: but we are to live on the principle of faith.

Now, I take it that it will be quite accurate to translate this word in Galatians 2: 20 like this—the Authorised Version reads, "I live by the faith of the Son of God"; a revised version might correctly read, "I live by the faithfulness of the Son of God." The Greek word may be translated with equal truth "faith" and "faithfulness." And faith on our part is never found except as it is linked with faithfulness on His part. If I may be permitted to quote Hudson Taylor again: you will remember, no doubt, the story how, while he was revising the translation of the Ningpo Testament, he came upon that word in Mark 11: 20, "Have faith in God," and looking at it in Greek, he said to himself, "Surely that could be translated, 'Hold the faithfulness of God'"; and the thought was revolutionary in Hudson Taylor's experience. If I may give my personal testimony, it has been revolutionary in my own case. If I look at my faith, I am easily discouraged, I can only think it is very weak and very small; but when I think of the faithfulness of Christ, it is very strong and very great; and as I think and count on His faithfulness, and not on my own faith, my faith takes hold of His faithfulness, and my need and His great fulness meet. His faithfulness provides the power and the grace, my faith applies the power and the grace.

Last October, in China, I was in the far western city of Chungto, where missionaries had gathered together for a few days of quiet waiting upon God, and it was my privilege to open the Scriptures to them; and we prayed together over their problems and discussed the progress of the Gospel. In a lighter moment between the intense seasons of prayer we were teasing each other a little, as I think was truly permitted. Among the group was a woman missionary from London, and somebody began to say something rather derogatory concerning London, to tease and to provoke her; and the dear missionary said in reply, "Now don't you say anything about London, for in London you can turn the tap and get water." Well, that may not mean very much to an audience in England, but when all your water has to be carried from a well, and then boiled before you can drink it, I began to understand— after three months under those circumstances—what a thrill it must be to a missionary from a tropical country to go to any American or British city and turn a tap and draw cold, fresh, sparkling water. In London you can turn the tap and draw the water; that is all you have to do, except to pay the water rate! The Corporation or the Water Board collects and conveys the water, and all we do when we are thirsty is to turn the tap and drink, and when we are thirsty again to turn the tap and drink again, and so the more we thirst the more we draw the water.

That is the secret of the blessed life, drawing continually at the fountain which has been opened for us; nay, it is far better than that, we do not go to a tap and draw the water—"Whosoever drinketh of the water that I shall give him shall never thirst; but the water that I shall give him shall be in him a well of water bubbling up unto everlasting life." So after the self-life is out of the way, and as occasion comes of dying to self, those fountains will be opened afresh, and our lives will be blessed and refreshed and made a refreshment; and we shall drink, and drink abundantly, and drink again, and out of us shall flow rivers of living water day after day in every place, to the glory of God and to the refreshment of many. Having made such a profession, God invites us to such a life.

O BREATH OF LIFE

O Breath of Life, come sweeping through us,
  Revive Thy Church with life and power;
O Breath of Life, come, cleanse, renew us
  And fit Thy Church to meet this hour.

O Wind of God, come bend us, break us,
  Till humbly we confess our need;
Then in Thy tenderness remake us,
  Revive, restore, for this we plead.

O Breath of Life, come breathe within us,
  Renewing thought and will and heart:
Come, Love of Christ, afresh to win us,
  Revive Thy Church in ev'ry part.

O Heart of Christ, once broken for us,
  'Tis there we find our strength and rest;
Our broken contrite hearts now solace,
  And let Thy waiting Church be blest.

Revive us, Lord! Is zeal abating
  While harvest fields are vast and white?
Revive us, Lord, the world is waiting;
  Equip Thy Church to spread the light.

BESSIE PORTER HEAD

IV
THE SPIRIT-FILLED LIFE

The long-hushed crowd had passed from
                Keswick's tent,
  And I crept forth to solitude,
To muse and ponder much in deep content,
  Mid lonely fell and wood.

Deep into Barrow's glen I took my way;
  The trees shed down their greenest shade;
The lofty cascade in the dying day
  Its softest music made!

Thus let me live in joy and even in tears;
  My life, like this, a ceaseless song;
A day of heaven lent from the eternal years;
  Nor missed in yon bright throng!

                J. ELDER CUMMING.

THE SPIRIT-FILLED LIFE

THE yearning aspiration of most earnest Christians is summed up in the phrase "The Spirit-filled life"; but to the majority, alas, it is a wistful longing only, never satisfied and finally regarded as little more than a mirage. Keswick's transforming message, which sounded out with electrifying effect, was that the "life more abundant" set forth in the New Testament is no unattainable ideal, but the pattern of life which God would have all His children to enjoy. His purpose is to bless us abundantly, and make us a blessing. The gift is ours, by grace through faith. The fulness of the Spirit is His provision for us, equally with justification. The fruit of the Spirit might be borne in every Christian life.

Like other aspects of the Keswick message, this has several facets. Clear presentation of the Scriptural teaching concerning the Person and ministry of the Holy Spirit is a first necessity: that every believer is born of, baptized, sealed and indwelt by the Spirit; but not all enjoy His fulness. That is not because God withholds this boon: rather is it that we fail to receive. The governing principle in this matter, as in all spiritual experience, is "according to your faith be it unto you." Keswick therefore calls for an act of surrender; a yielding up of all that hinders; a receiving of the Spirit in His fulness by faith; a committal of life entirely to His will. And that "crisis" must be followed by the "process" of maintained faith and continual surrender to His will in the fulness of its realisation. "One baptism, many fillings" was a theme stressed repeatedly by Evan Hopkins and other speakers. For every duty and every demand of every day there is the enduement of the Spirit; sufficiency of grace for every need.

The Spirit-filled life is therefore no extraordinary experience and condition which will excite and elate: it is rather the true "norm" of Christian life. The emphasis of Keswick is not upon what this blessing means to those who receive it—the satisfaction and fruitfulness they enjoy; but rather, the glory it ascribes to God, and the satisfying of His heart, in the fulfilling of His purposes in and through His children. Therefore, along with addresses which set forth "the blessed life" we find a complementary emphasis that the life so portrayed is "the everyday Christian life."

First is a message of particular value, by Canon Harford-Battersby—and this time a Convention address: yet delivered, not at Keswick, but at the Glasgow Convention, 1883, a few months before his Homecall. It is not so strange as it may appear that, while none of his Keswick addresses was printed in full in *The Christian's Pathway of Power*, this one was reported: for at Keswick he presided, and gave brief messages from the chair, rather than full-length addresses (see p. 248) Glasgow Convention was in those early days given as much space in *The Christian's Pathway of Power* as Keswick: and to that fact we owe this treasured message by Keswick's first Chairman, on "The Blessed Life."

Very fittingly, the following address is by Dr. J. Elder Cumming, the principal sponsor of "Keswick" in Glasgow. He had attended the Convention at Keswick in 1882, and "the Lord had met with him, so as to effect a great change in his life and service." Held in high esteem in the Church of Scotland for his saintliness and learning, his advocacy of the Keswick message carried great weight "North of the Border." Through his ministry at Keswick, from 1883 to 1903, and through his books, he became widely known and beloved in England also. His massive square beard, snow-white—at least, in his later years—gave Elder Cumming a patriarchal appearance, which was offset by the twinkle in his eye. He tended to be "massive" in utterance; but his addresses were masterly in their presentation of the Scriptural doctrine of sanctification. Figgis refers to the favourable impression he made on his first visit, in 1883, and adds, "He was still more impressive when, two years later, he said . . ." and he quotes at length from the address here reproduced.

We go back five years, to 1880, for our next address, "Anointed with Fresh Oil," by E. W. Moore. "Few have touched the inner springs of this movement more powerfully than he," Figgis declares; and he adds, "The crucifixion of the flesh, and the life in the Spirit, made and make this minister of Christ a ministering angel to very many." This message, although not his first at Keswick, is the first to be fully reported.

Andrew Murray's final address in 1895, which caused his hearers to feel themselves "beneath the opened heavens," brings us, even in print and after the lapse of more than six decades, some touch of Keswick's "morning glory."

None at Keswick would have had the temerity to follow, in person, such a speaker as Dr. Murray: but his exhilaratingly inspirational message is aptly supplemented by the methodical discussion of "God's Gift of Holiness," by Evan Hopkins in 1899. This is an address quoted at length by Steven Barabas, in *So Great*

Salvation, as an example of this great teacher's unsurpassed gifts of logical presentation at the Convention's teaching.

In 1904 the Bible Readings in both tents[1] were given by speakers from America—Drs. A. T. Pierson and R. A. Torrey. This had not been intended; but Prebendary Webb-Peploe, who was to deliver one series, was at the last minute prevented from attending: so the Trustees turned to Dr. Torrey, President of the Moody Bible Institute, Chicago, who was paying his one and only visit to Keswick—during his greatly-blessed evangelistic campaign in this country—and he "responded in a way that was manifestly in accordance with the leading of the Lord." His four weighty messages on the Person and work of the Holy Spirit stirred the hearts of all who heard them, and the last, on "The Spirit of Burning," brought a touch of living flame to the Convention.

Dr. Pierson came to Keswick more often than any other speaker from America in that "turn of the century" era: he took part with almost unfailing regularity from 1897 to 1909, and assumed from the first, unobtrusively, a position of leadership unique in a speaker from overseas. Again and again we read of him guiding the proceedings in times of particular moment—especially in 1905, when a breath of revival from Wales swept through the Convention, and with it some threat of the excessive emotionalism which was manifesting itself at that time. "Though Dr. Pierson's association with Keswick did not go back over very many years," writes J. Kennedy Maclean, Editor of *The Life of Faith*, and Pierson's biographer, "it was chiefly through his connection with that movement that he was known in this country; and it was at Keswick, perhaps, more than anywhere else, that he possessed his kingdom and occupied the sphere fitting his great gifts. There he dominated the Convention by his spiritual and intellectual powers, and thousands hung upon his words with an intense eagerness for instruction and help that was never disappointed."

[1] With the growth of the Convention the tent, seating some 2,000, could not accommodate all who wished to attend the meetings, so during Keswick's second decade it became necessary to hold morning and evening "overflow" gatherings in the Pavilion—the public hall of Keswick. Thus it came about that two sets of Bible Readings were delivered each year, and two evening meetings were held daily except at the week-ends. In 1901 a second tent was acquired, and the two tents were in use in this fashion, until the invention of amplifiers made possible, in 1926, the unifying of the great congregation in one tent seating 3,500—later enlarged to accommodate 4,000, while a permanent-structure "extension" brought its capacity up to 4,500. In fine weather the total attendances, including hundreds sitting and standing around, reached and even exceeded 5,000. Continuing growth necessitated a "relay" overflow in the "small" tent for the evening meetings in 1952 and 1953. This did not prove popular, however; although in subsequent years relays to all parts of the country have been highly successful, in Keswick itself they seemed rather an anti-climax—a case of "so near and yet so far"! So in 1954 a simultaneous evening meeting was restored, in the small tent, after the pattern prevailing for so long.

Possessing the burning eyes of a prophet, "as we knew him in later years there was something stern and severe in the appearance and manner of the tall, lithe figure; but behind the seemingly forbidding exterior there beat a heart of pity and love. . . . One of the most memorable Conventions in which he took part was that of 1905, when all hearts were warmed and subdued by the mighty happenings in Wales, and when the spirit of prayer and expectancy laid its hold upon the assembled crowds. At the Wednesday evening meeting in the Skiddaw Street tent Dr. Pierson spoke on 'The Inbreathed Spirit,' and in the impressive hush which settled upon the gathering it was felt that the Spirit who formed the subject of the address was Himself in the midst of the waiting people, and was doing His convicting work." This is the address here reproduced.

Our last address by Evan Hopkins—his predominant influence at Keswick naturally demands for him a larger representation in this volume than has been given to any other speaker—comes from that same year, 1905. A large contingent from Wales had brought something of the glow and fervour of the Welsh Revival, and it seemed that the Convention was on the brink of a like "visitation from on high." Opinions are still divided as to what truly transpired that memorable year. Some feared that emotionalism would run riot; others affirmed that the Convention leaders "quenched the Spirit" and checked what might have become a nation-wide Revival. It is in that setting that this address must be read: orderly and instructional as ever, the "statesman" of Keswick shows what "The Fulness of the Spirit" really is and means, and how this inestimable blessing may be possessed. Here is wise and spiritual counsel indeed!

Campbell Morgan was a most valued Keswick speaker who nevertheless was not really a "convention speaker" as we customarily employ that term. He was essentially a Bible teacher—and a prince among such. His principal ministry at Keswick was the delivering of Bible Readings; and the story is told how, at his first visit, the crowds flocked to hear him, leaving the other tent half empty. It was a new experience for F. B. Meyer—himself one of the most popular speakers—to see another man thus preferred before him, and he remarked, somewhat wistfully, "He must increase, and I decrease." Every series of Bible Readings given by Campbell Morgan at Keswick was scintillating, but there seems general agreement that those on the Epistle to Philemon, in 1911, surpassed all: and the final address reached high-water mark. It should be remembered that "The Secrets of Power" came at the close of a series of studies, and contains allusions to what had gone before: but it is nevertheless complete in itself, and an example of Dr. Morgan's ministry at its best. In memory we can see him now—tall, emaciated, commanding; with a mop of auburn hair, later snow-white; immaculately dressed, and with the most pleasant voice, surely, that ever an orator possessed. Here was a preacher of a mould all his own: he made his distinctive contribution to, and left his indelible mark upon, Keswick.

W. Y. Fullerton was an Ulster man—truly Irish: Charles Inwood was only such "by adoption," having exercised his ministry in the Methodist Church in the Emerald Isle, but being otherwise essentially English. Fullerton had succeeded F. B. Meyer—whose friend and biographer he became—as minister of Melbourne Hall Baptist Church, Leicester; and later he fulfilled his most notable service to the Kingdom as secretary of the Baptist Missionary Society. Tall and with an air of authority, he was most kindly and approachable; and he won the hearts of all at Keswick. He spoke briefly at a missionary meeting there in 1908, but took a prominent part only from 1913; and Sloan says, "Probably in the years that followed his message was never clearer than in that first expository address"—here reproduced. Sloan adds, "The two addresses that he gave (in 1913) were characterised by touches of homely humour, which kept his audiences *en rapport* with him; and there were quotations from unfamiliar hymns such as we often heard from him in later years." He was a truly extemporaneous speaker, and one of the last to deliver the Bible Readings without notes. In this and other ways his ministry was reminiscent of that of Prebendary Webb-Peploe. With a small Bible in his left hand, he would turn from passage to passage, explaining and expounding in most fascinating and instructive fashion.

Two further addresses by American speakers follow: the first by Dr. A. C. Dixon, who had come to this country to succeed the Rev. Thomas Spurgeon—son of the renowned Charles Haddon Spurgeon—as pastor of the Metropolitan Tabernacle. During his brief ministry there Dr. Dixon spoke at Keswick in 1911, and in 1912 he gave a series of Bible Readings on the Incarnation, which Figgis describes as "very powerful." The third of these, on "The Glory of the Cross," was particularly impressive.

Who can capture in words the whimsical personality of yet another visitor from America, S. D. Gordon, of "Quiet Talks" fame? Squat and swarthy, he looked unprepossessing; but when he began to speak he captivated all by his charm and by the thought-provoking quality of his quietly-spoken message. His characteristic aside, "Are you listening?" was of course rhetorical, and no indication that his hearers' attention was wavering! He spoke at Keswick in 1910 and 1931, and on both occasions his final address was singled out as especially arresting. The latter is particularly appropriate here, complementing as it does Dr. Dixon's theme, in its consideration of "The Crowning Day" of Christ.

Like certain others before him, the Rev. J. Russell Howden was prejudiced against Keswick, having attended another Convention with which he was not at all impressed. The persuasions of several friends prevailed, however, and he went somewhat reluctantly to Keswick in 1910—and found it vastly different from what he had imagined! An address by Mr. Walter B. Sloan on the text, "When I saw Him I fell at His feet as dead," brought the young curate from Tunbridge Wells also to the Master's feet. He spoke at one early morning prayer meeting the next year, and henceforward became a principal speaker, especially "between the wars," until ill-health obliged him to withdraw from speaking, though he remains a member of the Convention Council. He had an exceptionally powerful voice, and it is said that when he spoke the amplifiers had to be switched off! Several of his Bible Readings and addresses are remembered as creating a deep impression: the one selected from the Convention of 1929 proved especially helpful "because of its lucidity, and clear indication that sanctification is the work of God," to a great number, including a missionary home on furlough from Burma—the Rev. A. T. Houghton, who is now Chairman of the Council.

Our last address on the theme of the Spirit-filled life is chosen for its historical interest as the first message ever broadcast from Keswick, in 1933. To Dr. W. Graham Scroggie was given the distinction, and the responsibility, of delivering the address on this notable occasion: and he set forth the Keswick message in its range and fulness—so far as time would allow—with characteristic lucidity. Here his sure grasp of the Convention message, his pithy manner of speech, and method of instruction through the presentation of striking antitheses, are excellently revealed. What more appropriate epitome of Keswick teaching could there be than the title of this address—"Abounding Life"?

To present the full range of the Keswick message, this volume should contain a fifth section, upon the call to service, which follows so naturally upon the call to surrender and sanctification. In its earliest years, indeed, the Convention leaders carefully excluded any missionary note from its message: it was feared that once any missionary element was admitted various societies might seek to "exploit" Keswick for their own purposes. However desirable it might be to present to young Christians the challenge of the unfulfilled commission, and to gain new supporters for missionary work, the Convention leaders dreaded any deflection from the supreme purpose of Keswick, in the promotion of personal holiness. But this, they soon found, could not be separated from its logical consequence in consecrated service: the missionary note sounded forth spontaneously, and came to be recognised as an integral part of the Keswick message. It is a stirring story, how this aspect of the Convention's ministry developed, until the great missionary meeting came to be the crowning occasion of the Convention week. What a glittering array of honoured names the records contain! Missionary pioneers, heroes and statesmen from all parts of the globe, representing all aspects of missionary witness among all types of people in all nations, have sounded forth on the Keswick platform the "Macedonian call" from their respective fields. Alas, none of these addresses can be reproduced, for none is preserved: for it has been the custom to report only the "teaching ministry" of the Convention.

The "outflowing" of blessing from Keswick, through the service of dedicated lives, however, has other channels besides the overseas mission fields. Consecration was never regarded as an end in itself: Keswick taught from the first that holiness must find expression in devoted service. It is significant that the first recorded Bible Reading at Keswick was on the theme of "God's Instruments." Bible Readings were an innovation in 1881, and the first was given by Mr. H. F. Bowker—who two years later succeeded Canon Harford-Battersby as Chairman of the Convention. He was Headmaster of Christ's Hospital, and very prominent in evangelical affairs. This initial Bible Reading is, however, unrecorded: but three were given on subsequent mornings by the Rev. Hubert Brooke, an eminent Bible teacher who later made the delivering of Bible Readings his especial sphere of ministry at Keswick—and elsewhere, at "daughter" Conventions. "Surely," says Figgis, "there never was anyone more eminently the right man in the right place than Mr. Brooke at a Bible Reading! His style, clear as a frosty night and bright as its stars, as full of vivacity as of solemnity, exactly suited the light touch of topic after topic from page to page, and book to book, of the wonderful Word of God." This address, then, is the first of all the *series* of Bible Readings which from that time onward have been the central feature of every Convention.

Perhaps of equal import as the missionary meetings, though less spectacular in character and effect, are the meetings for ministers, which from early times have resulted in transformed ministries—and through them, who can tell the "outreach" of

Keswick's influence and blessing? These gatherings are of a more intimate character than any others at Keswick, and naturally are not reported: it would defeat their end if the speakers were conscious that what they said would appear in print. Yet an exception to this rule was made in 1889, when the two addresses to ministers were reproduced in *The Life of Faith*. Here the Rev. Handley C. G. Moule—afterwards Bishop of Durham—and Dr. J. Elder Cumming discuss, respectively, "Essential Principles of Christian Service" and "Speaking for God." These fittingly conclude the record of "Keswick's Authentic Voice."

THE BLESSED LIFE

Canon T. D. Harford-Battersby, M.A.

Who would not wish to have been one of the company "on the mountain" (Matt. 5: 1–12), when He who is "the life" commended that life to His disciples? In seven verses (3–9) we have it portrayed in its sevenfold aspect, rising from its root in self-emptiness, or poverty of spirit, step by step, until it reaches its climax in the disposition which sheds peace and plenty around it, wherever it goes (Jas. 3: 18). Whilst, as the crown and seal of the whole, we have another pair of beatitudes setting forth the joy of those who willingly suffer and are persecuted for His sake, and for righteousness' sake (vv. 10–12).

Can you not imagine with what a feeling of despair these disciples, when they reflected on the contrast between themselves and the character here portrayed, would listen to these words of the Master?—except that His presence with them, and the hope stirred in them by His precious and encouraging promises, would be an antidote to that despair.

I remember, when I was a young Christian, how I used to examine myself by the pattern character here set forth, and how hopeless it seemed that such a character could ever be mine. I suppose this is an experience which most Christians have shared with me. Yet we know that the Lord did not draw this beautiful portrait of the life of one of His disciples, merely to incite hopes which could not be satisfied. It is evident that He set it before us as something which each of us, according to our measure, might and ought to attain to. In Himself was to be the perfect exhibition of the character which His own words recommended; but a reflection of the same character was to be found in all.

We ask, "How is this possible?" And the answer must surely be, "Only by setting about it in the right way."

What is that way? The precepts and example of Jesus Christ command the admiration of thousands. But few of them can tell us how these precepts are to be carried out; how that example is to be followed. Unless we know the Person, and understand something of the work of Jesus Christ, these precepts, that example, will be comparatively useless to us. Let me commend you to the work of an old Puritan writer, who was a favourite of some of your best Scottish divines, *The Gospel Mystery of Sanctification,* by Walter Marshall. These are his words: "One great mystery is, that the holy frame and disposition whereby our souls are furnished and enabled for immediate practice of the law, must be obtained *by receiving out of Christ's fulness,* as a thing already prepared and brought to an existence for us in Christ, and treasured up in Him; and that as we are justified by a righteousness wrought out in Christ, and imputed to us, so we are sanctified by such a holy frame and qualifications as are first wrought out and completed in Christ for us, and then imparted to us. And as our natural corruption was produced originally in the first Adam, and propagated from him to us, so our new nature and holiness is first produced in Christ, and derived from Him to us, or as it were propagated. So that we are not at all to work together with Christ in making or producing that holy frame in us, but only to take it to ourselves, and use it in a holy practice, as made ready to our hands. Thus we have fellowship with Christ in receiving that holy frame of spirit that was originally in Him; for fellowship is when several persons have the same things in common (I John I: 1–3). This mystery is so great that, notwithstanding all the light of the Gospel, we commonly think that we must get a holy frame by producing it anew ourselves, and by framing it and working it out of our own hearts."

The common idea of Christians is that with the help of the Holy Spirit we shall be able to accomplish, more or less perfectly, the work of our own sanctification, forgetting the clear testimony of God's Word, "Of Him are ye in *Christ Jesus,* who was made unto us wisdom from God, and righteousness, and sanctification, and redemption; that, according as it is written, He that glorieth, let him glory in the Lord" (I Cor. I: 30, 31, R.V.). It is a blessed thing when we are brought to see that the Lord Himself is to be not only our righteousness but our *sanctification* also: or, as another Scripture says, "What the law could not do, in that it was weak through the flesh, God, sending His own Son in the likeness of sinful flesh, and for sin, condemned sin in the flesh: that the righteousness of the law might be fulfilled in us, who walk not after the flesh, but after the Spirit" (Rom. 8: 3, 4).

Thus, as I have said, our knowledge of the precepts and example of the Blessed Lord must be supplemented by our knowing Him in His divine Person and perfect work. We must know Him as God's own Son, before whom every form of evil must quail; and we must know what His glorious work was which He undertook for us, *i.e.,* not only to get pardon for us guilty ones, but also deliverance and cleansing for us defiled ones from the power of sin in our nature, and complete union with Himself by the Spirit.

This and this only is God's method for our sanctification. I do not say that a perfect condition of sinlessness is attainable here by any of us, but I do say that, if we succeed in understanding and employing the right method, the attainment of holiness is no longer the hopeless thing that it was, but a thing which we find to be practicable, not according to our own feeble measures, but "according to the purpose of Him who worketh all things after the counsel of His own will" (Eph. 1: 11).

Take but one example out of the verses before us (v. 8). "Blessed," says Christ, "are the pure in heart, for they shall see God." In Mark 7: 21, the same divine and unerring teaching gives us this description of what the human heart is; what a fountain of impurity it is—"From within, out of the heart of men, proceed evil thoughts, adulteries, fornications, murders, thefts, covetousness . . ." etc. All these evil things come from within, and defile the man. How terribly true is this description. What confessions one may sometimes hear from those whom we believe and know to be the most earnest followers after holiness, of the tremendous outbreaks of impurity and corruption within, at the holiest seasons, and when engaged in the holiest exercises, making it appear that the "purity of heart" of which the Lord spoke is a thing utterly impossible. And yet it is so? Our Saviour says, "Blessed are the pure in heart," and adds, "for they shall see God;" thus teaching not only that the sight of God is a privilege which will be awarded to the pure, but also that there will be provided a way by which this purity is attainable.

What is this "way"? We have already seen that it is Himself. "The blood of Jesus Christ, His Son, cleanseth us from all sin." This cleansing cannot mean only pardon: it must refer to purity also. There was a time, perhaps, when we had to restrict it to the former; but the context of the passage in which this text is found, as well as the general tenor of St. John's writings, has convinced us that we ought not so to restrict it; that a purity of heart beyond what our natural thoughts could conceive is open to those who are willing to claim it, through the blood of Christ alone: and we are here to testify to this most blessed power of that blood, and we trust that our testimony will not be in vain, but that many will be led to put it to the test, by coming to be cleansed, and to realise what greater, fuller blessing there is for them in Christ, than any they have yet experienced.

BLESSED EXPERIENCE

Rev. J. Elder Cumming, D.D.

And a highway shall be there . . . and it shall be called the way of holiness—Isaiah 35: 8, 9, 10.

I AM going, dear friends, to take a great liberty with you to-day, and speak to you as if you and I were but little children seeking to know something more of blessed fellowship with God. I wish to speak of *Christian experience*. And the first thing I should like to illustrate is that there is a definite Christian experience, very blessed and very different from the ordinary state of struggle and defeat. I appeal to many who are here, some of whom have known long, and some have gone far in what has been called the higher, but what might be really the *humbler Christian life*; and they will be the first to testify that they can recall in their own experience a time when their Christian life was something so poor and so faulty; so full, not only of omissions but of commissions, that they turned from themselves continually with loathing and more than distaste; but that since there has happened a certain thing in their souls, to be afterwards described, there has been a state of heart perfectly different, wonderfully different, much more blessed than they had before, and answering exactly to certain needs and certain cryings of the heart.

For instance, in former days it could not be said of them that they had anything like a constant state of peace within. Continually cares were rising about all sorts of things. Dear friends, it is not an uncommon thing to see a Christian man or woman laden with care the whole day long. It seems to me most touching to look at the faces of a great congregation, for oh! that look of sadness, that look of unrest, that look of impatience, tells of a great want of peace within; so much so, that in the earlier stages of the Christian life I do not know that there is one cry that goes into the ear of the Blessed Master more continually from the hearts and lips of His people than this, "O my Master, is there no peace? no abiding peace? no deep peace for the soul that looks to Thee?" So, brethren, we are children come to our Father; and the prayer that we presented to Him in those early days was, "O my Father, is there such a blessing in Thy hand as peace for the heart of Thy children? Thou hast brought me, Thy child, to Thyself, and I know that my sins are taken away; but there are so many cares; so much bitterness; so many great and so many little sorrows in this daily life of mine! My Father, hast Thou such a blessing in Thy storehouse that Thy child might have?"

Our Father knew that the need of His child would be such, and He answered in that blessed word of the prophet Isaiah, "Thou wilt keep him in perfect peace whose mind is stayed on Thee, because he trusteth in Thee" (26: 3). And my heart, as of a care-laden child, just went to my Father, and said, "My Father, is it true that there is perfect peace for me? for that is exactly what I am wanting. My cares are so many and so bitter. Oh! if there be perfect peace, let me have it. That is the cry of my heart: I ask that perfect peace, because Thou hast promised it." Dear child of God, who art bearing thine own care, and feeling it so heavy and so grievous, wilt thou take that peace which comes from God's hand—a promise and a gift?

Then as a little child I needed something more. I was always making mistakes: in speaking and in walking, in reading and in thinking, making mistakes continually. And the cry of the heart then was, "Oh, if I had just somebody to guide me." There may be some veritable child here to-day, looking back to a sainted father or mother by whose advice they were always guided, to whom they might go at every turn. "My father, advise me what I am to do here; my mother, tell me—give me secret wisdom here. Where shall I go, and what shall I do?" Now you are without those helps; father and mother are gone: you are forsaken. Is there no one to go to? Oh, if we could find in our Heavenly Father a continual guide; oh, if that great distance did not divide us from Him; oh, if that infinite silence might become vocal with His voice —how blessed to me to have a guide like that, and to be able to go to Him always.

I turn, then, to God's Word; and if I did not realise the truth before, I find something there which seems new to me. I turn to Psalm 23, and in two succeeding verses I find, "He leadeth me beside the still waters," and "He leadeth me in the paths of righteousness, for His name's sake." And in another Psalm I find, "I will guide thee with mine eye." *Guide me?* O my Father, that is just what I am wanting. I accept Thy guiding, oh, how gladly. I did not know it was to be had; I did not think it was a real thing; but, oh, I have come now to take Thy every word for gospel, and God as my guide. Guide me; and if Thou wilt, I will ever look toward Thee. In looking at that face I can see Thine eye. I cannot get guidance unless I look there. Many a look of love and direction, and many a look of Thy divine wisdom, I should lose if I looked not on Thy face. Lord, I will look on and see something more than guidance; but meantime I want to be guided!

Child of God, are you willing to be guided by the Lord as a little child? Guided where He will, guided as fast or as slow as He will? Guided always by Him? Because if so, I can promise you a very different Christian experience from that which so many have, of mistakes and continual stumbling, knowing not where to go, and turning to everybody for advice which brings so little good.

But there is something more as a child that I require very much. I sometimes feel (you say) that I need keeping. Well, I need keeping, always; there never is a time, never a day nor an hour, that I do not need to be kept somehow. O my Father, canst Thou ever condescend to be the keeper of Thy children? Canst Thou keep me? I am sure Thou dost know how much it takes to keep me; but I do not know it. Thou dost know how bad, how false, how foolish I have been many a time, even since Thou hast brought me to the mercy-seat, and I have found pardon in the blood and rejoiced therein. I want Thy keeping always. I need this tongue of mine to be kept, which is a most unruly member. There is something within this heart which I need to have kept, that its affection may be pure for Thee. And those constant, busy, wandering thoughts—oh, Lord, those thoughts; there are so many —surely I cannot ask Thee to keep them, my Father; though I know something of Thy love; but Thou art so busy! Yet I turn to God's Word, and what do I find there—"And the peace of God, which passeth all understanding, shall keep your hearts and minds through Christ Jesus" (Phil. 4: 7). Oh, Lord; but it was not *my mind*: it was something more. I think my mind might be kept; but *all those thoughts*! Look again then, and you will find that, instead of being translated "heart and mind," it should be, "heart and thought"—"the peace of God which passeth all understanding shall keep your heart *and thoughts*."

O my Father, if Thou dost not keep my thoughts Thou wouldst not keep me at all: they would have dragged me away into further wandering; but if Thou wilt keep my thoughts, how gladly would I give them into Thy hand. *Heart and thoughts*, from this moment, dear Lord, take and keep for ever; go as deep as Thou wilt, my Keeper and my Lord! Child of God, have you taken Christ—will you take Christ this moment—to be the Keeper of your thoughts and your heart? He will keep them in His treasury—where is that? In His heart: there is room for you, yes! for every one of you!

Then I think that, as a child of God, I cannot go on unless I have something like victory in my life. I think I cannot get on with that old experience which, thank God, may be done with for ever. You say, I am constantly being overcome with terrible sins; and they seem to be so much more terrible than they once did; they seem to mean much more. And when I think of this grieving the Holy Spirit of God, and almost breaking that heart which on the cross was broken for me; oh, it does seem to me as if my heart would be crushed under it! I must (you say) have victory over sin. I dare not look Christ in the face, unless I have victory over the old habits of sin. Well, no one here teaches sinless perfection—you will not misunderstand me; but I must have dominion over all the evil habits of sin. My Father, canst Thou give me that just now, or shall I have to wait till I die before I get that victory? I turn to the blessed Word to see if I can find anything to reach me. I go to the first Epistle of John, and he tells me, "This is the victory that overcometh the world." I had been thinking about sin only, but here is the world brought in, too—"This is the victory that overcometh the world, even our faith." O my Father, that is exactly what my soul was crying for, and Thou dost know it better than I do; and Thou wouldst give me such victory that I shall bless Thee here and in eternity.

Then, as a child of God I need something more. It is astonishing how hungry the Lord makes one for His blessings; how we get boldness to ask more and more. "Father, I have something more to ask; I have received so many things from Thee already, but I want the greatest thing of all—I cannot get on *without Thyself*! It is Thine own business, after all. I have learned a secret to-day at least. I did not know how I was so distressed, so troubled, and so ignorant. I could not find out how it was; but I think I have found it out now. O Lord Jesus, it is because Thou hast been so much away. I have a house, but I cannot find Thee in any room. I come to conventions, and I hear speakers talking about blessing, but my heart is crying out for my own living Saviour. O my Father, I cannot do without Thee, and it is an awful thought to have to wait till I die. I may be many years here before I go; might I not have Thy presence now? Satisfy Thy child's heart. I find God putting into the heart of the Psalmist the desire that He intends to satisfy. 'Nevertheless, I am continually with Thee,' and if I am with Thee, Thou must be with me! I therefore take that word. Thou *wilt* be continually with me. The light of Thy presence with me, O Lord Jesus. Thy servant can desire nothing better! Holy Father, if Thou art with me, I shall never want anything more all my days. Give me Thyself, Thy continual presence by day and by night in my soul; not far away, but here: bring sunshine into my heart, O my Father, Thy little one asks Thee, Thy continual presence!"

o

Child of God, do you desire it? Will you take it as your Father's gift in answer to the cry in your heart? If you do, you will find here, too, a Christian experience totally different from the old one, the one which so many people have; one where there is no peace, where there is no guidance, where there is no keeping, where there is no victory, where there is no continual presence of the Lord Jesus.

The second thing I would like to dwell on for a little time is that this definite and blessed experience is entered for the most part by a definite step. You do not *grow into it*, as a rule. I doubt very much indeed whether anybody grows into it, but they often step into it unconsciously. A great many people, not knowing anything about Keswick, but truly men of God, have done so. It is so blessed to have seen them, without knowing it, walking in the light. But when you come to know the theory as well as the practice, it seems so much easier to step into it without the experience of troubles and difficulties before-hand. If the way is set before me, God directing me, I take it to-day. I find in the Bible how constantly men of God were entering by definite steps and by a sudden experience into a more blessed life than they heretofore knew. For instance, Isaac entered that life at the step of the altar. When he said, "I will; bind me, my father," he stepped into the humbler Christian life. Next we come to Jacob, poor deceiving Jacob. That sin of his is always rising up in my heart against him. I know that some people try to make little of it, but I cannot stand that sin of Jacob at Isaac's bedside, covered with skins and pretending that he is his brother Esau. However, the same man after many changes comes to Penuel, and there he stepped into the blessed experience I have been trying to describe to you to-day.

Then there is Job the Patriarch. Job, I think, did not begin by any means so high up as many people suppose. They take considerable liberties with the Hebrew when they make so much of the words describing his character at first. Job learned a great deal in the course of God's dealing with him, and at last came to see God and God's glory. Then he stepped into an experience quite different to anything he had had before.

Then Moses. Moses was a God-fearing man before, but what a difference between the bad-tempered youth who in a passion slew the Egyptian, and Moses the meekest of men. What made the difference? He did not grow into it; but, standing face to face with God at the burning bush, there fell something away from Moses' soul at the sight, and he stepped into the experience of the humbler Christian life. I might go on to tell of Elijah at Cherith. It was in the beginning of the famine, and as he sat beside that lonely brook he learned the lesson of his life. So, then, it is in the experience of Christians now. There are thousands of devoted Christians who know nothing of the experience I have spoken of. Yet many of them have been growing for forty years. And in some respects they are not much farther on than they were at first; while young boys' and girls' faces are shining like angels', children who have at one step taken God at His word and have stepped into the experience of liberty, peace, and joy. O children of God, it is nearer you than you suppose. The word is nigh thee this day. It is in thy ear; may it be in thy heart, and God speak it there.

I should like to remark, thirdly, that there is a considerable variety in the ways by which God leads us into this blessed life. Here are some of which we cannot speak at length.

The avenues to this blessed life are many. First of all it may be some definite hindrance taken away. It may be a mother, a child, a husband, or a wife that hinders you from giving yourself to God. Such a one taken away may be the step into this blessed life, almost before you know it. Secondly, a definite act of faith in difficult circumstances when you feel hedged up, all but crushed; you feel—My life is almost gone; and in that moment of agony, in that crisis of life, the soul may cast itself upon the Word of God and trust Him with a loving trust. That moment may be the step by which the soul enters into the humble life. Then there is the open confession of Christ. Let me tell you what that is in one word. Some of you are downcast—there are sad, unsatisfied faces, even at this convention. Your want of rest and peace comes from your never having opened your mouth and said boldly, "I am Christ's, and I am not ashamed that anybody should know it." An open confession of Christ is sometimes the key to the door which admits you into the most blessed experience of Christian life.

Then there is the fresh apprehension of some vital truth. My brethren, I shall never forget the blessing that came to my soul (it was one of many steps of blessing) when I first understood that the Lord Jesus was really coming back again to earth, and that that was the hope which was and must be my hope from that moment. But that is not the only one. Another vital truth seen clearly and vividly for the first time that is sometimes blessed by God, may be summed up thus—putting the Lord definitely in charge, and just giving Him the keys of Headship. You, dear Christian women, know what that means—take all the keys of your heart and your home, tie them all up together, and say, "Dear Master, they are Thine; take them and keep them, I shall never touch them again; but as Thou givest one key after another, I will use it and hand it back to Thee!" The keys of Thy heart, and of thy home, and of thy purse, put them all into the hand of the Lord Jesus. That hand is stretched down to you to-day in order to receive the gift of the keys. Will you give them to Him?

There is yet another way of entering into the fulness of the blessing of Christ. I shall never forget the impression made upon me by hearing from the lips of our dear friend Canon Battersby, now in glory, standing I suppose within a yard of where I am now, in the calmest and most thoughtful words, not carried away by enthusiasm or eloquence, but in the simplest words, the story of his own experience. He told us how at the Oxford Convention he lay awake a great part of one night during which he had a sight of the glory of the Lord. I asked him about it afterwards. He said, "It seemed no vision of outward sight, but something for the eye of the soul to rest on." He could not put it into words, but that sight he never forgot. One could almost see in his eye that the vision of the glory of Christ was resting there even to the end. That was the sight that Job saw; that was the sight that Isaiah saw; and it is the sight that some blessed souls are seeing still, whom God has fully taken, because they have fully given themselves to Him. O my Christian friends, for me, and for most of you, there remains that blessed sight: the glory of Christ (not hereafter, when He shall come again, but now), and that is the means by which the Lord may enable us to step into the fullest blessedness of that Christian experience that I have been so feebly describing to you. May God bless us with it.

ANOINTED WITH FRESH OIL

Rev. E. W. Moore, M.A.

I shall be anointed with fresh oil—Psalm 92: 10.

WE DO not want the experience of last year to live on to-day. Job says, "My glory was fresh in me." How we love fresh things. The world came fresh from the hand of the Creator. The wordling takes pains to obtain new things; but there is only one place where we can find real newness—in Christ. In Him "old things are passed away, all things are become new." In Him we are always secure of finding freshness—a life of surprises from the unfoldings of God; days of heaven upon earth.

I. What is This Oil?

(i) This oil is a *holy oil* (Psa. 89: 20). It is a solemn, an awfully solemn thing, to come to a convention for holiness. This oil has a deep meaning for us—a meaning which is connected with its mention in the Old Testament. Prophets, priests, and kings were anointed with oil, and in Exodus 30: 22–33 we read the directions, given through Moses, for the compounding of this sacred oil. It was the symbol of the Holy Ghost and, as "most holy," was never "poured upon man's flesh," and every man was forbidden, on pain of death, to "compound other like it." What a warning this is to us! Take care of unreal sanctification. Assure yourself that your anointing is real, and do not deceive yourself by any substitute for the divine anointing. Certainly you will not deceive others than yourself. God knows your heart, and He can distinguish between the true and the false. The world finds out, and the devils can tell the trusting from the professing Christian. The seven sons of Sceva called upon the evil spirit in a man, in the name of Jesus, to come out of him. But the evil spirit knew better; he was not to be imposed upon, and he is not now. "Jesus I know, and Paul I know; but who, are ye?" (see Acts 19: 13–17). He was more than a match for them—they fled out . . . naked and wounded; and if we have not a real sanctification we may preach and profess, but it will be the same thing now. May God make us real, at any cost! This oil is a holy oil used to sanctify all the vessels used in the service of the Lord; but it is something more.

(ii) It is a *uniting oil* (Psa. 133), "the precious ointment" of David's Psalm. Do you want to know the secret of unity—how Christians may really exhibit that unity which was Christ's desire for all, at His departure to His Father? How may they, so diverse in kind, attempt it? There is only one way: by the anointing of the Holy Ghost, falling from Aaron's head to the skirts of his garments. If it is falling on us and all our brethren, then we shall know how to love them. All one in the unity of the Spirit, we must love, we cannot help it; we shall not be frozen together, but melted into one; fused together, forgetting all but one thing— that we are Christ's. The one word of St. John, at Ephesus, was, "Little children, love one another," and when they asked him to tell them something new, he replied, "Practise it, and then I will." Yes, love—it is the anointing oil that secures the love.

(iii) It is a *gladdening oil* (Psa. 45: 7; 104: 15). Yes, a joyous face is the best possible testimony to the influence of the Spirit and the presence of Christ. A joyless Christian is a stumbling-block to the world and an offence to God. We are to be glad with Christ, and so glad we have Him that we cannot help being joyful. And above all things, we want Christ as a personally manifested presence. His presence is never known as a personal reality, except by the holy oil (John 14: 20). Is it so with you? The world has no influence on a soul satisfied with Christ. We want definiteness; we are often so like that throng at Ephesus—the most part know not wherefore we are come together! We want a deeper experience of Christ as our life. "Not I, but Christ." This is not done without a distinct work of the Holy Ghost; self in the dust and really surrendered—then Christ comes in, and you have an indwelling Christ. In all your difficulties there is no peace unless He lives in you in peace, and He is the Prince of Peace, and sheds it abroad. Where Jesus is, there is peace and purity and guidance. "The anointing which ye have received . . . teacheth you all things" (1 John 2: 27). A soul cannot be sure of divine guidance unless possessed by the Holy Spirit; when yielded up to the Holy Ghost, He guides: but it costs us our will. The way of man is Christ. "I being in the way, the Lord led me"—the way of holiness (Isa. 35: 8). I wish we were all in that way to-night. I saw a man the other day so glad—I did not need to be told that he had had some of the oil upon him. If Christ is in us, He will make His people glad.

(iv) It is also an *invigorating oil*. There was an old practice among the Greeks of oiling the runner or wrestler in the games, from head to foot. It was supposed to impart power and ease.

And the effect of the anointing oil is power. We need power for service. If we seek power for self-enjoyment, we shall miss the blessing; do not seek it as a possession, but for use. It is true we need to be endued with power from on high; He knows the difficulties we have to contend against, and the imperative demand for power in the work we have to do. Not every believer has received the full anointing of the Holy Ghost. "Tarry ye in Jerusalem till ye be endued with power from on high": without it there is no competency for service. There is a sowing time: but we may expect to reap at least one-fourth of what has been sown (see Matt. 13). Let us seek the anointing oil, that we may be "strong to labour." "They that wait upon the Lord shall renew —i.e. change—their strength,"—that is, *exchange*, into a different kind of strength: His strength. It is free, but it costs something: it costs *yourself*; you must give up yourself altogether as the condition of gaining Christ. It is because we do not go down into the place of death that we do not get it. We say we are weak, but we do not get low enough; it is to those who "have no might" —we cannot share His strength, but exchange ours for it: God must have spiritual work done by spiritual means. We have the sentence of death in ourselves, that we should not trust in ourselves. Then we are on the high road to resurrection.

(v) It is a *consecrating oil*. Anointed before God as prophets, priests, and kings, to carry out the work. We want to be centres of blessing, that blessing may flow out to all around. "I will bless thee, and thou shalt be a blessing." One function of the priests was to bless and intercede. I feel increasingly the need for intercessory prayer. Why the garden droops is because in the Church there is not enough prayer for souls. How often, how long, do we give Him no rest, being importunate with God, as a priest holding up holy hands? We are verily guilty in this matter. God turned the captivity of Job when he prayed for his friends. We are so selfish in prayer, we give only the margin to others! If the area is great, single out the soul and pray for that one every day definitely: indefiniteness is the death of prayer. For this we need a continual supply of oil.

(vi) It is a *confirming oil*. David was anointed three times. But you must be in the right place.

II. The Assurance of the Anointing. "I *shall be* anointed with fresh oil." Such presumption! Was it? God wills that kind of presumption that takes Him at His word. How many people come to the border of blessing, yet never get blessed. There is no crossing of the Rubicon. We say, "we freely all abandon," yet we never abandon anything. We mock God; so there is no blessing.

There is a time when you first discover the secret of anointing;

when you can say with assurance, "I shall be anointed with fresh oil." What is the secret?

(i) *God's faithfulness.* The Church of God knows it in her past experience. What God begins, He will finish.

(ii) *God's provision.* As the mail train runs it sucks up water as it goes, and so is supplied; but it must be on the right rail. We must be in the right attitude of soul and on the line of God's guidance, and the supply will come.

(iii) *Conscious communion with Christ.* It is one thing to be united, quite another to be in communion; and to *live* in such communion is more. To obtain this, there must be a daily and hourly maintenance of surrender of will. What hinders the union, prevents the hidden supply of oil? Any controverted point between you and God; any unbelief, any self-indulgence hinders. It is not enough to look down: we must *go down.* No worldly conformity, no pride of life; the oil only flows downwards, from the head to the skirts, and the skirts get most. God puts His best things on the lowest shelf, so that the children can get them— within reach of the little ones.

Full surrender and full trust sum it all up.

He holds nothing back! Remember the foolish virgins. Beware of a wick of Christianity and no supply—the outcome of outward trappings, but no oil. Have mercy on yourselves. God forbid that of any here should go forth the cry, "I know you not"— too late then. That day will be a surprise to some who, having not the Spirit of Christ, are none of His. To-night see ye to it!

THAT GOD MAY BE ALL IN ALL

Rev. Andrew Murray, D.D.

Then cometh the end, when He shall have delivered up the kingdom to God, even the Father; when He shall have put down all rule and all authority and power. For He must reign, till He hath put all enemies under His feet. The last enemy that shall be destroyed is death. For He hath put all things under His feet. But when He saith, all things are put under Him, it is manifest that He is excepted, which did put all things under Him. And when all things shall be subdued unto Him, then shall the Son also Himself be subject unto Him that put all things under Him, that God may be all in all—1 Corinthians 15: 24–28.

THESE last words are my text. What a mystery there is in the context! We are accustomed to speak of the two great acts of humiliation on the part of the Lord Jesus—His descending from the throne and becoming Man upon earth, a Servant among men; and His descent through the Cross into the grave, the depth of humiliation under the curse. But, oh, what a mystery there is here—that there is a time coming in the everlasting glory when the Son of Man Himself shall be subjected unto the Father, and shall give the kingdom into the Father's hands, and God shall be *all in all*. I cannot understand this; it passes knowledge. But I worship Christ in the glory of His subjection to the Father.

And here I learn one precious lesson, and that is what I want to point you to—that the whole aim of Christ's coming, and the whole aim of redemption, and the whole aim of Christ's work in our hearts, is summed up in that one thought—"that God may be all in all." And if that is true, of what infinite consequence it is that you and I should take the thought as our life-motto, and live it out. If we do not know that this is Christ's object, we never can understand what He expects of us, and will work in us. But if we realise where it is all tending to—that everything must be subordinated to that—then we have a principle to rule our life, which was the very principle of the life of Christ. Let us meditate for a little while upon it, with the earnest prayer: "O God, we hope to be present on that wondrous day, when Christ shall give up the kingdom, and when Thou shalt be all in all. We hope to be there to see it, and to experience it, and to rejoice in it throughout eternity. O God, give us to know something of it here this very night. Lord God, do take Thy place, the place Thou hast a right to take, and reveal Thy glory, that every heart may be bowed in the dust, and have but one song and one hope—*that God may be all in all.* O God, hear us, and may every heart be subjected to Thee to-night in full reality. Amen.

I said that this is what Jesus came into the world for. This is the object of redemption. This is what we must try to understand. And I want to point you to two thoughts: First, see how Christ, in His own life, realised and worked out this—"that God may be all in all." Second, see how we, in our lives, can realise it too.

If you look at the life of the Lord Jesus, then, you see that there are five great steps in it. An old authority uses the very significant expression, "The process of Jesus Christ." There is first, His *birth*, then His *life*, and His *death*, and His *resurrection*, and His *ascension*. In all these things you will see how God is all.

Look at *His birth.* He received it from God. It was by an act of God's Omnipotence that He was born of the Virgin Mary. It was from God that He had His mission, and He continually spoke of Himself as being sent from God. Christ had His life from the Father, and He ever acknowledged it. And it is the first thing that a Christian must learn from Christ. We do not want to look at our conversion, and say, "I did this," and "I did that," and, perhaps, to put between, "God did that for me"; but we want to take time in God's presence to say, "As truly as it was the work of Almighty God to give His Son here upon earth, through the Virgin Mary, His life in human flesh, so truly and really has God given His life into my heart." We have our life from God.

Look at the next step. *The life Christ had, as Man, to maintain,* He had to maintain it in the path that God gave Him. How did He do it? He tells: "I can do nothing of myself." He tells us that He did not speak one word till the Father had told Him. He just lived every moment of the day with this one thought: God is absolutely all, and I am nothing but a vessel in which God reveals His glory. That was the life of Christ—entire, unbroken, continuous dependence upon God; and God really was, in His life, every hour *all in all.* That was what Christ came to prove.

And notice that this was what man was created for—to be a vessel into which God could pour His wisdom and goodness and beauty and power. That is the nobility of the Christian. It is God that makes seraphim and cherubim flames of fire. The glory of God passes through them, and they have nothing in themselves. They are just vessels prepared by God, come from God, that they might let God's glory shine through them.

And so it was with the Son. Sin came in, the terrible sin, first, of the fallen angels, and then of man. They exalted themselves against God, and would not receive the glory of God, and they fell into the "outer darkness"; first the devils, and then man. And Christ came to restore man; and so Christ lived among us, and day by day He just depended upon the Father for everything. Notice, He would not touch a bit of bread until the Father gave it to Him. He had the power, and He was very hungry, but He would not make a stone into bread, though He could have done it, until the Father said, My Son, eat this. Christ lived a life of absolute dependence upon God, waiting for God day and night; and that is the Man who is one day, in glory, to effect it that God shall be *all in all*.

Then, next, He not only received His life from God, and lived it in dependence on God, but *He gave it up to God*. He did it in obedience. What is obedience? Giving up my will to the will of another. When a soldier bows to his general, or a scholar to his teacher, he gives up his will—and my will is my life—he gives up himself to the rule and mastery and the power of another. And Christ did that. "I came not to do mine own will." "Lo, I come to do Thy will." In Gethsemane He said, "Not my will, but Thine be done." Then He went further, and on the cross He carried out what had been settled in Gethsemane, and gave up His life to God, and He thereby taught us that the only thing that life is worth living for is *to give it back to God even unto death*. If you take your life and spend it on yourself, even partly, you are abusing it, you are taking it away from its noblest use. Oh, Christian, learn from Christ that the beauty of having life and will and body is that you can give it to God, and that then God will fill it for His glory. Yes, the Lord Jesus came and gave up His life unto the very death.

We have been talking about crucifixion and death more than once during these days. Just let me say this in passing—we must not always look at crucifixion and death as necessary only from the side of sin. That is only half the truth—the negative side. But we must look at it on the other side, the side of the Lord Jesus. Why did He give up that life unto death, and what did He get by it? He gave up His earthly life, and God gave Him a heavenly life. He gave up the life of humiliation, and God gave Him a life of fellowship and glory. Christian, do you want a life of fellowship with God, and of glory and power and joy, even here upon earth? Remember, then, that there is but one way to secure it. Give your life up to God. That is the only way. That is what Christ did. He gave up His life unto the very death, into the hands of God. Oh, do not you see that in the life of Christ, God was everything, God all in all? Christ worked it out, and proved most gloriously that God can be, and God must be, all in all.

Take the next step. *He was raised again from the dead.* What does the resurrection mean? If you want to understand that, ask first, what does the *cross* mean? Jesus parted with His life, and what does that say to us? He gave Himself up into utter helplessness and impotence to wait upon God, to see what God would do. He said, I cannot seize the heavenly life for myself; I wait till my Father gives it to me. The grave was His humiliation. "My flesh shall rest in hope." There He waited, until God the Father raised Him up in everlasting glory. The time of Jesus in the grave was a very short time—only a portion of three days; but if there is one lesson we need to learn from Jesus, it is the lesson of the cross. Give up yourself in utter dependence upon God, unto death. Lose everything, and God will raise you up in glory. Christ could never have ascended to sit upon the throne, never could have accomplished His work of preparing the kingdom that He could give to the Father, if He had not begun by giving up *Himself* and let God do all.

And it was even so, too, with His *ascension* to heaven, and His entering into glory.

Well then, the five steps we have been considering are these: Christ had His life from God; He lived it in dependence upon God; He gave it up in death to God; He received it in the resurrection from God; and He ascended to God and was glorified in it with God for ever.

And so, remember that the throne in heaven is not the throne of the Lamb of God alone; it is the throne of God and the Lamb. Jesus went to share the throne with the Father, and the Father was always the first, and Jesus second. Even on the throne of heaven our glorified Lord Jesus honours the Father as Father, and honours God as God. It is a deep mystery, but it is the blessed subordination of the Son to the Father. Let us meditate until our souls get full of the thought and the blessed truth. The one thing that God must have He gets, even from His own Son—subordination, subjection; and it is because Christ sits in this spirit on the throne of glory, that one day He can give up the kingdom to the Father.

Let us now take in this—which I said was my first great thought. The Lord Jesus came to remove the terrible curse that sin had wrought, the terrible ruin that had come by man's pride and self-exaltation; and He came to live out, during thirty-three years, *that God must be all in all.* And let me ask, in passing, did God disappoint Him? I tell you, no. God lifted Him to the throne of the everlasting glory, and to equality on the throne with Himself, because He had humbled Himself to honour His God. And if we want God to bless us, it is down in the place of dependence and humility that the blessing will be found.

But now we come to the second thought, and it is this: *Are we called to live, just as much as Christ did, that God may be all in all?* Is there any greater obligation on Christ to let God be all in all, than on us? Most people think so, but the Bible does not. The obligation ought to be greater on us, for He is the Son of the Father and God with God; but we are creatures of the dust. Oh, there can be no thought of our existence having been given for anything but just for the blessed object that God may be all in all in us and to us. But have we understood that, and have we expected it, and have we sought for it, and have we ever learned to say with Christ, "It is worth giving up everything, that God may have His place and be all in all"?

But how can we attain to such a life? All our teaching about consecration will be moonshine, unless it come to this—that God must be *all*. What is the meaning of our talking about giving ourselves as a living sacrifice? It cannot be, unless it is actually true that in our life God is *all*. What is the reason of so much complaint of feebleness, of failure, of lost blessing, of walking in the dark? It is nothing but this: God does not get His place among us. I do not say that of the unsanctified, and half-sanctified, but I say it of the best among us. God does not get his place. And I ask you to-night, O saints of God, to pray with your whole heart, that God would take His place in the life of every one of us, and that the inconceivable majesty of God and His claim upon us might be so revealed that we may sink as atoms in the dust, and say, "God, be Thou all, and take all, and have all." God help us to do so.

Now what are the steps by which the soul can be brought, in some measure, to live like Christ every day, so that God may be all in all? My answer is, first, *Take time and trouble to give God His place*. Study your God, meditate more upon your God than you have done, and try to find out what is the place that God desires to take, and do not be content with a sort of vague conception. Yes, of course there is the throne in the heavens, and God is there. For, remember, God is not only an outward Being, so to speak. There is a locality and a throne where the glory of God is specially revealed; but God has an inward being. He dwells even in nature, and how much more in the heart of His redeemed ones and saints! I want to get some conception of what is the place of God, and words can hardly tell. I can only say this: God is the fountain of all life. Every bit of life in the universe is the work of God. If you really give God His place then you will get, oh, such a humbling conviction, that there is nothing but what must come from God, that God fills all things. The Bible says He works all in all, and so you will begin to say, If God is everywhere and in everything, I ought to see Him in Nature, and in Providence, and in everything; I ought always to be seeing my God. The believer can come to that when he sees God everywhere, and then he begins to give God His place. He cannot rise in the morning without giving God His place, and saying: Lord God, Thou glorious Being, Thou art all in all. And then he begins to say to his fellow believers: My brothers, I am afraid that in our prayer meetings we do not let God take His place. We pray because we have a God to pray to, and we know something about God; but how little we in our souls realise the everlasting God! In our little prayer meetings the everlasting God of heaven is present, and if He gets His place He will take charge of the prayer meetings, and He will give blessing and He will work by His mighty power.

Oh, just think of it! Take our chairman, for instance. He guides our meeting, he calls on one to pray, and another to speak, and he tells us what to sing, and gives orders what is to be done. He has a little kingdom in this tent, and he manages it, and you are grateful for it. But God!—people do not allow Him to manage the convention, or the prayer meeting. Do not we thank God for the chairman and the speaker, and for every earthly gift? But, oh, that we might each learn to understand, in the convention, in the church every Sunday, in the prayer meeting, in the closet—I must give time to let my God take His place.

Will God do it? God is waiting to do it. *God longs to do it.* And then, not only in the closet and the prayer meeting, and the convention and the church, but just as one of you takes the place of master or mistress in your house, and you sit at the head of the table, and you order the servant, and you manage everything, so God is willing in my heart and in yours to take the place of Master and of God. Brethren, have we given this glorious God the place He ought to have? Let us in our heart say, "No." And God forgive us if *we* have taken the place that Christ's redemption has given Him, and that Christ wants to give Him in us. Let us come to-night, ere we part, and say, "God shall have His place."

I might speak still further, in this connection, of the church of Christ. Has God His place there? Alas! No. May God humble us and stir in us an unquenchable longing, that God may be all in all. That is my first lesson. Give God His place, but take time and take trouble to do it. Take heed and be quiet. The prophet says, "Be silent of all flesh before the Lord." Let the flesh be kept down. Wait, and give God time to reveal Himself.

Then the second point is, *How am I in my life to attain this,* "That God may be all in all," and to work it out and prove it? *Accept God's will in everything.* Where do I find God's will? I find God's will in His Word. I have often heard it reported that people have said, "I believe every word within these two covers has come from God," and I have sometimes heard it said, "I want to believe every promise between these two covers"; but I have not often heard it said, "I accept every commandment within these two covers." But let us say it. If you like, write in the front page of your Bible what I once wrote in the front page of a young man's: "Every promise of God in this Book I desire to believe, every command of God in this Book I desire to accept." That is one step in the way to let God be all in all. Give up your life to be the embodiment, and expression, and incarnation of the will of God.

Then, further, *accept the will of God, not only in the Bible, but especially in Providence.* I find thousands of Christians who have never learned that lesson. Do you know what that means? When Joseph's brethren sold him, he accepted God's hand in that, and it is written that when he went to Potiphar as a slave, "God was with him." He was not parted from God when he had to part from his home. I read of David that when Shimei cursed him, he said, in effect, "That is God." He saw God in that; he met God there in that cursing of Shimei. God was there all in all, because God allowed it. When Judas came to kiss Christ and betray Him, and when the soldiers bound Him, and when Peter denied Him, and when Caiaphas condemned Him, and when Pilate gave Him over, Christ saw God in everything. God was all in all; and so Christ could drink the cup, for He saw the hand of the Father holding it. Oh, let us learn, in every trial, in every trouble, great and little, to see God at once. Meet your God there, and let God be all in all. There does not a hair of your head fall without the will of your Father. Meet the will of your Father in every trial, in the deepest trial and the heaviest; the Son of God walks there. Oh, let God be all in all. And in the smallest trials—the servant who torments you, the child who hinders you, the friend who has hurt you by slight neglect, the enemy who has reproached you, who has spoken evil of you and robbed you of your good name, the difficulty that worries you—oh, why do not you say, "God is all in all. It is my God who comes to me in every difficulty. I will meet Him, and honour Him, and give myself to Him, and may He keep me!"

There are two great privileges of meeting God in a difficulty, and knowing Him. The first is that, even though the difficulty come through my own fault, if I confess it, then I can say, "God has allowed me to come into this fault, to come into this difficulty, in order to teach me a lesson. My God allowed me to come into it, and He must teach me to glorify Him in it." If a father takes his child to a distant place to school, the child trusts the father to provide for him there. It is not willingly that the father sends the child away from under his eyes. And if God brings you into a difficulty by an act of your own, then you can count upon it that God will give you grace to be humble and patient, and be perfected through the suffering and chastisement, that in everything He may take His place. You will be able to look at Him with double confidence when you can say, "It is Thou who hast brought me here, and not man, and Thou alone canst take me out of it." Oh, if you would only allow God to be all in all, in every Providence, what a blessed life you would be living! Nothing can separate you from the love of God in Christ Jesus. You have a wonderful place provided for you in His love. Oh! learn to take this as the key out of every difficulty—*God is all in all.* And in prayer, day by day, make it your earnest supplication that God may be all in all.

Then the third point. The first was, Give God His place; the second, Accept His will. The third is, *Trust His almighty power.* Trust Him every day. I wish I could tell you rightly what, in this convention, I see a glimpse of; and that is, that the whole of our Christian life every day is to be the work of God Himself. Paul speaks of it so often. "It is God that worketh in you, both to will and to do." The will and the desire to obey—that is God's work in you, and that is only half of it. But He will work *to do,* as well as *to will,* if you will own Him practically in your life as *all in all.* In Hebrews 13: 20, 21 we read: "The God of peace . . . make you perfect in every good work to do His will, working in you that which is well-pleasing in His sight, through Jesus Christ." Here is my watch. Now, as surely as the watch-maker has made that watch, and worked at it, and cut it, and cleaned it, and polished it, and put in every little wheel and every little spring— just so the living God is actually and actively engaged in the work of perfecting your life every moment. God is willing to work in our meeting, from half-past six to half-past eight, every moment; and why does He not work more powerfully? Simply because you do not prove His power, you do not fully give Him His place, you do not wait upon Him to do it. Tell Him: My God, here I am now. I give Thee Thy right place.

Now suppose a canvas could move about, and that when a painter came into his studio to paint an unfinished picture, it always removed to some other part of the room; of course then the painter could not paint a single idea. But suppose the canvas began to say, Oh, painter, I will be still; come and do thy work and paint thy beautiful picture—then the painter would come and do it. And if you say to God, Thou art the mighty Workman, the wondrous Workman. I am still. Here I am. I trust Thy power—oh, believe it, God will then work wonders with you. God never works anything but wonders. That is His nature, even in what we call the laws of nature. Take the simplest thing, a blade of grass, or a little worm, or a flower. What wonders men of science tell us about them! And will not God work wonders in my heart, and yours? He will. And why does not He do it more? Because we do not let Him. Oh, learn to give Him His place, to accept His will, and then to trust His mighty work.

> In Thy strength may I lie still,
> The clay within the Potter's hand,
> Moulded by Thy gentle will,
> Mightier than all command;
> Shaped and moulded by Thee alone,
> Now and ever more Thine own.

Is that true of you? God is willing to mould you as really as the potter moulds his clay. He will do it. Let us believe it, and trust His mighty power; and let us trust His power especially to do things above our conception, or above what we could ask or think. Oh, that I could give every brother and sister before they leave Keswick a shake of the hand and tell them—but without it I tell them—*God is waiting to do for you more than you can even conceive.* I pray you, every yearning of your heart, every message that you have heard, of which you have said, I wish I had that; every prayer you have sent up—oh! just believe that God is willing to work it all in you, and that He is waiting to do it; that in every difficulty, in every circumstance God is there to work in you. Trust Him and honour Him, and let Him be all in all.

And then, once again, if you would honour God, *sacrifice everything for His kingdom and glory.* If God is to be all in all, it must not be so much, I must be happy, and I must be holy, and I must have God's approval. No. The root principle of Christ's life was self-sacrifice unto God for man. That is what He came for, and it is a principle that every redeemed soul carries within him as unquenchable; but, alas! it can be smothered. But understand that your God longs to rule the world, and your Christ is upon the throne, leading you on as His soldiers, and wanting to bless you with victory upon victory. Have you given yourselves up to God's glory? Alas, alas! The soldier upon earth says, Anything for my king and country, anything when my general leads me on to victory. My home I leave, and my comforts;

I give my life. And are earthly kings to have such devotion, and you and I merely *talk* about the glory of God and His being all in all, when there is a call that we should help to prepare the kingdom for Christ to give up to the Father, and when Christ tells us He is waiting for our help and depending upon it?

Shall we not each say, God must be all in all; I will sacrifice everything for Him? May God help us to-night to make a consecration afresh of our whole being to the furtherance of Christ's kingdom. And whether it be in mission work far away, or in Christian work near at home, or whether it be that we do not know how to work, that we are poor weak worms—whatever it be, let everyone yield himself a willing sacrifice, and then Christ can and will use the very weakest for the glory of God.

If you want to take a word as your motto and watchword, let it be, "Sacrifice everything and anything for the glory of your God." And if you do not know what to sacrifice, ask Him. Be honest, be earnest, be simple, be childlike, and say, "Lord, every penny I have is Thine, and every comfort is Thine. If Thou needest it for Thy kingdom, I offer it to Thee." Oh, in eternity, will a man grudge having made himself poor for the bringing about of that majestic spectacle, when the Son shall say, in a new sense, "It is finished," and give the kingdom to the Father, that God may be all in all? Do you hope to be there? Do you hope to have a share in the glory of that august scene, and are you unwilling to-night to say, "Anything that I can do for that glory, Lord, here I am"? Give yourself up to Him.

And now, the last thought, and that is, *wait on God*. I have been speaking, and you have been thinking about God; that is one thing. But oh, to know God, in His glory, within our souls; that is another thing. I told you what you ought to do—that you ought to meditate and study, and try to form a right conception of the place God should occupy in your life. But that is not enough. You must do something else. I said, give yourselves up to the will of God, prove the power of God, and seek the glory of God throughout the earth. But the chief thing is, wait upon God.

And why must we do that? Because it is only God who can reveal Himself. Remember that when God came to Adam, or Noah, or Abraham, or Moses, it was God who came forth out of heaven and met them, and showed Himself in some form or other. That was under the old dispensation. And it depends to-day on the good pleasure of God to reveal Himself. Not an arbitrary good pleasure. No. It all depends upon whether He has found a heart hungering for Him. Oh, that God would give us that hunger, and teach us to cry like David, "My soul thirsteth for God." Wait upon God. Make that in your closet a part of your life more and more systematically. Do not be afraid if people say, Do you want to make Quakers of us? Let us remember that every portion of Christ's body has a lesson for us. I do not think one of you will suffer if you learn the lesson, in your closet, of keeping silence before God, just with one prayer: Lord God, reveal Thyself in the depth of my heart. And though you do not expect a vision, though you do not get a manifestation—that is not what *should* be sought; it is that the soul should open itself to God, and wait upon Him that He may come in. "Verily, Thou art a God that hidest Thyself." You cannot see Him always, but He will come in and take possession of you, if you are ready for His incoming, and will reveal Himself, and work mightily in you.

Wait upon God. In your prayer meetings let that be the first thing. It is the mischief of our prayer in our closet and prayer meetings, that we begin to pray at once, as if it was all right. "Oh yes," we say, "God will do it"; and we do not take trouble to let our souls worship in holy awe and reverence and childlike trust. We do not take time to say, Father, let it please Thee to come near, and to meet me.

Some have said of the convention—I think many—"Oh! if we could have more time for waiting upon God!" I think so, too. I am a stanger. I do not want to be presumptuous, or to take unwarrantable liberty, but I do want to say that if next year it were so ordered by God that those people who wished it could wait upon God in prayer, others being at liberty to hear the speakers if they so desired, then I believe the result would be one of wonderful blessing. The responsibility resting upon this body of believers is tremendous. We confess that many of us have got a secret which other Christians have not got perhaps. We do not judge, but we confess that God has taught us something wonderful. Let us confess it boldly. But then, if that is true, we must get still nearer God, and have more of God, in order to teach other Christians how they can find God. You cannot find God without waiting upon Him. "Wait, I say, on the Lord."

Those are the steps by which we can come to have it in our hearts and lives, that God is all in all; and the steps by which we can be prepared for taking part in that glorious company who shall be present on that magnificent occasion when Christ shall give up the kingdom to the Father, "that God may be all in all."

GOD'S GIFT OF HOLINESS

Rev. Evan H. Hopkins

For ye see your calling, brethren, how that not many wise men after the flesh, not many mighty, not many noble, are called: but God hath chosen the foolish things of the world to confound the wise; and God hath chosen the weak things of the world to confound the things which are mighty; and base things of the world, and things which are despised, hath God chosen, yea, and things which are not, to bring to nought things that are: that no flesh should glory in His presence. But of Him are ye in Christ Jesus, who of God is made unto us wisdom, and righteousness, and sanctification, and redemption: that, according as it is written, he that glorieth, let him glory in the Lord—1 CORINTHIANS 1: 26–31.

I WANT to preface my remarks by stating a difficulty which may be present in the minds of many here to-night. Let me read you a sentence or two from a letter that I received. "We are asked to accept holiness by faith in the same way that we accept justification by faith. Now that presents a real difficulty to my mind. Is not holiness a growth, a process, the result of the work of the Holy Spirit in the heart? Justification is something already complete; to accept it therefore by faith, is clear and intelligible to me. But sanctification being a process that can never be absolutely completed in this life, I cannot see how it can be received by faith in the same way that justification is received by faith."

That holiness is a process, of course, we all readily admit; that it is a progressive work of God the Holy Ghost in the heart, is clear and intelligible; but that that is the only aspect or even the chief aspect in which holiness is presented to us in Holy Scripture, we cannot for a moment admit. I would endeavour to show that before we are really ready to deal with sanctification as a process, we must know what it is to receive sanctification as a gift: and that gift is Jesus Christ. It is of the very first importance, if we are seeking holiness, that our thoughts should be fixed not upon *it*, but upon *Him*; not upon a thing like a process, but upon a person, the Lord Jesus Christ. And when that is established clearly in our minds we shall find that to receive Christ by faith as our holiness does not present any more difficulty than to receive Christ by faith as our righteousness.

Let us consider sanctification from three points of view—as an *attainment*, as a *gift*, as an *experience*. Now look at sanctification as—

I. AN ATTAINMENT. I would quote a remarkable sentence from Dr. Edersheim's well-known work on *The Life and Times of Jesus Christ the Messiah*. In his exposition of the Sermon on the Mount he shows the contrast between man's way and God's way of righteousness. He says, "Every moral system is a road by which, through self-denial, discipline, and effort, men seek to reach the goal." Now let us understand what that means. Here is an unregenerate man; he is earnest, he is religious, he is seeking salvation. Well, he has a starting-point, and there is the road before him. But what is his goal? Life, righteousness—and he is seeking to reach that goal by painful effort. Now what does Dr. Edersheim say in contrast to this? "Christ begins with the goal, and places His disciples at once in a position to which all other teachers point as the end. They work up to the goal of becoming the children of the kingdom. He makes men such freely of His grace; and this is the kingdom. What the others labour for, Christ gives. They begin by demanding, He by bestowing."

These are golden words. We have here a grand principle, and when we grasp that principle we have the key to the difficulty of what is meant by sanctification by faith. Take *righteousness*. How is Christ made of God unto us righteousness? My answer is, *by attaining it*. There was a time in our own experience as sinners when we put righteousness before us as the end to be struggled for, and we hoped to reach it as an attainment. We knew no other way of justification than by personal attainment. But when the light broke in, and our eyes were open to see the truth of the Gospel, what did we discover? We discovered this—that that which we could not attain for ourselves Christ had attained for us, and that He placed us at once in righteousness as our starting-point. Christ made of God unto us righteousness, Christ the end of the law for righteousness; and we started the Christian life by starting from that point. So that that which *to Christ* was an *attainment*, became *to us* by faith an *obtainment*. We did not attain it, but it is a righteousness which Christ attained; He Himself became of God unto us righteousness. It was God's gift of righteousness to us, and we received that gift by faith. Now if we are Christians, we perfectly understand that. That is the first lesson, and that is the key to the whole difficulty.

Now take *holiness*. How is Christ made of God unto us holiness?

I answer, *by attaining holiness*. It is scarcely possible for us to conceive of a man, *created* holy, if we take holiness in the highest sense of conformity to the will of God. Moral goodness really means *choosing to be holy*, and no man can be *made* to choose, or be made as having chosen; there must be the trial, there must be the probation, there must be the running the race—the goal must be reached. It was not in His incarnation that Christ was made of God unto us righteousness or sanctification. His incarnation was the starting-point. As Professor Godet beautifully puts it, "Jesus was by His miraculous birth placed in the same condition of purity and innocence in which the first man existed before the Fall; and that was so ordered that He might be able successfully to enter once more upon that pathway of progress from innocence up to holiness which had been the course originally open to man, but at the very outset of which Adam had fallen." Now, here was the second Adam, and what we may glory in is that Christ has reached the goal not only of righteousness, but of holiness. And if it is asked what is the distinction between righteousness and holiness, I take it that the answer is, righteousness is that which satisfies God's *law*; holiness is that which satisfies the Father's *heart*: and the Lord Jesus Christ came not only to meet the claims of the law, and a broken law, by His death and perfect obedience, but He came also to lead the ideal life, the life of the child with the Father, a life that perfectly satisfied His Father's heart. He has become holiness unto us; and He, as holiness, is as much the Father's gift to us as righteousness, and as we receive Him by faith as righteousness, so we receive Him by faith as holiness. He has reached the goal.

Look at sanctification as—

II. A GIFT. What do we mean when we speak of the Lord Jesus Christ as God's gift of holiness? Not a gift *added* to Christ Himself, but a gift included in the one great gift—Jesus Christ. You cannot divide Christ into parts. To receive Him is to receive all that He includes; and He includes "all things that pertain unto life and godliness."

But it is one thing to receive a gift, and it is another thing to know what the gift contains. You may have a large estate, and yet you may know nothing of the treasures that lie a few feet below the surface. Perhaps you own thousands of acres of land, and yet you are a poor man because you cannot pay your way. Now if below the surface there were large deposits of mineral wealth, what would be needed in order to enrich you and set you free from your bondage and difficulty? No addition need be made to your property, but simply the *discovery* of what you already possess. Not something added to it, but uncovering the surface and seeing what is already there. So it is with Christ. You cannot be a

Christian at all if you have not received Christ. It takes two to make a Christian—the sinner and Christ; that is the Christian. And every true believer has received Christ Jesus the Lord, and in that gift everything is comprehended, all that is needed for life and godliness. You have Christ, but how little have you actually realised as to what He contains!

When we speak of the blessing of holiness we mean that a revelation has been made, by the Spirit of God to the soul, of a fresh aspect of Christ. That is what we mean. Every fresh blessing along the path of faith is connected with some new unfolding of the Person of Christ to the soul. It is a revelation of what you already have in possession, it is true; but we know that it is a law in the spiritual life that Christ is to you practically what He is to your faith. You must know what you have; you cannot trust until you know. "Faith cometh by hearing, and hearing by the word of God," and the word of God tells us that which we have to believe. You not only see it, but you appropriate it. Now this is the grand principle that runs through the whole life. The Holy Spirit unveils Christ to us in fresh aspects, meeting the fresh or the deeper needs of the soul.

Shall I try to illustrate it to you in a familiar way, so that even a little child might understand me? In that chapter which we read just now, I Corinthians I, or part of it, you will see that the main subject, as I understand it, is *wisdom*. The Greeks gloried in wisdom, human wisdom. "Do you glory in wisdom?" the apostle would say. As he would say to the Roman, "Do you glory in power?" As he would say to the Jew, "Do you seek a sign—outward glory?" The Lord Jesus Christ is God's answer to each of these needs. *Wisdom*. Here is the wisdom of God—behold how the wisdom of God is displayed in redemption. "Christ is made of God unto you wisdom, even righteousness, and sanctification, and redemption." Wisdom is that which comprehends these three things. I give you a purse. Let me call that purse *wisdom*. What does that purse contain? Well, there is one sovereign, and we will call that "righteousness"; there is another sovereign, and we will call that "sanctification." Put these two sovereigns together; they must go together, as we see from a consideration of the original—"both righteousness and sanctification." But there is something else in the purse; it is a promissory note. You cannot cash it yet; it has reference to the future. We will call that "redemption." The two sovereigns may be used at once to meet the need of the present. But we have to wait for that which is included in "redemption." Now when you take the purse you take what the purse contains. Look at the application of this. What is my need? My need as to *position*: the first thing is to be put into a right position before God. Christ is made unto me righteousness—that is my *standing*, my judicial position. I stand before God in the very righteousness of God. Christ is the righteousness of God.

But a right position does not meet all my need. It is not realising my position that can give me sufficient power for either walk or work. Therefore there must be the other provision—He is made of God unto me not only righteousness but sanctification. That points to my need as to *condition*; dealing with my disposition, with my desires, with my thoughts, with my will, with my whole spiritual condition. You cannot have right character till you have got right condition, and the first thing is to get into a right condition; and when I receive Christ not only as my righteousness but as my holiness, the first step is taken to secure the right condition.

All this is in perfect harmony with all the other doctrines connected with the triumphant life. Let me touch on one or two of these.

Take *victory*. How important to understand what the secret of victory is. Many of us have been taught in times past to look at it in this way: the enemy is on the heights, and we are on the plain beneath. Our great spiritual foe occupies the victorious position; we are in the valley, and the conflict consists in seeking through God's grace to dislodge him. That is to say, we have to fight *for* victory. But there is a more excellent way: what is the *fight of faith*? It means this, that Christ has dislodged the foe, and has secured for us the victorious position, and that before we begin that fight we are privileged to take by faith the place of victory. So that the conflict consists in holding the victorious position by faith. "That ye may be able to *stand*," hold your ground, "and having done all, to stand." What is it that the enemy is seeking to do? To dislodge you. Now Christ puts us into the victorious position, the impregnable position, and He gives us an armour that we might be enclosed in Him, and we must take it by faith, and hold it by faith, and fight by faith *from* that victorious position. It is the fight of faith; and all this is in perfect harmony with what we have said about holiness. We begin with victory even as we begin with righteousness—and so let us begin with holiness.

So with deliverance. Many a one knows that there is present pardon, but they realise that they are in bondage to sin, in captivity, and they say, "O God, give me grace that I may deliver myself!" Oh, if they could only see that Christ has set us free, that Christ has given us deliverance, and we step into the deliverance by faith, and then walk in freedom. "Stand fast in the liberty wherewith Christ hath made us free" (Gal. 5: 1). So with holiness. "That we, being delivered out of the hand of our enemies, might serve Him without fear *in* holiness—(not for it; it is to be the very element of our service)—and righteousness before Him, all the days of our life." We have not to serve in order that we might attain holiness, but we have holiness in order that we might serve Him *in* it, and it is to be the very element of our activity. We must begin with it. So, if we want holiness, we must apprehend Christ as God's provision for holiness. We must receive Him as such before we are ready to walk so as to please Him.

Now we come to holiness as—

III. AN EXPERIENCE. Take three thoughts briefly. First, there is *the rest of His peace*. I do not mean peace of conscience—simply that blessed peace that comes when you know the burden is gone and your sins are forgiven—but a far deeper peace than that, a soul-satisfying peace, the peace of the heart that is satisfied with Christ. Not as our own attainment, not a self-satisfaction, but a satisfaction with Him because we are finding how fully He can meet the need, that need which we realise in the walk amid difficulty, temptation, and trial. It is when we are *satisfied* in Christ and with Christ that we find the secret of abiding, for then we have no desire to depart from Him. We know that sheep that are satisfied with their pasture do not wander. So with the soul that is satisfied with the Lord Jesus Christ—the world loses its attractiveness. But when you cease to be satisfied with Christ, then you begin to look around, and the old temptations come with their old power. To abide in the rest of His peace—here is the secret of abiding; it is the secret of being kept calm and still, not easily moved.

Then there is *the rest of His purity*. So long as we are struggling with the impurity within, there can be no rest. You know what it is to fight, hand to hand, with your evil passions. Oh, what an endless fight, what a hopeless conflict it is when you are struggling with your own evil passions! But when you let the Lord come in as your purity, the Lord as your holiness, to possess you, you enter at once into a new experience. God appeared to Moses in the burning bush. Why was it called a holy bush? There was nothing different in the bush itself from other trees in the wilderness. What made the ground on which it stood holy? There can be but one reason—because God possessed it. The Holy One had come down and made that bush His abode. There is only one Holy One, there is only one holy centre. We are holy as we are brought to that centre; we have no holiness when we get away from that centre, and cease to be possessed by the Holy One. Christ is the Holy One: "He is made of God unto us holiness";

let Him come and take possession. Here is a room full of darkness. What must we do to get rid of the darkness? Bring in the light! That is all. The burning light brings with it its own rays which dispel the darkness. There is the cause and there is the effect. The cause is Christ; the illumination that fills our souls is the effect.

We are not to be occupied with the effect, but with Him who is the source of all our purity; and yet we cannot but be conscious of an entirely new experience. Oh, the rest of discovering that the Holy One stills the tempest that has been going on within! Christ comes, and says, "Peace, be still," and we realise that we are delivered from sin's dominion, raised above these evil passions. There *is* a process, undoubtedly; but we are not occupied with the process. It is an endless process—it is more and more; and it is the work of the Holy Spirit all along, the Spirit glorifying Christ in our hearts, the Spirit enabling us to realise our need of Christ more and more, and then unfolding to us an infinite fulness in Him, and showing us how perfectly He can satisfy the heart that is longing for holiness.

And lastly, there is *the rest of His power*. Listen to the words, "Strengthened (or, being strengthened) with all might, according to His glorious power," nay, better than that, "according to the power of His glory." This is the power of Him who is on the right hand of God; He has poured out His Holy Spirit upon us. There is the power of His death; we see it on the Cross. But here is the power of His glorified life. *"Being strengthened"*—it is continuous —"according to the power of His glory" (Col. 1: 11). Nothing is difficult if the power you have is sufficient. Struggling is a sign not of power but of weakness. To get the power, all that is needed is the contact of faith. It is not by struggling we get strength; it is trusting, and then the power flows in as a stream. And then activity follows as the result. But it is activity without fret and friction and strain.

Here is the secret of victory. This is to be in the stream of a triumphant life; it is the life of the risen One. Oh, be occupied with Him. Do not be occupied with an *it*. If your thoughts are taken up with the process of sanctification, the work of the Holy Ghost in you, of course you will be continually feeling your spiritual pulse, and you will desire to be satisfied with yourself, and you will be occupied with an *it*. But if you see that Christ is your indwelling holiness, and you enshrine Him as such in your heart, you will know what it is to be satisfied only with Him. And you will then see the great purpose God has in all this, namely, "That no flesh should glory in His presence," and that "He that glorieth, let him glory in the Lord."

THE SPIRIT OF BURNING

Rev. R. A. Torrey, D.D.

W E HAVE time this morning for the study of but three or four names of the Holy Spirit. Turn to Isaiah 4: 4, "When the Lord shall have washed away the filth of the daughters of Zion, and shall have purged the blood of Jerusalem from the midst thereof by the Spirit of judgment and the Spirit of burning." In our Authorised and Revised Versions, Spirit is spelt with a small "s"; but, as many of you know, in Hebrew there is no distinction between capital and small letters, so that the word spirit, spelt with a small "s," is simply the thought of the translators. But I hold that these two words, translated "spirit," are the names of a person, the Holy Spirit.

"*The Spirit of judgment*"—What is the thought in that name? Jesus Himself tells us in John 16: 8–11, "When the Comforter is come, He will reprove the world of sin, and of righteousness, and of judgment." The Holy Spirit convicts of sin. You and I can never convict people of sin. "The heart is deceitful above all things, and desperately wicked"; and about as hopeless a thing as anybody ever undertook is to try to convince someone else that he is a sinner before God. You cannot do it. God does not ask us to do it, or depend upon us to do it. But there is One who can do it, and who does do it—the Spirit of judgment, the Holy Spirit. It is simply marvellous, the way that the Holy Spirit, in a moment, can come to a person who is utterly unregenerate, who has no consciousness whatever of sin, and can overwhelm him with a sense of sinfulness before God, and make him cry to God for mercy through Jesus Christ. That is what we need in our churches to-day—a cessation of any attempt on the part of us preachers to do what no preacher on earth ever could do, or ever did do, to convince men of sin; and a counting upon the Holy Spirit to convince men of sin *through* us. He does it, but He does it through us. When He is come to *you*, He will convince the world of sin.

In our own church in Chicago, the officers of the church met every Friday night for counsel and prayer, because there did not seem to be that direct conviction of sin that we longed for in connection with our church work. We prayed that the Spirit of God would come in mighty convicting power. Shortly afterwards I was preaching, and as I looked down underneath the gallery I saw sitting beside one of our deacons a great stalwart man in a flashy dress. I said to myself, "He is a sporting man"; and I was right in the surmise, as I learnt afterwards. Well, he sat there riveted throughout the service. When the meeting was over, we went downstairs to the after-meeting, and he also came. It was rather late before I got through dealing with the inquirers that night. About eleven o'clock the same deacon came to me and said, "Come over and speak to this man." It was that sporting man. He told me that his mother kept a gambling house, and that he had never been in a Christian service before. He added, "I had started out this afternoon to spend the time in gambling. I passed an open-air meeting, and there I heard a young man stand up and testify whom I once knew in a life of sin. I stopped to hear him, and when he was done I went on, thinking nothing. But some strange, mysterious power laid hold of me, and brought me back to the meeting. Then Deacon Young got hold of me and brought me here. And oh!"—the man sobbed and shook all over—"I am so miserable. I never felt this way before in all my life! I do not know what's the matter with me!" I said, "I can tell you what's the matter with you; the Spirit of God is convincing you of sin."

Not long after, sitting almost above the place where the man sat that night, I saw another man, with a great diamond flashing on his shirt front, and everything betokening him to be a man of the world. I said to myself, "There is another sporting man"; and so he turned out to be. As I was preaching he kept looking at me intently, and in the midst of the sermon, to drive the question home, I said, "Who in this audience will accept Christ to-night?" Quick as a flash the man sprang to his feet, and it rang through the building: "I will!" I was not there to save sermons, but to save souls, and so I dropped the sermon and drew the net. I asked, "Is there anyone else?" A white-haired Colonel, who had been sent out to America to get as drunk as he pleased, and who was kept in a Chicago hotel for that purpose, rose to his feet, with tears streaming down his face. What did it all mean? We had counted upon the Holy Spirit, the Spirit of judgment; and He always works when you count upon Him, and He works along the definite line that you count upon.

But there is another name for Him in this same passage: "*The Spirit of burning.*" What does it mean? In Matthew 3: 11 we are told that Jesus "shall baptize with the Holy Ghost, and with fire." In Acts 2: 3 we read that "there appeared unto them cloven tongues, like as of fire; and it sat upon each one of them."

In 2 Timothy 1: 6 we are told to stir up the gift of God that is in us, and the word for "stir up" means to *stir up into a flame* the gift that is in us. In other words, the Holy Spirit is a fire in the soul that receives Him. That is what we need—*fire*!

What does fire do? First of all, *fire reveals*. There is nothing in the world that reveals like fire. If I have a piece of metal like gold, there is one way of finding out whether it is gold or not. Put it in the fire. The final test of a diamond as to its quality is fire. About two years ago a friend of mine went to a diamond merchant and said, "How do you tell a real diamond?" "We have many tests, but if we cannot find out by other tests the final test is to put it in the fire." "I thought fire would ruin a diamond!" "It would the way you put it in, but we put it in so that the fire brings out its real quality." Fire reveals. We are told in 1 Corinthians 3: 13 that in the coming day of Christ, "the fire shall try every man's work, of what sort it is." What Christ will do when He comes, the Holy Ghost does to-day with the individual. He reveals you to yourself. One of the first things that come with the real receiving of the Spirit is such a revelation of oneself as one never had before.

I shall never forget one night in Chicago. God had given me for a text—I could not see any other, though I tried to get away from it—to preach on the Sunday evening: "He shall baptize you with the Holy Ghost, and with fire." I had the sermon thoroughly prepared, but not written. When Saturday night came, and the preparation was over, I knelt down to wait upon God for His blessing upon the sermon. I said something like this: "Heavenly Father, Thou hast bidden me to preach to-morrow upon 'He shall baptize with the Holy Ghost and with fire'—upon the baptism of fire. I do not believe I have it myself, and how can I preach on it earnestly if I do not possess it? Now, give me what I am going to preach upon as a practical experience for myself to-night, that I may preach upon it as I ought to-morrow night." God heard my prayer.

Do you want to know what first was given? Such a revelation of myself as I never had before in all my life! I never dreamt I was so full of vanity, personal ambition, pride, so utterly self-centred, and so everything else that a minister of the Gospel ought not to be. It was very painful, but it was very salutary.

And so it will be with us, if we receive the Holy Spirit as the Spirit of burning. He will give us such a revelation of self as will lay us in the dust. That is just what we want. It is a good deal better to have the fire of the Holy Ghost revealing the character of our work now, than to have to wait for that awful day for some, when the fire shall reveal their work, of what kind it is—"wood, hay, stubble," and it shall all go up in smoke, and they be saved, but so as by fire.

Fire refines, cleanses, purifies. There is nothing that cleanses like fire. If I have a piece of gold, and there is dirt on the outside, and I want to get the dirt off, I can take soap and water, perhaps, and wash it off. But suppose that the dirt is in the very metal itself, there is only one way to get it out—throw it into the fire! Just so with you and me. The filthiness of our outer life is easily managed. The water of the Word will wash it off without any trouble. But what about the filthiness inside? Where we most need cleansing is not in our outward walk, but in the inward life; and the power of the Holy Ghost will refine in a moment more than any process of human ethical culture will refine in a century. The ethical culture is a very slow process; the refining of fire is a very immediate and wonderful process.

Take the apostles, for example. Up to the day of Pentecost, how full they were of self-seeking! Up to the last supper there was quarrelling as to who was to be the greatest, and not one of them would wash anyone else's feet! Peter said, "I am the one of whom the Master said, 'Upon thee will I build my church'." John and James said, "We are His cousins!" Judas Iscariot said, "I am proprietor of the whole concern!" And someone else said something else, and no one would wash anyone else's feet, until our Lord had to gird Himself with a towel and go round and do it Himself. They were all full of self! But after Pentecost it was not self, but Christ. Before the crucifixion and before the resurrection, how full of cowardice they were! The apostle Peter denied his Lord three times with oaths, and all the rest of the company forsook Him and fled. But after Pentecost that same Peter stood up before the very council that condemned Christ to death, and looked them in the face and said, "Ye rulers of the people, and elders of Israel. If we this day be examined of the good deed done to the impotent man, by what means he is made whole, be it known unto you all, and to all the people of Israel, that by the name of Jesus Christ of Nazareth, whom ye crucified, whom God raised from the dead, even by Him doth this man stand here before you whole" (Acts 4: 8–10). What a change! That is what we need—the refining fire!

Fire consumes—in fact, it refines by consuming. In the wonderful picture of God's purpose concerning Jerusalem (Ezek. 24: 9–11), Jerusalem is compared to a cauldron put into a hot fire until her filthiness is consumed away. So it is with us. The fire of the Holy Ghost consumes those things within us which are displeasing to God—vanity, pride, temper, personal ambition, uncleanness of all kinds.

We once had in our Bible Institute in Chicago the most un-promising pupil we ever had in the women's department there. I knew her before she came, as a trustee of a seminary which she had attended in Massachusetts. When I received a letter saying she was coming to the Bible Institute, I said to myself, "What on earth does she want at the Bible Institute?" At the institution in Massachusetts she had resisted everything done for the spiritual well-being of the place; she was boisterous, headstrong, wild, high-tempered—everything that a Christian worker and a Christian ought not to be. Well, I went over to the superintendent of the women's department, who also knew her, and said, "So-and-so proposes to come to the Institute. I cannot understand it. She is utterly unfit for the life here." But we accepted her, simply because her uncle was one of the best friends of the Institute, and out of regard for him. She came, and after a little while she applied for membership in my church. I was finally persuaded that she was a child of God though she seemed to have only a dim flickering of life; and I said, "We will receive you into the membership of the church." I dared not bring her before the committee of the church but passed her in without that.

We require of every student of the women's department that every week they must go down, in and out among the poor and outcast, and minister to their need. We are not trying to raise up workers who shall go among the comfortable and rich, but among the outcast and poor. Many of them are going out as foreign missionaries, and what is the use of sending anybody for that who has not sympathy for those to whom they go, and the remedy for wretchedness and sin? This young woman did not like it. It is very unpleasant work to one who has not a heart full of love. One day she came down from one of those wretched tenements utterly tired and disgusted, and turned her back on the whole business and said, "I have had enough of it; I do not like it. I have no taste for it." She then went to the most magnificent mansions in the city and looked at them and said, "This is what I like; I have had enough of Townsend-street! This is what I like, and what I am going to have!"

In that rebellious mood she returned to the Bible Institute, went up to her room, and afterwards came and sat down at the tea-table. As she sat there the fire of God fell right where she was, and burned, and burned, and she sprang to her feet, ran across the room to a friend, and threw her arms round her neck and said, "Here is a volunteer for Africa!" The fire burned, and so transformed the girl's character, and her views of life, and her ambitions, and her very face, as the new life within glowed out from those eyes, and the whole countenance, that her best friends could hardly believe what they saw and heard. In a few weeks she went back to the seminary in Massachusetts, and standing before the old girls who knew her, with parting words she pleaded that every one of them would give themselves to Christ and surrender absolutely to His work. Transformed in a moment! How? By fire!

Some of you men have been fighting against temper for years, against pride and ambition and selfishness, and you have made no headway. But the Holy Spirit is the Spirit of burning; and this morning, here and now, if you will open your heart to the fire, and be willing that the fire shall burn, it will burn through and through, and burn up all the filthiness and scum.

Fire illuminates. We are told in John 5: 35, "He was a burning and a shining light" (R.V., "He was a lamp that burneth and shineth")—shining because it burned. There is no shining without combustion. Every bit of light in the world comes from fire. The light that is on your gas fixtures comes from the combustion of the gas; the light that fills this tent at this moment comes from combustion in the sun; all light comes from fire. And the fire of the Holy Ghost illuminates. A real reception of the Holy Spirit will, in a moment, illuminate the soul that has sat in darkness for years. A baptism of the Holy Spirit and of fire will do more to illuminate the dark mind than a theological education, and will do more to make the Bible an open book than anything else that can happen. How many people go to theological halls and come out sometimes more than half infidels concerning the miraculous element in the Bible, the virgin birth of our Lord, the teaching of our Lord Himself as to the future destiny of the wicked, the cardinal doctrines of Christianity, and the substitutionary atonement of Jesus Christ! And then comes the day when, not through reading, but by the direct touch of the fire of God, the darkened heart is illuminated, and the heresies and errors and doubts go up in smoke and disappear, and the light of God shines, and a real baptism with the Holy Ghost and with fire makes glory to shine through every page of the Bible.

Take, for example, that young woman to whom I have already referred. I was away when all that happened, and when I came back a few days afterwards my secretary, now a missionary in South Africa—that is what we want our secretaries to become—said, "Mr. Torrey, have you heard what has happened to 'Jack'?" That shows the character of the woman, that she should be called "Jack." I said, "No," and he told me. I was going out, between the church and the Bible Institute, through the gate, and who should be coming down the street to enter the gate but "Jack" herself. She looked into my face, and her eyes danced;

her feet danced, too—the first time in my life I almost knew what it meant to "dance before the Lord." I do not object to that kind of dancing, but I object most strenuously to indecency, and I claim that the modern dance, which admits of familiarity and contact between the sexes, should not be permitted in decent society. That girl could not keep her feet still. She said, "Professor Torrey, have you heard?" "Yes," I said, "I have heard"; and she poured out her heart, and added, "And, Professor, one of the best parts of it is this: the Bible is a new book. I hated to read the Bible before; but God has given me such a wonderful revelation from His Word!"

Many of you to-day, if you told the honest truth, would have to admit that the Bible is the dullest book you read. You read it because you have to, but you would rather read trashy modern novels than the Bible. But when you receive the fire of God, glory will shine through every page, and you will want to give your time to the one book.

Fire warms, fire makes to glow. You go and stand before an open furnace, and hold in your hands a bar of iron. What a disagreeable, unpleasant, repulsive thing a bar of cold iron is! There is no beauty in it. But throw the bar of iron in through the open door of the furnace, and soon the fire in the furnace gets into the iron—a dull red, a brighter red, and then glowing.

How cold and unattractive you and I are by nature! But when the Lord Jesus takes us, and plunges us into the fire, we begin to grow warm, and then hot, and then we glow with the love of God, the love of Jesus, and with love for perishing men. I believe that is one of the greatest needs of the Church of Christ to-day—men in the pulpit that glow, men and women in the pews that glow! What cold things we preachers are, anyhow! We stand up and preach sometimes with the most faultless diction, our sentences are most logically constructed, our argument is mainly unanswerable; we preach on the most solemn themes—heaven, hell, judgment, sin; and our audiences sit there and admire, and go out saying, "What a remarkable sermon that was!" But nobody was converted. Why? Because we convince the intellect, but we do not melt the heart. When the preacher is on fire with the Holy Ghost, people do not go out and say, "What a wonderful preacher he is!" They go out with melted hearts, tearful eyes. That is what we need—the man in the pulpit all aglow! Wesley was such a man, Charles G. Finney was such a man, D. L. Moody was such a man. If we were men like that, men of fire, all England would be on fire in a few months. We can be men like that. The Spirit of burning is what we need in our pulpits and pews.

P

That is what we need in our choirs. One goes and listens to some singing, beautiful from an aesthetic standpoint, but nobody ever thinks of being converted under it—they just go and hear the music. But when one sees, as I have seen, a choir with the Holy Ghost in them, people do not say, "What beautiful singing!" They fall on their knees and cry to God for Christ's sake to have mercy on them. That is what we need—choirs baptized with the Spirit of burning.

That is what we need in our Sunday-school classes. We have so many helps to-day for the preparation of our lessons, the teachers know all about the geography of the lesson and the historical setting—and a great deal that is not true, besides. But there is not the fire. Sometimes you come across a plain old lady who has been teaching a class for the last fifty years, and has not been able to buy those helps. She is better without *some* of them—not *all* of them. But she sits there, and in the old-fashioned way, now out of date, teaches the lesson, and she glows with the fire of God, and, one by one, her scholars are led to Christ. That is what we need—the Spirit of burning!

Fire generates energy. The man of science tells us that, given heat, he can generate every form of energy. "Cloven tongues, like as of fire, and it sat upon each of them"—and then what power there was! Three thousand people converted in a day! A man takes me through a great factory, and this factory has the best machinery for turning out what it produces. He shows me a great engine of a hundred horse-power that will turn every wheel in this factory. I go upstairs, and there is the machinery, and the whole thing is in gear. I turn to the man and say, "Did not you say that this was the best machinery in England for producing what you turn out, and that there was power in that engine to turn every wheel in this factory?" "Yes, sir." "Then look here—the machinery appears magnificent, and everything is in gear, but there is not a wheel moving in the establishment! Will you explain it?" "Yes, come downstairs again." He takes me into the engine-room again, throws open the doors, and says, "Look in there! There is the explanation; no fire in the fire-box!" I go to many of our modern churches, and what beautiful architecture! what grand organs! what matchless choirs! what an eloquent preacher, speaking like an Apollos! The machinery all the best—but not a wheel in the whole institution turning for God! What is the matter? No fire in the fire-box! We need the fire of God as individuals and churches; we need the Spirit of burning.

Fire spreads. Some years ago, in 1872, in Chicago—I was not there then—a woman was milking her cow, and there was a little lamp of oil, a little flickering flame. The cow kicked over the lamp, and the flame kindled a wisp of hay, and another wisp, until all the hay in the stable was on fire, and the next building was on fire, and the next, and the next! The fire spread over the river to the main part of Chicago, and swept on until, within a territory one mile wide and three miles long, there were only two buildings standing. The little flame from that lamp had laid Chicago in ashes! If the fire of God shall fall in Eskin Street tent now, you may be only a little wisp of hay, but if it sets you on fire, the fire will communicate itself to another, and that to another; it will burn on and on, till the remotest part of the earth is touched by the holy fire of God. That is what we want.

I was going to speak about the Holy Spirit as the "oil of gladness," and as the Comforter, or rather, Paraclete, ever present, always at hand to help us in every emergency of Christian life and service. But I will not dwell upon that.

"He shall baptize you with the Holy Ghost and with fire." Who can have it? Everyone of us. You say, "I am unworthy!" Is there anyone that is not unworthy? The great turning point in my life was when I was brought face to face with this text (Matt. 3: 11). I knew I had been baptized with the Holy Spirit before that, and God had used me; but the two words that rang in my ears were, *with fire*. I knew that if there was anyone on earth that lacked fire it was I. I was cold in that sense; my students did not love me; I think they respected me, but they were afraid of me, and hardly dared to come to me with questions. They would go to almost anybody else in the Faculty before they would come to the head of the Faculty. But with that text before me I knelt down and said, "O God, I need fire!" And you need fire; and then you will have lips that glow, hearts that glow with love to God, love to Jesus, love for the perishing. That is what we want in Keswick, and to take away from Keswick. We can have it. In the upper room the disciples got it while they were sitting. We sometimes have the impression that it was while they were on their knees. It says, "And it filled all the house where they were sitting. And there appeared cloven tongues like as of fire, and it sat upon each one of them."

We can see the fire in this tent now—not with the natural eye. It seems to me as if the fire was just brooding over every person in this tent. Do you want it? It will burn. Do you want it? It costs. I was talking to a man yesterday about having love for souls, and I said, "Do you want it?" He replied, "Is it very expensive?" It is the most expensive thing in the world. If some of you get it, you will not be in England twelve months hence; you will be in Africa, China, or somewhere else. Or if you are in England, you will leave your beautiful home and go down and live in the slums—some of you, not all of you. Love for souls is very expensive, but it is wonderfully glorious. Do you want the fire? You can have it. The tent is full of it. *Open your hearts and welcome it.* But you must be absolutely willing that the fire burn just as it pleases; you cannot dictate to it.

THE INBREATHED SPIRIT

Rev. A. T. Pierson. D.D.

THAT we are in the presence of Christ is becoming so really and manifestly a matter of consciousness to some of us, that I am not quite sure I ought to speak. In the Ladies Meeting this morning, without any appeal, a spirit of self-sacrifice took possession of those who were in attendance. One sister desired to give the last thing she had to the Lord, and she gave a silver clasp. And others, without any attempt at an appeal for sacrifice, followed, until sixty-eight offerings from personal ornamentation, and over ten pounds in money, were offered to the Lord in that small meeting.

Personally, I have been on my face before God, wondering whether I ought to speak at all. I am not going to lead you in prayer, I am going to ask you to bow your heads and ask for two definite things—first, that I may be enabled to speak, or to keep silence, just as God will: and, second, that you may hear whatever I speak in His name, or whatever He speaks in my silence. Then, as He may lead, I will say a few words. (After silent prayer Dr. Pierson continued):

Now let us hear His word. Let me read the 19th and following verses of John 20, "Then the same day at evening, being the first day of the week, when the doors were shut where the disciples were assembled because of the Jews, came Jesus and stood in the midst, and saith unto them, Peace be unto you. And when He had so said, He showed unto them His hands and His side." Why? Because upon those wounds were based the peace which He spake to them. "Then were the disciples glad, when they saw the Lord. Then said Jesus to them again, Peace be unto you: as my Father hath sent me, even so send I you. And when He had said this, He breathed on them . . ." That is not the Greek word: it is not "breathed on them," but "breathed *into* them." "And when He had said this, He inbreathed into them, and saith unto them, Receive ye the Holy Ghost."

This is the first message to the assembled disciples after He rose from the dead. Nothing is more wonderful in the New Testament than this message, when you take it in all the surroundings of its utterance. Here is the risen Christ, having risen no

more to die, death having no more dominion over Him. He is
meeting His disciples now, together in the assembly, for the first
time after His resurrection. And He says to them three things.
First, "Peace be unto you"; second, "As my Father hath sent
me, even so send I you"; third, "Receive ye the Holy Ghost."
The first is a message of peace, the last is a message of power, and
the middle one is a commission. Peace founded upon the blood
of the cross, a testimony founded upon the salvation that comes
by the blood, and power for the testimony to be given. It might
truly be said that, beyond this, in the New Testament there is
not a new idea: it is all here. And everything that this means
may come to you in this tent to-night.

Look at the word "receive": it is one of the leading words of
John's Gospel. He tells us in chapter 20 and verse 31: "These
things are written that ye might believe that Jesus is the Christ,
the Son of God; and that believing ye might have life through
His name"—eternal life through believing. What is it to believe?
Look in the first chapter and verse 12: "To as many as received
Him, to them gave He power to become the sons of God, even
to them that believe on His name." Believing is receiving, and
receiving is believing; and the simplest act that God enables us
to do is the act of receiving. When He says "Peace be unto you,"
all you have to do is to receive it; when He says, "I send you, as
the Father sent me," all you have to do is to receive the commission; and when He inbreathes the Holy Spirit, all you have to
do is to breathe in what He breathes out. It is reception throughout.

Jesus stands among us in His risen power, and He says, showing
His hands and His side, "Peace be unto you. All you have to do
is to receive my peace, on the basis of my death." And immediately He says to you, as soon as you receive His peace: "I
send you now, as the Father sent me, to tell what you have
received; and here is the power to tell it: Receive ye the Holy
Ghost."

Now, if you look in Acts 2, you will find that the same thought
is brought before us there. When they were all with one accord
in one place, "suddenly there came a sound from heaven as of a
rushing mighty wind." No, it is not "wind," it is "breath"
—that is the Greek word; "there came from heaven the sound as
of a rushing mighty breath, and it filled all the house where they
were sitting. . . . And they were all filled with the Holy Ghost."
Here is God breathing, breathing a rushing mighty torrent of
breath; and, in that torrent of breath, they are all filled.

Now, see what this means, and what it involves. The Lord
appears before us, to-night, as the same yesterday, and to-day,

and for ever. He shows us His pierced hands, He shows us the wounded side, and He says: "Peace be unto you. Pardon is free; death has brought life—will you have it? Atonement has brought pardon—will you have it?" You can be immediately reconciled to God, through the death of His Son, and you can have the peace of God, now, this moment, if you will receive His peace. Having received His peace, begin at once to tell others what a Saviour you have found. Recommend them to come to the same crucified but risen Christ, for the same peace. There is your commission. And where is your power? He inbreathes the Holy Spirit; He says, "Receive ye the Holy Ghost"; and now you are qualified for your great commission.

Now, we talk about the profound things of God, and they are very profound; but it is quite as marvellous that they are so simple. There is not a child that is able to understand anything, that cannot understand these three things. Here is a crucified Christ, who has borne your sins in His own body on the tree, and you may go and tell what you have found in Jesus; and here is the Lord saying, "All you have to do is to receive now the Spirit I impart, and you shall be qualified for your work."

What do you do in the act of breathing? Two things—you create a vacuum, and you fill the vacuum. You could not breathe in if you did not breathe out; the lungs must be emptied of air, before you can take in air. If you want the Holy Spirit, abandon every other dependence, and then appropriate the sufficiency. Now, what are the effects of breathing? The effects of breathing are very simple: they are comprehended in this—what is in the air outside comes into the lungs inside; and the same life-giving properties that are in the atmosphere are in you. You received the Holy Spirit; and here is the stupendous effect—the life which is in God becomes the life that is in you. You put the iron in the fire, and presently the fire is in the iron. The effect of putting the iron in the fire is, that that which is peculiar to the fire becomes peculiar to the iron. And the result of your receiving the Holy Spirit is briefly comprehended in this—that that which is peculiar to the Spirit becomes peculiar to your own spirit.

Take this thought and trace it through the New Testament. Take the Acts of the Apostles. There the atmosphere that enveloped them was the holy atmosphere of God; they breathed it, they were filled with it, they were qualified by it for all their activities. Go into the Epistle to the Romans, and there, in chapter 8 and verse 2, "The law of the Spirit of life in Christ Jesus hath made me free from the law of sin and death." This breath of God that comes into you is, first of all, the breath of life; and if you read Romans 8 through, you will find that in

the thirty-nine verses there are twenty-nine references to the
Holy Spirit. The Holy Spirit is there represented as the Spirit of
life, teaching you, like a little babe, to walk with God; teaching
you, like a little babe, to talk with God. For what is "Abba"?
It is the Arabic word for "Papa." And what is "Papa"? It is
the first infant prattle, which can only deal with consonants and
vowels that do not need teeth for their pronunciation. "Abba"
is "Papa"; it is the Holy Spirit taking the child into which He
has breathed life, and turning the child's attention to God; He
hears the child say "Papa", and the little one has learned the
dialect of heaven. As the Spirit teaches us to walk and to talk, He
directs our spiritual intelligence to the right objects. That is
spiritual-mindedness; and then the mind is fixed upon divine
things, just as an affectionate mother turns the growing intelligence of the child to the things that are best calculated to
awaken and nourish the finest order of thought and affection.

Now, if you turn to 1 Corinthians 6: 17, you read, "He that is
joined unto the Lord is one spirit." When you take in the breath
from the Lord Jesus Christ, His life passes into you, His Spirit
weds your spirit; and now you are bound to participate in His
nature—His Spirit is His nature. This, the wedlock of the divine
Spirit with the human spirit, is one of the most stupendous
conceptions presented to us in the Word of God. If you read the
Epistles to the Corinthians carefully you will see that the Spirit,
entering into us and wedding our spirit, is there treated as mould-
ing and shaping our whole spiritual life. So that we can, in our
measure, reflect the attributes of God—His wisdom in our
knowledge, His righteousness in our morality, His order in our
obedience to Him, His unselfishness in our service and love, His
sanctity in our holiness. It is all there in the two Epistles.

Now, when you go to the Epistle to the Galatians, what do you
find? That this Holy Spirit, which has become the Spirit of life
to you, as in Romans, and the Spirit of unity with God, as in
Corinthians, is the Spirit who fosters in you such holy desires that
the desires of the flesh are overcome. There is a remarkable
passage in chapter 5:

"The flesh lusteth against the Spirit, and the Spirit against the
flesh; and these are contrary the one to the other, so that ye may
not do the things" under the Spirit's influence, which you would
incline to do under the influence of the flesh—which I take to be
the idea. Isn't it stupendous that lust should be ascribed to the
Spirit? "The flesh lusteth against the Spirit, and the Spirit against
the flesh." Why, has the Spirit lusts? Certainly. What are lusts
but overmastering desires? The lusts of the flesh come up from
the lower realm and drag the man down; the lusts of the Spirit

come down from the higher realm, and draw the man up—that is the difference. What are the lusts of the Spirit?

Love, joy, peace—Godward; gentleness, goodness, long-suffering—manward; fidelity, meekness, humility—selfward. Love puts hate down, joy puts gloom down, peace puts discontentment down. These virtues are the Spirit's lusts, to quell the lower lusts. That is the way the Spirit masters the lower by the higher. So it is a wonderful revelation. You have the love of God in you, and you are one with God by the Spirit wedding your spirit; and now that Spirit frames in you desires like God's, these desires quell and expel the lower desires. And that is the secret of a holy walk with God.

Then you come to the Epistle to the Ephesians, and oh, stupendous mystery! we are there taught that the Spirit of God, received unto us, lifts us to God's level in the heavenlies. It is the climax of all revelations in the New Testament, about the fact of the Spirit taking possession. Look at it for a moment. You breathe the breath of the Holy Spirit imparted by Christ, and the life that God lives you live. You come to Corinthians, and see what God sees; in Galatians you love what God loves; in Ephesians you live on the level of God: and what is the effect? Why, you sway the sceptre that God sways, for, in the Epistle to the Ephesians, you have the grandest revelation of the power of a child of God. Look in chapter 6: "We wrestle not against flesh and blood, but against principalities, against powers, against the rulers of the darkness of this world, against wicked spirits in the heavenlies." And yet over these consummate foes by which we are encompassed, with Satan at the head—probably the grandest being God ever created, without exception—against all of these we clothe ourselves in the armour of God, and simply stand and defy them all. It is a remarkable conception—the life of God in me, so that I live as He lives; the wisdom of God in me, so that I see as He sees; the love of God in me, so that I desire what He desires; the victory of God in me, so that I win as He wins—that is the effect of the reception of the Holy Spirit.

We could follow it all through the New Testament, and show that there is not an Epistle which does not manifest to us some new and glorious revelation of what it is to have the Spirit possess us and control us. The life that is impossible to you in the natural man and the carnal man, becomes possible in the spiritual man. "The things which are impossible with man are possible with God," and "all things are possible to him that believeth." Do you know what the power of these spiritual lusts is, to control and subdue the lower?

I remember, as I stand here—it is twenty-seven years ago—that once, in Michigan, I and my three children were in the water over half an hour, in instant peril of drowning. One of those children with me in the water was the beloved one who fell asleep in India a year ago last November. She was a little child; and when she came out of the water and went home to her dear mother, who knew nothing about the peril until it was all over, she took pen and paper and with trembling hand, wrote: "God having saved me to-day from drowning, I give myself henceforth to Him." When, in India, she had almost died two days before she actually departed, a companion said to her, "Louise, you almost left us yesterday. If God had called you, would you have been glad?" "Oh! wouldn't I," she replied. The Spirit had awakened such desires after God, that when He called she leaped like a tired child into her Father's arms. The thought of her, and of that escape from imminent drowning twenty-seven years ago, almost overpowers me as I stand here. I cannot but feel that, as to you, my friends, I have risen from the dead. I have been spared twenty-seven years to make this address in Keswick to-night. I might have died then. (The whole gathering here broke into the singing of "Songs of praises I will ever give to Thee." Dr. Pierson continued):

Now, I want to make a practical application of the things that I have said to you, with trembling voice. I want you to realise what is means when Jesus stands among us, stretches forth His pierced hands, shows us His wounded side, and says, "Peace be unto you."

Do you know how abundantly God pardons? You remember how, a few years ago, when Adolf Beck was in prison because he was confounded with another man; you remember how, when his innocence was confirmed, the Government tried to make some amends for the disgrace and shame that had come to him and his family. I put it down as one of the most remarkable human illustrations of which I have ever read, of what God's forgiveness is. Mr. Beck received from His Majesty a free pardon, the effect of which is much greater than can be conveyed by the word "pardon" in its ordinary sense. This comes from the Home Secretary; and what does he say? Hear his words: "A free pardon issued by the King not only forgives crime, but wipes out the whole conviction, and obliterates every stain which the law had ever attached to the alleged offence." That is what God says to you now, as he offers you a free pardon—not only forgiveness, but something more: all that appertains to the past wiped out, every stain of guilt obliterated. Are you a sinner here to-night unforgiven? Jesus stands among us, in His risen power; and He says, Here is a free pardon for you, wiping out conviction, abolishing penalty and judgment, and obliterating every stain. What does the Lord say to us to-night about power? My beloved friends, if you will receive the Holy Ghost, power is yours. I do not care at all about your feelings; it is a fact, irrespective of your feelings.

In the days of what was called "the underground railway" in America, we used to get the poor fellows from the South away from slavery by secret means, hiding them in cellars and garrets, and conveying them at midnight across the land, from one hospitable house to another. A poor fellow had found his way to Canada. Blessed be God, when he stepped on English soil he became a free man. As the train moved on into Toronto, Harriet Tubman, herself an emancipated slave, who had helped hundreds of others to freedom, went in and saw the poor fellow crouching down in a corner, mortally afraid that some slave owner or slave catcher might be after him. "Joe, you fool," she said, "what are you cowering there for? You have shaken off the lion's paw; you are a free man on free soil. Praise the Lord, Joe!" And when we see some sinner who has accepted Jesus Christ, and has had this free pardon, crouching down and cowering as though he were in the power of the world, the flesh, and the devil, we feel like saying, "You fool, you have shaken off the lion's paw; you are a free man. Praise the Lord!" I want you, if you have accepted Jesus Christ, to cast your doubts away, to cast away all your fears, all your hesitation, and just to believe in your freedom, and to publish to the world your declaration of emancipation. Yes, beloved, Jesus is the same yesterday, and to-day, and for ever.

Did you hear the beautiful anecdote of my friend J. F. Stuart, President of the Christian Commission established to help soldiers in hospital or on the battlefield dying of their wounds, to find Jesus? He had permission to go within the lines. Once, at midnight, he appeared on the outskirts of the Union Army. The sentinel challenged him to give the password. "Washington," he replied. "Not correct, and my orders are to shoot every man who does not give the password." "Then let me go to headquarters and get the password; for I must have been misinformed." He was allowed to go, and came back: "Give the countersign," said the sentry. "Potomac." "Right, enter the lines." "And now," said Mr. Stuart to the sentry, "now that I have given you the right password, may I ask whether you have the right password to heaven?" "Oh yes, Mr. Stuart; it is, 'Jesus Christ, the same yesterday, and to-day, and for ever.'"

And so, beloved friends, I say to you to-night, He is the same Saviour that He was on the Lake of Galilee; He is the same Saviour that He was in the upper room amongst those disciples.

He has the same pierced hands and the same wounded side. He
offers the same invitation to receive a free pardon, to accept a
glorious commission, and to accept an adequate and all-sufficient
power. Will you receive Him? Will you live the life that He lived?
Will you know the truth that God knows? Will you love the
things that God loves? Will you get somewhere near God's own
level, and know something about the power which God sways?

THE FULNESS OF THE SPIRIT

Rev. Evan H. Hopkins

I BELIEVE that many have come with longing hearts, and with a definite purpose to know what it is to be filled with the Holy Ghost. Let me pass on to you, beloved, what the Lord has taught me upon that subject.

There are two simple questions that I want you to consider. The first is, How to be filled with the Spirit. And I would say:

I. *Recognise that you have the Spirit.* I do not say realise. You are not conscious, it may be, of that fact; but recognise that *you have the Spirit.* You say, Give me the Scripture. Well, look at 1 Corinthians 3: 16, "Know ye not that ye are the temple of God, and that the Spirit of God dwelleth in you?" Do not dishonour the Holy Ghost by failing to recognise the fact that you are indwelt by Him.

And notice three things: Who He is, where He is, and what you are in relation to Him. Who is He? He is the personal Holy Ghost; not a mere influence, but the Spirit of God, equal with the Father and the Son. Where is He? He "dwelleth in you." You say, "What an attainment! I suppose those Corinthian Christians had made a marvellous progress in the Christian life." What kind of Christians were these Corinthians? We have only to read this epistle to find that the majority of them were carnal Christians. "I could not speak unto you as unto spiritual, but as unto carnal, even as unto babes in Christ." And yet he says of them, "Know ye not that ye are the temple of God, and that the Spirit of God dwelleth in you?"—not that He dwelt in you once, years ago, but that He is in you now. Let us begin where God would have us begin: recognise that fact. It is a grand thing to stand upon God's facts.

What are you in relation to the Spirit? "Know ye not that ye are the temple of God"—a place appropriated, set apart, and marked out by God, in which the Spirit is to dwell. Now, may God the Holy Ghost bring us all to that point. Do not wait and say, "But I do not realise it. Let us have prayer that we may realise it." I do not say that at all. God begins with you just where you are; and you say, "I do not realise it." Well, begin by recognising it, upon the warrant of God's own Word.

461

The next point is:

II. *Put away from you every evil thing.* Take these passages and look at them; listen to the command, and obey it. For instance, in Ephesians 4: 25–31 we have this direct command, "Wherefore, putting away lying . . ." and so forth. What are the things to be put away? All untruthfulness, all evil tempers and dispositions, all dishonesty, all impurity of thought or word, all evil speaking. Remember that those are the things to be "put off"—not kept under, mark you. It is not a case of trying to keep them under and confessing them, and leaving them where they are. Some people think that when they have confessed their failures the thing is done, the matter is settled; but they do not put away the cause of their failures, and that is what God is commanding them to do.

You say, "But isn't that a very dangerous doctrine? Do you mean to say that they are, so to speak, absolutely separated from me, just like a man who takes off his coat and lays it on one side?" I *do*; that is the force of the command. But I like to remember another truth, namely, that while every man is born into the world with an evil *nature*, not one of us has been born into the world with an evil *habit*. Mark the distinction between evil habits and the evil nature. Read Ephesians 4 from verse 24 to the end, and observe that they are all evil habits. A habit? Why, of course it is something that you wear. Take off the habit, then; lay it aside.

We heard this morning about the sycamore tree, and it was taken to indicate an unforgiving spirit. It had to be rooted out, and evil habits have to be rooted out, absolutely rooted out. The Lord can do it.

Well, now, let me give you another passage, Colossians 3: 8, 9. Write it out and put it before you; not simply to criticise it, or to make a Bible reading of it. Let us take these passages, write them out, look at them, and do what God tells us to do. Another passage, 1 Peter 2: 1, says, "Laying aside all malice, and all guile, and hypocrisies, and envies, and all evil speakings": laying aside, getting separated from them. And you can put down James 1: 21. Mark also Hebrews 12: 1, "Lay aside every weight." Look at the weights. They are not sins necessarily; they may be quite lawful in themselves. I have no doubt that God's Holy Spirit is now speaking to you, and you say, "I suppose that thing is a weight." Yes, you know all about it; it *is* a weight; it *does* interfere with your progress and your growth. "Other people do it." Yes, but is it a weight, a hindrance to you? Lay it aside. "Well, I have been praying about it. I believe in progressive sanctification, and I am going to do it gradually." Ah, that wont do; this is not a gradual, but the instantaneous side of sanctification. If you lay aside a weight, it drops. There is let-go faith as well as lay-hold faith. I do not need to put my finger upon it; I want the Holy Spirit to do that. It may be that, at the end, some of you will be coming to ask whether there is any harm in this or that. I am not going to answer you. Settle it with God, and give Him the benefit of the doubt. Put away from you, therefore, *every evil thing*. You want the fulness of the Spirit. Well, now, this is God's way. We have to clear the way.

The next thing is to yield unreservedly every part of your being to Him—your thought, your habits of thought, your imagination. And your thoughts very much depend upon what you read. We get into habits of thinking, we get into grooves, we permit certain streams of thought to flow through us. Now, all this has to be changed. You cannot change these things yourself, but you can yield them all to God. Put your whole inner being into His hands—your thoughts, your desires, and your resolutions; put them all into His hands, to be preserved by Him, and to be ruled by Him, to be used by Him. You can yield at once. "Oh, but then I always thought that, if I have to be filled with the Spirit, I have to wait." Wait! wait for the Spirit? Where is the Spirit? He came down, at Pentecost, to the Church; He came to you when you were converted; He is in you to-night. Why should you wait for the Spirit, then? You can wait *on* the Spirit, but you have not to wait *for* the Spirit: He is here.

Then, I would put it this way—believe, in order to receive. You remember how, in Psalm 27: 13, it is said, "I had fainted, unless I had believed to see . . ." You believe, in order to see; and you have to believe in order to receive. What does it mean? Giving a reception to the Holy Ghost. He is not far off, He is close to you. You have not to wait for Him, but you have to wake up to the fact that He is God. You may never have really honoured Him as God, He who has a claim upon you, He whose place is the throne of your heart. Now, give Him a reception, a royal reception, to-night. Honour Him, and get down in the dust before Him; open the door of every chamber of your being; bring the keys of every department of your life, put them into His hands, and do not reserve anything. Oh, how often you have brought all, except one or two. You say, "Ah, but that is such a little chamber. It is only a little drawer, *I* want to keep back that key." You have never really, then, given Him the reception that is due to Him. He is your Proprietor; you are His property, and He wants to come and live in His home. You are His home, and He wants to walk through every part of your being, to possess you, rule you, satisfy you, and use you. Believe, I say, to receive, and let Him have His right place. When the answer comes, you will find that

it is *not so much an outpouring, as an infilling*, a welling up of the
fountain within you. You had the Spirit before, if you are a
believer. But now He fills you.

The next thing I would say is, Praise Him, thank Him, that He
has done it. You say, "But I don't realise it." God knows all
about that. It is delightful to realise, but He has given us something else, that is, faith. God says, "Now I give you believing
instead of feeling"—and you have to begin to believe that He
has done it. *Now* praise Him; go away from this tent praising
Him. By and by you will find that it begins to work, that it is a
reality.

That is the first question. Shall we now look at the other
question? *How to have rivers of living water flowing from us*—that is
the other side. What is this blessing? Oh, it is a far greater blessing than the first, because it is more blessed to give than to
receive. When the fulness begins to flow out, then you realise what
you could not realise before—a deeper joy, a clearer vision,
greater power and more courage. There is *believing to see*; there is
believing to receive. Now we come to that other side, *believing to
give*. I think many of us need to have that emphasised. "He that
believeth on me, as the Scripture hath said, out of him shall flow
rivers of living water." It is very beautiful, when we look at the
original. "He that is putting faith in me," points to a continuous
believing condition of the soul. It is not, "he that believed on me
when he was converted"; not "he that believed on me when he
entered into eternal life"; but it is, "he that is believing on me
now"—just as you are breathing now, and will keep on breathing
while you continue this natural life. You must be a definite
believer for the stream to flow out of you. There are a hundred and
one things that seem to be against this practical outlook on life.
That is just where faith comes in. The Spirit's outflowing needs
believing on our part, just as much as the Spirit's inflowing.

My last thought is this—

III. *That the fulness of the Spirit does not dispense with the trial and
the exercise of faith.* Faith is not now replaced by feeling. The soul
that is filled with the Holy Ghost does not *feel* full; there is no
self-sufficiency. You may think it will be a very easy thing for you
to come out when you have the fulness of the Holy Ghost. But it
will not be an easy thing to come out, *apart from faith*—that is the
point. And it must be without feeling, again. Right along
throughout the whole life there will be the testing, there will be
the trial of faith, and there will be the need of the perpetual
exercise of faith just as at present, only on another level. Many
of us are thinking, "If I get the fulness of the Spirit, I shall have
plenty of power, plenty of wisdom, plenty of knowledge, and I

shall have a very easy time." Well, the full life *is* the easy life. "My yoke is easy." But it cannot be apart from the exercise of faith. Ease comes by believing, and by having your own emptiness met by His fulness.

You have an impression, too, that if you only get this full life, you will not need to be so vigilant and prayerful, or to be looking up for power. Well, look at Acts 4. Here were men, after Pentecost, who had been filled with the Holy Ghost; but how childlike and dependent they are, how conscious of their own nothingness and weakness! "And now, Lord, behold their threatenings; and grant unto Thy servants that with all boldness they may speak Thy word, by stretching forth Thy hand to heal; and that signs and wonders may be done in the name of Thy holy Child Jesus. And when they had prayed, the place was shaken where they were assembled together; and they were all filled with the Holy Ghost, and they spake the word of God with boldness." You see how weak, how conscious of their nothingness, how utterly dependent they were upon the Lord, after Pentecost; how they had to pray, how they had to exercise faith, how they realised the power of the Name, and how conscious they were that, apart from God, they must fail.

And this will be your experience and mine, right on to the end. But, oh, to know that God is here and in us, that we have the fulness of God! You see the paradox—"As having nothing, and yet possessing all things," God's strength being made perfect in our weakness. Do not say, "I am waiting to feel full, to have an experience that is to thrill my physical being, and that shall correspond to the experience of some others of whom I have heard, and then I shall be equipped." No, it is by faith. Believe! And if the cleansing, and the separation from things that hinder have been right up to the light that you now have, then the Holy Ghost *has* come—He *has* possessed you; and we will go forth and praise Him, trusting Him to use us.

THE SECRETS OF POWER

Rev. G. Campbell Morgan, D.D.

L ET ME remind you, in the briefest way, of the general scope of
our study. We have been considering the letter of Paul to
Philemon, attempting to learn its *essential message*, in order
that we may hear its *abiding appeal*. In this consideration of its
essential message we have seen that its central teaching for us
consists of the pictures it gives us of Christianity in its outworking.

I remind you of what we said by way of introduction, as to the
relation of this letter to three others, viz., those to the Ephesians,
the Philippians, and the Colossians—the four constituting the
letters of the first imprisonment. I suggested at the commencement that the letter to Philemon was written, if I may put it
that way, in the atmosphere of the other three. The great truths
which the apostle was writing in the three are illustrated in the
one. Incidentally, during that imprisonment Onesimus came,
was begotten of the apostle in his bonds, was sent back to Philemon with this letter; and through the letter I see the values of the
great things taught in the other epistles.

I want, then, briefly and in outline only, to speak of *the abiding
appeal* of the letter. If its central teaching consists of the pictures
it presents of Christianity in its outworking, its abiding appeal is
that of *its revelation of the power of Christ* in the inworking of that
power.

The appeal of the letter is implied rather than declared. It is
so peculiarly local. It had to do with this one man, these two men,
and the groups surrounding them: and I think all of us have felt
how powerful the appeal of the letter is to us. I repeat, however,
that it is implied rather than definitely stated. The pictures of
these individual Christian men, and the pictures of them in their
relationships with each other, and that final picture of the whole
Church, interested and co-operative—these pictures in themselves create an appeal to our own hearts. The supreme revelation is that of the power of Christ. That is the revelation which we
have as we look at Paul revealed in this letter; at Philemon as here
seen; and in that wonderful change in Onesimus, in which he
became no longer the unprofitable, but the well-profitable. It

is the power of Christ which is the supreme matter. To those, therefore, who share the life of Christ, these pictures call; and their call is surely to abandonment of that life, that like results may follow.

In conversation with some, in the intervals between these meetings, we have said to one another, "Yes, we have seen the glory of all this in these men; but the glory as we have seen it in them has been a revelation to us of our own shortcoming and our own failure in many of these respects." It is in that sense that the pictures of these men must make an appeal to our hearts. Paul triumphing over circumstances in his fellowship with Jesus Christ; triumphing over the mere right of a true authority in the power of love; triumphing over high and holy inclination in the interest of the Gospel, in a yet higher motive of desire and determination to serve Philemon: we have seen these things; and as we have seen them our hearts have cried out after the realisation of them.

I want to speak to you quite frankly, and—if I may put it this way—as a witness, rather than an advocate. My own recent study of this one-page letter produced at first in my heart the feeling almost of despair. As my own life came into contrast with the lives of these men as revealed in this letter, one was constrained to cry out in this regard also, "Who is sufficient for these things?" Yet, beloved, the answer to such an enquiry is already in your hearts; and all I desire to do is to take you back again to the things with which you are so familiar. Believing as I do that this letter was written in the mental mood, shall I say, of Ephesians, Philippians, and Colossians, I but remind you that in them we have revealed the secrets by which we also may triumph as these triumphed. In these writings we have the revelation of that power whereby we also may be changed from the unprofitable to the well-profitable life. In these we find the secret of that inner life which consists, as to its root-principle, in faith toward the Lord Jesus Christ, and, in its ultimate expression, in love to Him and to all the saints. In these are the secrets. Therefore what we need in order to hear the appeal of the letter, is to be conversant with the teaching of these *three* letters.

You will immediately see that all that can be done this morning is to remind ourselves of their general message to us; of their general revelation. I think that the best way to do that is to take from these three letters what I would suggest to be, in certain applications at least, the central words of appeal. Let us turn to these. Before doing so, let me now say that if the Holy Spirit this morning may bring to us a real vision of our resources as revealed in these epistles, instead of going away presently feeling that we have not attained to the level of these men, and that we cannot, we shall go away overwhelmed with the infinite resources at our immediate disposal in Christ Jesus. That seems to me to be the great value of this line of study. I bring you this morning into the presence of a veritable ocean of resources, so that whatever the lack, it is answered immediately and overwhelmingly in the provision that is made. When we look at these truths we do not wonder that Paul was such a man as he was: we wonder that we have failed at all!

The three verses, then, that I shall direct your attention to in the epistles are these very old and familiar ones. First in Ephesians 5: 18, "Be not drunken with wine, wherein is riot, but be filled with the Spirit." Then turning to Philippians 2: 5, "Have this mind in you, which was also in Christ Jesus." Turn on to Colossians 3: 16, "Let the word of Christ dwell in you richly in all wisdom."

I said a moment ago that these are the old and familiar central words of these three letters. We come back to them not so much for exposition, as for careful meditation, and an attempt to grasp their significance in the light of their context. I should like to say this also, before looking a little more closely at them. I suggest to you that the central one—that is, the one in the Philippian letter—is the one that no man can obey by trying. "Have this mind in you, which was also in Christ Jesus." It is the impossible word of the three, hardly indicating responsibility, although stated in such form as to reveal responsibility. But we must not begin there. The other two, I think, do reveal our personal and individual responsibility. "Be filled with the Spirit." "Let the word of Christ dwell in you richly." In proportion as we are obedient to these two injunctions, we are obedient to the central injunction. In proportion as we know what it is in truth to be filled with the Spirit, and that the word of Christ shall dwell in us richly, in that proportion, all unconsciously as to effort and endeavour, and I think to our growing amazement, we shall have the mind of Christ.

I do not think it would be quite fair to apply my illustration too far, but I suggest to you that there is here this thought at least concerning our relation to the Lord, the thought of Spirit, of mind, of consciousness, and of body in some sense. "Be filled with the Spirit," the Spirit of Christ. "Let the word"—and the Word was incarnate, and the fulness dwelt in Him corporeally—"let the word of Christ dwell in you richly." With what result? Where we are in true fellowship with these two facts of our Lord's Person, we have the mind of Christ; there is a natural result. Therefore let us turn to these verses and notice two or three things generally concerning them again.

Take the Ephesian letter and the word there, "Be filled with the Spirit." Let us remember that the word was addressed to the saints—you find that in the opening words of the letter. The word in Philippians, "Have this mind in you," was addressed to the saints. The word in Colossians, "Let the word of Christ dwell in you richly," was addressed to the saints. That is to be remembered at the outset, that these great words are not words addressed to those who have no relationship with Christ; they are words to the saints. With that I shall not further deal, but ask you to bear it in mind.

Now take this first word, "Be filled with the Spirit." It must be interpreted, I say, in the light of the context, in the light of the whole message of the letter to the Ephesians. The letter has very many values and applications with which I am not dealing now, but I would summarise it by saying that in the letter the apostle was dealing with the heavenly calling of the Christian Church, and with the application of that truth to the earthly conduct of the Christian Church. You remember the bare outline of the letter, how it is naturally divided by the injunction at the commencement of chapter 4, "I therefore, the prisoner in the Lord, beseech you to walk worthily of the calling wherewith ye were called." I would myself like to keep the word "vocation" there in some senses—"the vocation wherewith ye were called." That vocation has been revealed in the first three chapters, and the "walk worthily" is revealed in the second of the three chapters.

In the first three chapters the apostle deals with the predestination of the Church; with its edification, or building, by God in the processes of time; and reveals that wonderful and over-whelming glory of its ultimate vocation, the vocation that stretches far out beyond these changing scenes of time—the eternal vocation. All this is dealt with in the first part of the letter. Turning from that, he begins to show what the earthly conduct of people who have this calling ought to be. In the first half he impresses upon us the truth that the Church is other-worldly; in the second half he shows the effect that will have upon the activity of the Church here in this world, and during the period of her tarrying here.

In view of these things—the ultimate heavenly glory and the present earthly conduct—this is the central word, revealing the all-sufficient power of those who are thus called, and who are thus to behave: and the all-sufficient power is this, that they be filled with the Spirit. Now as I said a moment ago, we are in the presence of a great ocean of resources. I just select now from the letter only those things that help, as I think, to interpret the real value of that word, "Be filled with the Spirit." Let us read the references relating directly to the work of the Spirit, as they appear in this letter. There are nine of them. I do not mean to say there are no other references to the Spirit, but there are nine revealing very distinctly the relation of the believer to the Spirit and the Spirit to the believer, as to our life and work. The first—and I must not stay with the context—is found in 1: 13–14, "In whom, having also believed, ye were sealed with the Holy Spirit of promise, which *sealing* is an earnest of our inheritance, unto the redemption of God's *own* possession, unto the praise of His glory." Let us take out of that rich statement this one thought, "sealed with the Holy Spirit."

I turn to the second chapter, verse 18, "For through Him we both have one access in one Spirit unto the Father." The second word taken out of the whole truth is this, "access in one Spirit unto the Father."

In verse 22 of the chapter I read, "In whom ye also"—of course he is writing to the Ephesians—"are building together for a habitation of God in the Spirit." I take out this, "habitation of God in the Spirit."

Passing on to the third chapter, in verse 16, in that wonderful prayer of the apostle, I find these words, "That He would grant you, according to the riches of His glory, that ye may be strengthened with power through His Spirit in the inward man; that Christ may dwell in your hearts through faith." Out of that whole statement, take this as the simple word now to be noted, "Strengthened with power through His Spirit."

Coming to the fourth chapter, I read, "I therefore, the prisoner in the Lord, beseech you to walk worthily of the calling wherewith ye were called, with all lowliness and meekness, with longsuffering, forbearing one another in love; giving diligence to keep the unity of the Spirit in the bond of peace." "The unity of the Spirit."

Those passages indicate the privileges of our life in relation to the Spirit. Now we have these revealing our responsibilities. Mark them carefully. In 4: 30, "Grieve not the Holy Spirit of God, in whom ye were sealed unto the day of redemption." In 5: 18, "Be not drunken with wine, wherein is riot, but be filled with the Spirit." In 6: 17, "And take the helmet of salvation, and the sword of the Spirit." And in verse 18, "Praying at all seasons in the Spirit."

Now, my brethren, if the reading of those passages shall bring to your mind the consciousness that I am facing, or asking you to face, a theme all too large to be dealt with, well, that is exactly all I hope to do! But now mark this thing. The central word, I suggest, is this: "Be filled with the Spirit." Now interpret that by the general teaching of this letter on the subject of the Spirit. I turn aside from the teaching of the letter in other respects. What do I learn from this letter concerning the Spirit and my relationship to the Spirit as a child of God? First, that I am sealed by the Spirit. That is the sign and symbol of property—that I belong absolutely to God. That is the first thing. That sealing takes place in the very moment and act of regeneration. It is God's answer to belief: when we believe we are born of the Spirit, and in that fact sealed by the Spirit as the property, the possession of God. And that sealing is the earnest of my inheritance. You know the significance of the word "earnest" there.

Now is that all? No. If you are reading the context mentally as I am going on, you know that the apostle is dealing with these people and showing how they have been brought into union with Hebrew Christians, so that the two have been made one; and gradually he is leading up to that little statement about the unity of the Spirit. But what next? "We both have our access in one Spirit unto the Father." The Spirit seals us the property of God, but by the Spirit we are brought to the Father, into an actual, personal, immediate relation with the Father. By the operation of that Spirit we become the dwelling-place of God in the Spirit. I think the thought is an ultimate one, the completion of the whole Church; but it has its immediate application. Yes, let me put it this way: through the Spirit we have access to God, and He has access to us. We become the dwelling-place of God through the Spirit.

Then the apostolic prayer reveals a possibility. We are strengthened with power through the Spirit. And in order to the full understanding of our privileges we are to keep the unity of the Spirit, i.e., to keep in mind, to keep in view—not to keep in the sense of guarding or garrisoning; not that we are to defend it, but that we are to recognise it, to know it, to be conscious of it, to live in the power of it. It is not the uniformity of the body, which matters little; not the unanimity of the mind, thinking of the mind as of mere human conviction and opinion. These things have changed and varied. It is the unity of the Spirit, which has never been destroyed nor can be. We fail when we fail to keep that in view; but that is the ultimate thought.

Now glance once more over the ground. What is this? Sealed by the Spirit as belonging to God; through the Spirit having access to God immediately; by that Spirit God having access to us, to work in us to will and to do of His good pleasure—that is the thought; so strengthened with power or might by that Spirit, and each individual forming part of that great whole of the Church, so that the whole life of the Church is ministering to the life of the one, and the life of the one is making its contribution to the well-being of all; and all this through the Spirit.

Now that is almost mechanical. Oh that the wind, the very Spirit of God, may breathe upon the thing until we see all that it suggests! If we do, we shall see that all that these men were, surely we also can be, if these resources are at our disposal in Christ.

What, then, are our responsibilities? "Grieve not the Holy Spirit." May I translate that, "Cause not sorrow to the Spirit of God," for that really is the thought of it. It is the revelation of the tender, brooding love of our Father, in and through His Spirit, and of the fact that we can grieve Him. It does not mean *vex*, in our sense of the word sometimes, which is only another word for an evil temper; but "do not cause sorrow to . . ." That is our first responsibility; and the final passion for holiness is a desire not to grieve the heart of God. "Grieve not the Holy Spirit." Have such a sense of His love that is tender and compassionate, and that is wounded and capable of pain in the presence of our failure—have such a sense of that, as not to grieve Him. "Be filled with the Spirit" is the central word for interpretation.

One would like to go back to other passages, but I am not going! The figures of speech have been made use of on this platform, and in this great Keswick Convention for many years, that I think you are very familiar with them. Are you a child of God? Then you have the Spirit. But, alas, we know the difference between the life born of the Spirit—a spiritual life, and yet not filled with the Spirit—and the life that *is* filled with the Spirit. And the responsibility is always upon ourselves and never upon God. The filling of the Spirit is a continuous matter, a constant inflow and a constant outflow: the vessel filled by the inrush, and serving by the outflow. But for reasons which we know in our hearts, and which it is not mine to deal with in this Bible Reading, we are away from the source, away from the inrush of the stream; never losing the Spirit, if we are the children of God, but losing the fulness, losing the joy, losing the power, losing the influence. Yet we may be perpetually full, always being filled, and always overflowing. That is the privilege and responsibility of the child of God.

Then with regard to the conflict, "Taking the sword of the Spirit, which is the Word of God." And may I, in a parenthesis, say, "always remembering that the Word of God is only valuable as we remember that it is the sword of the Spirit." If the Word of God be only *my* sword, I cannot use it; but if I remember that it is the sword of the Spirit, and that the Spirit makes use of no other offensive weapon in our great warfare than this, then I shall know the value of it, and shall use it.

Finally, "Praying in the Spirit." I must repeat the thing that is in my mind. This outline is altogether too hurried, but my hope is that especially some of my younger brethren and sisters will take this letter and, leaving the larger teaching, follow that line; and remember that all these were the things in the mind of Paul, and especially in the experience of Paul, when he wrote that letter, and triumphed as he did. He did it through the power of the Spirit, that Spirit through whom he had access to the Father, through whom God had access to him, who was in him the very power of God. By that Spirit the triumph was wrought.

Beloved, that Spirit is not only at our disposal, if we are Christian men and women: He is our indweller. Do we halt and say, "Yes, but——" Well, let us settle that "Yes, but" between ourselves and God. If we know the thing that comes after that "but," that is the thing we are responsible for removing, in order that there may be the inflowing of His Spirit through His Word.

Then I propose to turn to the Colossian Epistle for a moment, and again only to suggest a line for future consideration. In 3: 16, "Let the word of Christ dwell in you richly in all wisdom." That was addressed to the saints; and I think we must remember that it was written to these Colossian Christians in view of the truth concerning the fulness of Christ and the filling of the Church in Christ, that being the great theme of the letter. May we not summarise the letter by citation of these words: "For it was the good pleasure of the Father that in Him should all the fulness dwell;" and "in Him ye are made full." He was not *made* full; in Him the fulness *dwelt*. We are made full in Him. Now in view of that truth the central word is this, "Let the word of Christ dwell in you richly." But what does the apostle mean by "the word of Christ"? I suggest that this must be interpreted by what, for lack of a better word, I will describe as the Christology of the Colossian letter. That is "the word of Christ." As Christ Himself is the Word of God, so here, for our reading and our understanding of Christ Himself, we have "the word of Christ." Is there anything more wonderful in the whole New Testament than the presentation of Christ that we have in the Colossian letter?

As to His Person, there is that passage so full of wonder in 1: 15-19. I am afraid one must not stay to speak of it. I only remind you of it, and ask you to meditate upon it. "Who"—the reference is to Christ, according to the context—"is the image of the invisible God, the firstborn of all creation." So he runs on. Summarise the passage: as to God, "the image of the invisible";

as to creation, "firstborn," sustainer of it; as to the Church—mark the difference—"firstborn from the dead." A more wonderful thing even than the fact that He is creator and sustainer of all creation, is the fact that He is the Head of the Church, which is His body; and He is that because He is "firstborn from the dead." That is the word of Christ, the fact concerning Christ, the truth about Christ. The truth massed by the apostle in this wonderful sentence all has to do with His Person. And then immediately following there is the purpose, as he goes on in verse 20, "Through Him to reconcile all things unto Himself." There we have a passage—I will only speak to myself—altogether too high and too profound for final exposition, concerning the reconciling work of the Lord.

Then the apostle moves on to make the application; and you have the teaching in Colossians of the threefold mystery. There is first the mystery of the Church. Then he passes within, the mystery "which is Christ in you, the hope of glory." And a little further on he comes to the central thing, the mystery which is Christ. You notice the relation of these three things, beginning with the whole Church, the mystery of the Church, the fact that the Church is a mystery—something hidden from ages, but now revealed. And what is this Church? If you want to know, take the mystery that lies within it, "Christ in you," in the individual, so that the Church consists of all those of whom it is true that the Christ is in them the hope of glory. But in that statement is a profounder mystery. What is that mystery? Christ Himself. What is the mystery of Christ Himself? "Image of God," "Firstborn of creation," "Firstborn from the dead," "The word of Christ," and that Christ in the individual, and those individuals constituting the whole Church: let that word dwell in you richly. Let it be more than intellectual apprehension; let it be volitional inspiration, and mastery; and all that God wills for us will then be realised by us.

Remember now, that presents to us the all-sufficient provision for our realisation of the purpose of God. The all-sufficient provision is Christ; the all-sufficient power is the word of Christ, as in us by the Spirit. That Christ presented in the Colossian letter, the word of whom we have heard and believed, is administered and realised within us by the Spirit of God. Then how dare we say, "Who is sufficient for these things?" The answer is patent—Christ is sufficient for these things; Christ by the Spirit in us is sufficient for these things; and when Christ is in us by the Spirit, and has full right of way within us, we are sufficient for these things. Or, in the language of the apostle, "I can do all things through Christ which strengtheneth me."

I turn for a brief moment, then, to the Philippian central word, realising, as I said at the commencement, that this is the outcome of our obedience to the responsibilities suggested in the other two. "Have this mind in you, which was also in Christ Jesus." Again it is addressed to the saints, as the first verse shows us. It was spoken in view of the fulness of life, and fulness of joy, at the disposal of the believer in Christ; revealing the all-sufficient power —the Spirit; the all-sufficient provision, the Christ Himself; and now the perfect pattern.

How are we to interpret this word of the apostle, "Have this mind in you, which was also in Christ Jesus"? Here is the next thing, the sublimest, in some senses, of all, of which there can be no doubt, for he immediately goes on, "Who, being in the form of God . . ." Then you have that wonderful unveiling that follows, not now to be dealt with in detail, but to be glanced at. Will you notice three things here—and oh, let us do it solemnly, putting off our shoes from our feet, for surely this is holy ground, to come even to read these inspired revelations of the mind of Christ. We have the mind of Christ revealed in its attitude in verse 6. We have the mind of Christ revealed in the activity which results, in verses 7–8; and we have the mind of Christ revealed in the authority which is consequent upon that activity, in verses 10–11.

Reverently, then, let us observe first the attitude of mind described: "Who, being in the form of God, counted it not a prize to be on an equality with God." That is a passage admittedly, I think, somewhat difficult of expression in our tongue. May I venture this as an interpretation, not a translation: "Who, being in the form of God, did not count that as something to be snatched at and held for self-enrichment; did not count His high, eternal, inherent dignity something to be held for Himself." Oh, infinite is the mystery, and the light is too bright for the feebleness of a sinner's sight! That attitude of mind—how can I understand it? Only in the measure in which I follow the activity resulting; and that you have in the verses following: "But emptied Himself . . ."

I confess that in reading this passage I am reluctant to touch upon anything that sounds like theological controversy. Yet at the same time, this passage has been the scene of so much false teaching concerning our Lord that I do think it is important that we pause, as we go through, to observe this, that from beginning to end the person is the same. Whoever the person is here referred to in the first place, that person persists through all the processes. He "emptied Himself," but that does not mean that He ceased to be Himself in any sense. He did not cease to be Himself when

He stooped, when He came to this amazing level to which we shall reverently follow Him. He "emptied Himself"; and I think the next verse explains that—"taking the form of a servant." Put that back in relation to the earlier phrase of the original position: "Being in the form of God . . . emptied Himself . . . taking the form of a servant." The change was from one method of manifestation to another method of manifestation; from that of sovereignty to subjection, from that of essential Deity which could not be revealed to men, to that of service in communion with humanity, through which human eyes might see what otherwise could not be seen. But the Person is unchanged. Or briefly, Christ did not divest Himself of Deity when He stooped. He emptied Himself of one form of manifestation, taking another. And what form of service did He take? Not that of angels. "Being made in the likeness of men." Brethren, we can read it, and re-read it, and we ought to; and ponder it, and bow in the presence of it. We can never grasp it; at least, I think not. The stoop is infinite.

Yet follow. "Being found in fashion as a man, He humbled Himself, becoming obedient even unto death." He went lower than the necessity of essential, pure humanity, in which there is no place for death. Humanity apart from sin should have known nothing of death. Metamorphosis, change, transfiguration—that is the word by which ideal humanity in the economy of God would have passed from the preparatory stage to the higher stage beyond; and our Lord's life in that sense reached its consummation in the Mount of Transfiguration. But He "became obedient unto death," for which there was no place in His life so far as His holy Personality was concerned.

Then that one phrase, "the death of the cross." I love increasingly the holy, reverent reticence of these New Testament writers, as Matthew, "There they crucified Him"; and I dislike growingly all pictures of this crucifixion, and all attempts to deal with details. "The death of the cross."

And with that issue? "Wherefore"—It is a very human thing to say, but it always seems to me that the apostle, overwhelmed, and hardly able to write, breaks away from the process to the issue: "Wherefore also God highly exalted Him, and gave unto Him the name which is above every name; that in the name of Jesus every knee should bow, of things in heaven and things on earth and things under the earth, and that every tongue should confess that Jesus Christ is Lord, to the glory of God the Father."

"Have this mind in you." How? "Be filled with the Spirit." "Let the word of Christ dwell in you richly." And do not evermore be trying to find out whether you have the mind of Christ; the people you live with will find that out!

Well, beloved, what is the final thing? A return to that which is pre-eminently practical that this little letter to Philemon says to us. I think it says this, first of all. It teaches Christian workers to-day that evil things in human life are to be dealt with by the transfiguration of individual Christian lives; that all social wrongs are to be put an end to by changing of men. Our business is for evermore to be finding Onesimus; and our greatest work is expressed if we are able to say, "I have begotten Onesimus," *i.e.*, in the leading of individual men into right relationships with Christ. In the training of such men for true life in the world, we are making our contribution, and the only contribution that can be made toward the bringing in of the Kingdom of God.

These two other practical words came to my heart from the letter; first, this relationship with Christ transfigures all other relationships. You say there is a sense in which there is very little application here, because slavery is done away? Well, will you rather please to say that it ought to be done away, and meditate that sentence of mine when this service is over! At any rate, remember this, that the Christian man and the Christian woman, truly Christian, have their relationship changed to their servants, to their masters. There is no single relationship of human life, either that of blood, or of household responsibility, or of commercial life, that ought not to be changed entirely in the case of men and women who are related to Jesus Christ. I am not going to deal with details of application: it is the principle I am after.

Now turning that round, our relationship to Christ is tested by other men by our relationship to them. It is not the thing I tell my boys they ought to be, that approves my Christianity; it is what I am to them. If Paul had instructed Onesimus according to the law of Christ, and had himself contradicted it, that would have been the supreme blasphemy. You agree? Then so also is it with us. Unless we know what it is to have the life changed by this power of Christ, we can bear no powerful testimony to the power of Christ.

But let the very last word be on the positive side, for the cheer and help of such as have seen something of the vision, and are almost afraid in the presence of it. Beloved, all this is ours. If we will but appropriate by faith and by entire dedication, we also may become the Lord's Onesimi, Philemons, yea, Pauls, so far as all these were Christ-men, mastered and held by the Lord Himself.

CHRISTIAN LIFE AND CHRISTIAN LIVING

Rev. W. Y. Fullerton

IN these morning meetings, which I share alternately with
Canon Joynt, it is our purpose to take, as the continuous
subject, Roman 5–8, one chapter each day. Neither of us will
pretend to give a full exposition of the whole chapter. Indeed,
the purpose is not so much expository as to open out the Christian
experience that lies behind the doctrine of these chapters. What
we shall try to say—I think I speak for my brother as well as
myself—is the message peculiar to this place, the distinguishing
message of Keswick. If we can find the message for which this
tent is more particularly identified, in this great imperial epistle,
where, if anywhere, the doctrine of the Church is set forth in
ordered sequence; and if we find that what is known generally
as the Keswick message is altogether Pauline, I think that any
criticism that may arise in the heart of any who have come here,
perhaps, for the first time, may at once be stilled. If the doctrine
is not Pauline, I for one do not want to have anything to do with
it.

There are some of my friends who, when I speak to them at
other places, say, "We can get the blessing of Christ at home, as
well as at Keswick; there is no need to go there for it." To that,
of course, I gladly assent. Thank God, the fulness of grace can be
received anywhere. But then, while I give a whole-hearted assent
to that, I always follow it with another proposition, and that is
that you can get the blessing at Keswick, too! It is too late for you
and me to question whether we are to be at Keswick or elsewhere.
The command, of course, is for the present moment; and we are
here. Let us abandon ourselves to the Spirit of God, then. Let us
open our minds to the truth of Christ as it shall be set forth in
these words, written by the Spirit long ago for our instruction and
edification.

We begin at chapter 5. The previous chapters have opened up
the sin of man, the failure of man, and God's great way of redemption. The subject of sanctification does not begin until the
sixth chapter, but we are in the region of experience in the fifth.
Now, we should all remember, and always remember, that
behind every great doctrine of the Bible lies an experience; that

behind every great word of the New Testament there lies an experience. If you meet with the phrase "justification," do not think it is a mere philosophic term; it is a word that is chosen by the apostle, under the guidance of the Spirit, to express something that he, in the deepest recesses of his nature, has experienced.

Our subject in this fifth chapter is Christian life and Christian living. You see, they are not quite synonymous. Of course, the whole includes the part; but sometimes we forget it. Now, Christian life is the whole, and Christian living the part. It is Christian life that is opened to us in this chapter; it is not something exceptional or abnormal; it is not something reserved for a select few; it is not the higher Christian life; it is just Christian life; and anything that is different is something else, or something less. What you and I want is not something exceptional; we want to know what Christian life is, and what Christian living may be; and then we want to go out recognising the life, and living it.

If you open the chapter and read it through, the thing that I think will inevitably occur to you will be that the Christian life is an abundant thing. Again and again you have it, "Much more"; "not only so . . ." The first thing about the Christian life, therefore, the foundation thing and the crowning thing, is this: *it is a life of God's grace.* You have that in many a verse. At the end of the chapter, in verse 20, you have, "Grace did much more abound"; and in verse 2, "The grace wherein we stand." If you are an accurate thinker, you will see that the word "grace" is used in two senses, just as the word "Keswick" is used in two senses. I find that some of my friends take a ticket to Keswick; and then you come to what you call a "Keswick." You use the word with a double meaning. Now, grace is the thing God gives us, and grace is the effect of the thing God gives us; and the Christian life is a life of grace. A great French preacher said long ago that for the supreme moment when God meets the soul of man, a new word is necessary; and that new word has been found: it is "grace." A distinguished English preacher, now with the Lord, said that the world never discovered the great word grace. It is a foreign language; it is the speech of infinite love.

That is exactly it: "grace" is the speech of love. A love that looks up is adoration; love that is level is affection; but love that descends is grace. As a friend of mine well says, "Grace is love out-loving love." That is Christian life; the Christian life of grace. It begins with grace; it continues with grace; it ends with grace. My friends sometimes tell me that we are going to be awarded our place in heaven according to our works. Well, our works may be some guide to it, but when you get your glory it will be grace still. You begin with grace, without any desert on

your part; and you will never have any desert. What you know of
God is of grace; if you learn any more it will be of grace. Because
you have grace, you will get more grace. It is one of the finest
arguments possible—I have often been compelled to use it before
God—that if God has given me grace, that is the great reason why
He should give me more, else all grace of the past will be lost,
for I cannot continue for ten minutes if God refuse me grace now.
If He has given me grace these years, I may plead with Him to
give me grace still.

The Christian life is a life of grace. The man who once gets a
conception of what God's grace is, will find that all differences in
rank and position and station will disappear. The great sinner
here this morning and the respectable sinner are alike—they
need grace. Some men may know more than I; some men may
have a better position that I have; some men may have a greater
capacity than I; but this man, and that man, and the other, all
need grace. We are on the same level; and there can be no class
or caste in the Christian Church when we are under grace, for
grace is such a great thing that there can be no difference between
those who receive it. The Christian life, then, is a life of grace.

The next thing, if you read the chapter, is that the Christian
life is *a life of faith*. On God's side it is grace, on my side it is faith.
"Being justified by faith." Of course, that is a necessary corollary
of the other. Thank God, the only thing that can receive grace is
faith. I cannot receive grace by my works, or by my experience;
it must be just faith. God shows His grace, and I believe it;
God gives His grace, and I accept it.

What is faith? Now you ask one of those very simple questions
that is exceedingly difficult to answer. It is so difficult, that in
the whole of the New Testament there is no definition of faith.
It is one of those axioms, a thing taken for granted. You are,
indeed, told in one place what faith does; you are told what is the
effect—"Faith is the substance of things hoped for, the proof of
things not seen." That is not a definition, but a description. The
only place that I know of where there is an attempt at a definition
is in the Apocrypha, in a very beautiful passage in the book of
Ecclesiasticus, where it says that "the love of God passeth all
things for illumination, and the fear of the Lord is the beginning
of His love; and faith is the beginning of cleaving unto Him."
You cannot better that: "Faith is the beginning of cleaving unto
the Lord." Now test yourself. Have you that faith? Have you
received that grace? You will never make an advance in Christian
living unless you start right. You will never be able to build your
building unless you lay a true foundation. The foundation is
grace, and the first course is faith.

There are two great objective realities around which grace and faith gather. If you read the chapter you will find constantly recurring "the One," the one Man Jesus Christ. Why, that is how grace comes to us. "Grace and truth came by Jesus Christ." The Christian life is a life that has Christ as its centre and Christ as its fulfilment. "In due time Christ died." He came at the right moment. "He was raised again for our justification." It is on the fact of Christ we build. I know there are people today who say it does not matter about the historic Jesus; the great thing is Christ in the heart. Now it is impossible for you or me to live the Christian life without believing in the historic Jesus. I believe that Jesus was born into this world, lived in this world, died here for my sin, and was raised from the dead. I have no difficulty in believing that He came into the world in an extraordinary way when I find that He went out in an extraordinary way. Our faith is built on the fact of Jesus Christ.

But there is another objective reality. Once in this chapter, and for the first time in this Epistle, and not again until you come to chapter 8, do you find mention of the Holy Ghost. It is a sort of side issue; it is a thing that is just mentioned incidentally, in verse 5, where we read about "the love of God shed abroad in our hearts by the Holy Ghost, which is given unto us." That is another fact. Christ died and rose, and the Holy Ghost has been given to us. Do you believe that? Have you got as far as that? God the Holy Ghost given; and, of course, you take what is given. You must not suppose that God gives a gift that you are not expected to accept. The Holy Ghost has been given.

Let us advance still one step more, and we find two other things answering to this series of truths. Christ came to reveal God's love. "God commendeth His love toward us, in that while we were yet sinners, Christ died for us." Christ came to reveal that at the centre of everything there is love. That is commonplace to you and me, because we have believed it so long, said it so often; but if it were not a commonplace it would thrill you to the marrow of your bones to think that at the centre of the universe there is not only a great law but a mighty heart, that God loves and that God is love. I believe in the Trinity not because it is a well-ordered theological dictum, but because I need the Trinity. I need to know God, and I can only know God in Jesus by the Holy Ghost. Christian life is built there.

One of the finest women I ever met, a Unitarian, seeking peace of heart, was led to Christian faith by this verse, when it was shown to her—and I remember the look of peace that came when she believed it: "God commendeth His love toward us, in that, while we were yet sinners, Christ died for us." When I asked her

Q

the question, "How could God commend His love to us if some-body else died for us?" she saw that He who died must be the same as the God who loved. It is impossible for me to commend my love to you by another man doing something for you. If I commend *my* love, *I* must do it; and if God commends His love and Christ dies, Christ and God are one, and I discover that love lies at the heart of God, and love is grace, and love is Jesus.

On my side I have faith—faith that comes by the Holy Ghost, and welcomes the Holy Ghost; and the result of that is that He sheds abroad in my heart the love of God—not my love to God, but God's love to me: so that, men and women, Christian life is God's heart in my heart. That is reducing it to its last analysis: God's heart in my heart; the love out of God's heart shed abroad in mine, and remaining there by the Holy Ghost.

> Oh, for a heart to love Thee
> More truly as I ought;
> And nothing place above Thee,
> In word, or deed, or thought.

Now about the Christian living: for that is what we have come up here to discover. How can I live the Christian life? There are a great many people who never live life at all; they are just trying to live. They spend all their days trying to live. They are like a man who is going to a meeting, and finds a crowd at the door. He fights his way through the crowd, and goes home thinking he has been at the meeting, whereas he has only been fighting in the crowd outside, trying to get in. There are some people who have never learned to live the Christian life; they are only struggling to live it all the time.

What is Christian living? Well, we take the Revised Version of this chapter; and I think there is not one of us here but quarrelled a little with the Revisers the first time we read it; but we will cease our quarrel because, after all, they are right. They are not always right! "Being therefore justified by faith, let us have peace with God through our Lord Jesus Christ." "Let us have peace with God." "Well," you say, "we *have* peace with God!" But the earliest versions give it, "let us have peace"—and I believe that is the right version, because it is the earliest we possess. But I also believe it because I could not imagine anybody altering the phrase, "We have peace," to the other phrase, "Let us have peace"; but I could well imagine people altering the phrase, "Let us have peace" to the other, "We have peace." Now that is the whole question of Keswick. The difference in the original word is only the difference between a long "o" and a short "o." It is not much, but the whole of the success of Christian living is in small adjustments. You are a theologian, and you say, "We have peace." I agree; indeed, we need not quarrel about it, because it says it in the chapter, in verse 11, "through whom we have now received the reconciliation." It is the same thing. "We have peace." Yes, but let us have what we have; let us live while we live. "Let us have peace," and enjoy peace. Let us, being justified by faith, accept the great reconciliation once for all; accept it once for always. Let us accept it every day. Let there be no longer in my heart any distrust of God; let there be no more dread of the future; let there be no more alienation of heart, or estrangement of life. Let me have peace with God.

I would search my heart and yours, my friends, and ask you quite frankly, Have you peace with God? Have you a grudge against God for anything? Have you controversy with God on any point? If you think that God is the God of grace, how can you have anything else but peace with Him, who will do much better for you than you could do for yourself? Can you say that He has done all things well? Very humbly, I dare to say it about myself. I would have nothing different, as far as God is concerned, in all the past. He has done right. All that God has done, all that God permits, all that God demands, all that God requires, is right. "Let us have peace with God." Shall we pause a moment? Search your hearts. Are you absolutely at this moment at peace with God about the past, and about all you know of the future? Yes! Thank God! Very well, go on then.

The second thing in Christian living is—again we will have to change the form of it—"Let us rejoice in the hope of the glory of God" (v. 2). So Christian living is a life of hope. We are not pessimists; we are optimists. We have hope of glory, hope of God's glory. God is going to be glorified in the future; He is going to be glorified in heaven; He is going to be glorified on the earth, and the will of God is to be done on earth as it is in heaven. God is going to be glorified. "Let us rejoice in the hope of the glory of God." However great your blessing to-day, it is not sufficient unless you look forward to the great hope of the future. We all need the thought of glory. We all need to rejoice in it. Things get into proper perspective then. The things of to-day appear very small when we are rejoicing in the hope of the ultimate glory of God, and are quite sure we shall have our share in it; when we are able to say that in spite of everything, we know that we shall arrive. "What time what circuit first, I know not, but I shall arrive."

> More happy, but not more secure,
> The glorified spirits in heaven.

Shall we go out of this tent like that, rejoicing in the hope of the glory of God?

I met a hymn two or three days ago. I do not know who sings it, but it has struck me ever since. The first verse runs like this:

> I'll sing the glories of the Lamb,
>   A hundred years to-day:
> My eyes shall see the great I AM,
>   A hundred years to-day.

It is true if we are in Christ. A hundred years from now all Christ's people in this tent will be in front of His glory. How little things on earth should seem, how poor and paltry all earth's trials, in the light of a hundred years to-day. But, my friends, it may be next week, it may be to-morrow, it may be even to-day. What a fool I shall be if a make myself unhappy about anything this morning, when this evening I may be in glory. Christian living is to rejoice in the hope of the glory of God.

"Yes," you say, "that is well; but there are a great many things that lie between me and that." Now, go on again. "And let us exult—glory, rejoice—in tribulations also." We make a profound mistake if we think that by one step into some blessing at Keswick we are going to get rid of all life's trials. We make a mistake if we think that any blessing may mean a short cut to ease. God will allow the *tribulum* to go over the grain, and separate the wheat from the chaff. We shall have tribulation. As Peter tells us at the end of his first epistle, "After ye have suffered awhile, ye are to be called to glory." He prays that we may be made perfect before the suffering. We are not made perfect through the suffering only, though there is a perfection that can only come by the great process. But we must suffer, and tribulation will bring joy when we see that it is working for us. It works. "Tribulation worketh patience"—an active patience; "and patience, experience"—trial, proof; "and experience, hope: and hope maketh not ashamed, because the love of God is shed abroad in our hearts by the Holy Ghost, which is given unto us."

Right in the centre of our Bible there are five books of experience—the Book of Job, the Psalms, the Proverbs, Ecclesiastes, and the Song of Solomon. I think if you will take this category of Paul's about what tribulation does, and put it alongside these books of experience, you will find that the Old Testament and the New Testament experience is very similar. You take the book of Job. "Tribulation worketh patience." Can you describe it any better than that? You take the Psalms. "Patience worketh experience." The Psalms form the book of experience *par excellence*.

"And experience worketh hope," because you know that God deals in strict equity; God rewards good and punishes evil. The man who lives for God is sure to have God's favour. You see it all in the Proverbs, where the righteous are blessed and the wicked are condemned. "Experience worketh hope, and hope maketh not ashamed," because you know that there is a divine order in the world. Hope brings courage. And if you go to Ecclesiastes, and find that under the sun there is nothing but vanity and vexation of spirit, yet you are courageous, because you have a hope of something eternal, something that lies behind; the final thing is love shed abroad in our hearts, which is the song of songs greater than Solomon's.

There are three things more. We go on to verses 9 and 10. The Bishop of Durham,[1] in all the beautiful things he has said, has never said or written a more felicitous or suggestive phrase than when, in his commentary on Romans, he translates, quite simply, without any emphasis or comment, the word which we have as "saved," as "kept safe." Nobody can dispute the accuracy of that, but nobody ever did it till he did it. You know, you can always tell the difference between a wise man and a foolish man when some truth is simply said. The foolish man, when he hears something quite simple, says, "Anybody could have thought of that!" The wise man says, "What a wonder I never thought of that before!" Now it is a wonder we did not think of it before. Let me read it: "Much more then, being now justified by His blood, we shall be kept safe from wrath through Him. For if, when we were enemies, we were reconciled to God by the death of His Son, much more, being reconciled, we shall be kept safe by His life." That is Christian living—safe because we are kept safe; safe because Jesus Christ is round about us. Saved from the wrath, we never more come into judgment, because we are shielded and accepted in the Beloved. Saved from the temptations and difficulties of this present time, because we are encircled by the life of Jesus.

More than once I have had to argue with Christians who had long read their Bibles as to the meaning of that expression, "in His life." I find that some have said it means the earthly life of Jesus; that we are saved by Christ's example. Now does that commend itself to you? No! Well, I do not think it will commend itself to anybody with a spiritual instinct. We are saved by the life of Christ on earth indeed; but it is His present life, it is His heavenly life, it is the life of the Living One who died. For Christ is not dead: He was living before, and He is living now; and it is the life He is living now that saves, for He is the life eternal. As

<hr>
[1] The Rt. Rev. Handley C. G. Moule, D.D. See page 27.

the apostle John says, "the eternal life was manifested, and we have seen it." We are "kept safe" because we are kept saved; not because we are strong, not because we have great will power, not because we know the doctrine, not because we have experience, but because we are in the centre of His life, "kept safe by His life."

> Safe from corroding care,
> Safe from the world's temptations,
> Sin cannot harm me there.

I know a man whose guard was broken down in the presence of sin, who had the occasion presented to him to sin; and at that very moment there came between him and the sin an impassable barrier, so that he could not do the thing that he would. It was the life of Jesus. You know men like that! You found it impossible to sin, not because your will was against the sin, because your will was broken; then to this child that had trusted Him, who had turned the responsibility of life over to Him, Christ came, and in His life saved you, tempted, tried, struggling as you were. This is the way of deliverance: we are "kept safe in His life."

Now let us go on again. There are two things more. Christian living becomes a very wonderful thing. "Let us have peace with God"; "Let us have hope in the glory of God"; "Let us exult in tribulation also"; "'Let us realise that we are kept safe' in Christ's life." You come, then, to the next verse, "And not only so, but let us also joy in God through Jesus Christ our Lord." "Let us joy in God." Christ sent seventy disciples out on a great embassy. They came back full of triumph, because they said the devils were subject to them; and Christ said, "That is joy; but rather rejoice that your names are written in heaven." That is a higher joy. But at the moment when Christ told His disciples that, He Himself had the highest of all delights. "Immediately"—and Luke is the narrator—"in that hour, Jesus rejoiced in the Holy Spirit." It is a great thing to rejoice in success in service; it is a greater thing to rejoice in the fact that your name is written in heaven; but greatest of all is it to rejoice in the Holy Ghost, God present. It is greater than service, for it is the foundation of service; it is greater than heaven even, for it is the assurance of heaven. Rejoice in God.

In the greatest catechism that ever was written, which is the Westminster Assembly's catechism—there is not a Scotsman here who will quarrel with that statement; and I am not a Scotsman, but I agree with you—the first question is (and you can always judge a catechism by its first question): "What is the chief end of man?" You all know the answer or, if you do not, you ought: "Man's chief end is to glorify God, and to enjoy Him for ever." Is not that splendid? The only thing that has caused any trouble is the comma in the middle. That leads people to suppose that this present life is to glorify God as best you can, and when you get to heaven you are going to enjoy Him for ever! It would have been a great thing if the comma had been left out: "Man's chief end is to glorify God and to enjoy Him for ever." Now you had better drop the comma. And though I would not suggest an addition to the answer, really what I would like to say would be: "Man's chief end is to glorify God and to enjoy Him for ever and to begin both now." Begin glorifying God now, and begin enjoying Him now.

In one of the church missionary magazines this month, Mr. Oldham makes a very suggestive remark. He says that he has been looking at a manuscript that is going to appear in a book as to the present-day motives of missionary work; and he is struck by the omission of one thing. It is written by an expert; but while the emphasis is laid very strongly on duty, there is nothing said about the motive of joy. We used to go to God's work because we were so glad in God. Now that is the great motive still. "Let us joy in God," not only in God's doings, but in God. Are you glad in God? Are you glad when you think God is nigh? Does the very withdrawal of God's face cause a shadow to you? Let us be glad in God. "God my exceeding joy," as the Psalmist puts it.

A German writer talks about an Englishman, whose name I will not mention, as "a God-intoxicated man." Mr. Hubert Brooke told us about God-possessed men last night. God-possessed men and God-intoxicated men! Oh, to rejoice in God; to get to know God so much, to get to dwell in God so constantly that while you rejoice in everything God has made—and who can help rejoicing in the beauty of this beautiful world, this homely mother earth; who can help rejoicing in the fair and lovely things that enrich life, and all the things that make life beautiful?—most of all you shall rejoice in God. Then it is easy to sacrifice; then it is easy to serve; then it is simple to live—

> For glee of God, knowing no wish nor will,
> World-heedless; whatever vintage fill
> Earth's jewelled cup,
> The cup-bearer so splendid,
> That for very ecstasy
> His wine we spill.

And we spill it gladly if we may but look at His face. "Let us rejoice in God." "You will be knowing something of the joy unspeakable," said Dr. Bonar to a man he was visiting. The man looked up with radiance in his face, and said, "It's more than that; it's joy unthinkable." "Let us rejoice in God."

Now, one thing more. Oh, if Christian living only came up to this level, it would be good indeed. Test yourselves whether you come up to it. Have we peace with God? Do we rejoice in hope of God's glory always? Do we always rejoice in tribulation, because of what it is doing in God's hand for us? Do we rejoice because we are perpetually kept safe? Do we rejoice in God because God is God, and God is ours? But there is another blessing still. Do we know what it means: "Much more they who receive abundance of grace and of the gift of righteousness shall reign in life by one, Jesus Christ"? We are to be kings. Christ makes us kings and priests. We are to be kings; we are to reign in life if we live the Christian life. Every man, every woman is to be, in a very real sense, under Christ, the captain of his own soul, the master of his own fate. You are not to be a slave, but to reign.

There is a chapter in Joshua—chapter 10—which is very interesting because it talks about the sun and the moon standing still. The great thing about that was not that the sun and the moon stood still, but that Joshua had enough confidence in God to command them to do it. We miss the point of things many a time! In that chapter we read about five kings who were hanged by Joshua in a grove. But Romans 5 is also a chapter about five kings: sin reigned, death reigned, grace reigns, Christ reigns, and I reign. If sin reigns, death is always on the throne, and I am under their feet: I am a slave. But if Christ reigns, Christ is on the throne, and I am on the throne, too, I reign in life by One, the only One, Jesus Christ, the One to whom I owe all. He makes me a king.

> 'Tis His grace His people raises,
> Over self to reign as kings.

Yes, we reign over self-interest, over self-indulgence, over touchiness, over sensitiveness. We forget self. We reign over the body. Woe be to a man if his body reigns over him! John Foster said about his body, "I will conquer it or quit it!" It was a great resolve, but let us understand how we are going to do it. You cannot quit it, and if you try yourself you cannot conquer it; but there is way.

Christian living also means that you are to reign over your circumstances; not to be a driftwood on the wave, swirled here and flung yonder, but to reign over circumstances and make them subject themselves to you; not to be bitter if you are chastened, not to be desperate if you are forsaken, not to be always under the tyranny of worry and little bothers, but to have God's peace in spite of all; not to be subject to the world's fashions—not even spiritual fashions. You will reign, so that you will not be subject even to Keswick fashions—if there are such things! Be yourself, be your better self, be your new self, be yourself in Christ, as Christ is to be the Head of the new manhood. All centres round Christ. You are to reign over death, so that you will neither be afraid of death nor of dying. I have known people who were not afraid of death, but very much afraid of dying. You are to reign over death, so that to you, as to Anselm, the word will come as you pass, "I appoint unto you a kingdom." For that is what Christ is doing to His Church. He is calling out of the world those who are to be His rulers in His Kingdom; those whom He can make kings, and say to one, "Have authority over five cities," and to another, "Have thou authority over ten cities." We are to reign. Oh, to think that there might be more than a thousand kings and queens here this morning! You a king, I a king! How is it to come about? How am I to get this conquest over those things where I need victory? How am I to conquer them, press them down, tread upon them? I cannot. It must be God's way, not mine. How? "They which receive abundance of grace." Not they that get plenty of it, but they that receive the grace that is abundant—receive it, that is all.

The word "receive" is the middle word. There are three words for "receive" in the Greek tongue. Now, the middle word is the word here. It is the same as "Receive the Holy Ghost." It does not mean to receive as you received the light this morning. You could not help yourself. The light shone, and it just came to you. Your eyes are made to see, and you passively received it. That is not how you receive grace. You receive grace rather as you received your breakfast. You did not remain passive and have your breakfast. You received the thing that was willingly given you. You do not receive grace in the third way, of struggling to get it, wresting it from an unwilling hand. God is eager to give His grace; His cross proves that love must have an outlet. Love seeks me, and I hold out my hand, and, as I take, I rise from abjectness, and stand before God a king, reigning in life by One; and that is Christian living. May God lead us into the simple and open secret!

THE GLORY OF THE CROSS

Rev. A. C. Dixon, D.D.

To-day we enter the Holy of Holies of our Christian faith. Three Scriptures serve as the key-texts of our study. The first is in Luke 23: 33–35, "They crucified Him . . . and the people stood beholding." The second is 1 Corinthians 2: 2, "I determined not to know anything among you, save Jesus Christ, and Him crucified." The third is Galatians 6: 14, "God forbid that I should glory, save in the cross of our Lord Jesus Christ."

The tragedy of the crucifixion is one thing; the deeper meaning of the cross is quite another. In its tragedy it is repulsive; in its deeper meaning it is the most attractive thing in all God's universe. We may learn something from the tragedy. As we stand under the cross, and listen and look, we may love and live. As we listen we really hear the voice of the cross speaking toward God: what the cross has to say to heaven. It is the voice of prayer, "Father, forgive them; for they know not what they do." The cross of Christ is a prayer to heaven for the forgiveness of a lost world, even for those who killed Him. If we bear any unforgiving spirit toward anybody, let us bring it into the light and heat of this prayer of our Master; and never refuse to forgive until somebody treats us worse than they treated Jesus, if we would be like Him.

As we listen, we hear again the voice of promise, "To-day shalt thou be with me in paradise." The only door to paradise, here and hereafter, is the cross of Christ. I have met people who ignored the cross, to whom it was an offence, and they mocked at the "religion of the shambles"; but I have yet to meet one such who has deep peace and joy of soul. Paradise enters into us, and we into paradise, through the cross of our Lord Jesus Christ.

And as we listen we hear the voice of physical need, "I thirst." The cross of Christ is the appeal to God for the body as well as the soul. There is redemption of the body; and every need of the body—its hunger, its thirst, its infirmity—finds expression, so to speak, Godward, through Christ on the cross.

Again, as we listen we hear the voice of the soul's deepest need, "My God! My God! why hast Thou forsaken me?" That is death—separation from God; that is hell—"Depart from me." And He "tasted death for every man."

490

That little word "Why?" is a dangerous word to use when we are in the furnace and on the cross; to ask God the reason for things. It often makes us stumble; but if you will follow the example of the Master, you will always be safe. "My God! Why?" Cling to God while you ask the question, and sooner or later it will be answered. The mistake is that "Why?" should sometimes make us turn our faces away from God in the times of our crucifixion.

Then we hear the voice of human love, "Woman, behold thy son! Behold thy mother!" Through the cross of Christ, about all there is in motherhood, and fatherhood, and childhood, and wifehood, has come to us. You do not find the home really where the cross has not touched. Dean Farrar points out the fact that in all the classic literature of the ancients there is not a reference to the joys of childhood, just because they had no joys; they were chattels and slaves. And there is no reference to the joy of wifehood; and an ingrate is the man who may thank God for home and all that means, and not accept Jesus Christ on the cross.

Then, as you listen, you hear the voice of victory, "It is finished." The work of atonement is done. "Father, into Thy hands I commend my spirit," the note of victory still. And it is right there where the death of the Christian, the physical death of the Christian, begins. He does not have to say, "Why hast Thou forsaken me?" That is death; but Jesus died for him, and he can look up and say, "Father, into Thy hands I commend my spirit." The dying of the Christian is just the commending of the spirit, redeemed by the blood of Christ, into the hands of the Father.

We might look about the cross and learn something. "The people stood beholding," some of the religious—priests—wagging their heads and mocking. Those who wag their heads and mock still at the cross of Jesus are sometimes the most religious.

There was a group of women with just enough religion to make them miserable. They have come along. After faith has failed, their love holds out, and it brings them near the cross. Oh, friend, it is better to have enough faith and love to make you miserable than to have none at all; and if you will keep near the cross, in it you are near the Lord.

I love to look at that sturdy Roman centurion, as strong a man, perhaps, as Roman civilisation produced. He has a duty to perform; he has the papers in his pocket, and as an officer he must perform that duty. He is intellectually convinced. "Surely this is a righteous man," and by-and-by, "This is the son of a god." But he keeps right on with the crucifixion; and I know men of clear intellect, who are intellectually convinced of the Deity of Christ, but they keep right on with the crucifixion. They do not join with those that worship and praise.

As we look above the cross at that inscription, we learn something. It is in Greek, and Latin, and Hebrew—the language of culture, the language of power, and the language of religion. "The place for learning is not above the cross," says an old Puritan, "but at the foot." It got into the wrong place. Yet it teaches a great lesson, that what the culture of the Greek needs, and what the sturdy Roman needs, and what the religious Hebrew needs, is the cross of Jesus Christ. What your culture needs, and what your strength needs, if you have any, and what your religion needs, is the cleansing power of the precious blood.

On the way to Damascus Paul had a vision of the glorified Christ, his first view of Him. But he never gloried in the glorified. He came back in the light of the glorified to the crucified, and said, "God forbid that I should glory, save in the cross."

When Leonardo de Vinci had finished his great painting of the Last Supper, he took a friend with him to criticise it, and as the friend looked at it he said, "The most beautiful thing in your picture is the cup." The artist took his brush and wiped out the cup. He said, "Nothing in my picture shall attract more attention than the face of my Master." And that was the religion of the apostle Paul. "Nothing in my preaching, in my character, in my mission, if I can help it, shall attract more attention than the cross of Christ. God forbid that I should glory save in the cross."

It is the glory of the cross that we ask the Holy Spirit to help us talk about now for a few minutes. We can put it, as far as it can be put, in one word, the word "sacrificial." In Christ and the cross there is the glory of *sacrificial love.* Love sometimes just enjoys itself, and it may not be sinful under certain circumstances. That is the tendency of human love, the first tendency, it may be; but love enjoying itself is not glory. It is love giving itself in sacrifice for others that has about it the halo of glory. When you behold Christ on the cross you have seen God. God has power, God has wisdom, "God *is* love." If you would have a clear vision of God in the glory of His love, you must see Him in Jesus Christ on the cross. He is more glorious there, even than in the power of the resurrection, important as that is; but the resurrection is just the stamp of heaven's authority upon the gold of God's love, that makes it coin current between earth and heaven.

I have been interested, as I have read the Scriptures lately, in noticing how God takes it for granted that He loves us. He just expects us to read it between the lines everywhere, and see it when He does not mention it. I decided to preach a series of sermons on that little text, "God is love." Well, I said, "I will take Genesis, and unfold the love of God in Genesis." What was my astonishment to find that Genesis has not a declaration of God's love in it!

The word "love" occurs thirteen times, but there is no reference to God's love. There is retribution, there is righteousness, there is power, there is justice, declared; but God seems to take it for granted that we know He loves us. "Well," I said, "I must get my first sermon from Exodus." It is not in Exodus! If it is, I wish you would drop me a postcard and give me the place! "Then," I said, "we will have a good time in Leviticus." It is not in Leviticus! There is no declaration of God's love in Leviticus. "To be sure it is in Numbers!" It is not in Numbers. In Deuteronomy there is an unfolding of God's love almost as in the book of John. It comes like a flash of light from heaven. "Well," I said, "I will make up for lost time when I reach the New Testament. I will preach a sermon on the love of God as declared in the Gospel of Matthew." I read it through without finding it. There is no declaration of God's love in the Gospel of Matthew. You know it; He does not have to tell you. Everything in it whispers love, without His mentioning it, and all the more emphatically. "Well," I said, "my sermon must be on Mark." It is not in Mark! "Well, then, I must go to Luke." There is only one incidental reference in Luke, "Ye Pharisees pass over judgment and the love of God" (11: 42), just incidentally. If it overwhelms you, as it did me, it will bring you to tears—the first declaration, not intimation, and not inference, but the first declaration of God's love in the New Testament, is John 3: 16, a sunburst upon mid-night, a revelation at one stroke of God Himself. "For God so loved the world, that He gave His only begotten Son."

Then we have the glory of *sacrificial light*. "I am the light of the world." Light tends to display itself, of course; but the glory of light is in its sacrifice. These beautiful mountains are sacrificed light. The sun gives off its light as upon an altar, and the light is taken up into leaf, and flower, and grass, and forest. If the sun should cease to be sacrificial, there would be no more light, and no more beauty, and no more fertility. And "if the light that is in you be darkness, how great is that darkness."

What is light? How did we get it, anyhow? Geologists tell us that during the carboniferous era the great forests took in the sunlight and wove it into fibre of branch, and trunk, and roots of the trees. Then there came convulsions, and these forests were buried out of sight, and the coal-beds were formed, imprisoned light. We dig out the coal, and we put it through a process of combustion, and the fire lets the light loose that the forest took in from the sun. That is the way the Lord Jesus becomes light: not by the Sermon on the Mount, but by Calvary; by the process of combustion on the altar, ablaze for us. Then He turns round and says, "Ye are the light of the world." I made a little sermon once, taking that text, on Christians as reflectors of light, and it was a cold sermon! Reflection is a cold process. You cannot raise a crop by moonlight; you must have it warm from the sun. It does not say, "Ye are reflectors of light"; it says, "Ye are the light of the world." How do we become light? "I beseech you, therefore, brethren, by the mercies of God, that ye present your bodies a living sacrifice, holy, acceptable unto God." We take in from the Sun of righteousness the rays of light, as the forest took it from the sun in the heavens; and then by a process of combustion, by the sacrificial spirit on God's altar, we are light as Jesus was light, and that is the glory of the Christian's life.

Then we have the glory of *sacrificial truth*. "I am the truth." Truth carries a sword; truth has to fight. The Lord said in a sense He sent a sword. "My peace I give unto you; not as the world giveth, give I unto you." The world gives peace by compromise or surrender, as Napoleon got it at Waterloo. The Lord Jesus Christ gives peace by victory, as Wellington got it at Waterloo. "My peace I give unto you; not as the world giveth." When a man wants a drink of whisky, the world says, "Get peace by going into the public-house and taking it"; but Christ says, "Get peace by conquering your thirst." "Not as the world giveth." Yet the glory of Christianity is not in the sword. It is truth on the altar, truth aglow with sacrifice, truth that is willing to die, truth that refuses to defend itself, while it dies for the untruthful.

We have also the glory of *sacrificial power*. Power exerts itself— and it ought at times. We must admire the omnipotent power of God, as we see it working in so many ways. But power exerting itself is not glorious, compared with power withholding itself. "Thinkest thou that I cannot now pray to my Father, and He shall presently give me twelve legions of angels?" But if He had so prayed, the glory of Christ had been eclipsed. Oh, the power that held back while love worked; oh, the power that refused to exert itself while Jesus Christ went to the cross in weakness for the salvation of the weak!

We have, again, the glory of *sacrificial holiness*. Now holiness is apt to cultivate itself, and none too much! It is well to cultivate it, in public and in private. Use every means possible for the promotion of holiness. But I submit that even holiness cultivating itself is not as glorious as holiness sacrificing itself on the altar for God; holiness giving itself in loving sacrifice for the salvation of others. If you will turn to a Scripture, you will have that suggested. "Being justified freely by His grace through the redemption that is in Christ Jesus: whom God hath set forth to be a propitiation through faith in His blood, to declare His righteousness for the remission of sins that are past, through the forbearance of God; to declare, I say, at this time His righteousness: that He might be just, and the justifier of him that believeth in Jesus" (Rom. 3: 24–26). The cross of Christ is the declaration of the righteousness of God. Join that with Romans 5: 8, "God commendeth His love toward us, in that, while we were yet sinners, Christ died for us." The cross of Christ is the commendation of His love, and the declaration of His righteousness; and Jesus Christ died because God is righteous as well as loving.

That brings us to the glory of *sacrificial mercy*. Mercy is a species of injustice, of unrighteousness. The moment a judge begins to be merciful, he ceases to be just; and the moment he begins to be just, he ceases to be merciful. I repeat, mercy is a species of injustice; and no man can be just and merciful unless justice has somehow been satisfied. There is an official justice. The Governor of Massachusetts is permitted to set free a prisoner from the State prison on Thanksgiving Day every year. Governor Guild went down and selected the wickedest man he could find and set him free, because there were some extenuating circumstances. It was an act of mercy, but certainly not of justice.

Judge Kerr, of North Carolina, sat on the Bench and heard the case of a thief who had stolen. He recognised that thief as a man whom he had known in boyhood. They had gone to the village school together; they had played on the green together, fished and hunted together. After the case was tried, and the man was found guilty, Judge Kerr pronounced sentence upon him. He was either to go to prison or pay a fine, I think it was of £20. When the sentence had been pronounced, Judge Kerr looked into his face and said, "My friend, you may not recognise me, but I recognise you. I am John Kerr that played with you on the village green, and I am going to pay your fine for you." He took out his cheque and wrote the amount, £20, and let his friend go free; and the man went out wiping his eyes, with a broken heart. Judge Kerr was just, and yet the justifier of that man by keeping the law. He could be merciful because he was just. If God begins to be merciful without the satisfaction of His justice, He loses the throne of His righteousness. The glory of the cross is that there is sacrificial mercy linked with justice, so that God can be "just, and the justifier of him that believeth."

Then there is the glory of *sacrificial life and beauty*. Stand with me at the door of the hospital in Brooklyn, New York. There comes a working man in his Sunday clothes, red-cheeked, vigorous, athletic. With a quick step he enters the hospital, to spend the day with his only boy, sick in the hospital. You admire that man's vigour, the beauty of his life. After three or four hours you see him come out of the hospital, supported on each side by a nurse. He looks as pale, almost, as if he were dead. Why? The doctor said, "There is just one thing that can cure your boy, and that is fresh blood in his veins. If you are willing to give some of the blood out of your healthy body, I will assure you that the boy will get well." That rugged working man bared his arm, and said, "Take it all, if need be, that the boy may go home to his mother!" He gave up the blood of his body for the life of his child. I say that that man, pale and emaciated, hanging on the arms of the nurses, was more beautiful than before—not vigorous life showing itself in strength, but sacrificial life giving itself for others. That is the beauty of patriotic life, philanthropic life, Christian life, that gives itself for others. I would like to paint it if I could, and put it on my study wall.

Two little girls in a Western State, overtaken in a blizzard and blinded, lost their way. Father and mother looked for them all day and all night, and next evening at four o'clock they were found, frozen to death. The elder child, about eleven years of age, had taken off her outer coat and wrapped it round her little sister, and then had taken off the undercoat and wrapped it round her, and then put her arms round her and tried to keep her warm, forgetful of herself. Oh, the beauty of it! first the repulsion of it, and then the beauty of it. And Jesus Christ on the cross is the most beautiful picture in the most repulsive frame that this world ever saw. In its tragedy it is repulsive; in its deeper meaning it is attractive.

That brings us to light on three or four Scriptures. We can just barely mention them. "I, if I be lifted up, will draw all men unto me." There is the magnetism of sacrificial love, and light, and truth, and holiness, and all the attributes of God and perfect man. "I, if I be lifted up, will draw," draw for forgiveness, draw for cleansing, draw for transformation. There is something in one, when he begins to feel himself guilty, that draws him toward the One that can pardon. There is something in one who feels himself defiled that draws him toward the fountain that can cleanse. There is something in one who feels himself weak, that draws him toward protecting power. "I, if I be lifted up, will draw."

Then that Scripture in John 12: 24, "Except a grain of wheat fall into the ground and die, it abideth alone: but if it die, it bringeth forth much fruit." Those cultured Greeks came wanting to see Jesus. Philip told Andrew about it, and then they two took them to Jesus for an introduction. What did our Lord say? "I am glad to see you; I am glad to have you see me"? Not a word of it. He said, "Except a grain of wheat fall into the ground and die, it abideth alone. Philip, Andrew, if your Greek friends see me now, they will not see Jesus at all. They will see the perfect man, the incarnate God, but they will not see Jesus. The only way to behold Jesus is to see me in the process of dying. Except a grain of wheat fall into the ground and die, it abideth alone. I have come to this world to save the lost, and it is by the power of death that I can multiply myself." You can keep the wheat in the barn, protected from weather and weevil, but you will have no crop. You can sow it out in the field, and harrow it in, and go ten days from now, and it is not worth a sixpence. It seems to have been lost. Its value is lost, but it has died with a view to the harvest. "Except a grain of wheat . . . die, it abideth alone."

You are not having any converts? Are you dying? Is the sacrificial heart of Christ beating in your heart? The Church of Jesus Christ is not being multiplied as it should; the harvest is not great. What is the matter? Have we reached the principle and incarnated it into our lives, of the cross of Jesus? That Scripture, then, has deeper meaning, "If any man will come after me, let him deny himself, and take up his cross, and follow me." Live the sacrificial life, be upon your Calvary, crucified with your Lord, and the grains of wheat will be multiplied. But if we spend our time protecting ourselves, and strengthening the remains, and looking after the ninety and nine while the one wanders off into the desert and mountains of death, we will wither, we will cease almost to exist, the candlestick will be removed. If we would multiply, let the glory of the cross fill our hearts and master our lives.

Just one word more. "Worthy is the Lamb that was slain to receive power, and riches, and wisdom, and strength, and honour, and glory, and blessing" (Rev. 5: 12). Let us step inside the gates ajar, and look and listen. As we look, we see a throne, and in the midst of the throne "the Lamb, as it had been slain." The throne of heaven is occupied by the slain Lamb, risen from the dead. Heaven is ruled by the sacrificial principle of the cross of Christ. If John should meet James on the streets of glory and ask, "How much do you think Paul is worth?" James would not think of gold, for they pave the streets with it up there! He would not think of banknotes and wealth of earth. He would just think, "How much is Paul like Jesus Christ on the cross?" His worth is in proportion to the similarity between him and Jesus Christ on the cross. "Worthy is the Lamb that was slain." When we adopt heaven's standard of worth, and live up to it, you need not go to heaven; it has come to you. You need not have golden streets to walk on; and can tramp the cobble-stones of London in a London fog with heaven in your soul. "Worthy is the Lamb that was slain." The coronation of Jesus Christ as Lamb of God makes heaven here and hereafter.

R

I heard in my boyhood the story of your noble Queen Victoria. It is familiar, doubtless, to every Englishman, but it stirred my childish heart. She sat, in her Coronation week, in the Royal box, while Handel's *Messiah* was being played. The lady-in-waiting went to her and said, "Everyone in the room, when they reach the 'Hallelujah Chorus', will rise and stand till the music ceases, except the Queen." It is the Royal etiquette that the Queen should keep her seat. The music continued, sweeter and fuller, sweet enough for heaven, I think. When the "Hallelujah Chorus" was reached, the people rose and stood with bowed heads. It was noticed that the Queen was deeply moved. Her lip quivered, her eyes filled with tears, her body trembled, until they came to that burst of melody, "King of kings and Lord of lords." Then, in spite of Royal etiquette, the young Queen stood up, and with bowed head remained standing until the music ceased. A nobler, queenlier thing she never did.

I heard that when Canon, afterwards Dean, Farrar was acting as chaplain to the Queen, he visited her when she was ill. She had been reading a pamphlet or book about the Second Coming of the Lord, and she said, "Chaplain, what do you think about the Second Coming of the Lord?" I do not know his reply, but as he left he said, "Your Majesty, why have you asked me that question?" "Oh," she said, "I wish He would come while I am alive, for nothing would give me more pleasure than with my own hands to give Him the crown of Great Britain and India!" In her young womanhood, with life before her, she crowned Jesus King of kings and Lord of lords; and now in her old age, with grey hairs and many cares that she has borne, she wants to give Him every crown that God has given her.

One of the most thrilling moments we ever felt was in a convention of the Christian Endeavourers, when Dr. Clark, the President, rose with a piece of yellow paper fluttering in his hand, and said, before about 20,000 young people, "I have a telegram from Japan." There was silence in which you could hear your heart beat. He stood there and read it—just three little words, "Make Jesus King!" We were silent, and then applause after applause burst forth, and the people wept as they looked into each other's faces. To a Japanese that means something, "Make Jesus Mikado!"

To-morrow we will have something to say about the Coronation, but while we are waiting for the Coronation to come, let us crown Him here. While He tarries in the coming in glory, let Him come in grace. Let us enthrone Christ the Lamb of God in our hearts and lives, and heaven is begun.

THE CROWNING DAY

Dr. S. D. Gordon

On His head were many diadems—Revelation 19: 12.

W E MEN measure things pretty much by time, by clocks and calendars. In every home there is a clock, and maybe most of you have a watch in your pocket or on your wrist. In every business there is a calendar; and both clocks and calendars are dominated by the same thing—the sun. Clocks and calendars revolve round the sun.

The Christian Church throughout the world goes through the year by what is called the church calendar. The Roman Church and the Greek Orthodox, the State Churches and the Free, the Primitive Churches, the Protestant, go through the year by the church calendar. And the church calendar is dominated by one Personality—Jesus.

We remember Christmas as the time when Jesus was born among us, as one of ourselves. We remember the Lenten season as the time of sore stress and temptation on the part of Christ in the wilderness. We have Good Friday marked off as the day when He climbed the hill of the cross, on His own feet, by His own choice, and was done to the death for all men, as only He could be done to the death. We remember Easter Sunday as the day when He scorned the imperial Roman seal, and rose up through the rock of the new-hewn tomb, and when the angels rolled away the stone, that men might see He was no longer there. We remember Whit-Sunday as the day when Jesus, crucified on earth, and crowned in heaven, flooded down His "other self," the Holy Spirit, at Pentecost. But I want to remind you very simply that there is to be a new day in the church calendar; it is a future day; it is the crowning day that is coming by and by.

> Our Lord is now rejected
>   And by the world disowned,
> By the many still neglected,
>   And by the few enthroned:

But soon He'll come in glory!
The hour is drawing nigh,
For the crowning day is coming
By and by.

"And there shall be upon His head many diadems."

I remember as vividly as though it were yesterday one evening in London—dear old smoky, dirty, foggy, lovely London—I remember an evening in the Albert Hall when it was full to overflowing; it was a gathering of races, a world gathering, a racial gathering. The olive-tinted face of the Chinese was there with the slant of his eye; and the keen, quick, nervous Japanese was there; and our own kinsfolk of India were there; our brothers from the African Continent were there; and from up and down the Continent of Europe; the flaxen-haired Scandinavian; the dark-eyed Italian and Spaniard; from Holland and Belgium and Switzerland; Teuton and Latin, all sorts of folk. There were between six and eight thousand in that racial crowd; they spoke many languages; they knew many angles of life. I can shut my eyes and go back in thought to the Albert Hall thirty-seven years ago when on that evening they all stood and sang, "All hail the power of Jesus' Name." How they sang it! Your good old British tune brings out the ringing emphasis. I can hear them now singing in every language of the earth, "Crown Him Lord of all." It seemed like an anticipation of that wondrous day that is coming when He shall be crowned Lord of all.

This old earth of ours has had some remarkable coronation scenes. Before the revolution in Russia, when a Czar had died and a new Czar came into succession, the custom was this. The officials, the titled folk, the military men, and the leaders, met in the Kremlin Church, in Moscow, and as the crown of the Czar rested upon the head of the incoming Czar they all stood in their brilliant apparel, and flashing their swords in the air they cried out joyously and loudly, "The Czar! The White Czar! Who is comparable to our Czar?" Sixty years ago a company of kings and princes and generals met in that famous hall in Versailles; they spent three or four days very earnestly conferring. Then a wondrous scene took place, as these kings and princes and generals picked out a man, William, King of Prussia, and they put him upon the elevated platform, and they all stood around him, and they flashed their swords in the air, and they took the crowns from their heads, and they cried out, "All hail to William, the first Emperor of the new united German Empire." Sixty odd million people took up the cry, back and forth it rang. "All hail to William, the first Emperor of the new united German Empire." A wonderful scene. But, softly—are you listening?—these coronations, famous as they have been, pale away into insignificance in comparison with the day that is coming, the crowning day of the King of kings, when "There shall be upon His head many diadems."

Have you ever noticed the choruses in the Book of Revelation? Have you ever counted the choruses of John's Revelation, the Revelation of Jesus to John and through John? Have you hushed your heart to listen to the choruses of Revelation? Our friends who love music, they ought to turn a bit to Revelation, the last book of the Bible, for it is the music book. It is the story of Christ crowned, which includes the chaining of the pretender prince.

The music begins in the bit that is marked off as chapter 1. John has begun to write down his story of what came to him at Patmos. Then all at once he gets a vision of the face of Jesus, and he bursts out in a ringing solo, in the major key. "Unto Him that loved us, and washed us from our sins in His own blood." Then you turn to chapter 4. There is a quartet, it is called the quartet of the living creatures. Listen with the ears of your heart, and you hear the quartet singing their song. Then in chapter 5 there is what I might call the sextuple quartet; six times four. The twenty-four leading men take up the song of the quartet—you can hear the quartet still singing back yonder; then swinging into the front is the sextuple quartet of leaders, taking up the same song; and back and forth they sing it.

Then as their music softens away in the distance, though you still hear it, there is the angel chorus. John tried to count them. John was fairly well up in mathematics; he counted ten thousand, and he had to multiply that by ten thousand; and even though he may have had a post-graduate course in mathematics, all figures on earth give out at some time or other; and he simply had to say, "and thousands of thousands." The angel chorus; there they are, a great sea of faces; the ringing sopranos and the contraltos, the deep rhythmic thunder of the bass, the ringing out of the tenors; back and forth they take up the song; and they are singing the same song as those before.

Then in the same chapter there is the creation chorus. Now we do not think of creation singing, do we? Paul talked about creation groaning and travailing in pain. We do not think of the animals singing. We know the birds do. Somebody has said that all the sounds of creation are in the minor key. We speak of the sighing of the wind. We speak of the moaning of the dove. We speak of the sighing of the sad sea waves. There is the minor note in all real music. But here in heaven all creation takes up the song, the angels' song. By and by that softens away as a new chorus swings in, and the minor note is deep here, and touches your heart.

It is the martyr chorus of chapters 6 and 7. They are scarred and maimed, they show in their bodies the marks of their sufferings for the sake of Jesus. That song takes hold of your heart. Some of these dear folk from the far-away lands, they will understand; and some folk in the Homeland, that we do not call martyrs, but they are. They will never speak of it themselves, but we can feel the rare music of the martyrs' chorus as they take up the song of the others, and sing it out loud and clear.

And then by and by as that softens away there is the virgins' chorus, that is in chapter 14, the chorus of the pure ones, those who have been washed and made pure; they sing the song that nobody else can sing. Back and forth they sing, until the very vaults of heaven seem shaken by the music of the pure ones made pure in the one way that purity can come for those who have known the taint of sin. Then, ultimately, as you turn to chapter 19, you will get the combined chorus. It is the Hallelujah Chorus. Listen—the solo, the quartet, the sextuple quartet, the angels, the creation, the martyrs, the pure ones—all together they sing back and forth. John loved music, and he tried to describe it. He was a martyr himself. So on the rocky isle of Patmos, he says, "I must really tell the folk what it sounds like, though they will never get it into their hearts till they hear." He remembered how on many a night on the isle of Patmos the Aegean Sea had roared. He recalled how the waters of the Aegean Sea had swept up on those rocky shores of Patmos. John said the music was like the mighty waters of the sea. The Hallelujah Chorus. What are they singing? Will you listen with your hearts? Shut your eyes and listen. There are variations in the music; there are variations in the words. But the undertone of the strain throughout is this, "Crown Him! Crown Him Lord of all!"

But who is this? Who is this to be crowned? Will you hush your heart? Look yonder—a stable, the cattle, a young mother, the Babe, born as none other, before or since, a Babe in a manger, in the new-mown hay, sharing a place with the stock. It is He! Look again. A little hamlet village on the hillside. A Carpenter in a shop, at a bench, with the odour of the pine shavings and the sawdust, with a bit of a garden at the back of the house. It is He! Look again. The olive grove. And the Man so human that He longed for human fellowship. But He must go on alone; there could be no fellowship with Him in what He is going to do on the morrow. He is on His knees; He is on His face; and already some drops of the blood of the Son of God are fertilising the very soil of the earth. It is He! And on the morrow after Gethsemane. There He hangs on the cross, done to the death, by His own choice, for all men. It is He! In Joseph's tomb, buried in the soil of the earth. Ah, but lift your hearts. The tomb is sheer empty. It is He!

> Sinners in derision crowned Him,
>   Mocking thus the Saviour's claim:
> Saints and angels crowd around Him,
>   Own His title, praise His name.
>
> Crown Him! Crown Him! angels, crown Him!
> Crown the Saviour King of Kings.

One other word. (Are you listening with the inner ears of your heart?) Who will have part in the crowning? Who will have share in that gracious, wondrous, coronation day? Those who crown Him now Lord of all will have a share in that wondrous crowning day by and by. My heart has burned as I have heard one and another say that they have crowned Him Lord of all. We do not really crown Him, as has been said many times, Lord at all until we crown Him Lord of all. I know that the heart that broke once on Calvary has been gladdened these July Keswick days as one and another has taken the crown of his own will, and has voluntarily put it upon the brow that once was so scarred with the thorns, but now is glorified; that crown, of one's own choice and will, that many a one here has placed upon that brow. If there be some here who know Jesus as Saviour, but you have not really crowned Him as King, there is an invitation open now to swell the chorus; there is still room in the great coronation chorus if you will crown Him Lord of all in your will and life. And my other friend listening here so kindly who has never taken Jesus, perchance, even as Saviour, you can economise the time; you can take Him as Saviour, and also crown Him as King in your life: it can be one transaction. Who will have share in that great coronation day? Those who crown Him now.

This story came to me from Africa, from an English missionary who had been there for years. He had led many to accept the Saviour. And as Christmas time drew near he had taught the people about the giving of gifts at the glad Christmas season. And he told them that they were to bring their gifts to the church, that the Jesus message might go to the tribes around who had not yet heard the blessed Jesus Name. It was Christmas Eve. They had met in the little chapel. The Communion Table was spread, and one after another came up and laid his gift on the table. Very homely gifts they would have seemed to our eyes, yet they were gifts of love. Here comes a man with a bundle of heavy-weighted wheat, and puts his gift on the table. Here is a bit of embroidery. Here is a bit of fruit. Very humble gifts they were.

By and by the missionary saw a young woman, just budding into rare young womanhood, come in very shyly up the aisle as though she feared she might be noticed; very softly and quickly she put a bit of something on the table, and she moved shyly and modestly away. The missionary was startled to find what her gift was; it was a bit of silver, equivalent to 3s. 6d. That might sound very little to us, but there it was almost a fortune; it was immense wealth. He knew the girl, and he naturally wondered how she got such wealth, and he felt as if he ought to have a word with her in a gentle, fatherly way afterwards when there was an opportunity. Later on he saw her, and he said, "I saw your gracious gift. But where did you ever get so much?" And her dark eyes filled up; and if an African can blush, she blushed. And with a flush on her face that revealed the flush in her heart, she said, "I had nothing to give. And Jesus has meant so much to me; He is everything to me; and those folk over there, they do not know Him; and my heart was heavy at the thought that I had nothing to give. And I found a man in a neighbouring tribe who wanted to buy a slave, and I sold myself to him, and that was the money I got, and I brought it." And her eye flashed out again, and with a bit of a tremor in her voice, she said, "Jesus gave all for me. I am so glad to give myself for Him, that others may learn of Him." I do not know whether the missionary spoke of the possible difficulties involved in slavery. But I do know this. That she will have part in that crowning day that is coming by and by. May we be in the fellowship of that sister of ours who gave herself to Him that others might know of His love. As we bow, let us join that blessed fellowship all anew.

GOD'S GIFT TO BELIEVERS

Rev. J. Russell Howden, B.D.

Be filled with the Spirit—Ephesians 5: 18.

G OD HAS been showing us life as He would have us live it.
Now the question which has brought us to Keswick is,
"How is it to be realised?" Remember that all life begins
as a gift. Natural life is a gift. You do not make yourself live;
you live because you had to; you had no option in the matter.
And in similar fashion your Christian life, the new life that is in
Christ, is a gift. You could not make yourself live, though when
you were born again, in that supreme moment of your experience,
all the emphasis was necessarily placed upon you and your definite
acceptance of Jesus Christ. And yet when you looked back upon
it you discovered that it was not so much what you did as what
He did. Life is a gift to be received. John 1: 12 declares that to
"as many as received Him, to them gave He the right to become
the sons of God, even to them that believe on His name." There
is no other way of being born again. That is the mystery and the
wonder of the new birth.

Then if you have been born again, remember that is only the
beginning, not the ending. After birth comes growth, and growth
is just as much a gift as birth. You cannot make yourself grow.
"Which of you by taking thought can add one cubit to his
stature?" You cannot make yourself grow naturally. You can
hinder it by foolish habits, by self-indulgence, and by wrong-
doing. You can stunt and spoil the development of your life, or you
can promote it by obedience to God's laws. Growth itself depends
upon factors you cannot command, and cannot even fully understand. And so it is in spiritual things. Growth also is a gift of
God. And this growth into such a life as has been set before us
so graciously and so winsomely, we can hinder; or, by God's
grace, we can seek to obey the laws that govern it.

What are the laws? If you will turn to Ephesians 5: 18, you will
see it all summed up in one sentence, "*Be filled with the Spirit.*"
Notice two or three things about that. First of all, observe that
the verb is *passive*—"Be filled." It is nothing you have to do; it
is rather something you have to let God do. God comes and He

bids us let Him have His own way with us in growth and development, even as He had His way with us in the new birth. You were
born again when you received Jesus Christ. When you received
Jesus Christ you received God; and when God received you, you
received the Spirit of God. If you are Christ's, you have the Holy
Spirit. But there is a difference between having the Holy Spirit
and being filled with the Spirit. It is a difference, not of kind, but
of degree; and the reason for our stunted development is that we
have not been willing to let God come into our lives and do in us
that which we could never do for ourselves. Some of us have been
striving for such a blessing as this. We have been struggling and
wrestling to attain it. We have been full of good resolutions and
good desires, and we have striven and struggled to bring these
resolves to the birth. But nine times out of ten we have failed,
and all the time God has been saying to us, "Be still and know
that I am God."

Then it is not only passive, but the verb is *imperative*—"Be filled
with the Spirit." It is a command. It leaves you and me no option
in the matter. It is just as much God's command as any other
command. God does not propose that there should be two classes
of believers—those who are Spirit-filled and those who are not
Spirit-filled. The fact of the command being given shows only too
clearly that there is a need for it. So many of us have but little of
God in our lives, and so little of that practical setting forth of
God's beauty in life and conduct, and so little real desire to be
pleasing to Him. Therefore we are to be filled.

Also notice that the verse is in the *present tense*, and the present
tense in the grammar of our New Testament always implies something which has a definite beginning, and leads on to a course of
events and of experience and of happening. You are to be filled
with the Spirit this morning. But the blessing of this morning will
not do for the needs of to-morrow. The blessing of to-day will not
suffice for next week; and it is your privilege, dear child of God,
to keep on being filled with the Spirit, God continually pouring of
His fulness into your heart, and you continually receiving it, and
continually, by His grace, transmuting that fulness into the expression of life and character and personality.

You say, "Well, how is this to be done? What am I to do to be
filled with the Spirit?" You heard the answer to that last night,
God saying to us all in the words of the Lord Jesus and through
the lips of His servant, "Follow me."[1] Many I doubt not, by His
grace, did it. We began last night, as we had never done before,
to follow Him—and He filled us. Look in John 7: 39, there you
read of the inescapable condition which is necessary to being filled

[1] The speaker was referring to an address by Mr. A. Lindsay Glegg.

with the Spirit—"For the Holy Spirit was not yet given; because
that Jesus was not yet glorified." When you glorify Jesus, then God
gives you the Holy Ghost.

It is put in so many different ways—presenting your bodies
a living sacrifice; following Jesus Christ; making Jesus Christ
King. But they all mean the same thing. They all mean the
yielding of your will to God. And please observe that this is the
reason why God gives us such a command as this in Ephesians
5: 18. He will not act without you. He will not drag you; He will
draw you. He will not force you; He will persuade you. This
command includes these two elements, God's appeal to you, and
your response to His appeal. Personality is the supreme earthly
gift of God to man. God has made you a person, and He will
never obliterate your personality. That is the work of the devil,
not of God. God has made you a person, and faith is relationship
with a person. Faith is the relationship of you with God, of the
sinner with the Saviour, of the child with the Father, of the
creature with the Creator. And all the way through it is the
same.

If you and I are ever to be filled with the Spirit, it must be on
a similar basis of personal relationship between ourselves and God.
God invites; we respond. The Lord Jesus says, Follow me. And
as we follow, then this other thing happens, this miracle divine
takes place in our lives: we are filled with the Spirit. And you
say, "That is just where my difficulty comes in. I find it so hard
to follow."

Let us set it out in this sequence. If I am to be well-pleasing
to God, I must be filled with the Spirit. If I am to be filled with
the Spirit, I must follow the Lord Jesus—unreservedly, without
hesitation or argument. And you say, "It all ultimately comes
back to me, and does it not ultimately depend upon what I do?
And that is the very thing I cannot compass. It is here I am most
helpless and crippled. It is just because I cannot do it that I have
no victory in my life and no joy in my heart and no bright witness
for Christ. You are shutting me up in a vicious circle. Is there no
escape from it?" Turn over to Philippians 2: 13, "For it is God
which worketh in you both to will and to do of His good pleasure."
So you see that all the way through it is most surely His work.
All the way through it is man's responsibility, and yet all the way
through it is God's grace poured out upon the soul. If you decided
to follow Christ last night, that was of God. Have you tried even
to rise up and to go after Him? That was of God. Have you recognised and learned to rejoice in the evidences of God's working in
your own soul? Do not sit down and mourn over your own
ineffectiveness. That strange stirring of the heart as you listened

to the message, it was God at work leading you into all the fulness of His grace and power. It is God that worketh in you the willing and the doing of His good pleasure. That deep, unconscious movement and reaction of your own soul to the divine call—it is all of God. That is where grace comes in.

That is the Gospel to announce, the Good News for the Christian as well as for the unsaved, the Good News for the saint as well as for the sinner. It is all of God from beginning to end. Just as surely as the new birth was of God, so truly your consecration, your sanctification, your holiness, your infilling of the Spirit will all be of God all the way through. And as He has brought us up to this point in our convention, bringing us face to face with His unescapable and drastic claims upon heart and life, and to what ought to be our ambition for life, He brings to us this command, which is to be the means by which all this can be realised—"Be filled with the Spirit." And the condition of filling is that you should crown Jesus; and your crowning of the Lord Jesus itself is the reaction of your own will to the divine strength. Have you ever seen a mother trying to teach her baby to walk? Its little legs are kicked out, and the whole body is tense with the excitement of the effort that is being put forth to walk. Yet underneath the weak little arms are the mother's strong hands. The baby thinks it is doing it all, but it is mother who is really at the back of everything. It is like that with God. Remember that much more than you want to be filled, God wants to fill you. Much more than you want to be ambitious, He is ambitious for you—your life to live for Christ, and your lips to speak for Him. When Jesus comes, as perhaps He soon will, you will stand before His judgment seat unashamed because you have sought to please Him. What is God's ambition for you?

And it is God who gives you His Spirit, and He will fill you now. And it is God who Himself will enable you to fulfil the conditions upon which alone He can fill your life with the Holy Spirit.

So as we bring our meeting to a close, shall we just venture on Him in faith? Shall we say to Him in our hearts, "Thou hast spoken these things to me, and as I place the crown of my life at Thy feet, as I yield my all to Thee, I do believe that here and now, according to Thy Word, Thou wilt fill me with Thy Spirit." You may not feel anything—well, I hope you don't, and I hope you won't; because your filling, as your saving, does not in the least depend upon what you feel. It depends upon God's fact, not upon your faith. And when you dare, in the absence of all feeling and all emotion, to believe what God says, He fulfils His word. If you are willing that He should thus take your life and fill it and use it, He will do that which He has spoken to us of.

ABOUNDING LIFE

Rev. W. Graham Scroggie, D.D.

I am come that they might have life, and that they might have it more abundantly—John 10: 10.

ON Monday, July 28, 1875, there was inaugurated in this place what is now universally known as the Keswick Convention. During this period the number of persons who have attended these annual gatherings cannot, in the aggregate, have been less than 200,000. These have been drawn from every part of the world, and have been representative of every Protestant denomination.

All who have attended Keswick will know what it stands for, but there are numberless people besides who think of the convention in various ways: some with mere curiosity, some with a noncommittal interest, and some more critically. And so it may be well, at this the commencement of another season of holy convocation, to recall and reaffirm what has been the distinctive message of Keswick throughout these years, and what immediately we are here for, ever remembering that a movement must be judged by what it professes and undertakes to do, and not by what lies outside its scope.

Of course there are some things that are taken for granted: things which, though not our distinctive message, are the foundation and warrant of it: such truths, for instance, as the evangelical doctrines of the Person and work of Christ, His real humanity, His proper Deity, and His atoning sacrifice on Calvary. Also the need and adequacy of the Gospel in this world of sin; and, as being our first source of knowledge of these things, the veracity and authority of the Scriptures of the Old and New Testaments. These truths are not Keswick's distinctive teaching, for they are held and taught by all branches of Evangelical Christendom; but here they are assumed.

What, then, it may be asked, is the distinctive message of this movement? A former distinguished leader was once asked what was the difference between a conference and a convention, and after a moment's reflection he replied, "A conference has a subject, but a convention has an object." As applied to Keswick, that is not a mere epigram, but a great truth. This convention has an object, and that object is nowhere so briefly and adequately expressed as in the words of our text, "I am come that they might have life, and that they might have it more abundantly." Here Christ distinguishes between "life" and "life more abundant," and it is for the interpretation of this distinction, and that we might know experimentally this maximum life, that we are now gathered.

'Tis life, not death, for which we pant;
More life, and fuller, that we want.

We cannot but have been impressed in our reading of the New Testament, especially of the writings of Paul and John, with the high level on which their thought moves when dealing with the subject of the Christian life. Phrase after phrase stands out in mystic grandeur of truths which have their origin in heaven, and their home in the human heart: such passages, for example, as, "For me to live is Christ"; "I count all things but loss for the excellency of the knowledge of Christ Jesus my Lord"; "I am crucified with Christ: nevertheless I live: yet not I, but Christ liveth in me: and the life which I now live in the flesh, I live by the faith of the Son of God, who loved me and gave Himself for me." And accompanying such passages as these, are others which point the way to the realisation of the blessed secret, such as, "Let us go on unto perfection"; "Being confident of this very thing, that He who hath begun a good work in you will perform it until the day of Jesus Christ"; "Be filled with the Spirit"; "Know the love of Christ, which passeth knowledge, that ye might be filled unto all the fulness of God"; "Having therefore these promises, dearly beloved, let us cleanse ourselves from all filthiness of the flesh and spirit, perfecting holiness in the fear of God." And there are yet other Scriptures which show the need of these, and which illustrate the fact that one may have life, and yet not have abounding life; that one may have the assurance of spiritual union with Christ, and yet be a stranger, for the most part, to that communion which is alone the outcome of obedience and trust.

Two illustrations will suffice. Remonstrating with the fickle Galatians, Paul says, "Are ye so foolish? Having begun in the Spirit, are ye now made perfect by the flesh?" Better-instructed Christians than they were are making the same mistake; and the matter is of vital importance, for we can never rise to the level of experience set forth in the foregoing texts so long as we are providing substitutes for the Holy Spirit.

But perhaps the immediate point is best illustrated by the

words of Peter at the time of his vision at Joppa. He saw, as it were, a great sheet let down from heaven, full of creatures clean and unclean, and when bidden to rise, slay, and eat, he replied, "Not so, Lord." How glaring a contradiction stands fixed in those words! He who says, "Not so," should never add "Lord," and he who truly says "Lord" never will say "Not so."

From these, and such-like passages of Holy Scripture, we must sadly acknowledge that Christians in general have been, and are, content with an experience far removed from the divine ideal. We have made the intellectual apprehension of truth a substitute for the power of it in our hearts, and are in danger of regarding Christianity as a philosophy rather than as a life. Christ is the complete answer alike to every false ground of hope, and every false theory of life. The answer to legalism is "Christ died for us," and the answer to licence is, "We must die with Christ." Religious belief is not enough: there must be moral change. It is the discrepancy between our profession and our experience that needs looking to; and we must deal with it, not in the twilight of past attainment, but in the noontide of divine possibility. The Christ, who dying did a work for us, now lives to do a work in us. "I am come that they might have life, and that they might have it more abundantly." There is great need that the truth be broadcast that abounding life is possible; and it should encourage us to know that in the experience of a multitude it has been, and is, actual.

All Christians have what the New Testament calls "eternal life," for without this one cannot be a Christian; but not all Christians have entered into the experience of abounding life. There can be relationship without fellowship; there can be union without communion; there can be life without health; there can be privilege without enjoyment; there can be movement without progress. One may war and yet not win, may serve and yet not succeed, may try and yet not triumph; and the difference throughout is just the difference between the possession of eternal life, and the experience of abounding life; the difference between "peace with God" and "the peace of God"; the difference between obtainment and attainment. Abounding life is just the fulness of life in Christ, made possible by His death and resurrection, and made actual by the indwelling and infilling of the Holy Spirit. It is not the will of God that we should be as fruitless trees, as waterless clouds, or as savourless salt; but that we should fulfil the highest functions of our Christian calling. Christ's promise is that He will slake the thirst of all who come to Him, and His purpose for those who come is that "out of their vitals shall flow rivers of living water."

The trouble and tragedy is that the Church has been content to live between Easter and Pentecost; on the right side of justification, but on the wrong side of sanctification; on the right side of pardon, but on the wrong side of power. The difference between the world and the Church is in the relation of each to Calvary. But it is not enough that the Church and the Christian be on the right side of Easter, which has brought us forgiveness and life; we are called also to the experience of Pentecost, which offers to us abounding life—life which is characterised by trust, and peace, and rest, and joy, and love, and power, and victory. We are as unable to live this life in our own strength as we were unable, in the first instance, to save ourselves by our own efforts; but He who began a good work in us can and will perfect it in all who yield to Him. A mechanistic psychology denies what it cannot explain, but the joyful experience and witness of a host of Christians, from the apostolic age to the present time, has been that "the law of the Spirit of life in Christ Jesus hath made us free from the law of sin and death."

If one is living before Easter, the Christ of the New Testament is not in his experience at all: he is spiritually dead. If one is living between Easter and Pentecost, Christ is in his experience as Redeemer and Saviour: he has spiritual life. But not unless one is living from and in Pentecost is the Lordship of Christ a reality to him, or can he enjoy spiritual health, which is holiness.

No one can but be impressed by observing the change which Pentecost wrought in the experience of the apostles. In the betweentime from Easter to Pentecost two things characterised them: fear, and a lost sense of vocation. We see them first behind closed doors for fear of the Jews, and then later, Peter, who had been called to high apostleship, said, "I go a fishing!" and the others said, "We also go with thee." No one can live the abounding life who is in the grip of fear, or who has failed or ceased to believe that God has for him a programme of life.

This between-experience has been the trouble from the beginning. It is illustrated by Israel in the wilderness between Egypt and Canaan, and by Paul's subjection to self, between his deliverance from the guilt of sin and his freedom from its power, as set forth in the Roman letter. It is this that is taught by the apostle's threefold analysis of men as "natural," and "carnal," and "spiritual." The "natural man" has not reached Calvary at all; the "carnal man" is on the right side of the cross, but has not reached Pentecost; and the "spiritual man" has entered by Pentecost into the Kingdom which is "righteousness, and peace, and joy in the Holy Spirit." The carnal Christian has spiritual life, for he is spoken of as a "babe in Christ," but there is little or no spiritual growth. He is like Lazarus, who, though raised from the dead, was yet "bound hand and foot with grave-clothes" until deliverance came. Is not this sadly illustrative of the experience of many Christians, people who are in bondage to fear, or doubt, or self, or sin? Yet freedom is our inheritance; we are called to the liberty of the sons of God. It will be a great day for each of us when we penitently acknowledge that we have not been what it has been God's purpose to make us; and it will be a greater day when we dare to believe that we may become all that it is in His power to make us.

It is this aspect of truth which Keswick exists to emphasise. The movement is not ignorant of, nor indifferent to, the social implications and obligations of the Gospel; but it is held and taught that the value of our outward activities is determined by the reality and depth of our inward experience; that it is the man who is entirely right with God who is best qualified and equipped to help his fellow men. It was not until after Pentecost that the disciples socially applied the Gospel; and it was not until after Pentecost that they were fired with enthusiasm and determination to carry the Good News to all mankind, whatever the cost might be: and ever since then, the Church's greatest days have been when she has lived and wrought in the power of Pentecost, which is normal Christianity. The Christian Church has plant, and organisation, and money, and learning, and much besides; but all this can be of no avail if she lacks Pentecostal power. We have banked more on prestige than on prayer; we have organised more than we have agonised; we have allowed ritual to obscure reality; we have thought more of conferences than of consecration: in short, we have displaced the Holy Spirit, and it is high time that we recognised the cause of our spiritual stringency.

The way out, and only way out, is by a return to Pentecost, which is the source and secret of abounding life.

But nothing effective will be done so long as we think in terms of the Church as a whole. We must be personal if we would be practical, for the Christian Church is only the aggregate of all Christians, and it cannot be better than the spiritual experience of those who compose it. The experience of Christians is not necessarily Christian experience. Christian experience is what the New Testament reveals, what Christ by His holy Passion has made possible, and what the Holy Spirit yielded to makes actual: but the experience of Christians is, too often, one of dispeace, of joy-lessness, of prayerlessness, of worldliness, and of defeat: and can anyone imagine that such an experience as that is Christianity! If Christ has called us to holiness of life, it is because He has made it possible; and if we will dare to believe that, and to draw upon our resources in Him, we shall experience in our hearts and demonstrate to others the reality of abounding life.

The sum, then, of what we have endeavoured to say is just this, that it is the intention of God that Christ shall be not only Saviour, but also our Lord; that we shall be not only justified, but also sanctified; that we shall be delivered not only from sin's guilt, but also from its power; that we shall not only live, but live triumphantly.

By Christ's death and resurrection, apprehended and trusted, we enter into eternal life; and by whole-hearted yieldedness to Christ as Lord and Master, we enter into the experience of abounding life. The yieldedness becomes a reality when, renouncing all known sin, and looking to Christ to accomplish in and through us by His Spirit, what by His death He has made possible, we follow on in love and obedience.

The evidence and expression of such an attitude will be in Christlikeness of character, and in sacrificial service for men. For the exhibition of such a life as that, the world is waiting; and surely the experience of such a life must be the devout desire of each of us. Then let us believe Christ when He says He came that we might live like that; and let us believe that He has given to us His Holy Spirit for its realisation. Here and now in this evening hour, let us claim our inheritance.

We need not wait for Him. He is waiting for us. In this place and moment He is offering Himself to us as the source of strength and satisfaction, as well as the place of safety; and if we will but receive Him, fear will be exchanged for trust, doubt for certainty, ineffectiveness for success, defeat for victory, and sadness for joy. We have tried trying and have failed; why not now try trusting? We have wrought in our own strength and have found it to be weakness; why not now take hold of His strength? The faith we once exercised for the possession of divine life, let us now exercise for the experience of abounding life; and as Christ met us then, so He will meet us now. May our attitude in the quiet of this tent, in this evening hour, be one not of yearning, but of yielding; not of struggling, but of resting; not of asking, but of taking. Let us go out to live the abounding life. May it be so, for His Name's sake.

GOD'S INSTRUMENTS

Rev. Hubert Brooke, M.A.

WHEN we see *how* God has chosen us, and *why*, we have a grand encouragement to expect that His will shall yet be truly fulfilled in us and by us. He has chosen us *in our folly*, that by being *wisdom in us* He may put to shame them that are wise. He has chosen us *in our weakness*, that by being *strength in us* He might put to shame the things that are strong. He has chosen the *base things and despised*, that He might bring to nought the *noble after the flesh.* He has chosen us as *"things that are not,"* nonentities, that by being *in us existence*—our life—He might bring to nought the things that are.

No complaint is more often heard than this: "I am so weak, and so unfit to do this work, or that." Thus you bring to God as an *excuse for not doing* His will, what He calls *the reason for doing it*. How often is it with us, after we have come to Christ, as with the stony-ground hearers in the parable: we see difficulties, persecutions, troubles in the way, if we should give ourselves entirely to God; and then we say, "We cannot do it." He tells us to come out wholly on His side, and we say, "We can't come out on His side." Now the fact that "you can't" is just the reason why God has chosen you to do it. We say we are weak; but that is just the reason why God chooses us, that He in us may be strong. You say you are so unholy; but that is just the reason why God chooses you to be holy. All through the history of His people God has followed the same plan. He chose the nonentities, that He might be *everything in them*.

(i) Turn to Exodus 3: 4–13; 4: 1–13. There we have God calling Moses, to deliver His people out of the bondage of Pharaoh. He says, "I have heard their cry by reason of their taskmasters (verse 7); come now therefore, and I will send thee unto Pharaoh, that thou mayest bring forth my people . . . out of Egypt" (verse 10). And Moses at once gives four excuses, four reasons in his own nothingness, why he should not go and do God's work. "Who am I, that I should go unto Pharaoh, and that I should bring forth the children of Israel out of Egypt?" (verse 11). "But, behold, they will not believe me, nor hearken unto my voice." "Oh my Lord, I am not eloquent, neither heretofore nor since Thou hast spoken unto Thy servant; but I am slow of speech, and of a slow tongue." "Oh my Lord, send, I pray Thee, by the hand of him whom Thou wilt send" (4:1, 10, 13). And God, instead of using Moses only, sent Aaron with him. Those reasons which he brought to God to show his incapacity for the service to which God called him, were just the very reasons why he was chosen to do it. He had to bring six hundred thousand slaves out of the land of bondage in the face of difficulties, and he thought *he could not*. God said to him, "What is that in thine hand?" And he said, "A rod" (4:2). Only a piece of dry stick, but with the power of God it should work wonders. Moses, with no eloquence, and a rod, was all that God wanted. By that dry stick God brought forth the Israelites.

Now see, God wanted Moses with his inability to speak, *with the rod*. God calls us to some service for Him. We begin to reason. We say we have no eloquence, no power; we cannot do this and that. God wants us *with what we have*. He says to us, "What is that in thine hand?" We answer, "A book—the Bible." "Go then," He says, "I will be with that Book; with that rod of my mouth I will smite the earth," and "comfort my own people" (cf. Isa. 11:4; Psa. 23:4). With a mind and body of no power, *and the rod*, He will free the slaves.

(ii) In 1 Samuel 17 we read how the Philistines were encamped against the men of Israel, headed by Saul. Day by day Goliath, the champion of the Philistines, defied the armies of God; David at once offered to go, in the strength of the Lord, to conquer him. Saul must first gird him with his own armour, but it was a hindrance to him; and now mark, David had to lay aside all the armour, and with what did he go? "And he took his staff in his hand, and chose him five smooth stones out of the brook, and put them in a shepherd's bag which he had, even in a scrip; and his sling was in his hand: and he drew near to the Philistine" (v. 40). And all the powers of the adversary fell before him. Our great adversary is the devil. How many try to put on the devil's own armour to fight him with. They try with all the powers of human intellect to meet the Goliath of this world. We have to learn that one little stone, and the power of God, is enough.

We have to do as the Master did—He took three smooth stones, with which to foil Satan. One for the wilderness: "Man shall not live by bread alone, but by every word that proceedeth out of the mouth of God"—and Goliath was beaten *there*. One for the pinnacle of the Temple: "Thou shalt not tempt the Lord thy God"—and Goliath was beaten *there*. One for the mountain top, where the devil showed Him the glory of all the kingdoms of this world: "Thou shalt worship the Lord thy God, and Him only shalt thou serve"—and Goliath was beaten *there*. We look at the adversary of our souls, and we seek for power with which to meet him; but we have to learn that we are to be as children, holding God's sling in our hand, the rod of God, and the smooth stones from the river of the water of life: and *then* all the power of the enemy shall fall.

(iii) 1 Kings 17: 9. God told Elijah to go to Zarephath, for there He had commanded a widow woman to sustain him. What had the widow woman to sustain him with? Had she barns and storehouses? Elijah might have asked her, "What hast thou in thine house? What is that in thine hand?" "As the Lord thy God liveth, I *have not* . . . but a handful of meal in a barrel, and a little oil in a cruse." Only a handful of meal and a little oil, but with the power of God it was sufficient to sustain them all. Those are the people God wants. Those who "have not"—who are nothing. He wants you to be the framework to set Christ in, that He may be seen, not *you*. Does He tell you to feed numbers with only a little word, a little corn that you have ground for yourself out of His Word, mixed with a little of the oil of the Spirit? Then go and feed them; fear not; He will increase the supply.

(iv) 2 Kings 4: 1–7. "Now there cried a certain woman . . . unto Elisha, Thy servant my husband is dead . . . and the creditor has come to take unto him my two sons to be bondmen. And Elisha said, What shall I do for thee? *What hast thou in thine house?* And she said, Thine handmaid hath not anything in the house save a pot of oil." And Elisha told her to go in with her sons, alone with God, and shut the door; then to spread out all her nothingness, all her empty vessels, before God, and there to get a supply from Him for years to come. Nothing save "a pot of oil"—a heart indwelt by the Holy Spirit—a vessel sanctified. That's enough for God. Go alone with God when the creditor presses hard on you for your members which you have yielded to God; spread out all your emptiness, all your nothingness, before God. A little heart in which the Spirit of God dwells; it is all you have, and it is enough; He will fill your emptiness. We look in the face of our difficulties, and we are babes against them. What are we to do? "Know ye not that your body is the temple of the Holy Ghost?" your difficulties: go alone with God, and claim His power, the power of the Holy Ghost, who dwells in you, and you need fear no difficulties, and dread no threatenings any more (Acts 4: 24–31).

(v) Just notice how God's prophets felt their own weakness. Isaiah, a man "of unclean lips." God wants such a man, that He might purge his sin, and send him forth a vessel meet for the Master's use. Jeremiah cried, "Ah, Lord God, I cannot speak, for I am a child." God wanted a child for His prophet, that He might put His words into his mouth. Amos said, "I was no prophet, but I was a herdman and a gatherer of sycamore fruit." He thought He could not speak, but the Lord took him as he followed the flock, and said, "Go, prophesy unto my people Israel." Their words were the axe to cut down the enemies of God, and they themselves were the handle; God swung it—He was the power. God swung the axe, and hewed down His enemies. The prophets were the handle, I said; and what was the handle made of? Of the wood of a dead tree. They were living trees once; but they had been cut down themselves first, that they might be used to cut down others, and then God's power wielded them.

(vi) Turn now to the New Testament—Mark 6: 37. The Lord Jesus, surrounded by the famishing multitudes, said to His disciples, "Give ye them to eat." "How many loaves have ye?" They began to look about them, and reckon up what they had. Not much. It never takes long to count up what *we* have! Five loaves and two fishes. It seemed little, but it was enough for God, and His power made it enough for all, until all did eat and were filled, and they took up of the fragments twelve baskets full. At the marriage in Cana of Galilee there appeared to be one great want—wine. The mother of Jesus turned to Him and said, "They have no wine." She acquainted Him with the need, and there left it. His was the power; she knew it, and therefore, addressing the servants, she said, "Whatsoever He saith unto you, do it." What had they? A row of empty vessels; and no wine. Six waterpots of stone. Jesus saith unto them, "Fill the waterpots with water. And they filled them up to the brim." It was enough, and the feast was supplied with wine. Empty vessels, with pure water poured into them, that was all; but they manifested forth His glory. So it is with your hearts. Only empty vessels into which God has poured a little of the water of life. Use them, and at His command it shall be changed into the wine of the Holy Ghost, and they shall manifest His glory.

(vii) It was just the same with the apostles. It was said of them, "These that have turned the world upside down, have come hither also" (Acts 17: 6). They were only men as others, but God chose them to turn the world upside down. The world's way is to place itself at the top, and God underneath and out of sight: but by them God reversed the order; they put God at the top, and the world underneath. How did they do it? What had they to do it with? "What is that in thine hand?" Three weapons, "weakness," "fear," and "much trembling," *with the Spirit* (1 Cor. 2: 3). They saw but little to encourage them at Corinth. God said, "I have much people in that city." And they went to work with those weapons, nothing of themselves, all of God; and they turned the world upside down.

All God's work is done like this. But in order thus to be used by Him, these three things are necessary:

(a) *Faith*, to believe what God says; and that when God says a thing He means it.

(b) *Surrender*, to allow that God knows best.

(c) *Obedience*, that sees what God requires, and *does it*. Ah! that is the point. When God shows you a thing, go and do it; do not wait for power, it is not yours, but God's. It was so with Peter on the water. It was not till he let go of the ship, that he felt God's power. *Let go!* Let go of yourself altogether, and then you will have power. We must say at once, "I have no power, but God has chosen me to do it." That is enough. He will use you. When you see God leading you out and telling you to do some work, you are just like Isaac going up the hill with Abraham. They had the fire and the wood, and Isaac turns to his father and says, "Behold the fire and the wood, but where is the lamb for a burnt offering?" Where is the lamb? You are the lamb. Your body to be offered a living sacrifice to God. God's will is the altar, the Spirit the fire, and you are the lamb that shall be consumed on the work of God.

So then, every command that comes from God requires these three things: belief, surrender, obedience. And if you are to be His servants, useful servants, see to it that you fulfil them. But who are the best servants? St. Paul exhorts servants to be obedient to their own masters, and to please them well in all things, *not answering again* (Tit. 2: 9). When a father tells a child to do a thing, he does not like him to answer again; and when God tells a child of His to go and do some great work, he is not to answer again. Not to question whether he is able or not. When God tells you to go and do something for Him, don't question, don't answer again; Moses did, and he had to share the service with his brother, instead of being used alone by God. Is not this the point where we lose the precious sense of God's communion, when we answer again? You hear God's voice calling you to do something, and instead of doing it at once you answer again. You think you can't do what God tells you; you hesitate, and then you answer again. You see one who knows not God; God says, "Speak," and you answer again, and the opportunity goes. Don't stop to find the word when God says, "Speak." Open your mouth before you have got the word, and it will come, and you will rejoice that He has used you. Never answer again when God calls you to service.

We see how God uses the weakest. We have known what it is to come "just as I am" to be forgiven; now why not come "just as I am" to be sanctified and made "meet for the Master's use, prepared unto every good work"? God wants us just as we are, for service. Will you not let Him have you just as you are to-day, that He may do as He likes with you, and use you just as He chooses?

ESSENTIAL PRINCIPLES OF CHRISTIAN SERVICE

REV. HANDLEY C. G. MOULE, M.A.

I am Gabriel, that stand in the presence of God; and am sent to speak unto thee—LUKE 1: 19.

THESE words are the utterance, not of a man, but of an angel. But we always pray that the will of God may be done on earth as in heaven. So we may gather many a precious lesson for Christian work in general, and the ministry in particular, from what the Scripture reveals to us of the holy angels, their life and conduct and attitude; what they are, and what they know themselves to be. We shall find this verse to be a case in point. Here is an angel, a blessed spirit from before the throne, come to speak to the aged Zacharias in the Holy Place of the Temple. He is asked, so to speak, to produce his credentials to the astonished, bewildered, awe-stricken man. And his reply is simply this, "I am Gabriel, that stand in the presence of God, and I am sent to speak unto thee."

Now there is something in every part of this angelic word which speaks to the heart of the minister of the Lord Jesus Christ, and reminds him of essential principles of the ministry. I might dwell upon the angel's *name*—Gabriel, God's man; God's personal, energetic servant. But I would rather look at once at his description of his service and of its inner secrets. And herein, first, at the word, "I stand in the presence of God." They form indeed a motto for us! Dear brethren of the ministry, observe its every word.

(i) "*In the presence of God.*" The existence of Gabriel was an existence in the presence: and ours must be so, too. You probably know that beautiful hymn which we owe to the pen, or rather to the regenerated soul, of a Hindu lady, Miss Ellen Lakshmi Goreh—the hymn beginning, "In the secret of His presence how my soul delights to hide": a hymn which every minister of Christ would do well to know by heart. Now the truth of that hymn is the law of the angelic life. Gabriel is what he is as abiding in the presence, as knowing face to face his eternal King, his Maker, Master, Friend, Father, All.

(ii) But observe again: "*I stand in the presence.*" Mark the word! He does not say, I *rest* in it, or even I only *abide* in it, but I *stand* in it. Here is the attitude of the servant. He is admitted to the *sanctum*, not to the outer Holy Place, but to the Holiest; not to the King's gate only, but to the King's own chamber. But therefore, inasmuch as the King is there Himself, the servant stands there, while the Master sits. Here, then, this blessed angelic spirit describes the law of his being. Thus he is, wherever he is. Is he locally in heaven? Or is he locally in Nazareth, carrying the annunciation to the virgin; or at Jerusalem, with his message to Zacharias? The law of his being, equally and everywhere, is this, "*In the presence,*" and "*I stand.*"

My brother in the ministry, we too must be there; and we too must be so. Never, never let us get out of that attitude of the soul, the position of a standing servant, whatever from other points of view our blessed attitude of privilege may be.

That attitude is immortally permanent for Gabriel. After nearly nineteen centuries, he is in it still to-day. His glorious personal existence is going on at this moment; and at this moment there is no relaxation of his standing in the presence. And *we* may be very sure that we are never to be released from our standing there. Oh, let us look up, that this law may be written in our hearts! Let me do so, do you do so, I humbly beseech you. Let the innermost secret of the ministry be this, for yourselves, for ourselves: "In the presence I stand."

(iii) Then he goes on, and says, "*I am sent.*" I am not about to speak upon the great principles of the ministerial commission as regards its side of authority. I am about to speak of it (for this seems to me to be the supremely important point), from the side rather of subjection, of servitude, of belonging, of our being indeed, as regards ourselves, "nothing, nothing." "*I am sent,*" says the archangel; not, "I come," merely, but "I am sent." I stand in the presence, a servant there. I enjoy indeed such a blessed sight of the Master's face as makes His true servant in unspeakable reality His friend. But still, I am eternally His servant; and with regard to thee, to whom I am speaking, I am a servant *sent*, simply sent. I am not come with a message which I have thought fit to bring; I am ordered to bring it. I have not come to lord it over thee, my human brother; to look down on thee, trembling yet holy Zacharias. I am simply "thy fellow servant"; "I am sent."

Just now, in seeking to lay this message upon my own heart before attempting to lay it before you, I was thinking over that beautiful picture in Genesis 24, one of the noblest episodes in the divine book—the picture of Abraham's servant. There he was, a very honourable servant, a man to whom Abraham talks as to a confidential friend, and whom he sends off on his errand with so much equipage and dignity that you find Rebekah, with the natural and noble courtesy of the East, addressing him as "my Lord." He is received with distinguished honour into the house of Laban, asked his errand. And then he speaks with the quiet dignity of one who cares only to seem what he is: "I am Abraham's servant"; Abraham's bondservant, *Ebed*, δοῦλος. Yes, that is what he was. Abraham had either actually bought him, or he was the son of a bought bondservant of Abraham's, "born in his house," as we read elsewhere (14: 14). Under conditions of society then permitted by God, he was Abraham's piece of property, as truly as any one of his camels was; and he said that he was so. This dignified, noble-hearted man, the man who was justly trusted by his human master (such a master!), who entered so nobly into his master's point of view, who had drunk in the spirit of an Abraham—all he said of himself was, "I am Abraham's slave," and "I am sent." He was on his master's business, not his own. He was in fact assisting to shut himself out of a position and wealth which otherwise apparently might have been his (15: 3).

My friends, that is a very noble picture; but shall we not bring it close home to ourselves? Shall we not see to it that *we* do not seek to pass ourselves off before the flock as anything but the bondservants of the Lord, and therefore their bondservants, their δοῦλοι, for Jesus' sake (2 Cor. 4: 5)?

Come back now to Gabriel; consider again the attitude of this blessed immortal bondservant of God. Listen to him again, with all the heart. His own utterance speaks of an annulling, an abeyance, an exclusion of self out of his serving life before the throne. We do not think of seraphic lives as unhappy, as unsatisfied, as stunted and confined. We can think of nothing more gloriously free and noble, in the vast worlds of created being, than the angel-life. Yet its law is an absolute servitude, a *standing* in the presence, and a being *sent* exactly where the Lord wills, and in order to say what shall bring glory, not to the messenger, but to the Lord. From self-glory the angels, with mysterious dread, always shrink back. It was a like-minded brother of Gabriel's glorious family who said, "See thou do it not; for I am thy fellow bondservant" (Rev. 22: 9).

My brethren, there is little risk doubtless lest anyone should fall down to worship us; but let us see that we fall not down to worship ourselves. We will see to it; by the infinite grace of God, which can indeed possess us, it shall not be. We will entrust it to His power that it shall not be. Whatever our blessed work of ministry brings us—and it does bring often weariness, and sometimes reproach, does it not also bring surprising kindness and allowance for us, on the part of dear brethren to whom we minister?—whatever, I say, ever comes to us as ministers of Christ by way of praise, or acceptance, directly or indirectly, we now resolve in our Master's name that it shall not be put into our own purse, for that is theft; it shall be passed over at once to Abraham to whom it belongs. We will not accept behind our Master's back any secret and surreptitious bounties. We can possess nothing, for we are ourselves possessed.

I say this because I desire myself to hear it; and I know that you will welcome it. Let us each say it to himself. Let us all, when we can, say it to one another, and keep ourselves in mind of it. Yes, dear and honoured brethren in the ministry of Christ, no surreptitious bounties, no secret contributions to self-complacency, must be accepted by the true bondservants of the heavenly Master from that Master's friends. It shall not be. We are above it, we are outside of it, because we belong to Him. Whatever He has given us to be, or have, or hold, for Him, we will now and evermore be giving back at once to Him that which is His own.

So I leave these words from the angel's voice for our guidance, strength, and blessing. Be it the inmost thought of each pastoral heart: "I am Jesus Christ's bondservant, and nothing else; and that in the fullest sense of the words. I am simply sent, a man under authority. I have come to you, not to be your lecturer, still less to 'do your speculation for you.' I have come to bring a message to you from One who is absolute for me, and absolute for you."

And now, dear and honoured brethren, let us follow up the words by singing a hymn which is very precious to me in this connection—"Oh! to be nothing, nothing." Never shall I forget the message it carried to my own soul when it was sung at the end of the first convention which I attended, that of 1886.

The hymn "Oh! to be nothing" was then sung.

SPEAKING FOR GOD

Rev. J. Elder Cumming, D.D.

M R. MOULE, in words so difficult to follow, has drawn some lessons for you to-night from the words of an angel. May I draw another lesson from what was said to one of the greatest of God's earthly servants—"Go thou near, and hear all that the Lord our God shall say; and speak thou unto us all that the Lord our God shall speak unto thee; and we will hear it, and do it" (Deut. 5: 27). And then, having taken the meaning of the verse, go back and read the two verses immediately preceding (verses 25 and 26): "Now therefore why should we die? for this great fire will consume us: if we hear the voice of the Lord our God any more, then we shall die. For who is there of all flesh, that hath heard the voice of the living God speaking out of the midst of the fire, as we have, and lived? Go thou near, and hear all that the Lord our God shall say." So that, if I read this verse aright, it is a confession on the part of Israel that God's presence is too awful to draw near; that they dared not go and hear; and that God's servants are commissioned, and expected, and called on, nay, that it is their special function and duty, to draw near unto that fire which Israel cannot approach, that therefore they may hear and speak. First let me say a word or two as to what is implied in the passage, and then let me turn to a practical question that I should like to speak on. In this passage, then, I think there are three leading points—

(i) *What ought to go before speaking?* "Draw thou near, and hear." How near? You remember the lovely verse of the hymn—

> Near, so very near to God,
> Nearer I cannot be,
> For in the person of His Son
> I am as near as He.

This is true of our position in Christ, as saved ones represented by Him who stands for us in the presence of God; but practically, as the servants of God, how near should we be to God? If you are in Christ Jesus, and if Christ be in you, how near are you to God? Can you be nearer?

Definitely, then, we are to take this position before we ever speak for God—*I in Christ, and Christ in me.* "Draw thou near, and hear." Notice, God speaks in fire. God speaks in consuming fire. God speaks in awful fire. When God's fire touched the sacrifice of old, it consumed it. It consumed nothing but what it represented, sin. God speaks in fire. His fire, when it touches sin, consumes it; and if there be in your heart or mine conscious sin as we stand in the presence of God, He speaks in fire; it is an awful fire!

Then, *God speaks only in solitude.* We must be alone, utterly alone —God and my soul together: otherwise I cannot hear His voice. And God speaks only to a soul when it waits, and waits patiently, silently before God. Oh, brethren, do not you and I know some of those solemn moments? Our hearers may not reckon on what has taken place. There has been a mountain-top not far from the study. There must be a mountain-top, where God, and God in fire, makes Himself heard, if we are to speak as this passage points out to us.

(ii) Then, *what sort of speaking ought it to be?* All that the Lord speaks to us, and only what the Lord speaks to us. Remember— let *us* remember (for I desire more to be spoken to as I speak, than to speak to you)—let us remember that it must be an individual message *to ourselves* before it can be a general message to any. We must hear God's voice; and oh, the solemn obligation to keep nothing back of what God tells us, though often we are tempted to do so. I know not that there is a more common, a more subtle, a more dangerous temptation for the servant of God than to keep something back—a word, it may be, that God says; but surely there is no greater mark of a faithful servant than that he should deliver his message just as he receives it. And sometimes I fear that if such a rule were in operation, sermons and addresses would be much shorter than they are! *Only what God speaks to ourselves.*

We see what should go before the speaking, and what sort of speaking is laid down here. Now—

(iii) *What is the object of speaking?* This, and this only, that the people should hear God's voice; should hear *it,* not our voice in it. Oh, would to God that we could so speak from day to day that our voice were not heard; and would to God that the people did not hear us, but heard the voice of God through us, and then that they do what He commands: the one great command of God being, Believe in Jesus. "This is the word of God, that ye believe in Him whom He hath sent"; and the other and great command is that a believer should obey.

And now may I say, in a word, what seems to be the special relation of these solemn truths to our present gathering at Keswick? What does it mean? Shall we bear in mind, dear brethren, that this convention and everything that it has in view, is for a practical object? I thank God that you will find nothing new in the teaching from this platform; that you will see that evangelical writers for generations have said it all; that you have been taught it at a father's knee or by a mother's voice. But it is not the question of an old or a new theory; it is the question of a fact in life: and this series of meetings, it seems to me, has no real object, or carries out almost no good purpose, if it does not bring you and me face to face with this question, Do I personally know what it is to be kept in the hand of Jesus Christ? Nay, more; I venture to say that there is an insidious danger in our apprehending too well the theory before we have entered on to the experience; but may I add, secondly, that the experience which these meetings have in view is, in the case of a large number of Christians, a distinctly new experience for them; by which I mean it is possible to be a Christian long, and to be an assured Christian, and to have generally the character of a Christian, and yet to know almost nothing of those things that have been taught here during these past few days.

The change from a Christian life that is unrestful, self-seeking, occasionally victorious, and occasionally cast down, is a most remarkable change for every man who has really experienced it; and I know that I speak in the hearing of many who can testify that they were Christians for years and years, but that until they came to a crisis in their life and passed through that crisis, to know of the unspeakable peace and power of God in their soul, they had no practical knowledge of the things that are spoken of here. I am sure there are many who are prepared solemnly and thankfully to testify that there is a great difference, an unspeakable difference, between the lives that men have lived as Christians in days gone by, and the lives that Christians are permitted to live by the power of Christ.

Then I should like to say once more, that there is such a definite experience in the Christian life as being filled and possessed by the Holy Spirit of God; that it is possible to live as a Christian without being possessed and filled by the Spirit of God; but that after having passed into a certain definite state—however it is passed into, consciously or not—there is such an experience as the New Testament over and over again describes as being filled with the Spirit of God, which makes a remarkable difference to the man who has known it; and that that is the experience we are needing? We all ask for the Holy Spirit, and until that Spirit of God so fills us, God cannot use us as He would like to do.

One word of caution I should like to give, and it is this. It does not seem to me to be possible for a man to be filled with the Spirit of God, until God has first cleansed the man. If you say, How far cleansed? I repeat in a sentence, what has been often said: we teach no sinlessness here. We have known no sinless man. We find in the record of the Church, and in the record of God's Book, no story of a sinless man save Jesus Christ. Understand that this is our firm position, which we defend as faithfully as any. But, on the other hand, how far the holiness of the soul may go, under the power, and the presence, and the teaching of Christ, I dare not say. I have seen no limit on God's part. We are not straitened in Him. Alas, alas, we are straitened in ourselves.

And may I add one word? I know the humbling experience, and you know, brethren, the humbling experience, through which God leads men to higher and deeper blessing. We must kiss the dust before it is possible for God to fill us with His Holy Spirit; and if we are willing to kiss that dust which is at Jesus' feet, then God undertakes to keep, and fill, and bless us. Are we willing to take that place? We have sung that hymn which always seems to me to be so solemn—"Oh! to be nothing, nothing." I know not what your experience is, but I know mine has been that while one seeks honestly and sincerely to sing that hymn, yet when men treat us as if we were nothing, there is a certain movement within the soul. We ask to be nothing before God, and also to be nothing before men. Are we quite willing that God should take us at our word? Is there one of us who would feel no pang for a moment, if God took him at his word, as he sang that hymn, or offered that prayer? But it is a true prayer, and a needful prayer, and a blessed prayer, all the same. "Oh, to be nothing, nothing." And I believe the only way that can be done is when Christ fills the soul of the man who welcomes Him and His indwelling; when Christ so fills the soul of that man and shows him the face of God, that he abhors himself in dust and ashes.